Chasing Je
and John

Chasing Jeb Stuart and John Mosby

The Union Cavalry in Northern Virginia from Second Manassas to Gettysburg

ROBERT F. O'NEILL

McFarland & Company, Inc., Publishers
Jefferson, North Carolina, and London

Library of Congress Cataloguing-in-Publication Data

O'Neill, Robert F.
Chasing Jeb Stuart and John Mosby : the Union cavalry in Northern Virginia from Second Manassas to Gettysburg / Robert F. O'Neill.
p. cm.
Includes bibliographical references and index.

ISBN 978-0-7864-7085-3
softcover : acid free paper ♾

1. Virginia — History — Civil War, 1861–1865 — Campaigns.
2. United States — History — Civil War, 1861–1865 — Campaigns.
3. Virginia — History — Civil War, 1861–1865 — Cavalry operations.
4. United States — History — Civil War, 1861–1865 — Cavalry operations.
5. United States. Army of the Potomac. Cavalry Corps.
6. United States. Army — Cavalry — History — Civil War, 1861–1865.
7. Stuart, Jeb, 1833–1864. 8. Mosby, John Singleton, 1833–1916.
I. Title.

E470.2.O53 2012 973.7'455 — dc23 2012018423

British Library cataloguing data are available

On the cover: *Passing Through the Pickets* (courtesy Dr. Ken Lawrence); Union Cavalry Flag © 2012 Clipart.com

Manufactured in the United States of America

McFarland & Company, Inc., Publishers
Box 611, Jefferson, North Carolina 28640
www.mcfarlandpub.com

This book is dedicated to
John Divine, Charles Jacobs, Brian Pohanka and,
most especially, to my dad, Robert F. O'Neill, Sr.

Let us now sing the praises of famous men,
Our ancestors in their generations, ...
Some of them have left behind a name,
So that others declare their praise.
But of others there is no memory;
They have perished as though they had never existed;
They have become as though they had never been born, ...
But these also were godly men,
whose righteous deeds have not been forgotten...

— Ecclesiasticus 44:1–10

Table of Contents

Acknowledgments

My wife Teresa is always first and foremost, rather than last but not least. Researching and writing this book has been a long process and she has been with me at every turn with her full love and support. She has made, and continues to make, many sacrifices so that I can continue to chase my dreams. Over the life of this project she corrected hundreds of computer problems of my own creation. She also offered solutions that prevented a few dozen others, and, at the end, gathered the photographs and arranged my files into a final format for publication.

I claim no expertise on John Mosby or his military career, but I was very lucky to have the full support of Horace Mewborn, of New Bern, North Carolina. He is the authority on John Mosby, as well as the men of the 43rd Battalion, Virginia Cavalry. I could not have considered nor could I have completed this project without his untiring assistance. He read the earliest drafts of the manuscript and challenged a number of my interpretations. In the end we agreed to differ on several. Still, he never hesitated to open his files, or to patiently answer or to research any of my innumerable questions.

My greatest debt may be owed to William Miller, of Churchville, Virginia. Bill has edited some of my work in the past, and, aware of my propensity to mangle the English language, he continues to answer my pleas for assistance. That he agreed to read several chapters of this manuscript a second time confirms a friendship that I value greatly.

Jim and Judy McLean are the proprietors of Butternut & Blue, one of the country's premier Civil War bookshops. They generously opened their own files and shared information that saved me countless hours of work locating several of the documents that enrich this narrative.

An early version of this book included an extensive amount of material on Elijah White and his 35th Virginia Battalion. Though most of it was left on the editing room floor, the late Charles Jacobs, of Montgomery County, Maryland, was most generous with his time, sharing the efforts of his own research on White and his command, answering numerous questions, reading several early chapters and guiding me and some friends to the many sites associated with Lige White in Montgomery County. Charles was the authority on Lige White. The 35th Virginia Battalion is now in the very capable hands of Horace Mewborn. Though working on his own study of the command, Horace, as he did with the 43rd Virginia Battalion, opened his files whenever I asked.

I am indebted to many librarians, archivists and staff members at a host of libraries, universities, historical societies and other institutions across the country. First and foremost I offer my thanks to Michael Musick and to all of the staff at the National Archives who have assisted me. Dr. Richard Sommers and the archivists at the United States Army Military History Institute, in Carlisle, Pennsylvania, have been exceedingly helpful over the years.

Richard Baker provided patient last-minute assistance as this project neared completion. Paul Carnahan at the Vermont Historical Society and Jeffrey Marshall at the Bailey/Howe Library at the University of Vermont were especially helpful during several days spent at each location.

This project took me back to Michigan several times, where I was ably assisted by Dr. Frederick Honart and his staff at Michigan State University, Sue Husband at Western Michigan University, Jennifer Wood at Central Michigan University, as well as the librarians and staff at both the Bentley Historical Library and the William L. Clements Libraries at the University of Michigan. I also extend my gratitude to the staff of the State Archives of Michigan, as well as to the staff at the Burton Room, Detroit Public Library, and to John Gelderloos at the Grand Rapids Public Library.

All requests for assistance were handled promptly by Julie Holcomb at Navarro College, Sharon Steinberg at the Connecticut Historical Society, Danielle Rougeau with Special Collections, Middlebury College, and Kerin Shellenbarger at the Historical Society of Western Pennsylvania. I also extend my thanks to the archivists at the Lavinger Library, Georgetown University, the Missouri Historical Society, the New York State Library and Archives, the Davidson Library, University of California, Santa Barbara, and the Department of Special Collections, at Wichita State University.

I am indebted to the inter-library loan staff at several libraries, including the Fairfax County Library in Fairfax, Virginia, and the Flathead County Library, especially the librarians at the Whitefish Branch in Whitefish, Montana. But this book could not have been completed without the tireless assistance of Ester Brandt at the Eureka Branch of the Lincoln County Library, Eureka, Montana. She has been my lead sleuth for the last several years and has never failed me.

Robert E. L. Krick gave the manuscript a critical reading, and his wife Julie deciphered my rough sketches to create the excellent maps for the book. Clark "Bud" Hall and his late wife, Deborah Fitts, read several of the early chapters and Bud shared his files on the Chantilly area. Arnold Blumberg read an early draft and offered incisive advice. Eric Wittenberg read a late draft and provided helpful advice. Roger Hunt untangled several misidentified images and kindly provided the image of Col. Richard Butler Price. Jim Nolan, the leading authority on John Buford, came to my rescue several times. Bruce Venter shared his files on the postwar life and career of Lt. Col. Allyne Litchfield. Robert Trout, the authority on Jeb Stuart and the members of his staff, answered several pleas for help and advice. Taylor Chamberlin, of Waterford, Virginia, answered numerous questions concerning Loudoun County. National Park Service historians John Hennessy, Frank O'Reilly and Scott Hartwig provided valuable advice and assistance whenever I called.

My family has always supported my endeavors and they continue to do so wherever they may be in the country. Our parents encouraged all of us to ask questions and, as they were able, they provided the avenues for us to follow as we sought to answer those questions. My brothers, Tim and John, along with John's wife, Amy, have been especially supportive of my wife and I while on research trips in Michigan. Tim and John, along with my sister Theresa, have each conducted research for me on short notice when I could not return to Michigan. John, a lieutenant colonel in the United States Army, and his good friend, Freddy Armstead, also spent a day at the National Archives on my behalf when I could not get back. Maj. Eric Shepherd assisted us on another visit to the Archives.

Numerous trips back East, necessary to complete the research for this book, awaited my wife and I after we moved to Montana. Many very good friends offered their hospitality and support, including Helen Morrison, Gigi Brown, Mike and JoAnn McDaniel, Scott and Linda Culver, Bob and Sherry Allison, Steve and Rosanne Hardgrove, Ted and Mary Doran, Frank and Marie Doran, Larry and Vicki Moser, Andy Johnson, Dick Crosby, Doug Graves, Kevin Holmes, Fred Kessel, Daryl Davis and Dan Horton. Writing can be a rather a lonely affair but each of you made the research aspect of this project truly rewarding. Thank you seems inadequate.

Closer to home, Mike and Jolene Workman, as well as Earlene and Royal Cushman of Eureka, Montana, and JR and Julie Hemp, of Columbia Falls, Montana, have each helped to advance this project.

A special note of thanks to Marshall Krolick for the phone call that started all of this, and for his continuing friendship.

Dr. Ken Lawrence, of Orwell, Ohio, very kindly allowed me to use the image that appears on the cover. Ken was a re-enactor for many years, portraying a trooper in the 6th Ohio Cavalry. Ken commissioned the painting, which includes a likeness of one of his ancestors, Capt. Delos Northway, who served in the regiment.

A final thank you goes to all of the men and women who ride across these pages — the heroes and the cowards, the romantics and the rogues, the educated and the unlettered, the blue and the gray. It is their story and only they know how close I came to the truth. I hope they recognize that I gave it my best on their behalf. The mistakes are mine.

Preface

When I moved from Detroit, Michigan, to Annandale, Virginia, in the spring of 1977, I was looking forward to pursuing two goals—a career with the Fairfax County Police Department and exploring the rich Civil War history of Northern Virginia. I arrived with an interest in the Union cavalry and a Yankee's disdain for John Mosby.

In reply to a random letter to the Chicago Civil War Roundtable I received a phone call from cavalry historian Marshall Krolick. Marshall put me in contact with the late John Divine, of Waterford, Virginia. John, who was justly known as "the Sage of Loudoun County," was an avid admirer of John Mosby as well as a man who had lived his entire life in a region that had seen more than its share of the Michigan Cavalry Brigade. For about sixteen years John was a patient mentor who opened many doors and introduced me to many historians who have helped to guide me in the years since. Like John, several of those friends, including Charles Jacobs and Brian Pohanka, are no longer with us. Others like John Hennessy, Horace Mewborn and Clark Hall continue to shape my knowledge of the war, especially the events in Northern Virginia.

Each of them encouraged me to take advantage of my proximity to the National Archives. That daunting edifice on Pennsylvania Avenue in Washington, D.C., is a true national treasure, but a treasure ignored by too many. It is intimidating, and it does not reveal its secrets quickly or easily. Thankfully, John provided me with a key. He introduced me to Michael Musick, at the time the senior archivist in the Old Army Records section. Over the years Mike patiently answered innumerable questions and helped to unravel and decipher the filing systems developed many years ago that are unique to the archives. Now retired, Mike graciously continues to provide assistance whenever I ask. This book is the result of one of those questions.

In the late 1990s I approached Mike with a question totally unrelated to any aspect of this book. After I explained the avenues that I had already explored, he suggested that I check a massive collection of microfilm rolls, titled "Telegrams Collected by the Office of the Secretary of War." The answer to that particular question still eludes me, but it was while searching that collection that the idea for this book was born and grew to fruition. I had, over the years, developed a fair appreciation for the vast amount of material that was not included in *The Official Records of the Union and Confederate Armies*, or the more recent *Supplement to the Official Records of the Union and Confederate Armies*. This collection drove the point home.

I found that the records of the lesser commands had been largely ignored, in particular the records of the command known as the Defenses of Washington and later the Department of Washington. Over a period of several years, as I copied and arranged hundreds of telegrams from the officers in this department, a narrative slowly emerged. These were the men who had battled John Mosby during the first half of 1863, the first six months of his storied career, and they had never been recognized.

I had also spent many weekends exploring John Mosby's haunts and skirmish sites with John Divine and Horace Mewborn, and a good-natured rivalry had developed between us, based solely on our regional or sectional perspectives. As we debated the many aspects of Mosby's career the disdain that I had brought with me faded, and I grew to admire the man. The following is a blend of perspectives, shaped during many hours on his trail, along the backroads of Northern Virginia, as well as those spent in the Archives, uncovering the paper trail of the men who pursued him and who have, unfortunately, been forgotten.

Introduction

In 16th century Ireland there existed an area around the city of Dublin that was under English control and known as *the English Pale* or simply *the pale*. The word pale meant stake or fence, and *to go beyond the pale* meant to venture beyond the security of English law and protection. During the American Civil War the Federal army established a pale around the nation's capital by erecting a massive system of forts and earthworks through Maryland and Virginia. As this system was completed additional troops, infantry, cavalry and artillery, were deployed to create a defense in depth, extending well beyond the inner circle of fortifications. While the inner line was fixed, these exterior lines of outposts and picket posts moved as dictated by military necessity. These sentinels stood watch beyond the pale.[1]

Following his defeat at Second Manassas, Maj. Gen. John Pope was instructed to fall back to the interior line of fortifications. There his Army of Virginia was consolidated with the Army of the Potomac. There was no time, however, for a long period of rest and rehabilitation, as General Robert E. Lee led his victorious Army of Northern Virginia into Maryland. To counter Lee, President Abraham Lincoln called upon Maj. Gen. George McClellan. Gathering the troops most able to endure another grueling campaign, McClellan moved into Maryland just days after his summons from the president. Left behind were thousands of men who had seen the hardest service and the worst of the fighting under Pope, including all of Pope's cavalry.

Within a few months many of these men rejoined the main army, including two of the three cavalry brigades that had seen service with Pope. The third brigade remained on the outskirts of the capital for ten months, finally rejoining the Army of the Potomac at the end of June 1863, as it again marched north in an attempt to counter Lee's second invasion. This brigade had been led at Second Manassas by Brig. Gen. John Buford, and included the 1st Michigan, 1st Vermont, 1st West Virginia and the 5th New York. Two of the regiments, the 1st Michigan and 1st West Virginia, had been severely pummeled in the last minutes of the battle in a sharp fight at Lewis Ford. On September 10, 1862, McClellan tapped Buford to serve as his chief of cavalry, and command of the brigade fell to the colonel of the 2nd Pennsylvania Cavalry, Richard Butler Price. During their ten months attached to the command known as the Defenses of Washington, and later designated the Department of Washington, the men of Price's brigade served as the tripwire along a line of picket posts extending throughout Fairfax County, Virginia, from the Potomac River north of the capital and around to the Occoquan River south of the city. In time other regiments, including the fledgling Michigan Brigade, arrived and shouldered much of the burden, but Price's brigade remained the backbone of the mounted force that stood watch beyond the pale.[2]

Surrounded by Virginia and the border state of Maryland, the loyal residents of Washington, D.C., as well as the president and his senior government and military officials, lived with a near constant fear of an attack against the city. Beyond the possibility that Lee would launch a concerted infantry assault against the forts protecting the city was the more realistic threat that he would send James Ewell Brown "Jeb" Stuart and his cavalry to make a strike against the capital. By the third week of October, Stuart had twice proven that the Army of the Potomac, especially McClellan's cavalry, was no obstacle to his troopers. After the two armies returned to Virginia in the fall of 1862, there was no reason to believe that Stuart's next foray would not be against the city or its environs. The first line of defense against such an attack was the cavalry attached to the Defenses of Washington.

Though Stuart always loomed in the back of their minds, these troopers also faced a more immediate threat from men they termed guerrillas and bushwhackers. By the winter of 1862 these groups included duly mustered soldiers from the 4th Virginia Cavalry, including the Black Horse and Prince Williams companies, the Iron Scouts of the 2nd South Carolina Cavalry, and Elijah V. White and his 35th Battalion Virginia Cavalry. These units operated behind the lines, targeting Union lines of supply and communication and conducting harassing attacks against Union pickets. Acting independently of these official operations were Southern cavalrymen home on furlough, who found it expedient to kill a lone sentinel as a quick means of obtaining a fresh horse and new equipment. Civilians also chose to prosecute their own private war by killing Union pickets and harassing small patrols. And while wise men, safely ensconced behind the lines, struggled to define how these different groups fit within the accepted rules of warfare, there were no distinctions along the front lines. Legal and academic niceties aside, these men remained guerrillas and bushwhackers to the troopers who guarded the pale.

In late December 1862, Jeb Stuart crossed the Rappahannock River with 1,800 men, and struck out across Prince William and Fairfax counties before being turned aside on the doorstep of the capital. Though the least celebrated of his raids, Stuart had again demonstrated that he posed a very real threat. Riding with Stuart on this raid was John Mosby. The young scout was a relative unknown at that point in the war, but that was about to change. When Stuart passed through the town of Middleburg, in Loudoun County, he elected to leave Mosby, along with a handful of men, behind to conduct harassing attacks against the Union lines. During the next six months John Mosby justly earned the nickname Gray Ghost, and he did so largely at the expense of the men from the 1st Michigan, the 1st Vermont, the 1st West Virginia and the 5th New York.

John Mosby and his 43rd Battalion Virginia Cavalry are well documented, though always from a Southern perspective and judgments are based largely on postwar accounts. During the war Mosby spent little time detailing the accomplishments of his command. The reports that he wrote were generally lean on details. Once the war was over, however, he became a fierce defender of his reputation and that of his men, writing numerous books and articles and hundreds of letters. Memoirs and reminiscences written by several of his men have further developed the history of the 43rd Battalion. These postwar accounts form the framework upon which all later histories of Mosby's military career have been constructed.

This study will examine the first six months of his partisan career from a Union perspective, using a vast, untapped reservoir of war date documentation that was excluded from the *Official Records*. History cannot truly be told from just one viewpoint, and while this is not an attempt to change history, it is an effort to fill in some of the voids, to balancing the record with accounts written by men from both sides.

This account will focus on the cavalry brigades attached to the Defenses of Washington, following the Union defeat at Second Manassas. In March 1863 these brigades were organized into a division led by Maj. Gen. Julius Stahel. Just over three months later, and on the eve of the bloody crucible at Gettysburg, Stahel was relieved, and his division was transferred to the Army of the Potomac. The transfer forced a sweeping reorganization of the Union Cavalry Corps. All three of Stahel's brigade commanders were either removed or relegated to their regiments. In their stead came George Custer, Elon Farnsworth and Wesley Merritt. From that day on the Union cavalry never looked back. Consigned to history's dusty attic, however, were the officers who had been replaced or demoted. This work is an attempt to dust them off, and to bring them back to life, if only briefly.

1

August 30–November 30, 1862

"Buford's cavalry are entirely used up"

On September 2, 1862, Maj. Gen. John Pope led his battered and disheartened Army of Virginia toward the fortifications that ringed the city of Washington, D.C., following his defeat at Manassas, Virginia. Trudging east along the Leesburg Turnpike as it climbed Munson's Hill the men observed Maj. Gen. George McClellan riding out to greet them. McClellan had, that morning, been given command of all of the troops gathering around the capital as well as those who manned the network of forts and entrenchments that gave the residents of Washington an uneasy measure of security. The two general officers spoke briefly along the turnpike before Pope took his leave and continued on into the city. Tasked with restoring order and relieving the continuing threat posed by Gen. Robert E. Lee and his Army of Northern Virginia, McClellan remained to meet the soldiers.[1]

In the immediate wake of Pope's defeat, the overriding concern of the citizens of the nation's capital was, "Can Washington be taken?" The editor of one Northern paper determined that it would be "*impossible.*" Others disagreed. The safety of the city and the government had been a pressing concern from the earliest days of the conflict, but not since the raw Union forces had been defeated on the same ground in July 1861 had the fear been so high. While Pope's army had not been routed, as the Federal army had been thirteen months earlier, it was still disheartening for loyal citizens to watch the beaten army march by.[2]

In late August and on the eve of battle, an officer who had just arrived in the capital city observed, "The air of this city seems thick with treachery; our army seems in danger of utter demoralization.... Everything is ripe for a panic." Now, Secretary of War Edwin Stanton ordered that the surplus ordinance held at the Washington Arsenal be sent to New York. Ships were reportedly standing by to evacuate President Abraham Lincoln and his senior officials, while gunboats lay at anchor in the Potomac River. One resident assumed that the "formidable" looking craft would "shell the town in the event of the Confederates gaining possession of it." In the days following the battle at Manassas, General Lee, in a conscious effort to increase the tension, purposely marched his army into Maryland along a line east of the Blue Ridge to threaten Washington and Baltimore, and indeed the unease crept north with him. Soon, officials in Philadelphia began evacuating vital documents and treasury funds to New York. The worst of the furor settled down once it became apparent that Lee did not have designs on attacking the capital, but that did not become apparent for several days. The threat of a Southern cavalry raid against the city remained for many months.[3]

The ranks of Pope's three cavalry brigades had been especially decimated by hard service during his campaign. In the immediate wake of the battle but when Pope had still desperately needed his cavalry to patrol his front and flanks he was advised by generals John Buford and George Bayard that there were not five horses per "company that could be forced into a trot." Now, as the weary horse soldiers arrived along the line of fortifications they were directed to guard the approaches to the city; George Bayard made his headquarters at Falls Church, with instructions to patrol the northwestern sector of Fairfax County, while John Buford's men secured the southern approaches through the city of Alexandria. On September 5, McClellan determined these two brigades to be "entirely used up," and that neither was available to render him any immediate assistance in the coming campaign. The troopers began to see limited service within a couple of weeks and Bayard's brigade rejoined the army before the end of the year, but Buford's command, whose ranks had been especially depleted, would not rejoin the Army of the Potomac for many months.[4]

McClellan did not help the recovery effort when, on September 10, he selected Buford as his chief of cavalry, a largely administrative position that almost certainly wasted the talents of the veteran soldier. In his stead Richard Butler Price, colonel of the 2nd Pennsylvania Cavalry, took over command of the brigade by reason of seniority. The fifty-four-year-old Price was a shipping merchant from Philadelphia, who had begun raising the regiment in the fall of 1861. The Pennsylvanians had arrived in Washington by late April 1862, and were ordered to Buford's command in early August. The unseasoned unit was then detached and assigned to escort the armies supply train, and while it was involved in several minor skirmishes it had not seen the debilitating service endured by the rest of the brigade. Price would prove to be a poor replacement for the talented Buford.[5]

The senior regiment was the 1st Michigan Cavalry, which was organized in Detroit during the first summer of the war. The regiment had been mustered that September and left for Washington, D.C., at the end of the month, under the command of thirty-nine-year-old Col. Thornton Brodhead. The command was assigned to Maj. Gen. Nathaniel Banks's Corps, Department of the Potomac, in December, and posted near Frederick, Maryland. Once Banks initiated the spring campaign, in conjunction with McClellan's offensive against Richmond, the regiment was divided; two battalions remained with Banks and saw service in the Shenandoah Valley, while the third, led by twenty-one-year-old Maj. William Atwood, accompanied Col. John Geary on his campaign through Loudoun and Fauquier counties. The regiment was reunited in early July, shortly after the War Department combined the several small commands that had served in and around the Shenandoah Valley into Pope's Army of Virginia. In the closing weeks of Pope's campaign the Wolverines surprised Maj. Gen. James Ewell Brown "Jeb" Stuart and several officers of his staff while they slept at a home in the small hamlet of Verdiersville. Only a timely warning from John Singleton Mosby, then a volunteer aide to Stuart, had allowed the officers to escape. Still, several vital documents were captured which allowed Pope to escape an attack planned by Lee for the eighteenth of August. Just over a week later Brodhead's troops nearly captured both Lee and Maj. Gen. James Longstreet on the streets of Salem [present day Marshall], Virginia.[6]

The 1st West Virginia and the 5th New York had also been raised and mustered during the first summer of the war. Eight companies of the 1st West Virginia served with a succession of commanders in the Shenandoah Valley during the spring and summer of 1862 before being assigned to Buford's brigade. The regiment's companies were distributed throughout the several commands, with just three companies seeing any sustained action during the Shenandoah Valley campaign and again at Second Manassas.[7]

Col. Othneil De Forest, a graduate of Yale University and a stockbroker prior to the war, led the 5th New York Cavalry. Along with the 1st Vermont and 1st Michigan, the New Yorkers had fought a sharp skirmish in the streets of Orange Court House on August 2, and accompanied the 1st Michigan on the reconnaissance in mid–August that had nearly netted Stuart and his staff. In the last days of the campaign the regiment was assigned to escort duty.[8]

The 1st Vermont was organized and mustered in November 1861, and left the state the following month, but with only ten companies rather than the full complement of twelve. The men had wintered at Annapolis, Maryland, alongside the 5th New York. In February 1862 their colonel resigned, and over the next few months several men would take command of the regiment, but the steady turnover did little to develop and maintain the efficiency of the regiment. The Green Mountain Boys sustained especially heavy losses in May 1862, as the Federal military situation in the Shenandoah Valley deteriorated, but the outfit recovered and fought well at Orange Court House.[9]

On August 30, the 1st Michigan, along with the several companies of the 1st West Virginia, was overwhelmed, in a sharp, bloody encounter with Stuart's cavalry near Lewis Ford, in the closing moments of the battle of Second Manassas. John Buford had been wounded in the knee, possibly by a spent ball, and several of his staff officers had also been wounded. Colonel Brodhead had been mortally wounded in a hand-to-hand duel, and two majors and ten other officers were wounded or captured from the 1st Michigan alone. The Wolverines sustained an additional loss of 11 men killed, 14 wounded, 6 wounded and captured and about 85 captured or missing for a total loss of about 130 officers and men or about one-third of the men who had entered the fight. Colonel Brodhead lingered for several days with two bullets through his chest and lungs before he died on the second day of September. The brigade suffered a total loss of 265 men killed, wounded and captured. As Stuart later crowed to his wife, "We knocked Buford's Brigade into Bull Run."[10]

A week after the fight at Lewis Ford one of the Wolverines observed, "Our regiment is somewhat disorganized probably [from] losing so many officers and men." Foremost was the lack of seasoned senior officers. Most of the men who were captured or reported as missing were paroled at Gainesville on or about September 2, and after spending the requisite period of time at parole camps in Maryland and Ohio they returned to the regiment. The captured officers were sent to Richmond to await their exchange, and most were released by the end of September.[11]

Lt. Col. Joseph Copeland had gone home on leave in the early summer after an extended illness had prostrated him in May. His absence further exacerbated the command problems within the regiment, which would be under the command of Maj. Angelo Paldi for several weeks. Paldi had survived his own brush with death or capture at Lewis Ford and was lucky to still be with the regiment. During the fighting he was under the control of three Confederate soldiers who, intent on stripping off his shoulder straps, neglected to seize his saber. The major was able to draw the weapon and disable his captors long enough to escape. In the aftermath of the defeat at Manassas the regiment was stationed at Fort Blenker, north of the city of Alexandria, Virginia, and Major Paldi assured his men that they would remain within the defenses of Washington for "a month or six weeks at least." In the end they remained for the next ten months.[12]

That the cavalry remained tethered to the capital was due, in part, to a continuing shortage of remounts. Priority was given to the mounted units assigned to the Army of the Potomac. The regiments refitting near the capital received remounts only after the orders from the army had been satisfied. Ten days after the battle of Antietam a trooper in the 4th New York counted over 400 men in his brigade alone who were still awaiting horses, and he saw "no prospects of getting any" soon. When Price's brigade stood an inspection a couple of weeks later fewer than 200 horses were deemed fit for duty. In mid–October the 1st Vermont Cavalry, numbering over 900 men, had only 112 serviceable horses. General Banks, who was then still in overall command of the defenses, was forced to go through McClellan for his approval prior to sending his requests for remounts on to the quartermaster. On the tenth of October, Banks implored McClellan to approve his latest request for fresh horses, and warned that his cavalry was "in danger of breaking down entirely." The following day Banks advised McClellan that he was unable to establish his picket lines as instructed. He warned the army commander that without mounted pickets to protect his infantry he would be forced to withdraw his troops from Fairfax Court House and Centreville. McClellan finally took notice, and 1,000 horses were diverted to the capital "in advance of all other requisitions."[13]

By mid–September, however, the cavalry had begun expanding their operations, though in limited numbers. On September 20, Colonel Price led an expedition, including detachments from the 1st Michigan and the 1st Vermont, as well as a section of artillery, west toward Ashby's Gap in an attempt to locate and capture a Southern supply train reported to be in that vicinity. Price marched only eight miles the first day, and was further slowed over the next two days when he encountered large numbers of sick and wounded Confederates in the towns of Aldie and Middleburg. After issuing paroles, the Yankees continued toward Upperville and Ashby's Gap, skirmishing with Southern pickets all along the route. On the morning of September 22, Price's advance guard, about 270 men of the 1st Vermont, came upon the rear of the wagon train, and the 130-man escort from the 6th Virginia Cavalry. After a sharp fight the Virginians "broke in great disorder." The successful clash of arms may have been good for the morale of his men but Price was forced to admit, "The object of the expedition, I regret, was not accomplished"—the time bought by the Virginians allowed all but a handful of the wagons to escape. Though his report suggests otherwise, Price appears to have been in no hurry to reach Ashby's Gap, and he failed to press his advantage once the Southern troopers fled. In what may have been Price's only encounter with enemy troops during the war, he was content to cede control of the fight to his subordinates. Still, for the next ten months Price, as brigade commander, sat in judgment of junior officers who had either failed in combat or who were perceived to have failed. His verdicts were harsh and several men were dismissed from the service and tainted as cowards.[14]

As a result of Pope's defeat and the subsequent consolidation of his army with the Army of the Potomac, changes in the command structure were common. Throughout the war an ever-changing number of major and subordinate commands were responsible for the defense of the capital. On September 2, the command known as the Defenses of Washington came under the purview of General McClellan as a military district of the Army of the Potomac. The official designation was the District of the Defenses of Washington and this title remained in effect until February 2, 1863. When McClellan assumed command the district included the ring of forts that protected the city. These fortifications were divided into two subordinate commands, the Defenses South of the Potomac in Virginia and the Defenses North of the Potomac in Maryland. On September 8, Nathaniel Banks, who was too sick to remain with his corps, assumed the immediate though temporary command of the district in McClellan's stead when McClellan moved north with the main army.[15]

On September 5, Maj. Gen. Samuel Peter Heintzelman, commander of the Third Corps, Army of the Potomac, was relieved of his command. Four days later he was assigned to oversee the defensive line around Washington south of the Potomac, a move that immediately rankled McClellan who asked that the order be suspended. Once McClellan was informed that the move had been made at the direction of both Halleck and Lincoln he relented in his officious demands, but he immediately included these troops in a plea for reinforcements that he made on the eleventh. McClellan would continue throughout his remaining tenure with the army to try, unsuccessfully, to pry Heintzelman loose. In late October, Heintzelman assumed temporary command of the entire defensive perimeter while Banks was on leave, and he officially replaced Banks in mid–November.[16]

Samuel Heintzelman entered West Point at the age of seventeen and graduated in 1826. A veteran of the Mexican War, in which he received a brevet for gallantry, he was promoted to the rank of brigadier general of volunteers in May 1861, and to major general a year later. Wounded at Bull Run in July 1861, his personal bravery was never questioned but his record in command was lackluster at best. "A stern man of blunt speech and abundant energy," Heintzelman was touted by the press as "No carpet soldier, petted by political favor," but one subordinate, Brig. Gen. Philip Kearny, dismissively called him "a weak old fool." He was "small in stature, with a stern, rather unkempt appearance, a full beard and long, thin hair." He was also, as a biographer described him, "a refined and cultured family man, a patron of the arts, lover of Shakespeare and the opera, amateur astronomer, meteorologist, geologist, naturalist, inventor, violinist, and a better-than-average cartographer." Lincoln had promoted him to corps command in the spring of 1862 over the objections of McClellan, and the fact that "he could be argumentative, proud, prickly, self-centered, and excessively vain" did little to ease their differences. His tenure as a field commander, both on the Peninsula and at Second Manassas, had been uninspiring, and though he retained hope of being offered the command of the Army of the Potomac, his opportunity for an active command had come to an end. Now, physically worn-down after weeks of cam-

Maj. Gen. Samuel Heintzelman led the Third Corps, Army of the Potomac, during the Peninsula and Second Manassas campaigns. In the fall of 1862 he was transferred to the Defenses of Washington, South of the Potomac River, and in February 1863 he assumed command of the Department of Washington, Twenty-Second Corps (Library of Congress).

paigning, he established his headquarters at Arlington House, the home of Robert E. Lee, just across the river from the capital.[17]

Several promotions within the 1st Michigan Cavalry brought much needed stability to the regiment. Maj. Charles Town, "a worthy man and a good officer," was promoted to colonel. His promotion had been reported in camp as early as October 10, but it was not announced officially until the end of the month. Just over a year later most every officer in the Michigan Brigade endorsed a petition on Town's behalf, describing him as "prompt and energetic ... brave and dashing ... a good disciplinarian ... [and] a gentleman of high sense of right and all the strongest and purest patriotism." Town, who had been wounded five times at Lewis Ford, was thought by one officer to have "always sought death on the battle field." If so, it may have been, initially, in response to the death of his wife in November 1861, and later as a means of escaping the increasingly debilitating effects of the tuberculosis that would claim his life after the war.[18]

Town recommended that twenty-six-year-old Peter Stagg be promoted to fill his former position as battalion commander, but when the time came in early December to fill the lieutenant colonel's position, vacated by Joseph Copeland, Town was reluctant to select a candidate "owing to the delicacy [of] having myself been promoted over my seniors." The matter was resolved when the regimental officers signed a petition on December 7, requesting that Stagg be promoted. In less than a month the "feisty young" officer from Trenton, Michigan, had risen from captain to lieutenant colonel. When Town's deteriorating health forced him to resign in 1864 he recommended that Stagg be appointed to replace him, assuring state officials "that the honor of the 'old Flag' is safe in his keeping."[19]

When the Army of the Potomac finally moved back into Virginia in late October it was preceded by General Pleasonton's cavalry, sparking a series of sharp engagements across the Loudoun Valley. When Pleasonton requested additional troops on October 28, General Heintzelman sent George Bayard with his brigade. Three days later Bayard, along with his brigade, was officially transferred to the Army of the Potomac. Heintzelman was clearly disappointed to see the brigade leave, noting, "I fear they won't return. This will leave us almost without cavalry." On November 5, President Lincoln, frustrated over McClellan's agonizingly slow advance, relieved the army commander and replaced him with Maj. Gen. Ambrose Burnside.[20]

The onset of winter and the health problems created when horses spend hours standing in wet snow and mud did not bode well for the mounted service that was now reeling from an outbreak of disease that ravaged the army's horses, including greased heel and sore tongue. On November 8, a trooper in the 5th New York mentioned that the regiment had received only 17 horses when they needed 300. The next day, Nelson Taylor, 9th New York Cavalry, reported "about half of our horses are sick some with the Distemper and some with the Black Tongue and new deasseas."[21]

On November 19, Heintzelman, in an effort to get his "much scattered" cavalry "in hand again," announced his intention to reduce what he termed "quite a small force at Leesburg," to little more than a mounted picket under the command of Maj. John Hammond, 5th New York Cavalry. Hammond was to establish a line of outposts back to Lewinsville, in Fairfax County, from where Major Charles Taggart, 2nd Pennsylvania Cavalry, would create an interior line of pickets. Several days of heavy rain, however, forced Heintzelman to reconsider. In the event of an attack, Hammond's troops around Leesburg would be cut off at Goose Creek, which was at flood stage, so Heintzelman ordered him to fall back to Dranesville. Taggart was then directed to establish the line through Dranesville, north to the Potomac and connecting with the infantry pickets at Frying Pan, four miles to the south. Still, Heintzelman encouraged Price to push his patrols "as far out on all the roads as [you] can with safety to give us timely notice of any movements of the enemy."[22]

Colonel Price's brigade, now numbering just over 1,700 effectives, manned a picket line that stretched from the Potomac River, north of Dranesville to the hamlet of Accotink, north of the Occoquan in lower Fairfax County, roughly 30 miles. Nearly 600 men, from seven regiments were headquartered around Dranesville, a village of "not more than 20 dwellings." Though the town was by no means substantial it was a vital point in the defensive line as two key roads, the Leesburg-Georgetown Turnpike and the Leesburg-Alexandria Turnpike converged there. Colonel Percy Wyndham, detached from the 1st New Jersey Cavalry, now commanded another 700 men at Chantilly. The other 400 men from Price's brigade were divided between the outposts at Annandale and Accotink. The troops guarding the capital were, at least temporarily, in an entirely defensive posture.[23]

On November 26, Union commanders renewed their calls for additional cavalry in the wake of an attack by Maj. Elijah White and his 35th Virginia Battalion against a Northern outpost at Poolesville, Maryland, two days earlier, and Halleck reiterated the long-standing order that the Potomac River "should be well picketed with cavalry." In Virginia, Union scouts reported that Capt. Robert Randolph's Company H, 4th Virginia Cavalry, known as the "Black Horse," was in Warrenton, their home turf, while three other companies of the regiment were stationed near Waterloo Bridge on the upper Rappahannock River. Other reports placed smaller detachments of Southern cavalry at Aldie, Dover and Purcellville in Loudoun County.[24]

When Maj. Gen. Franz Sigel, commanding the infantry in Fairfax County, requested additional mounted troops to protect the Orange and Alexandria Railroad [the present day Norfolk and Southern Railroad], Heintzelman's initial response was that he had none to spare, but an hour later he sent a follow-up message to Sigel informing him that he was sending 200 troopers, probably from the detachment posted at Annandale. Shortly thereafter Heintzelman received a request from Burnside for cavalry to assist General Bayard in guarding the telegraph line in the vicinity of Occoquan, and he was forced to inform the army commander that he did "not have even one company to spare," even though Price had 270 men at Accotink, a few miles north of Occoquan. That these men were not available suggests that they were occupied escorting the pontoon train that was moving overland to Falmouth to aide Burnside's crossing of the Rappahannock. This caravan of wagons had been delayed at Occoquan by high water several days earlier but reached Burnside late on the twenty-fifth. On the twenty-eighth, Burnside again requested that Price assume responsibility for protecting the telegraph line between Occoquan and Alexandria, and Heintzelman was now able assure him that he had the necessary troopers to carry out the task. In addition to the other demands placed against his lone brigade Price was now charged with ensuring the safety of the main line of communication between the army and Washington through Fairfax County.[25]

On November 27, Brig. Gen. Julius Stahel, now in temporary command of Sigel's cavalry, as well as the several cavalry outposts in western Fairfax County, and headquartered at Chantilly, received orders to make a reconnaissance into Clarke County. Stahel was to cross the Shenandoah River and verify reports that Maj. Gen. Thomas J. "Stonewall" Jackson had occupied Winchester. Around two o'clock the following morning the cavalry set out in a "cold drizzling rain" along the Little River Turnpike toward Aldie. Stahel rode at the head of about 450 men, from nine regiments, divided into two battalions. Following the cavalry was an infantry brigade from the Eleventh Corps. Arriving at Aldie shortly after sunrise, Stahel left the infantry to hold the vital road junction there and continued with his cavalry through Middleburg to Rector's Crossroads. From there, while the main column enjoyed a short rest, Stahel dispatched two scouting parties, one toward Upperville and Ashby's Gap while a second, led by Capt. Ulric Dahlgren, rode south toward Salem. Beyond a brief skirmish with pickets from White's 35th Battalion at Ashby's Gap, the day was uneventful.[26]

The following morning was "cold and bracing" and a light snowfall greeted the Yankees as they headed north, striking the Snickersville Turnpike near Mountville. The column turned west along the pike heading for Snicker's Gap and the Shenandoah River. Stahel again split his command, sending Colonel Wyndham into Snicker's Gap, while Captain Dahlgren took a small detail and scoured upper Loudoun County.[27]

As Wyndham's troopers descended the west side of Snicker's Gap they observed enemy pickets along the far side of the river. Completely unaware of the Yankee's approach, the Virginians were lounging near the riverbank with nearly all of their horses unsaddled. While Stahel and Wyndham deployed carbineers along the bank and prepared an assault force from the 1st Michigan and the 5th New York to charge across the river, the surprised Rebels from the 35th Battalion, attempted to engage the Federals in conversation to determine who they were and to stall for time while a rider was dispatched to alert the remainder of the battalion that was bivouacked several miles farther west.[28]

Once Stahel's men were deployed, his skirmishers opened fire as Capt. Abram Krom and his detachment from the 5th New York plunged into the cold water, accompanied by a detail from the 1st Michigan. The Confederates snapped off a few hasty shots before running for their horses and spurring frantically for the main camp. "Charging with a real Wolvereen yell," the Federals climbed the far bank and in what one of them later described as "a bold and splendid dash" pursued the Virginians "so closely into camp that they had no time to communicate our coming." According to Frank Myers, a captain in the 35th Battalion and in command of the outpost, a lieutenant and about 20 men were captured in this initial attack, while Northern accounts suggest that most of the Southerners made it back to the main camp. Ordering out flankers who were instructed to search every house within a mile of the road, and with a strong detail left to secure the river crossing, Stahel hurried the remainder of his force toward Berryville.[29]

After pursuing the fugitives for several miles, the Yankees "came suddenly upon White's camp and dashed in yelling like demons." A correspondent riding with the Federal column wrote, "I have heard of scenes of confusion that 'beggars all description,' but never had the pleasure of witnessing such a perfect bedlam of excitement before." Myers claimed that all of his men were packed and ready to leave when the Yankees arrived, except for an officer who was sick in his tent. Myers also claimed that all but one of his wagons made it to safety. Union accounts suggest that several men were surprised in their tents and captured, and

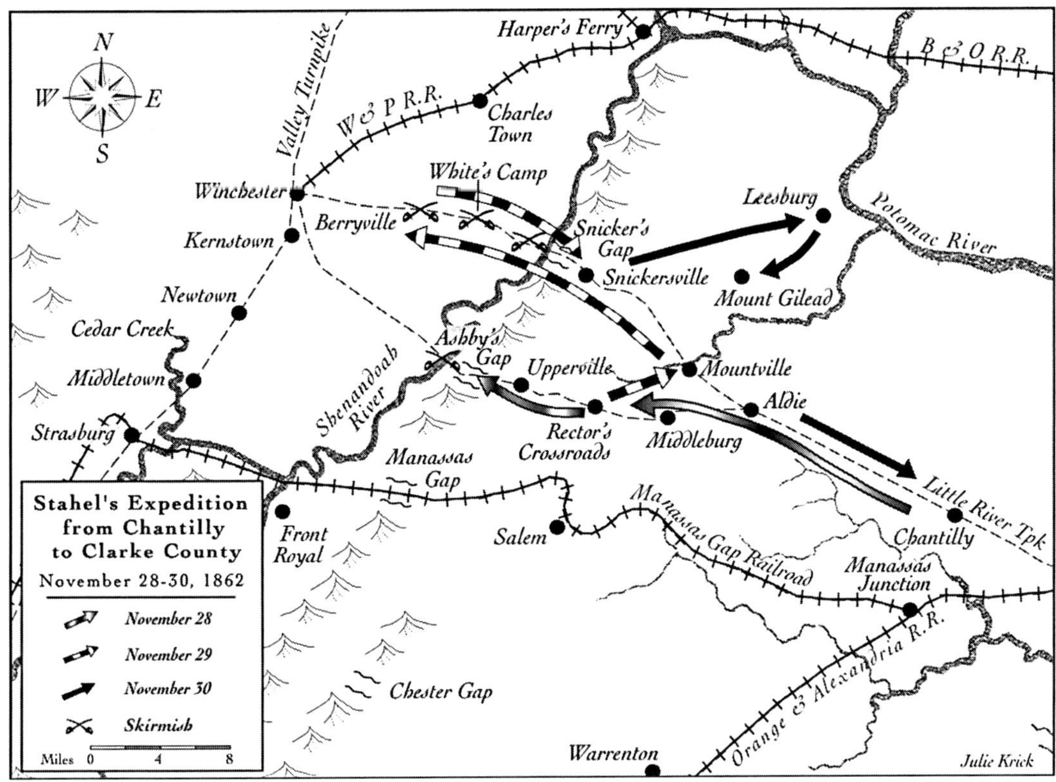

though several wagons were driven to safety, the majority were captured. The Yankees gathered up abandoned weapons as well as several flags, termed by one correspondent as "the notorious Bob White's colors." Worn-out horses were exchanged from among the 50 or so captured, and as many as 60 head of cattle were herded back across the river.[30]

As soon as the Yankees had appeared along the river a rider was sent to warn White, who was ill and resting in a home just over a mile from the river and about a half mile north of the Berryville pike. White, along with the trooper, fled minutes before the Federals came into view. Reaching the turnpike, White was attempting to rally the fugitives from the camp when he was shot in the thigh. Wounded for the second time in just over two months, White stayed in the saddle as he urged his men to stand and fight.[31]

The town of Berryville, in Clarke County, numbered about 500 residents in 1862, "most of them professional people, merchants, mechanics, and laborers." It had seen much of the armies but little of the war until now. Once the situation at Myers's campsite was stabilized Stahel left Wyndham to police up the prisoners and property while he led about 100 men, in pursuit of the fleeing Confederates. Reaching the outskirts of town, Stahel reformed the men into a column of fours, ordered them to draw their sabers and with a bugler blowing "Charge" the men dug in their spurs and galloped into Berryville from the east.[32]

Two miles west of the town lay the camp of the 12th Virginia Cavalry, commanded by Lt. Col. Richard Burks, who had no warning of the attack until the enemy reached the outskirts of town. He was then able to get about 100 men into the saddle and under the command of Maj. Thomas Massie, they set out to meet the Federal threat. As the head of the Union column neared the west end of town it was brought to a halt by fire from civilians and soldiers shooting from doorways and windows. As the Federals responded to this fusillade they were thrown into confusion when Massie's column plowed into them. Men and horses went down in the road and the fighting intensified as Confederates, including fugitives from White's camp, now struck the flanks of the Federal column from side streets. One Rebel raked his spurs across a Union soldier who was pinned under his horse hollering, "Lie there and die, you damned Yankee." "Women appeared to be transformed into fiends and appeared greatly amused as they fired their revolvers at the Yankees." In the aftermath of the fighting the intensity of the fire that had been observed coming from civilians left many of the Federals bent on burning the town, an act of revenge that was prevented by Stahel.[33]

Some of Massie's men now struck the Federals from the rear, but the Union rear guard wheeled around to meet the new threat. At the same time help arrived when one of Stahel's staff officers galloped up with a platoon of men fresh from policing the camp site. The Confederates were now caught between two fires and the battle dissolved into a "tug of war," that spread throughout the town. Stahel, prominent in a black cape adorned with a bright red collar, found himself surrounded by Confederates at one point, but was rescued by several officers before he could be taken away.[34]

With the weight of numbers now against them, the Virginians turned and fled toward Winchester, where word of the fighting "caused great excitement among the citizens." One claimed that orders were issued to evacuate the town. Wagons loaded with military supplies were moved to safety while the troops in town, supported by a battery of horse artillery, took up defensive positions along the turnpike to the east. Just one week earlier Unionist resident Julia Chase had recorded her wish that "the Federals may dash in and cause a skidaddle."[35]

The victorious but weary Yankees had no further designs on Winchester, however, and Stahel ordered his command back to the river. Once across they paused for a brief rest near Snickersville, allowing several scattered parties of soldiers to rejoin the column. At ten o'clock that evening they set out for Leesburg and then turned south to Mount Gilead, arriving at five o'clock in the morning. After a few hours of well-earned rest they resumed their march and reached Chantilly around 8 P.M.[36]

White claimed that the Federals were 800 strong while Myers vastly overstated the size of Stahel's cavalry at 1,200 men, "all superbly mounted." Myers further claimed that his men were hindered in their flight from the river by "indifferent horses" and were easily captured, a statement that is belied by numerous Federal accounts of Yankees exchanging their own worn-out animals for healthier Southern mounts. One Northern reporter stated that the actual number of horses captured could not be accurately determined due to the large number of them already being ridden by Union troopers.[37]

White reported the loss of two officers and the unit doctor captured along with twelve men missing and one wounded. Lt. Col. Burks tallied his losses at seven captured and three wounded, one of them mortally. Federal claims of casualties inflicted were generally inflated and ranged anywhere from 30 to near 100 killed, wounded and captured. Stahel lost one man killed, one mortally wounded along with four or five men with lesser wounds and as many as fifteen captured.[38]

Stahel had gained a significant victory over a command that had tormented Union forces in Northern Virginia throughout the year. Further, he had determined that a full brigade of Southern cavalry held Winchester, while also confirming that Jackson had vacated the area several days earlier. In all respects the foray was a significant morale boost for the worn down Federal troopers. The victory elevated "the character of our cavalry as soldiers," and allowed the men to boast that they had defeated "the famous White's cavalry," or as Myers later mocked Stahel's Hungarian accent, "dat dam Bob White." The victory must have been especially sweet for the men of the 1st Michigan, as they had helped to defeat the 12th Virginia, which had delivered part of the final crushing blow at Lewis Ford.[39]

In the almost three months since the debacle at Lewis Ford, John Buford's former brigade had undergone significant changes. Forced to remain behind, on the outskirts of the capital, while their comrades pursued the Army of Northern Virginia into Maryland, the men had seen their ranks swell as comrades returned from hospitals and parole camps. The regiments were already so broken up, however, between the several large outposts that the men could not yet appreciate their rebounding numbers. The outbreak of disease that had ravaged their horses in the fall had been overcome, and as bureaucratic obstacles were surmounted following McClellan's removal from command fresh horses were finally arriving in adequate numbers. Significant challenges lay ahead, but Stahel's victory, deep in enemy territory, had restored the Northern troopers' confidence. A further boost to their morale lay just over the horizon, as a fresh brigade of cavalry would soon be heading to the capital from Michigan.

2

"For special service in mountainous districts infested by bushwhackers"

Lt. Col. Joseph Copeland and Capt. William Mann were absent from the 1st Michigan Cavalry during the late summer and early fall of 1862. Joseph Copeland, who looked older than his forty-nine years, had served as a judge for 13 years in Michigan, including eight as a circuit judge and justice on the state supreme court. He was a stern, dour looking man with a zombie-like glare that must have been disconcerting to defendants and attorneys in his courtroom or to young officers called to stand before him. He saw hard service during the spring and summer campaign in the Shenandoah Valley and had led the cavalry for several weeks in Brodhead's absence. One of his officers described Copeland under fire near Winchester on March 23, sitting "upon his horse while the bullets flew about his head like hail stones, as cool as though he was sitting on the judge's bench trying a criminal for petit larceny."[1]

William Mann, born in Sandusky, Ohio, accepted a commission as captain in the 1st Michigan Cavalry on August 12, 1861 at the age of twenty-one, and resigned on July 5, 1862. An ambitious officer, Mann saw his service to this point of the war as an apprenticeship under the tutelage of both Brodhead and Copeland. On June 21, 1862, Mann submitted what he later referred to as a "scheme" to Secretary of War Edwin Stanton to raise a new regiment of cavalry. Recognizing that his youth and lack of ties to the state of Michigan might be a potential drawback Mann sought Copeland's support by offering the former judge the colonelcy of the proposed regiment. Copeland may have first broached the idea with Michigan governor Austin Blair in June while home on an extended sick leave. Mann submitted copies of his plan to both Stanton and Blair.[2]

Captain Mann's detailed proposal outlined raising a regiment of "good marksmen or 'Sharpshooters,'" and suggested that their accuracy with firearms be "the test of their fitness" for the unit. They were to be armed with "some good rifle — breechloading, if one of sufficient range can be found — and Colts Navy Pistols." Copeland later added that the men should also be equipped with hatchets, while the press reported that each man would carry a brace of pistols. In Mann's proposal "good swift horses" were to be purchased "with especial attention to the service intended," to which Copeland added a proviso that the animals were to be "procured in Michigan." Both officers asked that one company of artillery be permanently attached to the command and Mann, very presciently, laid out the merits of such a unit and the manner in which he envisioned it being used on the battlefield. He outlined using the men as skirmishers, who would ride to the point where they were needed, dismount and fight on foot. Both officers targeted the "roving, marauding, straggling parties of the enemy" that had harassed the Federals as they operated in the Loudoun and Shenandoah valleys that spring and summer. Specifically they named Turner Ashby's and John Hunt Morgan's units as examples, and explained that though they were "to a great extent undrilled militia, yet being armed with long range sporting rifles, mounted upon lightly equipped and fast horses ... they are able to make incredible marches, seeming to be almost omnipresent." In the opinion of the two officers, "Our cavalry armed generally with sabres & pistols are not effective against them, as they will not stand a charge or even allow us to approach within pistol shot, and with our heavily equipped horses, we are not able to run them down." To counter this problem Copeland and Mann proposed that this unit would be lightly equipped and "forage largely on the enemy." One local paper explained that the unit was designed "for special service in mountainous districts infested by bushwhackers," and that it was to be "patterned after the famous Ashby Cavalry." In truth Ashby's light cavalry hardly resembled the mounted light infantry concept that Mann described.[3]

Mann saw a need for units of this nature even if the war came to a rapid close, suggesting that the enemy might retreat into "the mountains and interior districts" and continue a guerrilla war "for some time." He suggested that his "Mounted Sharpshooters" be raised from several western states as opposed to one particular state, a stipulation that Copeland struck from his memorandum. In these two plans, which almost certainly originated with Mann and which Copeland later adopted with slight changes, the men foresaw the predominant tactics that the cavalry of both sides would employ over the last years of the war. But their idea of lightly equipped men chasing down small roving bands of guerrillas and then dismounting to fight on foot presupposed that their opponent would also choose to stand and match arms with them. In this regard the two officers showed a complete lack of understanding of guerrilla warfare and the hit-and-run encounters that the guerrillas preferred. Time would prove that arming the men with a brace of reliable revolvers and teaching them to rely on these weapons while rapidly closing with their enemy was a much more effective method of dealing with the guerrilla threat. The longer, more cumbersome rifles, regardless of their breechloading or repeating characteristics, proved to be very poor weapons in these short, deadly clashes, at close quarters.[4]

Col. William Mann, 7th Michigan Cavalry. As a captain in the 1st Michigan Cavalry, Mann proposed to raise a mounted regiment for the purpose of combating the escalating guerrilla problem. That regiment ultimately became the 5th Michigan Cavalry (USAMHI).

Once Stanton approved the idea, Mann requested that Copeland leave all matters concerning the organization of the regiment to him. The younger officer later claimed that he raised and mustered both the Mounted Rifles and the battery of horse artillery in eight days, and news accounts confirm that in just nine days over 800 men were in camp at Detroit while the remainder had been asked to delay their arrival until barracks and other accommodations were completed. The 1st Michigan Cavalry had earned an enviable reputation during the spring and summer campaigns (the disaster at Lewis Ford was still to come) and their record had been broadcast by local papers under banner headlines describing their accomplishments as "brilliant" and "splendid." This notoriety, combined with the fact that several other officers from the regiment had agreed to accept commissions in the new unit, certainly did not hurt enlistments. With Copeland in Washington, "seeking to secure a Brigadiership," Mann, through "hard work and close attention to drills and discipline in a few weeks made a magnificent command of these men." Other accounts dispute Mann's contention that Copeland played no role in recruiting the regiment, and while Copeland was indeed lobbying for promotion he was also struggling to insure that the men were armed in the manner that he and Mann had envisioned.[5]

Brig. Gen. Joseph Copeland, commander of the Michigan Brigade. During the summer of 1862, Copeland, then lieutenant colonel of the 1st Michigan Cavalry, supported Mann's plan to raise a new regiment, and ultimately gained a promotion to brigadier and command of the brigade. He lost that command to George Custer in late June 1863 (USAMHI).

Under President Lincoln's call for additional troops that July the state of Michigan was tasked with recruiting almost 12,000 men. Congressman Francis Kellogg then obtained permission from Stanton for an additional two regiments of cavalry to be raised under this quota. The situation took a turn, however, when Blair elected to count these new enlistees toward the state's quota under the July call for volunteers and Mann's First Mounted Rifles became the 5th Michigan Cavalry. In an attempt to mollify Mann, Blair reportedly offered him the colonelcy of the 6th Michigan Cavalry that was being organized at the same time, and after due consideration Mann accepted. Within hours, news of this arrangement reached the political patrons of the latter regiment, including Congressman Kellogg, and they rushed to Blair's office to protest the appointment of an officer who was neither from Michigan nor from the city of Grand Rapids where the new companies were organizing. After several hours of discussion a compromise was reached in which Mann again agreed to step aside and accept the colonelcy of the 7th Michigan Cavalry. Once Kellogg and George Gray, a resident of the city and Kellogg's choice for the colonelcy of the 6th, were satisfied, the issue of Mann's residency was no longer a concern, even though the 7th was also using the city of Grand Rapids as a gathering point.[6]

Several hundred volunteers were turned away once the rolls of the 5th were filled and many of these eager young men found their way to Grand Rapids where the 6th was being organized. On October 13, the regiment was mustered and the "overplus" was then directed to the nearby camps of the 7th Michigan. Jacob Coburn, who had given up a partnership in a law practice in Big Rapids, Michigan, to join the 6th spoke of his fellow recruits in a letter to the editor of the local paper. "I think there are none but have come determined to do their duty, and conduct themselves as becomes 'American Soldiers.'"[7]

Corporal Coburn thought Col. George Gray "very popular among the soldiers," but others found him "too severe." James Kidd, a lieutenant in the regiment, spoke of the Irish attorney as a polished speaker with a keen wit, but who also had an "irascible temper," a sharp tongue and who "was something of a martinet." One dissatisfied trooper saw Gray as "a poor fool," and concluded, "he is Irish & that is enough." Though Mann later claimed that he had been asked to assume the colonelcy of the regiment until being moved aside for political reasons, contemporary accounts suggest that a regular army officer was considered to lead the 6th with Gray serving as lieutenant colonel. Kidd believed that Capt. George Custer, then an aide to General McClellan, was angling for the position. Custer did appear in the camp of the 5th Michigan the following spring seeking the colonelcy of that regiment which was then vacant, but there is some evidence to confirm Kidd's speculation that his name had come up earlier.[8]

A petition was circulated among the officers of the regiment seeking their endorsement of George Gray for the colonelcy and, "though the feeling was general that it would be better for him to retain the second place and have an officer of the army, or at least one who had seen service, for our commander" the officers signed the petition and Gray was promoted. An item in the Detroit *Free Press* addressed the political bartering between Governor Blair and Congressman Kellogg over this position — it was an election year after all — and while not naming any of the officers involved the report suggests that the process was not as clean as that later described by Mann. The petition may have been a back door means of accomplishing what the two politicians could not agree to directly. The paper also mentioned that a young, unnamed, staff officer who was then in Detroit was seeking the colonelcy. Custer was not in Detroit at the time but he was on leave shortly thereafter when McClellan was relieved from command. The paper's assertion that the officer was then in Detroit may also have been an error. Whoever the paper may have been referring to, George Custer had petitioned Governor Blair for a command as early as January 1862.[9]

Congressman Francis Kellogg. Representing western Michigan, Kellogg, who had served briefly as colonel of the 3rd Michigan Cavalry, was instrumental in raising the 6th and 7th Michigan Cavalry regiments and in the formation of what became known as the Michigan Brigade (Library of Congress).

After spending the last weeks of 1861 in Ohio, as well as in Monroe, Michigan, recovering from an illness, Custer was back in Washington at the end of January pondering his future when he chose to introduce himself to Governor Blair. Mentioning that he had once been a resident of Monroe and that he still regarded the town as his home, Custer declared his "earnest desire to serve with the troops from Michigan." Stressing his West Point training and decrying "the law in the regular service which requires graduates of the Military Academy to be placed in the lowest grade of commissioned officers," Custer asserted — in words similar to those later used in the *Free Press*—that "it is reasonable to suppose that a graduate of the Mil. Academy is better qualified to exercise command over troops and to enforce discipline than one of equal natural talent but of inferior preparation and accomplishments." As to his own experience he concluded, "I have had more perhaps than most junior officers," and that experience, combined with his academy education, "fill me to hope to command a regiment." Stating that he preferred to lead a cavalry regiment but willing to accept any vacancy Custer acknowledged, "I should feel highly honored in accepting it and should use every means in my power to repay my country not only the debt which every citizen owes, but that one incurred by being the recipient of an education at her hands." The nature of Blair's response, if any, is unknown, but George Custer's hope of commanding *one* of Michigan's regiments was never realized.[10]

Col. George Gray. After much political wrangling, Gray, an attorney from the Grand Rapids area of Michigan and a friend of Kellogg's, was appointed to command of the 6th Michigan Cavalry (courtesy Grand Rapids History & Special Collections Archive, Grand Rapids Public Library).

The ease with which the 5th Michigan had been recruited and organized, combined with the number of regiments then being organized in other states, placed an overwhelming demand on the abilities of the armories and the quartermaster to supply them with weapons and equipment. The state adjutant general wrote a series of letters in August to both the quartermaster and ordinance departments in Washington, as well as to Governor Blair, outlining that the 5th Cavalry would soon be ready to take the field but for a complete lack of "clothing, arms & equipment." That these shortages continued into the fall is evidenced by Copeland's appeal of October 24: "My regiment is full numerically, but not fully clothed or equipped. We have no arms except for the Battery.... We are without camp equipage of any description."[11]

Colonel Copeland had specifically requested that the Mounted Rifles "be equipped with the best breechloading repeating rifle," and he had personally battled to ensure that the men received the new Spencer repeating rifle. Production problems, however, severely hampered the ability of the Spencer Repeating Rifle Company to fulfill several outstanding contracts including the contract to arm Copeland's regiment. In mid-September Copeland was informed that he would have to settle for French rifles and Sharps carbines. Infuriated, Copeland engaged Blair as well as John Robertson, the state's adjutant general, to press the issue with Stanton and Brig. Gen. James Ripley, Chief of Ordinance in Washington. The combined pressure resulted in Ripley informing Copeland a month later that he would receive the Spencer Rifles "as each hundred is made." Still, delays continued to plague production of the weapons. While Copeland expected to receive the first delivery in early November the first of the rifles was not shipped to Detroit until December 2, arriving after the regiment had left for the nation's capital.[12]

The weapons had fascinated local correspondents since they first announced that Copeland had been granted authority to raise the regiment. "From the manner in which it is to be armed it will undoubtedly be one of the most valuable and efficient regiments in the service," declared one editor in September. The same paper later pronounced that the new regiment was "to be armed in a particular manner, so as to cope with the famous rebel cavalry under General Stuart." By December 6, 1862, a limited number of the weapons had arrived and the curiosity of the press was satisfied as they finally had an opportunity to examine them, leading one correspondent to assert, "it is the neatest weapon we have seen." The command had received the very first of the rifles that were produced, "hence no regiment is armed so well as this regiment," though it would be weeks before the entire allotment arrived.[13]

Colonel Gray's regiment was armed initially with .44 caliber Colt revolvers and sabers as well as French rifles. By early 1863 these rifles had been replaced by 300 Spencer rifles that had been allocated for the 5th but were no longer needed by the time they were manufactured due to attrition within that regiment. Burnside carbines, a single-shot breechloading weapon that Ambrose Burnside had invented prior to the war, supplemented the Spencers. This weapon was produced in large numbers, lagging behind only the Spencer and the Sharps carbines in total production. The Burnside received mixed reviews from the troopers in the field, though, in general, most approved of the weapon and some actually preferred the Burnside over the Spencer because of its lighter weight.[14]

Governor Austin Blair. A staunch abolitionist and an early supporter of Abraham Lincoln, Blair had, at times, a contentious relationship with Congressman Kellogg as each sought to control the process by which the Michigan regiments were raised and officered (Library of Congress).

Four days after the 6th Michigan was mustered into service in Grand Rapids the officers and men of the 5th Michigan presented William Mann, now a lieutenant colonel, with a Kentucky thoroughbred—"a noble animal" in Mann's words — in recognition of his efforts and kindness while helping to organize the regiment. After a brief trip to Washington, Mann returned to Grand Rapids to take command of the 7th Michigan, a regiment that he was told already exceeded 1,000 men in camp. Instead he found just over 200. Consumed by his desire to be senior to Gray, a hope that was now gone, Mann admitted to being downcast and considered resigning his commission but "ambition, tastes, nervous energy, or patriotism, whatever it may have been, would not allow this view to prevail." Determined to succeed he hired a brass band to stir the hearts of young men at enlistment rallies, and when the first enlistees were mustered on November 14, he gave them furloughs and encouraged them to go home and seek additional recruits. In short he "made all the noise possible" to draw men into the ranks, but it would be several months before the 7th Michigan could be fully mustered or, as he put it, before he could be mustered as colonel. It was not until July 1863, that the regiment reached its full strength of 12 companies.[15]

During his time in Washington, Mann had seen to the armament of the regiment, guided by his mounted rifles or mounted infantry theory. Short-barreled British Enfield rifles were ordered, along with Colt revolvers and light cavalry sabers that the men would secure to their saddles to enhance their ability to fight on foot. By late November several crates of weapons had arrived, but the men were disappointed to find that they were muzzleloaders and "not the same kind that were promised." None of these weapons appear on early ordinance returns for the regiment, the records showing instead that the Burnside carbine was distributed on a limited basis in early 1863. The returns suggest that Mann's attempt to equip the 7th Michigan as mounted infantry did not last long, but instead it became a light cavalry or saber regiment whose men were never supplied with carbines in large numbers.[16]

In an attempt to speed recruitment in the regiment the editor of the Detroit *Advertiser & Tribune* spoke of Mann as "one of the best cavalry men we have in the State," describing him as "a young officer of daring and activity, who moves about with open eyes and is never caught napping," and concluding, "No one who enlists in his regiment will be disappointed in the picture we have drawn of him." And indeed Mann was a man of energy, enthusiasm and ideas, although one of his non-commissioned officers stated that he was more comfortable in the presence of his division commander than he was around his colonel. Mann continually sought new methods of bolstering the morale of his men. He supplemented the pay for his band members out of his own pocket, and later, as the regiment was preparing to head to Washington, he created what he called the "Guard of Honor." This was a small group of men, one from each company, selected for their "great courage, sobriety and physical development," that were entitled to wear a special medal that he commissioned. These men, who were honor bound not to consume alcohol, helped maintain discipline in the ranks and usually rode with the colonel while on the march. The creation of this unit may have developed after a band of intoxicated soldiers from the regiment created a drunken "fracas" in Grand Rapids, resulting in property damage to homes and businesses as well as minor injuries to several soldiers and citizens. "Such events," reported a local paper, "cause increasing ill will between the soldiers and citizens," and Colonel Mann was called on to "correct the evil as far as possible."[17]

In an attempt to bolster Copeland's quest for a brigadier's star and to nurture *esprit de corps*, Congressman Francis Kellogg raised the idea of brigading the three new regiments together. "The officers & myself would like to have these troops constitute a Brigade & have Col. Copeland [appointed] to the command of them." The local press immediately endorsed the idea of a Michigan cavalry brigade. "Let all who have a desire for cavalry service at once volunteer," one editor declared, "as this branch of the service is destined to play no mean part in the events of the next few months. In the event of [these] regiments being brigaded, we feel sure that they will win a name for Michigan such as she nor any other State has won."[18]

While they waited for orders from the War Department that would determine their future, the men of the 5th and 6th Michigan drilled incessantly, by company, battalion and regiment. They spent months learning the intricacies of dismounted drill, and the recruits in the 6th learned how to handle the saber. After their horses arrived, the men added mounted drill to their daily routine. Gershom Mattoon of the 6th noted that the first shipment of horses for the regiment were divided by color to distinguish the different companies and within days the men were riding across country. On November 20, the men of the 5th had "cause to morn the loss of one of her most promising young officers." Company K was returning from drill several days earlier when the officers decided to run their horses. During the race Lt. Henry Pettee's animal stumbled and fell on top of him, causing fatal injuries.[19]

Early in the fall one of the men in the 7th Michigan described an evening dress parade involving more than 1000 men on horseback and declared, "It looks pretty nice to see them all in one line, but it is not so easy to be in one line." Rebecca Richmond, a resident of Grand Rapids and a cousin of Elizabeth Bacon, the future wife of George Custer, could observe the cavalry camps from her home and noted that "the evolutions of the troops furnish entertainment for me, to say nothing of the fine brass band which performs daily at dress parade." By late November, however, even though bad weather and the constant drilling by thousands of men and horses had churned the camp grounds into a sea of mud, Gershom Mattoon was confident in telling his family, "It begins took look quite military around here," as the men supplemented their drilling by building barracks to see them through the winter.[20]

On November 26, Governor Blair notified General Halleck that the 5th and 6th Michigan were ready to take the field and he inquired, "to which army do you want them sent?" Orders arrived the same day directing the 5th Michigan to head for Washington, and they left Detroit on the fourth of December. As the 6th prepared to leave there was a great deal of grumbling and dissatisfaction among the men after they learned that they would not be paid until they reached Washington, but a dinner for the men, prepared by the ladies of Grand Rapids may have eased the complaints. On December 10, the regiment left Camp Kellogg. Neither regiment had as yet received their full complement of arms, but unlike other regiments that had been hastily raised and assembled under the same call for troops that summer and then thrown into the crucible of combat within days of organizing, these young men had had the benefit of several months of drill, as well as time to grow accustomed to the routines and rigors of camp life. Only the test of battle would make them soldiers and as they arrived in the nation's capital "the thunder of Burnside's guns" along the Rappahannock River at Fredericksburg "welcomed" them, promising that the ultimate test was not far off.[21]

Just as the men were hustling through camp packing their equipment and writing their last letters home it was announced that Joseph Copeland had been promoted to the rank of brigadier general. Later, after the general's death, Mann would be publicly critical of him for having spent months in Washington lobbying for the appointment while Mann and others saw to the organization of the regiments back in Michigan. Though this criticism was largely unfair, the appointment was the result of an effort that had taken several months.

Copeland had secured endorsements from politicians, prominent citizens and business leaders as well as from fellow officers, including Mann, who called him "an excellent officer," and declared, "it will be my highest pleasure to serve under him as commander of the Brigade."[22]

Undoubtedly Copeland understood that the opportunity to secure a brigadier's commission would be enhanced if the three new regiments were brigaded together, and so he combined the two goals into one package that was repeatedly presented to the War Department. "The officers and men of the Michigan 5th, 6th and 7th Cavalry are desirous of being formed into a Brigade, and to have Col. Copeland ... to command them," the editor of the Detroit *Advertiser & Tribune* told Stanton in mid–November. "Col. [Copeland] has earned some reputation as *the real* commander of the Mich. 1st Cavalry, although only 2nd in rank. This with his efficiency in organizing the 5th Cav., and his *known* devotion to the cause in which he is engaged, added to his capacity, lead his friends to hope that he may receive the appointment asked for." Now as the new recruits headed off toward an uncertain future their morale was bolstered by the news that a veteran cavalry officer would be there to lead them when they arrived.[23]

3

December 1–December 20, 1862

"The same old coon"

"It's pretty tough on soldiers in the face of an enemy standing picket these cold nights," Alfred Ryder reminded his friends in Michigan. The picket posts scattered around Dranesville had been established for some weeks and Charles Johnson, 1st Michigan, was certain, that regardless of the weather, the men enjoyed better health "out in the field than when in camp." Johnson and his comrades pondered their future as rumors moved through the camp that the regiment was to "be discharged for there is not men enough to constitute a Colonels command left in the [regiment]." Other gossip had the men being ordered into the capital to patrol the city as some were already doing in Alexandria. One detachment was ordered to meet a pontoon train of 75 wagons on the morning of December 5, at the corner of King and Patrick streets in Alexandria. The Wolverines were to escort the pontoons as far south as Aquia Creek, the main supply depot for the Army of the Potomac. Colonel Town was further directed to have another battalion of men from the regiment report at Fort Runyon that same morning to protect a herd of cattle that was also en route to Aquia. This latter directive came after Brig. Gen. Daniel Sickles, commanding the Second Division, Third Corps, now at Falmouth, advised that the cattle would be in danger "from the Prince William and Stafford Guerrillas," and recommended that at least four companies of cavalry be ordered to escort the herd.[1]

As the winter months advanced Jeb Stuart increasingly dispersed his cavalry to ease the burden on his own commissary and quartermaster departments, and he authorized several companies to conduct guerrilla operations. One of these was Company H, 4th Virginia Cavalry. Another may have been Company H, of the 15th Virginia Cavalry, known as the Prince William Rangers or Chincapin Rangers. This unit was organized in May 1862, to serve as partisans and would do so for much of the war, even after they were assigned to the regiment that fall. That many of the men were from either Prince William or Fairfax counties made them a natural choice to conduct guerrilla operations in that region. Less well known was George Handley, Co. H, 1st North Carolina Cavalry, who was operating behind the lines with ten men, officially as a scout, but contemporary accounts confirm that he was also conducting guerrilla operations in this region.[2]

On December 9, Burnside ordered Maj. Gen. Henry Slocum to move his Twelfth Corps south from Harpers Ferry as quickly as possible, directing him to move by way of Leesburg, Gum Spring and Centreville to Wolf Run Shoals, a heavily used ford on the

Occoquan River. At the same time Maj. Gen. Franz Sigel was to move his Eleventh Corps out of Fairfax County, by way of Wolf Run Shoals, and linkup with the Army of the Potomac. He was to leave behind a strong rear-guard until Slocum arrived, but he was to take with him the several mounted regiments attached to his corps, including the 9th New York. In an effort to replace these troopers Colonel Price, along with the small command under Percy Wyndham, was ordered to extend his already overtaxed brigade and assume the duties that Sigel's men relinquished. Once Slocum reached the Occoquan he would be attached to Sigel, with the two corps forming the Grand Reserve Division under Sigel's command.[3]

On the eleventh Sigel had his command fording Wolf Run Shoals en route for Dumfries with his cavalry moving by way of Manassas Junction and Brentsville, protecting his right flank. He suggested that Heintzelman move another brigade of infantry up to assist the troops in southwestern Fairfax, and Heintzelman agreed, ordering Brig. Gen. Edwin Stoughton to move his brigade of Vermonters into positions along the Occoquan. To supplement Price's troopers Halleck directed that the recently arrived 5th and 6th Michigan Cavalry be prepared to take the field as quickly as possible.[4]

That evening, in anticipation of Sigel's arrival, a telegraph operator along with an escort of 25 men from the 10th New York Cavalry arrived in Dumfries to establish a telegraph office. The following morning as Sigel started his corps toward Dumfries he sent word that should the town be threatened by the enemy in superior force before he arrived the operator had the option of falling back either south to Aquia or north toward Occoquan. By the time the message arrived, however, it was almost certainly too late.[5]

Established in 1749 near the head of navigation on Quantico Creek and along the main north-south road, Dumfries was the oldest town in Prince William County and it enjoyed a brief but storied period when "it was considered to be one of the most prosperous communities on the eastern seaboard." Much of the town's success stemmed from the shipment of tobacco through its port, but when sediment began to fill in the creek, and other modes of travel, including the railroad, bypassed the town, it fell into a steady decline. In 1822 the county courthouse was moved and by 1862 the town, which had long since seen its best days, had become a source of constant ridicule for the troops who passed through.[6]

Capt. Charles Adams, 1st Massachusetts Cavalry, an acerbic Boston blue-blood who seemed to take great pleasure in speaking poorly of everyone and everything, described the town as "the most God-forsaken village I ever saw ... even the inhabitants ... seemed relapsing into barbarism.... The very dogs are curs and the women and children ... seem the proper inmates of the dilapidated log cabins which they hold in common with the long-nosed lank Virginia swine." A Southern correspondent made a similar observation earlier in war, concluding, "I have never seen a more desolate, God forsaken looking town." On December 12, however, this town, which appeared as though it "had been built at the creation of the world," would once again make headlines.[7]

Brig. Gen. Wade Hampton was a bear of a man from Charleston, South Carolina. He had served several terms in the state legislature and devoted much of his time to family plantations in both South Carolina and Mississippi, but he had no formal military training. At the onset of hostilities he had raised and equipped a force known as the Hampton Legion. Participating in all of the major engagements in the east he received minor wounds at First

Manassas and Seven Pines and was promoted to the rank of brigadier general in May 1862. Two months later he took command of a cavalry brigade with the proviso that he could return to the infantry if he so chose. He was offered the opportunity of returning to the infantry upon the death of fellow South Carolinian Maxey Gregg at Fredericksburg but he declined. He remained with the cavalry throughout the conflict, and rose to the rank of lieutenant general and the command of all of Lee's cavalry by the end of the war.[8]

In early December, Hampton, who had been harassing Union outposts along the Rappahannock, was instructed to make a strike at Dumfries in an effort to disrupt the flow of supplies along the Telegraph Road and to seize any goods that he might find in the town. He set out on the tenth with 520 men from five regiments that he split into two small brigades. Col. Matthew C. Butler was in command of detachments from the 1st North Carolina, 2nd South Carolina and the Cobb Legion Cavalry. Lt. Col. Will Martin led the second unit, including men from his own Jeff Davis Legion and the 1st South Carolina. After a late start on the tenth, they moved through the day on the eleventh and bivouacked for a few hours late that evening. In the morning they marched 16 miles and approached the town shortly before five o'clock.[9]

Brig. Gen. Wade Hampton led several raids against the Union supply line between the towns of Occoquan and Dumfries during the fall of 1862. These raids forced the Federals to alter their supply route just before Maj. Gen. Jeb Stuart launched his Christmas Raid, which was largely empty of success as a result (Library of Congress).

Hampton elected to send Colonel Butler in from the north while holding Martin's command in reserve along the Telegraph Road between the town and Occoquan. When Butler's men charged into the town they "found everything and everybody asleep," including the just arrived cavalry contingent that had taken shelter in a large shed alongside the main road. Once the town was secured and the telegraph lines cut, pickets were established and a rider was dispatched to notify Hampton, who was with Martin, of their success. The men then set about securing their prisoners as well as 24 sutlers' wagons "loaded down with almost every variety of goods, eatables, drinkables, confectionaries, buckskin gauntlets, boots, shoes, hats, choicest underwear, etc." Christmas had come a few weeks early for the Southern troopers.[10]

The jubilation was short-lived as his pickets alerted Hampton to the appearance of Union infantry on the horizon to the north, and he was forced to forgo an attempt to capture another body of enemy troops nearby. Burning two wagons that were without teams to pull them, Hampton secured his prisoners and had his command on the road three hours after they had entered the town. They spent the night at Morrisville, near the Rappahannock River, where they divided up the spoils of war.[11]

Sigel had his lead division on the road early and they soon came in sight of the Southern cavalry "hovering" north of the town. Uncertain if a rebel infantry force might be behind the cavalry the foot soldiers approached cautiously and then found the road blockaded to such an extent that it would have taken several hours to clear. They sought a side road instead, but made no better time slogging through thick mud. It was not until ten o'clock that they entered Dumfries, without engaging Hampton as was initially reported.[12]

The timing and target of this raid was remarkable but almost certainly not a matter of happenstance. Stuart's cavalry excelled at intelligence gathering and the men that he drew from the ranks to serve as scouts were without equal. Dumfries sat between the line patrolled by the Army of the Potomac and Heintzelman's southern-most pickets, and the heavily wooded terrain to the north and west became a haven for guerrilla activity over the winter. One unit in particular that operated almost exclusively in this area over the coming months was a rather loosely knit group of men drawn from Hampton's brigade known as the Iron Scouts. Their involvement in this attack is unstated but almost certain. They frequented the vicinity of Maple Valley and Greenwood Church, in Prince William County between Occoquan and Dumfries; an area where two Union stragglers had recently been captured and from where they could shadow George Bayard's cavalry brigade that was camped nearby. They may have learned from these prisoners that Bayard was awaiting the arrival of the pontoon train and the cattle herd, though it is unknown if either was Hampton's objective. When Bayard returned to Falmouth on the ninth the cattle were safely within the Union lines, but that Hampton crossed the river the very next day and struck the town during a very narrow window of opportunity following Bayard's departure and before Sigel's infantry arrived suggests the precise timing of the attack.

General Stoughton received instructions late on the eleventh that his brigade, consisting of the 12th, 13th, 14th, 15th and 16th Vermont Infantry, be ready "to march at two hours notice." Their camps south of Alexandria were soon a hive of activity as the nine-month men prepared to move closer to the front lines. Shortly after five o'clock the next morning the brigade was in motion, with the 15th Vermont in the lead. Seven hours later the men began arriving at Fairfax Court House, and went into camp just outside the town. Before the foot-sore men could even cook dinner, however, Col. Wheelock Veazey, commanding the 16th Vermont, was directed to have his men ready to move to Centreville in the morning to relieve a regiment that had just lost two men to guerrillas. This news heightened expectations that there might be "some excitement in picketing out there," and raised concerns in Stoughton's mind for their safety. He urged that at least one cavalry regiment be ordered to his assistance, using Centreville as an outpost and establishing their own line of pickets in advance of his infantry. In response, Colonel Price reminded Stoughton that the 5th New York Cavalry was headquartered at Chantilly and the 1st West Virginia at Centreville, under the overall command of Colonel Wyndham. To further allay the general's concerns Price dispatched Peter Stagg to Wolf Run Shoals with 150 men of the 1st Michigan, with a second detachment to follow shortly thereafter. Lt. Col. Joseph Brinton, 2nd Pennsylvania, was put in overall command of the mounted pickets covering the line from Wolf Run Shoals to the mouth of the Occoquan.[13]

Although Fairfax Court House had remained the county seat, there is little to suggest that the town made a better impression on the troops when they arrived than did the forgotten town of Dumfries, in Prince William County. With few visible reminders that it once possessed "considerable hereditary pride and importance," Fairfax Court House was seen as a town whose "glory had departed." "You cannot tell how awful it is for such armies to pass over a country," one Federal officer had remarked in October, and Fairfax Court House had seen much of the two armies. "The soldiers will destroy all of the fences and most of the outhouses.... All of the pews from the churches, pulpits, stairs and alters are taken from them. Even the floors are taken up and all the tables, chairs, stairways and gallery are taken for fuel from the old court house.... Almost everybody is ruined. If they are Rebs, Union soldiers delight to destroy. If they are Unionists the Reb soldiers delight to destroy their property. No one escapes." Lt. Col. Charles Cummings, 16th Vermont, thought there was "scarcely any other place in Virginia around which more or pleasanter associations cluster and linger than about this old place, but its fragrance is now flagrantly odious."[14]

As Stoughton's men settled into their news camps they watched as the road-weary veterans of the Twelfth Corps trudged past. George Benedict, 12th Vermont, described the continuing troop movements as resembling "moves on the big chess board of which States and counties are the squares and divisions and brigades the pieces." That evening Brig. Gen. John Geary's division lay along the Occoquan River with the remainder of the corps strung out behind him. In the morning Geary led his command across the stream, slogging through the mire along the road to Dumfries. After an equally difficult march Brig. Gen. Alpheus Williams bivouacked his division along the Occoquan, after establishing a forward position on the south side near Bacon Race Church.[15]

Heavy rains throughout the night and into the following day did little to ease the mood of the men as they learned of Burnside's defeat of the thirteenth. "The disaster at Fredericksburg affects us all deeply," Williams admitted. "I am as discouraged and blue as one can be, as I see in these operations much that astonishes and confounds me and much that must discourage our troops and the people." In the capital one officer watched as ambulances trains carried the wounded from boats to hospitals, all the while dodging fresh troops preparing to head south. "I would not be surprised to see all the available force around the Capitol ordered forward," he remarked.[16]

One of the new regiments swept up in the rush to reinforce Burnside was Col. John Irvin Gregg's 16th Pennsylvania Cavalry. The orders caught Gregg totally unprepared, as two-thirds of his horses were unshod, several companies were without saddles and his men who had just received their carbines the day before were without the shoulder slings necessary to carry the weapons. Moreover none of the men had been trained in the use of the weapons and Gregg, who was without even a map of the route he was to take, warned his superiors, "I am controlling a mob of undisciplined men without a single officer of experience to aid me." In the end reason prevailed and the order was rescinded. The 5th Michigan Cavalry was also instructed to be ready to move to Fairfax Court House on short notice. The men were "immensely pleased" to learn that they would finally receive their Spencer rifles, and they looked forward to getting "into active service as soon as possible."[17]

On the sixteenth Geary's division camped on the outskirts of Dumfries after a wretched march through rain and mud. At the rear of the column was the brigade commanded by Col. Charles Candy that had been given the miserable task of assisting the supply wagons through the axle-deep quagmire. The following day it took six hours to march the remaining two miles into Dumfries, after which Geary received disconcerting orders to return to Fairfax

Station. Candy's brigade arrived in the town about noon on the seventeenth and one officer immediately questioned, "What on the face of the earth ever made a sensible man pick out this place in early times for settlement, beats me, for if ever there was a God forsaken looking place it is this." When Geary returned to Fairfax Station he left Colonel Candy and his brigade behind to garrison the town.[18]

The steady flow of troops and supplies through the towns of Occoquan and Dumfries presented a target that Hampton could not resist. On the seventeenth, he pulled together 475 men from six regiments and crossed the Rappahannock headed east. The men were not informed where they were going but Maj. William Deloney, commanding the detachment from Cobb's Legion, was certain they were in search of "reliable information or catching Yankees." At daylight on the nineteenth Hampton was at Kanky's Store, along the Telegraph Road at the crossing of Neabsco Creek, where he captured two cavalry picket posts, totaling 35 men and one officer from Company F, 10th New York, along with eight wagons, but was disappointed to find all but two of them empty.[19]

Hampton now cast his eye on the town of Occoquan and divided his command into three columns, sending Major Deloney along the Telegraph Road while Col. Will Martin moved by his right. Hampton took the third column and advanced on Deloney's left, along the road by Bacon Race Church toward Wolf Run Shoals. All three converged on the town just as a supply train belonging to Sigel's corps was crossing the river. The execrable condition of the roads had forced Sigel to leave the majority of his wagons behind until the mud dried, and thus his wagons were only now leaving Fairfax. A rope or cable ferry carried travelers across the river, in addition to the more commonly used fords upstream. When Colonel Martin's troopers dashed into the town, about 9 A.M., they seized the ferry as well as the train guards, just as Hampton and Deloney arrived.[20]

From these captives Hampton learned that a large body of Yankee cavalry was expected to arrive shortly at Selectman's Ford, a mile and a half above the town. This was the newly organized and recently arrived 17th Pennsylvania Cavalry. Led by Col. Josiah Kellogg, the regiment was one of many now headed south to reinforce the army. Accompanying Kellogg was Col. Richard Rush and two companies of his veteran 6th Pennsylvania Cavalry, as well as a small detachment from the 12th Illinois Cavalry. To meet this threat Hampton sent Capt. Tillman H. Clarke, 2nd South Carolina, with 40 sharpshooters from his own command as well as from the Phillips Legion, to the ford as a holding force until all of the captured wagons could be ferried across the river. But Hampton's intelligence was only partly correct, and, with the wagon train not yet fully secured, he was surprised when the Pennsylvanians appeared on the far bank.[21]

Colonel Kellogg was equally surprised as he approached the town, and was met with a "brisk" volley of gunfire from Confederates posted along both sides of the river. Union pickets stationed at Accotink, five miles north of the river, had assured Kellogg that the road was clear. He was riding at the head of the column when Hampton's men opened fire from the woods bordering both sides of the road. Kellogg's horse was wounded along with a man riding alongside him before the Federals could react. This allowed Hampton to withdraw his men from the north side of the river and to secure the wagon that was already on the ferry. Kellogg and Rush now found themselves at a disadvantage as none of their men were armed with carbines; Kellogg's men carried only revolvers that had been issued just prior to leaving Washington, while the Pennsylvanians were armed with nine-foot-long lances, topped with an eleven-inch steel blade. Kellogg, with a detachment of men from the 17th Pennsylvania, and 20 men from the 12th Illinois, the only men armed with carbines, held the main road while Rush attempted to flank Hampton by way of Selectman's Ford. Kellogg engaged the Confederates briefly but he was again driven back by heavy fire and withdrew out of range. A sutler, who escaped capture by ducking into a home in the town and posing as a friend of the owner, noted that the "bullets were flying about the streets quite briskly."[22]

Reaching the ford upstream Rush found Clarke's sharpshooters posted on high ground along the far bank. As Rush deployed his men, Clarke dispatched a rider to notify Hampton of this new threat, and the general wisely chose to abandon any further attempts to secure the remaining wagons. Sinking the ferry and calling in his own pickets, he started his column toward Greenwood Church, leaving Captain Clarke with orders to hold the ford for an hour before retiring. Rush, who had few options once he reached the ford other than attack, sent his Lancers and a detail from the 17th Pennsylvania across the river but Clarke's small command fought a resolute delaying action, allowing the wagons to be moved to safety.[23]

"The same old coon," as one North Carolinian referred to Hampton, had done it again. He had pierced the very heart of the Union supply route so efficiently that the "careless" men of the 2nd Pennsylvania had informed Kellogg and Rush that the route through Occoquan was "quiet and safe." Once he was back within Confederate lines Hampton tallied his captures, including 150 prisoners, 20 wagons, several hundred horses and mules and one cavalry guidon, sustaining no loss himself. One other wagon was burned but the Federals recovered 12 before they could be ferried across the river.[24]

In the morning, Kellogg took half of his regiment and scouted the area through Maple Valley and Greenwood Church toward Brentsville but found no sign of Hampton's force. Colonel Rush spent the day raising the sunken ferry and interviewing residents of the town. It was his belief that the sutler's wagons were Hampton's target, and that Sigel's wagons "happening to be there at the same time fell into their hands" as well. He also suspected that one of the sutler's wagons was actually part of a smuggling operation that provided needed materiel for the Confederates. In view of this second attack against Burnside's supply line in a week, General Halleck ordered that all supply trains not sent south by water would travel through Maryland and be ferried across the river rather than risk capture in Virginia.[25]

On the eighteenth, Colonel Asa Blunt's 12th Vermont Infantry rotated to the forward post at Centreville to relieve the 16th Vermont. When they reached the crossroads the right wing of the command marched another three miles before reaching the picket lines along Cub Run. The 1st West Virginia Cavalry patrolled the "debatable ground" in their front, sending out daily patrols and "alone disputing its possession with the enemy." That very afternoon and evening the Vermonters received a taste of life along the front lines. First, they were informed that "a secesh soldier in citizen's clothes" was within the lines making inquiries about the strength of their pickets. A detail was sent after him but he eluded capture. A "suspicious looking box" was later located in a barn, but on closer examination it was found to be an occupied coffin. That evening gunshots among the cavalry pickets roused the men and sent them scrambling for their weapons and running for the stream where voices could be heard. Other shots were fired along their line before the excitement died away. In the morning a wild-eyed trooper came into camp claiming that Lige White's cavalry had attacked his post, capturing all of their horses and seven or eight men.[26]

Alfred Ryder, 1st Michigan Cavalry, explained to his father, "You may think [us too] near Washington to have trouble with rebles or be even anxious about them but it is a fact that we have a little fight with them nearly every day." The increasing activity along the outer picket line left Brig. Gen. John Abercrombie, commanding an infantry division posted in Fairfax County, fearful that the enemy might "make a cavalry dash along our line of pickets in the direction of Dranesville and commit depredations before the" infantry along the interior lines could react. He also noted that his pickets had arrested several "persons connected with the Rebel army (perhaps spies)," suggesting that his lines were being probed for weak points.[27]

4

December 21–December 30, 1862

"A raid into Yankeedoodledom"

As the Christmas holiday approached there was little reason for the soldiers stationed around the capital to rejoice. The disaster at Fredericksburg left the men despondent and angry. Writing from Dranesville, Lt. George Kilborn, 1st Michigan Cavalry, declared, "our hopes have been blasted once more, our fine army badly cut up, if not demoralized, and the Rebels made jubilant." Alfred Ryder wished his mother "a Merry Christmas," but groused that he would spend another holiday eating "Hard bread & Salt junk" rather than her home cooking. Homesick and certain that his military experience had taught him how to "appreciate a free life if I ever gain it again," he wondered where the next holiday season might find him. Darius Maynard spent Christmas Eve in the capital with several friends, inspecting the city and visiting various military and government officials, including President Lincoln. He enjoyed the holiday playing billiards and smoking "innumerable cigars," certain that he "was the only sober man in Washington."[1]

Some of Stoughton's Vermonters took time around the holiday to visit the nearby battlefield at Chantilly, "partly to gratify our curiosity and partly for the humane purpose of caring for the still unburied dead." They found the field littered with the debris of battle and "gave such burial as our means afforded." John Williams, 14th Vermont, undoubtedly spoke for all of the soldiers, in both armies, when he noted in his diary on Christmas, "I was more homesick today than at any time since I enlisted in the Army."[2]

Prior to the battle at Fredericksburg Jeb Stuart established his headquarters five miles south of town along the Telegraph Road. On the twenty-third he received a welcome visit from his wife Flora, as well as from General Hampton, fresh from his successful raid on Occoquan. If Flora had expected to spend the holidays with her husband, however, her hopes were dashed when he received orders from General Lee to lead another sortie behind enemy lines to "ascertain, if possible, his position and movements, and inflict upon him such damage as circumstances will permit." Soon after these orders arrived Stuart almost certainly sat down with Hampton seeking the latest intelligence of the Federal defenses around Dumfries and Occoquan.[3]

Stuart elected to take 1800 troopers, from the brigades led by Hampton, Fitz Lee and W.H.F. "Rooney" Lee, along with six guns. Eager to strike before the Yankees could fully recover from Hampton's latest incursion, Stuart had the men rendezvous near Brandy Station on the twenty-fifth. Among the men selected for the expedition from the Jeff Davis Legion was Robert McClellan, who recorded that they set out on "a grand scout.... We expect something great to come of it — perhaps, even a raid into Yankeedoodledom."[4]

On the day that Stuart received his orders, information was received in Washington that his cavalry was "at or near Leesburg." Other reports had Southern infantry advancing on Winchester, raising concern of an imminent attack against Harpers Ferry or Point of Rocks, Maryland. In response to the reports of cavalry in brigade strength near Leesburg, General Slocum was directed to send small scouting parties to Warrenton, White Plains, Upperville, Leesburg and Snicker's Gap to confirm the information. To counter the second threat Burnside suggested that Slocum return to Harpers Ferry, though Halleck recognized that the enemy was simply attempting to force Burnside into a "game of shuttlecock, by sending troops backward and forward to Harper's Ferry," and thus he left Slocum where he was. In the midst of this confusion, a frantic call came across the telegraph wire from the operator in Dumfries, "We are attacked by a large force of cavalry.... There are several dead before my door."[5]

During his Christmas Raid of 1862, Maj. Gen. James Ewell Brown "Jeb" Stuart, commander of the Cavalry Division, Army of Northern Virginia, elected to leave John Mosby and a handful of men behind to conduct guerrilla or partisan operations against the Union lines in Northern Virginia (National Archives).

Stuart moved into Fauquier County in three columns on the twenty-sixth, reuniting about sunset at Bristersburg for the night. In the morning a short march brought them into Prince William County. Stuart intended to cut a wide section of the Telegraph Road between Occoquan and Aquia Church, and he again divided his command into three columns. Hampton, moving along Stuart's left flank, marched almost due east through familiar territory to strike again at Occoquan. Fitz Lee was farthest south, comprising the right flank, and his orders were to cut the Telegraph Road below Dumfries near Chopawamsic Creek. He was then to turn north, uniting with Rooney Lee's center column in a strike against Dumfries.[6]

"Everything glided on quietly" until about noon when Rooney Lee struck a Union infantry outpost just south of Dumfries near a mill owned by Dr. Richard Wheat. Lee ordered Capt. Stith Bolling's Company G, 9th Virginia, to charge and capture the pickets from Col. Charles Candy's brigade of Buckeyes. The majority of the Federals were seized, but several escaped and warned the garrison. Candy sent Capt. Joseph Cook, with his detachment of the 1st Maryland Cavalry to investigate, but they were quickly turned back by heavy fire from Bolling's Virginians, who were now supported by the remainder of the regiment.[7]

Alerted to Stuart's intentions, Candy, whom the Southern press later referred to as "a low, vulgar scoundrel and petty tyrant," called out his brigade, sending the 7th Ohio forward to block the approach from the south. Col. William Creighton commanded the regiment, but he was in charge of the brigade picket line that morning, leaving Maj. Orrin Crane in command of the regiment. The 5th Ohio, led by Col. John Patrick, was ordered to support Lt. William Rogers and his section of guns of the 6th Maine Battery near the former courthouse. Lt. Col. Eugene Powell was initially directed to deploy his 66th Ohio to the right of the town to block any approach along the Brentsville Road. The 7th Ohio arrived just in time to relieve Cook's overmatched cavalry. Holding the Telegraph Road with their left flank Crane's Buckeyes locked their bayonets in place as they pushed forward. Once they encountered the sharpshooters from the 9th Virginia they poured "volley after volley" into their position forcing the Virginians to retire. With this immediate threat eliminated Candy ordered Crane to shift his position farther to the west.[8]

This was in response to Stuart sending Lt. Col. John Critcher to seize the Brentsville Road with his 15th Virginia Cavalry. Near the intersection of the Brentsville Road and the road past Dyer's Mill Critcher's men, including Capt. William Brawner's Prince William Rangers, surprised a picket force of 24 men of the 12th Illinois Cavalry, under the command of Lt. John Clybourn. Critcher deployed his men to attack the Federals from front and back simultaneously, but Clybourn was able to fall back into a patch of heavy brush, possibly on the farm of Mahlon Lindsley. The Yankees fought dismounted but were overpowered and captured, with only one man escaping to alert the Federals to the new threat.[9]

To the south, Fitz Lee cut the Telegraph Road as instructed and turned north with Capt. John Washington Bullock, 5th Virginia Cavalry, leading the advance. Within minutes Bullock encountered a patrol of seven men from the 12th Illinois, led by Sgt. James Crowe, who later stated that Bullock's men were wearing Yankee overcoats. Crowe sent one man spurring back to warn Candy, and then attempted to make a stand, but his small party was soon routed. Two men were captured and the remainder scattered, including the sergeant who escaped on foot after his horse was killed. Bullock followed this success by pushing his advance up the Telegraph Road and was rewarded with the capture of nine well-stocked sutler's wagons.[10]

Sergeant Crowe's squad was the link between Dumfries and the Union forces at Aquia and Falmouth, including the 1st Connecticut Cavalry that maintained a daily patrol north toward Dumfries. Possibly alerted by the brief exchange of gunfire when Crowe's patrol was overrun the Connecticut troopers captured Pvt. Hiram L. Leister, Company H, 2nd North Carolina Cavalry, near the home of Dr. James Ford, south of Chopawamsic Creek in Stafford County, and then noticed the tracks of Lee's brigade along the Telegraph Road. The prisoner bragged that Stuart, with a brigade of cavalry supported by artillery, was planning "to have some fun at Dumfries." As soon as he was notified of the situation Col. Alexander Schimmelfennig, commanding a brigade of the Eleventh Corps near Aquia, sent couriers to warn his superiors and ordered a fresh cavalry detachment to tail the Confederates. He also sought permission to march north with his command but it took five hours for his request to be

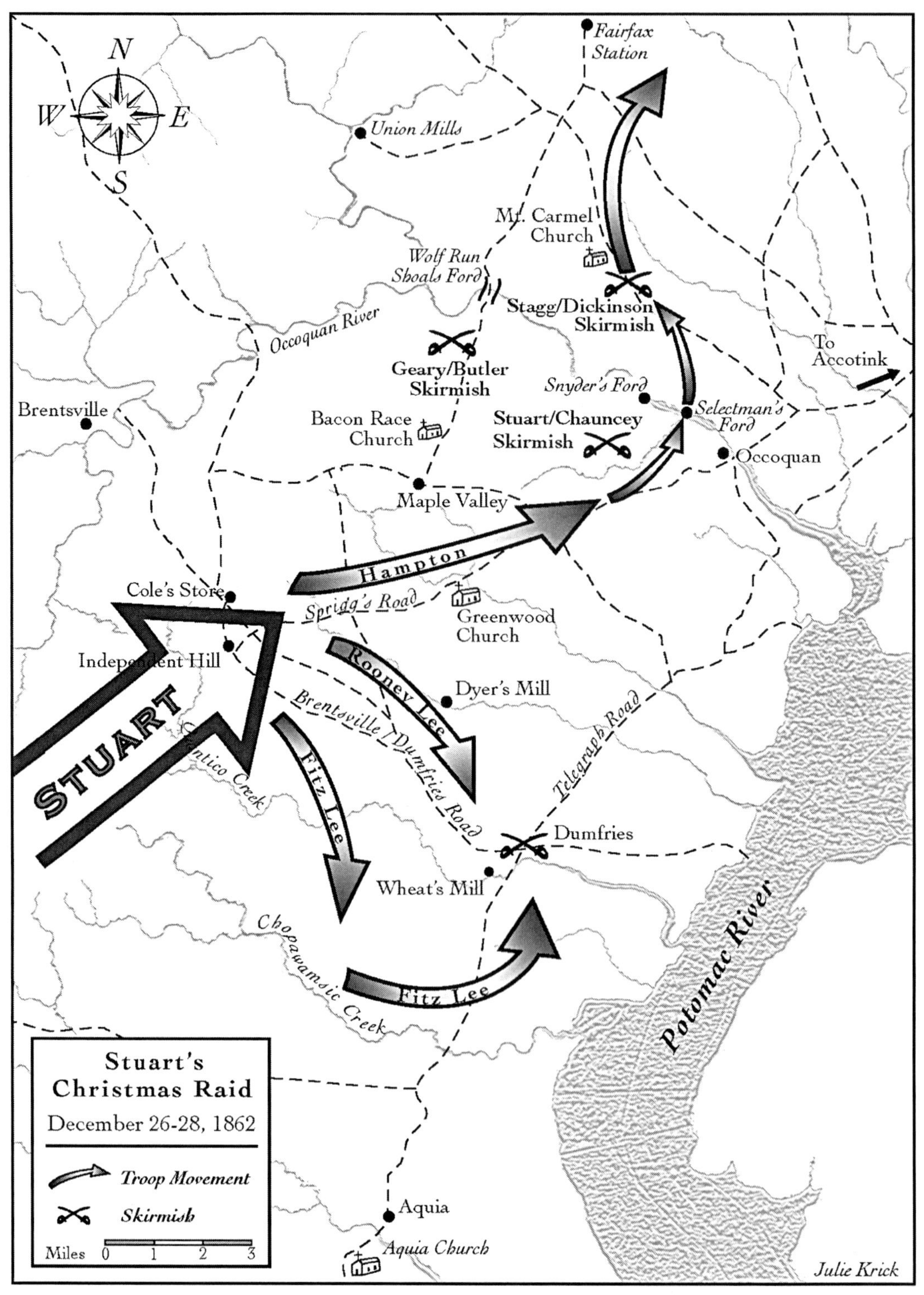

N
W
E
S
Fairfax Station
Union Mills
Mt. Carmel Church
Wolf Run Shoals Ford
Stagg/Dickinson Skirmish
Occoquan River
Geary/Butler Skirmish
To Accotink
Snyder's Ford
Brentsville
Bacon Race Church
Stuart/Chauncey Skirmish
Selectman's Ford
Occoquan
Maple Valley
Hampton
Cole's Store
Spridg's Road
Greenwood Church
Independent Hill
Rooney Lee
Dyer's Mill
Brentsville / Dumfries Road
Telegraph Road
STUART
Fitz Lee
Dumfries
Wheat's Mill
Chopawamsic Creek
Fitz Lee
Potomac River
Stuart's Christmas Raid
December 26-28, 1862
Troop Movement
Skirmish
Miles 0 1 2 3
Aquia
Aquia Church
Julie Krick

approved and by then it was too late. It was not until one-thirty the following morning that he was able to reach the vicinity of the engagement.[11]

When Fitz Lee arrived, Stuart determined to seize the town. He ordered Lee to divide his brigade sending the 1st and 5th Virginia to attack from the west while the 2nd Virginia crossed Quantico Creek and attacked from the south and east. The 3rd Virginia was held as a rear guard in the event that a Federal relief party should arrive from Aquia. Capt. James Breathed's section of the 1st Stuart Horse Artillery arrived with Lee and supported the attack alongside the guns of Captain Mathis Henry's 2nd Stuart Horse Artillery, which had been shelling the Federal positions for several hours. By this time Colonel Candy had deployed the majority of his brigade along high ground that dominated the town and gave his men every defensive advantage. The attack was to start on the left, drawing the attention of the defenders in that direction at which time the 2nd Virginia would cross the creek and seize the town. When Col. Tom Rosser, leading the 5th Virginia, and Col. James Drake, commanding the 1st Virginia, launched their attack, it quickly became evident that they would have no chance against the Federal infantry. One defender termed the assault "ineffectual," and stated that the Rebels were greeted by "a severe, unexpected fire" from the infantry that drove them back in confusion. The venture was almost immediately called off, but not before Captain Bullock, remembered as a "brave and noble spirit," was mortally wounded.[12]

According to Stuart the aborted attack cost Fitz Lee one officer wounded, in addition to Bullock, as well as one enlisted man, 12 men missing and the loss of three horses killed against the 50 men and nine fully laden wagons and teams seized earlier. In addition to the pickets captured outside the town the Federals lost about 30 men, including three men killed and 12 wounded. Northern news accounts reported that several buildings recently occupied by Union forces as well as "several other houses" in the town were "demolished" by the shelling from Stuart's gunners. The Confederates held their positions until dark when they withdrew along the Brentsville Road. Stuart, with Fitz Lee's brigade, continued to Cole's Store near Independent Hill. Rooney Lee took a more advanced position four miles to the east near Greenwood Church for the night. In order to prevent encumbering his command with the wagons and prisoners Stuart sent them to Culpeper, escorted by the 3rd Virginia under Lt. Col. William Carter. He was relieved of the task later that evening by Capt. Orlando Smith and a squadron of the 9th Virginia Cavalry.[13]

The road intersection known as Cole's Store was a natural point to encounter a strong picket force and as Hampton moved east that morning he observed 15 Union troopers posted nearby. He pulled 25 men from the ranks and instructed them to come in behind the pickets while he "drove them in" with an additional 20 men. The plan fell apart, however, when the larger party got lost and the majority of the Yankee sentinels escaped, leaving four men in Southern hands.[14]

Nearing the town of Occoquan Hampton split his force, sending Col. Matthew Butler with half the brigade by the Telegraph Road, while he approached the town along the river with the remainder of his command. Hampton hoped to be able to get into position to block the retreat routes out of the town before Butler launched his assault, but with daylight waning Butler galloped into the town before Hampton was in position, allowing the majority of startled Yankees to escape. In the words of one Virginian these "Pennsylvania [sour-kraut] Dutch cavalry ... skedaddled, firing their pistols off without being particular in which direction." For their trouble the Rebels came away with seven wagons and a handful of prisoners from the 17th Pennsylvania. Hampton sustained the loss of only man wounded, but darkness convinced him to rejoin Stuart at Cole's Store.[15]

As the day drew to a close the Federals attempted to sort out the scattered reports as they came across the telegraph wires. Late in the afternoon, as the fighting around Dumfries had reached a climax, the telegraph operator, based on verbal instructions from Colonel Candy, confirmed that the town was under attack but provided no specifics, asking only that reinforcements be sent "at once." In response General Sigel advised Slocum, at Fairfax Court House, to "send all the cavalry you have to Dumfries." He further suggested that a brigade of infantry and a battery of guns be advanced from Wolf Run Shoals in that direction, and he asked that Slocum forward a request to Heintzelman that he dispatch cavalry toward Brentsville to threaten Stuart from the rear. Sigel also instructed Julius Stahel to send any of his available cavalry to aid Candy. Other reports came in from Wyndham at Union Mills and Stoughton at Fairfax Court House that they could hear gunfire, but these undoubtedly did little more than add to the confusion. Wyndham offered to go after Stuart with his small command, but may have been told to hold his position until the situation became more certain. John Geary was instructed to move his infantry division from Fairfax Station toward Dumfries, while Alpheus Williams blocked the ford at Wolf Run Shoals. When Williams arrived he sent one brigade across the river to set an ambush, should Stuart attempt to cross at that point. After a long, "cold and uncomfortable" night the men were withdrawn in the morning, on the assumption that Stuart had retired.[16]

The reports that came in from the Union outposts along the Occoquan River did little to alleviate the uncertainty. Fugitives arriving from Dumfries erroneously reported that Candy had lost his artillery during the day's fighting, and doubled the actual size of the enemy force. In response to Hampton's previous raids Colonel Price had pulled the detachment of the 2nd Pennsylvania Cavalry posted at Lewinsville and sent it south to support the 80 men of the regiment stationed at Accotink. These troops listened to the firing from Dumfries throughout the afternoon but were unaware of the situation at Occoquan. Price now ordered the command, about 240 strong, to strengthen the pickets along the river, both at the town and upstream at Selectman's Ford. They arrived in time to fire a few hasty shots across the river as the Confederates withdrew.[17]

Stoughton's Vermonters listened to the sounds of gunfire move slowly northward during the day as the skirmishing developed first near Dumfries and later around Occoquan. The uncertainty of the situation left the men "in quite a stir" throughout the night. In Alexandria, the arrival of several frightened teamsters who had abandoned their wagons near Occoquan and fled with the teams created "considerable excitement" as well. The artillery fire reverberated in Washington, and combined with "exaggerated stories concerning alleged exploits of a body of Stuart's cavalry," produced "an intense ferment" throughout the capital.[18]

According to Lt. Channing Price, an aide to Stuart, the general canceled the expedition during the night, due to the worn down condition of his men and horses. It had not been the easy jaunt that Stuart expected. The reality was that the Confederates had gone to the well one too many times. The route through Dumfries had been closed, with the majority of the supplies now shipped by water or through southern Maryland, rather than Virginia. Stuart's own intelligence had let him down, as he was clearly not expecting to encounter a brigade of infantry in Dumfries. During the evening, however, Stuart received fresh, unspecified information from a man who had just come through Fairfax that changed his mind; the raid would continue. Rooney Lee's brigade had already started for the Rappahannock when Stuart received this information and he sent a rider to Lee with orders for him to return. Once the three brigades were reunited Stuart set out toward Greenwood Church, with his eye on Fairfax County. Reaching the church Hampton detached Colonel

Butler and his 2nd South Carolina with orders to move by way of Bacon Race Church, thus protecting the left flank of the main column.[19]

At dawn on the twenty-eighth, while Stuart was still pondering his options, Colonel Price sent Capt. Charles Chauncey across the Occoquan at Selectman's Ford with 150 men from the 2nd Pennsylvania, accompanied by a force of equal strength from the untried 17th Pennsylvania, led by Maj. Reuben Reinhold. They were acting on the belief that Stuart had retired during the evening. Once across the river Chauncey sent Lt. Alfred Byles ahead with a scouting party, while the main force proceeded up a steep hill and along a "single cowpath through thick woods." Leading the column was Company D, under the command of lieutenants David Leche and George Eckert. Chauncey estimated that after marching about six miles they entered the road from Wolf Run Shoals in the vicinity of Bacon Race Church, though this seems unlikely in light of other events that morning. Hampton recalled that he met the Federal force shortly after leaving Greenwood Church, suggesting that Chauncey marched in a more southerly direction after crossing the Occoquan, as opposed to the generally westerly direction that the Federal officer indicated. In either event just as the head of the Union column entered a broad open field Lieutenant Byles sent back word of the Confederate presence ahead but Chauncey refused to believe him. It was not until the entire column had exited the woods that Chauncey observed the Rebel pickets along a ridge to his front.[20]

Only ten of the troopers in the advance guard carried carbines and Chauncey ordered them to deploy in a skirmish line, while the remainder of the force moved into line for a charge. To his chagrin the carbineers refused to deploy as directed, milling about in confusion. Once Chauncey opened fire with his revolver, however, the men began exchanging shots with the enemy. Major Reinhold rode back to bring up the main body. Sensing the uncertainty in the Federal ranks, the Rebels let out a resounding yell and launched their attack. Chauncey later reported that the raw troops of the 17th Pennsylvania "deserted" him at this point, refusing to stand, even for a moment, though the casualty figures for the regiment belie this accusation.[21]

Confederate scribes universally overstated the size of the Union force with estimates ranging from 500 men to as many as three brigades, and most felt that the Yankees were already arrayed in a line of battle ready to make or receive a charge. When Stuart gave the order Major Drake and his 1st Virginia "let into them," followed by the 2nd Virginia, while Carter's 3rd and Rosser's 5th Virginia swung around and struck the Union flank. Caught by surprise and overwhelmed by superior numbers the Federals made a brief attempt to resist before the attack against their flank routed them and drove them back toward the river. "They gave one volley from their pistols, hurting not a man and then broke," Channing Price recalled.[22]

The initial attack cut off Chauncey and the advance guard from the main body. One of the first to fall was Lieutenant Leche. A sergeant who saw the officer go down attempted to go to his aid, but was confronted by "a powerful looking rebel," who struck him across the head with his saber and he barely escaped capture. As the fleeing soldiers reached the narrow, confined path through the woods "a jam and much confusion ensued." Several officers and a bugler attempted to rally the men but the arrival of Carter and Rosser against their flank sent everyone in a mad rush for the river. A number of men were knocked out of their saddles by tree branches as they galloped for the river. Reaching the "ugly woods" near the ford "they got into a tighter trap than ever," and the frantic men "made new roads through the thickets, and crossed the river at hitherto unknown fords."[23]

Lt. George Maxwell, 1st Michigan, was in command of the pickets guarding the ford, and according to Chauncey, he and his men "rendered valuable assistance" as the Pennsylvanians attempted to get back across the river. The Wolverines, aided by men from the 2nd Pennsylvania, held off the Rebels with a heavy fire long enough for most of the fleeing troopers to get across Selectman's Ford. Fitz Lee deployed sharpshooters along the south bank and sent men racing for Snyder's Ford upstream. Once the Yankees withdrew from the river Colonel Rosser led his regiment across the now abandoned "narrow and rocky ford," in what one officer termed "the prettiest affair I ever witnessed," and pursued the Federals through their campsite. The last of the fleeing Pennsylvanians observed the Virginians feeding their horses on Union forage while they burned the Federal tents.[24]

Confederate casualties were minimal, with the most notable being Lt. Col. James Watts, who was wounded in the groin. Estimates of the Federal losses vary widely, and cannot be verified with any certainty. Captain Chauncey believed that at least 50 men were captured. One postwar accounting states that the 2nd Pennsylvania lost 100 men in this fight, while a trooper writing just days later mentioned that only 26 men were taken. One officer was killed and one mortally wounded, but these are the only men listed in the published roster. Other accounts list one sergeant killed and four men wounded in the running fight. The 17th Pennsylvania lost at least 16 men, including one killed, four wounded, two mortally and 11 captured, two of them also wounded. Chauncey attempted to mitigate his defeat by asserting that 8,000 men had overwhelmed his small command. This estimate aside, the Federals were badly outnumbered and were easily routed by the well-coordinated Southern attack.[25]

As the firing died down along the banks of the river, the Confederates heard gunfire erupt near Bacon Race Church. Hampton had told Butler that he would meet him at the church, but the unexpected encounter to the east and subsequent pursuit that carried Fitz Lee's brigade across the river altered his plans. Hampton now sought to ride to Butler's aid, but Stuart refused, ordering him instead to cross the river and make another sweep for enemy supply wagons. According to Hampton, Stuart allowed that Butler could "follow if he could, or retire to camp." Stuart did send a rider to Butler, informing him of the change in plans and to assist in guiding the South Carolinians back to the main column, though Butler makes no mention that the courier ever arrived.[26]

Butler was not expecting to encounter the enemy in any strength and had instructed Lt. W.H. Perry, in command of his advance, to immediately attack any pickets that he encountered. His first brush with the Federals occurred within a mile of Bacon Race Church and Perry attacked without breaking stride, before realizing that he was up against a squadron sized force that showed no signs of being intimidated. Perry held his ground until Butler arrived and ordered the entire regiment to charge, anticipating that Hampton would support him at any moment. In the face of this attack, the Federals fell back and drew Butler up against infantry, supported by several cannon.[27]

General John Geary had reached the Occoquan near midnight, where his division went into bivouac. In the morning he crossed the river, en route for Dumfries, when his cavalry encountered Butler's South Carolinians and were driven back, losing three men. As Butler followed up his success, however, two sections of Capt. Joseph Knap's Independent Battery E, Pennsylvania Light Artillery opened with canister against the head of the charging column and the infantry "pored a volley into them." This persuaded Butler to break off his attack, causing the Federals "no more trouble" that day. The Confederates escaped with just two men wounded and the loss of several horses, leading Butler to suspect that the Yankees had elevated their guns too high.[28]

Butler, still counting on Hampton's imminent arrival, retired a short distance and prepared to make a stand by dismounting his sharpshooters. When it became evident that help was not going to arrive, however, Butler ordered his men back into the saddle and attempted to rejoin Hampton over the route that he taken that morning. Finding the road blocked by Federal troops he was forced to take a three or four mile detour and rejoined the brigade on the north side of the river. Hampton made a last futile sweep through Occoquan and departed as the sun dropped below the horizon, overtaking the other two brigades later that night near Burke's Station.[29]

While the fighting had been at its height at Selectman's Ford, Lt. George Maxwell sent a bugler back to Peter Stagg informing him of the crisis. Stagg gathered up 50 men from his 1st Michigan, alerted the nearby infantry commands that Stuart was across the river, and then rode toward the sound of the guns. Striking the Ox road near Mount Carmel Church and turning south the relief party found the road blocked by Capt. Henry Dickinson's company from the 2nd Virginia about a mile south of the church. Stagg deployed ten men on foot as skirmishers and sent them into the woods on either side of the road. The Wolverines then advanced about 600 yards when they encountered Dickinson, who charged and drove them back. Outnumbered, Stagg maintained contact while slowly falling back toward Wolf Run Shoals. Once Dickinson cleared the road Stuart continued north toward the Orange and Alexandria Railroad.[30]

Colonel Price forwarded Stagg's warning to Percy Wyndham, who was now en route to Dumfries with 300 men. Reaching the river at Union Mills, Wyndham learned that Stuart had crossed below him and was headed north toward the supply depots along the railroad. Wyndham turned his command around and retraced his march in an attempt to intercept Stuart. The Federal cavalry was badly scattered, however, and dispersed in such small numbers that there was little they could expect to accomplish against Stuart's force. The only realistic chance to bring Stuart to bay lay with the infantry.[31]

General Heintzelman knew shortly before six o'clock that evening that Stuart was within three miles of Burke's Station. He believed that Stuart planned to break through the Union lines between Alexandria and Fairfax Court House. He set his net by instructing General John Abercrombie to send three regiments and a battery from Upton's Hill to hold Annandale. A similar force was ordered to advance from Minor's Hill to take station between Falls Church and Fairfax Court House. Orders were also sent to Brig. Gen. John Slough, the military governor of Alexandria, warning against a "sudden dash" on the city and advising him

Lt. Col. Peter Stagg was an outstanding officer who rose quickly through the ranks of the 1st Michigan Cavalry. During late 1862 and early 1863, while Col. Charles Town was incapacitated by wounds and illness, Stagg led the regiment in the field. By the end of the war he had achieved the brevet rank of brigadier general (USAMHI).

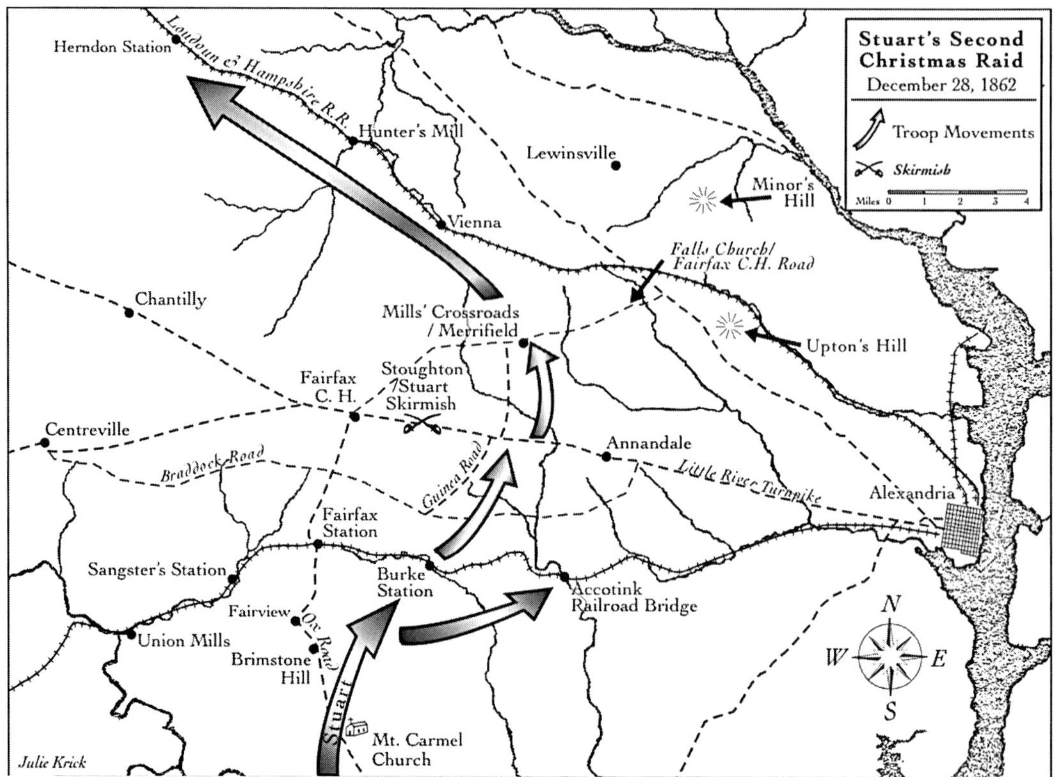

to disperse his troops to protect against it. What troopers could be brought together from the 11th New York Cavalry were instructed to assist Abercrombie, while Major Charles Taggart, 2nd Pennsylvania Cavalry, was pulled from his post at Dranesville and sent toward Fairfax Court House. Minutes after the telegraph line was cut somewhere west of Alexandria at 10:20 P.M. a courier arrived at Abercrombie's headquarters with instructions for him to oversee the deployment in person and to reestablish his headquarters in Annandale. Heintzelman's orders, however, made it clear that he was still uncertain as to the actual strength of the Confederate column, telling Abercrombie that it included cavalry and infantry and numbered between 4,000 and 8,000 men. Inexplicably, Heintzelman then advised General Slough that the column consisted of only cavalry.[32]

Abercrombie ordered Col. William Gurney to respond with three regiments from his brigade posted at Upton's Hill. Abercrombie then gathered five companies of the 11th New York Cavalry, led by Maj. Samuel Wilkeson, and headed for Annandale, arriving sometime after eleven o'clock. At the same hour the long roll was beaten in the infantry camps at Upton's Hill calling the men into the ranks and they marched the six miles to Annandale. Five hours later they were drawn up in line of battle across an open field, where there spent a very cold night waiting for some "rebel guerrillas."[33]

At midnight Brig. Gen. Robert Cowdin led the 22nd Connecticut, followed by the 11th Rhode Island and the 40th Massachusetts along with a battery, from their camps at Minor's Hill. John Morris, 22nd Connecticut, recalled that they were in "mud up to our knees part of the way." Reaching Mill's Crossroads [present day Merrifield] the brigade deployed in a large field and the majority of the men were allowed to sleep on their arms, while Morris's company spent the night on picket duty.[34]

The Union outer line extended from Fairfax Court House around toward the Potomac near Occoquan, and included Stoughton's Vermonters, Col. Frederick d'Utassy's provisional brigade as well as elements from Slocum's Twelfth Corps. Stoughton was notified at four-thirty Sunday afternoon that Stuart was across the Occoquan. By eight o'clock he had removed the military stores from Burke's Station and reinforced the troops guarding the larger depot at Fairfax Station. Shortly thereafter he lost telegraphic communication with the operator at Burke's Station. Though Wyndham was now posted between Sangster's Station and Fairview, immediately below Fairfax Station, he was not under Stoughton's control, leaving Stoughton hard pressed to meet the demands from his superiors that he send scouting parties in search of the raiders.[35]

The men from the Green Mountain State had listened to the sound of gunfire to the south since Saturday. Believing at first that they might be ordered across the Occoquan, they knew by late Sunday that "the rebs was a coming to Fairfax." Concerned for the safety of the depot at Fairfax Station, where Slocum had left only 400 men to guard his entire wagon train plus the military stores, Stoughton dispatched the 16th Vermont and three guns to secure the depot. Later that night Stoughton requested that d'Utassy send an additional two regiments and another battery to the station but due to the darkness of the night and unfamiliarity of the road network d'Utassy did not move until daylight, by which time the threat had passed. Fairfax Station was never in any danger, however, as Alpheus Williams, on his own initiative, sent one of his brigades along with a battery to provide further protection. Once Stoughton was notified that Stuart was near Burke's Station he deployed the remainder of his brigade "to prevent the enemy escaping" by way of the Little River Turnpike and Fairfax Court House. The orders reached his infantry about five o'clock, and the men were quickly issued sixty rounds of ammunition and two day's rations. Two hours later the 12th, 13th and 14th Vermont along with the 2nd Connecticut Battery moved through Fairfax Court House at the double quick, heading east along the turnpike. The 15th Vermont remained at Centreville.[36]

Stoughton posted his three regiments in an existing line of earthworks along the turnpike east of town. The 12th Vermont held the center of the line with part of the 13th to their left and several companies from both the 13th and 14th on the right. The remainder of the 14th Vermont was held in reserve, with the artillery positioned to command the turnpike. Stoughton pushed Companies B and G, 12th Vermont, and a squad of cavalry from the 1st West Virginia along the pike a half-mile out as skirmishers.[37]

Colonel d'Utassy strengthened his outposts near Union Mills, while Wyndham held the line of the railroad between Fairview and Sangster's Station. The cavalry officer also maintained patrols along the roads from Brimstone Hill on his left across to the railroad on his right. With a heavy infantry force blocking the road from Wolf Run Shoals, d'Utassy took the few mounted troops that he had, 60 in number, and deployed them to watch the open ground between the railroad and Centreville. His men spent a long, cold night and those who were allowed to sleep awoke to find their blankets frozen to the ground.[38]

Leaving the Ox road near Mount Carmel Church Jeb Stuart led his cavalry through the eye of a needle that continued to narrow as the night progressed. Approaching Burke's Station around 7 P.M., Stuart sent two or three men ahead to seize the telegraph office before the operator could get off a warning. Once this was accomplished Stuart instructed a man named Shepphard to work the telegraph key. Channing Price thought the situation "very ludicrous" as they listened to Union commanders "in great alarm" send orders that all supplies should be destroyed rather than allow them to fall into Southern hands. A detail from the 4th Virginia Cavalry was sent three miles up the line to burn the railroad bridge across Accotink Creek; while others inflicted what damage they could to the track near the station. During the several hours that he held the station Stuart sent a message to Union general Montgomery Meigs taunting him about the poor quality of the horses and mules that he was supplying to the army. Once this message was sent revealing his location Stuart had the wires cut and struck north, intent on capturing Fairfax Court House.[39]

Reaching Braddock road the troopers turned north on Guinea road, heading for the Little River Turnpike, with Colonel Rosser's 5th Virginia in the lead. Shortly after reaching the turnpike and turning west they came up against a scouting party led by Lt. William Cummings, 1st Vermont Cavalry, who challenged Rosser's men in the darkness. When the Confederates responded with the proper countersign, Cummings ordered one man to come forward but was greeted by the entire party. Reaching the lieutenant, one of the Virginians fired. Cummings avoided the shot by dropping to the ground but he was immediately captured. In the brief clash that followed three other Yankees were captured and the remainder bolted for the rear toward Stoughton's skirmishers, where they mistakenly reported that Cummings had been killed.[40]

The developing crisis found colonels Asa Blunt, 12th Vermont, and Francis Randall, 13th Vermont, attending a court-martial in Alexandria, ten miles east of Fairfax Court House. Mounting their horses together they set out at a gallop in an attempt to reach their commands, but became separated in the darkness. Randall, in the lead, met his regiment as they went into position east of the courthouse and received the cheers of his men. Blunt's horse quickly lost ground in the dash, however, and he was brought to a halt by Capt. Joel Erhardt, 1st Vermont Cavalry, who commanded the outpost at Annandale. The captain had sent Cummings up the turnpike only minutes earlier and the officer's wounded horse arrived back in camp just as Colonel Blunt reined in. Both officers now realized that Stuart had cut the road and that Blunt could no longer reach his command.[41]

The sound of the gunfire also served as a warning to Stoughton's men blocking the pike about two miles to the west. According to Lt. Col. Roswell Farnham, 12th Vermont, Stoughton received updates throughout the night concerning Stuart's progress and the near constant activity served to keep the men awake and "rather excited." About eleven o'clock a courier came in, followed almost immediately by "a dash of horsemen ... frightened half to death." These "scouts" as Farnham called them, advised, "they had been chased by the rebels." The infantry were ordered to load their weapons as "the faint tramp of cavalry" reached their ears from a point near where Farnham had posted his skirmishers.[42]

These two companies were under the command of captains Ora Paul and Ebenezer Ormsbee, and exhibited the steadiness of veterans, holding their ground as the excited troopers bolted through their ranks. Before the men in the entrenchments could carry out the order to load, the gray-clad troopers reached the skirmish line and were greeted by a volley from 100 rifles, "the first hostile volley fired by any portion of the Twelfth in this war." To the men at the barricade the volley erupted from the tree line as "a perfect sheet of fire into the road which was filled with charging cavalry." The Vermonters now expected the full force of the enemy to appear in their front, but the night suddenly grew ominously quiet.[43]

Stoughton called for Capt. John Yale and his company, 13th Vermont, to accompany him as he rode forward to investigate the gunfire along his skirmish line. "Our fun was spoiled," Yale complained when they determined "the rebs retreated after the first fire." The general called for a squad of volunteers to scout the enemy strength and position under the guise of a flag of truce. Sgt. Dan Hall, Company G, and six men responded and walked toward the Southern lines under the protection of a handkerchief tied to a bayonet. When the men observed the Southern pickets in the brilliant moonlight the sergeant was directed to proceed toward their lines alone, where he was met by "some 15 or 20 mounted men." After announcing that Stoughton wished to meet with Stuart, Hall was detained about fifteen minutes before an officer returned with word that Stuart would meet with Stoughton in the morning. After receiving Hall's report the entire party accompanied Stoughton back to the main line. Soon, large fires appeared in the woods around the Confederate position and the Federals could clearly see the troopers "passing to & fro before their fires." Stoughton, now realizing that Stuart had no intention of meeting with him, ordered his artillery to open and four to six rounds were fired "but without much affect," in the view of one man. Captain Yale believed the shelling convinced the Southerners to ride "off towards Vienna & that's the last we have seen of them." Scouts were again sent out and soon reported that Stuart was indeed gone. According to Lt. Robert Hubard, 3rd Virginia Cavalry, Stuart left the 3rd and 5th Virginia, under the command of Colonel Rosser, as a rear guard while he headed north with the remainder of his force, and it was Rosser who met Stoughton's flag of truce. As Hubard recalled, Rosser's two regiments followed Stuart within fifteen minutes of the Federals returning to their lines and before Stoughton ordered his guns to open fire.[44]

The 12th Vermont was sent back through Fairfax Court House to hold the road to Chantilly, while the other two regiments held their position until sunrise. In the morning the men went forward to observe the results of the brief clash. One prisoner was brought in along with a few weapons and a horse bearing a U.S. brand. Three dead horses lay nearby and it was thought that as many as eight men may have been wounded and carried off by their comrades. Southern accounts confirm that two men were struck by the fusillade.[45]

The Green Mountain boys were ecstatic after a long night "standing there in line of battle & cold as Greenland." "It was a bold raid," one declared, "but can have done them little or no good.... We have smelt gunpowder if we have not felt it and from the conduct of the men no apprehension need be felt that they will not do their whole duty if ever brought into action." Writing a long account for his hometown paper Theodore Benedict explained, "I have given so much space to this little skirmish because it is the thing of greatest excitement with us at present, and not, of course, for its essential importance." When Stoughton brought the men back to camp they dropped wearily into their tents and spent most of the day sleeping. Stoughton was "surprised" by the "coolness and enthusiasm" displayed by the men and Colonel Blunt commended his regiment, especially the skirmishers, regretting only that he had not been able to join them.[46]

Finding the road to Fairfax Court House blocked, Stuart turned north on a "by-road" or farm lane [now Prosperity Avenue] that crossed the Falls Church — Fairfax Court House road [Lee Highway today] just below Mills Crossroads, where he continued north to the line of the Loudoun & Hampshire Railroad [the Washington & Old Dominion Railroad and Regional Park today]. At Mills Crossroads John Morris and his company of the 22nd Connecticut had not been on the skirmish line more than fifteen minutes when he "heard the rumbling of artillery wheels and several thousand of Rebel cavalry ... passed across the Fairfax Road, about a mile ahead of us, and it turned out that they were the very fellows we were sent out to stop, and they were too soon for us by about half an hour as they usually are." General Cowdin held his position throughout the day, returning to Minor's Hill at seven-thirty on the evening of the twenty-ninth.[47]

Having now avoided the last significant threat to the safety of his command Stuart followed the line of the railroad past Hunter's Mill toward Herndon Station and then turned south for Frying Pan and Chantilly, arriving at the latter location at 10 A.M. There the men enjoyed a brief halt to rest and feed their horses. Stuart released four prisoners wounded in the fighting near the Occoquan, including Lt. Thomas Snyder, who was mortally wounded. Before he died Snyder reported that the general had been highly complimentary of Lt. David Leche and his efforts to resist the Southern charge near the Occoquan on the morning of the twenty-eighth. Stuart's weary troopers were soon back in the saddle heading west along the Little River Turnpike toward Aldie, where they spent the night.[48]

At Annandale, General Abercrombie held his position until evening, returning the infantry to their Upton's Hill camps around the same hour that Cowdin left Mill's Crossroads. General Slough was also notified that his troops around Alexandria could stand down. Abercrombie ordered what cavalry he had to head west toward Vienna and Hunter's Mill at 4 P.M. on the twenty-ninth, well behind the Confederate column. Two hours later Major Taggart reined up at Abercrombie's headquarters in Annandale, and reported that his small command had driven in some Southern pickets near Frying Pan, but realized that there was little he could do against Stuart's main body, at Chantilly. Abercrombie then sent Taggart to join the battalion of the 11th New York Cavalry, under Major Wilkeson, at Vienna. Moving through Fairfax Court House Wyndham encountered the tail of the Southern column near Chantilly and followed as far as Saunders' Toll Gate, but he was equally frustrated by his paucity of men. Captain Erhardt rounded up several stragglers from the 15th Virginia during the day as his Vermonters, along with a company of the 11th New York, searched the area between Burke's Station and Vienna.[49]

At noon on the thirtieth, Stuart resumed the march, and when his command entered Middleburg they were greeted by the sight of Confederate flags flying throughout the town, and young ladies cheering for Jeff Davis and the cavalry. The general reported that he had captured over 200 men, in addition to those killed and wounded. He had also seized an uncounted number of horses and mules along with other supplies. But the raid had clearly not been the success that he had hoped for. He garnered positive headlines, but not in the manner of his previous raids. Buoyed by accounts of Hampton's recent raids against the Union supply line Stuart hoped that by taking a larger force he might outdo his subordinate, but he failed. In his report of the operation Stuart appears to hold Hampton responsible for the failure due to his "numerous descents" upon the area "which had caused it to be abandoned." In the light of day, the damage that he had inflicted to the railroad near Burke was found to be minimal, the track being more obstructed than torn up and the bridge over the Accotink only slightly damaged rather than destroyed as Stuart reported. The damage was repaired the following morning by d'Utassy's infantry. The headlines and captured supplies soon passed from notice, and Jeb was left with the lasting results of the expedition, worn down horses heading into winter when forage and fodder were scarce and the beginning of a rift between him and Hampton as a result of his decision to abandon Colonel Butler on the twenty-eighth. With a rather quiet winter ahead of him allowing plenty of opportunity to write his report the general avoided the task until February 1864.[50]

From a Union perspective the raid was not the complete embarrassment created by Stuart's previous efforts. While Stuart had slipped the Yankee noose laid through Fairfax County it was the Federals who had dictated his path once he crossed the Occoquan, not Stuart. And while the Union cavalrymen were outnumbered at every point and unable to prevent his escape, they were not reduced to simply chasing after him, as they had done on the Peninsula in June and in Pennsylvania and Maryland in October. Instead, Heintzelman and his subordinates marshaled their infantry to protect vital supply depots, while employing cavalry to defend and patrol prescribed sectors as opposed to the entire route. Intelligence was disseminated quickly up to the point that Stuart cut the telegraph lines, allowing the infantry to be placed where it could be most effective protecting property and funneling the raiders out of the county.

Still, there were recriminations and accusations as officers sought to protect their reputations. Colonel Price, who had remained at his desk throughout the affair, was clearly feeling defensive when he told Heintzelman, "I am certain, Sir, there was no want of proper care and watchfulness on the part of the officers and men on duty" along the Occoquan. "I am *told*," he continued, that the line south from Occoquan toward Dumfries was guarded by the 17th Pennsylvania, laying any blame on the shoulders of those unseasoned troopers, when his own 2nd Pennsylvania was responsible for much of the same area. In truth it was not a matter of watchfulness that allowed Stuart to cross the Occoquan but weight of numbers. The raiders simply avoided the infantry and overran the outnumbered the cavalry that stood in their path.[51]

General Alpheus Williams complained that he could to do little because of the lack of cavalry on the front lines and alleged that 5,000 troopers were retained to defend Washington and Alexandria, while the men on the front line were "cut up into small parties of fifty or a hundred scouring around the country to little or no purpose." He claimed that he was not notified when Stuart crossed the Occoquan, as the Union troopers along the river "took the most convenient route to a safe place," failing to "even resist the crossing." In this last allegation he must have meant that he did not receive any official notification, as he admitted sarcastically that "a runaway cavalryman" did bring a warning that Stuart had crossed the river. Beyond the blatant inaccuracies of his allegations Williams was not in the chain of command for the cavalry posted along the river, and he was recalled to the area just hours before Stuart arrived. Still, it seems doubtful that the cavalry commanders along the river were not aware of his presence and failed to keep him abreast of the rapidly developing situation, if time and demands on their harried commands allowed. The manner in which Peter Stagg and other officers kept the infantry informed of the state of affairs in southern Fairfax County belies his assertions, while his claim that he alone was responsible for the safety of the Orange and Alexandria Railroad was simply untrue.[52]

In the dark days following the bloody defeat at Fredericksburg perception was more important than fact, however, and the perception among many of the men in the Union ranks was that their officers had, once again "been fairly outgeneraled." That Stuart had accomplished little was immaterial; he had passed through the Federal lines without incurring capture or a serious defeat. As one Vermonter concluded, "On the whole, I think it was an ingenious performance of Stuart." In the words of a companion the Confederates had given the Federals "the slip as usual."[53]

In his report Stuart maintained that he was able to create the impression "that another invasion of Maryland was contemplated," forcing the Federal cavalry into "rapid marches over the difficult roads ... in the fruitless effort to thwart me in my real intentions." Writing with the benefit of fourteen months of hindsight, this claim was easy for Stuart to make, and though accurate to a degree, on balance his raid was a failure. The impression that he left with the Union high command, however, that he could lead a raid against the capital at virtually any moment, was a result that Stuart could not fully appreciate. That fear would linger for months to come.[54]

When word of Stuart's expedition reached the Army of the Potomac, a trooper in the

3rd Indiana Cavalry predicted that the Confederate raid, combined with the recent success of other sorties against Union pickets, "will no doubt encourage them to a renewal of their old game of dashing in our rear.... The large amount of government clothing captured enables them to play frequent sharp games on our outpost pickets, and there seems to be no means by which such misfortunes can be avoided." He recounted for his readers how the enemy was not above dressing in captured uniforms and boldly riding up to a picket reserve post, claiming to be a relief squadron and then capturing the entire party or "very deliberately" calling in the pickets from their scattered posts and seizing them. The unnamed trooper could not know just how prescient his letter was. The men of Stuart's cavalry division had seized hundreds of Union uniforms during the month of December and one man in particular now intended to terrorize the Yankee sentinels that stood watch along the pale in Northern Virginia.[55]

5

December 29–December 31, 1862

"I thought I could make things lively"

On December 29, Heintzelman notified Burnside that Stuart would probably slip his noose, and indeed he did. Burnside had been pondering an operation that might raise the flagging spirits of his army and instill some initiative back into his, so far, disastrous campaign. On the twenty-eighth he had tasked Brig. Gen. William Woods Averell with leading a cavalry raid of his own. Averell proposed to cross the Rappahannock and Rapidan rivers, on the thirty-first, with 1,000 men and four guns and strike south across the James River. Depending on the circumstances that confronted him once he was across the James, he would head either for Suffolk, Virginia or the Union lines in North Carolina. He also proposed sending a smaller force of 250 men to capture a body of enemy cavalry reported to be wintering near Warrenton.[1]

Events immediately aligned, however, to thwart this enterprise. Word of the proposed raid reached Lincoln just as the War Department received information that Stonewall Jackson was planning to cross the Rappahannock below Fredericksburg and attack Burnside's left flank. Even though this report was deemed unreliable (Heintzelman noted that it was based on the sighting of a Federal cavalry detachment on the south side of the Occoquan and asserted in his journal, "I must find out what officer could circulate such a report") the president informed Burnside on the thirtieth that he should undertake no "general movement of the army" without his approval. The raid was canceled, but Averell was ordered to try and intercept Stuart near Warrenton, based on reports that the Confederates had last been seen headed toward Aldie.[2]

On New Year's Eve Averell acknowledged the change in plans but sought to convince his superiors to allow the raid to go forward as he would, undoubtedly, "be too late" to intercept Stuart. That morning at eight o'clock, a detachment of the 1st Massachusetts Cavalry charged into Warrenton, intent on capturing the "two companies of rebel cavalry" using the town as a base of operations. Captain Charles Francis Adams, the perpetually disgruntled commander of Company D, 1st Massachusetts, later told his mother that he "smelled a rat" as soon as the command approached the silent town. The absence of fire from the enemy force that reportedly held the town left him "feeling like a fool" as he led his men through the town at a gallop, "astonishing and delighting peaceful citizens." Adams remarked that the townsfolk were "very civil and certainly exhibited no signs of distrust or fear." After making a rapid search of the town and determining that there were no enemy soldiers in the immediate area, the men from the Bay State "turned round and left," feeling, as Adams reiterated, "like fools."[3]

Several miles out of town the Yankees "heard bells ringing and wondered what it was."

According to Adams, "It was a signal," to General Stuart whose troopers entered the town just two hours after the Federals left. The signal made the Federals realize just how close they had come to stumbling into Stuart's entire force, but Adams was also left to wonder what the outcome might have been if Averell, with a brigade of fresh men had greeted Stuart's saddle-worn command upon its arrival. The regimental historian for the 1st Massachusetts saw this reconnaissance as "discouraging to officers and men alike," another failure during "the gloomiest" period "that the Army of the Potomac ever knew." Stuart had "proved to be like the Irishman's flea — when we put our hand upon him he was not there."[4]

The target of the early morning dash into Warrenton was the Black Horse — Company H, 4th Virginia Cavalry. These men remained in Fauquier County on detached service, operating against the Union supply lines, and had elected to avoid a fight against the superior Federal numbers that morning. Once the Federals withdrew the Southerners returned and riders were sent to advise Stuart of their departure. Stuart had departed from Middleburg at 7:00 a.m., but had been warned of the Federal advance and had sent Fitz Lee, along with the prisoners and captured wagons around the town of Warrenton to the west, on their way to Culpeper Court House. Stuart remained out of sight but within striking distance, only entering Warrenton once it was clear. The general and his staff remained in town "for some time" until Rooney Lee and Wade Hampton moved through with their brigades, and then they took the road again, reaching Culpeper Court House that evening. The Southerners had not entirely vacated the area, however. Stuart had authorized ten men to remain behind.[5]

Both Jeb Stuart and John Mosby said little about the decision that led to Mosby's legendary career. Jeb Stuart never commented on the matter. Even in February 1864, when the general wrote his account of the Christmas Raid, by which time Mosby's exploits had made him a hero in the South and a demon in the North, the general remained silent, failing to publicly take any credit for his role in Mosby's early career as a partisan. Mosby, who became a prolific writer during his long life, also said little — summing up Stuart's decision to leave him behind in less than a paragraph. On the evening of December 30, 1862, Stuart had taken lodging with Col. Hamilton Rogers, at Oakham, along the Little River Turnpike between Dover and Middleburg. The following morning John Mosby approached the general, "and asked him to let me stay behind for a few days with a squad of men. I thought I could do something with them. He readily assented. I got nine men.... This was the beginning of my partisan career." In another account Mosby said simply, "I did not want to rust away my life in camp, so I asked Stuart to give

Col. John Mosby may not have been the most colorful guerrilla or partisan commander of the war, but he was clearly the most respected and effective, and he led the 43rd Battalion, Virginia Cavalry, to enduring fame (Library of Congress).

me a detail of men to go over to Loudoun County, where I thought I could make things lively during the winter months."[6]

The twenty-nine-year-old Mosby had grown up in Powhatan County, west of Richmond. When he was five or six years of age his family moved to a farm near Charlottesville, in Albemarle County. Though slight of stature and often ill, the young student was a scrapper who "never ignored a provocation." Sensitive in his youth to remarks about his size, or lack thereof, as well as comments about his poor health, he made it known that he was not to be trifled with. Though he earned a reputation as being "easy to bait and easy to beat," he was a voracious reader of novels by Sir Walter Scott and tales of Greek heroes, and he developed "a hair-trigger notion of personal honor." Those tales often influenced his later writing.[7]

In 1850, two months shy of his seventeenth birthday, Mosby entered the University of Virginia. Following a street fight between students and local youths Mosby drew the ire of the town constable, George Slaughter, who was attempting to quell the disturbance. When Slaughter attempted to arrest him, Mosby resisted violently, shattering a gunstock against the officer's head, and earning a ten-dollar fine. On March 29, 1853, Mosby confronted George Turpin and challenged him to explain some disparaging remarks about Mosby that Turpin had made to several mutual friends. Turpin had earned a reputation for violence, and he was not averse to using a weapon to ensure the outcome. When the two students met, Mosby had a six-shot Allen pepperbox pistol in his pocket and as soon as Turpin came toward him Mosby drew the weapon and fired, striking Turpin in the neck. Mosby returned home and was arrested that evening, charged with "malicious shooting," and "unlawful shooting." After a five-day trial Mosby was convicted of the lesser of the two counts, "unlawful shooting," and sentenced to spend one year in jail and pay a fine of five hundred dollars. After seven months in jail he was pardoned, and the fine rescinded.[8]

One of his advocates was William Robertson, the man who had prosecuted him. When Mosby expressed an interest in studying the law Robertson loaned him his law books, and upon his release Mosby continued his studies in Robertson's office. Gaining admittance to the bar several months later, the new attorney opened a practice in Howardsville, south of Charlottesville. There he met Pauline Clarke and the two were married in December 1857. The firing on Fort Sumter found the couple living in Bristol, Virginia.[9]

In late 1860 Mosby joined a militia company in Abingdon, Virginia, known as the Washington Mounted Rifles. The commander was William E. Jones, a future general. Another member of the company was William Blackford, who was later a member of Stuart's staff. Blackford recalled Mosby as "an indifferent soldier," who appeared to care little for the responsibilities of a soldier. On May 30, 1861, the company left Abingdon, and on July 9 the men reported for duty with Jeb Stuart's 1st Virginia Cavalry.[10]

Jones recognized something in Mosby and on the morning of July 21, as the two armies closed for battle, sent him, along with five other men, across Bull Run on his first scouting mission of the war. In September, Jones was promoted to colonel and took command of the regiment. Five months later Mosby was appointed regimental adjutant. A commission to 1st lieutenant followed soon after, yet two months later, following another turnover in the regimental command, Mosby resigned his commission and accepted a position on Stuart's staff. In the words of historian Jeff Wert, "The appointment began the most important association of Mosby's military career." Mosby later termed Stuart "the best friend I ever had," and he remained Stuart's staunchest advocate for the rest of his life.[11]

Stuart first took notice of Mosby in March 1862 when Gen. Joseph Johnston fell back from Centreville to the line of the Rappahannock, and Stuart, with his cavalry, provided rear guard protection for the army. When McClellan dispatched a column of infantry and cavalry to follow the Southern army Johnston needed to determine if the Union force represented a reconnaissance in strength or the van of the entire army. Stuart charged a musician by the name of David Drake from the 1st Virginia with the task, and Mosby volunteered to assist him. The men spent a night behind enemy lines and returned in the morning to confirm that the Federal force represented a reconnaissance only. In his report for this operation Stuart acknowledged Mosby for the first time, noting that he and Drake, "volunteered to perform the most hazardous service, and accomplished it in the most satisfactory and creditable manner."[12]

In early June, and with the Union army now on the doorstep of the Southern capital, Stuart asked Mosby to scout the Federal lines along Totopotomoy Creek. Riding behind the Union lines with three companions from the 1st Virginia, Mosby, determined that McClellan's right flank, including his supply line to the York River, was vulnerable. When he presented his report to Stuart the senior officer took the information to Robert E. Lee, who had only recently taken command of the army. Wary of basing a major offensive on the word of a man unknown to him, Lee directed that Stuart confirm the intelligence. The result is known to history as "Stuart's Ride Around McClellan," and it firmly established the reputation of both Stuart and his cavalry. Again, Stuart recognized Mosby for his "conspicuous and gallant service during the whole expedition."[13]

Calls for a guerrilla war rose throughout the South as soon as the echoes of cannon fire died in Charleston harbor in April 1861. Citizens in border states like Virginia soon recognized that they were now on the front lines and "would have to rally and turn back the invading Federals," while others in the deep South also responded to the threat and volunteered "to be employed on the border." Men forced to flee the Union occupation and abandon their homes eagerly answered the call for partisan or guerrilla units in part because it allowed them to return and defend their own land, once it became clear that the government could not protect every mile of Southern territory.[14]

The nature of this warfare quickly brought its advocates into conflict with military and government leaders, especially those trained at institutions like West Point, who frowned on guerrilla warfare and likened it to the manner of fighting practiced by "uncivilized peoples" rather than "the romantic knights of the American Revolution." When these guerrilla units began prosecuting their own private war against their neighbors, their usefulness was called into question. In an initial attempt to control the growth of these guerrilla or partisan outfits, the Confederate Congress "passed an act 'for local defense and special service,' in August 1861," which specifically avoided the term guerrilla, but as historian Daniel Sutherland observes, commanders of these units "would allow limited guerrilla activity without calling it such."[15]

The furor spawned by these units continued, leading the Confederate Congress to pass the Partisan Ranger Act on April 21, 1862, but only after a vigorous debate. This law granted President Jefferson Davis the authority to commission officers to raise partisan units to be received into the Confederate service and to be paid and provisioned in the same manner as regular army units. These outfits were governed by the same military regulations as the rest of the army, but there the similarities ended. The new units were entitled to be paid for any captured enemy munitions or arms they turned over to the army quartermaster and they could keep any non-military items that they seized. Yet the government also opted to institute national conscription at the same time. The result was that rather then curtail the number of guerrilla or partisan units, as the supporters of the Partisan Ranger Act had hoped, the drive for conscription actually drove more men into the ranks of these irregular units as a means of avoiding service in the regular army and allowing them to remain near their homes and families. Not only did this combination create problems for the army itself, but the Partisan Ranger Act met with mixed success in curtailing the evils that had led to its inception. Worse, as Daniel Sutherland explains, the combination of conscription and the Partisan Ranger Act led to the rise of the outlaw bands that "subverted the legitimate use of irregular war and sent the relatively contained pre–1862 guerrilla contest careening out of control."[16]

John Mosby first learned of the Partisan Ranger Act while serving with Stuart on the Peninsula, and he approached Stuart in July to discuss "the idea of starting a partisan life." He asked Stuart to give him "command of a small detachment," with the authority to operate in Northern Virginia. Stuart instead sent him to see Stonewall Jackson who had just been ordered to Gordonsville to meet the threat presented by John Pope. Thinking to save time, Mosby determined to take the train from Beaver Dam Station to Gordonsville. As he later explained, he was waiting at the depot, on July 20, when Lt. Col. Judson Kilpatrick rode up at the head of the 2nd New York Cavalry and "placed an attachment upon my body."[17]

He was a prisoner for "about ten days," before he boarded a steamer bound for an exchange point near Fort Monroe. Mosby spent four days on the ship, anchored in Hampton Roads observing a steady passage of troop-laden transports. A Southern sympathizer captained his ship and from him Mosby learned that the troops were Union reinforcements en route to join General John Pope's Army of Virginia. As soon as he was able Mosby personally delivered this information to Lee, and then resumed his trip to Gordonsville, but his hope of a partisan career was put on hold, as Jackson confronted the developing military threat in his front. It was less than two weeks later that Mosby, along with Stuart and his staff narrowly avoided capture at Verdiersville. "We ran ingloriously," Mosby admitted.[18]

Over the next few months Mosby was Stuart's constant companion and scout. On December 28, Mosby and a friend were scouting ahead of Stuart's column and among the first to encounter Captain Chauncey's Pennsylvanians. With a gush of hyperbole Mosby later described the action. We "went forward at a gallop, until we met a large body of cavalry. As no support was in sight, several officers made a dash at us, and at the same time opened such a fire as to show that peace on earth and good will to men, which the angels and morning stars had sung on that day over 1800 years ago, was no part of their creed." After the passage of so much time, Mosby had conveniently forgotten that it was Lee and Stuart who had ignored the spirit of the Christmas season. Mosby concluded his account of the skirmish by taking one last jibe at the Federals. "All the fun was over with the Pennsylvanians then. There was no more merry Christmas for them."[19]

By the end of the year Stuart had made up his mind to leave his friend behind. The area then termed the "debatable ground" would soon be known as "Mosby's Confederacy." The man who Stuart had once described as "bold, daring, intelligent and discreet," would not spend the winter rusting away after all. Mosby knew that the Union picket line around the capital, extending from the Occoquan to the Potomac, near Great Falls, was bound to have gaps and weak points, and he believed the troops that manned the line led an "easy, lazy life." He saw the potential for "a bountiful harvest." On the very day that Mosby received his orders from Stuart, Union general John Abercrombie sent a warning to Heintzelman. "I observed the pickets ... were not so vigilant as they should be; moreover they are in the habit ... of keeping up fires during the night, which ... must expose to view the position of the whole line of pickets as far as this practice extends." Abercrombie recommended that an officer be sent to visit the picket lines and "correct ... these improprieties, [to] prevent disastrous occurrences."[20]

6

December 31, 1862–January 13, 1863

"The war is to be more desperate and deadly"

When the men of the 1st Michigan Cavalry, attached to the outpost at Dranesville, returned to their camp on New Year's Eve they found the site had been destroyed, and they were forced to spend the first day of 1863 rebuilding their shelters. "I carried boards to fix up a shanty," Charles Johnson explained with disgust, "for the cowardly officer that was left in charge of the camp (while the men were chasing Stuart) was so afraid the rebs would come in and take him that he burned our tent up with a lot of others."[1]

The first of January was no holiday for the men of the 5th New York Cavalry either, as they abandoned their bivouac at Fairfax Court House and returned to their former position at Chantilly. On the second, a patrol from the regiment under the command of Lt. Edward Tolles was attacked by about 20 men near Hutchinson's Mill, west of Saunders' Toll Gate and just south of the Little River Turnpike. Hiram Earl, a private in Company F, gave his father a brief account of what occurred. "I was out the other day with the lieutenant and seven men and we was attacked with about twenty Cavalryman ... I had five shooting at me at one time. I shot four shots at them and then I had to run for my life." Two of Earl's comrades were captured in the brief encounter. A similar attack was carried out against the pickets of the 1st West Virginia between the mill and Centreville. Concern for their security following these attacks may have been the reason that the soldiers "burned a good many" of the Southern barracks that had stood in the area since the previous winter. Based on these encounters Lt. Col. Robert Johnstone, 5th New York, reported that the enemy were "not far beyond Cub Run," possibly intent on moving toward Vienna and "operating" against the outpost at Dranesville.[2]

Other scouting parties reported several hundred Southern cavalry in and around Brentsville, in Prince William County. None of the Federals identified the Confederate units that they encountered, but the Black Horse cavalry, posted in Warrenton, as well as the Iron Scouts, based around Brentsville, are the most likely culprits. It was the presence of enemy cavalry at Brentsville that caused the greatest stir. Reports on the fourth that as many as 500 Southern troopers were lingering in that area led to a flurry of worried telegrams from Colonel Candy in Dumfries, but by the end of the day the nervous colonel was convinced that "the emergency was not as great as supposed."[3]

Candy was undoubtedly on edge following an incident outside Dumfries on the third.

While patrolling toward the town four men from the 1st Connecticut Cavalry stopped at the home of Joseph Herndon, a member of the 9th Virginia Cavalry, who was on parole following his capture in September. Cpl. Michael Carver was in command of the group, which stopped at the home looking for breakfast. Herndon, who was present with his wife and young daughter, agreed to feed the men, but he denied that any other soldiers were in the house. However, Herndon's daughter admitted that two other soldiers were upstairs. The men debated the safest course of action and were in favor of returning to camp for assistance but Carver determined to take the men into custody. He and Private William Gates started upstairs when a door opened and several shots were fired. Carver was struck in the head and killed. Gates returned the fire before retreating out of the house, where he confronted Herndon, who claimed that the soldiers were unknown to him, but had come by asking to spend the night. In fact the other two soldiers were William and Thomas Warren, who like Herndon were members of Company A, 9th Virginia Cavalry. Thomas Warren was also on parole. As Carver's body was being carried from the house, the Warren brothers again opened fire before bolting for freedom.[4]

Unwilling to chase the men into the surrounding woods, Gates and his comrades headed back to camp where they reported the incident to Capt. Erastus Blakeslee, 1st Connecticut Cavalry, and Col. Alexander Schimmelfennig, commanding an infantry brigade. Blakeslee responded with the remainder of his company, along with a detachment of the 6th Ohio Cavalry, followed closely by Schimmelfennig and an infantry patrol. Arriving at the Herndon home and after being apprised of the circumstances, Schimmelfennig asked for the opinion of the other officers present as to what should be done. Clouding their thinking was their belief that "ten to forty men have infested the ... neighborhood ... dressed in blue, some in gray and some in citizen's clothes and were harbored in the farms of that neighborhood." The situation was further aggravated, in their view, by the fact that two of the men were paroled soldiers, who had committed an honor code violation, and they agreed, unanimously, that the home should be burned, "being a harboring place for bushwhackers." After an hour in which Mrs. Herndon was allowed to remove all of the family's effects, "except a few bushels of corn," the house and outbuildings were put to the torch. A number of residents from the area were also taken into custody, including Herndon's father.[5]

Maj. Freeman Norvell was in command of the 5th Michigan Cavalry when it left Detroit. He had been promoted to lieutenant colonel on December first and full colonel at the end of the month, but his addiction to alcohol was creating a measure of turmoil throughout the ranks of the regiment and it would force him to resign just two months later. On January 4, Lt. Col. Ebenezer Gould advised his brother that due to Norvell's battle with alcohol "Copeland has placed the command in my hands and I assure you I never had so difficult a task imposed on me." Gould thought Norvell "a man of immense military knowledge quick perception and clear headed were it not for this habit he would be one of the first *Cols* in the army." The regimental surgeon later explained Norvell's behavior in this instance as the result of "sheer nervous exhaustion," brought about by his concern for the final inspection and mustering of the regiment. Finding Norvell "prostrated" on the afternoon of December 30, a senior officer had "administered some brandy." The following day, "the day of the inspection," the doctor learned that Norvell had not slept, and he administered two doses of "brandy & water with morphine." The doctor later stated that the morphine had "an exceedingly irritating and injurious effect," on the colonel "exciting rather than soothing the nervous system." Though Norvell resumed command two days later and was promoted to full colonel Norvell did not regain control of himself. Several senior officers later stipulated that his drunken behavior continued until the fourth of January.[6]

On the fifth, Gould informed his wife that the regiment had just received orders "to pull up stakes and move to Fairfax Court House." He remained doubtful that the move would actually occur, however, and tried to reassure her that "there is no danger there but it is near enough to danger to make the men more attentive to their duties." That the regiment was expected to take the field was confirmed by Capt. Carroll Potter of Heintzelman's staff who advised Colonel Wyndham that the 5th Michigan Cavalry, "968 men for duty—all equipped except firearms will be ordered this day to report to you."[7]

Nearby, Capt. James Kidd, 6th Michigan Cavalry, was also chafing to take the field. He was finding it increasingly difficult to get the men to tend to their horses and their other routine duties. "I am becoming every day more and more a believer in the strictest form of discipline. Men won't '*do*' if left to themselves." Kidd thought the regiment "a fine one and undoubtedly could do good service in the field and there is where we ought to be." The men had received their sabers and about 60 revolvers per company, but they were still awaiting their carbines.[8]

That evening, January 5, 1863, the men assigned to the picket lines, the outposts and to the fortifications stretching through Northern Virginia were to learn that there was now a new threat to their welfare. If, as General Abercrombie had warned, the sentries did not become more vigilant and forego their warming campfires, then there would indeed be disastrous occurrences. The men were about to learn the price for their lack of discipline and vigilance.

A congregation of primitive Baptists established Frying Pan Meeting House in western Fairfax County in 1791. Named for a nearby stream, the church saw to the religious needs of both white and black residents as early as the 1840s. With the coming of the Civil War the church became an outpost that was briefly held by Confederate soldiers, before becoming a key point in the Union picket line around Washington. When the men of the 5th New York Cavalry moved back into the area on the first of January, they reestablished a post at Frying Pan as part of the line extending northward through Herndon to the Potomac River. On the evening of January 5, Cpl. William Barrows was in charge of six men from Company H on picket at the church. After the war, The Rev. Louis Boudrye, the regimental chaplain and historian, wrote that the regiment moved into this position on the first "to guard against the incursions of Mosby and his gang," when, in truth, the New Yorkers had not yet heard of John Mosby. Indeed, the men of the regiment had no hint that a new threat existed when the sun went down that day.[9]

"I had the good luck, by mere chance, to come across a forester named John Underwood, who knew every rabbit-path in the county." This is the extent of what John Mosby would later say about his association with the man he termed "a brave soldier, as well as a good guide." John Scott, an early chronicler of Mosby's military career, later stated that the two men met on the evening of Mosby's first raid. Scott described Underwood as a "short and thickset" man, with "a shock of white hair, which stood erect in unrestrained independence.

His whole appearance was that of a wild man, but his eyes, ever in motion, indicated watchfulness and an intelligent mind." Shortly after convincing Underwood to join his group and serve as his guide, Mosby led his men in the direction of Frying Pan Meeting House.[10]

"Surprise has always been an important element in warfare," notes historian Don Rickey. "A confused enemy is an ineffectual opponent. Some soldiers, when suddenly and unexpectedly fired upon ... became excited and unable to function effectively.... The demoralizing effect of surprise was increased when the troops had not been drilled, trained and disciplined." Throughout his career John Mosby used the element of surprise to his advantage, often against untrained troops, and when combined with the shock of a sudden cavalry charge his tactics proved virtually unstoppable.[11]

Under cover of darkness Underwood led the Confederates around the Union position at Frying Pan Church, so that they approached from the rear of the New Yorkers who were silhouetted against their campfire. Following a single pistol shot from Mosby the partisans rushed from the trees and captured the seven men, one of whom was reportedly wounded slightly when he attempted to flee. The prisoners, along with their horses and weapons, were quickly led away from the Union lines, and into Loudoun County. There, Mosby paroled the Yankees and presented his men with the captured property, including a full share to John Underwood. The following evening Underwood led Mosby and his men against a second outpost along Cub Run and captured several more members of the 5th New York.[12]

Leaving one man to stand guard over the prisoners taken at Cub Run, Mosby rode north toward Herndon Station and a picket post manned, according to Mosby, by the 1st Vermont Cavalry. The men had taken shelter in a home, leaving one sentinel outside. He was fooled into thinking that the approaching men were a relief party coming from the reserve camp. Once the man issued his challenge the Confederates charged, and, as Mosby later wrote, "it was all over with the boys from the Green Mountains." John Scott detailed a more exciting, yet fictitious, affair in which a battle ensued between the attackers and the men in the house, who were then tricked into surrender by Southern calls for the infantry to move up. Mosby denied this version of events, admitting that if the men had resisted "they might have driven us off."[13]

The following morning John Mosby paroled his prisoners near Middleburg, and then headed south to rejoin Jeb Stuart in the vicinity of Fredericksburg. Delighted with Mosby's account of his success, Stuart assented to his friend's request to return and resume his operations, this time with 15 men. On the eighteenth, Mosby led the men back north, through Fauquier County where he was greeted with skepticism after he explained his intentions to continue his attacks against the Federal pickets.[14]

The first news accounts of these events came out of Fairfax Court House on the evening of the sixth. The reports carried no details beyond the fact that "sixteen men were gobbled up last night by the Rebels." When Col. Percy Wyndham notified Heintzelman of the situation, he totaled the loss at 15 men, which Colonel Johnstone further detailed as five men from "our outpost at Cub Run on the Aldie Pike and ten men at the Frying Pan outpost ... the former at midnight and the latter at 4 A.M." Wyndham also voiced the need to strengthen the detachment at Chantilly. "It is impossible," he warned Heintzelman, "with my present command to cover the front which formerly a whole division of ... 2000 cavalry, were employed to picket, and unless infantry be sent to Chantilly there is danger of my losing some day a whole regiment." Officers along the picket line were told to "be very particular in sending instructions to the pickets tonight." The outposts were to be drawn in "as far" as thought proper and the men were to "be ready for all emergencies." Campfires were now prohibited.[15]

Wyndham was particularly concerned that the 5th Michigan Cavalry had not arrived as expected. He was informed that the Michiganders would be delayed in departing for the front due to the fact that they were not yet fully armed. In their place, Heintzelman directed the 18th Pennsylvania Cavalry to move immediately from their camps near Arlington Heights to Chantilly. On the January 8 the Pennsylvanians marched to near Jermantown, just west of Fairfax Court House, where they went into bivouac alongside a detachment from the 1st West Virginia Cavalry.[16]

Col. R. Butler Price advised Heintzelman that "several of the Bushwhackers have been taken and will be sent in," and, he urged, "I hope they will not be permitted to return again to commit similar acts." These unidentified men had been seized near Dranesville after firing on a picket post and had nothing to do with John Mosby. "The guerrillas are very active," warned Boudrye. "The utmost vigilance cannot secure us perfectly from their depredations. The only way to rid ourselves of this plague would be to ... arrest every male inhabitant able to carry a musket, and burn to the ground every building, including houses, where these bushwhackers reside or find refuge." The chaplain knew that the government was not prepared to resort "to so stern a punishment," but "if the war is to continue long this would prove to be true policy, saving lives of many of our brave boys."[17]

Without specifically referring to the latest incidents George Benedict, 12th Vermont, noted a similar change in attitude among the soldiers. "The war as a whole is to be more desperate and deadly in [the] future, because [it is] waged with a foe maddened by privations and loss of property, and especially by the President's Proclamation of Freedom. We have already ceased to hear much talk about 'playing at war.' It is owned to be *work*, and pretty earnest work now, and if it grows hotter as a whole, it will of course be the harder in its parts."[18]

When the 17th Pennsylvania was transferred to the Army of the Potomac at the beginning of the month, their reconnaissance role was assigned to the detachment of the 1st Michigan Cavalry, under the command of Lt. Col. Peter Stagg, posted along the Occoquan near Selectman's Ford, while the main task of the 2nd Pennsylvania Cavalry remained the protection of the telegraph line through southern Fairfax County. Stagg was also called on to help fill a gap in the picket line vacated by the 17th Pennsylvania between the town of Occoquan and Neabsco Creek at Dumfries. To aid Stagg several additional companies of the regiment stationed at Dranesville were sent to Wolf Run Shoals on the eighth.[19]

The furor created by Colonel Candy on January 4, concerning enemy activity around Brentsville, combined with the persistent activity of the Iron Scouts between Brentsville and Dumfries led to a heightened fear of attack from that region. On the sixth, an infantry officer advised General Stoughton, "I have almost positive information that a portion of Hampton's Legion intend to make a dash at my picket line between Woodyard Ford & Manassas tonight or tomorrow." Two days later Candy reported that one of his patrols had been attacked and one man presumed captured near Brentsville at two o'clock that afternoon. He reported that "bushwhackers and several small scouting parties of the enemy" held the roads around the town and he inquired as to what the cavalry at Occoquan was doing about the problem, if anything. It was apparently in response to these reports that Lt. George

Maxwell led a squad of six men from the 1st Michigan Cavalry across the Occoquan at Wolf Run Shoals on the ninth of January.[20]

The Iron Scouts, along with men from the Prince William Cavalry, Company A, 4th Virginia, boarded with local citizens in the area around Brentsville. On the ninth, about 20 men rendezvoused in response to a report that Maxwell and his Wolverines were approaching the town. The Iron Scouts, under the command of Sgt. William A. Mickler, 2nd South Carolina Cavalry, caught the Federals along the main street running through Brentsville. Sgt. Alonzo Wilcox, Company H, and Charles Hicks, Company F, 1st Michigan were killed, and William Teeples, Company C, was mortally wounded. Lieutenant Maxwell and the other two men were captured.[21]

On the eighth, Brig. Gen. William Averell had received orders to take the field, partly in response to the reports of enemy activity around Brentsville. He was also directed to confirm reports that the Confederates were attempting to rebuild the railroad bridge at Rappahannock Station. Averell split his force, sending scouting parties to Catlett Station and Brentsville, while Maj. Samuel Chamberlain, 1st Massachusetts Cavalry, took a second detachment to Rappahannock Station. A third squad, under the command of Lt. Leicester Walker, 5th U.S. Cavalry, was directed to scout the upper fords of the Rappahannock River. Averell reported that the men heading to Catlett Station got a late start on the eighth, and "were driven back to the lines," without giving any further explanation. Setting out again in the morning they reached Catlett Station by two o'clock in the afternoon, but found no evidence of enemy activity. The party that was sent to Brentsville reached the town at the same time on the ninth, where they encountered a squadron of the 12th Illinois Cavalry. They later ran into a second detachment from an unidentified Federal unit patrolling the road between Dumfries and Brentsville, but found no sign of the enemy that they were looking for. These two patrols were attached to a separate force under the command of Colonel Schimmelfennig, who was looking for a fight after several of his pickets had been killed. Later news accounts reported that Schimmelfennig had a skirmish with "50 to 70 Rebel cavalry" at Catlett Station, but one of the officers who made the trek admitted, "the expedition had no very particular results."[22]

Lieutenant Walker ran into a company of 40 Confederates near Grove Church and had a "brisk skirmish," but he was not deterred from his mission of scouting the river crossings toward Kelly's Ford. Major Chamberlain struck out at 8 A.M. on the ninth with 100 men from the 1st Massachusetts and the 5th U.S. Cavalry. Chamberlain ran into the Iron Scouts near Elk Run and drove them back in the direction of Catlett Station. In the process he recovered Lieutenant Maxwell and the men who had been captured in Brentsville. Chamberlain broke off any pursuit of the Southerners in adherence to his orders to determine the condition of the railroad bridge, which he found almost completed. Averell later reported, though Chamberlain did not confirm it, that one of the Iron Scouts was killed in their encounter. Averell further claimed that the guerrillas had attempted to kill their prisoners at the point they realized they would no longer be able to retain them. Captured by one of these patrols was Wyndham Lucas from the 4th Virginia Cavalry.[23]

Averell reported, erroneously, that the 20 men who had ambushed Lieutenant Maxwell and his patrol were all that remained of the 2nd South Carolina Cavalry. He also included in his report a statement that others would repeat many times before the conflict was settled. "There are ... many young rebels, who assemble, mount, and form scouting parties at the shortest notice," he explained. "Upon the approach of any superior force they are as suddenly transformed into idle, loitering citizens, without arms, and professing great ignorance of the country." The cavalryman declared that if given an additional regiment, "I will cause the arrest of all such that can be found between Brentsville and the Rappahannock."[24]

Brig. Gen. Edwin Stoughton, commander of the 2nd Vermont Brigade, was largely despised by his men. Few of them mourned his loss when John Mosby captured him at Fairfax Court House on March 9, 1863 (USAMHI).

On January 9, General Edwin Stoughton was told to shift three of his regiments to Fairfax Station, along with an artillery battery, to relieve Slocum's infantry. Stoughton was instructed to send his remaining two regiments to Wolf Run Shoals to relieve Colonel d'Utassy. A second battery of guns was assigned to support Stoughton at the latter point. Stoughton was also given the latitude to, "establish your HdQrs at the point most convenient to your command."[25]

Twenty-four-year-old Edwin Stoughton had graduated from West Point in 1859. Following a stint as colonel of the 4th Vermont Infantry, during which he saw service in the Peninsula Campaign, Stoughton went home on leave. While in Vermont his leave was extended so that he could "assist in organizing and drilling" the several new regiments then being raised in the state. He received another extension in October 1862, and was soon campaigning for a general's star. When his appointment as brigadier came through, to date from November 5, 1862, he was ordered to Washington. Though he was, at the time, the youngest brigadier in the Union service Stoughton's career was not untarnished. He had faced a court-martial the previous winter for visiting Washington without a pass, and had been convicted of conduct prejudicial to military discipline.[26]

On November 14, 1862, it was announced in special orders that Stoughton had completed his assignment in Vermont and was to report to General Heintzelman. A rumor that Stoughton was to take command of the 2nd Vermont Brigade spread quickly through the camps of the five regiments. He had not endeared himself to these men while supervising their training that autumn. Lt. Col. Charles Cummings, 16th Vermont, informed his wife, "The 'galliant' Brigadier has a great reputation in the army as a woman's man. He is probably the handsomest Brigadier in the army, or at least would be so called by the girls." Henry Willey, also in the 16th, wrote after the war, "A brigade had to have a general," and we had "a man named Stoughton." The young general drilled his men incessantly, and earned a reputation for being abusive. Willey remembered Stoughton's "most striking characteristic was his senseless profanity and West Point snobbery." He also recalled Stoughton's "ever memorable knapsack drill ... hour after hour ... often at the double-quick ... carrying our whole equipment which weighed around eighty pounds." A soldier in the 12th Vermont observed in January, "some of the boys would as soon shoot him as not."[27]

Henry Smith, 1st Vermont Cavalry, was happy to move from Dranesville to a less exposed position at Lewinsville on the seventh. "The rebels are most every night shooting at our pickets at Dranesville they have wounded three and captured five." At his new post he found a "good house warm rooms stoves bunks built up about two feet from the floor and hay in them to sleep on plenty to eat and more coffee than we can use." While Smith moved off the front line, William Martin and the 18th Pennsylvania moved up toward the front for the first time on the eighth. The march to Jermantown had been one of trepidation as "one hundred well drilled and armed rebel cavalry could have taken our hole regiment prisoners while comeing here we had nothing but our old sabers and twenty Carbines to a Company we had no ammunition to take." Two days later the 5th New York Cavalry joined the Pennsylvanians at Jermantown.[28]

The 5th Michigan Cavalry received the first shipment of the long awaited Spencer rifles on the tenth. Before the "splendid rifles" were distributed to the men, Colonel Norvell issued detailed instructions for their care and handling. "The commanding officer hereby cautions that they are a most expensive weapon and must receive the finest attention and care. No needless cocking, nor forcing back and forth the guard will be allowed.... A weapon injured through neglect or carelessness will be charged ... and deducted from the man's pay." The following day Lt. Colonel Gould noted the arrival of "some 600 rifles ... and if called again [to the front] we shall go." The weapons were distributed on the thirteenth, and Norvell started drilling the men with the rifles the following day. The men of the 6th Michigan began to receive their weapons as well. "There is some talk of us going into active service," John Farnill told his father. "We have drawed revolvers they are a pretty weapon I can tell you." A day later the men were issued their sabers.[29]

The demand for additional cavalry along the picket line continued after Brig. Gen. Alexander Hays took command of the infantry brigade formerly led by Colonel d'Utassy. Hays worked to have a supply of rockets issued and to devise a system of signals by which the outposts could warn of "actual or anticipated danger." He also sought additional cavalry, telling a superior, "I cannot sufficiently impress upon you the necessity of stationing some cavalry at this point which would be subject to my orders."[30]

General Hays made it a habit to ride his entire line on a regular basis, regardless of the weather or time of day. If his pickets could not sleep then he would not sleep either. His officers and men ignored this fact at their peril. On the thirteenth Hays was up well before daylight and rode out to observe one of his regiments at reveille. When he found them "napping ... they caught a lecture." Hays had spent a restless night as, according to his wife, one of his men had been killed on the picket line that evening. "The shots could be heard here," she informed her brother. This may have been a soldier in the 125th New York who was shot in the leg while standing guard.[31]

Later in the day Hays sent a telegram to Maj. Gen. Silas Casey concerning another problem that had been brewing for some time: "Col. Wyndham's cavalry makes a great deal of trouble, they will not obey orders and act entirely too independent to be of that service which they ought to render. If the cavalry stationed at and for the protection of Centreville would receive orders to report for special instructions to the commandant of the post of Centreville so that they would act in conjunction with his dispositions, their effectiveness might be insured which at present is apparently paralyzed through the orders they received 'not to obey any orders but Col. Wyndham's.'"[32]

Beyond the prejudice toward foreigners that was rampant throughout the army, the nature of Wyndham's military background was a singular irritant that grated his fellow officers. His exact age became a matter of dispute during the war but he claimed to have been born on February 5, 1833, on board a British ship bound for Calcutta, India. In December 1862 he detailed, for the benefit of the War Department as well as to further his chance for promotion, his military career. Unlike other European officers who had served for or against their own country in national wars of independence, Wyndham had served France, England, Austria and Italy as he sought promotion and action. Beginning his career in the Student Corps in Paris in 1848, he soon transferred to the Navy where he earned a promotion to ensign of Marines. He resigned less than two years later and volunteered in an English artillery unit, serving in Northern Italy, before resigning and accepting a commission as 2nd lieutenant in the 8th Austrian Lancers in December 1852. Following promotions to 1st lieutenant and Squadron Commander he resigned in 1860 and immediately accepted a position in the Italian Army as captain. Promotions to major and lieutenant colonel followed, and he reported that he was in command of a brigade when he took leave in October 1861 to come to America. Among the honors that he received was a Knighthood bestowed upon him by King Victor Emmanuel.[33]

In February 1862, "upon the special recommendation of General McClellan" the governor of New Jersey appointed Wyndham colonel of the 1st New Jersey Cavalry. That a man with his resume accepted a mere colonel's commission surprised the men of the regiment. That he accepted the position with a regiment that had "a reputation by no means to be envied, and ... fast verging not merely to disbandment, but to utter demoralization," was even more of a shock. Though initially thought to be "a thorough soldier," his men soon had cause to question their early conclusions. Wyndham was captured during a skirmish near Harrisonburg, Virginia, on June 6, 1862, when, according to his second in command Lt. Col. Joseph Karge, he ignored a warning that he was leading his regiment into a possible ambush. Exceeding his orders and proceeding on horses exhausted to the point of "waddling through bottomless roads," Wyndham advanced three miles until the regiment was engulfed in fire from three sides. Thirty-two men were lost, including one officer killed and two others captured along with Wyndham. The men also suffered the loss of their regimental standard.[34]

In the wake of this rout Wyndham was castigated in the press, with one New York paper blaming the defeat on his "bad conduct, neglect or disobedience of orders." A correspondent for *The New York Times* claimed that he was among those who had seen the enemy ahead and that he had personally warned Wyndham of the threat. Initially, the colonel was "loth to make any demonstration," pending orders from his superior, General Bayard. However when another scout reined in and suggested that the enemy force could be easily captured Wyndham remarked to the correspondent, "We'll have a little fun, then; would you like to see it?" At that the cavalry moved forward in what the reporter termed "a terrible piece of imprudence," by Wyndham. Several men from the regiment also weighed into the controversy. Charles Coffman could not fathom what had gone through Wyndham's mind. "Whether he could whip the *whole* of Jackson's army with his regiment, or whether he is tinctured with secesh; but the scout told him a brigade was there.... It was a marvelous thing that any one got out alive." Another trooper acknowledged, "Col. Wyndham receives all the censure and blame for the sad disaster that befell the First New Jersey Cavalry." After the war a Southerner, who derisively described Wyndham as "a soldier of fortune, but to fame unknown," admitted that while he led the charge "with considerable dash," he had failed to "observe that his men were not following him."[35]

The colonel was exchanged and resumed command of the regiment in August. In the weeks immediately following the defeat at Second Manassas, George Bayard was confronted with unrest among the officers of the 1st New Jersey, but the young general made it clear that he firmly supported the two senior men. "I trust Wyndham and love Karge, no one can hurt them in my estimation." Bayard then detached Wyndham from his regiment and assigned him to command of the cavalry outpost at Chantilly.[36]

After several months at Chantilly, Wyndham approached Heintzelman seeking the general's endorsement for a promotion. "Understanding that the names of a great many Colonels in the service, have been recommended to the *President* for promotion, I, not being acquainted with any political parties or persons of influence, naturally have no chance of being recommended in like manner. I would consider it a great and lasting favor, if you would use your influence in obtaining me a *position*, and if possible in your command." Shortly thereafter he lost his staunchest supporter when Bayard was mortally wounded on December 13, at Fredericksburg. That same day an opponent to his bid for promotion wrote to General Halleck. "He is probably not a safe man for the position either in principle or practice. There are many men who doubt his loyalty and I have it from a field officer of cavalry that Wyndham said to him ... that he would as [soon] fight for the Confederates as for the Union & that he would if our Gov't did not give him what he wanted." On the fourteenth Wyndham sent a hasty note to the Secretary of War, stating that his name had been submitted for promotion but claiming that he needed the document returned to him, "for the purpose of having other *names* and *approvals* [added] to it." If this flurry of correspondence failed to raise questions within the War Department about his fitness for command then Wyndham's actions in the field certainly did.[37]

Col. Percy Wyndham was both colorful and controversial. He had a volatile personality and clashed often with his superiors, as well as John Mosby (USAMHI).

Wyndham's immediate superior was Richard Butler Price, who had entered the service as colonel of the 2nd Pennsylvania Cavalry one month before Wyndham received his appointment as colonel of the 1st New Jersey. Price, with no military background, saw little front line service during the war. Content to let his subordinates take command in the field, Price spent most of his career in Washington, where he could critique their actions from the comfort of his desk. Wyndham, with his long military resume, bristled under this command structure. Following Stuart's Christmas Raid, in which Price had remained on the sidelines, Wyndham began looking for a way out. In addition to pressing for a promotion, he sent a telegram to Heintzelman on the sixth of January, in which he advised the general on the state of affairs at Chantilly and requested to "be placed under the order of Slocum or Stoughton." Wyndham was in the habit of shortcutting the chain of command and communicating directly with Heintzelman, and when the general and his staff responded directly to Wyndham, Price found himself completely in the dark. Angered by this abuse of military protocol, Price told Wyndham on the tenth, "You will in the future send anything intended for Headquarters Defenses of Washington through these headquarters." And, if this growing dispute were not enough of a distraction, Wyndham was, once again, the cause of unrest within his command.[38]

Col. Richard Butler Price was an ineffective commander who elected to spend most of the war behind a desk rather than in the field. Still, he was comfortable sitting in judgment of young officers as they struggled to combat the guerrilla problem in Northern Virginia (courtesy Roger Hunt).

When he received intelligence that the Confederates were rebuilding the railroad bridge at Rappahannock Station on December 31, Wyndham directed Col. Nathaniel P. Richmond, 1st West Virginia Cavalry, to make a reconnaissance to determine the validity of the information. According to a press account Richmond refused, citing "informality and the want of rations." Wyndham then ordered Richmond to report to his headquarters where, in an angry tirade, he called Richmond a "Coward." Three days later 46 officers, including several of field grade and one chaplain, forwarded a petition to Heintzelman requesting that Wyndham be relieved from command. The men charged that Richmond had been summoned to Wyndham's quarters, where behind a closed door guarded by a sentinel, "Wyndham did, without provocation, use abusive epithets to Col. N.P. Richmond and seizing him by the throat inflicted several blows upon his face and then ordered him to leave his room immediately." Shortly thereafter, and still in an apparent rage, Wyndham overtook Richmond, who was en route to Fairfax Court House to prefer charges, and ordered him back to his post. After a meeting between Wyndham and General Stoughton, Richmond was charged with disobedience of orders. In their petition, the officers alleged that Wyndham was in the habit of placing officers under arrest "without just cause." Ominously, the officers stated that in the future they would only report to his quarters "armed, for their personal safety."[39]

A week later the situation had not been resolved. Capt. James Penfield, 5th New York, and one of the men who signed the petition, noted in his diary, "Col. Wyndham does not suit the Officers & [is] obnoxious to the Whole Com'd." On January 18, Wyndham abruptly submitted a letter of resignation. One of the local papers speculated that Wyndham "became offended at being, to some extent, placed under the orders of Col. Price, his senior, whose duties in this quarter have kept him nearer this city." Heintzelman, who admired Wyndham, tried to save his career by recommending instead that he be transferred. "I think the interests of the service would be greatly promoted by relieving the Colonel from this immediate command." Suggesting that it might be best if he was returned to his own regiment, then attached to the Army of the Potomac, Heintzelman concluded, "Col. Wyndham is such an excellent Cavalry officer, when under the orders of a suitable commander, and has behaved so gallantly on frequent occasions, that I would most reluctantly see his resignation accepted. His services with the main army in the front, would I am satisfied be eminently valuable." Heintzelman's assessment aside Wyndham remained in command at Chantilly for the next several months.[40]

Nathaniel Richmond was placed under arrest on December 31, 1862, and remained so until he resigned on March 18, 1863. Two days later the officers of his regiment addressed another petition to Secretary of War Edwin Stanton, requesting that the order accepting his resignation be revoked. Referring to their colonel as "an accomplished cavalry commander," possessing "unflinching courage, and devoted patriotism," they asserted, "His resignation was prompted by that high sense of *Honor*, which should ever characterise an officer and a *gentleman*." At their urging Richmond had attempted to withdraw his letter while it was still "in the hands of Col. R. Butler Price," but due to "some unknown influence" it was forwarded and approved. Stanton and Heintzelman were in a bind as long as Wyndham remained, but following his transfer that spring Richmond was reinstated as colonel of the regiment.[41]

Thus, at the very point that John Mosby chose to begin attacking the outer picket lines the officers in charge of those lines were on the verge of open revolt. Colonel Price was either in Washington or at Fort Scott in Arlington, essentially ceding all direct control to Wyndham who was quarreling with both his superiors as well as his subordinates, and concentrating his attention on his own career. Colonel Richmond was under arrest, and the officers at the outpost were incensed and distracted by Wyndham's conduct. Further, the men of the 18th Pennsylvania were simply too unseasoned to warrant any confidence from the veterans in the other regiments. In the end, however, this situation played no significant role in the success of Mosby's ventures in early January, which may actually have helped to refocus the officer's anger against a new but now common enemy.

7

January 14–January 31, 1863
"Bush Whackers are all around"

As the month of January approached its midpoint and the soldiers in the Defenses of Washington suffered through the winter doldrums, doubt and anger were the pervasive feelings consuming their thoughts. Not only were the officers quarreling with each other, but the men in the ranks were questioning the commitment of their officers. Alfred Ryder, 1st Michigan Cavalry, may have been referring to lingering effects of the bloody defeat at Fredericksburg, now a month past, when he wrote, "I begin to feel as though I should be glad to have that day hasten that frees us from the service. I doubt our finil success.... It don't seem as though our officers designed to bring the war to a close but merely prolong it for the pay. The lives of millions seem to be nothing in the balance." Lt. George Kilborn, of the same regiment, was clear as to the reason for the disaffection. "The defeat at Fredericksburg and Gen. Stewart's *raid* with his cavalry through all our outposts overshadows everything. Confidence in the Civil & Military Leaders is below zero.[1]

The increasing number of alarms along the outer picket lines, which cost the men precious sleep, did little to improve their attitude. More often than not it was nervous cavalry pickets who created the problems and earned the enmity of the infantry. An infantryman, who was safely ensconced at Fairfax Court House, made light of the alarms at the expense of the cavalry. "Two or three nights ago," the soldier wrote on the fifteenth, "we were awakened by the beeting of the long roll at abot midnight they said they heard firing in the direction of Chantilly whare our Cavalrys pickets are stationed ... they swore it was some rebels but it might have been a Coon or a possum or something of the like."[2]

At Dranesville, Charles Johnson, 1st Michigan Cavalry, explained a very different reality to his mother. Referring to John Mosby's recent attacks Johnson explained, "we have had some trouble here we have had one post captured and two or three more fired on and wounding one man each time but our Major put a stop to that by arresting some of the citizens and telling them that he should hold one of the most prominent of them responsible for every man that was shot or taken from the command and since then we have been left alone."[3]

William Martin, 18th Pennsylvania Cavalry, stationed at Centreville, may still have been too new to take the danger seriously or he chose not to alarm his wife. "There is not much danger in standing on picket duty in this part of the country as the rebels are scarce about here ... there is generaly from ten to twelve of us stationed tolerably close together we have [three] reliefs [and] we have to set still on our horses for two hours at a time." Men like Captain Penfield who maintained a diary were less concerned about easing the fears of loved ones and often more accurate in the record they maintained. Penfield's terse entry that day was simply, "Some of the Va. & Penn. Pickets captured at Centerville." According to Colonel d'Utassy, a sergeant and nine men were "picked up" from a post along the Braddock Road. "The cavalry picket was scarcely half a mile from my infantry pickets but it seems that the cavalry had been surprised in their sleep." In his explanation to General Casey the colonel explained, "Capt. [Thaddeus] Freeland, [Company E] 18th Pennsylvania Cavalry commands pickets now but he is not to be blamed as his predecessor gave him absolutely no instructions and he did to my knowledge work to the utmost of his ability."[4]

Well to the south, near Belle Plain, a trooper in the 1st Indiana Cavalry elected to reassure the readers and family members back home as well. "It is quite natural that these marauders should be continually scouring the country between our lines and Washington, and so they have employed themselves for the last fortnight on our right flank." As he was posted on the opposite flank the trooper claimed, "Such raids are considered of no consequence here, and are sometimes not even heard of.... It is not worth the wear and tear of horseflesh for our cavalry to be jaunting over the country after these comparatively harmless marauders." Closer to where these "marauders" were active General Averell saw the need to request that infantry be ordered up to support his picket lines.[5]

In addition to the Iron Scouts the men most actively working against the right flank of the Army of the Potomac were the troopers from Capt. Phillip Williams' Prince William Cavalry and Capt. Robert Randolph's Black Horse Cavalry, of the 4th Virginia. Randolph informed his superiors on January 16 that his men had just captured two scouts from the 1st Rhode Island Cavalry. He also reported, "It is almost an impossibility to get into the Yankee lines now, his pickets are so close. They are very particular in not permitting citizens to go in or to come out, and for this reason I cannot find out as much as I did when I first came over, for then I went into their lines, and they permitted citizens to pass in and out." That same day two men from the 6th Ohio Cavalry were seized near Dumfries, and paroled by Lt. Alexander Payne of Randolph's company. Later in the month a civilian refugee reported to General Hays that Randolph had established a parole office in or near Warrenton, where Union deserters came "in squads to get paroled ... they are [then] advised which way to go to avoid our lines."[6]

With General Burnside preparing to launch a new offensive, General Slocum was notified on January 14 that he should have his men ready to move "at a few hours' notice." The immediate concern, for Burnside, Heintzelman and Halleck, was how replace Slocum's men once he headed south. Halleck was not going to allow the inner defensive circle to be weakened to provide troops to replace the Twelfth Corps along the outer lines. On the seventeenth, Burnside informed Halleck that Slocum was to move the next morning. Halleck concurred, but reminded the army commander that Heintzelman would not be responsible for the line beyond Occoquan, warning "these positions can only be held in weak force as outposts." Heintzelman actually felt that he could hold the line only as far as Wolf Run Shoals. Burnside then complicated the matter when he requested that Slocum be allowed to take the cavalry from the lines along Bull Run and the Occoquan when he pulled out. Slocum was concerned that he had but one regiment, the 12th Illinois Cavalry, assigned to his corps, and the majority of that regiment was posted at Dumfries with Colonel Candy. Three companies of the 1st Maryland Cavalry had been attached to Candy's force at Dumfries, but they had been re-deployed to the upper Potomac River on the tenth. The battalion of the 1st Connecticut Cavalry that had been assisting Candy had also just been ordered to Baltimore to join Gen. Robert Schenck's Eighth Corps. The only other cavalry that Slocum had were two companies, one each from the 1st Maine and the 1st Michigan. To correct this deficiency he sought, unsuccessfully, to obtain the 18th Pennsylvania, advising Burnside on the eighteenth, "I would be glad to have it ordered to join me." Slocum began pulling out of the lines the following day.[7]

Lt. Col. Roswell Farnham, 12th Vermont Infantry, was a lawyer and schoolmaster prior to the war. His letters provide a detailed picture of life along the picket lines. He became governor of Vermont after the war (USAMHI).

Stoughton relieved Slocum's veterans at Wolf Run Shoals on the twentieth, shifting the 12th and 13th Vermont, along with the 2nd Connecticut Battery to hold the vital crossing point, while the remainder of his brigade, supported by Battery H, 1st Rhode Island Artillery, held the depot at Fairfax Station. Over the next few days these men reversed the old Confederate earthworks on the far side of the Occoquan and dug new lines commanding the ford. Stoughton posted a platoon of men downstream at Davis Ford, advising, "It is so narrow as to be able to be crossed by only two abreast," and he assured his superiors that the fords to the north "are also perfectly guarded."[8]

Lt. Col. Roswell Farnham found the roads frozen, but so chewed up between Fairfax Court House and Wolf Run Shoals that the wagons were turned off the road and moved through the fields. That night the temperature rose, the skies opened and the condition of the roads deteriorated. "I don't know, of course, how the world's surface looked after the flood in Noah's time," Alpheus Williams confessed, "but I am certain it could not have appeared more saturated than does the present surface of this God-forsaken portion of the Old Dominion." The rain and mud quickly swallowed Burnside's new offensive, which went down in history as "The Mud March."[9]

As Farnham explained to his family, the 12th and 13th Vermont were now "at the front, that is there are no troops between us & the rebel forces.... When the river goes down we shall have to depend upon our pickets to apprise us of the approach of danger. I will explain to you what pickets are. About half a mile in front of us, within rifle shot of the river, are posted two companies of infantry. They keep out a dozen or twenty sentinels on the look out night & day.... Still nearer the river are the cavalry pickets, consisting of one, two or three horsemen who watch all the roads.... There are cavalry pickets on every road from Dumfries to Poolesville."[10]

General Hays repositioned his brigade as well, posting two regiments and a battery at both Centreville and Union Mills, and sending one regiment to Fairfax Court House. While overseeing this move Hays and his wife accepted an invitation to dine with Stoughton. "I found General Stoughton one of the handsomest, men I have ever met," Annie Hays declared, "well educated, his manners very refined, and only twenty-four years of age." She also noted that he "is elegantly quartered, has a large modern house, with many pieces of handsome furniture," but in an interesting aside she admitted, "but I prefer 'Union Mills,' it looks as if a soldier lived there." After dinner a twenty-piece band entertained the guests.[11]

On January 6, Joseph Copeland, now bearing a brigadier's star, was ordered to report to Heintzelman in Washington. The new general was assigned to command a new brigade consisting of the 5th and 6th Michigan Cavalry. Lt. Col. Ebenezer Gould was more than satisfied that both regiments were to remain together under Copeland's command in what he termed "Copeland's Cavalry Brigade." With the continuing demand for cavalry, Gould told his wife, "There was quite a strife among the generals who should get us we all worked as hard as we could to get with Gen. Copeland and [are] happy to have succeeded."[12]

On the nineteenth the two regiments passed through the city along Pennsylvania Avenue in a line "nearly two miles in length." They made a "fine show as respects the appearance of both men and horses," but the fact that the men of the 6th Michigan were still awaiting their carbines, prevented them from taking the field. Having witnessed the martial display, the editors of the Washington *Evening Star* wondered when the shortages that confined them to the city would be corrected. "Quite 2000 cavalry are here waiting for a portion of their arms that have not yet reached Washington. As they are new troops, we trust they are being industriously drilled by experienced officers." The paper also reported that a large number of the men already at the front were still not fully armed and urged, "Every nerve should be excited to correct this state of things."[13]

The officers, many of whom were experienced, did keep the men on the parade ground "drilling pretty hard," according to a trooper in the 5th Michigan. "We have ... saber exercise in the forenoon and battalion drill in the afternoon which keeps us in our saddles from 1 o'clock until nearly night." At the same time the Detroit *Free Press* was reporting that the 7th Michigan was "full to a minimum and ready to take the field. The arms, equipments, clothing, horses etc have all been given out to the men." With just enough men to field ten companies the regiment was mustered at Grand Rapids, Michigan, on January 27, but it was almost a month before the first detachment boarded trains for the long ride to Washington.[14]

The contingent of the 1st Michigan that remained at Fort Scott, along with the regimental headquarters detail, was also kept busy on the drill field. Three days a week under "the immediate eye" of Colonel Town, the troopers drilled until nine o'clock at night. The troopers manning the picket lines, however, many of them veterans, had little time or desire for drill. Restricted by a lack of suitable ground on which a large number of men and horses could practice their "Evolutions," or simply because the company officers chose not to press the matter the men grew lazy and earned the disdain of the infantry.[15]

Like the Michiganders, the 1st Vermont Cavalry was also headquartered at Fort Scott, while the majority of the regiment was scattered between posts at Annandale, Lewinsville and Dranesville where the men idled away the hours not spent on the picket lines. Charles Chapin admitted, "You never saw such a lazy set as the soldiers are.... I don't believe at any rate if I walk past half a mile I can hardly breath. I am not used to walking you know, but I can sit a horse six or eight hours a day and not feel it a bit." And though Chapin would brag "there is none like the Vt. cavalry," the steady, mind-numbing routine of endless picket duty, even in the face of mounting incursions against the outposts dulled their combat efficiency and instilled a habit of indolence that would cost the regiment dearly over the next few months. Even the regular reconnaissance patrols during the fall and early winter had too often been a matter of routine, lulling the men into the dangerous attitude of complacence reflected in Chapin's letter. While Chapin professed pride in his unit he was also comfortable bragging, if only to his brother, of just how lazy he and the rest of the men had become.[16]

The losses along the outer line of outposts continued on an almost nightly basis. On the seventeenth, an infantryman reported, "20 more of our Pickets taken last night," while an officer in the same brigade recorded the loss of 15 men during the night. And while these figures are hard to verify, and may reflect desertions as well, they do confirm an ever-increasing problem. On the nineteenth, Captain Penfield noted that another man had been seized from the 18th Pennsylvania, making a total of 10 men captured by "Bushwhacker[s]" that month near Hutchinson's Mill along Cub Run. Possibly in an effort to keep the men more alert, or simply to cut the number of horses that the government was supplying to the enemy, the commander of the 5th New York sent two companies out the following night dismounted. Their chaplain reasoned it was so "they might be better prepared for guerrillas should they appear."[17]

According to Richard Kenwell, 5th New York, the men of the 18th Pennsylvania "are the simplest men about the duties that are expected of them on picket that I ever saw." Even though the post he encountered was under the supervision of an officer, "One of our officers come round and caught the whole party in a house with their arms off while the sentry was upon his post without arms he having left his in the house with the party."[18]

Wednesday night, January 21, was, according to William Martin, 18th Pennsylvania, "the most disagreeable that we have seen since we came to camp it rained and stormed all night." Martin returned to camp that afternoon, after a night on the picket line, and had not been asleep long when the men were aroused at ten o'clock and ordered out of their tents. Word had been received that Lige White would attack at some point during the night. "We got up and got on our equipments, Martin recorded, "sadled our horses tied them to our [picket] ropes and got our ammunition loded our carbines formed into lines of battle in the woods close to the road we watched for the rebels till day light but they did not come." Martin declared that having lost a second night's sleep, "we intended to give them our best licks."[19]

Lige White was still in the Shenandoah Valley, and though there are indications that he was harassing the Federal lines around Harpers Ferry, it is not known if he had sent any of his men east to work the Union picket lines, but some group was clearly operating in western Fairfax County. The name of John Mosby was not yet widely known among the Federal troops, though the New Yorkers first captured by him would have identified him when they were paroled. White was still the name that was uppermost in the minds of the

Yankee sentinels, but the identity of the men who were conducting many of the hit and run attacks along the lines remains a mystery.[20]

Among the civilians who may have been responsible for some of these attacks was Richard "Dick" Moran, who resided in eastern Loudoun County. Moran began riding with Mosby in March 1863 and enlisted in June, but there are indications that he was conducting his own personal war before then. Following a fight near Hatcher's Mill, west of Middleburg, in April 1863, Julius Stahel referred to Moran as "the leading guerrilla near Dranesville." A month later he was referred to as "the notorious bushwhacker, Dick Moran." One correspondent alleged that Moran "delighted in shooting down the poor pickets after finding out their whereabouts in the day time." This reputation may have been earned while operating independently during the early months of 1863, when Moran was at least forty years of age. He was also the father of ten children, seven girls and three boys. The oldest of his sons would have been about twenty and may have ridden alongside his father.[21]

On the evening of January 23, Ambrose Burnside asked to meet with President Lincoln at his earliest convenience. Eleven hours later the general presented Lincoln with the option of dismissing several ranking officers from service in the Army of the Potomac, including Maj. Gen. Joseph Hooker, or accepting his own resignation. The president met with the army commander again two days later. Lincoln informed the general that he had decided to accept his resignation and promote Hooker to replace him. The following day General Burnside took his leave from the army.[22]

When John Mosby returned to Warrenton following his meeting with Jeb Stuart in mid–January, he dispersed his 15 men, and directed them to rendezvous on January 26, at Mount Zion Church, east of Aldie on the Little River Turnpike. While his men rested, Mosby scouted the Union lines in western Fairfax County. Old School Baptists built Mount Zion Church in 1851 following a disagreement "over doctrine" with the members of the Little River Baptist Church several decades earlier. It was a companion church to Frying Pan to the east. Mosby probably did not tell the men where they were headed when they left the church, but they followed him eastward along the turnpike, meeting John Underwood along the way.[23]

Just a mile north of the turnpike and three and a half miles across the Fairfax County line stood Chantilly Church, which Mosby knew housed a picket post of the 18th Pennsylvania Cavalry. Years after the war Mosby spoke of the "life of drowsy indolence" that the Union soldiers enjoyed along the lines surrounding Washington, and by all accounts the Pennsylvanians, as evidenced by Richard Kenwell earlier, were the simplest if not the most indolent. Kenwell did not identify the location of the post that he described, but as Mosby scouted the Union lines he may well have observed the same negligence by the men stationed at Chantilly Church.[24]

At four o'clock on the afternoon of January 26, Mosby attacked the outpost at Chantilly Church. The Pennsylvanians were caught unprepared; they had unbridled their horses and were feeding them when the Confederates, dressed in Union overcoats, rode up. When one of the Yankees attempted to escape Mosby shot him, but later apologized when he learned

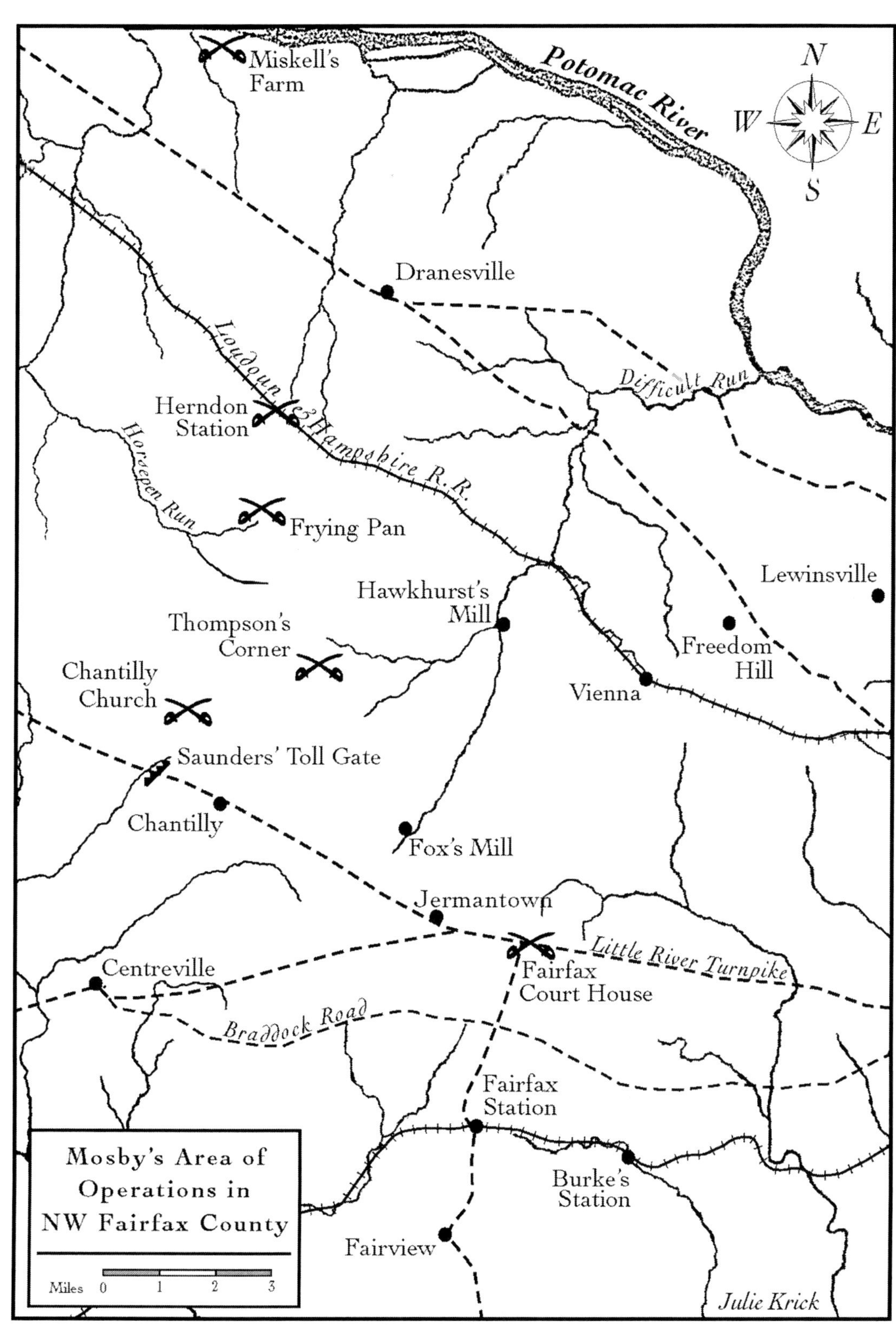
Miskell's Farm
Potomac River
N
W
E
S
Dranesville
Loudoun & Hampshire R.R.
Difficult Run
Herndon Station
Horsepen Run
Frying Pan
Lewinsville
Hawkhurst's Mill
Thompson's Corner
Freedom Hill
Chantilly Church
Vienna
Saunders' Toll Gate
Chantilly
Fox's Mill
Jermantown
Little River Turnpike
Centreville
Fairfax Court House
Braddock Road
Fairfax Station
Mosby's Area of Operations in NW Fairfax County
Burke's Station
Fairview
Miles 0 1 2 3
Julie Krick

that the soldier had no way to control his unbridled mount. The Confederates seized ten men, along with their equipment and horses, and herded them west to Middleburg, where they were paroled. The wounded soldier was released at a home about two miles west of the church. That very day William Martin wrote a letter to his wife explaining, "it costs the government about 250 dollars apiece to arm and equip each trooper in the service properly." By this estimate the partisans divided $2,500 in government property before they dispersed. Nonetheless, Mosby complained, "that unless the men were better armed and equipped it wouldn't pay to capture them." Mosby and his close friend Fount Beattie then went to the home of Lorman Chancellor on the east end of Middleburg to get some sleep.[25]

Whether it was the sound of Mosby's gunshot that alerted the Federals or word from a relief party that found the men missing is unknown, but Capt. Abram Krom and Lt. Albert Waugh soon led Companies E and G, 5th New York, in pursuit. They were ordered, however, not to go any farther west than Aldie, six miles east of Middleburg. Nine hours after the attack Colonel Wyndham set out with a force of 200 men from the 5th New York and 1st West Virginia. According to both The Rev. Boudrye and Captain Penfield, this second detachment of New Yorkers, under the command of Maj. John Hammond, acted independently of Wyndham and the West Virginians. This suggests that Wyndham either split his force to scour a wider area or his dissatisfied officers were attempting to preclude Wyndham from gaining any credit for the events that followed. In his very brief report, Wyndham appears to go out of his way to speak only in the first person, and thus refusing to credit the contributions of the other men.[26]

Near Arcola, Hammond encountered Krom's detail on their way back from Aldie, and the combined force then started for Middleburg. Just after daylight the Federals, with Captain Krom in the lead, charged into the town, rousing the citizens from their beds, "amazed at our early call." The troopers quickly drove the sleepy residents out of their homes in their search for the raiders. Five men were seized from a hotel, along with their horses from a nearby barn. The Yankees then took the opportunity to feed their horses on Southern grain before heading back to Chantilly with their prisoners.[27]

Mosby and Beattie awoke in time to flee from the Chancellor home and avoid capture. While the Federals were occupied searching the town and gathering up prisoners, Mosby and Beattie were busy rounding up as many of their own men as they could locate. Just as Hammond's rearguard was leaving, Mosby attacked with a handful of men from the west end of town. Hammond quickly wheeled his column about and drove Mosby and his comrades about three miles beyond the town, capturing another three men, including Beattie, whose horses fell on the ice-covered road. William Martin, who was not present, told his wife, "they gave the rebel capt a sharp race but his horse proved to fast for ours." The Federals lost one man captured in this skirmish along with three horses. Among the Southern prisoners were men from the 1st, 4th, 6th and 11th Virginia Cavalry.[28]

In the continuing battle between Wyndham and Price, the former drew Price's ire when he failed to promptly inform his superior about these events. "You will on receipt of this immediately inform me," Price directed, "of the circumstances stating what force you sent out and in what direction. All movement of the troops under your command you will report to these headquarters and if important to Heintzelman also." By way of reply Wyndham scribbled out a hasty four-sentence report, in which he cited the capture of 24 prisoners. All of the prisoners, including 14 believed to be Union deserters were incarcerated in the jail at Fairfax Court House before being transferred to Old Capitol Prison.[29]

Beyond the threat presented by bushwhackers and partisans the Union sentinels confronted a host of other issues along the picket lines. Colonel Candy was concerned about a smuggling operation run by three men he identified as "Davis, Smith and Cross," who were purchasing goods in Alexandria and transporting "them through the lines to Brentsville." In an attempt to have them apprehended Candy informed General Slough, the military governor of Alexandria, on the twenty-fourth, that when the three men were in the city they passed "themselves as sutlers belonging to the Army of the Potomac." That same day Col. William Doster, the provost marshal for the city of Alexandria, arrested a man who was identified in the papers as John B. Hunter. Hunter was held on suspicion of having betrayed a government scout to Stuart's cavalry during their raid through Fairfax in December.[30]

Alfred Ryder spent the twenty-fifth guarding several prisoners, including "an old man and his son, a lad of 12 years." They had been arrested for delivering government horses "over to the Secesh," including two horses captured after the soldiers riding them were shot. Still, Ryder "couldn't help pitying" them and gave them his own rations when he learned they had had nothing to eat for 24 hours.[31]

On the twenty-sixth Colonel d'Utassy led a patrol to Gainesville where he recovered a stash of rifles hidden in a barn. He also reported that two "Rebel cavalry" had seized a young man and some horses from a farm just outside his lines the previous day and taken him as far as Hopewell Gap before he was able to escape. At Wolf Run Shoals, Lt. Col. Roswell Farnham was grateful for the company of his wife, but would not let her ride through the camps as she had in Fairfax. In a letter to her brother Mary Farnham explained the reason for her confinement—"Bush Whackers are all around."[32]

When Ambrose Burnside met with Lincoln on the twenty-fourth he presented the president with the option of dismissing several senior officers from the army or accepting his own resignation. Joseph Hooker was Burnside's main antagonist in the army, and the president knew it. Still, Lincoln relieved Burnside and promoted Hooker, thinking that he had found in Hooker a man who would fight. The new commander possessed boundless self-confidence, but also a penchant for self-promotion and political intrigue that alienated many of his fellow officers, including Samuel Heintzelman. One of Hooker's most vocal supporters was Count Adam Gurowski, a Polish revolutionary who maintained the nation's most public personal diary from his home in the capital. Termed by one historian as "a crow cawing his omens," the former State Department translator delighted in lecturing and criticizing the Lincoln administration.[33]

"Hooker is in command! And patriotic hearts thrill with joy," Gurowski proclaimed on the twenty-sixth. Heintzelman, who was disgusted by the appointment, promptly told Halleck that he "could not serve under Hooker." By the next day Gurowski was aware of the disaffection in the officer corps and declared, "Let them go ... the hole in the army will be invisible. I am sorry that Heintzelman plays such pranks, as he is a very good general and a very good man." Heintzelman quickly sought to distance himself from Hooker by having his command designated as a separate department, beyond the control of the army commander. In an attempt to appease Heintzelman, Halleck told him to "wait a few days—

there may be other changes." Officially Heintzelman avoided mentioning his disdain for Hooker and presented his idea to Halleck as a matter of simple practicality. "Scarcely an order issued from the headquarters of the Army of the Potomac applies here," he wrote. "The duties being so different, cannot the defenses be made into a separate department with such limits as may be convenient?" Heintzelman reminded Halleck that his current area of responsibility stretched from the mouth of the Occoquan, north to Piscataway Creek near Annapolis Junction, west along up the Potomac River as far as the Monocacy River and then south to Goose Creek and along Bull Run Mountain through Aldie and Cedar Run, suggesting that he would be satisfied if the new department incorporated the same area.[34]

On the twenty-eighth General Copeland reported that all of the men in the 5th Michigan Cavalry were now equipped with sabers and revolvers and that 600 Spencer rifles had been distributed, with another shipment of 600 expected any day from New York. Sabers and revolvers had been issued to Colonel Gray's 6th Michigan, and Copeland had determined that the regiment would receive 400 of the rifles that he was awaiting from New York, along with another 150 revolvers, in an effort to hasten their move to the front. Two days earlier one company of the 5th Michigan had been sent into Virginia, with Copeland planning to rotate other companies to the front on a ten-day cycle, "to give our men an idea of active duty."[35]

The first of the companies to take the field was Company K, led by Capt. John Clark. His orders were to assist Stoughton, securing the supply depot at Fairfax Station as well as Fairfax Court House. Two more companies took the field on the first of February, when captains Eli Simonds and Stephen Purdy led Companies D and H across the Potomac River to Poolesville, Maryland, in response to a request from Heintzelman for additional cavalry to be assigned to the Potomac crossings.[36]

Though the mud and snow of winter made travel difficult, Colonel Wyndham was ill at ease following Mosby's incursion on the twenty-sixth, and the most recent redeployment of the infantry. He reported that there was "now no infantry within six miles" of his main post at Jermantown. Prior to Stoughton moving two regiments to the Occoquan, Wyndham had benefited from "infantry between the pickets and the camp & also a regiment in its immediate neighborhood." He warned Heintzelman, that with his troopers manning a line that stretched for fifteen miles, "a bold dash of the enemy with three hundred men might capture the pickets, and surprise, if not endanger the command." Based on intelligence gathered during his recent expedition to Middleburg, Wyndham believed that Stuart was planning another raid against his lines, which only increased his concern. Tabulating his losses for the month at 40 men, Wyndham requested that an infantry regiment be returned to cover his position or that he be allowed to withdraw towards Fairfax Court House "as a precautionary measure."[37]

Heintzelman rebuffed his plea, and asked why he should send cavalry to a post already held by infantry. He reminded Wyndham that two infantry regiments and a battery held the fortifications in his front at Centreville, and told him that he had little to fear as long as his men remained vigilant and his scouts stayed active. Heintzelman also directed Wyndham to immediately obstruct all the roads by which enemy cavalry could approach his position.[38]

The month of January ended much as it had begun, with attacks against Federal patrols and picket posts. At Dranesville, Dexter Macomber, 1st Michigan, noted the capture of several men from the regiment on the thirty first. "I am on picket on the Frying pan road." A corporal "has charge of the out side post on the pike towards Leesburg he has six men & at 3 P.M. he is attacked by John Mosby & 25 of his men." The Wolverines lost two men captured. On February 4, Mosby wrote a brief summary of his activities following his return to the area a week earlier, but made no claim of responsibility for the incident reported by Macomber. In concluding his report, however, Mosby expressed his belief that the outpost could be easily captured. "There are about 300 at Dranesville. They are so isolated from the rest of the command that nothing would be easier than their capture. I have harassed them so much that they do not keep their pickets over half a mile from camp." Macomber's erroneous statement suggests that John Mosby was now the man who predominated the concerns of the Union pickets.[39]

8

February 1–February 19, 1863

"There is a rebel captain ... by the name of Mosby"

In Grand Rapids, Michigan, recruitment of the 7th Michigan Cavalry lagged, and morale plummeted as the early enlistees spent months building roads and new barracks. Endless drill and the mindless routine of camp left the men feeling surly as they pondered their future. Their horse equipment began to arrive in mid–November, and by the end of the month the rifles and sabers had also reached camp. The men were satisfied with the quality of the sabers they received, but, as one soldier grumbled, the rifles were muzzleloaders, and not "the same kind that were promised us when we enlisted." All across the North and South, Ordinance officers issued similar complaints, but all would have agreed with recruit Edwin Havens, who observed, "The men will be hardest to get."[1]

By mid–December Havens was beginning to doubt Colonel Mann who had reported that 900 men had enlisted in the regiment. "I do not want you to think I do not believe what our Col. tells for he is respected as a *man* by his entire regiment. But there is something rather perplexing to hear his stories and not see the men." Within days, though, horses began to arrive, and the soldiers were encouraged that they appeared to be of better stock than those that had been delivered to the 6th Michigan. Their arrival broke up the daily routine, as the men groomed them twice a day, and made a mile long trek to water both morning and night. Soon, the noncommissioned officers were taking instruction in mounted drill, in preparation for training the privates. Still, as Havens observed the New Year he counted one hundred horses assigned to his company and only sixty men.[2]

The men bristled under Mann's insistence on discipline and military protocol, and they viewed him as a commander who was "playing out." Havens termed him "a very strict disciplinarian, and all style, very egotistical, and of a quick impetuous temper. He demands a great deal of respect from inferiors," and "a salute from every one who meets him and never returns one, and for myself I have just about quit saluting him.... At first I feared him.... But now I care for him no more than I would for the meanest scoundrel I ever met and respect him about as much." That they had not been paid was also "a fruitful source of complaint," but in the end the men questioned whether they would ever be allowed to contribute to the war effort. "All I would ask," Havens concluded, "is that I could be put somewhere where I could do what I enlisted to do, namely help get this country out of this fuss, but which I will never do as long as Col. Mann commands the 7th."[3]

The recruits were on the verge of open rebellion, and took out their frustrations by "stealing [from and] insulting the citizens" of Grand Rapids. Mann reacted by confining the men to camp, which only inflamed the volatile situation. The malcontents met on January 24, and vowed to defy the colonel. They would go into town regardless of his restrictions. Strapping on their sabers many broke past the guards and stormed into the city. Several men were arrested and confined in the guard house. Two nights later the structure mysteriously burned down.[4]

On February 1, Havens informed his parents that men were now "deserting every night and will probably continue to do so as long as we remain here." Though he continued to fault the colonel, Havens also allowed that Mann might be "unjustly accused." Did Mann simply possess a volatile personality or was the strain of raising the regiment affecting his judgment? Havens was astute enough to recognize that Mann had not yet received his colonel's commission pending muster of the regiment, and his letter of the first suggests that Mann may have been breaking under the strain. Constantly traveling between Grand Rapids, Detroit and Washington, Mann may also have been on the verge of despair as he watched his dream and military career fading away. Observing his colonel everyday, Havens saw "a kind, generous hearted man, who has not only his own, but the interests of his men at heart. But he is also very impulsive and does things and gives orders, which, in his calmer moments he is sorry for and many of them he afterwards modifies or countermands. This nature almost, if not entirely unfits him for the command of a number of men as he cannot exercise the amount of firmness necessary to perfect discipline."[5]

On the evening of February 1, John Mosby called his men together in Middleburg, and struck east along the Little River Turnpike. After taking dinner at the home of a friend, near Arcola, Mosby turned his command north; avoiding the pickets from the Chantilly outpost, and headed toward Frying Pan. He stopped at the home of Ben Hatton. A known Union sympathizer, Hatton had reportedly visited the Federal lines that afternoon and was persuaded by Mosby, on threat of imprisonment, to guide the men toward a nearby outpost of the 18th Pennsylvania Cavalry along Lawyer's Road, south of Herndon Station. Leaving their horses behind and using the light from the Yankee campfire as their guide, the men approached the post on foot and captured all of the dismounted men. Two mounted men, including Sergeant Lorenzo Headlee, attempted to escape, but were pursued by Ned Hurst and William Keys, using Yankee horses. Sergeant Headlee was killed and the second man captured. Fearing that the gunfire had alerted other pickets in the area, Mosby hustled his men and prisoners back toward the horses, where they watched a detachment of Federals gallop past in the dark. Once he felt it was safe, Mosby led his men back to Middleburg by a circuitous route.[6]

In his report of the incident, Mosby claimed that Colonel Wyndham had set a trap for him by placing a reaction force nearby, and that it was this force that had galloped past as his men huddled in the woods near their horses. Though generally accepted as fact, Mosby's claim is doubtful. Certainly Wyndham was by this time well aware of the threat that Mosby posed to his pickets, and, as events would soon show, Wyndham was both angry and frustrated with Mosby's method of warfare, but for Wyndham to have set a trap for the guerrillas near that particular outpost, when he was in command of a picket line many miles in length, suggests a degree of insight into Mosby's intentions that the Union officer could not have possessed. Short of a turncoat in Mosby's ranks, and it is almost certain that none of the men, other than John Mosby, knew where they were headed that night, the claim that Wyndham laid a trap for the guerrillas is nothing more than supposition. There had, however, been enough gunfire to draw the attention of either a routine patrol or a response from the reserve outpost. Most of the shooting erupted at the spot where Mosby had left two men to guard Ben Hatton and the horses. In the darkness, those men had scared themselves into thinking the other man was an enemy soldier and they engaged in a comical shootout with each other, in which "a fusillade" of shots were fired. The only victim of this exchange was the innocent Hatton, who was shot in the thigh. The two guerrillas abandoned Hatton and fled the scene before Mosby and the others returned.[7]

While there is nothing in the contemporary record to confirm John Scott's account, the officer in command of the reserve was required to send out patrols on a prescribed schedule to check on the forward pickets. The last patrol of the day went out at midnight and as this attack took place in the early morning hours of February 2, it is possible that it was this routine patrol that was nearby, heard the commotion and rode to investigate, but following the procedures defined by the army did not advance or pursue beyond the forward picket line.[8]

In his brief account of this raid William Martin addressed a major deficiency in the armament of the regiment. Referring to Mosby's earlier comments on the poor quality of the Merrill Carbines that the Pennsylvanians were issued, Martin recognized that the Union troopers would need revolvers if they were to successfully counter the sudden attacks of the guerrillas. Though the carbine was often more readily available than a holstered revolver, the long-barreled weapons proved cumbersome, and sometimes useless, in close quarter combat when the men had time to get off only one hurried shot. As Martin explained, we "need revolvers badly to compete with the rebels."[9]

At five o'clock that afternoon, the 1st West Virginia and 5th New York were ordered to meet Colonel Wyndham at Centreville. The patrol, about 500 strong, left Centreville at dusk, and, with the temperature plunging below freezing, the men rode toward Warrenton, arriving at midnight. Taking the sleeping town by surprise, Wyndham sent squads toward the Rappahannock while the main body made a hurried search of the town. The Federal troopers found numerous weapons, and some "warm beds," but no sign of John Mosby or his men. The "chilled" Yankees destroyed the weapons and turned for home, reaching their camps about noon.[10]

Following each of his raids Mosby retired to the vicinity of Middleburg to parole his prisoners and to dispense the captured horses and equipment. Wyndham's men had encountered and done battle with a handful of the guerrillas along the main road through town in late January, and he had undoubtedly learned that Mosby used the town as a rendezvous point prior to his most recent raid. Acting on this information the colonel, issued a warning to the residents of Middleburg, that he would hold them responsible for any further incursions against his lines. According to John Mosby, Wyndham declared that he was willing to burn the town. Following the capture of the Pennsylvanians on the second, Wyndham may have issued another similar warning. Having been roused from their warm beds by angry Yankees and then forced to duck for cover as the brief gun battle erupted in town at the end of January, the town's prominent citizens needed little persuading when Wyndham's second edict arrived. They promptly took their concerns to Mosby, asking that he discontinue his guerrilla war against the Federals. Mosby turned them down cold, declaring, "I unhesitatingly refuse to comply." In an attempt to mollify the people he admitted that, following a recent raid, the prisoners had been paroled in the town by "a misunderstanding of my orders." He then tried to assure the residents that they could not be held liable for his actions, based on his claim that his men had never occupied the town, but this seems rather empty, as he and Fount Beattie had spent the night there following the attack on January 26. The speed with which they later rounded up several companions that morning suggests that they too were bedded down nearby. That Mosby used the town as the rendezvous point on the first of February also belies this claim. The simple fact was that the young partisan had spent his entire life standing up to opposition, and he was not to be deterred now by Wyndham's threats or the pleas of the worried civilians.[11]

Mosby informed Stuart of the matter in his report of February 4, and included copies of his correspondence with the residents of Middleburg. Both Stuart and Lee endorsed the report as well as his handling of the Yankee threats without directly commenting on the matter. They also ignored his suggestion of a possible attack against the large Union outpost at Dranesville, choosing instead to simply commend him on his "prowess, daring, and efficiency." Stuart did take the opportunity to remind his superiors that his subordinate was still serving without a formal military commission, though that matter remained unresolved for another five weeks.[12]

On February 2, and in response to Heintzelman's request of January 26, the command known as the Defenses of Washington was removed from the control of the army commander and designated as the Department of Washington, with the troops forming the Twenty-Second Corps, under Heintzelman's command. His area of responsibility was confirmed as he had requested on the twenty-sixth.[13]

On February 5, the reorganization of the Army of the Potomac continued when General Hooker terminated his predecessor's system of Grand Divisions, and ordered that the army would return to the corps system established by Lincoln and McClellan. Hooker also directed that the cavalry be organized into a corps, under the command of Brig. Gen. George Stoneman. This brought to an end the disastrous policy of scattering the cavalry among the infantry commands, though it did not effectively end the equally troublesome tradition of dispatching large numbers of mounted soldiers to infantry commands as escorts and couriers.[14]

On the fourth, Wyndham directed Capt. James Penfield and 60 men to prepare for an expedition into Loudoun County. Undeterred by a "snow squal," Penfield led his men out at one o'clock the following afternoon. Moving as far as Aldie, the New Yorkers took shelter at Mount Zion Church for the night as the snow turned to rain and further degraded the treacherous roads. While the men warmed themselves, Penfield spoke with a scout from the Army of the Potomac who had recently encountered several of Mosby's men in Middleburg.[15]

In the morning the Federals entered Aldie, where their presence immediately raised fears among the residents that they were there to burn the town. Instead, Penfield set his men to searching for contraband and ordered one detachment to move north along the west side of Bull Run Mountain toward Leesburg. Observing a horse tied up outside the home of a Mr. McCarty, the Yankees surrounded the property and captured six of John Mosby's men. Confident that the Federals would not be out in such miserable weather, the men were inside "having a good time with the girls" when the New Yorkers came through the door. One of the Confederates was wounded in the encounter, and a postwar account mentions that one of the women was also injured. By midnight the Federals had the men secured at Chantilly, whence Lt. Col. Robert Johnstone, 5th New York, was pleased to report that the prisoners were "part of those under Mosby that have been attacking our pickets."[16]

Mosby called for his men to rendezvous again on the seventh at Ball's Mill, along Goose Creek in eastern Loudoun County. He learned of the incident at McCarty's when only a handful of riders arrived. Angry that the captured men had disobeyed his orders, Mosby set out toward his favorite hunting ground in western Fairfax County, where he encountered Dr. Francis Drake, struggling through the deep snow and mud. The doctor informed them that a roving party of Federal troopers had stolen his horse and medical equipment. The guerrillas rode off in pursuit and soon cornered the four culprits along the banks of Horsepen Run, which was nearly "impossible" to cross following the recent rain and snow. After watching one man nearly perish in his attempt to escape, the other Federals surrendered to their fate, and Mosby recovered the stolen property, including the doctor's medical equipment. The four prisoners, all from the 1st Vermont Cavalry, were paroled two days later. "A bold piece of business and worthy a better man than Mosby," was how Vermonter Charles Stone recorded the incident in his diary.[17]

Five days earlier Major William Wells, 1st Vermont Cavalry, had been put in temporary command of the outpost at Dranesville, and Colonel Price had admonished him that he and his men were to "exercise the *utmost diligence* in picket and patrolling duties." Price reminded him that several men "have lately been captured at your post — try to prevent a re-occurrence." Commanding a post of nearly 600 men from four regiments, if only for five days while the senior officer was on leave, may have been a heady experience for Wells, who told his brother on the sixth, "since I came here we have had no trouble at all." Despite his assertion to the contrary, four men from the 1st Michigan were captured near the outpost on the third of February.[18]

In a letter dated February 2, Sgt. James Somerville, 6th Michigan Cavalry, informed the newspaper readers in Grand Rapids that the regiment was still awaiting their firearms, and that they would not leave the capital until the weapons arrived. With the eager boastfulness of most untried soldiers, Somerville wrote that if the folks at home wished to know when the regiment took the field they need only "watch the telegraphic column: and, when they hear of something being done, then set it down that the Sixth have crossed the Rubicon." "We are anxiously awaiting our rifles — Spencer's repeating," declared another soldier. "When fully armed and equipped, I fancy we will look much like a Turk, 'armed and bearded to the teeth.'"[19]

When their weapons arrived later that week, the men were disappointed to learn that they had been issued Burnside carbines. A final shipment of 800 Spencers arrived the same week for the 5th Michigan, and once these were distributed the surplus was given to the 6th to supplement the other weapons. John Farnill informed his father, "we now have all our arms which are composed of the very best we have a splendid Sabre a Six Shooting Revolver together with the Spencer and Burnside Rifles." Farnill had apparently hefted both weapons and remarked that the Spencer is "a great Deal heavier Gun than the" Burnside that he had been issued. With either weapon he was confident that "we ought to do some execution."[20]

Orders arrived on the seventh sending the 5th Michigan to assist Wyndham on an expedition across Loudoun and Fauquier counties. Specifically, Wyndham was to send two columns of cavalry, a combined force of at least 1,000 men "to thoroughly scour the country" in his front, with one column following a route through Leesburg to Snicker's Gap, while the second moved south of the Manassas Gap Railroad across Fauquier County, clearing the right flank of the Army of the Potomac. In addition to the escalating guerrilla threat along the Fairfax County–Loudoun County border, reports of other attacks, along the right flank of the Army of the Potomac, as well as along the Blue Ridge, convinced Heintzelman to order this expedition. These latest incidents included the capture of a stagecoach carrying several Union officers on the sixth near Millwood, just west of Ashby's Gap, by men from the 12th Virginia Cavalry. In a running fight the following day, two companies of the 1st New York Cavalry recovered the coach and the officers. On the seventh, "a force of guerrillas, numbering 35 or 40 men," attacked a picket post manned by a lieutenant and 16 men from the 17th Pennsylvania Cavalry, near Hooker's supply depot at Aquia Creek, in what one soldier later referred to as a case of "midnight murder."[21]

The 5th Michigan left the capital early on the morning of the eighth and spent the night six miles west of Dranesville. After posting the men and setting out his pickets Lt. Col. Ebenezer Gould returned to Dranesville where he found that Col. Freeman Norvell "had been drinking pretty freely." In the morning, Norvell, whose hangover left him feeling "very squally," divided the column, which now included four additional companies from three other regiments, and offered Gould the opportunity to command one wing of the expedition. Under the pretext however, of instructing Gould in the finer points of leadership Norvell requested that the two officers remain together. While one column proceeded through Leesburg to Snicker's Gap, Norvell would move through Aldie to Ashby's Gap, where the two columns were to link up and then proceed to Manassas Gap to meet Wyndham.[22]

Lt. Col. Ebenezer Gould, 5th Michigan Cavalry. His letters detail the problems created by Col. Freeman Norvell's alcoholism, as well as his own efforts to assume command of the regiment (USAMHI).

Norvell and Gould set off in the morning accompanied by Alexander "Yankee" Davis, a Northern sympathizer, who resided near Aldie. Davis told them "who [the] secesh were and," according to Gould, "we sent out parties and searched their houses & took away all arms and ammunition." Gould thought the country "the finest I ever saw," and he told his wife, "I should love to live and die in it." They spent the night at a large plantation near Aldie, with the colonel "so drunk he could not stand up or ride on horseback." The next morning they moved through Middleburg, liberating a Union soldier from a local hospital and pushed on for Upperville, capturing six men, including a captain who was found hiding in "a hay mow," and a cattle buyer for the Confederacy who was carrying $8,000 in Southern script. The Federals also seized 40 horses and assorted weapons. They encountered several parties of "rebel pickets but," as Gould lamented, "they would not let us get near enough to try our rifles." Maj. Noah Ferry set an ambush for the enemy troopers who were tailing the column but they refused to chase the "stragglers" who were the bait.[23]

Amanda Edmonds, who had not seen the hated Yankees in many weeks, spent the morning hours visiting several friends and family members between Paris and Upperville. Just when she thought the day would remain quiet and peaceful, a cry was heard, "The Yankees are coming. The Yankees are coming." Within minutes, "the slumbering peace of Paris was suddenly aroused to a perfect volcano."[24]

By the time the Federals reached Ashby's Gap, Norvell was "so drunk as to require five or six men to take care of him giving orders without sense and neglecting those that were most necessary." Gould later reported, that as they were "in the face of the enemy ... I was compelled to take command away from him." Major Ferry noted that this difficult decision was reached only after Gould consulted the senior officers. According to Ferry, both Gould and the senior major were reluctant to relieve Norvell. It was only after Ferry, disgusted with their indecision, agreed to assume responsibility for their decision that Gould took the action. In his detailed retelling of the events Ferry suggests that Gould never took overt command of the column, ceding that instead to Ferry, possibly in an attempt to avoid any future repercussions.[25]

Captain William Williams led an advance guard into the hamlet of Paris. At the head of his column were lieutenants George Dutcher and Samuel Harris, who both claimed in

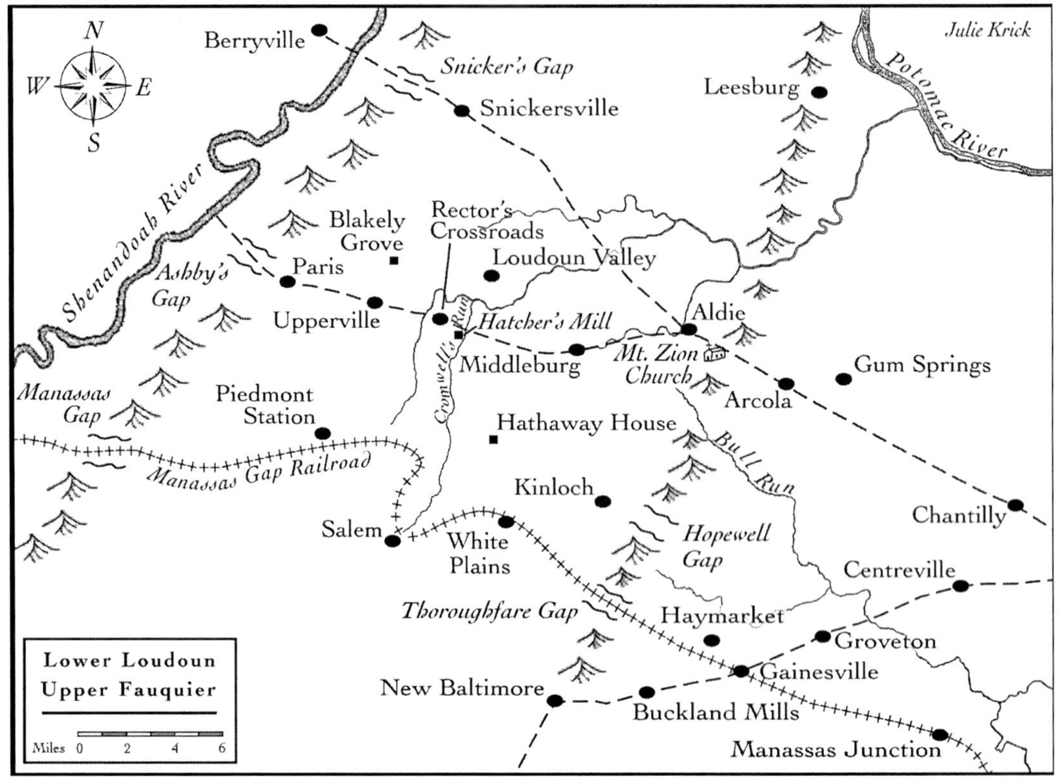

postwar accounts that they were "fired on by men in the houses." According to Dutcher, Gould ordered the men to return through the town after drawing the first fire, and as they complied they were "again fired on from the houses," with one of the balls penetrating Dutcher's left hand. "I ... was rather excited, and really did not notice the wound at the time," Dutcher wrote later. Once beyond the town Harris, who maintained that they "drove the rebels and bushwackers out of the houses and up the mountain," bound up his comrade's hand with a handkerchief, and Dutcher had it properly dressed later that night by the surgeon. The accounts by Harris and Dutcher were later disputed by Captain Williams, who affirmed, "There was no battle or skirmish [in Paris] the only gun fired was one that the company found in a house that was searched and found loaded." According to Williams, as well as one of his sergeants, the men accidentally discharged the weapon when they seized it.[26]

Edmonds, who made no mention of a "skirmish," stated that the soldiers immediately "commenced searching houses and robbing stables." As she and her sister attempted to protect their possessions within the house, "one vile rascal" took possession of Nelly, her horse. The young women were soon engaged in a valiant but futile struggle to retain the horse, saving only the saddle and bridle. As Nelly was led away, Amanda wished that the soldier's "brains might be kicked out.... Such a set of angry wolves never were seen before, among all the Yankees. These take the lead." She estimated that the residents lost $7,000 worth of property.[27]

Concerned by Norvell's deteriorating condition Gould and Ferry cut the expedition short, returning to Aldie, rather than attempting to link up with Wyndham. The 5th Michigan arrived back in Washington near midnight on the eleventh, having sustained only one casualty, that being Lieutenant Dutcher.[28]

The detachment that marched through Leesburg to Snicker's Gap was under the command of Capt. Josiah Steele, 1st West Virginia, and included Lt. Charles Stone's company of the 1st Vermont, along with two companies of the 18th Pennsylvania, and a detachment from the 1st Ohio Cavalry. Stone commented that they were intent on finding "Mosby & White," but they were hampered by high water at several points and forced to alter their route. After passing through Leesburg Steele turned south rejoining Norvell and Gould along the turnpike to Upperville. There Stone confessed, "the boys committed a depredation that fairly made me shudder," when they entered a tailor's shop where the owner also maintained a small grocery "and took everything he had." This kind of behavior led another soldier to conclude, "No wonder Mosby sought vengeance for such meanness." Leaving Upperville, Steele turned his squadron north and reached Snickersville at noon on the eleventh. After searching both the town and reconnoitering Snicker's Gap, the men returned to Leesburg, arriving at three o'clock. Attempting to reach Dranesville that night they were forced to turn back when they found Goose Creek still running high, but not before James Rush of the 1st Vermont drowned in the turbulent stream. Not wanting to risk further loss of life the column returned to Leesburg for the night, and reached Dranesville the next day.[29]

The Federals captured seven officers, as well as "250 guns, 60 horses and mules, and one woman," who was, according to Victor Comte, "so ugly that she could be left with the soldiers without any fear of being molested." In his opinion, "We had two men too many with us — the doctor and the chaplain. The doctor because he prevented us from drinking and eating what we wanted ... and the chaplain because he preached abstinence and forbade marauding." Comte remained unrepentant, telling his wife, "that both of them wasted their time, and I hope that they will not be with us on another expedition." Augustus Paddock, 1st Vermont, viewed the expedition as "quite a trip," during which the men "stole everything that came in the way."[30]

Wyndham's column, including the 5th New York, under Major Hammond, as well as a contingent from the 1st West Virginia, left Centreville at 10:30 A.M. on the ninth, marching through Catlett Station and spending the night west of Bristoe Station [modern day Bristow]. Two companies of the 5th New York were sent to make a late night scout through Warrenton, arriving just after daylight on the tenth. They captured and paroled two soldiers and seized some weapons and saddles before pushing on for New Baltimore, where they lost four men and horses to a small party of Rebels. The squadron continued to Buckland, where it captured one member of the 4th Virginia Cavalry, before returning to the main body. In all the circuit cost the squadron six men captured. Wyndham took the larger force "to near Rappahannock Station." He then traveled to Hartwood Church, where he made contact with the Army of the Potomac, continuing by way of Elk Run and Spotted Tavern. There he had a brief skirmish with the enemy, "wounding several & capturing two." On the eleventh the expedition passed within four miles of Falmouth, before turning north and spending the night near Stafford Court House. It returned the following day, passing through Dumfries and crossing the Occoquan at Wolf Run Shoals.[31]

In his first encounter with Southern civilians, Gould took obvious pleasure in making them uncomfortable and bragged of his boorish behavior to his wife. "I slept in the best houses without invitation and got my food ordering the FFVs to get it and paying them if I chose ... they endure this from both sides they say, and they don't know which is worst." Gould "ordered them about in the most civil manner I could," but confessed that by the end of the trip he was "quite indifferent" to the feelings of the local gentry. In a follow-up letter Gould explained to his children, "that the inhabitants suffer both by loss of property and some times loss of life — but this is not the worst feature of the war here in Virginia here neighbor is arrayed in deadly hostility against neighbor and sometimes brother against brother and father against son & son against father." Much of Gould's attitude was shaped by his discussions with "Yankee" Davis, who had described for Gould the true nature of the neighbor versus neighbor conflict that existed in Loudoun County, including a graphic account of a bloody encounter in his own house when a group of Southerners had attempted to arrest him the previous June.[32]

In his report of the operation Colonel Price informed Heintzelman that three regiments of Confederate cavalry were reported to be near New Market in the Shenandoah Valley. Price, who took no part in the expedition, also advised that Brig. Gen. William "Grumble" Jones was planning "to make a raid soon." Though Price discounted the report, stating, "it comes from no reliable source, merely country people's talk," there is evidence that it was based on fact. Lee was tired of Brig. Gen. Robert Milroy's presence in the Shenandoah Valley, especially his hard-handed treatment of civilians. On the thirteenth, Lee sent a directive to both Stuart and Jones indicating his desire that they attempt "to limit the operations of General Milroy ... if he cannot be dislodged." Jones was to report to Stuart, and using New Market as a base they were to interdict Milroy's line of communication and supply. Events along the Rappahannock, however, tied Stuart to the main army, leaving Jones to continue his harassing attacks on his own.[33]

Of more pressing concern for Price was the behavior of Colonel Norvell. When Price forwarded the reports of the expedition to Heintzelman he admitted that it had been cut short by Gould without reaching Manassas Gap as desired, and he included a list of charges that had been preferred against Norvell by Major Ferry. Price was uncertain as to how he should proceed, in part because he was bedridden due to illness and could not investigate the matter fully. Upon his return Norvell had submitted a written pledge that he would no longer drink "while in command," and he authorized his superiors to consider the pledge "an unqualified resignation if I under any circumstances violate this promise." Seeking the general's advice on the matter of a court-martial, Price informed Heintzelman, "Some of [Norvell's] friends desire that he should be allowed to resign." According to Gould, the colonel had turned against the senior leadership of the regiment, charging that they were conspiring "to oust him," and Gould admitted, "we are very much demoralized on account of this thing and it is injuring our regiment very much.... I hope it will be disposed of in two or three days." It was not, and by the twenty-third both Norvell and Copeland were appealing to Gould to speak to the officers in an attempt to resolve the matter. Though he felt strongly that Norvell should be removed, Gould sought to remain neutral but he found his position "exceedingly unpleasant."[34]

The disaffection with Colonel Wyndham continued to simmer as well. Though Wyndham had left the majority of the 18th Pennsylvania behind to picket for the infantry as he had been directed, General Hays complained to Heintzelman that this was not the case. Following a meeting with Heintzelman, Hays concluded, "Wyndham is played out, and new arrangements are expected on our lines." Colonel Price, who was engaged in his own battle with Wyndham, felt that Hays made the complaint in an effort to take control of the cavalry brigade, but it also appears that Price was content to allow Hays to press his agenda, concluding as Hays had, that "there will be no difficulty there after Col. Wyndham shall have been removed."[35]

Price was also planning to send Lt. Col. Peter Stagg, 1st Michigan, back to Warrenton in an attempt to deal with the 50 or so members of the 4th Virginia who continued to use the town as a base of operations. Price informed Heintzelman that Stagg "knows exactly where to find the hiding place of the Black Horse Cavalry." On the eleventh Price instructed Stagg that once Wyndham was within the lines, "you can start upon the expedition proposed, with such portion of your force as you may deem necessary leaving in camp enough for picket duty."[36]

On the thirteenth, Capt. Charles Snyder led 50 men from the 1st Michigan into Prince William County. After traveling six miles Snyder divided his command, leaving a squad of ten men, led by Lt. Peter Karpp, as a rear guard, while he continued toward Brentsville with the remainder. Frederick Schmalzried remembered that Snyder divided his command a third time, so as to approach Brentsville from two directions. Unbeknownst to the Federals, Sgt. William Mickler and a party of 15 Iron Scouts had spent the night on the west side of the Occoquan, intending to strike the Michigan pickets in the morning. Mickler also had ten men from the 1st North Carolina Cavalry, led by George Handley, and three men from the Prince William Cavalry. These men were just gathering at the rendezvous point when the smaller Union patrol was observed. Mickler immediately sent all of the men who were already in the saddle after the Yankees, and hurried the other men along as they arrived. After a sharp race through the woods, in which the Confederates became badly scattered, the Michiganders made a stand along a hillcrest in an open field. When Mickler heard the gunfire from the initial chase he ordered the men with him into their own frenzied gallop through the woods that again left the Rebels badly strung out. Arriving with only two other men Mickler immediately ordered a charge against the Yankee line. It was a contest of pistol versus carbine and the Confederates dropped three men, driving the remainder of the Federals from the field. In the ensuing chase two more Yankees were wounded and the remainder captured. From the prisoners Mickler learned of Captain Snyder's reconnaissance to Brentsville, and the fact that he was expected to return in a couple of hours.[37]

Though he knew that he would be outnumbered, Mickler decided to ambush Snyder's patrol when it entered a deep ravine, about three miles outside of Brentsville. The sergeant dismounted 14 of his men and deployed them along the crest of the embankment, concealed by thick undergrowth. Mickler held his other four men on horseback, with orders to charge the rear of the column once the shooting started. After allowing the advance guard to pass through the ravine, Sgt. Prioleau Henderson was to spring the ambush by a shot from his pistol, when the head of the main column was directly in front of him. At that point Mickler instructed the scouts to "give them every barrel of your pistols, and then run back, mount your horses and follow them." Henderson noted that what he saw as an ambush was viewed as bushwhacking by the Federals.[38]

An hour later the advance guard approached and was allowed to pass, before Henderson fired his revolver. This was followed by "shot after shot in rapid succession ... dealing death and destruction to the terrified enemy, from a foe they could not see." The Wolverines were driven to confusion as they attempted to escape the killing ground. Those not immediately struck down were chased all the way to the Occoquan before Mickler called off the pursuit and returned to the scene. There he found Sgt. Calhoun Sparks lying on the ground, holding his pistol on a Yankee still on horseback. In charging on the rear of the Union column Sparks emptied both of his revolvers before he was shot in the chest. Turning his horse off the road, Sparks passed out. He regained consciousness just as the Federal trooper rode by. Sparks disarmed him and was holding him at bay when his comrades arrived. Though severely wounded with a bullet through his right lung Sparks survived. Two other men, including Handley had their horses killed and one man was injured when his horse fell in the initial charge down the embankment.[39]

One of the prisoners was Frederick Schmalzried, whose horse "went wild" during the melee and threw him from the saddle. He and the others were allowed to ride to Gordonsville, where they boarded a train for Richmond. He was paroled three days later and sent to Annapolis to await exchange. From there he wrote a letter to his brother accusing the officers, namely Captain Snyder of being among the first to flee. "Had he been a man he would have turned around to lead & not one of the rebels would have escaped." By all other accounts, however, Snyder was a courageous officer who had been with the command from its organization. A Southern report credits Snyder with being the man who shot Sparks, when the South Carolinian called on him to surrender.[40]

The survivors of the ambush arrived back in camp in the early afternoon and Stagg notified General Hays about two-thirty. Hays grabbed a hurried meal and then rode to the Michigan camp. Setting out with 140 men, as well as an ambulance and a surgeon, the relief party arrived at the river only to find it dangerously high, but "with the hope that we might meet the rebels," they plunged in, and Hays received "a thorough wetting." After a ride of seven miles they arrived at the scene of the ambush, but found only dead horses and several wounded troopers, returning "without the opportunity of punishing the guerrillas."[41]

If Stagg made a report of this incident it has not been found, nor did the Michigan press cover the defeat, so it is difficult to know if Snyder's patrol represented Stagg's effort to destroy the Black Horse Troop or the Prince William Cavalry or if it was simply a routine reconnaissance. That Snyder set out with no more men than what Stagg expected to encounter in Warrenton suggests that this was not the effort that Stagg and Price had discussed. Alfred Ryder, whose horse was shot in the affair, thought that several men had been killed and told his father, "Death is a hard master unto whom we all shall haft to find sooner or later." Another trooper admitted, "we run into a nest of bushwhackers and they played cain with us."[42]

On the fifteenth the Federals made an attempt to ensnare Mosby and his men by means of a decoy ambush. William Martin, 18th Pennsylvania, explained, "there were about eighty cavalry out of the old regts went out several miles from camp they had six wagons loaded with the buck tails infantry ... our men done this to fool the rebs and put the cavalry in front and behind the waggons to make the rebles think they had something worth capturing in their wagons." The men spent the night about 15 miles outside the lines. In the morning, Martin continued, "along comes Mosby with about 14 cavalry they got tolerably close and the [1st West] Virginia cavalry as soon as they discovered them they made a dash on them and chased them some four or five miles but the rebel horses was to fast for them and they all got away." The men returned in the morning with only "a wagon load of chickens" for their trouble.[43]

The regimental historians of the 13th Pennsylvania Reserves Infantry, known as the Bucktails, describe a very similar scenario, taking place in March. "Early on the 9th, four men from each of the companies were ... [concealed] in four army wagons ... escorted by a plainly insufficient detachment of cavalry." After an uneventful day the men spent the night in a barn. "Hardly, however, was the expedition under way the next morning, when the cavalry in the advance ran into some of Mosby's men and immediately retreated upon the wagons. The Bucktails ... heard the cavalry come racing back, and naturally inferred that the guerrillas were in full pursuit. Leaping to their feet, they threw back the curtains of the wagons and blazed away." In this account the rebels were not as close as the infantry had suspected and retreated unharmed, but the historians include that the Yankees returned with "numerous chickens, ducks and various other delicacies."[44]

Southern versions place the event on or about the eighth of February. As described by John Scott the Federals spent the night near the home of Laura Ratcliffe, where a talkative Yankee seeking a glass of milk warned her of the scheme. Ratcliffe, then in her mid-twenties, was described by a Union officer as "a very active and cunning rebel," who was well known to the Union troops in the area. Alerted to the scheme, Ratcliffe set out on foot and warned Mosby in time to avoid the ambush. Mosby, however, later stated that he "was off on another enterprise & didn't see them," suggesting that Scott's tale about Ratcliffe warning the guerrilla leader is inaccurate.[45]

In Scott's version of the thwarted ambush Mosby, after being warned by Ratcliffe, headed for the Union picket lines, and struck a reserve post of the 1st Vermont Cavalry in the early morning hours of the sixteenth. Lt. Charles Stone, who was in charge of the post, noted with some humor, "Was relieved from picket little before time this AM by Capt. Mosby." Stone explained that one sentinel had been on guard but that he "gave no alarm until too late & we had surrendered." Guided by John Underwood, Mosby had dismounted his men and avoiding the lone sentinel, surrounded Stone's inattentive reserve force. "Dismounting & coming up on foot they had each man of us by the collar with revolvers at our heads before we had time to draw our own," recalled Stone. In his diary that evening Stone continued his account of his first day of captivity. "Without mercy we ran at full speed...."

After crossing Goose Creek we halted for breakfast ... here we expected to be paroled but the Capt. did not feel inclined to do us this favor ... we arrived near Aldie where spying some cavalry made a detour to the right and came upon the pike above the village.... The men thus far have been kind & treat us respectfully." After a halt for dinner the Green Mountain Boys continued their journey to Richmond, not being paroled until March. When the men of the 1st Vermont learned that Mosby was now sending his captives to Southern prison camps, rather than granting immediate paroles, one declared, "I shall show them some good runnen before they get me."[46]

On the nineteenth, William Martin penned a letter to wife in which he declared, "There is a rebel captain that stays back in the mountain by the name of Mosby that captures our pickets. The way that they do it the citisins turn out with him and they ... generally come in squads of from fifteen to twenty men they are armed with two revolvers a peace they surround our picket posts and cut off their retreat from the reserve." Though the guerrillas were better armed than the Pennsylvanians, Martin assured his wife that "our men are a getting [wise] to their tricks [we] draw in [our] pickets at dusk so that if they come again they will have to fight some."[47]

9

February 16–March 8, 1863

"It is their business to fight and if necessary die"

On February 16, Maj. Gen. Silas Casey requested permission to begin rotating the 6th Michigan Cavalry to the picket lines north of the Potomac River, relieving the two companies of the 5th Michigan that had been on duty there since the first of the month. His request was granted and on the nineteenth Companies I and M, 6th Michigan, took the field, reporting to Colonel Albert Jewett, at Rockville, Maryland. Jewett commanded a brigade, known as a Corps of Observation, posted along the banks of the Potomac River. Jewett was not pleased with the change, and he advised Heintzelman that the men of the 5th Michigan "are the most serviceable to me on [account] of [their] acquaintance with the country. They are under good discipline and energetic." The orders stood, however, with Company I moving to Poolesville on the twentieth, and Company M, remaining at Rockville.[1]

In Grand Rapids, orders arrived on the eighteenth for Colonel Mann to begin shipping his horses to Washington. The animals were loaded on train cars by noon the following day, and after enjoying "a sumptuous dinner, prepared by the ... loyal people of Grand Rapids," the animals, along with a guard of 100 men, were en route for the capital. On the twenty-third, following a ceremony in which each member of the colonel's guard of honor swore an oath to obey the orders of their superiors and "to abstain from the use of intoxicating liquors, they were each presented with a specially designed cross of solid silver, by the President of the local Ladies' Soldiers' Aid Society. The regiment then marched for the depot, where they boarded a train at noon, arriving in Washington on the morning of the twenty-seventh.[2]

When the two companies of the 6th Michigan left Washington, they did so in the midst of "a storm of rain and snow," which lasted for three days. Temperatures plummeted and snow fall estimates ranged between six and fifteen inches. Charles Hampton, 8th New York, termed the twenty-second, "the worst day I have ever seen in the service." After spending the night on picket Hampton made a six-mile trip to insure that the relieving pickets were properly posted, during which his "horse would sink nearly to its knees in mud & snow every step." Several men in the regiment had to have their frozen boots cut off when they returned to camp, while others had to heat their boots in the morning to pull them on.[3]

The weather did not deter "the bushwhackers and guerrillas," who, according to Henry Norton, 8th New York Cavalry, "trouble us a great deal." Cold, and often alone, the Union sentries struggled to stay awake on their posts. Under orders to remain in their saddles, the men found that the only way to stay warm and alert was to dismount and walk around. Yet this lack of discipline, and the mounting losses along the picket lines, drew the ire of Hooker, who sent a scathing note to the commander of his cavalry, Brig. Gen. George Stoneman, just as the storm was reaching its peak. Referring to outpost duty as a "sacred and important trust," he observed sarcastically, "If orders would make an army what it shall be this would be an army without fault. The orders must be obeyed."[4]

George Benedict determined, "Picket duty is decidedly rough at such time, and some mothers' hearts I know of would ache could they see their boys out on the picket line." An infantryman assessed all of his current miseries and declared, "This Reserve Picket business is played out." Many of the sentries only wanted an opportunity to take out their discomfort against their seldom seen enemy, including a trooper from New York who just wanted a "chance to skelp a Rebel." To relieve the tension the men sought distraction in regimental snowball battles, resulting in the "most fun we have had in a long time."[5]

The weather, which Colonel Price termed "boisterous," did not bring the war to a halt, however. A Federal scout reported on February 24, that Stuart was concentrated near Warrenton, and that along with Stonewall Jackson, who was erroneously reported to be at Staunton, he was going to make a raid into Maryland. Hooker, who saw such an attempt as "a physical impossibility ... at this season of the year," was forced to ask Heintzelman for help the following day when Southern cavalry struck his lines around Hartwood Church.[6]

Though Lee had hoped to send Stuart and Jones against Milroy's lines of communication in the Shenandoah Valley, Union troop movements forced Lee to alter his plans before Stuart departed. Lee had begun receiving reports from his scouts on the fourteenth suggesting that Hooker was breaking up the Army of the Potomac, and sending large detachments back to Washington as well as south to Suffolk, Virginia. Lee's uncertainty was caused in part by the withdrawal of the Pennsylvania Reserves to Washington, along with erroneous intelligence brought in by the Iron Scouts that General Hays was falling back from Union Mills to Washington. Due to the inability of his cavalry to penetrate the Union picket lines and determine the validity of the reports, Lee was forced to prepare his army to meet several possible Federal moves. On the fifteenth he instructed Stuart to consider striking a blow at the Union lines toward Washington rather than in the Valley. In a follow-up dispatch Lee was more emphatic, telling his cavalry chief to "suspend your movement in the Valley & see if you cannot ride into [Hooker] before he leaves."[7]

Stuart's first inclination was to pierce the Union lines at Dumfries, but word from Lee that the town was still secured by a brigade of infantry as well as cavalry dissuaded him. Instead, reports that large numbers of Federal cavalry had been withdrawn from near Hartwood Church, leaving behind only a thin picket line, appear to have determined Stuart's course of action. On February 24, General Fitz Lee led 400 men from the 1st, 2nd and 3rd Virginia Cavalry regiments across the frigid Rappahannock River at Kelly's Ford. After a day plowing through snow that one officer measured at 18 inches, the troopers encamped that evening at Morrisville. In the morning, guided by Captain Randolph's Black Horse, they routed the Union pickets from the 3rd Pennsylvania Cavalry and 16th Pennsylvania Cavalry near Hartwood Church.[8]

Throughout the day fighting rolled back and forth as Union reserves arrived at critical points, attempted to stem the Southern drive and were driven back in turn, until the Confederates pushed up against the inner lines manned by infantry. By late afternoon, having penetrated five miles through the Union lines and humiliating General Averell's cavalry division, Fitz Lee withdrew. He took with him 150 prisoners, in addition to those who had been killed or wounded, while sustaining a loss of only 14 men. He had also located the Federal infantry, allowing his uncle to make a detailed report of the Union position to President Davis the following day and dispel the rumors of a Union withdrawal. He left the Union high command angry and embarrassed.[9]

While General Stoneman's troopers slogged through now rapidly melting snow and mud "running liquid" in a futile attempt to throw a net around the enemy force, a flurry of telegrams raced across Union telegraph wires. Col. William Creighton, commanding the detachment at Dumfries, was immediately alerted to the possibility of an attack. He did little to dismiss these concerns when he reported his own belief that the enemy was contemplating an attack against the town. The Union response was further crippled when his reports were passed to Brig. Gen. Alfred Pleasonton, forcing the cavalry general to remain near Aquia with his brigade, until the situation was further developed at Dumfries. This prevented Pleasonton from riding to assist Averell, and in the recriminations that followed left Pleasonton open to unfair censure and reproach.[10]

A request also went to Heintzelman, asking that he send any cavalry that he could spare to cooperate with Averell's division in an attempt to prevent Lee from escaping across the Rappahannock. Hooker's request, that Heintzelman send troops "from Catlett's and Rappahannock Station," suggests a misunderstanding of the manner in which Heintzelman's forces were deployed, but Heintzelman immediately readied 600 men at Fairfax Court House and notified General Copeland to have the 5th Michigan and six companies of the 6th Michigan ready to march as soon as possible toward the river. Within hours the men were underway, but the long simmering dispute between Wyndham and Price now worked to hamper the effort.[11]

The crisis found Price in Washington and Wyndham in Alexandria. Price was not notified until 2 A.M. but he made arrangements to meet the two Michigan regiments at Fort Scott at daylight. Through a mix-up in orders the 6th Michigan actually started earlier than planned and departed from Fort Scott ahead of Price. When Price arrived he found a telegram from Wyndham advising that he would be taking the morning train from Alexandria, and the colonel galloped for the depot, arriving five minutes after the train departed. Price, who had shown little inclination to take the field for months, but who was now apparently eager to do so in an effort to silence Wyndham, was literally left standing at the depot and forced to explain the appearance of "any want of promptness ... or any unwillingness to take command," on his part. Wyndham, who understood that the mission's only chance to succeed was through a quick departure and a rapid march to the Rappahannock, found only delay awaiting him at the other end of the line.[12]

Wyndham, edgy and intolerant, arrived at Fairfax Court House ahead of the cavalry but quickly busied himself by sending angry missives in an attempt to determine when they would arrive. He also informed Heintzelman that 800 men had already departed for Manassas Junction, but reports of "a strong force" of enemy cavalry at Middleburg led him to instruct the Union commander not to proceed beyond Manassas Junction until he arrived with Copeland's Wolverines. Then his impatience turned to fury when he learned that Mosby had again victimized the troublesome 18th Pennsylvania Cavalry during the evening, with a force estimated "between 100 & 200" men. It was this report that generated the warning about the strong force at Middleburg. That a patrol numbering between 200 and 300 men from the 18th Pennsylvania had departed in pursuit of Mosby prior to Wyndham's arrival further reduced the force he could take out in his search for Fitz Lee.[13]

During the evening of February 25, Mosby set out from Rector's Crossroads with 27 men, intent on striking a large reserve post of the 18th Pennsylvania Cavalry, at Thompson's Corner, along the Ox Road, midway between Jermantown and Frying Pan. A local resident attempted to dissuade Mosby from making the attack, informing him that the post was manned by 100 men, to which Mosby replied, "if you are right they will suppose that a hundred at least have come to attack them." That this was exactly the case is confirmed by Wyndham's earliest report of the affair to Heintzelman. Nearing the outpost Mosby left his men behind while he reconnoitered the position. He hoped to surround the log buildings, including the Thompson home and a nearby schoolhouse, in which the men had taken shelter and take them from behind, but he was prevented by an alert picket who observed the Confederates while they were still "several hundred yards off." The sentinel snapped off one round that roused his comrades from their slumber. The Pennsylvanians attempted to fire a few shots as they staggered out of the building, but quickly fled into the woods.[14]

William Martin, who was a member of the regimental relief party, stated that the attack was made about 4 A.M. He arrived four hours later, to find the schoolhouse littered with "quite a number of sabres and carbines." With three pickets on duty outside, it was apparent to Martin that the men had relaxed their guard entirely and that Mosby attacked at the hour when the men were "pretty sleepy headed." Mr. Thompson acknowledged that only a few of their carbines actually discharged, leading Martin to again wonder when the front line soldiers would receive quality equipment, and most especially when his regiment would be armed with revolvers. That the guerrillas left the weapons behind confirms their disdain for the unreliable Merrill carbine. Just a couple weeks after this incident the regiment refused on two occasions to stand picket until they were "armed sufficient to fight." Though the men were inside stout log structures in which firing ports had been cut through the chinking, they immediately abandoned the buildings, according to Martin, and attempted to form a battle line in the open. If this was the case it seems likely that the men, who were awakened to gunfire and confused by the "terrific" yelling of their attackers, may have forgotten to properly cap their weapons. Whatever the case, once their weapons failed to fire the men fled precipitously, well before Mosby's men could cut off their avenues of escape. That they scattered in all directions is evidenced by the report of an infantry officer who reported that "the sole survivor" was in his camp near Centreville. Though Mosby reported that four Pennsylvanians were killed, Colonel Price confirmed the death of only one man, with two others wounded and five men captured. Abandoned to the Southerners were 39 horses, along with other assorted equipment and weapons.[15]

Some of the escapees reached the regimental camp at daylight, but the relief party did not leave until seven o'clock. Maj. Joseph Gilmer, 18th Pennsylvania Cavalry, pursued the partisans as far as Middleburg, and a couple men from both the 7th and 11th Virginia Cavalry regiments were captured, but, in Martin's view, Gilmer was "too slow" to achieve any positive results. Others went to the scene to recover the dead and wounded, including Lt. John Nelson, who was in command of the post, and who had been injured so severely, receiving a gunshot wound in both his right shoulder and right leg, that Mosby believed he had been killed. His leg was later amputated, but the bullet was never removed from his shoulder, causing him a lifetime of misery whenever he attempted to use a crutch to aid his mobility. Though it would be at least four months before he could leave his hospital bed and stand before his accusers, the condemnation of his actions began immediately.[16]

Heintzelman ordered an immediate investigation, telling General Hays to be sure and include "the name of the officer that was in command." At the same time Price sent out a similar directive attempting to identify Nelson. Price then fired off a second telegram to Lt. Col. Robert Johnstone seeking "further particulars," specifically "if it was a complete surprise and if any resistance was made," as well as "the present condition and whereabouts of Lt. Nelson." Though Johnstone had not yet spoken with Nelson, who he believed to be mortally wounded, he informed Price that the lieutenant had "disobeyed orders," failing to post his pickets as Johnstone had personally directed, and he condemned the men for running after "one discharge." Johnstone explained that he had shown Nelson where he could make a stand if attacked, but that it was his failure to post his pickets as ordered that had allowed his men to be surprised, a point that was more a matter of degree than fact. On the twenty-seventh several Northern papers announced, "An example will of course be made of the officer commanding this picket by dismissing him from the service summarily, for permitting this surprise to succeed." Price filed his final report on the matter on March 12, repeating Johnstone's assertions that the post had been completely surprised and that no defense had been made before the men fled. Again, the accuracy of these claims was a matter of degree more than clear fact as both Johnstone and Price made it appear. The sentinel had not been surprised. Still, a court of inquiry found against Nelson, but allowed him to resign due to his injuries rather than summarily dismissing him.[17]

Colonel Wyndham, who was in the habit of twirling his ten-inch mustache when angry or nervous, received the reports concerning the incident at Thompson's Corner while he waited at Fairfax Court House. Once again Mosby had victimized his brigade, particularly the 18th Pennsylvania, which was now being sarcastically referred to as "the famous 18th Pa. Cavalry." Though he may have inwardly burned to take his command after his tormentor, Wyndham's orders were to proceed toward the Rappahannock, in an attempt to corral Fitz Lee. In light of the continuing problems with the Pennsylvanians, his delay awaiting the arrival of the two untried regiments from Michigan may have set him to twirling his mustache at a furious pace until he could wait no longer. When the two new regiments reached Fairfax, about 2 P.M. on the twenty-sixth, Wyndham was already gone. The agitated colonel gathered "a portion" of the brigade at Centreville but got no farther than Bull Run, where he found the bridge out and the water so high that two horses drowned attempting to cross. He set the men to repairing the bridge, and returned to Centreville to wait.[18]

The Wolverines had been awakened at eleven o'clock the previous evening and ordered to prepare to march, but beyond that the task ahead was a mystery, and it appears that their objective remained a mystery to the men in the ranks. Lt. Colonel Gould dashed off a hurried note to his brother confirming that the leadership crisis within the regiment remained unresolved. Unaware as yet that Colonel Gray would be in overall command Gould warned, "if it should be our drunken Colonel I am afraid there will be some unpleasant scenes as some of the officers have said they would never go under him." Norvell had just submitted his resignation, but with letters of support from political patrons as well as General Copeland, who was troubled by the fact that no other field officers in the regiment had military experience, Norvell was allowed to resume command. In an effort to appease his angry subordinates Gould assured them that Norvell would not be the "principal commander," as he had been earlier in the month.[19]

Colonel Gray was ordered to ready three squadrons of his 6th Michigan and within minutes the camp "was astir and swarming like a bee-hive." The men "had apprehensions that some special work was at hand," as they had watched signal rockets launched from the Union camps in Virginia throughout the evening. They set out at 2 A.M. "amid a violent tempest of rain," that tormented the men throughout the day, and quickly dulled their enthusiasm for their first taste of active service. "Down through the silent, slumbering city the multitudinous tread of iron-shod horses awoke strange echoes, while the splashing raindrops and lowering clouds did not serve to raise the spirits," recalled Capt. James Kidd. The regiment halted briefly at Fort Scott to await the arrival of the 5th Michigan before setting out again, under the overall command of Colonel Gray, through Alexandria and Fairfax Court House before reaching Centreville at dusk. There the tired men stood in the rain all night, catching what sleep they could. "The following morning as we hadn't lain down we didn't have to get up," one of the men grumbled sarcastically.[20]

Joined by contingents from the 1st West Virginia, 5th New York and 18th Pennsylvania, the Michiganders set out the next morning at 6 A.M. By all accounts Wyndham set a punishing pace, moving "as fast as horses could go," refusing to pause but once for the men or animals to catch their breath. To Kidd, the colonel "seemed bent on killing as many horses as possible, not to mention men. The fact was," the captain concluded, "the newspapers were in the habit of reporting that Colonel or General so-and-so had made a forced march of so many miles in so many hours, and it is probable that 'Sir Percy' was in search of some more of that cheap renown." In truth Wyndham was simply following orders that sent him on a futile chase after Fitz Lee when he burned to go after John Mosby. The men never understood, and may never have known, that their mission was to prevent Fitz Lee from reaching the Rappahannock. Instead, they believed they were pursuing Mosby.[21]

Capt. James Kidd, 6th Michigan Cavalry. An outstanding officer, Kidd achieved the brevet rank of brigadier general by the end of the war. He was also a devoted chronicler of the Michigan Cavalry Brigade, both during and after the war (USAMHI).

Though his orders directed that he proceed to Rappahannock Station by way of Catlett Station, Wyndham amended the route due to "the flooded state of the streams," and the saturated roads. The command passed through Warrenton at a gallop that afternoon, ignoring the small squads of Confederate cavalry observed on the surrounding hills. The soldiers were anxious to confront the enemy but "Wyndham was evidently in too great haste to see good," groused one soldier. Leaving Warrenton Wyndham turned south, taking three regiments along the direct road past Hartwood to Falmouth, while Colonel Gray veered to the left with his two regiments and scouted an interior line toward the Orange and Alexandria Railroad. The command reunited along the railroad, spending the night on the north side of Licking Run.[22]

The march resumed at 6 A.M. the following morning, February 28. At least one regiment, the 5th New York, continued to Bealeton Station, before Wyndham turned the command east to Elk Run, on word that "a force of the enemy" was in that vicinity. There he learned that Fitz Lee had long since crossed the Rappahannock. With his food and forage exhausted he took the direct road to Falmouth, arriving at 2 P.M. with seven prisoners in tow, including two members of Captain Randolph's Black Horse, who were captured that day. The weary men and animals remained in the Falmouth area until March 2, in an attempt to "recruit" the horses.[23]

Shortly after arriving at Falmouth, Wyndham turned over command of the entire force to Gray, in the belief that the army had finally accepted his resignation, which he had first submitted on January 18. Whether Wyndham had submitted a second letter or simply asked that his previous request be reconsidered is unknown, but telegrams went out on February 28, notifying both General Hooker and the governor of New Jersey that "the order discharging Col. P. Wyndham ... by resignation has been revoked." Wyndham then submitted a request, from Falmouth, dated March 1, to Brig. Gen. Seth Williams, Assistant Adjutant General for the Army of the Potomac, that he be transferred to the army "being desirous of more active service than can be obtained in my present command." Hooker immediately endorsed the request and sought to have the colonel returned to his regiment. Wyndham then went to Colonel Gray, possibly with a copy of his request, now carrying Hooker's endorsement, and advised the colonel that he would be responsible for seeing the command back to Centreville. The saga took another turn that night when Gray and Hooker received the errant telegrams that had been sent on the twenty-eighth stating that the approval of Wyndham's request to resign had been revoked. Wyndham was ordered to resume his command and return with the column to Centreville. As his request for transfer passed up through the chain of command, an officer attached a note stating, "This is the officer who recently tendered his resignation, in consequence of difficulty with his superior officer." Wyndham was notified two days later that this latest request was "Disapproved." There is no reason to believe that this superior officer was anyone other than Colonel Price.[24]

The return trip from Falmouth was made at a more leisurely pace, but the conditions of the roads remained "almost impassable." The Wolverines reached their camps in the capital at nine o'clock on the evening of the third. By all accounts the expedition had been a disaster, described by Gould as "a wild goose chase all over eastern Virginia without any benefit to [the] government and some serious injury to men and horses." In his estimate "$6000 would not make up the damage to the regiment in horse flesh alone." Gray stated that his two regiments had "sustained great loss," with numerous horses left dead by the roadside while other men and horses had been left behind to return when and if they could. Kidd saw the effort as "a big raid on government horses, ruining a large number," and found after reaching the capital that only 22 of the 80 horses in his company were serviceable. The manner in which Wyndham prosecuted the march to the Rappahannock was based on the clear need for speed, but it had been futile from the start. That the officers and men in the Michigan regiments never understood the true purpose of the expedition reflected Wyndham's imperious style of leadership. The men of the 5th Michigan never forgot this march. In May, when word reached them that a regular army officer was seeking the colonelcy of the regiment 33 officers sent a petition to the governor requesting that the promotion be made from within the command. They cited their belief that regular army officers were intent only on their own careers and that "men and horses have been and will be sacrificed recklessly to obtain that object." In particular they referred to this expedition and the resulting loss in men and horses, "which we are still unable to get replaced," all "to gratify the pride and ambition of an aspiring officer of the Regular Army." Though Wyndham did not hold a regular army commission he had left that impression and the men never forgot nor forgave him.[25]

With the majority of the cavalry chasing after Fitz Lee, the infantry commands and the few horsemen left behind were forced to confront the continuing possibility that Stuart planned a much larger raid through northern Virginia and into Maryland, possibly against the Baltimore and Ohio Railroad. On the twenty-seventh Capt. Sam Means, commanding the Loudoun Rangers, a Union outfit raised in Loudoun County, reported that a large body of Southern cavalry, along with three pieces of artillery had moved into Leesburg, and though his report was deemed unreliable it added to the mounting concern that Stuart was preparing to launch a raid from Loudoun County. Means proposed sending an expedition from Harpers Ferry into Loudoun to verify the threat, and though his superiors were not convinced of its validity, the report was circulated among the surrounding commands. "Afraid there is some gas about this," commented one foot soldier. In the ranks of the 1st Vermont Cavalry, word that several noted troublemakers from the regiment had gone to a local home and committed "disgraceful and reckless crimes" had created "some excitement but the report that Stuart is making another of his cavalry raids through this vicinity is causing more still." The few troopers who remained at Centreville kept their horses saddled continually in order to promptly meet the expected attack.[26]

Maj. William Wells, 1st Vermont Cavalry, had earlier complained that there was no defensible line where his men were posted, and he created a flap with his superiors when he sent a proposal directly to Heintzelman requesting that he be allowed to withdraw his pickets to a superior position on the east side of Difficult Run. Heintzelman referred the matter back to Price with a warning to Wells, "When General Heintzelman wants Major Wells' advice he will ask for it." Price also ignored the problem, focusing instead on the fact that, yet again, a junior officer had gone over his head directly to Heintzelman. He referred the matter to Maj. Charles Taggart, commanding the outpost at Dranesville, who called all of the officers at the post into his office. After chastising them about the violation of protocol, Taggart dismissed the officers without the matter of the picket line being resolved. The proposal remained on Taggart's desk until the end of March when it was finally approved and the line contracted.[27]

Though Heintzelman privately doubted the reports of a possible raid, he questioned his commanders as to what each was hearing in their sectors, while instructing that they "observe increased vigilance." He also sent word to Wyndham at Falmouth that he was to return immediately. In response to his queries, General Stoughton advised Heintzelman that he had discovered a gap in the cavalry picket line of a mile or more between the Ox road and the Dranesville outpost, and urged that the matter be remedied. Lt. Colonel Johnstone agreed with Stoughton, but stated that the 1st West Virginia Cavalry, which was holding the line between Herndon and Centreville, was not strong enough to do so properly.

He recommended that the line be consolidated and removed closer to the infantry pickets until the manpower shortages could be corrected. Wells was then instructed to cover the gaps by means of patrols rather than stationary pickets.[28]

Stoughton further requested that all "women and other irresponsible persons" in the area around Fairfax Court House be compelled to either take the oath of allegiance or be "placed outside the lines." He was concerned that Southern soldiers were coming home while on parole and gathering intelligence or that family members were passing beyond the lines to keep Southern authorities apprised of the military situation in his area of responsibility. Stoughton was especially concerned that a man, "undoubtedly a spy," had been at the courthouse the night before interrogating his "servants minutely respecting the troops in the vicinity, asking if I kept my horse saddled in the night, and other suspicious questions."[29]

While also mentioning security concerns posed by refugees passing through his lines, General Hays reported that "the enemy continues to make night signals in the various gaps of the Bull Run Mountains," and, "small squads of Rebel cavalry reconnoiter carefully out of rifle range in my front." His reports, combined with another that a brigade-sized force, including Lige White's battalion, was near Aldie, continued to focus attention on the Loudoun Valley. Maj. Joseph Gilmer had examined the area on the twenty-seventh, when both Eliza Davis, wife of Yankee Davis, and Hamilton Rogers, a civilian who lived between Aldie and Middleburg, advised him that a battalion of cavalry was "in the vicinity of Aldie seeing to the thrashing of grain." Though Gilmer had only seen "the enemies videttes," both Davis and Rogers had warned him that his patrol was in danger of being cutoff by the enemy before he could get through the gap in Bull Run Mountain. Though Heintzelman remained skeptical he could no longer publicly ignore the threat and he authorized several separate scouting patrols to determine the validity of the reports.[30]

The smallest of these was conducted by the 1st Michigan. Dexter Macomber stated that the patrol only went about five miles beyond the lines "without seeing the rebels," but the officer in charge did report observing smoke and campfires along the mountains, corroborating the report from Hays. Major Gilmer took out between 150 and 200 cavalrymen from the 5th New York, 1st West Virginia and 18th Pennsylvania, while two companies of the 1st Vermont Cavalry, numbering about 50 men, under Capt. Franklin Huntoon, were called from the post at Annandale to conduct a third reconnaissance. Three separate patrols, each pulled from a different part of the line, and each heading for the same location was a recipe for disaster, and Price warned Gilmer in particular, to exercise caution to avoid a "collision with our own forces." Gilmer received his orders that evening, and the camp was soon a hive of activity as the able-bodied men prepared to leave by 1 A.M. With Wyndham still out and Gilmer preparing to set out, even the sick were instructed to saddle their horses to facilitate a rapid response in the event of an attack while the other parties were in the field. Amid the flurry of activity none of the men noticed two figures lurking in the shadows.[31]

Walter Frankland and James Ames had recently joined Mosby's small group at Rector's Crossroads, and though both would become two of his most dependable men, they had followed vastly different paths to his command. Frankland had served in the 17th Virginia Infantry from April 1861 until his discharge for health reasons in late 1862. After serving a stint in Richmond with the Provost Marshal, he had recently headed north seeking to join Lige White's 35th Battalion. While taking dinner at a home south of Rector's Crossroads, he was told by the homeowner "of a private scout named Mosby," who was then enjoying some success harassing the Federal pickets. Frankland determined to meet with Mosby before continuing his effort to reach White.[32]

James Ames was born in Bangor, Maine, and made his living as a sailor before joining the 5th New York Cavalry as a corporal in October 1861. The following spring he earned a promotion to sergeant, but he was, reportedly, angered later that year when President Lincoln announced his Emancipation Proclamation. Ames either walked away from his regimental camp near Jermantown or he elected to desert while the regiment accompanied Wyndham across Prince William County in mid–February. Either way he walked into Rector's Crossroads without horse or weapons on or about the twelfth of February, just after Frankland had met Mosby for the first time. Though his motives and intentions were a matter of immediate suspicion for the other men, Mosby took a liking to the big Yankee and quickly paroled him.[33]

By Frankland's account, he and Ames set out on the twenty-eighth to procure horses from the stables of the 5th New York. The hike took several days and the men arrived as Gilmer was preparing to depart. Once the main body was gone the two men sauntered through the camp and into the stables where the remainder of the horses were now saddled. All they had to do was bridle two horses and walk them out of camp. According to Frankland they then set out in an attempt to warn Mosby of Gilmer's expedition, but they were delayed by the terrible condition of the roads.[34]

Gilmer's orders were to conduct a reconnaissance, gathering as much information as possible by the use of "flankers and small detached scouting parties." Instead, he led his force directly to Middleburg, where, according to Southern accounts he surrounded the town and conducted a house-to-house search for Mosby and his men. After the war Mosby claimed that Gilmer set out at an early hour with the expressed purpose of reaching Middleburg before dawn in the hope of catching the guerrillas asleep, yet Gilmer's orders, according to Lt. Col. Johnstone, who was in command of the Jermantown outpost in Wyndham's absence, stated that he was not to cross Cub Run, a mile east of the Loudoun County border, until daylight. Whatever the case, as Mosby met his command that morning at Rector's Crossroads, three miles west of Middleburg, the only suspects that Gilmer had taken into custody were later described as six "old gentlemen."[35]

Mosby recalled that he received word of the Union incursion as his men gathered at the rendezvous point, and that he promptly set out with 17 men, looking "to pick up some stragglers." When he arrived at Middleburg, the Federals had already departed toward Aldie, and the partisans were surrounded by women and children greatly distressed at having seen the men led away. They told Mosby that Gilmer had forced the prisoners, including those who were on crutches, to "mark time" in the street by marching in place before they were led away. In a postwar account of this incident Mosby recalls setting off in pursuit of the Federals after listening to the "harrowing treatment of the old men." He wrote of the "pathos of the scene," the "tears and lamentations of the daughters," who had seen their fathers led away, and declared that "one of the vows of knighthood" was to "avenge the wrongs of distressed damsels." All of which made for a great story and helped to establish the enduring myth of the Gray Ghost, but forgotten in this version are comments that he had made earlier in his *Reminiscences*, when he spoke of exploiting the fact that there was a Confederate hospital in Middleburg. "I utilized" the patients who "were now convalescent," taking them on raids and returning them to the hospital, and "when the Federal cavalry came in pursuit they never suspected that the cripples they saw lying on their couches or hobbling about on crutches were the men who created the panic at night in their camps." Mosby's knightly chivalry was not quite as evident when he wrote rather coldly, "At last I got one of the cripples killed, and that somewhat abated their ardor." He also conveniently forgot his own vehement denial that he had ever used the town of Middleburg to suit his military needs. Moreover, it appears that the Federals did suspect the deception that Mosby thought so clever, (some of his prisoners were still being paroled immediately in and around Middleburg, and they would have been aware of the fact that men from the hospitals were participating in the raids, either from their own observation or comments made by their captors) and the town's folk paid the price for his cleverness while Mosby continued to deflect the blame, holding the Federals, in this case Major Gilmer, responsible. "It was not flattering to his men for [Gilmer] to suppose that the old men he had caught were the same men who had routed their best cavalry regiments.... But he pretended to think so," wrote Mosby.[36]

As Gilmer's expedition headed east along the turnpike toward Aldie, Captain Huntoon's Vermonters were approaching Aldie from the east along the same road. Huntoon was a veteran, who had been promoted from first lieutenant to captain of Company H in September 1862. Prior to joining the cavalry he had done a three-month stint with the 1st Vermont Infantry as a private. His counterpart that day was Capt. John Woodward, in command of Company M. Captain Woodward had received his commission on November 19, 1862, and his company, the last raised in one of the most senior mounted regiments in the army, joined the command in January 1863. He and his men had yet to see the elephant.[37]

The Vermonters observed Gilmer's column approaching them east of Aldie, and Huntoon and Woodward, unaware that it was a friendly force, deployed their men in a skirmish formation. Gilmer's advance guard was also mystified as to the identity of the troops in their front and fell back on the main body. On receiving their report Gilmer turned his entire command off the turnpike, without making any attempt to identify the men in his front, and continued along the road to Centreville that parallels the turnpike to the south. Sergeant Martin, who was not present, wrote that Gilmer abandoned the captured wagon and several of the prisoners, "and returned to camp with as mad a set of men as you most ever saw." Another Pennsylvanian dubbed the major's action as the "grand retreat of Major Gilmer." A few of his men were angry enough that they left the column and returned to the turnpike where they again encountered Huntoon, advising him of what had just occurred and that there were no enemy troops in Aldie.[38]

Mosby left Middleburg at a gallop with six men, leaving the others to follow at a slower pace. West of Aldie he ran into two of Huntoon's troopers who had been sent ahead to picket the turnpike toward Middleburg, and captured them without firing a shot, though one account claimed that both of their revolvers misfired. Huntoon, who felt that he had taken all the necessary precautions and who believed the road to be clear at least to Middleburg, allowed his men to rest and feed their horses. After unbridling their mounts, the men relaxed around the Aldie Mill and a nearby blacksmith shop. Completely at ease, based on the reports from Gilmer's men, some of the men lay down within the mill while Huntoon and Woodward took a breather outside on the front steps. A report of the affair, filed later that same day, claimed the Vermonters had observed a lone Confederate picket on the turnpike west of the mill but that he retired when Huntoon's pickets approached. A member of the regiment who was not present later wrote that his comrades were no more concerned for their safety "than were the citizens of ancient Troy on the night of her downfall."[39]

Mosby never questioned his two prisoners but immediately sent them to the rear, as he was then able to see several more men in the town, and assumed they belonged to Gilmer's command. Admitting that he "had no suspicion that any others were near," he ordered his

Sitting along the Little River Turnpike, the Aldie Mill, seen in this photograph from the 1930s, was a silent witness to countless engagements during the war, including a skirmish on March 2, 1863, between the 1st Vermont Cavalry and Mosby's partisans (Library of Congress).

men to charge. As they got closer they observed Huntoon's command lounging around the mill. Mosby, who still had only six men with him, then attempted to rein in his mount and retreat, but he was riding "a very wild horse" that he had difficulty controlling and which now carried him into and through the crowd of Federals at the mill. The men with him never knew that he had tried to retreat, and followed him with their revolvers blazing. As his horse was about to carry him into the midst of a second group of Yankees Mosby jumped off the animal, just as the remainder of his command came into view. The Vermonters in his immediate front mounted their horses and bolted for home, leaving the men around the mill to fend for themselves.[40]

In his report, written the following day, Johnstone credited the Vermonters with fighting well, but he admitted that they were not a part of his command and that he had not yet interviewed any of the survivors. Instead, he expended his wrath on Gilmer. In truth the men at the mill had not fought well, or in the words of one regimental scribe, "*very few*, stood firm." Most simply did not have a chance to fight. Huntoon was taken after firing one shot. Several dashed into the mill and hid among the grain sacks or in the hoppers, only to be rounded up at gunpoint. Captain Woodward did mount his horse and engage the enemy, emptying his revolver and then defending himself with his saber before his horse was killed. Pinned under the dead animal Woodward reportedly drew a small pistol and wounded William T. Turner, who may have fired at the captain while he was on the ground. Several accounts credit Mosby with being the man who either convinced Woodward to surrender or prevented the wounded Turner from killing him. One other Vermonter, Joseph Guertin, also drew notice for his stand. Severely wounded in the shoulder and groin, Guertin was said to have reloaded and emptied his revolver a second time, before mounting his horse and fleeing.[41]

Mosby captured 22 men and a like number of horses. Woodward's wounds were severe enough that he was paroled and left at a nearby home, from where he was recovered the next day. Guertin, the only other man wounded, was able to make his way back to Union lines. The one known casualty in Mosby's command was Turner, though several Union accounts suggest that five of his men were wounded. Gilmer was arrested the same night and court-martialed later that month. He was found guilty of being intoxicated and cashiered from the service in July. In the immediate aftermath of the fight William Martin wrote, "I am in hopes that our next Col. may be a sober man." Franklin Huntoon, who had been referred to a year earlier as "one of the finest officers in the Regiment," was charged with cowardice and summarily dismissed from the service on March 25, 1863, without benefit of a trial and while he was still a prisoner of war.[42]

Huntoon had at least one factor working against him, beyond the fact that he was never able to speak in his own defense. When Col. Edward Sawyer took command of the 1st Vermont Cavalry in late 1862, he issued an order directing that all of his officers report any government property then in their possession, to include horses and other equipment for which they had not reimbursed the government. This was, in Sawyer's words, an effort to combat the "thieving among the men" which he found to be "very common." Huntoon responded, in writing, that he did not possess a government horse, whereas several men and officers had filed detailed statements alleging that Huntoon had been stealing horses for months from government corrals as well from civilian farms. Capt. Henry Parsons accused Huntoon of telling him that taking a personal "horse *south* is utter folly," and "what on earth is the use of *buying* things." This last statement had especially angered Sawyer, and he recommended "that if ever there was a case justifying the unheard and immediate expulsion of an officer from the service, this is such a case." Sawyer's report may still have been sitting on Stanton's desk awaiting action when the reports of the fight at Aldie sealed Huntoon's fate. Huntoon continued to press the matter, however, and the order was overturned after the war, when he was granted an honorable discharge.[43]

Gilmer's men came back into the Union lines between Centreville and Union Mills, through the infantry pickets, spreading word that an enemy force numbering 800 men and led by Lige White had nearly cut them off. The foot soldiers were ordered to prepare for battle and surgeons laid out their instruments in anticipation for a fight. One infantryman told his wife, "The boys are ready for a fight any time the Rebs have a mind to attack them." Amid all the "bustle & confusion" a soldier in the 125th New York Infantry pointed what he thought was an empty weapon at a friend in jest and pulled the trigger, killing the soldier and wounding a second man. Beyond this tragedy the opportunity for a greater disaster was very real as Wyndham's troopers were returning this same afternoon from Falmouth. Hays passed along a report of an unknown force moving "along our front," and inquired, "Are our troops in front? For we fear a conflict with them." Wyndham was equally leery, sending word that he would be crossing at Wolf Run Shoals, and when Heintzelman forwarded his note to Hays it included the warning, "Be sure no accident occurs." Still, one of the artillery batteries fired several rounds across Bull Run thinking a party of guerrillas was on the other side. As night descended on the jumpy troops along the Occoquan and Bull Run it was only by a miracle that Gilmer's misconduct, combined with the erroneous reports of the previous few days did not lead to a disaster much greater than what befell the Vermonters at Aldie.[44]

Colonel William Creighton had been on edge for a week; since the first news of Fitz Lee's attack at Hartwood gave rise to rumors that Lee would assail the Union outpost at Dumfries. Though the Confederates had long since returned to Culpeper County, rumors of a roving force in Creighton's vicinity continued to circulate. In the midst of this uncertainty he was told that the 12th Illinois Cavalry, the only mounted unit attached to his command, was being transferred. Creighton protested, telling his superiors that while his infantry was strong enough to hold the town, "it would be impossible for him to protect the telegraph line" linking the Army of the Potomac with the military posts in Northern Virginia and Washington without cavalry. Their withdrawal would also prevent him from doing any scouting of the dangerous country toward Brentsville. His superiors tried to allay his fears, advising him that the most recent rumors of a Southern force near his outpost were generated by erroneous sightings of Wyndham's command as he moved through the area. But to allay Creighton's concerns, Alfred Pleasonton was instructed to maintain a patrol along the telegraph line and to realign his pickets to insure the safety of the wire. General Stoneman, who was prepared to send a reconnaissance force of 500 men into the area, was told to stand down, "until we have later and more accurate intelligence of the enemy's movements." The reports were confirmed shortly before 1 A.M. on the fourth.[45]

The 8th New York Cavalry was picketing a line extending through Maple Valley to Independent Hill, northwest of Dumfries. The pickets had been relieved near midnight by a detachment from Companies K and M, which promptly took shelter "more comfortably than wisely, in a deserted house." One, possibly two men were left on watch outside. The enemy approached on foot, and opened fire, killing the guards and then "poured in a rapid fire through the doors and windows," wounding three men, one mortally. Though several troopers escaped, at least ten others were captured along with their horses. It was the third time in two nights that picket details from the regiment had been hit in the same area, and the men suspected that the attackers were "either Stuart's or White's men, who had been piloted to their destination by some of the bushwhackers, who live in the immediate vicinity, and are always acting as spies, or engaged in shooting single pickets from ambush, a murderous sort of warfare that would disgrace a savage." A brief item in the Richmond *Dispatch* credited the attack to 16 members of "our cavalry ... lead by Mr. R. Farrow."[46]

Though the Army of the Potomac had assumed picket responsibility to a point northwest of Dumfries and the 12th Illinois Cavalry was not immediately withdrawn, the attack at Independent Hill served to keep Creighton on edge. "There is no unison of action," between the commands, he rightly complained, and he was incensed that he received word of the attack from a scout rather than an officer. Hooker was also furious. Now more than ever, with almost daily attacks against the picket lines, the cavalry could not afford to cast a blind eye at officers or enlisted men who neglected to perform their duties in a diligent and responsible manner.[47]

Stoneman was advised on March 6 that Hooker had learned of this latest incident "with great regret and astonishment," and Hooker instructed his cavalry commander to take immediate measures "to bring to trial all who are in any way at fault." The battalion of the 8th New York that had been holding that end of the line had joined the regiment only weeks earlier and was immediately withdrawn and drilled daily for the next three weeks in an attempt to improve both their efficiency and discipline, but there is no indication that any charges were filed against Capt. Vincent Smith, commander of Company M or any other officers as a result of this failure. The New Yorkers were relieved by the 3rd Indiana, whose commanding officer was sent out with the admonishment "that your command will meet with no disgraceful surprise, such as occurred the other day in the Eighth New York." "We made good and killed several bushwhackers," one of the troopers later boasted. Unfortunately, they also shot an officer from the 8th New York who did not heed the commands of a picket promptly enough.[48]

General Averell, still angry over the conduct of his troops during the recent attack at Hartwood Church, issued his own directive the same day. "The arms and equipments of those enlisted men and all government property in the possession of officers who surrendered to the enemy without being wounded in the recent skirmish ... will be charged against them on their next muster role.... The spectacle of men with superior arms and equipment enlisted in the just cause yielding themselves prisoners ... without a struggle to a gang of yelling rebels, with old shotguns and horse pistols, is revolting to contemplate ... the officers and men of this Division must come to the understanding that it is their business to fight and if necessary die wherever they meet the enemy." The men were again on notice that the punishment for failure was going to be as harsh and as immediate as the danger they faced along the picket line.[49]

On March 7, Col. Tom Devin, 6th New York Cavalry, who was in temporary command of Pleasonton's division, recommended taking "the necessary course for ridding the country in the vicinity of our lines of the roving parties of the enemy who now infest it." He proposed that a "vigorous beating up of their haunts" would "clear the country of them, and give some relief to our pickets now continually harassed both in body and mind by unremitting attacks of the enemy." Though his suggestion came to naught his men were equally frustrated with the nature of the war on the picket line. The Southerners who placed great stock in the tradition of chivalry in the cavalry were now viewed as "a detestable set of cowardly sneaks who should have been shot at sight without challenge."[50]

The enemy remained just active enough along the Occoquan and Bull Run to keep the men on edge there as well. When Captain Woodward was brought back from Aldie he reiterated earlier reports that Lige White was indeed roaming through Loudoun County with 400 men, securing the early wheat harvest. Other accounts placed a smaller force in the vicinity of Manassas, intent on making a raid across either Woodyard Ford or Wolf Run Shoals. This latter report gained credence when two members of the 1st Michigan were captured in that area on the fifth. On the seventh, Maj. Melvin Brewer, 1st Michigan, made a reconnaissance to Brentsville, but returned "with out seeing any rebels." General Hays was "satisfied that there are organized bands of guerrillas, or spies, around Manassas Junction and throughout the country beyond Bull Run, from whose assistance and information the scouts of the enemy are enabled at times to approach our lines with impunity." To alleviate the threat he recommended, "that all able-bodied men, who have escaped conscription, and who cannot give satisfactory evidence of their loyalty, be arrested and brought within our lines."[51]

On March 8, Colonel Price was contemplating another expedition into the region, but exactly what he intended is unknown, as his plan was never put into effect, for several reasons. The horses had yet to recover from Wyndham's reconnaissance to Falmouth. One observer said they "look as if they came from Egypt during the seven year's famine," and many still needed shoeing after the punishing expedition. Quartermasters were also experiencing difficulty getting the heavy forage wagons to the forward lines along roads that remained "next to impossible." The cavalry sought to alleviate the threat to solitary or stationary picket posts by drawing in the lines at night and covering much of the ground by means of patrols, but this only served to increase the workload on the already worn out men and animals. At Lewinsville, Charles Chapin counted only 32 men at the post. Noting the new patrol policy he remarked, "there is so few of us we have to be sent out almost every night."[52]

Picket duty in Fairfax County remained "severe," in the opinion of most, as they faced "one continual round of disturbances and alarms." The lack of sleep, constant tension, and a continuing onslaught of "snow, rain, frost and mud" all took a toll on the men, both in mind and body. The only bright spot for the infantry was that the unremitting rain kept the men off the drill field during the day. As the pickets took their posts on the evening of March 8, 1863, they faced another miserable night standing in the rain. Warm temperatures caused fog to form in low-lying areas, making their task as sentinels even more trying. The men who were lucky enough to be off duty that night and out of the weather awoke in the morning to learn that John Mosby had "carried off" a general.[53]

10

March 9, 1863

"It was the best raid of all"

John Mosby now rode at the head of 29 men, who were called from their comfortable quarters and warm firesides to rendezvous at Dover, just west of Aldie, on Sunday, March 8, 1863. Mosby disliked Percy Wyndham intensely, and had ever since the colonel had issued his ultimatums to the residents of Middleburg earlier in the year. By closely interviewing prisoners and scouting the routes into Fairfax County, Mosby had fleshed out a plan to kidnap Wyndham from his headquarters at Fairfax Court House. Mosby never identified himself as the man who "interrogated" General Stoughton's servants on the night of February 28, but he did state that he had "accurately ascertained the number and disposition of the troops" in the vicinity of the courthouse. He credited one of his most recent recruits, James Ames, who came to be known as "Big Yankee" Ames, as his most valuable asset in planning the venture. Beyond his personal knowledge of troop dispositions and picket posts, Ames was a man who just might be able to talk his way past any troublesome guards with his heavy Maine accent. As Mosby drew up the plan in his head he knew that he would not be able to follow any of the major roads into or out of the county, but his confidence in guide John Underwood remained unshakable. By early March it was simply a matter of waiting for the right weather to aid his attempt, and the fog and rain on March 8, provided the conditions that he was waiting for.[1]

The men proceeded east along the Little River Turnpike to a point near Saunders' Toll Gate, where they turned south, picking their way through gaps in the picket line, and struggling to keep together in the gloomy darkness as they followed remote farm paths through the forests. A gap of about three miles between Centreville and Chantilly had been reported as recently as March 5, "through which the enemy can pass," and this is exactly what occurred. Colonel Price had instructed Lt. Col. Robert Johnstone to close the gap, and though Johnstone had relayed the orders to a subordinate, he also dismissed the report as coming from a telegraph operator who "is more conversant with his [equipment] than with picket lines." If such a gap actually existed on the night of March 8, or if the raiders were just lucky in avoiding the stationary pickets as well as the recently instituted patrols remains unknown.[2]

Reaching the Warrenton Turnpike between the outposts at Centreville and Jermantown the Confederates turned east, following the pike for several miles, before turning south to avoid the Federal camps at Jermantown. Mosby then led his men south and east toward Ox Road, which brought them into Fairfax Court House from the direction of the depot at Fairfax Station. Though he had hoped to reach his objective by midnight, to insure that he was beyond the lines again before dawn, Mosby was delayed several times; first when his

Fairfax Court House, which was the scene of John Mosby's most famous raid, had also witnessed one of the earliest skirmishes of the war. Seen in this postwar photograph is a monument erected to the memory of Capt. John Quincy Marr, who was killed in a skirmish with Union cavalry here on June 1, 1861. He is believed to have been the first Confederate officer killed during the war. Lt. Charles Tompkins, 2nd U.S. Cavalry, was later awarded a Medal of Honor for the action (Library of Congress).

men became separated due to the weather and darkness and later as they cut the telegraph lines along the Warrenton Turnpike. On the way they encountered one or two pickets who were captured without a shot fired. He arrived at 2 A.M., two hours behind his self-imposed schedule.[3]

Each man had an assignment as Mosby sent small details to capture both Wyndham and Johnstone. Though Mosby never expressed the enmity for Stoughton that he had for Wyndham he elected to go after the general himself, while the other raiders were instructed to capture as many horses as possible from the nearby stables. Cloaked either in Union uniforms or with their Confederate gray concealed under dripping ponchos, it was an easy task for the raiders to silently capture the few guards they encountered. Ames was sent after Wyndham but found that the officer had left for Washington the previous day. Ames did not leave empty handed, however, as he found his former company commander, Capt. Augustus Barker, asleep in another room. After rousting Barker from his bed, Ames and his compatriots seized one other man as well as Wyndham's personal wardrobe, before heading back to the rendezvous point in the town square.[4]

With six men at his side Mosby rapped on the door at Dr. William Gunnell's home. When someone opened a window and enquired about the disturbance Mosby responded that he was an officer from the 5th New York Cavalry. Lt. Samuel Prentiss, 13th Vermont Infantry, opened the door, only to be roughly greeted by the armed men and quickly hustled back inside. He was asked where the general was and he led the way upstairs to the general's room, where Stoughton was asleep after having thrown a party that night for his mother and sister. The women were quartered, along with several members of his staff, at the nearby home of Edward Ford. Slapped out of his slumber, Stoughton was ordered to dress quickly and as they headed for the front door one of the raiders handed the general his gold watch.[5]

Once outside Mosby found that the two men who had been left on guard had met with their own success, rounding up seven troopers along with their horses. These men may have been the seven men captured from Company A, 1st Ohio. They were asleep in their tents when the Confederates began beating on the tent walls with their sabers. Once Mosby reached the square he learned that neither Wyndham nor Johnstone had been found. As they prepared to leave Mosby gave the men new assignments, selecting guards for the 33 prisoners, and men to ride herd over the 58 captured horses. William Hunter was charged with insuring that General Stoughton reached Southern lines. At three-thirty the partisans departed.[6]

Striking the Ox Road the now sizable party sounded like a squadron of cavalry, and as they rode past the home of Joshua Gunnell a man challenged them from an open window. Reveling in their success the raiders laughed off his demands, arousing the suspicion of the man inside. Mosby realized that only a senior officer would have the temerity to confront them and he sent two men into the home. Finding an officer's uniform the men realized that it was Johnstone who had challenged them, but his wife obstructed them long enough that Johnstone was able to escape, reportedly by hiding under a privy in his night clothes. Several of his aides were also reported to have fled the home "in a nude state."[7]

As they neared the fortifications at Centreville a couple of men, including Captain Barker made a dash for the Union lines, which led to several shots being fired. Though Barker was recaptured, several prisoners, including Lieutenant Prentiss, were able to escape in the darkness and confusion caused by Barker's attempt. Colonel Clinton MacDougall, 111th New York Infantry, later reported that this occurred at four-thirty. One of his sentinels heard the shot, and the command "close up," followed quickly by another voice asking, "What the devil did you fire that gun for?" The reserve posts responded just as a lieutenant in charge of the outposts that night approached and gave the countersign, thereby relieving any suspicion on the part of the pickets. MacDougall later theorized that Mosby's men passed around his position at exactly the same time that the lieutenant was occupying the attention of the guards. "I can attach no blame to any one," the colonel wrote, "unless it should be the [lieutenant] ... who returned too early (at least an hour earlier than he was instructed) had he been at his post ... it is possible he might have seen a body of horse men pass—as it proved they took an unfrequented path through the woods & passed around his post."[8]

Moving through Groveton the raiders continued to Warrenton where word of their success had preceded them, giving the town's folk time to turn out and prepare for their arrival. A celebration was in order and "Trays and baskets of cold bread and meats, and of crackers and cheese" were prepared and placed outside only minutes before the "long cavalcade made its appearance, and the pale blue livery of despotism left no doubt, the Yankees were near." The prisoners were allowed to help themselves from the "cold collation" that had been prepared, and though Stoughton refused the others "partook." When the party departed for Culpeper one scribe noted, that Mosby, while "well pleased with the result of his adventure, would have been better satisfied to take Wyndham, as this pseudo nobleman had sent him repeated messages, announcing a purpose to hang the Captain, when caught."[9]

In the immediate aftermath of the raid Price angrily queried Johnstone about how the Confederates had entered the Union lines. "Major Taggart informs me that your pickets do not unite with his [at Dranesville], as I ordered and as you assured Major Wells should be done.... If so there has been gross negligence." If Johnstone had indeed failed to correct the reported gaps in the line he chose to avoid the matter by pointing suspicion at persons in and around Fairfax Court House who may have aided Mosby. Price informed Johnstone that he could arrest those persons "if you have proof against them," but the colonel also informed Heintzelman that he would personally investigate Taggart's complaint, by inspecting the line of outposts for himself.[10]

A half-hearted attempt to catch the raiders was made by the 5th New York, but it never had a chance of succeeding. Captain James Penfield noted conspiratorially that Johnstone sent the men in the direction of "[Dranesville] & Herndon but is careful not to move in the direction they have gone." The confusion spawned by the affair led to the usual erroneous reports of enemy activity where there was none, as troops were reported advancing on Dranesville and suspicious signals were observed near Dumfries. By the end of the day, the Pennsylvania Bucktails were patrolling Fairfax Court House, order was restored and all that remained was to see whose reputations would suffer and whose would survive.[11]

It was quickly apparent that Stoughton's men felt little sympathy for their commander. Lt. Colonel Roswell Farnham told family and friends, "We feel ashamed altho' in no way to blame for the event," and he explained that Stoughton "had been respectfully warned of his danger." George Benedict echoed this sentiment, declaring, "none of the disgrace of the affair belongs to the regiments of this brigade. Gen. Stoughton was not taken from the midst of his command." Benjamin Hatch, 12th Vermont, was equally unsympathetic, stating, "he might have stayed with his brigade [but] he is so unpopular he must have his head quarters at the court house." A member of Stoughton's family later tried to defend the general against the criticism and asserted in a public letter that he had made his headquarters near the courthouse with the assent of General Casey. In fact, Casey had advised Stoughton on at least one occasion that he preferred the general to establish his "headquarters at Fairfax Station."[12]

Stoughton's reputation for "senseless profanity," led one soldier to declare, "when I advance into rebeldom I will have a better campaign than old Stoughton — he can swear as he please [now]." Henry Willey, 16th Vermont, remained critical of Stoughton well into his later years when he recalled, "after our none too short experience with him we ought not be blamed if we had no tears to shed for him." Another infantryman quipped, "that Gen. Stoughton was anxious to go to the front. He has gone at last, but not in a way particularly agreeable to himself." Even men who were not under Stoughton's direct command made light of his misfortune. "It was good enough for the Gen.," one unsympathetic cavalryman declared, "for he was putting on stile in town when his command was a long way off. Every body was glad of it. If they would take the pains to gobble up some of our stylish officers every night it would be a good lesson for them."[13]

General Hays could not help making light of Stoughton's demise either, telling his wife, "I was not the Brigadier General captured this morning.... It was your handsome young friend, Genl Stoughton. He, his men servants, his maid servants, and the Stranger within his gates; also all his fine horses and beasts of burden, are now enroute for Richmond." Days later Hays was still chuckling at Stoughton's misfortune, telling a friend that he had been captured along with everything "as appertains to a Brigadier General, viz, Guards, band, horses and servants, besides the usual assortment of 'tins, kettles, pans, piano, family carriage, and other cooking utensils.'" Hays believed, jokingly, that the raid was "conduct unbecoming officers and gentlemen," seeing the affair as "a slight to my horses and servants, as they are in every respect superior to those of Gen'l Stoughton." When Col. Asa Blunt was named interim brigade commander and directed to establish his headquarters at Fairfax Station, George Benedict remarked, "When *he* is pulled out of bed by guerrillas I will let you know."[14]

The Northern press was equally harsh toward the "stolen Brigadier." One correspondent stated that by staying at Fairfax Court House Stoughton "could have a good brick house to live in, while at the Station he would be compelled to 'dwell in tents' as did the rest of the brigade." Lt. Colonel Charles Cummings attempted to defend Stoughton from charges that he had had a "dalliance with a woman of easy virtue," namely Antonia Ford, whose parents owned the home where Stoughton's wife and sister were quartered. He also took up for Miss. Ford, whose reputation in his opinion was as "unspotted as that of any lady in Virginia," but in the end he found it difficult to get past Stoughton's extravagant lifestyle. Cummings predicted that George Stannard would be named as Stoughton's permanent replacement, declaring that he was "a plain, practical man with an abundance of good sense.... If he comes he will live in a tent like the others of his command, & if he is taken prisoner it will only be after a fight." Cummings believed that Stoughton was a ladies man who had been spoiled "by overweening friends." Admitting that he was "a good tactician, and disciplinarian [who] did much in these respects for the Brigade," Cummings could not overlook his belief that Stoughton was "far short of being ... a genuine soldier."[15]

The Federals also recognized the dash and daring that allowed Mosby and his men to beard the lion in his own den. "It must be said that they worked splendidly and very slyly," opined John Williams, 14th Vermont. Wheelock Veazey, colonel of the 16th Vermont, declared, "It was the best raid of all," while a Northern paper termed the affair "the bold, dashing and reckless raid of Mosby's guerrilla thieves." In the South, Mosby and his men were hailed as heroes. The raid became the defining moment of their careers, and spawned the legend of "The Gray Ghost." Both Stuart and Lee praised Mosby, with the latter proclaiming that he "has covered himself with honors." Stuart announced in general orders that the capture of Stoughton was a "feat, unparalleled in the war." The cavalry chief also recognized the other men who had ridden into Fairfax Court House that night. "The gallant band of Captain Mosby share the glory as they did the danger of this enterprise, and are worthy of such a leader."[16]

Though often referred to as a captain, Mosby held no official commission as such, but Stuart now acted quickly to correct the matter. On March 23, Mosby was informed that he had been appointed a "captain of Partisan Rangers," with the authority to raise a company of men. Two days later, however, Stuart counseled him to avoid the partisan designation, stating, "It is in bad repute." The cavalry chief suggested "Mosby's Regulars" instead, but it never took hold, and the command went down in history as Mosby's Rangers. After providing some brief instruction in the manner in which the company was to be raised, Stuart addressed a matter still to be resolved—"that unprincipled scoundrel Wyndham. Can you catch him?" In the end neither man would have the satisfaction.[17]

The following day nine citizens were taken into custody and sent to Washington, including Joshua Gunnell, who owned the home in which Johnstone resided, Edward Ford, father of Antonia Ford, and Thomas Murray, who owned the home in which Wyndham made his headquarters. Four other local men who had recently been released from prison were taken back into custody. Several others, including Jack Barnes, who participated in the raid, were arrested and charged with acting as guides for both White and Mosby. On March 13, Antonia Ford was arrested at her home and letters and documents were seized, including a "commission" from Jeb Stuart, dated October 7, 1861, naming her as one of his honorary aids. Miss. Ford was a very attractive young woman who had been the object of several young men's affections during the early days of the war. Once the area fell under Northern control, several officers made her parent's home their headquarters, or took rooms and meals there, including Maj. Joseph Willard, an aid to General Heintzelman, whom she would later marry. Though she had proudly passed on intelligence to Southern authorities earlier in the war, her involvement in the raid remains unproven. She remained in prison for six months before she took the Oath of Allegiance and was released on the orders of General Heintzelman. The other detainees were eventually released as well.[18]

11

March 10–March 17, 1863

"There is no evidence to show that the accused did not act with courage and zeal"

The events of March 9, as well as continuing reports that a larger raid, or raids, could be expected, convinced Northern military authorities that Wyndham's command needed to be supplemented to meet the perceived threat. On the tenth, Wyndham was informed that the 5th and 6th Michigan regiments would join him the following day, and the 7th Michigan was also instructed to prepare for a possible move to the front. Once the two senior units arrived Wyndham was to make another sweep of eastern Loudoun County. Though the immediate purpose of this patrol would seem to be in response to Mosby's foray, persistent reports from Milroy in the Shenandoah Valley of an enemy force moving on Winchester, as well as threats of an attack against the Baltimore and Ohio Railroad, or a strike launched across the Rappahannock from Culpeper County, may also have been the stimulus. General Halleck had requested that Hooker send a mounted force into the valley to investigate and breakup any threat to the Union forces at Winchester, but the army commander had refused.[1]

An expedition to Winchester was going to be a long, difficult proposition regardless of where the troops came from. Hooker claimed that it would disable his cavalry for six weeks, but he had other reasons to hold his troopers close to home. One of the army's chief scouts submitted his report of the recent raid at Hartwood Church on the eleventh, detailing a large gap in Brig. Gen. George Stoneman's picket line through which the Rebels "contemplate a raid," against the vital railroad bridge across Potomac Creek, in Stafford County. Stoneman was ordered to correct the gap, and, most important, if the raid should occur "not a man or horse of the enemy [was to] escape." The report also renewed concerns of an attack against Dumfries, and pointed out just how thin Stoneman's line was, as he attempted to cover an area stretching from King George County around to Independent Hill in Prince William County. With all of the mounted troops attached to the garrison at Dumfries occupied in patrolling the telegraph line, infantry commanders were ordered to keep their men "vigilant" and to assist the cavalry where possible. On the twelfth the nervous commander at Dumfries forwarded an erroneous report that the enemy had crossed "Kelly's Ford in force." When additional reports reached Halleck that Grumble Jones and John Imboden were moving against Winchester in division strength he again pressed Hooker to intervene.[2]

In the face of Hooker's refusal to send his cavalry toward Winchester the task fell to

Heintzelman, who was equally hesitant. He initially restricted Wyndham to patrolling eastern Loudoun County only, but he included a caveat that Wyndham was to leave a line of couriers at designated points along his route in the event that Heintzelman was forced to send him into the Shenandoah Valley. Copeland's cavalry left Washington on the morning of the eleventh, marching only as far as Fairfax Court House, where they remained three days before returning to the capital. Lt. Colonel Gould believed that the move was, in fact, instigated by Wyndham, who "broached to Heintzelman the proposition" of attacking Stuart's cavalry in Culpeper County. Wyndham did, in fact, propose a two-pronged assault, with Stoneman making a frontal attack across the Rappahannock while Wyndham moved into Stuart's rear and cut off his line of retreat. In Gould's view, "Heintzelman was so certain of Hooker's cooperation that he ordered us out before he got Hooker's answer," which, "was an utter refusal to have anything to do with it." The Wolverines took the news with "very bad grace as we thought we could have cut up [Stuart]."[3]

Halleck's attempts to prod Hooker into sending his cavalry into the valley continued for several days, infuriating the army commander, who took the issue to the Secretary of War seeking "unconditional orders" one way or the other. At the same time Hooker advised Halleck that he had just sent Averell, with 3,000 troopers, "to attack and break up the cavalry" reported to be gathering in Culpeper County. Halleck immediately backed down and on the morning of March 17, Averell launched an attack across the Rappahannock at Kelly's Ford. After an all day battle Averell retired across the river, satisfied that he had gained a measure of revenge for the recent embarrassment at Hartwood Church. Hooker, however, was disappointed in his cavalry, believing that Averell had acted conservatively from the very start and had not gained the decisive victory that Hooker had sought.[4]

Yet Hooker had no one to blame but himself. Averell explained that he had been forced to leave fully one third of his division to hold the river crossings in light of reports, which he received along with the orders authorizing his attack, that an enemy force numbering between 250 and 1,000 men was in the vicinity of Brentsville, in a position to threaten his hold on the river. He claimed that he had requested that just one regiment be sent to Catlett Station to hold this force in place but that his request was denied. According to Gould this was exactly what Wyndham had proposed to do with two brigades, and which Hooker had refused. Officially, Wyndham said only that his force was "not sufficient for the expedition which I had planned, [and] it is therefore given up."[5]

When the Wolverines learned of the battle at Kelly's Ford they were equally disappointed. James Kidd believed, "This was probably the work set apart for us but for some reason it was thought advisable to change the plan. Some say the streams were swollen so we could not cross some think a sufficient force failed to cooperate with us, and other stories are rife as to why *we* could not measure our strength with the celebrated [Stuart]."[6]

The demands for additional cavalry continued to increase following the raid on Fairfax Court House and recent reports out of Prince William County only added to the urgency. Mosby wrote, postwar, that his goal was to "use and consume the Northern cavalry in hard work," and he was doing just that, but he was not doing it alone. He also claimed that by making multiple attacks at different points along the Union lines in one night he was wearing down the pickets both mentally and physically. In truth, he had made multiple attacks in the same night only once, but his was not the only command harassing the pickets. Federal commanders tried to react and respond to every threat, real or imagined, over a vast amount of ground, stretching from the mouth of the Rappahannock River to the Shenandoah Valley and north to the Potomac River. Small hit and run raids at multiple points along that line were on the increase and were indeed wearing down the Union cavalry. In the minds of cautious Union commanders these small affairs validated the rumors of pending larger raids brought in by their scouts and often brought a horse killing response. Now, with enemy activity on the increase, and calls for a cavalry response on the rise as well, commanders were hard pressed to meet the demand with the troops on hand.[7]

On the thirteenth, Col. Clinton MacDougall mentioned to Hays "the great need of a force of cavalry" to be posted at Centreville. Though MacDougall sought at least 200 troopers, he was convinced that "had I had even fifty ... on the night of the late rebel raid ... I could next morning have followed up and captured the whole force." He had set his men to felling trees and obstructing "all the *paths* to Centreville," assuring Hays "that when they enter Centreville *we will not all be asleep*." Orders also went out to Colonel Blunt directing that his men erect additional rifle pits around the vital depot at Fairfax Station.[8]

The threat to Dumfries also remained. A Union scout by the name of John Skinker reported on the thirteenth that the men on "the picket lines, especially in the neighborhood of Dumfries, Occoquan & above," should remain especially vigilant. He reminded the high command of the threat posed by the Iron Scouts, "who know this country well ... and should be carefully looked after." At the same time Lt. Col. Peter Stagg reminded his superiors that the lack of communication between the army and the Department of Washington, first mentioned by Colonel Creighton, remained. Referring to the new line established to Independent Hill, Stagg complained, "I have heard indirectly that a new cavalry line has been established from Neabsco Creek in a northwesterly direction, will you please inform me where the western terminus is if you can else I might run into them by mistake." Price had "no official information" either, and was unable to give Stagg a definitive answer.[9]

The fourteenth brought a second report that Hampton's Iron Scouts were actively roaming the area between Brentsville and the Occoquan; specifically, that 250 men were in the vicinity of Bacon Race Church, "en route to the Occoquan," and another "three or four squads, numbering 80 to 100" men were patrolling between Brentsville and Dumfries. That same day Lt. William Smith, with his company of the of the 4th Virginia Cavalry, struck the picket line of the 2nd Pennsylvania Cavalry at Davis Ford on the Occoquan. A patrol from the same regiment of Pennsylvanians was also attacked nearby, losing one man killed or wounded and four captured. Stagg responded by immediately sending a detachment from the post at Wolf Run Shoals toward Accotink, along the Pohick road to determine the size and intent of the raiding party, but the trip was to no avail as the men got lost in the midst of "a very hard snow & thunder storm," and returned without encountering the infiltrators.[10]

Though the size of the raiding party appears to have been small and the damage it caused minimal, the sudden strike served to heighten the concern of Federal commanders along the Occoquan. Col. Francis Randall, 13th Vermont Infantry, immediately sent a telegram to Hays advising, "We suffer for a company of cavalry." Colonel Blunt sent a similar missive directly to General Casey, requesting "a company or two of cavalry." Wyndham used this incident, along with the other reports of enemy activity, in an attempt to keep the two Michigan regiments in Virginia. He explained that 300 of his men were on picket, another 100 were on a scout and the remainder "merely sufficient as a reserve to the pickets & to protect the camp," but his pleas fell on deaf ears as the Michiganders were sent back to Washington the same day. The following day the Pennsylvanians, captured on the fourteenth and now paroled, returned and reported that Fitz Lee was at White Plains, Hampton was scouting Prince William County and Stuart was in the vicinity of Warrenton."[11]

On the evening of the fifteenth, a seven-man patrol from the 8th Illinois Cavalry was ambushed about four miles north of Dumfries. The regiment was assigned to guard the telegraph between Dumfries and Occoquan and sent out a patrol about every seven hours. A trooper who had covered the route earlier that morning described the roads as the worst he had ever seen. For three miles the horses had forced their way through deep "frozen mud." By the time the evening patrol set out it had "commenced snowing accompanied by fierce thunder and vivid lightening." The men had reached the post at Occoquan and were headed back by eight o'clock when they were hit by what was believed to be a group of about 25 men, "lying in a marsh on both sides of a deep ravine through which they had to pass." When Capt. Elon Farnsworth responded to investigate he found four sabers lying in the mud where the attack had taken place. Scouring the area he returned with three prisoners, an officer and two privates one of whom was riding the horse belonging to the corporal who had been in charge of the captured patrol.[12]

General Pleasonton, who was responsible for the telegraph line north of Dumfries, requested that he be allowed to send one brigade to clear out "the rebel partisans and bushwhackers ... from the vicinity of Occoquan and Brentsville." Stoneman also sought more "stringent" measures, including "shooting, hanging, banishment or incarceration" of "every male inhabitant" in the area. Hooker urged restraint, however, advising his commanders to arrest and bring to trial any local men against whom they could prove a case. The Vermonters guarding the Occoquan were also debating the issue of revenge after the recent raid at Davis Ford, and at least one determined that there was nothing to be gained by burning the homes of the local populace and turning "the women and children houseless into the country," regardless of the loyalty of the male inhabitants.[13]

On March 16, John Mosby was at Rector's Crossroads. He had decided to make his next strike in the vicinity of Dranesville, and while waiting for his men to arrive he sent a note to Stuart predicting that he would "flush some game before returning." John Underwood had scouted the area over the previous couple of days and learned that the 1st Vermont Cavalry had recently established a reserve post at Herndon Station, numbering between 30 and 40 men. With his ranks bolstered by several new recruits, Mosby headed east with 50 men until he reached the vicinity of Ball's Mill, where he sought shelter for the night. In the morning they continued east, reaching the Loudoun and Hampshire Railroad at noon. Underwood then led the men through the woods so that they approached the depot at Herndon Station from the north, following the road from Dranesville as though they were a Union relief detail.[14]

That same morning Maj. William Wells, 1st Vermont Cavalry, wrote a note to a friend, assuring them, "Our pickets have not been molested for some time, all is quiet at the front." He went on to mention the capture of Stoughton, commenting that "his quarters were guarded only by a few men he should have had a company ... if he had they could not have captured him." Wells and two other officers then headed out to investigate a report that their men were plundering the homes around the depot. When the three officers arrived at the depot Mr. Nat Hanna, a local Union sympathizer, offered them dinner. With the exception of a couple of pickets the remainder of the men were relaxing around the depot and a nearby sawmill, awaiting the relief detail that was expected at any minute.[15]

About one o'clock Mosby led his men out of the woods and onto the Dranesville road at a walk. According to Northern accounts the men were wearing Union overcoats, furthering the deception that they were the expected relief party. While the majority of the Vermonters were occupied in gathering their belongings and packing their bedrolls, Mosby sent two men ahead who approached the lone picket and easily took him prisoner. The Confederates then charged, taking the Federals entirely by surprise. Though seven men escaped and carried word of the attack back to Dranesville, the rest were captured with but little resistance. Those men who sought safety in the sawmill were convinced to surrender when Mosby threatened to set the building on fire. One man was slightly wounded in the hip by a pistol shot.[16]

Wells and his companions had just finished their meal when the gunfire erupted around the station. Peering outside they saw Mosby's men rounding up the prisoners and two of the officers, Lt. Perley Cheney, who had arrived with Wells, and Lt. Alexander Watson, who was in charge of the post, rushed outside. According to William Brent, 6th Virginia Cavalry, who was riding with Mosby for the first time, the officers reached their horses and sprinted for safety. Brent and Jacob Fisher were both still mounted and gave chase. Fisher soon overtook Watson while Brent chased Cheney down the tracks. "I made it so hot for him with pistol balls that he attempted to get to the other side of the track to be out of direct range." In doing so Cheney's horse tripped on the rails and went down throwing Cheney, whose pistol landed beyond his reach. When Cheney tried to remount his horse, the saddle turned. As Cheney struggled with the saddle Brent rode up and took him prisoner.[17]

Major Wells and Capt. Robert Schofield hoped to avoid capture by hiding in the attic. They couldn't hide their horses however, and when the Confederates noticed them tethered in front of the home several men, including Big Yankee Ames, went inside. Finding no one, but seeing the table bearing the remains of a large meal, Ames went to the attic and fired a shot into the dark. Jolted by the sudden gunshot the two officers slipped off the beams and fell through the ceiling, into the midst of the men below. Concerned that the actual relief detail would arrive at any moment, Mosby hustled the men onto their horses, while Wells, also aware that any delay might bring help, did his best to stall. Mosby termed him "dilatory," while a Northern account referred to the major as "a troublesome prisoner," who "came very near being shot." Mosby sent 20 of his men to escort the prisoners into Loudoun County, while he and the remaining 30 men hung back as a rear guard. Within minutes the relief party arrived under the command of Lt. Edwin Higley.[18]

Edwin Higley had entered the military in September 1861, at the age of eighteen, shortly after beginning his sophomore year at Middlebury College. At a farewell dinner given by the school in honor of Higley and two other volunteers, he addressed his fellow students, stating, "I believe there is more work for me to do after the war is over. I do not go with the expectation of never coming back. I rely on God. If He wills that I survive, well; if not, 'tis well; I am ready to die." When he had sought his mother's permission she had told him, "Go, and may God bless you, keep you, and bring you safely back, but especially may you be kept from the evil influences around you, and may you never allow a spirit of revenge to remain for a moment in your breast." During his years of service Edwin Higley would have many opportunities to recall her admonishment.[19]

Higley had departed Dranesville at one o'clock that afternoon with 50 men to relieve Lieutenant Watson. Three miles out he dropped off ten men to picket a vital road junction, and had just resumed his march to Herndon Station when he encountered a trooper heading for Dranesville at a full gallop. The trooper informed Higley "that the force at the Station was all captured." Higley immediately sent one of his men back to Dranesville with the news, and with orders for the ten-man detail that he had just left at the intersection along with the ten men they had relieved to hasten after him. He then proceeded toward Herndon as quickly as possible. On his arrival he was told that the raiders had just left and "could not be more than a half-mile distant." Pursuing through thick woods for several miles the Vermonters came into an open meadow that extended about a half-mile to Horsepen Run. On the far side of the stream Higley could see Mosby's rearguard disappearing into another stand of trees. Splashing across the creek Higley, and those men still with him, reached a high point from where they had a good view of the country ahead, but there was no sign of the rebels. It was at this point that the lieutenant, after consulting with his non-commissioned officers, elected to give up the chase. Erroneous news accounts claimed that Mosby turned on his pursuers and chased them back across the creek. In the view of one member of the regiment, Higley "proved not to be the man for the occasion.... He came in sight of the rebels, came so near as to recognize the prisoners, and exchanged a few shots, but did not charge them.... He let a golden opportunity pass unimproved, and our regiment is again disgraced."[20]

Lt. Edwin Higley, 1st Vermont Cavalry, was branded a coward by his superiors and dismissed from the service for his actions near Herndon, Virginia, on March 17, 1863. Higley successfully fought the charges and regained his position within the regiment. After the war he served as a professor at Middlebury College in Vermont (courtesy Special Collections, Middlebury College, Middlebury, Vermont).

That evening Major Wells scratched out a brief note, telling his brother, "We are on the road to Richmond." The prisoners had been allowed to ride their horses and Wells stressed, "*We have been well treated.*" Many years after the war Lieutenant Cheney thanked Mosby for his "courteous" treatment, telling him that the manner in which the captives were treated belied the many negative connotations associated with the term guerrilla. The enlisted men were released near Paris, and sent north to Harpers Ferry. They would return to the regiment on the twentieth. En route to Harpers Ferry the men trudged past Amanda Edmonds, who noted with pleasure that they looked "quite humble, dismounted and on their way back to Yankeedom." The four officers were sent to Richmond where Wells may have had the opportunity to share his experience with Stoughton. Upon their return to Dranesville the men spoke "very highly of Capt. Mosby."[21]

In his report of the affair Maj. Charles Taggart censured Lieutenant Higley for failing to perform his duty, and he echoed the comments of other frustrated officers in urging "that all citizens near" the outposts be removed beyond the lines, in an effort to prevent further such occurrences. Higley was arrested and charged with cowardice, and, as was becoming the norm, dismissed without a hearing, but unlike the officers in previous incidents his case was re-opened and the verdict overturned. In his defense Higley gathered statements from several of the men involved, including the captured officers upon their return. Several problems within the regiment as well as the brigade became apparent, including the fact that both Colonel Price and Major Taggart had conducted a poor investigation of the affair, relying almost entirely on the statements of one or two disgruntled enlisted men and officers who were not present, including an officer not even attached to the Dranesville outpost. Price alleged that Higley had arrived at Herndon Station "in time to see the prisoners marched off," that the captive officers had beckoned Higley "to come to their rescue," and that he had refused even though "his men were anxious to charge the rebels." Higley believed that Taggart formed his opinion of the situation and Higley's conduct prior to Higley returning to Dranesville and without ever allowing him to offer an explanation. It was not until the captured officers were exchanged that the actual facts of the case became known.[22]

Three of the officers involved, Major Wells and lieutenants Cheney and Watson, along with several of the sergeants, signed affidavits declaring that the facts as reported by Taggart and Price were inaccurate, namely that Higley had never been within sight of the prisoners and that none of the prisoners had ever beckoned to him or to any member of his party to come to their rescue. Even Col. Edward Sawyer, the regimental commander, admitted that he had been misled by the "false reports of irresponsible privates," and it was now clear to him that Higley "could not have *overtaken*" the prisoners, "to say nothing of his chances of success in a fight with Mosby" and his rearguard. Bolstered by the statements and confidence of his fellow officers Higley presented a detailed statement of the problems that he was confronted with. He reported that it had been necessary to select "at random by detail," the 50 men and serviceable horses needed for the relief party "from twelve different companies, [with] no idea of order or discipline." He explained that "many of them were new recruits, [and] all of them had come but prepared for picket duty, and with no preparation for a march, much less for a race or charge." Higley further pointed out that all of the horses at the outpost "had been on less than half rations of hay and grain for many days," and many of those selected that day "were lame or otherwise unfit for travel," but that they were "sufficient for a tour of picket duty."[23]

Once he was advised of the attack at the station Higley saw that he would have to "exert [himself] to the utmost to keep my party from utter disorganization." The mud, which he termed "extremely deep," quickly told on the weaker horses, scattering his column as some men struggled to "urge their horses through the mud," while others sought reasons, legitimate or otherwise to drop out, and Higley found himself ranging the ever increasing length of the column in an attempt to maintain some semblance of organization. As he had never been to Herndon Station he had no familiarity with the road network. Reports that the enemy party numbered "two or three hundred" men did little for his confidence as he struggled to keep his men together. While he was at the rear of the column urging the stragglers along several men from what he termed the "old guard" who "did not strictly belong to my command," broke ranks and galloped ahead. It was these men, who were never identified, who later gave the erroneous reports to Price and Taggart. Upon reaching the station Higley learned that Mosby had only 50 men, and he continued his pursuit as rapidly as possible, but reaching the high ground beyond Horsepen Run, and with his efforts to keep his detail closed up having come to naught, he called off the chase, having pushed his faltering animals at a canter eight miles through the mud. Returning to Herndon Station he established his pickets and assumed the duties to which he had been assigned, stating that if he "had been the contemptible coward that my present position indicates, I could have halted [there]—thrown out my videttes, reported the capture of the post, and awaited the orders of the brave commander at Drainsville," referring derisively to Major Taggart. Instead, he attempted to recapture his comrades, and though he had "*failed*" and was "ready to bear the censure which that failure shall demand from any just and honorable tribunal," he was not ready to submit to the charge of cowardice.[24]

None of the captured officers ever made an official report of the engagement, indeed Heintzelman expressed on the twenty-sixth his frustration at his inability to obtain "a satisfactory report of the circumstances." Price's unpublished version of Higley's role in the episode was written on the twenty-first, but it did not address the capture of the post. Taggart's self-serving report, the only Union account appearing in the *Official Records*, was equally devoid of information, while highly critical of Higley. On April 2, both Halleck and Stanton endorsed the recommendation that Higley be dismissed from the service on a charge of cowardice, and it became official four days later. When the statements and petitions of Higley's friends and fellow officers were submitted to Price in late May, the 1st Vermont was no longer in his brigade, and he refused to reconsider his earlier decision. His refusal based simply on the fact that Higley was no longer in his brigade is understandable, but not if he took the time to read the statements and recognize the erroneous information and accusations upon which his decision had been based. Instead he reiterated that he had reached his decision after consulting with majors Josiah Hall and William Collins, 1st Vermont, and Col. Charles Town, 1st Michigan, though none of them had direct knowledge of the situation. Collins and Town were not even assigned to the outpost, and Hall flatly denied that Price had ever spoken with him about the matter.[25]

On May 22, and in response to an inquiry from Major Wells in which Wells termed Taggart's investigation of the affair "a jug handle report," Colonel Sawyer admitted, "The feeling against [Higley] in the regiment was very strong, and ... the most injurious stories were circulated and believed." Sawyer stated that Price only consulted him after he had made his report and admitted that based on Price's version, "I could not say a word against it, except to remark that it was hard to reconcile it with [Higley's] previous good conduct." When Higley approached his colonel for advice, Sawyer urged him to fight the matter and "immediately determined to help get him reinstated." For his trouble Sawyer now found himself under attack as the responsible party, but he continued to urge the lieutenant to fight the charges, and he encouraged Wells to offer the same advice. In response to a question from Wells as to whether Price blamed him for the embarrassment as well as Higley, Sawyer told him, "I never saw the report, but Col. Price repeated to me what he said was the amount of Taggart's report to him, and I could not see as it in any manner tended to injure you—or any other officer except. Lt. [Higley]."[26]

The issue ultimately went before a military commission headed by Brig. Gen. James Ricketts. In his summation Ricketts pointed out that Price had never investigated the matter himself, relying entirely on the report from Major Taggart, who in Hall's opinion was predisposed to find against Higley. "There was some ill-feeling existing between Major Taggart," who was in command of the outpost, but who was also a member of Price's 2nd Pennsylvania Cavalry, "and the officers of the 1st Vermont Cavalry." In Hall's opinion Taggart was responsible for the poor condition of the regiment's horses as, "The distribution of supplies for the men and horses was not equal," implying that Taggart gave preference to the men and animals from the 2nd Pennsylvania at the expense of the other units at the outpost. Colonel

Sawyer's second statement calling for a re-examination also should have borne some weight with Price, as he admitted that he had agreed with the initial decision to dismiss Higley based solely on Price's explanation and on no personal knowledge of his own, but now saw the injustice of the decision. In the end the commission concluded, "There is no evidence to show that the accused did not act with courage and zeal in his endeavors to overtake the enemy and rescue the captives," and recommended on July 8, that he be restored to the service. Seven months later Lieutenant Higley was still fighting for his back pay.[27]

After describing the defeat at Herndon Station to his father, one trooper concluded, "I am afraid that the First Vt. Cavelry will be rather small before long." A hometown editor opined, "if our Yankee officers and men cannot contrive sure ways to prevent being deceived, and to stop being surprised in such an easy way as they have been, they had better go home and have more wide awake men put in their places." An editor in Richmond related the events of the seventeenth and declared that Mosby "will get Wyndham yet, or make him die of watchfulness," but, in fact, Mosby was about to lose his opportunity to capture the man he most despised.[28]

12

March 17–March 31, 1863

"We are now to occupy the ground in which the guerrillas live and act"

By the end of the day on the sixteenth, it was evident that Col. Percy Wyndham had lost the confidence of one of his last supporters, when General Heintzelman noted with frustration, "I hope I will soon have a reliable cavalry officer." The Stoughton Raid had embarrassed the entire command, and it had forced Heintzelman to begin considering his options. The affair at Herndon Station convinced the general that a change had to be made. On March 21, 1863, Wyndham was relieved from duty with the department and reassigned to the Army of the Potomac, resuming command of the 1st New Jersey Cavalry. Named to replace him was Maj. Gen. Julius Stahel.[1]

Maj. Gen. Franz Sigel had been working with his political friends for several months to insure the promotion of both Carl Schurz and Julius Stahel to the rank of major general. Lincoln, not certain that he could gain the promotion of both men at the same time, requested Sigel's opinion as to which of the two men would be preferable. Sigel was of the decided "opinion that Gen. Stahel is the best man." For political reasons of his own Lincoln sought to promote both men, with the only question being how he could appease all three with an appropriate command. On January 12, he proposed that Stanton submit both names for elevation, Schurz to command the Eleventh Corps (Sigel was still in command of a multiple corps Grand Division that included the Eleventh Corps), replacing Stahel who would take command of a cavalry corps, yet to be formed. "They, together with Sigel, are our sincere friends; and while so much may seem rather large, anything less is too small. I think it better be done," Lincoln counseled. Still, either Stanton or Halleck balked, and on January 26, a frustrated Lincoln advised Sigel, "I have tried, in regard to Gen. Schurz and [Stahel], to oblige all around, but it seems to get worse & worse." When Schurz learned that only his name had been submitted for promotion he informed Lincoln that he would not accept the honor unless Stahel's name was added to the list, telling the President, "You will pardon me for this, for it has always been my principle to be true to my friends and to stand up to a word I once have given." Lincoln decided to table the decision, telling Sigel, "I believe I will not now issue any new order in relation to the matter in question; but I will be obliged, if Gen. Hooker consistently can, and will give an increased Cavalry command to Gen. [Stahel]. You may show this letter to Gen. Hooker if you choose."[2]

That very day, February 5, Hooker announced the formation of a cavalry corps, but Stahel's name was not to be found in the order. The negotiations were further derailed when Hooker, eliminated the cumbersome Grand Division system of his predecessor. Hooker's decision angered Sigel because it significantly reduced the size of his command. Sigel requested to be relieved on February 12, allowing Hooker to place Oliver O. Howard in command of the Eleventh Corps. In the end both Schurz and Stahel were promoted, and Sigel was left on the outside looking for a way back in.[3]

On March 13, Stahel was summoned to Washington to meet with Lincoln and Heintzelman. After their meeting, Heintzelman sent Stahel a note, stating, "nothing would afford me more pleasure than to have you assigned to my command. The cavalry service is now suffering greatly from the want of an officer of your rank, experience & well known soldierly qualities." When Stahel accepted Heintzelman's offer, Lincoln telegraphed Hooker, advising that both Stahel and Heintzelman were eager for Stahel to be transferred, if it met with Hooker's approval. Hooker responded in the morning, telling the President, "No serious loss will result to the service by the transfer ... provided Colonel Wyndham ... be ordered to join his regiment." On the seventeenth Stahel was promoted to major general and assigned to the Department of Washington three days later.[4]

When he assumed his new command, Julius Stahel-Szamvald was thirty-seven years old. Born in Hungary, he had served briefly in the Austrian army, rising from private to lieutenant. Later he was involved with revolutionaries (including Sigel) in an unsuccessful bid for Hungarian independence, and was forced to flee the country in 1849, when the revolution was defeated. Ten years later he came to the United States and found employment with a German language newspaper in New York City. In 1861 he had helped to recruit the 8th New York Infantry, also known as the 1st German Rifles, and soon commanded the regiment. He was promoted to the rank of brigadier general in November 1861 and saw service in the Shenandoah Valley during the spring of 1862. At Second Manassas he had led a division in Sigel's corps and in the confusion after that disaster he was one of several Union general officers who were erroneously listed as killed in the battle.[5]

In the fall of 1862 he found himself commanding cavalry for Sigel and Heintzelman, and was described by one trooper as "a very cool, decided man ... and we trust he may continue in the command he assumes, as it affords us great consolation in our present struggles to find that we are not abandoned by one whom we so highly value." The following summer Annie Hays, the wife of General Hays, described Stahel as "small, not very handsome, but looks as if he could fight; is the most unassuming Dutchman, I ever met." A sergeant in the 7th Michigan thought Stahel an officer "with the least possible style about him," and felt more comfortable in his presence than he did his own colonel's. James Kidd remembered Stahel in his postwar account as "a dapper little Dutchman," whose foreign staff officers "would have been 'dudes,' only there were no 'dudes' in those days.... They were dandies.... It is a pity we did not get a chance to see Stahel in a fight, for I have an idea he was brave, and it takes away in an instant any feeling of prejudice you may have against a man on account of his being fussy in dress, when you see him face death or danger without flinching."[6]

There was never any question of Stahel's personal bravery. He had led a charge at Thoroughfare Gap on October 18, 1862, and again at Berryville in November. On June 5, 1864, at the Battle of Piedmont, in the Shenandoah Valley, he suffered a gunshot wound while leading another cavalry charge; an action for which he was later awarded the Medal of Honor. But just prior to that battle Maj. Gen. David Hunter had complained, "It would be impossible to exaggerate the inefficiency of General Stahel." Yet, when Stahel was transferred to a less strenuous position to aid his recovery, Hunter expressed "his appreciation" for the general's "faithful, zealous and gallant services."[7]

General Sigel had selected Stahel to lead the cavalry that was assigned to his command in the fall of 1862. The move may have been an attempt by several German officers, including Sigel, to place Stahel's name before the press and to aid his advancement, an effort that was ultimately successful. His activity in the Loudoun Valley that fall had gained him front-page headlines. An item in *The New York Times* stated that "he is constantly on the move, and the artillery and cavalry at his command have had but little rest," and indeed he had proven more willing to keep his cavalry active than other officers of more renown. The correspondent also declared that he had "the ability and tact for the kind of service required here at this time."[8]

In the wake of Stuart's Chambersburg Raid in October 1862, and with no apparent background in the cavalry or in intelligence operations, Stahel found himself thrust into the midst of a crisis in which the safety of the capital was deemed to be at stake. He was the officer that others looked to for answers, and he failed, though not for want of energy. Following a seventy-mile circuit through Loudoun County on October 13, during which the enemy had never been encountered or directly observed in more than company strength, Stahel had accurately determined that there was no significant enemy force east of Ashby's Gap and Snicker's Gap. But that evening he allowed signal fires along Bull Run Mountain to convince him that his men had missed a large force of enemy cavalry preparing for a strike against Washington. Having now prolonged the crisis and heightened anxiety, he took the field again two days later. Reinforced at his request, he either sent or led his troops to each location where the enemy was reported to be, and responded immediately to the capture of a wagon train in Haymarket. Still, having now made two circuits of Loudoun County as well as western Prince William and northern Fauquier and not encountering any enemy force in strength, he reported, erroneously, on the nineteenth that 3,000 Southern cavalry had entered Loudoun County through Snicker's Gap days earlier, when, in fact, there was no Southern force of this size east of the Shenandoah River. Regard-

Maj. Gen. Julius Stahel took command of the cavalry division assigned to the Department of Washington in March 1863. In late June, the division was transferred to the Cavalry Corps, Army of the Potomac, and Stahel was transferred to the Department of the Susquehanna (USAMHI).

less of continuing claims to the contrary, the only legitimate difference between the two cavalry forces at this point in the war was their ability to gather and interpret intelligence. Without question, Stuart's October raid had proved just how inferior the Federal cavalry was in this regard, and Stahel, who had proved tireless in his search for information, had been found lacking in his ability to sift and interpret the intelligence that he collected.[9]

In this regard Stahel had plenty of company within the Federal ranks, but his willingness to take the field and spend long hours in the saddle appears to have impressed many of the men who rode with him. Upon hearing the news of his promotion in March, Maj. Charles Knox, 9th New York Cavalry, sent Stahel a letter at the behest of his officers. "The Field and Line officers of this regiment have requested to make application to you to have this Regiment again placed under your command." The New Yorkers had ridden with Stahel throughout the fall campaign, and Knox reminded his former commander, "Not a single road nor hardly a single by-path is unknown to us.... We are therefore peculiarly fitted for this region." Nothing came of the request, however, and the 9th New York remained assigned to the Army of the Potomac.[10]

On the evening of March 18, Heintzelman was summoned by Stanton and interrogated about the recent raids, including the capture of Stoughton. The exasperated general assured the Secretary of War that he had the situation under control, "but that it was impossible to make these volunteer officers do their duty." Three days later Heintzelman reorganized his department, assigning Stahel to command a newly formed three brigade cavalry division to include Wyndham's former brigade, now led temporarily by Col. Timothy Bryan, 18th Pennsylvania, a second brigade led by Colonel Price, including the widely scattered 2nd Pennsylvania, 1st Vermont, 1st Michigan and a squadron of the 1st Ohio. Joseph Copeland's Wolverines, the 5th and 6th Michigan Cavalry, were ordered to the front as the third brigade in the new division.[11]

After the war Mosby claimed full credit for the transfer of the Michigan Brigade. "What were called my depredations had caused another brigade of cavalry to be sent into Fairfax to protect Washington." Mosby had clearly precipitated the change in command, but the idea of stationing the Michigan regiments at Fairfax Court House had first been proposed on December 27, 1862, before any of the troops stationed around the city were aware of Mosby's existence. General Casey had reported the arrival and availability of the 5th and 6th Michigan that day, as well as the expected arrival of the 7th Michigan. It was Casey's idea that "a well organized and efficient body of cavalry, as this may become, stationed in the vicinity of Fairfax Court House would be very useful both in repelling raids from the enemy's cavalry and making raids in return."[12]

There was also a political aspect to the decision in that Lincoln needed to satisfy the German factions that were vital to the future of his administration and his successful prosecution of the war. Promotion alone for Stahel was not enough. Having recently been in command of an infantry corps as a brigadier, he now needed a command commensurate with his new rank, dictating that Heintzelman expand his cavalry force into a large division, and he did so by assigning the Michigan Brigade to Stahel. Mosby's persistent attacks may well have been a factor, but he was not operating by himself. Lost in discussions of Mosby's military career are the activities of the Iron Scouts, the Prince William and Black Horse companies of the 4th Virginia, and other units that were just as persistent. None of these units, however, benefited from the talents of determined chroniclers as has Mosby's command, and the accomplishments of those other units have been largely lost to history.

On March 21, Lt. Col. Peter Stagg received intelligence that Mosby would try and cross the Occoquan below Wolf Run Shoals during the night. In an attempt to thwart the raid Stagg sent a party of 50 men to lay in ambush along their suspected line of approach. Though the men spent a miserable night lying out in snow and rain, without success, Stagg's information was not entirely in error. At 3 A.M. a force, later described as numbering between 36 and 100 men, and including both soldiers and civilians, crossed the Occoquan and attacked the reserve post of the 2nd Pennsylvania Cavalry, at the home of Elizabeth Violett, along the Ox Road. Leaving their horses in the woods, the Confederates attempted to surround the outpost but were challenged by an alert picket. Wary of the "evasive answer" received to his challenge, the picket fired, wounding one man. In the ensuing skirmish three Pennsylvanians were wounded, and 20 were captured, along with a like number of horses. The remainder of the Federals escaped, by fleeing west to the camp of the 13th Vermont Infantry at Wolf Run Shoals. Three officers at the post "escaped by the aid of a colored woman." The Confederates fell back to the river, attempting to cross at Selectman's Ford, which was held by eight men. "A sharp skirmish" erupted and two or three of the attacking party may have been wounded, before the pickets were forced to retreat.[13]

When Capt. William Brinton, 2nd Pennsylvania Cavalry, arrived with the reserve from Accotink he crossed the river with 100 men and pursued as far as Bacon Race Church, before turning back. He reported that the raiding party consisted of 27 men from the 4th Virginia, most likely the Prince William Cavalry, guided and assisted by a large number of local citizens. One man, believed to have been the leader of the party, was seriously wounded, and left at the scene. Two other wounded men were found on the south side of the Occoquan. The Pennsylvanians lost three men wounded, in addition to the prisoners and horses. Weapons and other equipment were found scattered along the escape route to the church.[14]

All indications suggested that the raiders fell back in the direction of Brentsville, and Stagg, who had hoped to prevent the raid, was now called on to intercept the men, while Brinton reorganized the picket line. Stagg was unable to recall his own men quickly enough, however, so a call went out to the Army of the Potomac. That evening, Maj. Edmund Pope arrived in Dumfries, from Stafford, with several companies of the 8th New York. After acquiring an additional 80 men from the regimental reserve post at Dumfries, Pope set out for Brentsville at midnight on a difficult ride through thick fog. Reaching the town near daybreak the men found no sign of the enemy, and turned for home having traveled 50 miles, "through mud and mire in the fruitless pursuit of our wary foe." Heintzelman concluded his journal entry for the twenty-second with a terse comment on the number of men who had been lost, and, confident that Stahel's leadership would soon make a difference, he opined, "I hope they are the last."[15]

Though Stagg, Brinton and Pope had all come up empty, reports of enemy activity immediately along the Occoquan continued, including a sighting of 15 men across from Selectman's Ford on the night of the twenty-second. Colonel Randall set his men to building a boat, which he used to ferry two companies of the 13th Vermont across the river to investigate the activity in their immediate front, but nothing was found.[16]

Captain Brinton also re-interviewed the wounded officer captured at Mrs. Violett's,

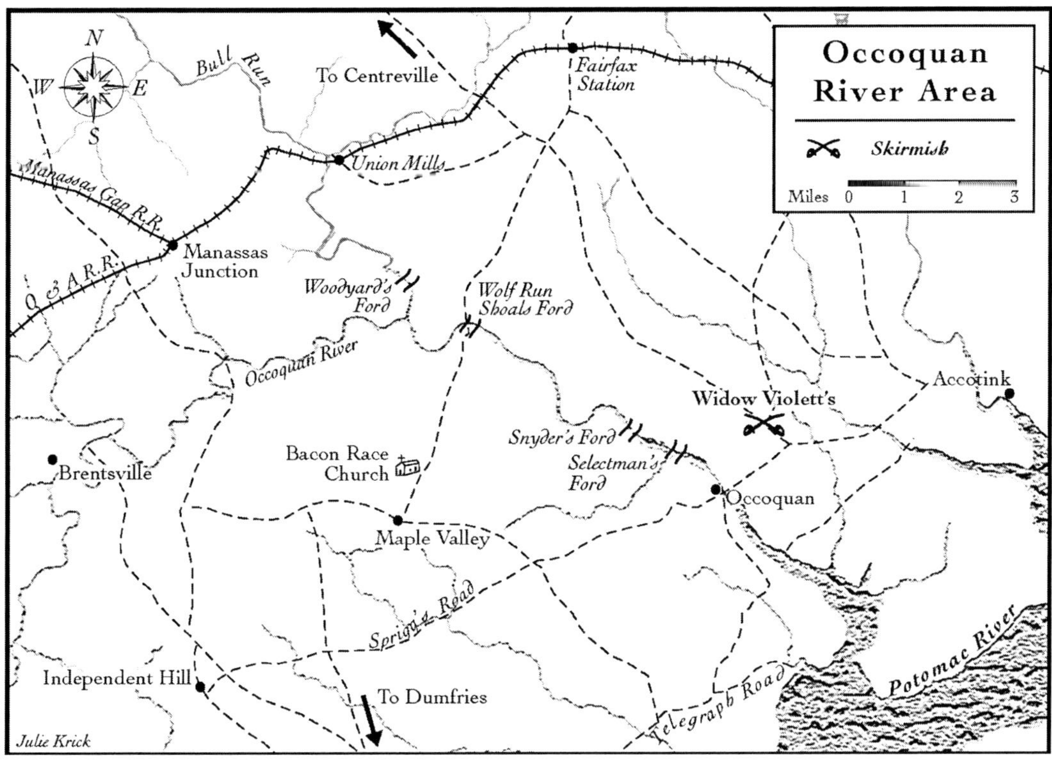

and though the man was not "disposed to give much information," he did admit that "quite a heavy force" of the enemy was operating in the area between Bacon Race Church and Brentsville. Based on this report Stahel planned to mount a larger effort on the twenty-fourth, using Stagg's 1st Michigan, supported by the available troops from the brigade at Jermantown. Lt. Col. Robert Johnstone was instructed to have his men ready at an early hour to assist Stagg in an attempt to scour the area between the Occoquan and Brentsville. Johnstone was to remain within supporting distance of Stagg, who was to move directly on Brentsville, possibly as bait. The plan fell apart for several reasons. Johnstone initially begged off, telling Price that his horses were "utterly unfit to march," and asking that, "if they must go," to let him know as soon as possible as he needed to recall them from picket. Then, while the details of the plan were still being hashed out, Mosby struck Johnstone's pickets at Chantilly. In the end, Johnstone arrived with two regiments but too late to coordinate with Stagg who made the effort alone. Though the men expected to "have some fun before they [got] back" the trip was without significant result.[17]

After the raid at Herndon Station on St. Patrick's Day, Mosby had disbanded his men and told them to meet again on March 23 at Rector's Crossroads. He had spent the intervening time in the company of John Underwood scouting Union positions around Chantilly and he had identified two reserve posts that he thought he could capture, given a sufficient number of men. When he found 50 or more waiting for him on the twenty-third he endeavored to try. He led the men east along the turnpike until they were within a few miles of the Union lines, where they turned off the road and continued moving east through fields and woodlots to avoid detection and to take the position from behind. Arriving within sight of his target, Mosby found the pickets alert and saw little chance for his original plan to succeed. Though Mosby later wrote that he then sent several of his men to run in the pickets, hoping to draw the larger force out, others have suggested that it was a random act of several of the more impetuous men who were with him that day. Either way, a handful of men charged the nearest group of Yankees who fled toward the camp. As the Confederates closed on them one of the New Yorkers was shot in the head and killed, either out of hand as the regimental historian later claimed, or as he turned to fire on his pursuers as one Southern account states. The death of their friend convinced the others to rein in their horses and surrender.[18]

Mosby observed this attack from the crest of a hill. While his men rounded up the prisoners below, Mosby watched as the larger reserve force reacted to the attack and formed their ranks to respond. Mosby led his men back to the turnpike as it presented the quickest means of escape, though it was also the road on which the reserve was now coming at full speed. Just east of Cub Run the road passed through a thick stand of trees, and it was here that several barricades had been erected across the road. Mosby concealed his men behind the barricades, and ordered them to charge as soon as the New Yorkers came into sight. The sudden turn of events caused the Yankees to panic and flee. Though Mosby wrote that the plan had been forced upon him by the fact that his horses were "very much jaded," they showed little evidence of this as the Rebels chased the Yankees back to their camp.[19]

Northern accounts universally speak of the men being greeted by a heavy, sudden fusillade of gunfire as they approached the barricades, while Mosby later wrote that this was one of the few times that he ordered his men to use their sabers. Once the New Yorkers fled, however, the men sheathed the sabers and drew their pistols. Edward Winters, who was captured, told his mother, "I had one Ball shot threw my coat sleeve and lots went so close to my head that I felt them I don't see how they ever all got by." William Brent, who was with Mosby, remembered that when ordered to charge, "we rushed upon them, and unloaded our pistols in their faces." Once they broke, "we were on them like bee Martins, popping them in their backs."[20]

As was often the case in mounted combat, the fortunes of war turned again when a second force arrived, this one a body of Union troopers from Frying Pan. This allowed the officers of the first group to rally their men, and the combined Federal column sent the Confederates running. The damage had been done however, and though they followed Mosby for several miles the Northerners soon broke off the pursuit. The 5th New York lost two men killed, one man mortally wounded and at least 30 men captured, including one officer, while Mosby sustained no loss. More important to the Federals than their casualties was their embarrassment when they realized that rather than riding into a prepared ambush at the barricades they had allowed themselves to be panicked by the very men they had been chasing seconds before. Sgt. Marvin Wight, who was not in the fight, laid much of the blame for the defeat on Maj. William Bacon, who had been promoted from lieutenant and regimental adjutant to major in November. He alleged that the "men broke and ran following the example of [Bacon] ... who never stopped till he reached camp." Wight credited the other officers with being "courageous enough but that is not all that is wanting to make an efficient officer." The regimental historian was more circumspect, concluding, "Every one felt mortified at the result of this day's work, and resolved to retrieve our fortunes on some more fortunate occasion."[21]

On March 23, William Rockwell, 5th Michigan Cavalry, received the disheartening news that the regiment might well spend the remainder of the war in the capital, "one of the miserablest muddy Countrys in the world, it cannot be beat for mud, and dead horses and [Crows] in flocks of hundreds. Take it altogether it is a miserable place." Moreover, if they remained they might "never be in a battle." If Rockwell and his companions were looking for a change of scenery the orders came the following morning when the brigade was ordered into Virginia, and this time they were going to stay. "I suppose we are now to occupy the ground in which the guerrillas live and act & we are to commence picket & outpost duty in earnest," opined Lt. Col. Ebenezer Gould. In the camp of the 7th Michigan the men watched rockets ascend around the capital as they prepared to march. Camp rumor, punctuated by the rockets and the sound of artillery in the distance, had it that Stuart's cavalry was "loose," reportedly having crossed Bull Run the day before, and Edwin Havens speculated, "I suppose we will have to go out and chase them into their holes."[22]

Within hours of receiving the orders the brigade left the capital for the last time, crossed the river and camped near Bailey's Cross Roads for the night. In the morning Lt. Col. Russell Alger, 6th Michigan, was sent to Vienna, Virginia, with four companies, in anticipation of an attack that night. The remainder of the brigade established their camps about a mile east of Fairfax Court House, on the twenty-fifth, with General Copeland commandeering the Ford home for his headquarters.[23]

The Wolverines believed they were responding to reports that Stuart was again raiding through northern Virginia. As early as the fifteenth, reports out of Winchester had placed Stuart near Snicker's Gap "with a large force of cavalry." Over the next several days, and in the face of all the evidence to the contrary, the rumors persisted. On the twenty-first Stuart was reported to be moving into Loudoun County, and Johnstone volunteered to send a patrol into the northern part of the county the following day, but events closer to home dictated otherwise. On the twenty-third Stuart was said to be in the vicinity of Nolan's Ferry, above Leesburg, but with the more immediate threat believed to be the force operating in Prince William County, along the Occoquan, Johnstone was ordered to take the 1st West Virginia and the 18th Pennsylvania and respond to Union Mills to assist Stagg in his move against Brentsville. Though Johnstone did not get his entire command across Bull Run before he met Stagg returning, his move weakened the northern picket line just as Stuart was believed to be moving east from Leesburg, and necessitated, at least in part the deployment of the Michigan brigade to Vienna and Fairfax Court House. Johnstone returned to Chantilly the following morning, allowing Stahel to meet any attack that might materialize with his entire division. Several of the infantry units were also shifted to further strengthen the forward lines. The 14th and 15th Vermont moved up from Fairfax Station relieving the 126th New York between Union Mills and Wolf Run Shoals. The New Yorkers marched to Centreville, where General Alexander Hays was ordered to concentrate his brigade.[24]

That night, with the supply depot at Fairfax Station now guarded by "but thirty men," Colonel Randall reported that "a small party of the enemy" crossed near Wolf Run Shoals, forced their way through his picket line and were believed to be making their way for the depot. In response Johnstone ordered a squadron of the 18th Pennsylvania to strengthen the guard detail at the depot. He also asked that the 1st Michigan be sent "to cut off the rebels if they attempted to recross at the ford." To support the cavalry Randall put half of his regiment on the march in an attempt to locate the enemy, but like so many others "it proved to be a false alarm."[25]

By now both Johnstone and Stagg must have felt like a cat chasing its tail, as Stagg also received a report from the provost marshal at Centreville that a party of guerrillas, coming out of Prince William County, would strike the picket line between Centreville and Occoquan in the morning. This report was deemed credible as it came from two of the soldiers, just paroled, who had been captured at Mrs. Violett's on the twenty-second, and Stagg responded by sending 50 men across Wolf Run Shoals in another attempt to intercept the guerrillas. This time the anticipated raid failed to materialize.[26]

On March 26, 3,000 of Stuart's troopers were reported between Warrenton and New Baltimore, and a squadron from the 6th Michigan was "routed out" just before midnight to verify the report, which also proved false. The following day Alger sent in word that he anticipated an attack at Vienna, and the main body of the 6th Michigan was sent to his support. On the twenty-eighth, the reports gained credibility after two men who were captured in Fairfax Court House divulged details of the intended raid. Stuart, with 5,000 men, they said, would attack the town, intent on capturing a contraband camp of 1,500 men employed as woodchoppers, as well as the troops stationed nearby. The two prisoners identified themselves as members of a scouting party that had been sent "to obtain information in regard to the disposition" of troops in the vicinity. They then expanded their tale to include a strike by Stonewall Jackson at Centreville. These details necessitated a further redeployment of troops to counter the threat. Two infantry regiments, the 127th and 144th New York were sent to Vienna, with orders to construct "light defensive works," while two additional regiments, the 25th and 27th Maine Infantry, were deployed west of Centreville, with orders to retire on the fortifications if attacked in force. The Vermonters at Union Mills were instructed to fall back to Fairfax Court House if necessary, while those blocking Wolf Run Shoals were to "hold out at all hazards." The division commander also instructed that "every unknown and suspicious looking person should be arrested and critically examined."[27]

Like so many other threats, this one failed to develop, but many of the men spent a sleepless night as events along the line continued to give the impression that an attack was imminent. At 6 P.M. rebels burned the Warrenton turnpike bridge across Bull Run, and two hours later a returning cavalry patrol reported that a party of enemy troopers were advancing from Manassas. Gunfire erupted at several points along the line, causing the troops at Vienna to be called out and formed in line of battle. In the confusion a man in the 111th New York was shot in the arm when he failed to respond to another picket's command to halt.[28]

Copeland's regiments had seen their share of activity since their arrival, as they were repeatedly called "to encounter some bugbear enemy." John Farnill, 6th Michigan, reported that his regiment had already been out "to or three times" scouring the country around the "Old Bull Run Battle Ground," and Gould told his brother on the twenty-ninth that he had just received orders that "will probably give us a night ride and possibly a fight for breakfast." Lt. Col. Allyne Litchfield, 7th Michigan, informed his wife that the "horses are all saddled and the men sleeping on their arms." They had been on one scout that morning and Litchfield declared, "This seems a little more like war than being in [Detroit] or [Grand Rapids]. As this was the regiments first deployment he admitted, "I would rather not fight our command till they are better prepared but the precision and good order with which they formed ... gave me confidence they would do all in their power." Years later one of Litchfield's men remembered that the excitement centered around John Mosby, "but Mosby was like Pat's flee, he was not there, at any rate we did not get our fingers on him, or our eyes either, so we bid farewell to the old cuss and went back to quarters — it was only a false alarm."[29]

On March 30, Stuart and Jackson were reported to be in the vicinity of Aldie. This caused Col. William Gurney, commanding at Vienna, to request that the remainder of his brigade be sent to his support. That evening, Maj. Melvin Brewer, 1st Michigan, reported that he had just returned from an extensive patrol to Manassas Junction. From there he had sent patrols to the western boundaries of Prince William County and found no evidence to suggest that any of the reports from the previous couple of days were true. A handful of Confederates were chased for several miles before being lost in the woods near Gainesville, and he reported seeing smoke in the direction of Warrenton, but he found nothing to substantiate the myriad rumors of the previous few days. Col. George Gray scoured eastern Loudoun County the same day. His report that no rebels had been found, combined with Major Brewer's report appeared to calm the many frayed nerves along the lines.[30]

It is likely that there was some concert of action between the Southern units operating against the picket lines to increase the pressure and strain on the Federals by striking repeatedly at multiple points. It is equally likely that the Federal intelligence system, such as it was, was overwhelmed by false leads, planted by the many deserters, and Southern citizens that were constantly passing through the lines, as well as misleading information that paroled prisoners were either told or allowed to hear. Not since mid–February had there been any discussion, for which evidence has been found, that Lee and Stuart were considering a raid into either northern Virginia or Maryland. Even a plan to send Stuart into the Shenandoah Valley to aid Brig. Gen. William "Grumble" Jones against Milroy at Winchester had been cancelled due to bad weather. On March 31, Lee did suggest sending Col. Thomas Munford's cavalry brigade into Loudoun County, but only as protection for commissary details sent to gather wheat and flour. Still, the rumors persisted, forcing the Federals to strain their resources to investigate them. And, while it may be said that the constant alarms served to keep the men alert, there was a point of diminishing return, a point at which tired men become less attentive due to lack of sleep, and frustrated with the annoying routine of false alarms amidst the continuing foul weather.[31]

In an effort to overcome the complacency of their men, officers were dispatched to conduct regular inspections. On March 20, a captain from the 5th New York Cavalry inspected the men along the entire line from Dranesville to the Accotink. He reported that 150 men "per day" were detailed on picket between Dranesville and Herndon Station, and he cited the men, horses and equipment as being "in excellent condition." He found the line from Herndon Station to Centreville manned by the 18th Pennsylvania Cavalry, with the men, generally, "not on the alert." He observed that their were horses saddled and equipment "in fair condition," but noted that their carbines and sabers had been condemned, "as worthless." The 125th New York Infantry held the line from Centreville to Mitchell's Ford and he found them in "excellent order — arms and equipment good — discipline good." The 1st Michigan Cavalry, picketing from Blackburn's Ford to McLean's Ford, was determined to be in "fair condition." To their south the 126th New York Infantry held the line to Yates Ford, and he judged them "well provided for an attack," and their "equipments and discipline fair." A unit from the Pennsylvania Reserves along with the 13th Vermont Infantry held the line from Yates Ford to Mill Ford and he passed them without complaint, saving his harshest assessment for the 2nd Pennsylvania Cavalry, whose men he labeled as "poor." Their equipment was maintained but he thought the soldiers undisciplined, "not well informed, [and] do not know their business," with some of the troopers unable to name their commanding officer.[32]

Orders also went out forbidding the men to pass any refugees through the lines "on any pretense whatever," other than contrabands. Too many of the recent arrivals were deemed to be "spies and dealers in contraband articles" who then return "to the Confederacy with valuable supplies and information." The historian of the 126th New York Infantry noted that many civilians in "forlorn condition" were affected by this policy and that the officers and men were sympathetic in turn, sharing their rations and that General Hays sent a wagon load of supplies beyond the lines to ease their plight. Still, if the soldiers deemed anyone suspicious they were taken into custody, and according to one of his soldiers, Colonel Randall sent "all citizens that he could get hold of to Washington for we are fully convinced there is no Union people here they are the worst kind of Rebels."[33]

Still, none of these precautions could entirely eliminate the threat of espionage, and while the rumors and reports focused Federal efforts on the expected raid north of the Occoquan, the guerrillas and bushwhackers struck the lines to the south near Dumfries. At least five men were wounded or captured between March 22 and 28, near the town. On the twenty-eighth, a scouting party from the 8th New York Cavalry, led by Lt. Murganzey Hopkins, was in the process of surrounding the home of a man named Atchinson, "a notorious & active Rebel," when Atchinson observed the troopers and warned three men in the house who escaped out the back. Hopkins arrested Atchinson, and charged him "with knowing of and assisting in Bushwhacking operations and of harboring & aiding Rebel soldiers etc, etc." This was part of an effort by Maj. Edmund Pope to "arrest the soldiers & Bushwhackers in this vicinity who are harbored & assisted by inhabitants near our lines."[34]

On the morning of March 29, Pope sent in a report detailing the shooting of Henry Norton, just after midnight, by a man Norton never saw until they were within 20 feet of each other. Both men fired, and though he was hit in the hand and lost a finger Norton dismounted and gave chase until he observed his assailant join two or three other men. He could hear them discussing how to get back through the lines as they ran. He fired on them as they fled into the darkness. Pope sent a detail of men on foot to search for the bushwhackers "without avail." Two hours later several more men were fired on as they darted across a road in the same area, and again Pope sent out a squad in a futile attempt to locate them. Later that day Pope ordered the arrest of three brothers, named Chapman, who lived nearby and who had "excited the suspicion" of his men over the previous couple of days. The major warned, however, of the overall difficulty protecting his men in the "dense undergrowth & forest as exists along our entire line."[35]

That afternoon one of Pope's patrols, numbering 16 men and led by Lt. R. James Colburn, was attacked eight miles north of Dumfries, by a force estimated at "one company or a small squadron [numbering] about 60 men." When the Confederates came into view Colburn immediately "formed line facing the road when the rebels ceased the charge and took a position opposite our party." The Rebels "formed line and immediately charged," after sending "a detachment down the road to intercept & prevent the escape of the" Federals. Six of Colburn's men were able to break through and reach Dumfries, though one man was killed, one mortally wounded and two captured. Initial reports indicated that Colburn and the remainder of his men were also captured, but, after scattering and concealing themselves in the thick undergrowth, they reached camp later that night. Union scouts learned shortly thereafter that a party of Rebels numbering "about 60 passed Brentsville P.M. about 5 [o'clock] and had two prisoners." Pope explained that he was unable to pursue the party in a timely manner due to his having "but 20 horses who were in condition or able to march all night," as well as the fact that he "apprehended [further] trouble from the Bushwhackers or the soldiers of the enemy on my lines." In frustration he reiterated his earlier warning, "If you have been over our present picket and patrol line you will appreciate the difficulty of protecting ourselves and the almost impossibility of preventing passage through our lines by dismounted men."[36]

With the 8th New York Cavalry unable to place a sufficient force in the field, the task of pursuing the guerrillas fell to Capt. Elon Farnsworth and the 8th Illinois Cavalry. Farnsworth set out from Stafford Court House at 2 A.M. on the thirtieth with 160 men. At ten o'clock he made "contact with eight or ten rebel scouts or guerrillas" near Bristersburg, "and commenced a skirmish or running fight which continued until dark and extended over twenty miles of country." As the Federals pushed north toward Weaversville, they encountered stronger parties of the enemy, numbering between 25 and 30 men who attacked them "on every side at once." Undaunted, Farnsworth continued four or five miles past Warrenton Junction [modern Calverton], before turning back through Catlett Station to near Brentsville, "where the skirmish ended." In the darkness Farnsworth headed south, moving west of Brentsville, until he reached a reserve post of the 3rd Indiana Cavalry at 1 A.M., and made camp.[37]

The Federals lost one man killed, one wounded and three captured, in what the chaplain later termed "a desperate engagement." Later in the day Farnsworth recovered these three men and seized several prisoners of his own. He reported that once his men had been disarmed "a man pretending to be a citizen and calling himself Arthur Woodyard took up a loaded carbine, cocked and aimed it at one of my men saying, 'Now you damned Yankee son of a bitch I'll kill you.'" The prisoners thought he would have done so if not stopped by one of the soldiers present. Woodyard, who was himself captured later in the day, was described by Farnsworth as "a bushwhacker and a dangerous man with a smooth tongue," who should "be severely dealt with." Among the Southern prisoners were James Dulin and Jack Shoolbred of the Iron Scouts. Sgt. John Towles, Company A, 4th Virginia Cavalry, who had been operating with the Iron Scouts as a guide was also taken, but escaped the following night as the command neared Dumfries, by dropping off his horse in the darkness. Four other men from the Prince William Cavalry were captured near Elk Run. Farnsworth believed that two Southerners had been killed along with one man wounded and captured. In total they took 11 prisoners, but were unable to recover the men from the 8th New York, who were already across the Rappahannock.[38]

13

April 1, 1863

"Mr. *Capt. Mosby*"

In his official account of the April 1, 1863, fight at Miskell's Farm, John Mosby described the 1st Vermont Cavalry as one of the Union's "oldest and best regiments," a statement that was only half correct. John Scott then propagated the erroneous story that Mosby and his men defeated a group of handpicked volunteers from the regiment. In time the 1st Vermont Cavalry would truly become an outstanding cavalry regiment, but in the spring of 1863 it was a command in utter turmoil, bordering on complete collapse in terms of efficiency, military discipline and morale. Internal strife throughout the officer corps of the regiment consumed the attention of the "shoulder straps." Focused on their own concerns, the officers ignored the enlisted men. With the resulting lapse in discipline the men became slovenly, and a malaise spread throughout the command. The recent defeats at the hands of the guerrillas only added to the dissatisfaction and disaffection within the regiment.[1]

The 1st Vermont Cavalry had been mustered into service on November 19, 1861, and had arrived in Washington, D.C., the following month with ten companies. After climbing down off the train, the men were marched a half mile to an old graveyard, where they were ordered to camp for the night, amongst the headstones. One man had already been killed and several injured falling from the train as it pulled into New York City days before. These omens did not bode well for any of the young men who had volunteered for the cavalry with visions of achieving fame and glory.[2]

The regiment had been raised under authority granted to Lemuel Platt, a fifty-year-old physician. Platt had initially proposed to the governor to raise a regiment of cavalry, but was turned down, as the state was not authorized to enlist cavalry. Platt then turned to Secretary of War Simon Cameron, who granted the request, extending a colonel's commission to Platt. Described as a man "of marked energy," Platt was a politician, doctor and farmer, but not a military man, and he soon lost his zeal for military service. Before his enthusiasm waned, however, he ensured that the men received the finest Morgan horses available in Vermont. He also approached the army about arming his men with the revolutionary Henry repeating rifle. In a letter written to Brig. Gen. George Stoneman, McClellan's chief of cavalry, on November 19, 1861, Platt advised that the New Haven Arms Company, which produced the weapon, was "proposing to furnish Henry's repeating rifle for my Regt." Platt termed the rifle "the most efficient arm I have seen, and I should be glad to have the Regt. armed with it." It would be many months, however, before the senior officers in the Ordinance Bureau could be convinced of the value of the new repeating weapons, and Platt's efforts failed. Instead, he settled for the Sharps carbine, which arrived in such limited numbers that only ten men per company were initially issued the weapon.[3]

When Platt tendered his resignation in February 1862, Capt. Jonas P. Holliday, 2nd U.S. Cavalry, was appointed as his successor. Seventeen years younger than Platt and a member of the West Point Class of 1846, Holliday would be remembered as "tall, slender, grave, a thorough disciplinarian and a spirited and sensitive gentleman." He immediately dedicated himself to the drill and discipline of the regiment, but just two weeks after his arrival the command was ordered to return to Washington, where it arrived on March 10, 1862.[4]

Two days later the regiment passed through Rockville, Maryland, en route to join General Banks in the Shenandoah Valley. The Vermonters arrived in Harpers Ferry on the twenty-ninth, departing again on the last day of the month to aid the beleaguered Union forces around Winchester. Moving south past Kernstown the troopers observed the detritus of the recent fighting, before linking up with General Banks at Woodstock on April 5, 1862.[5]

During the march that day, Holliday departed from the regiment and returned to Strasburg, accompanied only by a bugler and his orderly. Reining to a halt along Tumbling Run, and just a short ride from the Shenandoah River, Holliday sent first the bugler and then his orderly ahead with orders for his adjutant, Lt. Edgar Pitkin, to meet him there. Alone, Holliday then rode down to the river, tied his horse to a tree and shot himself in the head. Informing McClellan of the incident the next day, General Banks termed his death "very sudden and very sad." Though it is doubtful that Banks had had much interaction with Holliday he reported that the colonel had "appeared greatly depressed about the condition of his regiment," and in the opinion of the regimental officers "had been nearly insane for three weeks," due to some "personal disappointments not connected with his profession." The regimental surgeon later remarked, "All the business of conducting a regiment agitated the colonel." Casting a further shadow over the regiment was the accidental death of one of the soldiers who accompanied the colonel's body back to Winchester.[6]

In the aftermath of this double tragedy, Lt. Col. George Kellogg assumed command of the regiment. Kellogg was a thirty-six-year-old attorney from a prominent family in Brattleboro. The regiment's two majors were William Collins and John Bartlett. Collins was the only officer in the command with any prior military experience, having served several years in a British artillery unit. When Bartlett tendered his resignation on April 25, 1862, the regiment was left with only two field officers, Kellogg and Collins. Banks, not yet confident of Kellogg's abilities, divided the command between the two men, but the turmoil continued when Capt. Edward Sawyer, who was home on leave, took advantage of Bartlett's resignation and the fact that he, Sawyer, was then in Vermont, to finagle a promotion to major over seven senior captains. Unconvinced that Kellogg, Collins or Sawyer was qualified to command the regiment, Gov. Frederick Holbrook appointed thirty-one-year-old Charles Tompkins from the ranks of the regular army.[7]

One Vermonter described Tompkins as "a fine looking officer," and though it was said, postwar, that the men were "glad to have again at [their] head a 'regular' who knew his business," they may well have looked askance at Tompkins after the upheaval they had already endured. Years later Tompkins stated that he "found the regiment was improperly officered," with many of the best men "misplaced," in his opinion. He felt that then captain William Wells should have been a major, describing him as "a good man and a good officer," and that Addison Preston, "a stirring fellow," should have filled the position as lieutenant colonel. He also singled out both Franklin Huntoon and Henry Flint for praise, describing the latter as "a good man in every way — a fine man and soldier." Of the men in general,

Tompkins, thought only a few "were not good," and recalled that they "never growled or grumbled at their lot."[8]

The Vermonters were brigaded with the 1st Maine, 1st Maryland and the 5th New York, under the command of Brig. Gen. John Hatch. They saw their first combat on April 8, when a company led by Preston, skirmished briefly with some of Turner Ashby's cavalry near Columbia Furnace. Just after Tompkins arrived, disaster struck when Stonewall Jackson routed the Union forces scattered between Strasburg, Front Royal and Winchester in late May. The 1st Vermont had been broken up into several detachments: Tompkins's battalion was assigned to protect the baggage trains while Major Collins's squadron scouted the retreat route to Winchester along with Lt. Col. Calvin Douty and his 1st Maine Cavalry. Over the three day-period beginning on May 23, the regiment lost seven men killed or mortally wounded, seven others wounded and 85 men captured. Collins was wounded and captured, and Major Sawyer was injured when his horse fell on him. Several men, who were too severely injured to be moved, including Collins, were left in Front Royal by their captors and recovered at the end of the month. Adding insult to injury Tompkins was forced to burn all the wagons, one of which held the regimental colors.[9]

By the second week of June, the command had replaced the equipment lost in the retreat, and a shipment of Sharps carbines allowed Tompkins to fully arm four companies with the weapon. The regiment stayed in the Shenandoah Valley until early July, when it moved east of the Blue Ridge into the Virginia Piedmont to join Maj. Gen. John Pope's new command: the Army of Virginia. Brig. Gen. John Buford replaced Hatch, and the brigades were realigned in July, with Buford now in command of the 1st Vermont, 1st Michigan, 1st West Virginia and the 5th New York, but the senior leadership within the regiment continued to be a problem.[10]

Lt. Col. George Kellogg deserted his post and returned to Vermont in July, and eventually left the army. Neither of the majors would return until October and without the homegrown help of senior officers within the regiment Tompkins found his position increasingly difficult. Though he stayed with the regiment through Pope's tenure, Tompkins resigned on September 9, 1862, and returned to the regular army's quartermaster department.[11]

Edward Sawyer had returned to Vermont to recover from the injuries he sustained in the Shenandoah Valley, and he was still in the state when he was promoted to colonel to replace Tompkins. This further aggravated the raw feelings within the officer corps as Sawyer was again promoted over a senior officer. The popular Addison Preston was selected to fill the position of lieutenant colonel. Both promotions were effective on September 16, 1862, but before word of Sawyer's promotion reached the regiment, Capt. George Conger had the temerity to appoint himself regimental commander. When word of the official promotions reached the regiment on the sixteenth, Preston relieved Conger, who resigned shortly thereafter. Six days later Preston was severely wounded at Ashby's Gap.[12]

When Preston returned home to recover from his wounds, the regiment was left in the hands of the senior captain, Samuel Rundlett. The upheaval continued when Tompkins, the former commander, reported the continuing crisis in command to his new superior Montgomery Meigs, quartermaster general of the army, and Meigs referred the matter to General Banks, then in command of the Defenses of Washington. That Tompkins was so disgusted with "the abuses within the regiment," as to resign his colonel's commission and return to the regular army as a captain spoke volumes. Meigs sent a blistering four-page indictment of the regiment to the war department, in which he concluded, that, "in its present condition, its employment seems to be a waste of national treasure, and of the best blood of the State." An officer was quickly dispatched to examine the situation firsthand. His investigation centered on Sawyer and Collins, specifically whether their absence was authorized and whether they were, given the numerous allegations of their misconduct, qualified for command. Sawyer returned to the regiment during the investigation and was soon mustered out of the service without a hearing, "for inefficiency and neglect of the welfare of his regiment whilst a Major thereof." In the coming months this manner of discipline without a hearing would take hold in the army, especially in the cavalry and numerous officers were dismissed without a chance to defend themselves, but Sawyer's case included a clause that allowed him the opportunity to clear his name and seek reinstatement. In doing so he would further tear asunder the fabric of the regiment.[13]

Major Collins was now in command, and as Sawyer worked at organizing his defense, a personal feud erupted between the two men, both in camp and in the press. Collins was already under fire both privately and publicly for ordering an attack on May 24, near Middletown, Virginia, which resulted in heavy casualties both to his detachment as well as to the 1st Maine Cavalry. In an attempt to mitigate his culpability for the affair he wrote a self-serving report in which he attempted to lay the blame for the disaster on Lt. Col. Calvin Douty of the 1st Maine. Months later, Collins and Sawyer would reduce themselves to squabbling over more trivial matters, like the ownership of a horse, and whether Sawyer had spent time with several prostitutes while traveling from Vermont to Washington, D.C. In a letter to William Wells, who was in Vermont on recruiting duty, Sawyer sought his help to clarify the latter complaint and stated rather boldly that Collins would soon be "up the spout!"[14]

Sawyer, an attorney before the war, presented his case and was reinstated on December 20, 1862, but his personal victory did little to quell the feuding within the regimental command structure. By forcing the officers to take sides in his dispute Sawyer cast the seeds of further dissension and then sought retribution against those who had stood with Collins. Aligned against Sawyer were all of the officers that he had superseded on the seniority list. On January 8, 1863, two of those men, Collins and Capt. Joel Erhardt, each filed their own charges against Sawyer, reiterating many of the previous allegations, including embezzlement, misuse of government property and conduct unbecoming an officer for his alleged cavorting with "strumpets." General Heintzelman received the complaints and his aide, Capt. Wesley Merritt, was detailed to investigate them. In the end Merritt and Heintzelman felt that none of the charges could be substantiated, and Sawyer again prevailed. But it was also clear to both men "that Col. Sawyer is not ... either in a military, moral, or social point of view, all that the regiment deserves in a [commanding] officer. Col. Sawyer's lack of experience is greatly against his being regarded with favor, by officers of the regt., who served in the field while he was absent sick, or recruiting — officers who claim with reason, a superior knowledge of military matters. This want of good feeling materially interferes with the discipline & efficiency of the regt."[15]

In the end Erhardt sought to resign, and though Heintzelman disapproved the request, General Halleck approved it effective February 4, 1863. Captain Rundlett resigned in mid–March and Captain Huntoon was cashiered on March 25, ostensibly because of allegations arising following his failure against John Mosby at Aldie on March 2, though the ill will between he and Sawyer may well have played a role in the final decision. Capt. John Woodward escaped similar censure for his role in the fight at Aldie, possibly because he was badly injured in the affair, but the fact that he had signed a resolution in support of Sawyer, whereas Huntoon had remained a vocal opponent, suggests that regimental politics may well have played a role in Huntoon's demise. The dissension might have ended when Major Collins resigned in May, but Sawyer continued to antagonize his fellow officers as he found one reason after another to avoid duty in the field, leading several of the senior men who had initially stood by him to now turn against him. In the end, however, he remained in command of the regiment until April 1864, when he resigned.[16]

With the men of the regiment scattered among several outposts in the winter and spring of 1863, and with the attention of the officers diverted by the constant bickering, John Mosby could not have moved against a more hapless regiment than the 1st Vermont Cavalry. At some point the military discipline of the men had to be affected by the many distractions within the command, as well as the lack of attention from the officers. As Charles Chapin had confessed January, "You never saw such a lazy set" of men. After the war an officer admitted that "the First Vermont was no more fit for picket duty than hell was for a powder house." Comments of this nature, combined with the unbridled dissension afflicting the officers, as well as a complete lack of leadership and direction from Price and the suspicion of favoritism fostered by Major Taggart cast serious doubt on any description of the regiment as "efficient." In truth it may have been the least efficient regiment within the department at that time.[17]

Historian George Benedict explained that operations along the picket line were "conducted under a singular system or want of system. The picket details were made up of squads from different regiments. The picket reserves consisted of similar fragments, under officers who were commonly strangers to most of the men." Benedict observed, "Dissensions prevailed among the officers; there could be little *esprit de corps*, where the organic unity, both of the regiment as a whole and of the companies, was so broken up, and the morale of the troops in all the cavalry regiments suffered seriously. The arrangement of picket stations could hardly have been better adapted to encourage the operations of Mosby, and it was not surprising that these were often successful." Lieutenant Higley's statement that he had to draw from the entire regiment to find just 50 men and horses able to stand the picket duties at Herndon Station on March 17, confirms Benedict's assessment. In time William Wells would lead the regiment back to respectability, but he was still sitting in a Southern prison on the first of April, when the command suffered its worst defeat of the war.[18]

Following the capture of Wells on March 17, Maj. Josiah Hall took command of the regimental detachment at Dranesville. As Wells had requested weeks earlier, the picket lines were finally withdrawn at the end of March to the east side of Difficult Run, and the main camp was established at Freedom Hill, eight miles southeast of Dranesville, on March 30. This was accomplished during a driving snowstorm that dumped ten inches of snow over the area.[19]

John Mosby called for his men to rendezvous at Rector's Crossroads on the last day of March. When he arrived he found 69 men, most of whom were total strangers to each other. Among the group were several infantrymen disabled by wounds and several cripples who tied their crutches to their saddles. The size of the force arrayed before him suggested to Mosby that now might be the time to strike the "strong outposts in the vicinity of" Dranesville. He knew that this would be the most dangerous raid yet attempted, but he was confident that with his "usual good luck," and his trusted cadre of men by his side, including Dick Moran, William Hibbs, John Underwood and Big Yankee Ames, that he would succeed. Still, he thought it best to change the time of his attack to dusk. When he arrived at Herndon Station he learned that the Yankees had withdrawn their pickets behind Difficult Run. Like Wells, Mosby recognized the natural barrier that Difficult Run presented and knew that it would be "hopeless" to attempt an attack across the stream. He chose to fall back along the Leesburg Turnpike, making a brief stop at the home of Henry Green, where Dick Moran elected to remain and visit with the family. Mosby and the others continued along the pike and spent the night at a farm that has gone down in history as Miskell's Farm. The property was near the confluence of Broad Run and the Potomac River, and Mosby hoped to find plenty of forage there, along with water for his horses. Arriving about 10 P.M., the men unsaddled and fed their horses, washed down a hasty dinner with some hard cider and bedded down. Mosby posted no sentinels along the approaches to the property, although several men remained awake to guard the animals.[20]

During the evening, a citizen brought word to the officers at Freedom Hill that Mosby was at Dranesville. Capt. Henry Flint gathered all of the available men —148 troopers from six companies. His orders were "to rout or capture [Mosby] if practicable." Flint was, by all accounts, a competent officer, who had been cited for bravery on two previous occasions. His reputation as "one of the most resolute officers in the regiment" appears to have made him a good choice to lead the men on March 31, but there is no evidence that he had ever led a force of this size. Flint's reputation aside, the continuing strife among the officers of the regiment, as well as the fact that the men were drawn from six companies and several outposts, suggests that Maj. Josiah Hall, an experienced battalion officer, would have been a more sound choice. Flint's second in command was Capt. George Bean, whose character had already been questioned once and would suffer again as a result of the coming engagement.[21]

Flint departed the outpost at 2 A.M. on the first of April, and proceeded up the Leesburg Turnpike to Dranesville where he split his force, so as to take the town from both ends at the same time. Captain Bean, with 50 men, moved to the far end of the town and the charge was then coordinated by a gunshot. Learning that Mosby had long since moved on, Flint continued west along the muddy, snow-covered turnpike to the Henry Green home, where Dick Moran was spending the night. Moran was in the kitchen when the Yankees approached and he immediately ducked under the stairs until the Federals were gone. Once they were out of sight Moran mounted and set out across the fields to warn his comrades of the approaching Union column.[22]

At the farm, Mosby had his back to both Broad Run and the Potomac River, across which he was able to discern activity in the Union camps that morning. Moran found his commander in the barnyard, less than "a hundred yards from the house." Moran alerted Mosby and his comrades by yelling, "The Yankees are coming," as he galloped up to the house. Running for the cover of the barn, Moran and Mosby observed the Vermonters emerging from a belt of trees and passing through a gate into a large field, later estimated by Price at 150 acres in size. At the far side of the field was the barnyard, surrounded by "a high and strong rail fence." In his report of the affair Price claimed that Flint divided his force as he came across the field, leaving Captain Bean with 100 men as a reserve. This division, if accurate, seems unwise, as the initial information credited Mosby with having at least 60 men, and it is doubtful that Flint would have intentionally approached with a smaller force. Bean made no reference to a formal division, stating later that his company, numbering just 25 men, was in the rear of the column, and was still passing through the timber when gunfire erupted at the head of the column. Lieutenant Josiah Grout, 1st Vermont Cavalry, writing postwar, supported Price. Grout stated that Flint placed him in charge of the carbineers at the head of the column and that Bean "was to have charge of the balance of the command, acting as a support." Though most of the earliest Federal accounts of the fight appear unreliable, two points are generally consistent — that Flint designated Bean to act as a reserve, and that Flint then attacked without giving any further instructions. Flint also failed to reform his column, which had become spread out along the road from Dranesville and again as it passed through the first of two fences around the property. Sgt. Horace Ide believed that there was no reserve force, but that all the men "came into the field as possible." Josiah Grout, whose account is the most detailed, confirms that the men, cold and tired after six hours in the saddle, were strung out in a long column of twos as they approached the farm. He claimed that Flint ordered the men to attack with the saber and only directed Grout to "engage the enemy with the carbineers who were in front," at the point that Grout was "passing [through] the gate" and into the field. Grout also claimed that Capt. George Bean was left, with as many as four companies, to act as a support force. Both Grout and Ide were in the advance, but the difference in their recollections almost certainly reflects their ability to know of what they wrote. Grout, in command of the carbineers, spoke directly with Flint.[23]

Several of the Confederates recalled that the Vermonters in the front rank unleashed a volley from their carbines, "splattering bullets into the front of the barn and the boards of the fence," but Horace Ide, one of the carbineers, makes no mention of any such effort. He stated that the men were so cold and their fingers so "numb" that "we could not handle and fire our revolvers and carbines with the rapidity of men who had not been exposed to the weather."[24]

Other accounts suggest that Flint knew he had Mosby in a cul-de-sac from which he could not escape, and thus ordered his men to charge with the saber as soon they cleared the fence and entered the barnyard. George Benedict later claimed, "*If* Flint had halted and used his carbines, a number of the enemy could doubtless have been put *hors de combat* and the rest driven from their partial shelter," a statement suggesting that few men relied on the cumbersome carbines. Captain Bean said simply that "all was confusion" as the lead ranks entered the field, and rather than reforming his men, as others have described, Flint led them in a disorganized saber charge toward the point where Mosby was rallying his own men.[25]

Sergeant Ide claimed that Grout "suggested" to Flint that he reform the men before making the attack "but was overruled." Grout later explained that as they approached the farm, Flint had indeed ordered the men to use the saber, but then, as Grout passed through the gate, in his estimation about 800 feet from the barn-yard, Flint instructed him "to move quickly up toward the yard and engage the enemy with the carbineers who were in front." "In executing the movement," Grout continued, "an effort was made to create a new formation as near in line as possible, from the formation in column of twos ... without coming to a halt. In traveling over the soft field and forming anew in this way, some confusion showed itself, which when in line, had brought us too near the enemy for the best results from carbines against pistols, being within pistol range." Only the men in Companies D and I were carrying carbines, and the confusion may have resulted when Grout attempted to move these men to a position from where they could use their weapons to advantage. Samuel Chapman, who was with Mosby that day, confirms this account, stating that the

Vermonters "were not in close formation, but had spread themselves out with considerable intervals between each man, in order to catch us." Chapman's description has led to the belief that the Vermonters extended their line to the left and right in an effort to cut off any escape.[26]

"Probably forty of the detail had reached this position, and were giving the best fire possible, and taking patiently a lively return," Grout recalled. "It was a hot place. The enemy, using pistols, had more shots than we. We were in close proximity, separated not more than [100 to 130 feet] from each other." Under this galling fire several men, including Sgt. Carlostin Ferry, dismounted and attempted to tear an opening in the fence. In Grout's view two of these men were killed and the others driven back by "the storm of bullets and splinters." It was at this point that Captain Flint rode up, urging the men to "Tear down the fence, boys, and get at them with the saber." By this time the carbineers, "who [had] behaved with a coolness and deliberation born of the dress parade," had been joined by the men from Companies B and C, led by lieutenants Eli Holden and Charles Woodbury. Grout believed that only about "half of our detail came out of the woods into the field where the fighting was done." Yelling for the men in the rear to "Come on," Flint was hit by five bullets and punched out of the saddle.[27]

Just as Flint toppled from his horse, Mosby ran to the gate and threw it aside, yelling for those men who had already mounted to charge. He then accepted a horse given to him by Harry Hatcher and followed them through the gate, while the men who remained behind the fence continued to fire into the ranks of the enemy with their revolvers. According to Grout, "Mosby poured his whole force out upon our right flank and into our rear," suggesting that Grout deployed his men to attack the fence, rather than attempting to surround the house and barnyard and cut off the escape of the partisans, as Chapman claimed. Mosby's attack forced Grout to attempt to re-deploy his men to confront "this new movement of the enemy ... but the enemy were soon behind, around, and all amongst us." Routed by Mosby's attack, the Vermonters raced back across the field toward the gate at the wood line. This gate, which was designed to close on its own, and which had been secured in the open position, was closed when the frightened men reached it.[28]

In Colonel Price's official report of the affair Flint rode back to urge on Bean's reserve just after the Confederates began pouring out of the barnyard. Flint then returned and "whilst endeavoring to rally his men, who had been scattered, he was killed." Ide makes no reference to any such action by Flint, stating only that he was one of the very first men killed. These accounts also claim that both Grout and Holden were wounded in the immediate aftermath of Flint's death, leaving the men essentially leaderless. Grout, however, recalled that he conferred briefly with both Holden and Woodbury and attempted to organize a counterattack against "the enemy, who were needlessly firing into our men cornered at the gate." All three officers then attempted to rally the men at which point "a smooth faced rebel boy" confronted Grout by pointing a pistol at his head. Grout swung his saber at the boys head and sunk in his spurs, but in escaping the one enemy he now found himself in the midst "of a dozen or more" at the gate.[29]

Bunching up in front of the narrow opening the Vermonters found that the gate would only open inward, thus the mass of men and horses pressing against it prevented their escape until it simply yielded to the weight bearing against it. With the attention of the Yankees concentrated on escaping through the narrow opening, "the remorseless revolver was doing its work of death in their ranks." Though Mosby viewed the saber as an "obsolete weapon," other men, like Sam Chapman, who had emptied their revolvers, now drew their sabers and began slashing at the men milling around the opening. The bloody melee in the field and around the gate lasted only minutes. Grout swung his saber at one man's head just as another partisan shot him in the right side. In the confusion the rebels didn't realize that Grout had been gravely wounded. Unable to dismount, he was seen as failing to comply with their demands and one man attempted to push him off his horse. It was only with the aid of his comrades that Grout was helped from his horse and carried to a point of relative safety. During this melee Lieutenant Holden "had a piece of his scalp taken off with a Sabre."[30]

Once the Yankees finally cleared the exterior gate they fled toward Dranesville. A resident of the town, who had noted the arrival of Mosby the previous evening, observed the panicked flight and remarked in her journal, "We have the pleasure of seeing the Yankees flying down the road with Moseby's men at their heels." The only officer credited with attempting to rally them was Lt. Charles Woodbury, who was shot in the head and killed before he had any chance of succeeding. In the end at least 77 men were captured. Three men were killed outright and three others died of their wounds over the next two days. The majority of the dead and wounded, including Captain Flint, and lieutenants Grout and Holden, came from just three companies, C, G and I. The manner in which the casualties were dispersed throughout the six companies as well as the nature of the casualties suggests that Captain Bean may have held two companies, A and G, in reserve, while the men of I and D made the initial attack, supported by Woodbury and Holden with Companies B and C. The heaviest loss was in Company I, indicating that they attacked the interior fence line closest to the barnyard gate and took the brunt of Mosby's counterattack in their right flank. Mosby lost four men wounded, one of whom later died.[31]

Once the survivors from Flint's command reached the outpost at Freedom Hill, Major Hall started with a relief party that brought in the bodies of the dead as well as the less seriously injured. Several men, including Lieutenant Grout, were temporarily left on the field due to the severity of their wounds. Three of the men died over the next two days. Lieutenant Grout would recover from his injuries but he never returned to the regiment.[32]

In his account of the fight Grout spoke highly of his fallen captain, declaring that Flint "patriotically, conscientiously and fearlessly gave a generous, noble life to the cause. He died in the noisy rattle of a sharp little battle, foremost in the desperate charge." Grout placed the blame for the disaster squarely on the shoulders of Captain Bean, repeating several damning comments from Colonel Price's report. But much still remains unknown. Any plan that Flint had in mind as he approached the farm died with him in the opening moments of the fight. Clearly, however, he made no reconnaissance to determine the nature of the position he was attacking or to verify any of the information that he had been given or gathered along the route. A question that will linger, unanswered, was what effect, if any, the recent punitive actions taken against both Captain Huntoon and Lieutenant Higley, both of whom had failed in their recent encounters with Mosby, may have played in Flint's decision. Did he rush into a hasty, ill-conceived attack in order to avoid the accusations that damaged the careers of those men?[33]

At some point that day, and almost certainly unaware of the events that had transpired many miles to the east, twenty-year-old Lucy Buck, of Front Royal, made the following notation in her diary: "Truly Captain Mosby is making to himself a name and bids fair to rival Ashby." Indeed John Mosby had climbed another rung on the ladder of Southern heroes with his victory at Miskell's farm, and some may have taken hope that a legitimate successor to Turner Ashby had arrived. If there had been any lingering doubts about John

Mosby's leadership this victory banished them. His growing reputation had encouraged almost 70 men to respond to his call, and enough horses and weapons were captured to arm and equip each of them. He had turned imminent defeat into a stunning victory over a force twice his size, and inflicted more casualties than he had men in his command. He had also received a valuable lesson: his failure to post sufficient pickets had nearly spelled disaster, but as he later pointed out his "authority over the men was of such a transitory nature that I disliked to order them to do anything but fight." On April 2, the Confederate Congress confirmed his promotion to "major of Partisan Rangers," which General Lee forwarded by courier on the fourth with "pleasure."[34]

The defeat at Mosby's hand was not the new beginning that either Heintzelman or Stahel had hoped for, and Stahel was unrelenting in expressing his displeasure, citing "bad management on the part of the officers and the cowardice of the men" for the debacle. The heavy loss of officers further stunned the command still reeling from the divisions within their ranks, and only added to the "mortification and exasperation" felt throughout the regiment. The widely erroneous initial accounts of the fight that appeared in several Vermont papers prolonged the pain. "I cannot conceive any possible defense for Captain Bean, though I would gladly do so, as every loyal Vermonter would," wrote one editor in Rutland, who concluded, "Military men here condemn him." Caught, as he was, at the very back of the Union column as the lead elements turned and fled from the Southern charge, a truly objective observer would have to wonder just what Bean could have accomplished to save the command that was already routed, but there were no objective observers. Bean's letter of rebuttal to Price's allegations contains so few specifics as to his own actions that it suggests either a complete lack of knowledge as to what took place at the head of the column or a degree of culpability that he knew he could not overcome. His claims that he made several attempts to rally the men were ignored, while Price's allegation that Bean "made no effort to check the enemy, or rally the retreating men," as well as the equally damning assertion that he "was the first man in camp," stuck, and Bean was dismissed on April 28, 1863. That Sergeant Ide, who was taken prisoner in the fight, saw Bean's dismissal as a result of the "government need[ing] a 'scapegoat,'" suggests that he disagreed with Price's judgment. The absence of a hearing, regardless of the verdict, left many unanswered questions. Price's report, which almost certainly reflects his bias as well as that of Major Taggart against the regiment, has to be read carefully. Price concluded with the accusation that Cpl. James Kelley, Company A, though "well mounted and far out of reach of the enemy ... stopped and gave himself up. This confirms a rumor which I had before heard (of which I have no proof) that some of the men of this regiment had declared they would give themselves up, for the advantage of the parole." With this accusation Price was impugning more than the reputation of just one man.[35]

On the evening of April 1, Lt. Col. Gould, 5th Michigan Cavalry, explained to his brother "there is constant excitement and turmoil" in the camp, that forced him to awaken the men several times over the previous nights. "We are taking Secesh sympathizers and laying them away in the Old Capitol prison so rapidly that we shall depopulate the country pretty soon yet the man Moseby is playing his pranks with the Pa., Va., & Vermont cavalry almost every day, but keeps away from my men." Gould saw two reasons for this, "our destructive" seven shot Spencers and "our alertness on duty." Referring to Mosby's success at Miskell's farm, Gould declared, "Our boys are very anxious to have a brush with him."[36]

At half past noon on the first, Maj. George Newcombe and three companies of the 7th Michigan left Fairfax Court House in a routine attempt to "intercept" Mosby. They made a circuit to the west as far as Bull Run Mountain, returning twelve hours later with but one prisoner. The men saw several "flocks of nice fat 'mutton,'" but as Edwin Havens observed, "our object was to take either White, Stuart or Moseby and not inoffensive cattle and sheep." It was not until the men returned to camp that they learned of the fight at Miskell's farm and heard the rumor that Mosby had been "killed in a hand to hand combat" with Captain Flint. Thus, in his next letter home, Havens dropped Mosby's name, telling his father "we have to be on the alert at all times as Stuart and White are like the Dutchman's flea, [and] turn up where we least expect them."[37]

14

April 2–April 23, 1863

"Citizens except ... when they are the terror-inspiring band of Capt. Mosby"

The rumor that Mosby had been wounded or killed quickly took hold throughout the Union camps around Washington. William Martin, 18th Pennsylvania, observed "a good deal of rejoicing at the news of Mosbey's death as he and his party have kept three regts of cavalry uneasy all winter." With Mosby gone, Heintzelman determined to "break up his band of Marauders." A soldier in the 6th Michigan, writing for his hometown newspaper told his readers "a band of rebels under one Capt. Mosby," has been committing depredations, "and it seems to be the intention of our officers to put a stop to his proceedings."[1]

By the morning of April 3, the 5th and 6th Michigan were under orders to take the field with three days cooked rations. Captain Andrew Duggan was directed to respond with Company B, 1st Michigan, from their camps along the Occoquan River, to further bolster the force that also included elements from the 1st West Virginia, 5th New York and the 18th Pennsylvania. General Joseph Copeland led the expedition out at three o'clock that afternoon, marching as far as Aldie, where the men spent the night; but they got little rest, as they were ordered to stand to horse "nearly all of the time."[2]

Leaving Companies A and E, 5th Michigan, to scour the countryside around Aldie, Copeland headed west, "in a pelting snowstorm," reaching Middleburg by sunrise where the men "had a chance to see the workings of secesh sentiments on the softer sex," as nearly all of the men of the town "had skeddadled." Ordered to search for "horses and contraband goods," as well as any of Mosby's men, they were denounced as "Michigan guerrillas." As several men led a horse out of one house, where an attempt had been made to conceal it "in an inner apartment," the woman of the house taunted them as cowards, declaring, "Our men capture their horses; they don't steal them." The Wolverines thought this "a rather thoughtless boast in behalf of Southern chivalry, inasmuch as Moseby is famed for such gallant acts as shooting pickets and despoiling Union citizens." The search of the town produced only a few horses, and while the farms held "immense quantities" of hay and grain, the men took only what their horses could eat, as they had no means of transporting the feed, but chickens and sheep were another matter.[3]

While in Middleburg information was received that there was a rebel camp several miles south of town, and Col. George Gray and his 6th Michigan were sent to investigate. One of his scouting patrols, consisting of four troopers, including Cpl. Albert Dimond and Pvt. James Foe encountered three men about a mile west of Middleburg. Two of the men were reported to be in civilian attire while the third wore a Union military hat. The men were Capt. Daniel Hatcher, and his brother Sgt. Maj. Harry Hatcher, of the 7th Virginia Cavalry. The third man was "Big Yankee" Ames. When challenged by Dimond the three men fled west to near the Hatcher home at Hatcher's Mill, in an apparent attempt to draw the Yankees farther away from their supports. When the Federals reached the mill a second group of four men rode into view, and all seven men participated in the fight that followed.[4]

In John Scott's account the Hatcher brothers and Ames turned and galloped toward the oncoming Yankees, with both sides firing their revolvers when "within a few paces of the point of collision." Ames was immediately hit in the right shoulder and Harry Hatcher's horse was killed as he crossed the bridge over Cromwell's Run. Private Foe was killed instantly by a shot to the chest, and Dimond was shot three times, in the right wrist, the left arm and left leg, but escaped. Scott recounts that the other Yankees were wounded and two horses captured, but neither point can be verified, and it is doubtful that any of them, especially Corporal Dimond, would have escaped if he had been unhorsed. Both of the Hatcher brothers were also wounded in the affair, according to Scott. Lt. Colonel Gould, still anxious to test the Spencer rifles suggested, "If our boys had used their seven shooting rifles they would have done better," though, in truth, the rifle was not the answer in the kind of fight that his men found themselves.[5]

The Wolverines were furious when Private Foe's body was found completely stripped near the road, "having been killed by some lurking fiends in human shape." "These are the kind of men that Mosby commands," Capt. James Kidd explained to his father. "Citizens except ... when they are the terror-inspiring band of Capt. Mosby. Our boys killed one rebel and wounded another so that we would be even if one of our men were not worth a dozen of these miserable 'Bushwhackers.'"[6]

The men of the 5th Michigan left to hold Aldie had better luck, rounding up about 40 prisoners, several in Confederate uniforms while others were taken wearing Union overcoats. A couple of men on crutches were seized, as Mosby's practice of accepting injured or disabled men, who brazenly strapped crutches to their horses, as several had done on April 1, continued to put local citizens at risk of arrest. One of the Michiganders recalled a conversation with a citizen who stated that so many of Mosby's men wore Union blue that when a column of mounted men approached it was impossible to discern who they were until they were close enough to "recognize features." The soldier concluded, "One thing is certain, the citizens must compel [Mosby] to leave the country, or we will bring them in and hold them accountable."[7]

The anger and fury of the Northern scribes was matched word for word by the Southern press. In a letter to the Richmond *Sentinel*, a resident of Middleburg cried, "Since [General John] Geary's occupation of this country, no such brutal ruffians have appeared among us, and we were not surprised to recognize among them some of the 1st Michigan Cavalry, who, a year ago, gave us our first experience of Yankee rules.... Their course up the turnpike was marked by scenes of violence and outrage: every horse taken ... every citizen seen arrested ... all quiet citizens ... *but not one soldier*!" As the column of horsemen withdrew back toward Aldie "some fiends" started a fire in a store in the center of Middleburg. General Copeland was said to have watched the fire before he rode off without objection. Only when a later group of officers arrived including a "Col. Johnson" were men "compelled to extinguish the fire." For his actions the colonel earned the gratitude of the correspondent who asked, "So, if Mosby ever catches Col. Johnson, give him the softest place in Libby prison."[8]

On Sunday, the fifth, Copeland returned to Fairfax Court House, herding 61 prisoners and more than 50 horses and mules through "a violent storm," described by one local as "the worst storm of the winter." Copeland believed that his men had seized five of Mosby's personal horses and captured Dick Moran, the man who had brought the warning to Mosby at Miskell's farm, but both claims were untrue. Seven of the prisoners were later said to have admitted a "connection with Mosby's gang," and several of the horses were believed to have been taken during the Stoughton raid. As the Federals vacated the Loudoun Valley, one resident concluded, "Things are looking darker and darker for our unhappy and unpro tected people." Gould was frustrated that the guerrillas would only shake their fists at his men, while remaining beyond range of his rifles, but he voiced a bit of grudging admiration when he observed that Mosby "is ubiquitous." Major Noah Ferry, 5th Michigan, was as frustrated as Gould, but with the lack of effort exhibited by his own commanders rather than Mosby. "Had I been on trial in Michigan for whipping a lame idiot and stealing his dinner, I should not have been more mortified and ashamed." In lieu of a large expedition thrashing through the countryside in search of the guerrillas, Ferry offered to take 100 of own his men "and not return until I had captured or killed Moseby and his whole gang. But that wouldn't be military and could not be allowed"[9]

Several smaller columns supported Copeland's expedition by scouring the area along his flanks. Maj. Melvin Brewer, 1st Michigan, led a patrol through Hay Market, New Baltimore and Warrenton. The men found no evidence of an enemy presence until they reached New Baltimore where they encountered Lt. William Smith and his party of the 4th Virginia Cavalry, but Smith elected to retire without challenging the Wolverines. Capt. Josiah Steele, 1st West Virginia, probed the country north of the main column. Early on the fourth he passed through Dranesville and reported that he drove Mosby out of the hamlet. Attempts at pursuit were hampered by, what one soldier termed the "damndest" storm of the season, that dumped ten inches of snow throughout the region.[10]

In the first week of April General Heintzelman ordered an inspection of the entire picket line from the Occoquan to the Potomac River. For the most part the men were found to be fully alert and with a thorough understanding of their orders, though the men of the Vermont Brigade were reported as "not very attentive and poorly instructed in outpost duty," and with a "great chance [for] improvement." Nor was the inspector impressed with the layout of the line held by the 5th Michigan, which he described as running "through a thick growth of pine wood, making it a dangerous line." For the most part, however, the cavalry along Difficult Run earned high marks, a point confirmed by John Mosby who set out on the sixth, the same morning that the inspecting officer filed his report, to scout the Union lines for "an assailable point," but found them "guarded by large and vigilant bodies of cavalry," forcing him to "to explore new fields of enterprise."[11]

By the second week of April the snow was gone, the sun was drying the roads and General Hooker was preparing the opening moves of his spring campaign. His plans required that the Orange and Alexandria Railroad be reopened through Prince William and Fauquier counties, and necessitated several changes within the Department of Washington. On April 10, Colonel Price's brigade was rotated off the front lines and moved back toward Fairfax Court House for thirty days, relieved by Copeland's Michigan Brigade. The 5th and 6th Michigan were posted between Centreville and Vienna, while 200 men from the 7th Michigan, under the command of Lt. Col. Allyne Litchfield, took over the line vacated by the 1st Michigan along the Occoquan, the remainder of the latter regiment being held in reserve.[12]

The initial task of providing security for the work details along the Orange and Alexandria Railroad was given to the 1st Michigan Cavalry. At the same time Col. Asa Blunt and Gen. Alexander Hays were instructed to prepare their brigades to take the field, and rumors soon raced through their camps that they were heading south to join the Army of the Potomac. Hooker then notified General Halleck that he could no longer be responsible for the security of the telegraph line between Occoquan and Dumfries and Stahel tasked Litchfield and his detachment of the 7th Michigan with protecting the wire. Heintzelman's instruction to Stahel included a stipulation that he was "to remove all disloyal persons from the vicinity of the line." Stahel was also informed that Gen. John Abercrombie's infantry had been withdrawn from Vienna. Those troops immediately returned to Alexandria, where they boarded transports for Fort Monroe on the fifteenth. Abercrombie remained with the Department of Washington, and took command of the division formerly led by Silas Casey two days later. Other minor changes included the transfer, at Col. Timothy Bryan's request, of the 18th Pennsylvania Cavalry, from Johnstone's Brigade to Price's Brigade, replaced by the 1st Vermont.[13]

The heavy spring rains caused havoc with Hooker's plans to send his cavalry, led by Maj. Gen. George Stoneman, on a raid deep into Southern territory to cut Lee's lines of supply and communication, and the dispirited troopers found themselves penned along the north bank of the Rappahannock River for two weeks. In an attempt to keep the men active, Stoneman sent scouting parties toward Warrenton to "obviate [the] difficulties" caused by bushwhackers operating in that vicinity. In several encounters over four days, at least 13 men from the 4th Virginia were captured. On the eighteenth, troopers from the 8th Illinois and the 3rd Indiana ran into a squad from the Black Horse near Orleans and captured, among others, Lt. Alexander Dixon Payne, who was credited with putting up a desperate fight before he was "obliged to yield." Though he had almost killed Capt. John Southworth, 8th Illinois, in single combat and succeeded in crippling the Union officer's horse, Payne noted that he was "treated with much courtesy & kindness," by his captors. That evening Payne met with Col. Benjamin "Grimes" Davis, who accused the Virginian of commanding bushwhackers. "I understood to enlighten him," Payne explained, "and denied for myself and company the commission of any act by which we could be classed as bushwackers."[14]

The storms also prevented Stahel from surveying the Orange and Alexandria track to the Rappahannock. He was directed on the seventeenth to escort engineers from the railroad to a point from where they could observe the railroad bridge across the Rappahannock but high water had washed out several other bridges, including the bridge across Bull Run.[15]

The Federals were not the only troops frustrated by high water on the seventeenth. John Mosby assembled 100 men at Upperville that morning with the intention of interdicting Gen. Robert Milroy's lines of communication and supply between Winchester and Harpers Ferry, but he got no farther than the Shenandoah River before he was forced to turn back by rising water. He returned through upper — Loudoun County, passing through Waterford and Bloomfield just ahead of a Union patrol led by Maj. Thomas Gibson, 14th Pennsylvania Cavalry. Gibson, who also reported the creeks as "unfordable," had no luck cornering Mosby but he did capture several of White's men, including Charles Cooper, a man who "admits having shot pickets," and who Gibson recommended be tried for "for bushwhacking and horse stealing." Prevented first from penetrating the Union lines along Difficult Run and now by the rising Shenandoah River, Mosby still made headlines.[16]

In the third week of April several Northern newspapers carried a story reporting that "a squad of Mosby's Rebel guerrillas" had seized a man by the name of James Harvey Sherman from his home near Dranesville in the early morning hours of April 17, and hanged him. Under the headline "A Murder by Guerrillas," readers were informed that Sherman was a detective in the employ of Col. Lafayette Baker, the head of the Federal Secret Service, and they were treated to a letter from Sherman's wife, beseeching Baker, "in the name of eight small children," to do what he could for her husband as well as her family "left destitute" by his capture. The letter was dated on the day of his capture, and the accounts reported that Sherman was "summarily" hanged the following morning. Editors called for two accused Southern spies, currently held in Old Capitol Prison, to be hanged in retaliation.

James Sherman, formerly of New York, had served as a guide for Gen. John Geary during his march through the region in the spring of 1862, and later investigated reports of smuggling and fraud for Colonel Baker, who relied upon Sherman for both his abilities as a detective as well as his knowledge of the citizens in Loudoun and Fairfax counties. In February Sherman and a second detective were involved in a shoot-out between Leesburg and Berlin in which a Southern officer was reportedly killed and Sherman was wounded. Both detectives were captured and immediately paroled. On April nineteenth, Charles Chapin, 1st Vermont, reported this latest incident to his brother, referring to Sherman as "One of our Union Scouts," and concluding, "there has been a reward of $5,000 offered for" for his capture, "so he will be hung I am afraid." Thomas Smith, historian of the 11th New York Cavalry, referred to Sherman as one of "the guides and spies" who had assisted the regiment on several occasions. Smith recounted an earlier attempt to capture Sherman, in which Sherman's seven-year-old son "walked four miles through the forest" to warn him that their house was surrounded. His capture on the seventeenth appears to have been precipitated by the Union withdrawal to the Difficult Run line, which put his home outside the lines. On April 21, Colonel Gray was instructed to determine "the name of the officer who allowed Sherman to pass outside our lines," suggesting that some effort was made to investigate the circumstances of his capture. Gray later reported that Sherman had crossed Difficult Run by the turnpike bridge on the evening of the sixteenth, with the permission of Lt. John Newton, 1st Vermont Cavalry. Though even Gen. Heintzelman believed that he had been hanged "without judge or jury," it was eventually learned that Sherman had not been executed but that he was incarcerated, eventually escaping from prison in Salisbury, North Carolina, in 1865. What remains unknown is exactly what role, if any, John Mosby or any of his men played in his capture, but Mosby had been in and around Dranesville on several occasions since the first of April, and several of his men continued to operate in the vicinity.[17]

On the eighteenth, Albert Greene, 1st Vermont Cavalry, penned a letter to his brother suggesting that he and others in the troubled regiment were still not adhering to the strict discipline required of the men while on picket. Forced to stand watch through a night of unrelenting rain, Greene confessed, "we had orders not to have any fire," but "we made up our minds that we would have a fire any way rebs or not we did not care if old Mosby did come." The men of the post simply felled some trees in order to blockade the ford they were guarding and then built a warming fire. Greene then went on to ridicule the men from Michigan. "Theas darn michigans we call them Michiganders are so fraid that they don't know what to do they are new comers they have not been out only three or 4 months."[18]

Friction between the regiments developed shortly after Copeland's men arrived. The Vermonters found themselves having to seek permission to pass through the lines manned by the Wolverines, even if they wanted to draw water from the nearby stream. Horace Ide, 1st Vermont, believed that it was an attempt to force the veterans to make their purchases from the Michigan sutlers, which Ide viewed as "invading our rights in a way that we did not like and great indignation was expressed there at." The result was a late night raid on the sutler's tent in which most of his goods disappeared. This combined with an incident in which one of the Michigan pickets shot at a soldier from the 1st Vermont soon had the entire camp on edge and the officers fearing a mutiny, but according to Ide, once the "obnoxious sutler left, the guards were more lax in enforcing the orders, and peace was established."[19]

While some of the Wolverines may have been uneasy standing watch in the thick timber, others, like Capt. James Kidd, pushed the limits of the freedom enjoyed by officers. On the seventeenth, Kidd and two lieutenants were out checking their lines when they elected to cross Difficult Run and "came near riding into a 'Hornets nest' of rebels." Kidd decided that the three men would explore the road they were on, when, after several miles, they "concluded to enquire where the road led & were informed by a woman that we were going to Drainesville where Mosby's whole force is said to be." Having "no desire to meet any great number of Mosby's men single-handed," and having "no business outside the Pickets," the three men headed back to Difficult Run. They had found tracks, however, suggesting that three "rebel patrols" had scouted their lines the night before, and as Kidd explained to his father, "The difficulty is they always know where we are what we are doing, and how many there are of us. We know comparatively nothing of them and have to find them in their own haunts."[20]

Orders or not it was less than militarily prudent for an officer in charge of a picket line to not have a thorough knowledge of the country and the road network that he and his men were charged with securing. Less than one month later Capt. Charles Adams, 1st Massachusetts Cavalry, described the tour of the lines that he was given near Hartwood Church by the officer that he was relieving. Adams explained that the officer led him through fields rather than roads with the result that when the quick tour was over, "I no longer knew where the river ran, which was north or south, or indeed where I was. My mind was a jumble of fords, hills and roads." Attempting to reorient himself that evening Adams discovered that he was "in an awful maze." Adams also echoed, almost word for word, Kidd's comments about the citizenry "who know the country and we don't, and every man is a citizen or soldier, as the occasion offers." One of Kidd's fellow Wolverines would not be as lucky as Kidd and Adams while making a similar ride.[21]

Lt. Robert Wallace, 5th Michigan, elected to ride outside the lines on Sunday morning, April 19, accompanied by Pvt. Samuel Earle, to gain some familiarity with the local roads. In the vicinity of Hawkhurst's Mill, along Difficult Run, the men were surprised, and quickly surrounded by a party of Confederates who stepped out of the woods. With every avenue of escape blocked the two men surrendered. Their captors were a squad of men, including John Underwood and Walter Frankland, detailed by John Mosby to scout the Union lines in that vicinity. Several stories quickly circulated through the Northern papers claiming that Wallace and Earle had disobeyed orders, going outside the lines for "a better dinner than camp rations afforded," and erroneously placed the capture near Centreville. That account was retracted and an apology of sorts offered when a member of the regiment offered another version of the capture, though according to Wallace's own postwar account it was equally incorrect. Wallace and Earle, along with several other prisoners, were escorted to Upperville where Wallace reported that he was treated very kindly, especially after a local resident remembered him as the officer who had previously prevented his home from being looted. Wallace remembered Mosby as "a clean cut little man, with a clear, bright eye and looked the man he was." The lieutenant was also surprised to find his captors represented "a better class than is usually found in the ranks of either army." Samuel Dushane, formerly an officer in the Louisiana Tigers and now riding with Mosby acquired Wallace's saber, presented to him when he left Michigan. When Wallace explained how much the presentation saber meant to him Dushane replied, "I may get it back to you some time." Dushane was wounded and captured less than one month later and requested that his captors return the weapon, which reached Wallace the following winter.[22]

Wallace recalled in his memoirs that he and Earle joined several other soldiers recently captured by the same squad, and other Union accounts confirm that Underwood and the others had enjoyed additional success. John Farnill and Charles Emmons, 6th Michigan, and Charles Chapin, 1st Vermont, all mentioned losing men from their regiments during this time span, though none can be identified with certainty. John Scott also recounts that a Yankee surgeon was captured at the home of a young woman that he was courting. Still, at least one man in the 1st Michigan, now posted at Fairfax Court House, was feeling rather secure, claiming, "We are just vain enough to indulge in the notion, that *Mr.* Capt. Mosby would find it somewhat embarrassing if he tried to come in here just now, with the hospitable intention of escorting one of our Michigan commanders to Southern parts, a hospitality he bestowed upon a former commander of this post."[23]

On April 20, the movement of troops continued as Hooker resumed preparations for his spring campaign. On the sixteenth, the Ohio Brigade, that had garrisoned Dumfries throughout the winter, received orders to rejoin the Army of the Potomac, and it departed four days later. It was supplanted, in the short term, by a detachment of cavalry under the command of Col. Alfred Duffie. Most of the troopers were dismounted, and those who arrived with horses were under orders not to use them, as they were worn down and "must be recruited." In addition, only 95 of the 1,000 men were equipped with carbines and attempts to rearm the men were hampered by the miserable condition of the roads. To avoid further delays the weapons and other provisions were shipped by water. During the transition, however, Duffie ran afoul of his superiors, possibly due to the condition of his command and the resultant delay in relieving Slocum's men, and Col. John Irvin Gregg replaced him.[24]

On the eleventh, Brig. Gen. George Stannard was ordered to the Department of Washington, and he assumed his new position as commander of the Vermont Brigade on the twentieth. Forty-two years of age, Stannard had served as lieutenant colonel of the 2nd Vermont Infantry, and later as colonel of the 9th Vermont. Two days after the infamous Fairfax Raid and the capture of Stoughton, George Stannard was promoted to brigadier general. In an early assessment of the new brigade commander several soldiers noted the obvious contrast with the ostentatious Stoughton. "He is received rather differently from Stoughton.

Every one seems glad that we have him, and are prepared to like him. He is plainly dressed, wearing his old uniform with new shoulder straps," and the soldier concluded, "Drunkard officers will have little mercy at his hands." In one soldiers view Stannard "don't look so 'gay and festive' as Stought used to with a plume in his cap and a shawl crossed over his shoulder parading the streets of Fairfax with a — Well I wont say what — But she proved a foe instead of a friend." Soldiers who saw Stoughton as a "quick tempered & fractious dog," were relieved to hear that their new commander was "not much like Stoughton." Noting Stannard's utter lack of flamboyance one soldier observed, that "like the rest of us [he] lives in a 'cotton house' and eats off of a *tin plate*," and is thus "very much more *popular* in the brigade." Yet the urgent need to protect the Orange and Alexandria Railroad left Stannard with little time with which to become familiar with his new command before it was on the move.[25]

On the twentieth, General Abercrombie was reminded that work crews would begin repairing the railroad the following day, and his infantry was given the task of guarding the workers, as far as Manassas. Heintzelman notified Brig. Gen. Herman Haupt, superintendent of the railroads, that it would "be impossible" for men from his department to secure the track all the way to Rappahannock Station, and he urged Haupt to seek additional help from the Army of the Potomac. Still, Heintzelman informed Stahel that he would assume responsibility for the safety of the trains that would soon be Hooker's lifeline. A detachment from the 1st Michigan, commanded by Lt. Col. Peter Stagg, accompanied the workers as far as Bristoe Station, and a warning was sent to Stoneman's cavalry at Warrenton Junction to "prevent a collision" between the two commands. Though one arriving soldier was amazed at the extent of the damage "a long that Railroad," Heintzelman's claim on the twenty-second that the track was repaired as far as the Rappahannock, and that trains were already en route to supply Stoneman's cavalry at Warrenton Junction, suggests that the track itself may have been relatively undamaged. This immediately prompted Stahel, who appears to have been unaware that Stoneman's presence at Warrenton Junction was forced by continuing weather delays and never meant to be long term, to request that Stagg be allowed to withdraw, and that Stoneman assume full responsibility for the safety of the line. Heintzelman instead directed Abercrombie to send infantry to Bristoe Station, with orders to construct several blockhouses at that point, "as it is desirable that you get along with as small a guard as possible." The first infantry to be dispatched was Col. Wheelock Veazey's 16th Vermont. In the end both the cavalry and the infantry remained.[26]

15

April 24–April 30, 1863

"General Stahl and his miscreants"

On April 24, Ernest Yager, Heintzelman's chief guide and scout, reported that Southern authorities were under the impression that Stoneman's move to the river was designed to draw Lee to Warrenton allowing Hooker to cross the Rappahannock unopposed at Falmouth. Indeed, as early as April 2, Lee had advised President Davis that he expected Hooker to use deception to aid a crossing of the river near Falmouth, and Lee intended to counter the move by making a thrust against the Union forces at Winchester. As a first step Lee sent Rooney Lee's cavalry brigade to the upper Rappahannock on the fourth to reinforce the cavalry already guarding that section of the river and to allow Fitz Lee's brigade to move into Loudoun County to quickly gather all the supplies and forage possible. Once Stoneman moved his cavalry to the river the Southern army commander assumed that his intentions were to strike for the Shenandoah Valley. Lee then alerted Grumble Jones to the possible threat and advised that Stuart would move with two brigades to assist him. The need to shift Stuart, however, was negated once the heavy rain prevented Stoneman from affecting a crossing. Still, the idea prevailed at Confederate headquarters that Stoneman intended to cross the Blue Ridge while Hooker moved his army to the Peninsula. Lee, who doubted that Hooker would uncover Washington, prepared to make an aggressive move of its own by May 1, preferably against General Milroy at Winchester.[1]

The threat presented by Stoneman's presence along the Rappahannock gave Stuart an opening to urge that his division be reinforced. On the twentieth Lee promised to do all that he could, asking Davis to release Beverly Robertson's brigade from duty in North Carolina. Lee also advised Stuart that Capt. William Brawner's company had been authorized, as Stuart had requested, to join Mosby. Lee suggested that Stuart might retain Brawner, at least in the short term, or order Mosby and Brawner to stay close, protecting Stuart's left flank.[2]

By the twenty-third, Lee had been made aware of the Union troop movements between Centreville and Union Mills. Lee was also aware that the Orange and Alexandria Railroad was back in operation, possibly as far south as Bealeton and that Union troops were now posted along the line to defend it. But Lee remained perplexed about Hooker's intentions. His confusion was caused in part by reports that Union troops were moving west toward Centreville and south toward Dumfries, while other reports advised that transports were carrying Union troops south down the Potomac River. Lee suggested to Stuart that John Mosby was in the best position to sort out the conflicting reports. On the twenty-fifth, Lee was still pondering Stoneman's intentions, and he believed that it was only a fear of Southern cavalry plunging "into the rear of their army" and cutting their lines of communication that prevented Stoneman from advancing. "Should he cross into the [Shenandoah] Valley nothing would call him back sooner than such a move on your part," Lee told Stuart. Lee suggested as an alternative that should Stuart opt to pursue Stoneman then "Mosby & the Black Horse might be let loose in their rear." Mosby had already suggested an operation into Fairfax County in order to determine what troop movements were taking place behind the fortifications at Centreville. Stuart initially endorsed the proposal, but the following day, April 26, Stuart pointed Mosby toward the railroad.[3]

In the last several months John Mosby had earned the full faith and confidence of both Lee and Stuart. He was now a man that both officers relied upon as a scout. On April 26 Stuart instructed Mosby, "Information of the movements of large bodies of troops is of the greatest importance to us just now. The marching or transportation of divisions will often indicate the plan of a campaign."[4]

Stuart was especially interested in a strike at Warrenton Junction, which was seeing regular rail traffic by that time. The cavalry chief suggested that Mosby attempt to capture a train at a point far enough away from the large Union camps to allow him to escape with his "plunder and prisoners." The Orange and Alexandria Railroad was now averaging 104 cars a day through this area with as many as 175 on the busiest days. To insure the safety of these trains Stoneman posted Brig. Gen. William Averell's cavalry division along with

The Orange & Alexandria Railroad near Union Mills, Virginia (Library of Congress).

Grimes Davis's brigade between Warrenton and Warrenton Junction. Brig. Gen. David Gregg's division along with John Buford's brigade held the line at Warrenton Junction.[5]

If Julius Stahel had thought that his new position with the Department of Washington was going to be the easy, relaxed posting that it had proved for others he was quickly learning otherwise. As he responded to orders shifting his cavalry along the length of his line from Dumfries to the Potomac River as well as westward along the Orange and Alexandria Railroad, he was now asked to send patrols toward the Blue Ridge. This was in response to a Southern raid against the Baltimore and Ohio Railroad in West Virginia launched on April 21, by the combined forces of Grumble Jones and Brig. Gen. John Imboden. By the twenty-fifth, the intentions of the raiders to strike the railroad were apparent to the Union high command. Local garrison troops were directed to meet the threat presented by Jones and Imboden, while Stahel was asked to "look out toward the Blue Ridge and the Valley." Additionally, specific information had been obtained from a prisoner, who had reportedly been close to Stuart, detailing the location of Fitz Lee's brigade in western Fauquier County. It was also believed that several brigades of Southern infantry were moving through Fauquier Country as well. Stahel was tasked with verifying these reports.[6]

The Federal high command discounted the notion that Lee might try to strike the rear of the Union army once Hooker crossed the Rappahannock, and Stahel was allowed to relieve the majority of the 7th Michigan from their task securing the telegraph line between Occoquan and Dumfries. Leaving behind only a small patrolling force the Wolverines proceeded to Bristoe Station for railroad security and scouting duty, relieving most of Lt. Col. Peter Stagg's 1st Michigan. As they departed the Wolverines warned the residents "that if any injury is done the line the nearest neighbor will be punished." Upon his arrival at Bristoe Station Col. William Mann, commanding the 7th Michigan, was instructed to "clear out the small parties of Rebels," and establish his cavalry in a position from which they could protect the railroad, preferably from a point south and west of the line. Before heading west Lt. Col. Allyne Litchfield got off a quick letter to his wife explaining that he expected to "guard the RR and pick up Guerrillas."[7]

The larger part of Stagg's detachment returned to Fairfax late on the twenty-fifth, after a dangerous crossing of Bull Run, which was still out of its banks. Once in camp they learned that their comrades had been on the alert all night as they "expected Old Mosby might call on us ... he being inside our lines somewhere with his command." In fact the partisan had been tirelessly seeking an avenue by which to get at the Yankees for several days. On the twenty-second his men had laid in ambush near Harpers Ferry hoping to strike a patrol from the 14th Pennsylvania Cavalry, but after waiting all day they departed for home that evening, having made an 80 mile round trip for naught. On the twenty-fifth Mosby and 18 men attempted to cross Difficult Run, but were turned back by high water. It was not for want of effort that Mosby's efforts had come to nothing, but the spring rains did not distinguish between combatants.[8]

Late on the twenty-fifth, five of Mosby's men stopped for the night at the home of Charles Utterback near Warrenton. Shortly thereafter a patrol from the 8th Illinois Cavalry, under the command of Capt. Elon Farnsworth surprised the men. In the ensuing exchange of gunfire two of the men escaped, two were captured and one man, Tom Turner, was mortally wounded. Known as "Kinloch Tom" to distinguish him from William "Maryland Tom" Turner, he had joined Mosby less than a month earlier with a recommendation from Stuart. Following his son's death, his father, Edward Turner, expressed his concern over his son's choice. "This announcement was anything but agreeable to me. In the first place I did not respect the service in which Mosby was engaged. Its object was mercenary rather than patriotic." Written after his son's death these comments may or may not truly reflect the concern his father felt in late March, but the elder Turner knew first hand the price that his neighbors paid for the actions of Mosby and the other groups operating in the area. On April 5, he had remarked on the success that the guerrillas were enjoying but he also knew that the Federals would keep large details in the area to counter the problem. "This being the case," he noted sadly, "the people of this country will doubtless suffer much." A week later Mrs. Ida Dulany echoed these comments in her diary as she explained how Mosby's men quartered at her home near Upperville. "The impression seems to be that we are protected by them from the Yankees, but I fear it is just the reverse for after every raid by Mosby's men there is retaliation by the enemy, in which the citizens suffer severely, as Mosby and his men must always get out of the way, seeing he is always out-numbered."[9]

Upon his receiving the intelligence that Southern cavalry and infantry had moved into Fauquier County, as well as a request to make a demonstration toward the Blue Ridge, Heintzelman ordered Stahel to investigate, advising him "you [are] to be absent long enough for you to make a satisfactory reconnaissance for the object proposed." Stahel was given little time to organize his force before Heintzelman began prodding him, desiring to know if the expedition had already taken the field. Stahel responded that he would leave that night, April 26, sending out two columns, one to proceed through Dranesville and Leesburg and the second through Chantilly and Gum Spring, with both proceeding as far as the Blue Ridge. In response to his request for clarification as to whether he was to enter the Shenandoah Valley, Heintzelman replied that he was not to cross the Blue Ridge with the main body of his command, but that he was to send scouting parties to obtain the desired information. Heintzelman also overruled Stahel's plan to send a column through Leesburg, "unless you know there is a body of the enemy there." Instead Stahel was to concentrate his strength on a line through Aldie toward Front Royal.[10]

Stahel was with General George Stannard on the twenty-sixth, and the orders appear to have caught Stahel by surprise. The two men inspected the 7th Michigan Cavalry, followed by a review of Stannard's infantry. Immediately upon returning to camp the troopers of the 7th Michigan were ordered, "to pack up everything and be ready to move within an hour." At eleven o'clock that night the regiment pulled out, reaching Union Mills five hours later. Taking but a short break the regiment moved through Manassas Junction and then followed the railroad to Bristoe Station. The men remained in the dark as to the purpose of the move, though rumor had them joining Stoneman "to make a dash to the rear of the rebels." Their optimism quickly vanished, however, when they learned that they were destined for more guard duty. Allyne Litchfield planned to take the men out as quickly as possible, writing, "I would like to meet and whip somebody for the benefit of the ... Regt as it would give encouragement for all the hard work we have to do."[11]

Stahel wanted to station the regiment at Brentsville as it was believed to be a base of operations for several of the guerrilla bands in the area, but Heintzelman urged him to hold it closer to the railroad. If he wasn't going to hold the town, however, Stahel needed to at least insure that it no longer housed a threat while the main body of his cavalry was in the field, and he instructed Colonel Mann to make a sweep through the town in the morning. Mann set out before daylight on the twenty eighth, with his guard of honor and 44 men. The Yankees charged down the town's one street at 5 A.M., before turning back to search the buildings. According to Sergeant Havens the main street included "a court house and jail, what was once a tavern, a store, a stone church and a dozen dwellings." The patrol turned up little of note. As Havens remarked, "Our scout amounted to seeing the country, [and] a pleasant ride."[12]

At daybreak on Monday, the twenty-seventh, Stahel started toward the Blue Ridge with 2,000 troopers, one battery of artillery and five days' cooked rations in the men's haversacks. Unaware that the larger goal of the operation was to clarify reports that enemy cavalry and infantry had moved into western Fauquier and Loudoun counties, the men in the ranks were convinced that they were out "for the purpose of capturing Mosby," or, as one quipped, "Mosby had made several raids on our pickets and must be looked after." Just beyond the picket lines and near Cub Run the advance guard chased five rebels, capturing three. One of them was armed with a carbine taken from the 18th Pennsylvania, but as the other two were carrying double barrel shotguns they claimed they were squirrel hunting. In actuality the three men, John "Jack" Barnes, Albert Wrenn and Peachy Taliaferro, were members of Mosby's command intent on stealing horses from the Yankees at Fairfax. Barnes had been taken prisoner following the Stoughton Raid and had just rejoined the command after his release from Old Capitol Prison, to which he soon returned.[13]

Reaching Aldie the column surprised a second squad of Confederates and chased them for a mile, seizing three more of Mosby's men, Thomas Green, Lycurgus Hutchison and a man listed only as Thompson when their horses fell, leading one to exclaim, "It was a d—d *Yankee horse*." The Federals captured another seven men in Middleburg, one of whom was discovered moaning in bed, claiming that he was too sick to move but when the covers were withdrawn he was found to be in full Confederate uniform, including boots and spurs.[14]

The Federals then galloped down the main street through Middleburg, before searching "in vain for any armed chivalry: alias squirrel hunters." Several men were spotted along the heavily wooded slopes of the ridge one mile west of town, but Stahel refused to let his men be lured into another chase. Instead he called for his artillery and briefly shelled the woods, drawing the derision of Southern chroniclers like John Scott, who described Stahel as opening "a concentrated fire, very much to the destruction of the saplings and the grievous injury of the trees." A correspondent for the Richmond *Sentinel* observed the occupation of the town by "General Stahl and his miscreants," and likewise mocked Stahel and his gunners, attributing the shelling to the actions of "a youngster who rode slowly before them, out of rifle range, bowing and waving his hat to the advancing column. Such insolence was not to be borne: so they planted their cannon and shelled the woods ferociously." Was Stahel, in fact, being "prudent" as Scott sarcastically referred to him? Neither Scott nor Mosby were aware of the overriding reason for the reconnaissance, that two brigades of Southern infantry as well as cavalry were reported to be in the western part of the county. Stahel may have been attempting to develop the enemy position with a reconnaissance by fire, a method more famously attributed to Brig. Gen. Governor K. Warren at Gettysburg later that summer. Rather than acknowledging that Stahel was attempting to prevent a surprise encounter with a much heavier force, Southern scribes assumed that he was simply on another punitive expedition to exterminate the guerrillas, and saw his behavior as ludicrous.[15]

A Northern correspondent for the New York *Tribune* reported that Capt. Abram Krom, leading the advance guard from the 5th New York, encountered increasingly stiff resistance along the six mile route from Aldie to Middleburg, and that as many as 60 men had retired into the woods from the streets of Middleburg as the New Yorkers entered the town. The reporter, who almost certainly tilted the numbers to favor the Northern perspective, recounted that only one section of guns was deployed, sending a few "compliments" whenever the enemy made a show of resistance. William Martin, 18th Pennsylvania, counted a total of "eleven shots." The fusillade apparently did little to ease Stahel's concerns and he prohibited his men from building campfires.[16]

Stahel sent scouting parties toward the gaps of the Blue Ridge the next morning, while a third party was sent south toward White Plains. Again, the accounts differ. None of the Union records indicate that any of these patrols encountered resistance, while John Scott relates, fictitiously, that Stahel advanced toward Upperville the next morning with the bulk of his force, including his artillery and that he was brought to a halt and persuaded to retire by a group of "five or six men" led by Tom Richards. Richards, who became one of Mosby's most trusted subordinates, was likely ordered to shadow Stahel that morning, and he may have tangled with a reconnoitering party that Stahel sent toward Upperville. Meanwhile, Mosby gathered as many men as possible for a strike against the railroad as ordered by Stuart. Amanda Edmonds, who faithfully recorded the military activity in and around Ashby's Gap, noted on the twenty-eighth that the several Confederates who were quartered at her home "set sail to look after the enemy," but she does not mention whether any of "the blue devils" ever made an appearance.[17]

About noon on the twenty-eighth, Stahel turned his men south toward Salem and White Plains, with flanking parties led by Capt. Abram Hasbrouck, 5th New York, and Lt. James Lynch, 2nd Pennsylvania, searching the homes along the route. The reporter who accompanied the column claimed that a man named Duncan, who had served as a guide for Mosby on the Stoughton Raid and who had more recently harbored Big Yankee Ames after he was wounded at Hatcher's Mill, was one of the men captured that afternoon.[18]

Mosby meanwhile had gathered 80 men at Upperville and moved through Salem, ahead of Stahel, toward the Manassas Gap Railroad. Reaching Thoroughfare Gap, Mosby was informed that Stahel was on his track and about one hour behind him. Diverting from his intention to cut the railroad Mosby turned toward the Union force, which Scott, listed as numbering 2,500 men. Mosby likewise increased the size of the Federal column to 4,000 troopers. Reaching a hilltop near White Plains, Mosby watched as Stahel rolled his guns into battery and deployed his cavalry for battle. Mosby and Scott both wrote that the two sides confronted each other for an hour before Mosby elected to retire. According to Sgt. John Jackson, 5th New York, "it was quite dark" when the Federals arrived, and though they knew that Mosby had been in the area that day, "he kept out of our sight." John Scott locates this standoff near Kinloch, the home of Edward Turner. Turner was home caring for his son, who was paralyzed and dying. In his diary Turner remembered that the Federals appeared "Late in the afternoon," while "Mosby's Company of 120" arrived "About the same time," and took a position near Turner's "ice pond." The two lines were "little over a mile apart ... and approached to within a few hundred yards of each other." Realizing that "The odds were too great to risk a battle ... Mosby," according to Turner "retreated rapidly toward" the mountains. William Martin also thought the Confederates "got away right fast," allowing a prisoner to escape as they fled.[19]

The Federals did not pursue Mosby, but, according to Turner, set about "plundering the people." About 6 P.M. the Northerners arrived at the Turner home. Ignoring the pleas of the family, a Union officer, described as "a rough and unfeeling man," insisted on examining their son's wound and eventually returned with a surgeon who was tasked with determining if Tom was fit to travel. Satisfied that he was "too ill to be removed" the men left empty-handed. The confrontation was certainly difficult and Mr. Turner leaves a heart rending account, but the following year, and not many miles away a less thorough group of soldiers left John Mosby, who identified himself as an officer in the 6th Virginia Cavalry, lying in a home with a wound that they wrongly assumed was mortal. Tom Turner died the following day.[20]

Stahel turned his column back toward Middleburg, arriving after midnight. After disbanding his men, Mosby rode into Middleburg and spent the night at a nearby home. Upon being awakened in the morning he was surprised to find Stahel's command encamped in the surrounding fields. "The Major-General and I had been running away from each other a whole day and night, and then came very near sleeping together," Mosby recalled with some humor. Upon being questioned as to why he had not attacked Stahel during his night march to Middleburg, John Scott has Mosby replying, "I knew nothing of it, and I had no right to suppose an idiot had been placed in command of two brigades of cavalry and four pieces of artillery." Mosby does not make this statement in his own account, but he does relate more than a passing knowledge of Stahel's route back to Middleburg, claiming, that Stahel, fearful of a confrontation, avoided the roads, cutting across fields and farm trails, while destroying bridges and felling trees to hamper any pursuit. Though Stahel's thoughts and motives are unknown, there is nothing in the record to confirm this last claim. The *Tribune* reporter stated that the roads had been turned to mud by rain earlier in the day, causing the guns to become stuck in the mire. "The column was halted until the pieces were extricated, and then moved on in silence and in darkness until it reached Middleburg." If the roads were in such bad shape the fields were certainly no better, and while the statement that they moved on in silence may suggest a fear of attack it certainly belies any claim that they were destroying bridges and felling trees.[21]

Passing through Aldie in the morning, Stahel allowed the men to spend the day relaxing east of the town, or, as the Richmond *Sentinel* declared, "carrying on their work of pillage." Near dark Dick Moran led four men in a dash against the Union pickets. According to the account, Moran attempted to deceive the slumbering Yankees into believing that he rode at the head of a large force by shouting, "here they are, General! Bring up the reserve." That version has the Yankees scattering, "leaving the ground strewn with overcoats, blankets, corn, [etc.] never looking back to see who was after them." Northern accounts suggest that Stahel already had the men in the saddle and headed toward Fairfax when Moran struck. Dexter Macomber, 1st Michigan, noted that Moran attacked at dark and captured one man. The Wolverines prepared "to fight the bushwackers but they scatter & get away [and] we continue our march." Charles Johnson, also a member of the 1st Michigan, explained that his regiment had drawn picket duty, with Company B, supported by 20 troopers from the 2nd Pennsylvania guarding one stretch of road. As the troopers were being drawn in at dark Moran and his men hit the rear of the column. An orderly sergeant and ten men turned back to meet the attack "and checked them." It was at this point that Moran apparently yelled, "General! Bring up the reserve," as the sergeant, thinking the attackers were being reinforced fell back on the remainder of the company a half-mile off. Disgusted that the lieutenant in charge had failed to support the counterattack, Johnson wrote that he was found, along with the other 30 men "whare his neck was perfickly safe." Moran, satisfied with his harassing attack, also withdrew.[22]

The main body was already on the move when this skirmish occurred, and by 3 A.M., April 30, the men were back in their camps around Fairfax. Estimates of the number of prisoners brought in vary from 35 to 75. The *Tribune* reporter concluded his accounts of the expedition by stating "that Moseby's force proper consists of about twenty-five men; that with the neighboring farmers and innocent citizens his band can be augmented to about three hundred," and that when needed he could request "reenforcements from White and Stuart." The reporter did not claim that Stahel had "totally exterminated" this force as Mosby asserted in his *Reminiscences*.[23]

Mosby and Scott were, in part, justified in their criticism of Stahel's leadership. He had taken a substantial body of cavalry, supported by at least four guns, in an attempt to verify reports of infantry and cavalry moving along the line of the Blue Ridge in force, and it was this information that influenced the manner in which he conducted the operation. However, rather than pushing to Ashby's Gap with his entire force and sending scouting parties into the Shenandoah Valley as instructed, it appears that he did not proceed much beyond Middleburg with his main body, sending his scouting parties only as far as Ashby's Gap. Once he swung back toward Bull Run Mountain he again let caution take hold. Both Mosby and Scott explain his fear with references to the disastrous losses inflicted on the attacking Persians at Thermopylae by the small band of Spartans almost 24 centuries earlier. Writing the day that he returned to Fairfax, William Martin confirmed their belief, stating that once the captured soldier escaped from Mosby and reached the Union line near Kinloch, the Union officers believed that Mosby was attempting to lure them through the gap and into a trap laid by Jeb Stuart with 8,000 men. Had Mosby planted the idea and then allowed the prisoner to escape? Stahel had shown no such apprehension when he led a charge through the gap the previous October, but perhaps the fear of an unseen enemy, for which he had found no evidence, had governed his actions from the first afternoon when he had shelled the woods west of Middleburg and had left the reconnaissance bereft of any value. It is doubtful that Mosby was aware of the true motive behind the expedition, and the information that Stahel was acting upon, but he couldn't help to perceive Stahel as an idiot as he watched him shell empty woods, deny his men their evening campfires and then run from ghosts. The search of western Loudoun and Fauquier counties had been so cursory that any claims suggesting, "the object of the expedition [had] been attained" were empty.[24]

The Northern accounts of the expedition all indicate that Stahel's purpose was to eliminate John Mosby and his partisans, suggesting that the men in the ranks never knew that Stahel's actual purpose was to clarify the reports that Southern infantry and cavalry had moved into western Fauquier County. Calls for retribution against the guerrillas only served to inflame the growing animosity in the region. "Hanging is certainly too good for these citizen-bushwhacking murderers," the *Tribune* reporter concluded, "and it is to be hoped that an example will soon be made of this class of part thief, part marauder, but no soldier." A correspondent for the Richmond *Sentinel* concluded his account of the expedition with a plea from the residents of Middleburg. "'How long, oh Lord, how long!' is the cry that comes from our violated firesides, from our outraged country."[25]

The entire affair may have been for naught as Union scouts from the Army of the Potomac reported on the twenty-eighth that the Confederate cavalry, thought to be advancing through Fauquier County was either guarding the Rappahannock River near Kelly's Ford, or had moved into the Shenandoah Valley to assist Jones in his strike against the Baltimore & Ohio Railroad. In truth both Fitz Lee and Rooney Lee's brigades were in Culpeper County, and were contesting Stoneman's advance as he finally got his cavalry across the river. Hampton, who the Federals believed was with Jones in the Shenandoah Valley, was actually in southern Virginia, between Lynchburg and the North Carolina border, preparing to rejoin the army. On the thirtieth, with Stoneman now across the river, but before Stahel had returned to Fairfax, Hooker asked Heintzelman if he would extend Stahel's patrols along the Orange and Alexandria Railroad as far as Rappahannock Station. Heintzelman replied that he could not as he did not expect Stahel to return for several days. When Heintzelman learned that Stahel had returned earlier, the commanding general promptly instructed Stahel to assume the security of the railroad in Stoneman's absence.[26]

On April 27, General John Abercrombie made some minor adjustments to his infantry lines to compensate for the lack of cavalry protection while Stahel was in Fauquier County: Abercrombie temporarily moved the 111th and 125th New York regiments north to hold the Ox Road between Jermantown and Frying Pan. With the majority of the cavalry pickets having been removed, the infantry experienced several alarms over the next couple of nights as small parties tried to pierce their lines. According to William Martin what cavalry remained on the line had been instructed not to challenge any intruders, allowing them instead to pass through the thin outer line and up against the stronger infantry lines. Abercrombie also discussed with Stahel the most effective disposition of the infantry assets that were then available in the hope of strengthening the outer line. Both men felt the line was too extended for the number of men on hand, especially the sector from Chantilly to the Potomac. Abercrombie sought Heintzelman's approval to move the troops then stationed at Upton's Hill and Minor's Hill forward, to bolster his right flank. Ignoring this request Heintzelman reminded Abercrombie on the twenty-ninth that his most pressing concern was now the railroad. "You will *hold Bristoe Station*."[27]

16

May 1–May 9, 1863

"He came in like h—l and went out like damnation"

On May 1, with Hooker having launched his spring campaign, the security of the Orange and Alexandria Railroad became paramount. Herman Haupt, head of the military railroads, instructed, F.P. Lord, his superintendent at the Alexandria Depot, "we will operate any road at any time where the service requires it if military protection is afforded it, but not otherwise without positive orders from the commanding general." Lord was concerned about the safety of a train carrying troops from Wolf Run Shoals to Bristoe Station. As a precaution, Lt. Col. Allyne Litchfield was instructed to "send strong patrols directly up the railroad to Warrenton Junction to note condition of track as a train with regiment of infantry will go up to take post there." Litchfield was further advised to picket the line from Warrenton Junction to Catlett Station and to "await the arrival of the train." Haupt saw no need for further safeguards, but he advised the engineer to run the train "carefully as some damage may have been done" to the track. The orders to establish an infantry force along the railroad came from Halleck, prompting Heintzelman to remark, "I ordered it although I told him my force was nearly broken up. I have also to send cavalry to cover them." That task went to Othneil DeForest, colonel of the 5th New York Cavalry, who now led Stahel's 3rd Brigade. He complied the same day, moving his three regiments to Bristoe Station.[1]

Before noon the following day, May 2, the 12th Vermont Infantry was packed and on the road, marching from Wolf Run Shoals to Union Mills where they boarded the train for Warrenton Junction. Arriving at 4 P.M. the men jumped from the cars and eight companies marched south, establishing a camp about three miles below Warrenton Junction near Midland. Two companies headed north to hold Catlett Station. As they became acquainted with their new surroundings the faint sounds of the battle at Chancellorsville reached their ears, reminding the men that they were "not quite so safe [here] as at [Wolf Run Shoals]." Though construction crews from the 16th Vermont may still have been employed near Bristoe Station, much of that regiment was back at Union Mills and Lt. Col. Roswell Farnham recognized that his regiment now represented the only "infantry within twenty one miles."[2]

In the midst of the battle at Chancellorsville, Hooker continued to fret about the integrity of his supply lines. Orders went to Col. John Irvin Gregg at Dumfries directing him to begin patrolling the railroad as far as Bristoe Station, but he could not comply as his horses had been sent to Dumfries to recuperate. "The condition of our horses will not permit of our sending patrols as far as Bristoe Station. I could not send them *over four or five miles* to patrol, they are in *very* poor condition." Hooker also directed General Averell to dispatch one regiment to begin "patrolling the country between the Aquia Railroad and that of the Orange and Alexandria," against the threat of guerrilla activity. Up the line at Bristoe Station, Litchfield and 30 men had gone on a late night chase after a party of "the *Black Horse*," based on a report from an escaped prisoner. "I pushed on," Litchfield told his wife, "with some prospect of a brush but failed to see anything." Colonel DeForest also took a detachment from his brigade on an uneventful scout to Rappahannock Station.[3]

Lt. Col. Allyne Litchfield, 7th Michigan Cavalry. Through his letters, Litchfield left a vivid record of life in the regiment until he was captured in March 1864, during the controversial Kilpatrick-Dahlgren Raid. He spent the remainder of the war in a Southern prison camp (USAMHI).

At her home east of Upperville, Ida Dulany closed out her diary entry for May 1 by recording, "Mosby left for another raid yesterday, his object being to burn some bridges; it is a hazardous business and I feel anxious for the result." Her information was confirmed the next day by Bradford Smith Hoskins, an English soldier of fortune riding with Mosby, who remarked, "Met at Upperville; marched to Warrenton, and bivouacked about four miles below; intention to burn a railway bridge at Catlett Station." That Mrs. Dulany was aware of his intentions suggests that Mosby was either not as guarded as he had been earlier in the year, or, that he had misled his men about his purpose. Mosby says nothing in his *Reminiscences* about burning a bridge or making any attempt to interdict the railroad whatsoever, stating instead that he left Upperville with 70 to 80 men intent on riding to the sound of the guns at Chancellorsville. After spending the night near Warrenton, Mosby headed south in the morning hoping to strike at the tail of Hooker's army near one of the river crossings, and "to contribute my mite of support to the Southern cause." With many of the men riding with him for the first time, he hoped to further entice them by striking at heavily laden Union supply wagons. En route, however, he heard a bugle, suggesting that a cavalry camp was nearby that "we might sweep through as we went along." He then caught a solder from the 12th Vermont Infantry, who informed him of the infantry encampment nearby, and who confirmed that there was a cavalry camp along the railroad as well, "and so I made for that," Mosby wrote, and in doing so "I committed a great error."[4]

Estimates of Mosby's numbers that morning vary, with some accounts stating that he had as many as 98 men. His ranks included 20 men from the Iron Scouts as well as an unknown number of troopers from the 4th Virginia's Black Horse. Sam Chapman, who later became one of Mosby's company commanders, recalled, postwar, how the men in "the regular army were quite ready to criticize our methods," and that "Mosby was quite anxious to give these gentlemen a taste of our warfare upon the first opportunity." According to Chapman, once he heard the bugle "Mosby's face lighted up as he said: 'You can have your fight now in short order.' The temptation was too great to resist." It was simply not in Mosby's nature to pass up a fight.[5]

According to Lt. Colonel Farnham, the bugle that alerted the guerrillas belonged to his infantry. "He heard our bugle & supposed that we were cavalry." Coming in sight of the infantry encampment, the Confederates seized three of the Green Mountain Boys, who "were out straggling around camp." The three men later escaped, or were released. They reported that "Mosby had questioned them & becoming satisfied that we were infantry said he wanted nothing to do with us & turned towards the Junction." Iron Scout Prioleau Henderson remembered that the enticing bugle actually led the guerrillas to charge into the infantry encampment, learning, "to our dismay" that it was an infantry outpost. "Fortunately we did not lose a man."[6]

Whatever the actual sequence of events, Mosby turned his men back toward the horse soldiers three miles up the line at Warrenton Junction. Riding out of the woods on a "warm and pleasant" morning they observed a detachment of the 1st West Virginia Cavalry, numbering between 70 and 100 men, lounging around the cluster of buildings. Many of the horses had been turned out to graze without either saddles or bridles and the men were occupied in "currying, some watering, some playing 'poker,' some playing 'euchre.... In fact," as one of the troopers recalled, "all were in that particular state of inattention to be easily taken by surprise, and sure enough it came." As the Confederates rode out of the woods, the West Virginians took them for a relief detail from the 1st Vermont, an assumption based on the fact that the men in the front ranks were wearing blue jackets and were calmly walking their horses toward the Yankees. Three hundred yards out Mosby erased all doubt by ordering his "invincibles" to charge. In the words of one West Virginian the guerrillas charged, "With yells, hideous and defiant, perfectly conscious of their advantage, and never dreaming of defeat." As the Confederates drew their revolvers and sunk in their spurs, the Federals threw down their cards and currycombs and ran for their weapons.[7]

Despite accounts stating that they only "fired a few shots, then surrendered," the West Virginians mounted a "stubborn" fight, considering the position they found themselves in. The Southerners were slowed by a "miry" stream, allowing most of the Yankees to take cover within the buildings, while about 20 of the men who were caught too far from the buildings were cut off and the majority of them were quickly captured. One private fled on horseback toward the railroad, chased by three men. Reaching the embankment he reportedly turned and drove his saber into the head of his nearest antagonist and then escaped when the horses of the other two pursuers stumbled and fell.[8]

Pvt. Thomas Harlow was singled out as the man who killed Madison Templeman, a Texan who had gained a measure of notoriety as a scout and spy for the South. An early entry on his service record shows Templeman "detailed as a guerrilla," and later as a "general scout," who drew notice from then Brig. Gen. John Hood for "gallantry and valuable service as a courier" at Antietam. To the Yankees he was "the famous rebel spy Templeton," who was remembered by one Vermonter as a man who had come into their camp the previous October peddling and singing "patriotic Union songs ... [who] talked very eloquently and patriotically to the boys." The New York *Herald* reported that "having discharged his pistol" Templeman approached Private Harlow and with "inconceivable effrontery" demanded his surrender. Pretending to comply, Harlow drew his revolver as if to surrender it, then shot "and killed the bold desperado." In another version it was Templeman who, after surrendering, shot his captor before being killed by the dead Yankee's "exasperated comrades."[9]

While some of his men dashed off in pursuit of the fugitives, Mosby turned his attention toward the Federals that had taken cover in the buildings and were now pouring a hot fire into the Southern ranks. The loyal Virginians who had run into the smaller outbuildings found that they provided little protection and were easily persuaded to surrender. The one-and-a-half-story main building, later described as being 30 feet by 50 feet in size and which now housed the majority of the Yankees, proved more of a fortress and it was apparent to Mosby that he would need to overcome their resistance quickly if he was to avoid a prolonged, bloody fight. One of the Iron Scouts stated that they faced "a sheet of fire, from doors, windows and everywhere else" as they galloped up to the building. "I have been under some pretty hot fires, and participated in some hard battles," Prioleau Henderson declared, "but that blaze of fire from rifles and pistols, in my very face and nostrils that day, exceeded all that I have ever encountered." While some of the attackers drove the defenders away from the windows by galloping up and firing into the house, Mosby ordered others to dismount, charging the house on foot or using the now vacant outbuildings as cover while they returned the fire of the defenders. Sam Chapman briefly took cover below one of the windows and used his saber to slash at the gun barrels that protruded above his head.[10]

Mosby, whom Henderson recalled "standing in front of one of the windows, firing shot after shot into the foe," demanded their surrender. The officers inside, including Lt. Col. John Krepps, Maj. Josiah Steele and Capt. William McCoy, refused and Mosby ordered Alfred Glasscock to set the building on fire. In quick order, however, both Steele and McCoy were wounded, Steele mortally, and the majority of the men inside were driven upstairs by the heavy fire directed through the windows on the main floor. While Glasscock piled hay against the building, a handful of his comrades, including Sam Chapman and John DeButts, ran through the open door and into a hallway with rooms to either side and a staircase leading to the second story. Standing at the foot of the stairs, Chapman again yelled for the Yankees to surrender. The men upstairs, along with those in the room to the right, dropped their weapons. The men in the room to Chapman's left were protected by a closed door and briefly held out until John DeButts began firing through the door, reportedly killing the man who was barricading it with his body. DeButts and his comrades then pushed their way into the smoke filled room where a brief but deadly gun battle ensued. Those outside heard "continual firing" for several minutes before the West Virginians dropped their weapons, possibly at the insistence of the officers who had surrendered minutes before.[11]

As the Yankees were being herded outside and the guerrillas scrambled to gather up weapons and to attend to their wounded, Henderson heard what he thought was "a volley of musketry, and looking up, I saw it was a regiment of Yankee cavalry, and the noise I heard was their horses' feet striking the railroad iron, as they crossed the tracks not fifty yards from where we were." Like the West Virginians only minutes earlier, the Southerners "scattered around in every direction," running for their own horses, while still trying to retain their plunder. According to Henderson, "the last I saw of Mosby and [Sgt. William] Mickler that day, and for some days to come, they were trying to rally and form the men. But they did not succeed in doing so." Sam Chapman was still collecting the weapons surrendered by the men in the house "when the cry was raised," and he was caught with such "an armful of pistols" that he "could hardly walk." Dropping his burden he ran past the men who moments before were prisoners, grabbed his horse "and rode off with all the others."[12]

Much of Mosby's success to this point in his career has to be attributed to audacity, superb scouting and meticulous intelligence gathering. He and John Underwood were especially tireless in their attention to scouting Union positions, but at Warrenton Junction Mosby had failed to reconnoiter, and now he paid the price. Whatever his intentions when he left Upperville, whether it was to interdict the railroad, as had been requested, or to strike the tail of Hooker's army, as he later stated, he had stumbled upon a target of opportunity and he attacked impulsively. He did so in contravention of an earlier warning from Stuart, that he conduct his operations against the railroad "far enough away from a brigade camp" in order that he be able to escape with his "plunder and prisoners." The 5th New York and a party of the 1st Vermont were camped within a half-mile of the scene of the fight, in an area of generally level, open terrain and none of the Confederates knew they were there. Further, Mosby had again neglected to establish an adequate security or picket detail as he went into the fight, allowing the hard-charging Federals to take him entirely by surprise, at the very point that John Scott described him as being the "undisputed master of Warrenton Junction."[13]

Sgt. John Jackson, 5th New York, stated that the men were in the saddle and formed for the charge within three minutes of hearing the firing. Lt. Frank Munson remembered that in his haste two of his horses ran off before he could saddle either of them. Getting a saddle on a third horse he headed for the scene with only one girth strap buckled. He believed that only 40 men made the initial counterattack. Before "fleeing in disorder" the Confederates unleashed one ragged volley that failed to slow the New Yorkers who "descended like an avalanche upon the guerrillas." Edwin Havens learned that the West Virginians had been herded to a point about 100 yards from the main building when the New Yorkers appeared, charging around the smoldering station house from two directions. "They did not perceive the 5th until nearly on them and on receiving the charge broke and ran to the four winds leaving behind all but three of the prisoners," along with their wounded. Colonel DeForest, Maj. John Hammond and Capt. Abram Krom led the Federals in a chase of eight to ten miles toward Warrenton. One of the Yankees who did not escape in the initial confusion was Cpl. Corneilus Shannon. After fleeing for several miles his captor turned to fire at Krom and Shannon knocked the revolver out of his hand and took the Southerner prisoner in turn. Krom may have been the "fine-looking captain" who challenged Chapman with his saber. "He and I exchanged blows," Chapman wrote later, "but [Richard] Montjoy shot him, and got his fine bay horse." The bullet struck Krom in the corner of his right eye, traversed his nasal passages and lodged against his left jaw. Lieutenant Munson was shot in the leg and shoulder during a duel with several Rebels, but took some satisfaction in seeing one of his assailants taken prisoner.[14]

Chapman recalled that "about one-fourth of our men" were taken prisoner in their flight back to Warrenton. One man was killed and three others mortally wounded. Another fifteen were wounded and taken prisoner, including Samuel Dushane, who had captured Lt. Robert Wallace weeks earlier and who now sent Wallace's sword back through the ranks as he had promised. Dushane later complained to a hospital steward "of the unmerciful manner in which [the Yankees] killed his horses, as he had four shot under him in his endeavor to escape." About 30 men were taken prisoner.[15]

The men of the 12th Vermont were alerted "by a frightened telegraph operator" who fled from the station in the early moments of the attack, as well as by one of the three men who had been captured that morning and who had escaped on horseback once the cavalry arrived. The foot soldiers then rode a train back to the station and observed "the bodies of a dozen dead horses strewn around" the station house as they jumped from the cars. George Benedict had "hardly taken twenty steps" before he came across the body of Madison Templeman sprawled in the dirt. He found another 17 wounded "butternuts" and several unwounded prisoners lying near the house, the inside of which "was strewn with wounded men, among them Major Steele."[16]

Several Northern accounts claimed that Mosby had been either wounded or killed, though all of them were nothing more than wishful thinking, as was Stahel's claim that the fight had "resulted in the complete annihilation of Mosby's command." The widely reported rumor that Mosby had been wounded or killed resulted when a prisoner identified a sword laying on the ground as belonging to the guerrilla leader and exclaimed, "That's Mosby's sword. My God is he killed, too!" Eager for any good news in the escalating war with the partisan, Stahel hurried off several dispatches to the New York *Tribune* and *Herald* as fast as reports came in from the scene, including the claim that Mosby had been wounded. Yet after months of embarrassing failure the exuberance of the officers and men is understandable. As Edwin Havens told his parents, "Moseby was compelled to fly at his best speed to save himself as he is getting pretty well known by these regts., and they would be very happy to become the possessors of his body dead or alive." The following day Roswell Farnham confidently assured his wife, "I don't think we shall have anything more to disturb us at present." Stahel issued a statement thanking the men of DeForest's brigade for their "promptness and gallantry," declaring, "Deeds like these are worthy of emulation, and give strength and confidence to the command."[17]

The enthusiasm of the men was tempered, however, by their own losses, including one killed and several mortally wounded. Major Steele would linger for almost a month before he died. A total of seventeen men from the 1st West Virginia were listed as killed or wounded, including Capt. William McCoy who was shot through the chest. Lt. Col. John Krepps, who had been troubled with medical problems for the past eight months, resigned just over a week later, ostensibly on a medical disability. At least four men in the 5th New York were wounded, one mortally. Among them were Captain Krom, and lieutenants Frank Munson and Samuel McBride.[18]

Sergeant Havens remained at the station that afternoon as part of a ten-man detail led by Capt. Alexander Walker. It was the first time any of the men had seen the destruction wrought by combat. Havens observed the "hard looking" prisoners and several of the wounded, including Dick Moran, who had been shot through the throat. "He it was who led the charge on the 1st [Vermont Cavalry]" at Miskell's farm. "Some of the men were quite fine looking fellows, but they had no regularity of uniforms being clad in everything they could find." Surrounded by the dead horses and the detritus of battle, Havens informed his family, "the house is full of ball holes and on the walls inside is the following inscription 'Sunday May 3rd 1863, Major Moseby charged on the 1st [West] Va. Cav. He came in like h—l and went out like damnation.'"[19]

John Scott, who always viewed the glass as more than half full when it concerned Mosby, saw the action at Warrenton Junction as both "a victory as well as a disaster," but he admitted that the disastrous second half of the fight "had the effect of damping the ardor of the 'Conglomerates' to such a degree that only 37 men met Mosby" at his next rendezvous a week later. "They had been instructed by that event that war, even with [Mosby], was not an uninterrupted flow of victory, and that, if they made a habit of going with him, they would have blows to receive, as well as blows to give." Sam Chapman viewed the fight as "our first disaster," which "grew out of overconfidence," and like Scott, he saw the setback as teaching the men "a useful lesson." Or, in the opinion of one Union officer, "an occasional defeat makes a good soldier a better fighter and knocks a coward out." Mosby did not file a report on the fight until after a subsequent action in which he more fully complied with the wishes of his superiors to cut the flow of supplies to Hooker's army. His statement "that we had captured nearly the [entire 1st West Virginia Cavalry] (about 300 officers and men)" may have been his honest belief or it may have been an attempt to mitigate his first defeat, as the weight of evidence suggests that he outnumbered the West Virginians that he swept down upon that morning. In later years he stuck with his claim to have "taken three times my own number prisoners," and stated that he only fled the field when confronted by "10 times my own number." He did admit that the attack "was a mistake ... even if I had been completely successful ... [as] I had no idea whether I was attacking a hundred or a thousand men." Concluding his account he wrote, "I learned wisdom from experience, and after that always looked before I took a leap."[20]

On the day before the fight, Amanda Edmonds had watched seven young men ride away from her home to meet Mosby in Upperville, and she had spent an anxious night after first receiving word of the fight. She was later relieved when she learned that "our crowd came out safe." She had earlier made the acquaintance of Madison Templeman and upon hearing of his death remarked that he "was a brave and useful man." Sgt. William Mickler and his Iron Scouts had also stayed nearby prior to the fight and she admired Mickler as well, "partly for the high estimation in which his men hold him."[21]

Later in the day, May 3, and again on the fourth, orders were issued to Abercrombie's and Stahel's brigade commanders to have their men "ready to march at a moments notice with three days' rations." In part this was in reaction to the fight that morning at Warrenton Junction, but these men had also been listening to "Hooker's guns" at Chancellorsville and thought the directive may have been issued in the event "disaster overtakes Hooker." The initial order included those troops already stationed along the railroad, but after Mosby's attack Heintzelman amended the orders to preclude those troops from any move to assist Hooker.[22]

Though disaster did befall Hooker, Heintzelman's infantrymen were again disappointed, for they remained in their camps frustrated and idle. But Heintzelman now believed that Southern cavalry threatened the bridge at Rappahannock Station and he instructed Stahel to "send out some more cavalry to prevent [its destruction.]" Stannard and Abercrombie were also told to "increase the guard" at the bridge by sending another infantry company from Warrenton Junction. Still, railroad officials remained leery of leaving their trains for any period of time within the disputed area.[23]

On Wednesday, May 6, a flurry of orders and telegrams clogged the wires as Heintzelman again shifted his troops to meet the reported threat to the bridge at Rappahannock Station. The bulk of the 12th Vermont Infantry, along with a section of the 1st Rhode Island Artillery, were to be shipped south to that point, but heavy rain had damaged the bridge across Bull Run, delaying the necessary transport for at least a day. Still, two companies of the 12th Vermont covered the distance to the bridge on foot, acting "as a sort of advance guard," pending the arrival of their comrades. In the meantime Colonel DeForest was responsible for the security of the span across the Rappahannock. Heintzelman believed that his lines were now stretched to the breaking point once he assumed responsibility for the bridge some 50 miles in a direct line from his headquarters, and eight miles south of Farnham's current position below Warrenton Junction.[24]

Though by most Union accounts Mosby and his "conglomerates" had been "terribly whipped" at Warrenton Junction they still remained a focus of concern, not just for the troops now posted along the railroad, but also for those in the Shenandoah Valley. On May third, a Union patrol out of Dranesville scouted the turnpike corridor through Middleburg and returned with the news that Mosby had been reinforced to a strength of 200 men and that he would soon receive four pieces of artillery. The following day Union troops attempted to ambush a party of the guerrillas. Upon relieving the 1st West Virginia at Warrenton Junction, Lt. Colonel Litchfield was told by one of their captains that he could lead Litchfield to an area nearby where "50 or 60 Rebs" were sheltered in the trees. Litchfield set out with 100 men and came in sight of the rebels with their "horses hitched to trees," but instead of charging them immediately as he intended he allowed the unnamed captain to talk him into trying to lure them into a trap. Sending a handful of men into the woods as if on a routine patrol, he held back the remainder, but the Southerners refused to take the bait and fled.[25]

On May 7, Litchfield led a squadron in search of oats for their horses. Arriving at the farm where he had been told he could obtain the oats, Litchfield sent a lieutenant and ten men to the house while he remained a short distance away with the remainder of his force. A group of "8 or ten 'rebs'" then charged out of the woods intent on capturing the men at the house and stumbled upon Litchfield and the reserve. After an exchange of ineffective volleys, the rebels fled, with one man screaming, "as though [he] had been struck." Havens learned on this patrol that the soldiers he viewed as guerrillas made their homes with local families and not in a military camp, leading him to repeat the now familiar suspicion "that every man is a guerrilla, farming in the day time and prowling around at night."[26]

The same afternoon Capt. Robert Randolph and 30 men from his Black Horse caught six soldiers from the 5th New York Cavalry, including Capt. Zolman McMasters, out in the open between Catlett Station and Bristoe Station. After a running battle, the Virginians captured one of the New Yorkers when his horse was killed, and a second man drowned attempting to ford Bull Run, which was near flood stage. The prisoner was paroled the same day at Greenwich, and when he reached camp the following morning he reported that Randolph was using the small hamlet as a rendezvous point for his company. In fact, Randolph was no longer commanding the Black Horse, but was probably back in the area looking for a horse, as his had been killed days earlier at Chancellorsville. Lt. William R. Smith was now leading the company from the 4th Virginia Cavalry.[27]

Once the bridge over Bull Run was repaired, trains were able to shuffle troops along the line downstream, allowing the bulk of the 12th Vermont to move south to Rappahannock Bridge about 2 P.M. on the seventh. The 15th Vermont was also relocated, replacing the 12th Vermont south of Warrenton Junction. Roving bands of guerrillas were still making their presence felt: one group obstructed the track between the 12th Vermont's new position and the section patrolled by the Army of the Potomac. Hooker instructed General Pleasonton to maintain the necessary patrols along the line, and he told the cavalryman, "You will put to death any person tampering with the road without authority." The foot soldiers were ordered to finish the block houses being constructed along the line "with as little delay as possible."[28]

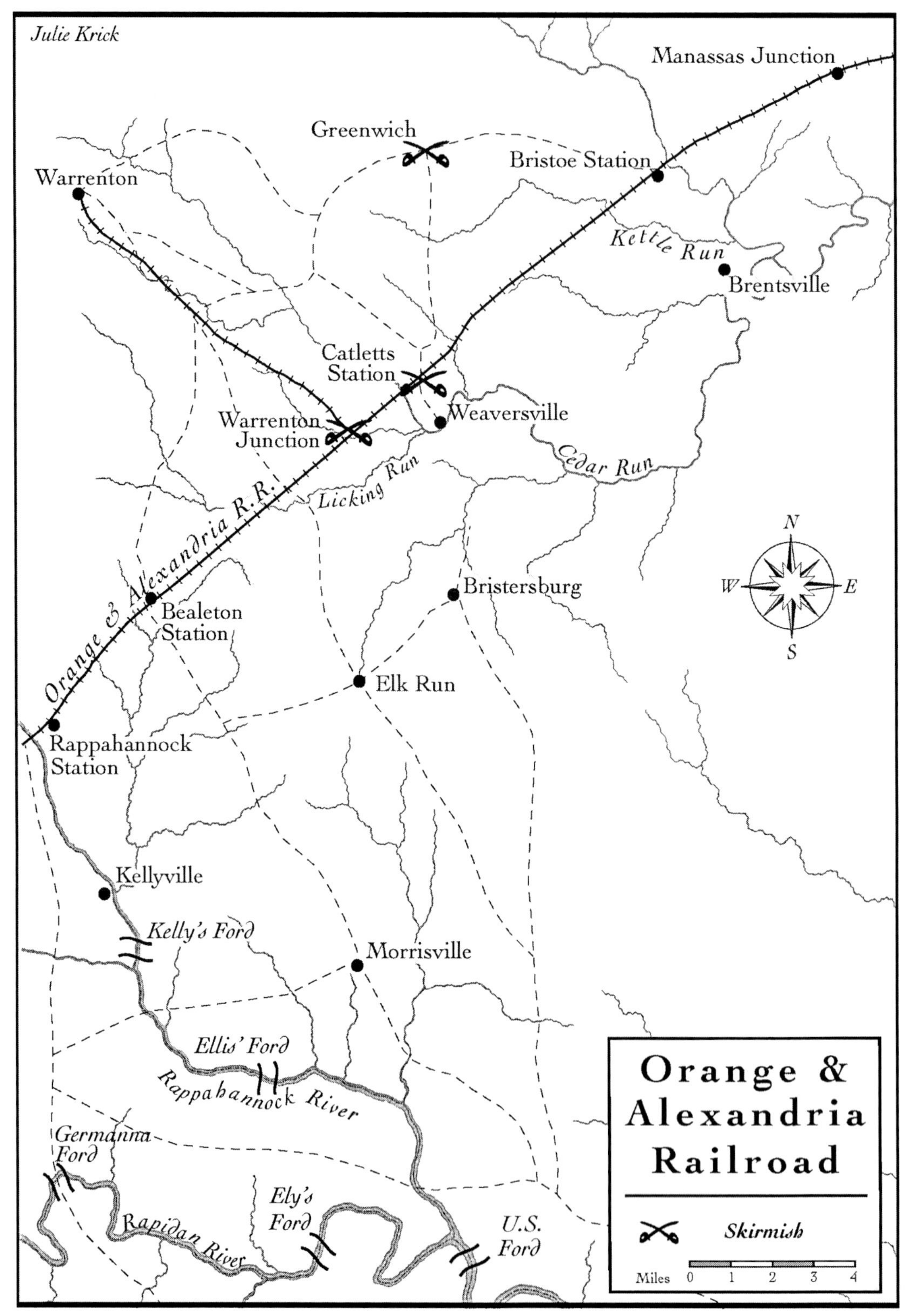
Julie Krick
Manassas Junction
Greenwich
Bristoe Station
Warrenton
Kettle Run
Brentsville
Catletts Station
Weaversville
Warrenton Junction
Cedar Run
Licking Run
Orange & Alexandria R.R.
N
W
E
S
Bristersburg
Bealeton Station
Elk Run
Rappahannock Station
Kellyville
Kelly's Ford
Morrisville
Ellis' Ford
Rappahannock River
Orange & Alexandria Railroad
Germanna Ford
Ely's Ford
U.S. Ford
Rapidan River
Skirmish
Miles 0 1 2 3 4

General George Stoneman reached the Rappahannock on the seventh, "very much exhausted" after his raid, but the high water prevented him from immediately crossing the river. In an effort to assist the weary troopers, Heintzelman ordered Colonel DeForest to concentrate his brigade at Rappahannock Station while General Abercrombie assumed responsibility for the upper end of the line. Stahel also planned to send the 2nd Pennsylvania Cavalry from Fairfax Court House to Warrenton Junction.[29]

On Saturday morning, May 9, Stahel ordered DeForest to move the 7th Michigan to Bealeton Station. They arrived in time to observe the approach of the cavalry corps, with Brig. Gen. David Gregg's division in the lead. Sergeant Havens gazed in admiration as the troopers came into view, commenting, "it was the grandest sight I ever saw." The sheer number of men left Litchfield awestruck, but their appearance was another matter. "You can imagine the condition of men and horses after being saddled and ridden for 7 days," Litchfield told his wife. He believed that he would remain at Bealeton Station for two weeks before Stoneman's men could assume responsibility for the area, but within a couple of days the regiment was back at Warrenton Junction.[30]

That same day Heintzelman issued an order directing Stahel "to seize as soon as possible all horses between the Potomac and Rappahannock Rivers and the Blue Ridge except those within our interior lines." It was hoped that this measure would help "to eradicate thoroughly the system of irresponsible guerrilla warfare practiced within" the area, but Mosby struck again before Stahel could act on the directive.[31]

17

May 10–May 13, 1863

"Those Bushwackers fire on you as they would fire on a sparrow"

General Stahel assumed that George Stoneman would remain along the line of the railroad, securing the ten miles of track between Rappahannock Station and Cedar Run. Based on that understanding, Stahel ordered DeForest to withdraw to the north, establish his base at Bristoe Station and secure the line between Cedar Run and Bull Run. But Stoneman then ordered his saddle-worn troopers back to the supply depots near Falmouth. This forced Stahel to amend his orders to DeForest. He was now instructed to hold his brigade at Warrenton Junction and to resume patrolling the line from the Rappahannock to Bull Run. Stahel was also acting on the belief that Stannard's infantry was guarding the bridges that carried the track over the numerous streams. It was in the midst of this confusion that Mosby conducted his first operation against the railroad.[1]

Mosby gathered 30 to 40 men at Upperville on May 9, and set out in the direction of the railroad. The following morning, Sunday, May 10, he found the bridge at Cedar Run unguarded and burned it. Mosby then turned north, and just south of Kettle Run his men removed a couple of rails before continuing to the span across Kettle Run. There, as they applied the torch to the bridge, a southbound train appeared carrying 60 men from the 16th Vermont Infantry. As the train approached the crossing, the bridge was "blazing in high style," and one soldier estimated that it would have been impassable in another ten minutes, but the Vermonters quickly extinguished the fire by smothering the flames with dirt. The guerrillas watched from a field a quarter of a mile away. Leaving several men to secure the bridge the Federals re-boarded the train and continued south, as Mosby and his men "filed into a piece of woods & disappeared." The train had only proceeded a half mile before it was again brought to a stop by the section of track that Mosby had removed. Though Mosby reported that the train derailed, one of the soldiers on the train stated otherwise, writing that the damage "was soon remedied and we passed on."[2]

As the train again headed south, the foot soldiers gazed upon the massive cavalry camps, the same camps that Mosby had successfully skirted as he moved north from Cedar Run to Kettle Run. Hugh Henry, 16th Vermont, had observed DeForest's men near Warrenton Junction, "but the most impressive sight I ever saw was three divisions (near 20,000) of Stoneman's Cavalry" farther down the line. "For two or three miles both sides of the [railroad]," he told his mother, "was a perfect sea of men & horses banners fluttering, trumpets blowing and long [wagon] trains just forming into line." But with Stoneman, DeForest and Stannard each thinking that someone else was guarding the bridges none had done so, and

Mosby had again found the chink in the Yankee armor. As the train approached Cedar Run, the Vermonters found an infantry detail now guarding the bridge "which they had discovered burning & succeeded in saving." The guerrillas had captured two of these men but seeing them as "a bad investment ... of time and trouble" had paroled them almost immediately. Upon their return they reported that Mosby had "near a hundred" men, but the more astute Henry surmised correctly, "I believe they were mistaken as a body of cavalry looks to number more than they really do."[3]

By finally striking at the railroad Mosby had done as Stuart had requested, but this was not the warfare that the partisans had come to expect, nor was it the kind that would continue to draw men into Mosby's ranks. On the heels of the defeat at Warrenton Junction the men who had answered Mosby's call to rendezvous at Upperville on the ninth were looking for a quick, easy strike that would result in captured horses and weapons. Burning bridges after a long ride may have helped the war effort but it was not putting money in their pockets and they termed the operation of May 10 "a water-haul," or a failure. Mosby claimed that the Federals were forced to "suspend" operations along the line "for two days," which, according to John Scott "paid Mosby." Nothing found in the records of the Orange and Alexandria Railroad supports this claim. Rather, the records confirm Hugh Henry's assessment that the damage was trivial and that any necessary repairs were completed the same day.[4]

As Stahel reacted to the raid and attempted to sort out the confusion over who was responsible for each section of track, he warned DeForest that another attempt to burn the bridges would "undoubtedly" be made that night, and the colonel was instructed to maintain frequent patrols. Later in the day, and after a flurry of telegrams between Heintzelman and Hooker, the latter acquiesced and agreed that his cavalry would assume responsibility for the railroad from Rappahannock Station to Cedar Run. Heintzelman then allowed Stahel to withdraw his cavalry north of Cedar Run. Heintzelman also wanted to allow General Abercrombie to withdraw his infantry, but Stoneman failed to take Hooker's order seriously and left only fifty men behind as pickets. While waiting for the cavalry to sort out their responsibilities, the infantry were told to redouble their efforts to complete the blockhouses, and to block "all by-paths and roads ... so as to interrupt the passage of cavalry."[5]

On the eleventh Heintzelman reissued his directive of May 9, ordering Stahel to seize all the horses between his picket lines in western Fairfax County and the Blue Ridge. This time, however, the order specified "Brentsville and vicinity," attributing the recent problems along the railroad to "Bushwackers & guerrillas which calls for the necessity of executing the above order as soon as possible." The horses were to be "appraised and certificates issued to the owners that could be redeemed for cash payment once the owners established "their loyalty."[6]

With this edict in mind Col. William Mann, 7th Michigan Cavalry, approached Stahel about the possibility of making "a raid to Warrenton," followed by a sweep through the Loudoun Valley. The general gave him "a very curt reply" denying the request, and ordering him instead to report to DeForest. This was due in part to the growing concern that another attack would be launched against the railroad, a fear possibly heightened when guerrillas, said to have been Mosby's men, struck a Union hospital at Bristoe Station and captured ten men. When these men were released they perpetuated the story that Mosby had been wounded in the fight on May third, but "only slightly in the shoulder." That the story continued to thrive suggests there may have been some hint of truth to the rumor, or, more likely, that the guerrillas were playing to the gullibility of the prisoners.[7]

An excited picket roused the camp that evening when he galloped in shouting that the guerrillas were right behind him. Within minutes DeForest's entire brigade was in formation awaiting orders, with the exception of the troopers in the 5th New York who immediately charged toward the threatened point on the line. Sergeant Havens had heard about their similar response on the third "and deemed it incredible before seeing it done." He believed the threat was only a few bushwackers who had seized a trooper "straggling outside the lines." This alarm prompted Stahel to reconsider Mann's request, however, and he authorized the colonel to make his proposed sweep with 130 men. Litchfield saddled his fastest horse in the hope of getting "after Mosby."[8]

Setting out at first light, the 7th Michigan charged through Warrenton at 6 A.M., but, according to Sergeant Havens, they "saw no rebs although I believe that had we searched we might have found some." Mann led his column on a jaunt of about 40 miles through "New Baltimore, Buckland Mills, Greenwich, [and] Auburn." Litchfield judged the trip "delightful," during which he chatted with some "pert secesh ladies, took some horses, [and] gained some valuable information." Havens, however, was disappointed with the effort and began to doubt his officers. After the quick dash through Warrenton, in which no effort was made to actually search for the guerrillas thought to be housed there, Havens noted, "Our boys are all anxious to meet them and swear that our officers are afraid to lead them on against Mosby and I must confess that it does look a little like it."[9]

It was at this time that another name crept into the daily telegrams of Union officers along the upper Potomac River near Harpers Ferry, as well as Loudoun County, and that name was John Mobberly. An imposing man at six feet tall and near two hundred pounds Mobberly remains a curious enigma. One biographer writes that he was "known as captain, lieutenant, common soldier and 'common bastard' during his Civil War career, [who] was to many people a lamented hero. To others, he was just possibly the worst man who ever lived in Loudoun County." The roster of Lige White's 35th Battalion shows that he enlisted on September 15, 1862, deserted almost two years later and "was assassinated 4/5/65," two months shy of his twenty-first birthday. A roster for Mosby's 43rd Battalion shows that he enlisted with White on January 11, 1862, had a horse killed under him at Brandy Station on June 9, 1863, and served with John Mosby on at least one occasion. Mobberly also prosecuted his own private war, "Preying on friend and foe alike." Like many other young men who led colorful yet brief lives that skirted both sides of the law and which generally ended in a blaze of gunfire, Mobberly's life remains a fertile ground for historians to probe and ponder. To the Yankees, who generally misspelled his name as Mobley, he was simply another bushwhacker or "guerrilla desperado," whose business was "stealing and robbing and killing pickets."[10]

On May 11, Mobberly was reported to be in Loudoun County with 70 men, "capturing horses and impressing citizens. Gen. William Morris, commanding an infantry brigade at Harpers Ferry, attached to Maj. Gen. Robert Schenck's Eighth Corps, forwarded this information but advised that he had no suitable force to send after him. As a relative unknown, the name Mobberly became Mosby when Schenck forwarded the report to Halleck the following day. News accounts of the day continued the error when correspondents in Washington copied Schenck's telegram under the headline, "The Guerrilla Mosby Still Prowling About." Now, in addition to requesting assistance from Maj. Gen. Robert Milroy in the Shenandoah Valley, Schenck sent a note to Halleck asking, "Cannot Heintzelman hurry off some of Stahel's force in that direction to help catch the rascals?" Heintzelman, who was still trying to secure Stoneman's assistance along the railroad, now told Hooker, "I have pressing need for all my cavalry to the [north].[11]

The immediate response came from Milroy, who ordered the 1st New York Cavalry to cross the Shenandoah River and deal with the problem. On the morning of May 12, Capt. William Boyd led 200 men through Snickersville to Purcellville, where he divided his command, sending a detachment under the command of Capt. Frederick Hendricks through Wheatland and Waterford, while he continued to Leesburg. The command reunited in Leesburg at six o'clock that evening. In the morning Boyd again split his force, sending Capt. Abram Jones, with four companies, south along an interior line through Philomont to Middleburg, while Boyd took the remainder to Aldie, reuniting in Middleburg later in the afternoon. From there Boyd took the direct route along the turnpike to Upperville, while Jones swung north to Bloomfield and then south to Upperville. Reunited once again the men camped for the night between Upperville and Paris with four captured soldiers as the only reward for their effort.[12]

Boyd returned to Upperville in the morning, May 14, again splitting his command into several columns, after he received reports that about 40 of Mosby's men were in the town. Over the next four or five hours the Federals chased after guerrillas who taunted them from the hilltops, losing three horses killed, and one man seriously wounded in several small skirmishes. After recalling his scattered squads Boyd headed north, through western Loudoun County before crossing the river at Shepherdstown, with eight prisoners in tow. When Col. Andrew McReynolds completed his report of the expedition later that afternoon he concluded that there was no organized Southern force in the county, but only scattered groups belonging to Mosby and White, along with a local he identified as George Gaither. He also suggested that a concerted sweep of the county, by his own 1st New York, along with Sam Means's Loudoun Rangers and aided by a contingent from Stahel's division, would "clean that section pretty effectively."[13]

Lige White's command had spent the winter in the Shenandoah Valley, where under the watchful eye of Grumble Jones and Lt. R.T. Watts, the battalion adjutant, the men and officers had turned to drill and discipline. The men resented being attached to the army, and chaffed to return to independent duty in Loudoun County, and while they never lost the raw edginess that made them such a fearsome fighting unit the several months of army discipline served them well. Still attached to Jones' brigade, the 35th Battalion had spent the previous month operating against the Baltimore and Ohio Railroad in West Virginia, and as a unit was nowhere near Loudoun County, but a combination of events now led Union officials to believe that the battalion was once again operating along the Potomac River on Washington's doorstep.[14]

McReynolds's account came on the heels of a report from Col. Albert Jewett, commanding a Union brigade stationed along the Potomac River in Montgomery County, Maryland. Jewett reported, "One of White's guerrillas, a deserter, who has just crossed the river reports that about 400 of the enemy are on the slope of the mountain about three miles west of Leesburg and about 500 at Upperville." Heintzelman's adjutant confirmed, "Your telegram with regard to the position of White's guerrillas just received." Mobberly's small squad of men, possibly all from White's battalion, had just become White's entire command, and, the adjutant continued, "Stahel has ordered [Lt.] Col. Stagg of the 1st Michigan with all the available force he could gather—400 men—with orders to intercept White or Moseby if he is there as reported or if he can be found." Stahel also enjoined Stagg "to arrest every secessionist" that he should encounter. But as Stagg was potentially facing a force over twice his size, Heintzelman warned Schenck that "it is not considered safe to allow them to proceed too far, and in consequence will be of little assistance to the detachment of the First New York sent out by you, as our forces are so far apart." McReynolds's superiors did not receive his report, that only a handful of men were roaming the upper county, until after Stagg took the field. The Wolverines followed Boyd's New Yorkers through Leesburg, arrested a couple of persons and returned on the fifteenth, having failed to find evidence to support the reports. John Mobberly had departed the region, most likely unaware of the consternation he had caused or that his forays were being credited to others.[15]

When Stahel notified Heintzelman that he was sending Stagg into Loudoun County he stated, "I would like to have sent a stronger force but I have not yet got them as Colonel Price will inform you." While Heintzelman worked to secure additional assistance from Hooker, to guard the railroad that was supplying Hooker's army, Stahel was struggling to adequately man two picket lines: the forward line from Union Mills to Rappahannock Station with four regiments, and the interior line from the town of Occoquan through Prince William and Fairfax Counties to the Potomac River with just over five regiments. Poor intelligence and staff work throughout Heintzelman's department, combined with the guerrilla's practice of striking at as many points along these lines as possible may have again brought the situation to a crisis point, and the infantry did little to alleviate it. Just after Stagg left on the thirteenth Heintzelman received a complaint from the officer commanding the infantry detachment at Vienna that all of the mounted pickets around his camp had been removed, leading Heintzelman to ask Stahel, "Cannot you leave ten or fifteen men to cover the infantry?"[16]

Brig. Gen. David Gregg had not withdrawn his entire command to Falmouth, as some may have believed, but the fact that he left only one small squadron to guard the railroad between Rappahannock Station and Cedar Run provoked the prickly Heintzelman. Brig. Gen. John Buford picketed the river below the station, and while Hooker had pointedly told Stoneman that he wanted Buford's men ready to take the field again as soon as possible, Buford found himself with problems beyond tired troopers and worn-out horses. On May 12, Buford reported the area between Hartwood Church and Bealeton Station as "infested with some irregular cavalry that is excessively annoying," and he admitted, "our efforts to overhaul them so far have proved abortive." The historian for the 6th Pennsylvania Cavalry dubbed the area, specifically Morrisville, as "the worst region for the operations of murderous guerrilla bands we ever found." That Buford was responsible for picketing a line 35 miles long with his lone, under-strength brigade, while dealing with the hit and run attacks against his sentries afforded him "very little opportunity" to refit. Buford's other pressing need was forage for his animals if he was to have them ready to assume offensive operations in a timely manner, and that meant keeping the railroad open. To that end Stoneman agreed to cooperate with Stahel, and he instructed General Gregg to send three regiments to relieve DeForest on the fourteenth, finally allowing Stahel's brigade to regroup near Warrenton Junction and relieving some of the strain on Stahel's outer line.[17]

The relationship between Joseph Hooker and George Stoneman grew increasingly strained as Hooker sought to make Stoneman the scapegoat for his own failures during the recent campaign. On May 12, Stoneman was asked to make a full accounting of his raid, as well as the current condition of his men and horses, and he was instructed to have them ready to take the field again as soon as possible. Stoneman also learned that William Averell had been relieved and that his command was now led by Stoneman's chief rival, Alfred Pleasonton. Adding to Stoneman's concern was the ongoing confusion over exactly who was responsible for the security of the railroad between Rappahannock Station and Cedar Run. In the opinion of one officer Stoneman had returned from his raid to find "that his rivals have been intriguing against him and have been trying to have him superseded in command of the [Cavalry] Corps." At the same time Pleasonton was being touted as "a man of ideas," and "the man to lead our cavalry." Stoneman not only learned that he would get no opportunity to rest his men but he was also thrown immediately on the defensive as he tried to save his position. In the end he may simply have been too tired to fight his enemies. Worn down by ailments inflamed by his recent raid, he took medical leave on May 22, never to return to the Army of the Potomac.[18]

Just before the 1st Michigan went on the scout through Loudoun County, regimental adjutant Darius Maynard expressed his feelings concerning the defeat at Chancellorsville, as the true extent of the debacle became known. "It is really depressing to feel that after such a destruction of precious human life, *nothing* is gained, but prestige to our enemies. Our papers try to make a cheerful view apparent to the public, but they hide the realities in vain, to us who know the result so perfectly. We are again a defeated army." Maynard reported that the discipline in the regiment was improving, and that when not otherwise occupied they passed their time "playing ball ... [and] riding horseback," but those distractions seem to have done little to ease his own depression. "Our division is picketing as usual. Some think we shall move farther south ... in a few days while others are positive that we remain here a month or more. I feel almost as if I didn't care particularly *what* we do now."[19]

The very nature of the war along the picket line tended to demoralize the men. It was not only ugly but it was also more personal, a more man-to-man conflict than that experienced by the foot soldiers who fought in long battle lines many yards from their opponent and where each individual soldier was soon masked by clouds of smoke and gunpowder. The personal war that these men experienced would not be easily forgotten. Instead it would smolder through another year before it exploded in the Shenandoah Valley in 1864.

As Victor Comte explained to his wife, "Our lives are in danger every moment without having the satisfaction of even defending ourselves. Those Bushwackers fire on you as they would fire on a sparrow." When caught, the guerrillas claimed, "They're revenging themselves," a rationale that the Union soldiers soon exploited. "What a fine revenge they get. When a picket-man is killed we plunder their whole farm." Comte detailed an incident in which he and three other men were ordered to "guard a so-called Union house." Later that night the sentinel on duty outside fired at "3 armed men coming toward" him. A volley of pistol fire "dispersed the Bushwackers," and then Comte went to look for the owner of the house and his two sons. "I couldn't find anyone but had recognized those three men to be the very owners of this farm which I was guarding." Speaking of those he termed bushwhackers, Comte concluded, "They are night owls who watch for their prey very patiently."[20]

Ebenezer Gould, lieutenant colonel of the 5th Michigan, also had concerns. "Everything is looking blue with us and uncertain." He was tired of being tethered to the capital, but he was more frustrated with the deteriorating command situation within the regiment. A complete breakdown within the 1st Vermont had been averted once they were transferred out of Price's brigade and the majority of the regiment moved to Warrenton Junction. The move had helped to quell much of the infighting within the ranks of the officer corps, but now Gould found himself in the midst of similar situation as the officers of the 5th Michigan took sides in the question of who should run their regiment.[21]

Colonel Freeman Norvell had, in February, forced his officers to take sides on the question of his remaining in command. Now Norvell and General Joseph Copeland turned to Gould to resolve the matter. Gould, who was personally disgusted by Norvell's behavior, tried to remain the voice of reason, but he also had his eye on Norvell's eagles. Norvell had submitted his resignation on February 25, and it was accepted on March 6, but the position had remained vacant. Copeland had requested that if Heintzelman should accept Norvell's resignation that he allow it "to take effect at some future date upon the appointment of his successor." Heintzelman thought otherwise, and the regiment had now been without a colonel for several months.[22]

By spring, Gould believed that his regiment was being victimized by the colonel of the 6th Michigan, George Gray, and he voiced a complaint very similar to that expressed by Maj. Josiah Hall against Charles Taggart during the investigation into Lieutenant Higley's conduct in March. "Gray who is an *Irish hog* will always command me and my men as he is now doing.... As we are now situated the regiments have to go on picket together and Gray of course commands. He places his officers where they have the easiest time and feeds his men & horses and lets mine suffer." Only after Gould took his complaints to a higher authority did his regiment receive adequate rations of food and forage, but in doing so, he believed he had brought "Gray & [headquarters] down on me." If there is a proper Cavalry man in Michigan," he wrote, "who is not a drunkard [then] it would be better for me that he should be appointed at once."[23]

Several days later the regiment received a visit from another contender for the colonelcy, a man who fit Gould's stated criteria perfectly and Gould resigned himself to the possibility that he would not receive the desired appointment. "There is a new applicant," Gould told his brother on April 26, "a Capt. Custar from Monroe who has been here and says that he came at the request of the governor.... I saw him and became satisfied that he had assumed from the gov's manner that all he need do was to make the request and the commission would be given. I don't know as anything now can be done." Gould was hoping that his brother Amos, an attorney and a prominent businessman in Michigan, would visit the regiment during an expected visit from the governor to help plead Gould's case. That hope lingered until early May when Gould noted, "My impression is that [the governor] intends to appoint the man from Monroe at least I fear so." But George Custer, who had garnered endorsements from Pleasonton and Hooker, as well as Stahel and Heintzelman, did not receive the appointment. The possibility that a lieutenant from West Point might fill the position over an officer from within the ranks raised the hackles of Michigan men throughout the army. The junior officers within the regiment wanted nothing to do with a West Pointer, and 33 of them signed a petition imploring the governor not to appoint an officer from the regular army who would do nothing but "recklessly" sacrifice the "men and horses" in furtherance of his career. Governor Blair listened and a disappointed Custer returned to the army. On May 9, Copeland appealed to Michigan's Adjutant General John Robertson, stating, "It is important for the good order and discipline of the Regiment that a Colonel be appointed without delay," yet still the position remained vacant. In the end, Gould, who had refused to take decisive action in February when Norvell's misconduct had endangered the command, did not receive the appointment.[24]

Among the other aspirants actively seeking the position was Lt. Col. Russell Alger, of the 6th Michigan Cavalry. Alger had moved to Michigan from Ohio while engaged in the lumber business. He had first entered the service as a junior officer in the 2nd Michigan Cavalry at the age of twenty-five. On July 1, 1862, he was wounded and captured at Boonville, Mississippi, escaping later in the day. While recovering he maintained a regular correspondence with Governor Blair, advising that he had "purchased quite a large military library and am doing all I can to advance myself in its knowledge." He generally closed his letters, by expressing his "great desire to command" a regiment from the state. On October 27, 1862, he resigned his commission in the 2nd Michigan, and accepted the lieutenant colonelcy of the 6th Michigan Cavalry.[25]

As early as January 8, 1863, Blair had expressed to Alger the possibility of his assuming the command of his former regiment, the 2nd Michigan. There was opposition from within that regiment, however, and nothing came of the idea. On May 4, Alger contacted Blair and presented his case for the colonelcy of the 5th Michigan. A month later Blair selected Alger over Custer and Gould. In his letter of thanks to the governor, Alger remarked that the officers of the regiment appeared ready to put the internal strife of the last months behind them and "assist me in bringing the reg't up to its proper standard."[26]

There may also have been a degree of tension beginning to infect the relationship between the two senior officers of the 1st Michigan. Col. Charles Town had struggled with the effects of consumption for months, and his decision to remain at Fort Scott following the Second Manassas campaign may have been directly attributed to his weakened condition. The historical record does not show that he took an active role in the leadership of the regiment again until April 1863 when unit regrouped at Fairfax Court House. His first appearance before the regiment was at a dress parade on April 17, during which he "made a great speech," steeling the men for the coming campaign. But as one of his soldiers observed he was "near gone with the consumption. He says that he knows he has but a short time to live and that he would like to die at the head of his regiment. He is a desperately brave man beyond question." His eagerness to lead his men into battle one last time may have led to the angry missive he sent to General Stahel on May 14, after learning that Peter Stagg was to command the regiment on the reconnaissance into Loudoun County. "Taking into consideration the fact that I am the Comd'g officer of this Regt. and that all the *available* men of the Regt. are ordered upon the expedition I would most respectfully inquire if I am held by my superior officers to be incompetent to take command of it when it is ordered to the *field*." Town's competence and bravery had never been questioned. Stahel's decision to let

Stagg command the reconnaissance was almost certainly made with Town's debilitating medical condition in mind, but Town's bitter response to what he saw as a personal affront was just one more piece of evidence that the many months of picket duty combined with the nature of the war that these men were fighting were taking their toll on the morale of the men.[27]

18

May 14–May 27, 1863

"These skulking Bushwackers are all we have to [deal] with at the present"

On the morning of May 14, Col. William Mann left camp with four companies of his 7th Michigan on what Sgt. Edwin Havens termed "another raid." Several days earlier, Mann had received information concerning the whereabouts "of some 12 or 14" guerrillas "whom he hoped to arrest. He sent out four separate detachments in an attempt to cordon off the area where the men were believed to be residing, before moving in to affect their capture. The plan ended in a bloody shootout, however, when the colonel observed several horses in the yard of a home, known to the men as Marsteller's Place, and he sent in four men without first reconnoitering the location or establishing a perimeter. Sgt. Asa Isham, then nineteen years of age, was in command of the men who approached the home. Isham, who worked briefly for a Michigan newspaper before the war, would become a prolific writer after the war. In addition to compiling a history of the regiment, he also authored numerous articles chronicling his military experiences, including an account of his visit to Marsteller's Place. He called the piece: "The Story of a Gunshot Wound."[1]

In his article Isham described approaching the door of the home with his comrades and being confronted by ten men who opened fire at a distance of "not more than five feet." When it was over three of the Federals, including Isham, were either dead or seriously wounded and the fourth had fled. One of the Confederates was later found hiding outside and killed, and in several accounts the owner of the residence is also listed as killed.[2]

Though several families with the last name of Marsteller lived in both Prince William and Fauquier Counties at the outbreak of the war, and in close proximity to the line of the Orange and Alexandria Railroad, the location of this incident is difficult to determine with certainty. Prioleau Henderson refers to the home several times as the Marstella home, and it was to this home that he fled following the fight at Warrenton Junction. In his account of this incident Henderson recalled that six members of the Iron Scouts were on the front stoop of the home saying their goodbyes to the owner's "five pretty daughters" when the Yankees rode up and demanded their surrender. As the women ran inside the scouts opened fire, shooting "five or six" Federals out of the saddle before fleeing themselves.[3]

Two privates, Alexander McClain, who was mortally wounded, and Aaron Kitchen, who received a gruesome wound to the mouth and neck, accompanied Isham when he approached the home. The fourth member of the party, who was accused of fleeing, was an unnamed sergeant. A Surgeon Donnelly treated McClain before he died and in his report Donnelly mentioned nothing about searching for weapons, but stated that McClain "was shot by a Rebel Guerrilla Assassin, whilst approaching a house to purchase milk having been in the habit of going there for that purpose." William Gage, another member of the regiment, later recalled that the Marsteller home had been "visited on other occasions" by men from the command.[4]

The member of the Marsteller family who was killed was unnamed but he was found hiding in some bushes near the home after the rest of the command rode up and was shot immediately. He was simply unlucky. According to Lt. Col. Allyne Litchfield, a corporal had stopped "to attend to a call of nature," when he observed the man "peeking round a tree." The trooper calmly "caught up his rifle which lay by him and fired." After arranging his clothes the corporal went over to where the man lay and observed that he had been hit in the head and killed instantly. He was unarmed and according to his sisters "had never taken up arms on either side. But," as Sergeant Havens explained, "he was found in bad company and received a punishment which perhaps should have been given to others." "There is no doubt that this house was a rendezvous for rebels," Havens concluded.[5]

William O'Brien, who arrived just after the shooting, observed that all four government horses were killed in the hail of gunfire. He recalled "there were three pretty looking girls there not only looking good but handsome as most all Virginia girls are," but they expressed no sympathy for his wounded friends, instead they "were in high glee," wishing that "more of our men lay there with them." Once their brother's body was brought in their "tune changed," according to O'Brien. Several of the men clamored for the house to be burned, "but the Colonel would not let us," O'Brien lamented. Litchfield confirmed that both he and Col. DeForest were initially in favor of burning the home, but relented "after learning all the dreadful circumstances." With no wagons available two of the wounded men rode back to camp, a trip that must have been especially excruciating for Isham, who was shot in the groin. McClain was paralyzed from the neck down by a shot in his lower back that severed his spine and he died eight days later.[6]

The Federals believed that the Southerners involved were members of the Black Horse Cavalry. The Iron Scouts generally eluded mention in Union reports and as a group may have been unknown to the Federals at this point in the war. When members of this outfit were captured they were usually referred to as belonging to Hampton's Legion. That the Wolverines thought the Black Horse was responsible may also have been based on the fact that three members of the 7th Michigan were captured on the thirteenth while "carelessly strolling about a mile from camp." Those men were paroled by a captain in the Black Horse Company and returned to camp on the fifteenth.[7]

That the men of the Black Horse were cutting a wide swath through the region is evidenced by their strike against a small supply train on the morning of the fourteenth on the Ox Road near Mount Carmel Church in southern Fairfax County. The wagons had departed from the camp of the 13th Vermont near the home of the widow Violett and were en route to the supply depot at Fairfax Station. This suggests that Captain Robert Randolph may have remained with the company after returning home to replace the horse lost at the beginning of the month and conducted operations in Fauquier County, while Lt. William Smith continued to work the line of the Occoquan. In this case it was Smith who caught the empty wagons two miles from camp, cut the horses and mules loose, mounted his eight prisoners, including two sergeants from the 13th Vermont, on the captured animals and rode back across the river. Shortly thereafter a horseman rode into the Union infantry camp and alerted them to the strike. An attempt was made to recover the prisoners but once the foot soldiers reached the point where Smith had crossed the river they realized that they had no chance of catching men on horseback and returned to camp. The immediate suspect was John Mosby, and it was not until the prisoners, who were paroled near Gainesville, returned to camp on the sixteenth that their comrades learned the identity of the real culprits. But Randolph and Smith were beginning to draw their own notice as evidenced by an order to Col. Benjamin Davis on the seventeenth, in which Stoneman referred to "bushwackers or men detached from what is known as the Black Horse Cavalry." Stoneman desired all of them "put out of the way—no matter how, so they are gotten rid of."[8]

Union officials credited both Mosby and John Mobberly with a successful dash through Charles Town on May 16 that resulted in the capture of a company of men from the 2nd Regiment Maryland Potomac Home Brigade, under the command of Lt. George Summers. In truth Capt. Roger Preston Chew, commander of the Ashby Battery Horse Artillery, led the attack, assisted by one of his lieutenants, John W. "Tuck" Carter along with Lt. Gowan Philpot, 7th Virginia Cavalry, and about 45 men. Chew hit the town about one o'clock in the morning catching the Federals asleep and within minutes he rode off with 56 prisoners and 75 horses. General Morris suspected Mobberly, but General Schenck again struck through Mobberly's name and inserted Mosby when he forwarded Morris's information, while telling Morris that he did not believe "Mosby's rebel cavalry can be in Charles Town." The following day Lieutenant Philpot, who was escorting the prisoners through Fauquier County, was attacked in turn by troopers from the 13th Pennsylvania Cavalry and the 3rd West Virginia Cavalry, and though the officer commanding the Federal detail was killed the Virginians were routed and the prisoners and horses recovered. A second Union column, which had been dispatched from Berryville, encountered a Southern force near Berry's Ferry and routed it after a vicious fight. Twenty-three gray-clad troopers were reportedly killed or captured. Several of these men were members of Mosby's command at the time.[9]

Suspected of being at several widely scattered points, John Mosby was in southern Prince William County, having left Rector's Crossroads on May 15 with 25 men intent on disrupting Hooker's supply lines along the Telegraph Road below Dumfries. Moving through New Baltimore and Greenwich the next day the men spent that evening east of the railroad, before heading for Dumfries in the morning. Mosby considered attacking a train but found all of them too heavily guarded. He was also rebuffed in his attempts to penetrate the Union lines east of the railroad, where one of his men noted that they had been fired upon by infantry. "Without having effected anything" the men spent the evening of the seventeenth at the farm owned by Moses Lynn, about seven miles west of Dumfries.[10]

On May 11, Col. John Irvin Gregg returned to his regiment and was replaced in command of the remount camp at Dumfries by Maj. Claude White, 3rd Pennsylvania Cavalry. Before leaving, Gregg had struggled to find enough healthy horses to meet the demands placed on him by Col. George Blake, his superior posted at the supply depot at Aquia Creek. On the second, Gregg had informed Blake that his horses could not march "*over four or five miles*" and were "in *very* poor condition." The following day, in response to a request for additional men, Blake could only send 60, and he told the army commander, "I have no horses fit to put a saddle on in the several commands (Blake's or Gregg's)." Several days earlier, Gregg had barely found 100 horses from the 4th New York and 6th Ohio to meet a request, and he admitted that most of his patrolling was conducted by dismounted men.[11]

On May 12, Major White attempted to capture a party of guerrillas who had robbed a courier the previous day, but the best he could do was send out 60 dismounted men in the futile attempt. He did arrest several criminals preying on his soldiers in the area and mentioned the arrest of a man he identified as Benjamin Krigler, who had been singled out by a paroled soldier "as one of the Bushwackers who captured" him and two companions earlier. By the thirteenth, White was able to resume limited mounted patrols, and under the leadership of Maj. Augustus Pruyn, 4th New York Cavalry, these patrols brought in seven prisoners over the next three days.[12]

According to White, it was his cavalry pickets who had fired on Mosby and his men on the seventeenth and not infantrymen, as the Confederates believed. After the exchange of gunfire Major White dispatched Lt. Alvah Young, 16th Pennsylvania Cavalry, with a scouting party to track the guerrillas, but he ordered Young not to engage them. Young soon confirmed "that it was 'Maj. Moseby' with about 45 men" who had engaged the pickets, and Young notified White of this by courier. White promptly sent Major Pruyn back out with 60 men to assist Young, but the courier got lost and led Pruyn eight miles in the wrong direction. Before Pruyn realized the mistake, Young had located Mosby's men camped around the Lynn farm and, contrary to orders, attacked.[13]

Mosby would later admit that he had taken a risk by allowing the men to relax at a point within the enemy's lines, but explained that he went against his better judgment as "we were tired and hungry." The men had finished dinner and were lying around in the yard with their horses unbridled when the shout went up "that the enemy was coming." In his eagerness Young had allowed his men to become "strung out for a long distance," and rather than reforming them prior to his attack he yelled for them to draw their sabres and charge. With enough warning that his men were able to bridle their horses Mosby immediately launched a counterattack. Again Southern lead bested Yankee steel and Young and several men around him went down in the first volley. After what Mosby termed "a pretty sharp hand-to-hand fight," the Yankees broke and fled, and Mosby, recognizing that fortune had smiled on him again, elected not to pursue but turned for the friendlier confines of what was becoming known as "Mosby's Confederacy." By the time Major Pruyn reached the scene the Confederates were long gone and his own horses were in no condition to press the pursuit. Though the Federals believed they had wounded five of Mosby's men and killed three of his horses the guerrillas escaped unharmed, while Young, in addition to his own serious wound, had lost two men killed, two wounded and three captured, along with the loss of six horses. Mosby's escape coupled with the casualties sustained by Young resulted in what Major White termed "a double disaster" at the Lynn farm.[14]

Two days later Mann and Litchfield both mistakenly reported that Mosby had been "whipped," and had "retreated in great haste." They believed that he had retired by way of Gainesville and Thoroughfare Gap, with his "horses completely jaded." Mann also assumed that Mosby would "likely be quiet a day or two," and he requested permission to go after him. The two officers eagerly sought their own confrontation with the guerrilla leader, and Litchfield told his wife, "I wish I could have the job of catching him.... And Moseby *can be caught.*" He also mentioned that Stuart might make an attack across the Rappahannock, but complained, "These skulking Bushwackers are all we have to [deal] with at the present." For the time being Mann's request went unanswered, but Col. Alfred Duffie was ordered by Stoneman to "clear out the bushwhackers and guerrillas in the country lying between Morrisville and Dumfries," and he was instructed "to take every horse and animal found in the district capable of being used for such purposes." He was also to seize all firearms and warn the residents that whenever "guerrillas or bushwhackers are found ... within their premises, their houses will be burned to the ground and their property confiscated."[15]

On May 14, and just as the responsibility for the protection of the Orange and Alexandria Railroad was thought to be resolved, Hooker informed General Halleck that he no longer needed the railroad to supply his army, with the exception of the cavalry that was detailed along its length. Having resumed his former position along the Rappahannock fronting Fredericksburg, Hooker would draw the bulk of his stores through the depot at Aquia and over the Richmond, Fredericksburg & Potomac Railroad. Stoneman was now able to withdraw Buford's brigade, which Hooker was still eager to recruit, and replaced it with Col. Luigi Di Cesnola's brigade, under the temporary command of Col. Eugene von Kielmansegge, of the 1st Maryland Cavalry. Yet a report from Kielmansegge dated May 18, relates the toll that the recent raid had taken on Stoneman's cavalry. From his three regiments the colonel could count only 346 men with horses healthy enough to guard the five river crossings that he was responsible for, while also dealing with the infestation of guerrillas that Buford had reported a week earlier.[16]

With General Gregg now holding the line below Cedar Run, Halleck suggested that Heintzelman withdraw his infantry from their forward positions, especially at Rappahannock Bridge, and he queried Heintzelman as to the possibility of releasing some of his infantry to reinforce Hooker. Heintzelman replied with a detailed accounting of the manner in which the 53,000 men (32,000 effectives) under his command were distributed. Eliminating those guarding the railroad between Washington and Baltimore, as well as the garrisons holding the extensive network of 56 forts and batteries along the line, Heintzelman had Stahel's cavalry division, numbering fewer than 4,000 men, and Abercrombie's 8,500 infantrymen. One of Abercrombie's brigades was holding the supply depot at Fairfax Station and supplying a labor and security force for the Orange and Alexandria Railroad. Of the remaining 7,000 men Heintzelman gave the following distribution, reflecting the distribution of the infantry as planned but not yet fully implemented: two regiments (13th and 14th Vermont) at Wolf Run Shoals, two (15th and 16th Vermont) at Union Mills, four (39th, 111th, 125th and 126th New York) at Centreville, two (25th and 27th Maine) at Chantilly and the 12th Vermont holding the railroad from Bull Run to Cedar Run. To send Abercrombie's division to Hooker would, in Heintzelman's words, mean abandoning "to the enemy all the country up to the fortifications on the south side of the Potomac," including the Orange and Alexandria Railroad, the Occoquan and Bull Run. Halleck concurred. The infantry would remain.[17]

To complete the consolidation of his brigade, General George Stannard asked Superintendent John Devereux for the use of two trains to move the 12th and 15th Vermont from their advanced positions along the railroad on the eighteenth. When the new deployment was completed the following afternoon, the 12th Vermont held Bristoe Station with five companies, with two more stationed at Catlett Station and three at Manassas Junction. Alongside the infantry at Bristoe Station was the main encampment of DeForest's cavalry, from where Silas Mason, 5th New York, told his mother, "We have to keep our horses saddled all the time so as to be ready any moment for an attack but I don't think there is over 500 Rebel cavalry this side of the Rappahannock and they couldn't whip one side of our brigade."[18]

Rumors continued to keep everyone wary. One of the latest had an unidentified party of rebels heading for Chain Bridge, one of the key spans into the capital. In his journal entry for May 20, Heintzelman stated that information had been received from a reliable source just in from Richmond that a picked force of 1,500 Southern cavalry, disguised with Union uniforms and aided by "the countersign they expect to get from a disloyal colonel," was planning on entering the capital and kidnapping Lincoln, Stanton and Secretary of State William Seward. Whatever the source of the report it led to the famous order, erroneously attributed to the threat posed by John Mosby, that the guards on the Virginia side of the bridge were to remove "a few planks" from the span at night and replace them "again in the morning." According to Lt. Col. Roswell Farnham, and others, the planks on several bridges were removed in anticipation of this raid. A Washington insider, writing after the war of the numerous rumors that plagued the capital during this period, includes the threat of an attack by Lee through Dumfries, but makes no connection linking Mosby to this threat. Heintzelman instructed his aide, Maj. Joseph Willard, on May 11, and again on the twentieth, to examine the security of the bridges in the event of "a cavalry raid," but he made no mention of Mosby in particular or guerrillas in general. Contemplating these reports one trooper concluded, "If [Stuart] will only select a cool comfortable kind of day I don't care how soon it comes.... I believe we can clean him out with the division here."[19]

Colonel Mann remained eager to prosecute the war and attempted to have his entire regiment united at Bristoe Station, where he hoped the command would remain—"at the front," where, he told his superiors, "there is work to be done." The next night, May 22, Litchfield sent out the Guard of Honor, led by lieutenants Daniel Littlefield and James Birney, in an attempt "to trap a few Guerrillas." Though they listened to men moving around during the night none came near enough for the officers to spring the trap. In the morning, however, a group of soldiers, believed to be from the Black Horse, captured a patrol from the 1st Vermont and were heading back with their captives, when they passed by the Wolverines' position, "quite well pleased with their exploits. But," as Sergeant Havens quipped, "'there is many a slip twixt the cup and lip.'"[20]

As Havens described it, the Virginians had captured two men and were chasing their horses and a third man when they ran into the Michiganders, who promptly opened fire. Taken completely by surprise the Southerners "'bout faced and started on the back track' right smart." The Yankees chased them until they came upon the Rebels who had been left behind to guard the captives near the railroad embankment. Using the embankment for cover the Yankees opened fire "at close quarters" driving off the second party of Virginians and rescuing the Green Mountain Boys. Though it was believed that three of the Rebels had been wounded, Litchfield was skeptical stating, "Our men were somewhat excited and out of truth doubtless aimed too high." Recounting the incident to his wife, Farnham termed the area "a most unpleasant place to be. There is no chance of a general fight, that will result in anything, but the men are in danger of being waylaid & murdered by guerrillas."[21]

The twenty-fourth was "hot, sultry and smoltry" according to one trooper, but the atmosphere in Washington was thick with more than just the typical summer humidity as rumors of a raid persisted. One benefit of the furor was that Secretary of War Stanton authorized Heintzelman to immediately draw a thousand fresh horses from every available source to insure that all of Stahel's dismounted men were back with their regiments as soon as possible. The reports now focused attention on the southern approach across the Occoquan, through Accotink toward the supply depots at Alexandria, and planks were removed from the bridges into the city of Alexandria as well as the nation's capital. Heintzelman took advantage of the situation to try and recoup the infantry who had been transferred from his department but his pleas were for naught. Gen. John Barnard, Heintzelman's chief engineer for the defenses ringing the capital also took the opportunity to point out the difficulties he was having completing the network of fortifications south of the city. In particular Barnard complained about the difficulty maintaining a sufficient force of paid laborers to complete the work, while thousands of contrabands were kept busy toiling over less vital tasks. According to Litchfield this complaint was remedied immediately "and contrabands without number were at once set to work on the defenses of Washington."[22]

Julia Wheelock was a nurse attending to the sick and wounded in both Alexandria and Fairfax Court House. She along with several other civilians had toured the battlefield at Chantilly on the twenty-first of May but General Abercrombie refused their request to tour the Bull Run fields, as that "country was overrun with guerrillas." Returning to Alexandria amidst this latest scare she admitted, "I hardly knew the place.... New lines of fortifications had been thrown up, the streets stockaded, and cannon were even placed in position."[23]

The thought that Stuart was going to launch a major raid toward the capital or points farther north persisted for weeks, fueled in large measure by the concentration of his cavalry in Culpeper County. Stuart had sent word to Grumble Jones on the twenty-third to return from the Shenandoah Valley and rejoin the cavalry division in Culpeper, and it was only three days later that Union reports noted the Southern concentration between Culpeper Court House and Brandy Station.[24]

Heintzelman asked Stahel for an assessment of his division's ability to respond to a raid, particularly a foray from the south across the Occoquan. Stahel's response reflects the effectiveness of Mosby's campaign to strike at as many points along the Union picket line as possible. On the twenty-third Mosby was said to have "established pickets" between Warrenton Junction and Catlett Station, a point from which he could threaten the railroad. Three days later, and miles to the northeast, his men launched two harassing attacks against the pickets of the 6th Michigan Cavalry on Lawyer's Road.[25]

In his response Stahel did his best to sound confident that his men could handle any threat from Mosby or Stuart, but there is a hint of weariness reflected in his letter, suggesting that Stahel now fully realized the difficulty of his position, as he attempted to counter each threat, while still responding effectively to the many demands made against his division. Clearly, Stahel felt that he was now weakest along the line of the Occoquan, remarking that the best that he could hope for was to alert the officers in Alexandria and Washington in the event the enemy pressed an attack from that direction. Having ceded much of the responsibility for this region to the Army of the Potomac, he was attempting to cover Prince William County by means of "two strong scouting parties." He was more confident of resisting an attack from the west through Fairfax County, but the Orange and Alexandria Railroad remained a point of contention.[26]

Over the last few days while both Halleck and Stanton attempted to insure that the troops defending Washington were fully prepared to resist an attack, they had also attempted to erase any further possibility of confusion concerning responsibility for the protection of the railroad, and to free up as much of Stahel's division as possible for a counterstroke in the event that a raid actually materialized. Brig. Gen. Alfred Pleasonton, now in command of the cavalry corps, told Brig. Gen. David Gregg, on the twenty-fourth, that he was responsible for the security of the line. The wording of Pleasonton's order, however, remained rather ambiguous as to the point at which Gregg's responsibility terminated and Stahel's began. Instructed to also recoup his division as quickly as possible, Gregg explained the nature of the problems that confronted him, including the fact that his division, reduced to less than 2,000 effectives, was now holding a line of almost 40 miles long, over which they were "drawn out like a thread." Several of his regiments had not yet rejoined the command following Stoneman's raid, and attempts to supply his men were haphazard at best, depending upon exactly where the regiments were stationed. He had less than 1,000 men posted along the railroad between Rappahannock Station and Cedar Run, and it was these men who were his greatest concern. The constant picket and patrol duty took a continuing toll on his horses and, in the face of orders otherwise, he requested that he be relieved of the responsibility for the railroad, at least until his men could draw needed supplies and equipment and until their horses were again serviceable. Unable to comply, Pleasonton sent Averell's former command, now led by Colonel Duffie to assist Gregg, while Buford, who still needed 1,400 remounts, was ordered to Dumfries to deal with the guerrilla problem in that area.[27]

But by the twenty-seventh when Stahel responded to his superiors, Heintzelman as well as both Hooker and Pleasonton must have thought the maddening issue of the railroad resolved but Stahel saw it otherwise. Clearly the onus for an adequate response in the event of an attack would fall upon Stahel's shoulders, and as both Heintzelman and Barnard had done he took advantage of the situation to try and improve his own position. It was not that Stahel's men were ill equipped and in need of fresh horses as were Gregg's men, but, like Gregg, his men were "so scattered that it would be difficult ... to concentrate them in due time where circumstances might require a strong force." And though he claimed he was not seeking "to shorten [his] line," he did request that Pleasonton assume more responsibility for the area between the Rappahannock and the Occoquan. Still, the Hungarian remained confident that his division was "in perfect readiness," and that "no sudden surprise nor any disaster can befall them."[28]

By May 27, the residents of Washington were said to be "very feverish" over the threatened raid. Hooker's intelligence bureau was reporting that Stuart now had three brigades, led by Fitz Lee, Rooney Lee and Wade Hampton, totaling almost 5,000 sabers between Culpeper Court House and Kelly's Ford. That afternoon Colonel Mann advised that one of his patrols, led by Lt. Colonel Litchfield, had moved through the Warrenton area and confirmed a "concentration of large force at Culpeper & towards Waterloo for speedy raid." Litchfield had set out near midnight to scout the terrain through Thoroughfare Gap toward Warrenton and the Rappahannock. Lt. Col. Addison Preston led a second column from the 1st Vermont Cavalry. Near Salem, Litchfield divided his force of 150 men, sending two companies to link up with Preston at White Plains. Continuing with the remainder of his detachment through Salem a flurry of shots rang out as the men pursued a handful of Confederates through the town. Though his men claimed to have been fired on from one of the homes, Litchfield was dubious, and when the troopers were unable to determine exactly from which building the shots emanated he was satisfied to warn the residents that in the event of a similar occurrence he "would lay the whole town in ashes." If Litchfield doubted from where the shots had come from Sergeant Havens did not. The building, in his view, "proved to be a school house," occupied by about fifteen "scholars" and a female instructor who "evidently held the 'Yankees' in great detestation as she seemed very anxious to prove by the many sarcastic remarks she made while submitting to the searching of her house which was made much more severe than it might have been." Both Havens and William O'Brien reported that an election was to be held in the town that day, but, O'Brien quipped, "we put a stop to it, our votes carried the election." Litchfield did learn "that Moseby had passed through the day before with a piece of artillery which the tracks in the road leading to the town fully confirmed." though "only 3 or 4 men were with the piece" at the time.[29]

Litchfield then pressed on for White Plains, where he met Preston. While the two officers conferred the men adjusted their saddles, tightened their girths and allowed their horses a quick feed. This interlude came to an end, however, when Confederates showed themselves near the base of a mountain just out of rifle range. Realizing that they needed to get through Thoroughfare Gap, which was currently held by an advance detail of only 25 men, led by Capt. Daniel Darling, 7th Michigan, the Federals mounted quickly and made for the narrow pass. As the first squadron galloped past Darling's men they were fired upon by an unseen foe scattered amongst the rocks ahead. Preston was in the lead and sent word for Litchfield to come up with a contingent of dismounted men armed with carbines, as none of his men had any. Litchfield sent 75 men scrambling over "the rocky bluffs with alacrity and for a little time there was music," he told his wife. But he was also disconcerted by the fact that they were "walled in by mountains this being one of those huge cuts of nature just wide enough for a [railroad], a stream and a road ... a perfect hiding place and strong hold for an enemy."

Sergeant Havens was not one of the men selected by Litchfield but minutes after the skirmishers advanced Havens handed the reins of his horse to another trooper, "borrowed a carbine and set forward at 'double quick.'" Joining his comrades, Havens and a dozen others were told to advance over Pond Mountain on the south side of the gap. After crossing Broad Run the men splashed up the far bank with their "boots full of water." They reached the top of the ridge without encountering any opposition, though gunfire echoed below them throughout their ascent. As he came over the top of the ridge, Havens learned that "the rebs had retreated and I hadn't seen them." Down below, Preston ordered a saber charge against the fleeing rebels, resulting in the capture of a man described as "a Mexican ... who had recently joined Moseby." According to Havens he was a former member of the 1st Georgia Cavalry and had been an artillerist in the opening engagement at Fort Sumter. The prisoner admitted that 40 men had contested the Union advance, all of them being recent additions to Mosby's command. According to Mann's report the Confederates lost two men killed, and three wounded, one mortally in addition to the prisoner. Two of Captain Darling's men were captured, but according to William O'Brien, one of the two men escaped after knocking his guard "from his horse with an old sabre." Officially Mann listed only two horses killed and two injured. After riding about 60 miles the Federals returned to their encampment that evening, with a total of six prisoners and 15 captured horses.[30]

Litchfield viewed the reconnaissance as one "of considerable magnitude." Not only had it given many of his Wolverines their first taste of combat but they also confirmed that

Stuart was concentrating his forces near the Rappahannock. Of more immediate importance to Litchfield, however, was the verification that Mosby had received a cannon. This had been rumored in the Union camps for several weeks, and it had been followed by reports that the guerrilla chief had been reinforced with 100 "picked men from Stuart's command," along with two staff officers sent to consult with Mosby. How the earliest report of the cannon arose is unknown, as Mosby did not officially request the "mountain howitzer" until May 19. "I think I could use it with great effect, especially on the railroad trains," he told his superior. Not only had the Federals now confirmed that Mosby had indeed received a cannon, but the information derived from the Confederate prisoner also confirmed that he had received reinforcements, though not in the numbers originally reported, and the intelligence from the prisoner appears to verify the report that Stuart sent two staff officers to accompany the cannon and men up from the south.[31]

According to the prisoner, the men who had contested the pass "belonged to Capt. Farleigh's command." Days earlier, on May 22, Maj. Bradford Hoskins noted in his diary the arrival in Mosby's camp of "thirty men of Hampton's Legion ... under Capt. Farley." These accounts suggest that the two officers sent by Stuart were Capt. William Downs Farley and his younger brother Lt. Henry Saxon Farley. William "Will" Farley was one of Stuart's most trusted and daring scouts, who also served as a volunteer aide-de-camp with the honorary rather than official rank of captain. He and his brother were from South Carolina, and while much remains unknown about both men it is certain that the elder brother had traveled to South Carolina in the spring of 1863, thus missing the Chancellorsville campaign. Exactly when he left and returned is also unknown, but he almost certainly rejoined the army in the company of his younger brother. Henry had attended West Point but resigned in November 1860. Following the outbreak of hostilities he held commissions in both the infantry and artillery, and, as the prisoner mentioned, he had been attached to one of the batteries that had fired on Fort Sumter. Henry officially resigned his commission in the artillery on May 30, 1863, and is known to have been on temporary duty with Stuart less than a month later. While Fount Beattie is credited with escorting the gun to Mosby and Sam Chapman is said to have trained the men who later manned Mosby's cannon, it seems reasonable that Stuart would have sent an artillerist to accompany the gun. That both officers along with the reinforcements were from South Carolina further confirms their identity. How long either man stayed with Mosby is unclear, though the lack of any further mention in contemporary accounts suggests that their stay was brief.[32]

19

May 28–May 30, 1863

"Grand Rebel Raid expected"

Union patrols scouted possible avenues of Southern approach through Stafford County, as well as routes through Aldie and Leesburg. None of them found any evidence that a raid was underway; though the authorities remained convinced that Stuart's concentration in Culpeper County signaled an advance in the near future. Even the engineers for the Orange and Alexandria Railroad were on the alert, with one log entry for May 27 stating, "Grand Rebel Raid expected today." Orders were issued that "no bodies of troops however small [were] to pass within our lines without being stopped and examined by an officer. "This" was an attempt "to prevent rebels in our uniforms and with the countersign from passing in."[1]

Though the patrols found little evidence to support the persistent rumors in the region east of the Rappahannock, reports of Confederate activity across the river continued to heighten concern with Halleck, Hooker and Heintzelman. On May 28 General David Gregg reported that the Southern cavalry pickets had been relieved during the evening by infantry, suggesting that the raid was now imminent, and he warned his superiors that his diminished force along the river would "not be able to offer strong resistance" unless it was supported. Gregg's warning immediately caught the attention of General Joseph Hooker. In an attempt to impede a rapid advance across the river Gregg was ordered to destroy the bridge at Rappahannock Station as soon as possible. Pleasonton then instructed John Buford to advance his brigade to Bealeton, to take command of all troops in the area and to "drive the rebel scouts and parties in the neighborhood of Warrenton and Sulphur Springs across the Rappahannock." Hooker also detailed Maj. Gen. George Meade to bolster the cavalry pickets along the river with infantrymen from his Fifth Corps.[2]

One day earlier Pleasonton had explained in detail the depleted condition of his command, and he had advised Hooker that Gregg's division was down to fewer than 2,000 serviceable horses and that Buford counted just over 800 serviceable horses for a brigade numbering 2,400 men. By Pleasonton's tabulation, the effective strength of the entire corps was only one-third of what it had been in March. In an attempt to partially alleviate this shortfall Col. Judson Kilpatrick, who had remained in the Northern Neck region following Stoneman's raid, was ordered to rejoin the army immediately, following a route "through one of the richest portions of Virginia," from which he was expected to seize every horse possible.[3]

In a follow-up directive to Buford, Pleasonton instructed that he was to "drive the enemy out of his camp near Culpeper and across the Rapidan, destroying the bridge at that point." Buford was staggered. Not only was he to launch an attack across the Rappahannock with his under strength brigade, but he was expected to drive at least three Southern brigades, if not the entire division, across the Rapidan River, and then press his advance toward the Blue Ridge in an attempt "to ascertain the true object" of the Southern concentration. "I am at a loss to know how to proceed," he responded. Buford was all soldier, however, and after again mentioning his lack of forage and rations, he only requested clarification as to where he was to return once his mission was over. Pleasonton offered little by way of further direction in his reply, telling Buford, "You will not return to Dumfries," and by reiterating his previous instructions, to which Buford replied simply, "I'll do my best." Buford then dashed off a telegram to the quartermaster, requesting 5,000 horseshoes to his own specifications. Alluding to the difficult task before him, Buford closed by stating, "I am trying to get in a fix to make a mark."[4]

In the short term Pleasonton had few options with which to counter the threat of a raid. Hooker's cavalry was stretched as thin as Stahel's, and, like Stahel he seized this threat to the capital as an opportunity to bolster his force. Not only did he make a second request that Stahel be directed to scout toward the Shenandoah Valley, but he also boasted to the Secretary of War that his cavalry would "pitch into [Stuart] in his camps ... if General Stahel's cavalry were with me for a few days." Stanton did not deny his request out of hand but forwarded it to Halleck, Heintzelman and Lincoln. Halleck pointed out that Hooker could not ask on one hand that Stahel be sent into the Shenandoah Valley while claiming at the same time that he would use him to make an attack against Stuart in Culpeper County. Further, the presence of Meade's infantry along the Rappahannock meant that Hooker would again have to rely upon the Orange and Alexandria Railroad to supply the men. This would curtail Stahel's ability to assist Pleasonton as his men were charged with the security of the track. Most important, Halleck was not prepared to relinquish the only mounted force assigned to the protection of the capital. "If it be removed," Halleck told Stanton, "there will be no force in front to give notice of enemy's raids on Alexandria or Washington." Hooker's request was denied.[5]

Hooker must have also sent an inquiry directly to Stahel, who detailed by way of reply the disposition of his command, stating that DeForest's small brigade was now guarding the railroad from Kettle Run to Bristoe Station, Copeland's command held the line between the Little River Turnpike and the Potomac River and Price was in reserve at Fairfax Court House. Stahel also had detachments scattered from the Occoquan to the Shenandoah Valley, further depleting his overall effectiveness.[6]

In an attempt to stave off Hooker's efforts to steal his division away from Heintzelman, the Hungarian may have gone directly to the press. On May 28, an editorial was printed in the New York *Tribune* concerning Stahel's division. It had been written three days earlier, the very day that Hooker was in Washington making a direct appeal for reinforcements. The writer, who referred to Mosby's command as no more annoying than "the everlasting singing and occasional stinging of a [mosquito]," petitioned officials in the administration as well as the military to "bring a little plain practical common sense" to the problem. Rather than tying Stahel's cavalry to picket lines or wearing out horseflesh on "daily and nightly scouting parties," they should be allowed to clear "the whole region of everybody capable of bearing arms." The writer ridiculed the administration for a policy that released "the bushwackers, picket-shooters, and horse-thieves, who are sent in as prisoners." As an alternative the correspondent appealed for the picket lines to be abandoned and that Stahel's force be "united and left free to act" against the "farmers and citizens and the few soldiers [who] band themselves together to ride over the country plundering and killing." The writer declared, "Gen. Stahel would soon rid the country of Mosby and his gang, not by chasing them ... but by killing or capturing them."[7]

The Union pickets were increasingly on edge. An unknown band of guerrillas had recently made a night attack against a picket post manned by troopers from the 5th Michigan. In the confusion, the Wolverines had shot at some of their own men as they chased the guerrillas through the woods, leading one soldier to declare, "They shoot at men verry careless down here. A fellow ain't safe any where with so many men with loaded rifles scattered all threw the woods. I shall be glad when I get to a civilized Country once more."[8]

On May 28 Maj. Luther Trowbridge, 5th Michigan, explained another incident of near fratricide in the Michigan Brigade. Trowbridge had been asked to clarify why a company from the 6th Michigan Cavalry, had been allowed to pass through his picket line in violation of the standing order that no body of mounted troops be allowed to enter the lines without a thorough examination. The major explained that his men had in fact challenged the company officer, Capt. Peter Weber, twice but that neither Weber nor any of the men at the head of the column had heard the command over the noise created by the horses and equipment. Emphasizing the tense situation along the lines Trowbridge found that his troopers should have fired on Weber as the orders instructed, while also holding Weber at fault for not stopping at the picket line "whether ordered to do so or not." Concluding his report Trowbridge stated, "In passing through the lines at so great a distance from any vidette, without halting, he subjected his command to a fire which he would have received, had the vidette done his duty."[9]

After a midnight summons to Stanton's office to discuss Hooker's plea for Stahel's cavalry, Heintzelman returned to his headquarters on the morning of the twenty-ninth to coordinate his cavalry's efforts to uncover Stuart's plans while continuing to secure the railroad and the approaches to the capital. Before long he was en route to Halleck's headquarters with the latest reports from Stahel so that the two men could compare them with the intelligence coming in from Hooker.[10]

Stahel reiterated that there was no enemy cavalry east of the Blue Ridge, but he updated his superiors on the recent skirmish at Thoroughfare Gap and the intelligence that his men had uncovered concerning the reinforcements sent to Mosby. He also reported that Mosby had probed his lines near Dranesville and along the Little River Turnpike earlier in the week. Stahel's scouts were certain that Mosby intended to make another larger raid within a few days. As to a possible raid by Stuart, Stahel had learned that Dr. Jesse Ewell (brother of Confederate general Richard Ewell) was "making arrangements for the pasture of a large number of horses," at his rather secluded property along Bull Run Mountain, giving some credence to local "conversation that Stuart is to be this side of the Blue Ridge within a week." In response Halleck warned the cavalryman "to be exceedingly vigilant against raids to cut the Orange and Alexandria Railroad and into Alexandria. If made they will be quick and rapid."[11]

That evening the enemy probed the picket line of the 7th Michigan at Bristoe Station. Sergeant Havens was posting the relief force about eight o'clock when the men at a nearby post fired two shots. He responded immediately and was informed that two men had ridden past and failed to respond when challenged by the pickets. Soon several more shots were heard farther down the line. As Havens questioned each man it was clear that two men on horseback had probed each of the three posts by riding "up quite slowly and deliberately but not halting when ordered." When one of the intruders attempted to fire his revolver at Pvt. Henry Allen it failed to discharge, but when Allen fired back he heard a cry of "O God," as the man "tumbled out of his saddle." The gunfire caused Allen's horse to bolt and by the time he returned to the scene the Rebels were fleeing on one horse, with the wounded man draped across the saddle. The camp was kept awake throughout the night, and about midnight Havens led a patrol of eight men along the railroad toward Warrenton Junction "but discovered nothing."[12]

On May 29 Mosby rendezvoused with "about forty men" and what he called "my little gun," at a farm four miles outside of Middleburg with the sole intention of striking the Orange and Alexandria Railroad. He was by now intimately aware of the number of Union troops guarding the line and judged the attempt "not only hazardous but foolhardy." After stopping for their evening meal near Greenwich the men continued another couple of miles in the direction of the railroad, possibly spending the night near the Marsteller home. Mosby did not say whether he sent any men to probe the Union picket posts that night but it seems likely that the consummate scout would have done so. Sam Chapman's comment that the "railroad was so well guarded," and the patrols so active, "that the track was hard to get to," suggests that it was Mosby's men who exchanged shots with the Union pickets that night.[13]

About 7 A.M., Saturday, May 30, a southbound supply train, numbering ten cars, pulled out of Alexandria, carrying supplies and forage for the troops posted along the line below Manassas Junction with a termination point at Bealeton Station. An engineer by the name of Sheafer was in the cab of his engine, the Fred Leach. The train picked up a security detail of 25 men and one officer at Union Mills, before continuing south. Men from the 12th and 15th Vermont generally furnished these details, and on this morning the troops came from Companies F and G, 15th Vermont, led by Lt. Eldin Hartshorn.[14]

Mosby later wrote that he was awakened by the sound of reveille in the nearby Union camps, and that he quickly moved his men, by way of a narrow trail through the woods to "within a hundred yards of the railroad." He assigned men to cut the telegraph wire, while others pulled the spikes anchoring a section of rail so that an oncoming train would be thrown from the tracks near his location. The accounts vary as to whether the rail was removed entirely, moved just enough to damage the train or loosened and then left in place to be removed at the last instant by means of an attached wire. Sam Chapman, a former artillerist with the Dixie Artillery, and "one of the few men in the Command who knew the difference between a Howitzer and a saw-log" was in charge of the 12-pound howitzer.[15]

According to Sergeant Havens, the train reached his location near Bristoe at nine-thirty, dropping off mail and rations for the men as well as forage for the horses before resuming the trip to Bealeton at ten o'clock. Havens believed the train had only proceeded another two and a half miles, reaching the area where he had turned his patrol around earlier that morning, when he heard the first round fired by Chapman. Lt. Colonel Litchfield stated that the train was just five minutes beyond the station when he "heard the report of a cannon." His statement that Mosby had taken possession of a cannon had apparently been met with skepticism by some of his fellow officers, who deemed the information "a hoax," but Litchfield now felt vindicated, exclaiming, "There says I is my gun firing into a train." In his report of the affair, written the next day, General Stannard placed the derailment at "9:40 A.M.... two miles this side of Catlett Station where the woods come down close to the railroad."[16]

Most Union accounts state that a crewmember in the locomotive saw the rail being pulled out of position by means of an attached wire and that the engineer attempted to stop the train, but was unable to do so in time as it was on a downgrade. Mosby said only that the "locomotive glided from the track," while Chapman credits the engineer with stopping the train before it derailed. Scott Laughlin, who was one of the guards on the train, does not state either way, but intimated that the engineer's version was designed to put his own conduct in the best light possible while denigrating the actions of the guards.[17]

Lt. Eldin Hartshorn, 15th Vermont Infantry. Lieutenant Hartshorn was in command of the troops guarding the train that was derailed by John Mosby near Catlett Station. After the regiment was mustered out of service, Hartshorn enlisted in the 17th Vermont Infantry and quickly earned a commission. Following the war he entered politics in Iowa and served as governor of the state (courtesy Vermont Historical Society).

Chapman recalled that once the train came to a stop the guards fired "one ineffectual volley," before he fired a round that scattered them. The Vermonters were certain their volley killed one man but in truth the only casualty was a horse. It was then that Chapman fired what the Yankees believed was "grape & canister" at them, and Lieutenant Hartshorn reportedly gave the order for his men to retire. Scott Laughlin, who stated that all of the negative reports concerning the behavior of the guards emanated from the engineer, declared angrily, "he did not stay long enough to know how the guard did act." Still, Laughlin was certain "we could [not] have saved the train, for they could easily set it on fire with shells in spite of us." Others disagreed; including a soldier in the 12th Vermont who concluded that the train could have been saved if Hartshorn "had showed fight." Edwin Hall, 15th Vermont, stated that Hartshorn ordered his men to fix bayonets after their ragged volley, but that the sight of the guerrillas bearing down on them on horseback convinced the officer that a stand would be fruitless. "The Lieut not being a fighting man ... told them to run and save themselves if they could which I recon they did without further orders." The men of the 12th saved some of their scorn for their chaplain who had been on the train and made such good "use of his legs," that "we have not heard from him sense," or as another crowed, "the best joke of all was that our chaplain ... is probably in the hands of the cavalry as a straggler. So we shall not have any preaching today." A bitter Laughlin thought, "It would have pleased a great many very much" if some of the guards had been killed, but the only casualties were a newsboy and the fireman. An employee of the railroad further disparaged the members of the guard, writing in a log, "the guard *15th Vermont* run in every direction wonderfully demoralized and not only disgraced themselves — but the whole regt."[18]

After speaking with the crew of the train and Henry Rollo, the newsboy, Stannard determined that Mosby had two field pieces. Rollo had broken his leg jumping from the train and was unable to escape. Hiding in some undergrowth alongside the tracks he believed that Mosby had "two iron field pieces in the woods." His statement along with a description of the rate of fire from Chapman's gun led to the erroneous belief that the Confederates used two cannon. "From the character of the discharges, two coming in quick succession followed by two more after a short interval it was inferred that the artillery consisted of two field pieces." Stannard, who wrote his initial report before he spoke with any of the guards, reported that once the train derailed his soldiers "fired upon three or four rebels in the edge of the woods, who constituted the only hostile force then visible. A number of carbine or revolver shots were returned from the woods indicating the presence of a rebel force of some

Catlett Station, along the Orange & Alexandria Railroad. Scene of a famous raid by Jeb Stuart in August 1862, it was near here that John Mosby derailed a train on May 30, 1863 (Library of Congress).

size." Stannard believed the guard fled "after two discharges of shell or grape, which passed through some of the cars," but that none of the rebels made any attempt "to pursue or capture the guard or any of the persons on the train, all of whom escaped to the woods uninjured."[19]

In November 1862, Union general Herman Haupt had issued a memorandum explaining that the most "expeditious mode of ... rendering locomotive engines useless to an enemy ... would be to fire a cannon-ball through the boiler." With a hint of humor he continued, "Cars are readily destroyed by burning. On this subject no instructions are necessary." The train that Mosby had just derailed was hauling fresh fruit and shad, along with several sacks of U.S. Mail as well as miscellaneous sutler's stores, in addition to forage. While their comrades rushed from cover to loot the cars, Sam Chapman ordered his gunners to roll the howitzer forward "to within thirty feet of" the locomotive, with the intention of putting a round through the boiler. Chapman admitted that he did this out of "ignorance of the destructive capacity of steam," and it was not until Richard Montjoy yelled that they would "all be scalded to death," that the gun was moved back to a safer position before it was discharged. Even at 75 yards Chapman declared, "such a noise and spray of steam never enveloped us before." Mosby then ordered his men to retire. Stannard, again apparently referring to the testimony of the newsboy, stated that once the guard fled "a party of twenty mounted rebels, came to the train, set the cars on fire, let the steam out of the engine and after a short stay departed." Stannard makes no mention of Chapman firing into the boiler and concludes his report by stating that while the train was destroyed, "the engine [was] not badly damaged," an assessment at odds with Mosby's and Chapman's accounts.[20]

In the cavalry camps the 5th New York was formed in line within three minutes of the initial discharge, and set out one minute later "across the railroad track, making a circuit to the right, in order to get in the rear of the enemy." Lt. Col. Addison Preston reported that he was en route to the scene within ten minutes with 125 men of the 1st Vermont. Litchfield timed the response at five minutes, with Col. William Mann in overall command as the ranking officer, though the detachment from the 7th Michigan was the smallest of those involved and draws no notice in the accounts. Ten men from the picket line were sent directly to the scene but arrived too late, suggesting the speed with which Mosby carried out the attack. Though his "blood boiled to be in it," Litchfield was told to "double the picket and hold the camp against all h-ll." Stahel stated that 170 men responded to the raid in total, the vast majority from the 1st Vermont. Clearly it was not an entire brigade as Mosby later estimated, though it may have appeared so as he counted the flags of the several regiments arrayed against him later that morning. What is certain is that Preston's Vermonters alone outnumbered the Rebels three to one. Mann and his Wolverines aside this would be a fight between Mosby and his two primary antagonists, the 1st Vermont and the 5th New York. Stannard reported that one of the cavalry detachments encountered the guards and train employees "about a mile from the scene." The troopers secured the men and brought them back, but "whether this was to secure their assistance, or as an arrest for misconduct I am unable to learn."[21]

Mann led his party directly to the scene of the attack, which he reached in about thirty minutes. There "with some difficulty" they picked up the retreat route coursing through "thick pine woods," and followed it for three miles. The men from the 5th New York, led by Capt. Abram Hasbrouck, raced across country through fields and woods as they sought a point of advantage in the rear of the retreating foe. Shortly after they entered "a narrow rocky road where three horses could scarcely walk abreast," several of their flankers came back with the warning that the enemy was making a stand with the cannon to their left front. Hasbrouck immediately ordered the men to tear down the fences bordering the lane, thus allowing them some room to maneuver when a shell landed in their midst killing Lt. Frazier Boutelle's horse. Union sergeant John Jackson confirmed Mosby's opinion that this shell "scattered" the New Yorkers before Chapman could put a second round into their midst. Hasbrouck reformed the men in the woods a mile to the rear, allowing Mosby to continue his retreat. To cover his withdrawal Mosby ordered James Foster and a handful of men to make a mock charge in the direction of the retreating Yankees, recalling him once the main body was back on the road.[22]

Hasbrouck's indecision angered at least two of the men with him, Lt. Elmer Barker, 5th New York, and Lt. Daniel Littlefield, 7th Michigan, who accompanied Hasbrouck as a guide at Mann's direction. Littlefield swore angrily when Hasbrouck stopped to tear down the fences rather than make an immediate attack and he "swore worse" when the shell landed in their midst. Barker, who later admitted, "I was nothing but a boy anxious for a fight," confessed to superceding Hasbrouck once the men had reformed by ordering, "By fours from the right, trot, march," and set off after the guerrillas with about 30 men following in his wake.[23]

Barker took off at a dead run following a trail of items looted from the train for three or four miles and his men "were well strung out when" they collided with Mosby's rear guard blocking the trail on the far side of a tight bend in the road concealed in a belt of timber. It was such a close affair that Barker and two enlisted men riding alongside were unable to halt and ran right into the Southern ranks. The rear-guard included, by Barker's count, Mosby, British soldier of fortune Bradford Hoskins and three other men. Mosby recalled that this fight took place on more open ground from which he was able to observe the enemy closing in upon him from several directions, and that he had six men by his side as the Yankees rode into his ranks, sparking "a fierce hand-to-hand fight." At the first fire Cpl. Joseph Worster and Pvt. George Jenkins, were wounded at Barker's side. Worster went down when his horse was killed and a pistol ball struck a folding knife in his pocket and drove it into his thigh. According to Sergeant Jackson, who was farther back in the Union column, it was Jenkins who mortally wounded Hoskins. Hoskins confronted Jenkins with his saber and demanded he surrender. Jenkins, who had already been shot in the left arm, replied that he "'couldn't see the point'" and shot Hoskins. As Mosby recalled the event Jenkins was shot in the left arm immediately after his duel with Hoskins. The entire affair lasted only a few seconds but those seconds seemed like "hours" to Barker who was now the only able-bodied man confronting the guerrillas. Having emptied his revolver Barker was barely fending them off with his saber when help arrived, and the two sides broke contact.[24]

Mosby now sent James Foster ahead with orders for Chapman to make a stand at the home of Warren Fitzhugh, near the village of Greenwich. Sergeant Jackson described it as "a strong position up a narrow, rocky lane, quite steep to where the cannon was planted," on "a level plateau." As the Yankees again rode into view, Chapman knew that this was to be the last stand on what had been a long, trying day for the men of both sides. When Barker bellowed, "Will you go with me and take that gun," Jackson recalled that some gripped their reins tighter and replied "We will," while others "faltered and fell back," but Jackson couldn't fault them, terming the job at hand, "no desirable undertaking." Along the hill crest Chapman found the same hesitation among some of the newer men in his own ranks. As had happened in other raids there were men who rode only for the profit, but as

Mosby's stalwarts steeled themselves for the final blow, Chapman and his gunners drew their pistols and "threatened" the laggards until they fell in alongside the veterans.[25]

Years later Barker described making only one charge against the position, and thought that he was within 20 feet of the muzzle when Richard Montjoy yanked the lanyard discharging a blast of canister that killed three men and wounded several others. Two of the balls struck Barker in the left thigh, another ripped a stirrup off his saddle and several more struck his horse, which still managed to carry Barker to safety. "Repulsed ... but ... not disheartened," the survivors fell back just as Preston and Mann reached the scene. Mosby recalled a more sustained confrontation in which successive charges were made by both sides while Chapman's howitzer continued to throw lead in the Yankee ranks until the Vermonters arrived. Mann ordered Preston to launch an attack from the front and right flank, forcing the Confederates to divide their fire. Lieutenant John Hazelton and Sgt. Daniel Hill led men from two companies in the main attack back up the narrow lane, while Preston attacked from the Rebel's flank. The bloody melee around the howitzer was over in minutes as Chapman fired his last round into a horse at the head of the column, "which passed lengthwise through his body before bursting." Moments later Mosby received a saber blow across the shoulder "that nearly knocked" him out of the saddle. He dispatched his assailant with a pistol shot and raced for safety. Those who were still able followed Mosby, with the Yankees in pursuit as far as their tired horses would take them. Chapman and Montjoy found that their horses had run off, and, the two men stuck by the gun to the last. Chapman was shot in the thigh and Montjoy captured, but their gallantry drew the admiration of most of their captors, including Preston, who highlighted Chapman's heroics in his report. Even Litchfield, who was not present, singled out the two "gunners who fought well till they were knocked down." Yet as the smoke started to dissipate a wounded trooper confronted Chapman and threatened to shoot him, claiming that Chapman had shot him in the closing minutes of the fight. Restrained by his comrades, the unidentified bluecoat later sought out Chapman and apologized for his behavior, admitting, "I would not have talked so but I was confounded mad." Leading the men from Vermont in the final charge were bothers Job and Stephan Corey. In the confused fighting around the gun Job was killed and Stephan fired the shot that knocked Chapman out of the fight.[26]

Stahel reported a loss of four men killed and fifteen wounded, with at least three men killed and five wounded in the 5th New York and one killed and six wounded in the 1st Vermont. Havens mentioned that one man in the 7th Michigan was slightly wounded by a spent ball in the knee. A second member of the regiment, having charged past the gun, was shot in the leg and captured. He was later paroled by Lt. William Smith, 4th Virginia Cavalry, and walked 15 miles back to camp where the bullet was removed. Though admitting that he had been "routed," Mosby did not dwell on his losses. Union accounts list as many as six killed, twenty wounded and ten captured. The names of seven prisoners were listed in the Northern papers, while the wounded were paroled on the field. Bradford Hoskins died of his wounds during the early hours of June first. Three days after the fight, Mann informed his superiors that scouts from Buford's command had returned to the scene, possibly on the thirty-first, and "found & buried three more rebel dead. This makes their loss ... to have been six killed instead of one as reported by me." Most of these men remain unidentified.[27]

The fight near Greenwich was the second time in a month that these troopers had seen the backs of Mosby and his men as they fled a contested field, and it gave the Yankees reason to believe they had turned a corner in their war with the guerrillas. The victory, which helped to ease the lingering sting of previous defeats, must have been especially satisfying for the men of the 1st Vermont "Moseby is about used up he has been whipped every time of late," Litchfield boasted. Sergeant Havens, who had doubted Mann's capacity for leadership months earlier, now declared, "We have some gallant and noble officers as ever left the state and they have men upon whom they can depend to follow where they may lead. Col. Mann is in command ... and those who saw him ... say that fear has no place in his mind." The young colonel enjoyed the moment with his men, crowing to his superiors, "Whipped Mosby like the devil. Took his artillery," which he immediately referred to as "our cannon." Thinking that he could not state the case any better Stahel purloined Mann's comments and repeated them in his dispatch to Heintzelman. The press credited the mounted force in general, stating it "has shown its mettle in various parts of the country, and in no one instance has it displayed more bravery and determination than in this last fight with Mosby." But then the correspondent went too far, assuming, "General Lee will not be likely to trust Mosby again with artillery." Mosby, who dismissed the Union claims of his defeat, stated later that Stuart reassured him that he would send him another gun if he would sell it "for the same price." Stahel saw the gun as the ultimate symbol of a hard won victory over his nemesis, and he requested to be allowed to "retain the howitzer in my command."[28]

The following day four companies of the 12th Vermont escorted a repair crew to the scene to "repair the track & clear up the rubbish." One of the soldiers "had a good chance to look the property all over & saw the place where they placed the cannon in the woods & got some of the cotton they used for wadding." He confirmed that Chapman had "sent shell & solid shot whizzing through the engine ... and the whole train was destroyed." The track was quickly reopened, however, and "the cars are running again — but Uncle Sam is several thousand dollars worse off than he was before the raid."[29]

20

May 31–June 12, 1863

"I fear that he is trying to get my cavalry"

The first reports of the fight to reach Heintzelman's headquarters were taken as confirmation that a Southern raid was indeed underway, and the general was instructed by Halleck to have his troops ready to move at a moment's notice. An erroneous report, from General Alexander Hays, of enemy cavalry advancing along the Warrenton Pike may have also briefly heightened fears of a larger attack. Stahel quickly calmed Hays by sending 200 men of the 1st Michigan to bolster his pickets. General Buford also moved up to the outer defense line between Colonel DeForest and General Gregg. Early reports that Mosby had burned one or two bridges along the line were also determined to be erroneous when the track was examined and the wreckage cleared the following morning. Stahel reported that the situation was now stabilized.[1]

The most important result of Mosby's attack was unintended, and went, generally unnoticed, but it may have had the most important impact on the coming campaign. Five men from Colonel Sharpe's Bureau of Military Intelligence under the command of Capt. John McEntee had just been attached to Pleasonton's cavalry corps and sent to Bealeton Station, arriving on May 29. From there the men were to infiltrate the enemy lines, while McEntee processed their reports in an attempt to improve the accuracy of the intelligence reaching army headquarters. But the furor created by Mosby's attack forced McEntee to pack up and "operate out of his shirt pocket," limiting his ability to complete his mission.[2]

On Sunday, May 31, Darius Maynard wrote a long letter home, reporting the prevailing opinion that a Southern move was afoot. "There is no doubt but that we shall receive a call either from [Lee] or Gen. Stuart with his Cavalry.... I confidently believe that twelve hours will find this whole division under arms & *very lively*. If Lee is on the march he will not stop, nor can he be checked, until Pennsylvania or Maryland & possibly Ohio are invaded." His closing view, that "the events of the coming week must be of lasting effect to our cause," was expressed exactly one month too soon.[3]

On June 1, John Buford reported that a Union reconnaissance force had returned the previous day from a patrol of the upper Rappahannock. He tried to reassure his superiors that no additional enemy forces had moved into the region, "save those who have been here all winter." Still, while the troops on the front line tried to convince their superiors in the rear that there was no evidence to substantiate the rumors of a pending raid, preparations continued unabated. Col. Charles R. Lowell was instructed to send half a company from his 2nd Massachusetts Cavalry to bolster the pickets at Fort Reno and the other half to Fort Lincoln, both on the Maryland side of the capital. The interior defenses were inspected to insure that the men were alert and prepared for whatever the South might send their way.[4]

Stahel was directed to send a squadron of troopers to the depot at Burke Station, where they were to meet a "Mr. Roberts who will inform the commander as to the location of quite a number of strangers now in the neighborhood of Accotink." Once found all of the strangers were to be arrested. Stahel sent Maj. H.B. Van Voorhis, 18th Pennsylvania, with a patrol to investigate the report. He returned on the second with three prisoners in tow, and enough tools and weapons to suggest that the men were bent on the destruction of property. After observing the prisoners, a New York correspondent took the opportunity to issue another refrain of the now familiar call for a methodical cleansing of the area. "Nothing but a complete scouring out of this whole region, interspersed with an occasional hanging will give any security" to the Federal troops in the vicinity.[5]

Still, for all of the bitterness that many soldiers felt over the personal nature of the war along the picket lines, as well as the howls from the press corps for the occasional hanging, there were moments that gave hope that some measure of humanity remained in the region. In late May a party of troopers from the 18th Pennsylvania Cavalry visited the home of William Thompson, the scene of one of Mosby's raids in February in which the Pennsylvanians had been his victims. Thompson had been arrested following that incident but, according to Martin, he had been released when he agreed to act as a spy for the Federals. Having again aroused the suspicions of the Pennsylvanians, his home was now searched and incriminating documents were discovered, including maps of their current and former camps, as well as letters from John Mosby. In light of the evidence against him Thompson was again arrested and returned to Old Capitol Prison "to act Union spy there a while." Though the date of his arrest is uncertain, Mrs. Thompson was in some medical distress by May 29. Colonel Gray requested an army surgeon for her, and General Stahel advised that he would send one. Stahel enjoined Gray, "You will be kind enough to see [Mrs.] Thompson is not unfairly disturbed. No officer or soldier has the right to enter any house or take any horse without your special permission or order." In part, Stahel's remark was in reference to an earlier complaint from Mr. Thompson accusing an officer in the 5th Michigan of not only stealing a horse but also using "insulting language" while he did so. On June 3, Thompson was released, suggesting either the serious nature of his wife's medical condition, a lack of evidence or both. Less than two weeks later, Stahel again contacted Gray on Mrs. Thompson's behalf, instructing that she was to be allowed to "remove her effects to Fairfax Court House."[6]

Stuart had done little of an overt nature to give life to the persistent speculation of a Southern raid, beyond the initial concentration of his division in Culpeper County, which was done at Lee's request as a point from which Stuart could "better observe the enemy." The cavalry chief had reviewed the three brigades already in Culpeper County on May 22, but this had drawn little notice from the Federal high command. It was not until May 27 that positive information was received from Union scouts that Stuart was in Culpeper County with three brigades, numbering almost 5,000 effectives, and that Grumble Jones was en route from the Valley with his brigade, as directed by Lee four days earlier. This report also mentioned that Lee's army was under marching orders to a destination not supported by the Southern railroad system, in other words he again intended to cross the Potomac River. According to historian Edwin Fishel, this warning did not reach the authorities in Washington until June 8, due to a "malfunction of clerical machinery." Within a matter of days both Jones and Beverly Robertson would arrive to round out Stuart's division. But if the Federals were having difficulty divining, interpreting and communicating the intentions of the enemy, so, to, were Lee and Stuart.[7]

In a letter written to Stuart on May 23, Lee confessed to being unable to "determine" the intentions of the enemy, and asked Stuart to remain ever vigilant while at the same time devoting his "attention to the organization and recuperation of" his command. "I do not wish to let an opportunity escape of dealing the enemy a blow should one offer," Lee stated emphatically, but his overriding concern was the health of the cavalry, and he warned, "you had better not undertake an expedition at present." Four days later, Lee sent a note to Maj. Gen. Arnold Elzey, commanding the troops around Richmond, in which he warned Elzey to be prepared for a Northern cavalry raid against the city. This belief was based, in part, on the movement of Stoneman's cavalry to the line of the Orange and Alexandria Railroad to support Stahel, which, combined with statements from captured soldiers and other sources, was taken as a preliminary move against Richmond. Both armies were now preparing for a raid against their capital city and both were wrong. That same day, May 27, Lee reiterated to Stuart the importance of timely, accurate intelligence from his scouts if he was to successfully counter any Northern movement. He suggested that the information void had him groping around in the dark, sifting through erroneous reports. Lee lamented his failure to discover Hooker's intentions and hinted that it might be best if he fell back in order to better defend Richmond.[8]

What remains unknown is the extent of disinformation, if any, that the two sides may have been leaking in an effort to mislead each other. After Lee's warning reached the capital, Confederate Secretary of War James Seddon thought that Union spies were deceiving Lee, but he also found it difficult to argue with the "judicious" process by which Lee reached his conclusions. Lee admitted to the possibility of deception and misinformation in a letter to Seddon on the thirtieth, but like Halleck, Lee simply could not ignore the threat. Writing to Stuart on the thirtieth, Lee asked his cavalry chief to consider releasing Lige White's battalion for independent duty in Loudoun and Fauquier Counties, possibly as a means of bolstering the scouting force and thus the information obtained from that region. The following day, Lee received an invitation from Stuart to attend a second review of the cavalry division. Lee declined, but he complained, again, about the "contradictory" information coming into his headquarters and his frustration at being unable to foresee and counter Hooker's next move. Possibly as a gentle means of reminding Stuart that the vital task at hand was not another review Lee stated, "I think a cavalry expedition must be on foot, unless they are moving up to Fauquier ... for the purpose of grazing. If you can find out this is so, and that they are in detached parties, they can be easily broken up." Otherwise, "I think you had better hold yourself in reserve *en masse*, recuperate, and at the proper time throw yourself with force on a vulnerable point." Lee was clearly relying on Stuart for help, and as yet not receiving any.[9]

As Lee suspected, a Federal movement was afoot. John Buford had moved into Fauquier County with the intent of determining Stuart's intentions, to determine if enemy forces had occupied the county beyond those small bands that had been based there for months and to recruit his horses. If Stuart could confirm this to be the case he had the go ahead from Lee to make an offensive move. Wade Hampton had reported, however, that Hooker was not planning to take the offensive. His information, combined with reports out of Richmond that the perceived threat to the capital from Union forces on the Peninsula had also dissipated, convinced Lee to proceed with his own plans for an invasion of the North.[10]

By June 3, the troopers on both sides of the river were edgy and eager for a fight. When Col. Thomas Owen, 3rd Virginia Cavalry, took a force of 300 men to scout the Rappahannock River, between the Hazel River and Waterloo Bridge, it is doubtful that he had any idea that he would initiate the first skirmish of the Gettysburg Campaign. Near Fox Ford he observed a picket force from the 1st Massachusetts Cavalry numbering 30 men and two officers, led by Capt. Daniel Gleason. As the men glared at each other across the water, Owen opted to send across Capt. William Field's squadron, 3rd Virginia, to capture the New Englanders. What he got was more fight than he could handle as Gleason and his outnumbered men repeatedly charged the head of the Southern column. Gleason later declared that, before he was sabered over the crown of his head he had "cut, slashed and stabbed to my heart's content." Owen was forced to send another detachment across to succor Field's beleaguered command, and Gleason's men were convinced to yield. By the time Union supports arrived, Owen was back across the river. Yet earlier that morning, and miles to the southeast near Fredericksburg, Robert E. Lee issued the orders that started his infantry moving north, on a path that ended in Pennsylvania. Lee was on the move.[11]

Though it would be several hours before dust trails along the horizon alerted Hooker to the activity across the river, inconclusive or conflicting reports from Union scouts continued to arrive at headquarters but shed little light on the situation. One suggested that Lee's army was still too weak to move, while another speculated that if Lee did move, he would head south. Most of the reports had either Stuart or Lee, or both, headed north, and sooner rather than later. Scout John Skinker concluded, "[Pennsylvania] will, more than likely be the point." Throughout the day men toiled with pick and shovel along the lines from Centreville to Manassas and Union Mills in a last attempt to improve their fortifications as the "Expectations of a rebel raid" reached a fever pitch.[12]

Edwin Havens looked forward to the raid with eager anticipation. He had been in charge of a ten-man detail that escorted the able-bodied prisoners captured at Greenwich to a holding cell at Fairfax Court House. The men from North Carolina allowed "they had rather be Union prisoners than Secesh soldiers.... But Moseby's men were saucy as turks and expressed their opinions quite freely that they would soon have the opportunity to return us the same civilities that we were then showing them." Havens longed for a confrontation with Stuart, telling his family, "I often wish he would come this way, we would do our best to make his visit agreeable to him if fighting was what he came for." While Havens would have to wait another month to confront the famous cavalryman, Mosby was not content to wait and was already working his way through the Union outposts, intent on striking the interior portion of the lines where the men had been undisturbed for too long.[13]

On the afternoon of June 3, Mosby with between 30 and 50 men, including John Underwood, set out for Frying Pan Church. The larger part of the command halted at Fox's Mill, along Difficult Run six miles from the church, while Underwood led five men into the Union lines picketed by the 5th and 6th Michigan. Mosby's plan was for Underwood to make a quick strike against a small outpost while he waited with the main body to ambush the larger Union reaction force that he hoped to draw out. It was near five in the morning and Mosby was just starting to doze when Underwood struck a patrol from the 5th Michigan along Lawyers Road.[14]

Capt. Smith Hasting, 5th Michigan, was making an inspection of the outposts, along with two other men, including Victor Comte. They had just encountered a relief detail numbering ten men, when Hastings stopped to speak with the men at the next picket post along the line. Lying in the woods nearby Underwood observed the perfect opportunity to create maximum confusion, while also giving Mosby the opportunity he was looking for, and he opened fire as the ten-man detail passed in front of his position, wounding a corporal and one horse. Forty yards away Hastings and his men turned around in time to see the horses of the relief party plunging and rearing while the sergeant in charge struggled to rally his men. Underwood immediately broke contact and raced back toward the mill, followed by the angry men of the relief-detail who snapped off a few hasty shots from their carbines before going in pursuit. They were followed by Hastings and his two men. With the die now cast, word reached Mosby that a third Union force, thought to number 100 men, was already en route to the scene. The men immediately on Underwood's heels lost him in the thick woods that had always made the Lawyers Road line dangerous, and the situation quieted down until near eight o'clock.[15]

There were, however, still two Yankee patrols in search of the partisans; Capt. Abram Vanderburgh, Company F, 5th Michigan, was moving along the Ox Road [modern day West Ox Road] toward Frying Pan Church, while Colonel Gray, with one company from both the 5th and 6th Michigan, headed north along Lawyers Road, and then west on the Fox Mill Road to the church. About halfway there Vanderburgh elected to cut across country toward the Fox Mill Road, coming into the road behind both Gray and Mosby. "Our detachment passed the rebs about 75 strong in the woods," recalled Frederick Corselius, 5th Michigan. "They followed just out of sight expecting to surprise & overbear us with numbers when we reached open country; but Co. F joined us just as we got to Frying Pan." Writing after the event Corselius described a situation in which he knew that Mosby was trapped between the two units, or as he termed it, "Moseby's cake was all dough," though it is unlikely that anyone knew where Mosby was until he opened fire.[16]

The confusion that Mosby created was still apparent days later when several of the men attempted to explain what occurred. Mosby was clearly aware of his predicament and elected to attack anyway. Slipping into legalese he recalled seeing "The party of the first part" halt at the church, just as he "overtook" the rear of Vanderburgh's column and attacked. John Farnill, 6th Michigan, described a situation in which the road dust generated by Gray's column became impenetrable once Mosby's men charged out of the woods, leaving the men at the church completely blind as to exactly what was happening. Mosby, who had no intention of waiting for the dust to settle, dashed out of the surrounding trees and sliced through the scattered ranks of Vanderburgh's company wounding one man, gathering up seven prisoners and shooting a number of horses before he "broke for the woods." "That was the end of our first battle," noted Victor Comte succinctly. By striking the rear of Vanderburgh's column before it exited the woods, Mosby completely neutralized Gray's larger force in the open ground around the church. Mosby later asserted that this would have been his "last day as a partisan commander," if Gray had immediately counterattacked, but Union accounts written in the wake of the fight make clear that Gray's only option was to charge through Vanderburgh's ranks, creating further confusion possibly leading to disaster and thus he hesitated. It was not until Mosby was long gone and order restored that Gray led his men in a half-hearted pursuit. Though Union accounts mention that several of the guerrillas were either killed or captured, the only known casualty was Dr. Lawrence Alexander, a volunteer surgeon who was taken prisoner. The Union captives were recovered by a patrol from the 5th Michigan, the following day.[17]

Jeb Stuart and the threat of a raid remained the prevailing concern for Halleck, Hooker and Heintzelman. On the fourth, Col. Albert Jewett mentioned that loyal residents north of the Potomac River were "much alarmed" over "unmistakable evidence from the enemy's sympathizers that a raid is to be made in this section." Alexandria remained a hive of activity, as existing rifle pits were improved and new ones constructed. The troops at Wolf Run Shoals labored to complete a new line of fortifications to block the crossing.[18]

Col. George Sharpe had received word that Beverly Robertson's brigade of North Carolinians had reinforced Stuart, but Sharpe's scouts were unable to penetrate the Southern screen along the river to confirm this intelligence. What a handful of men could not do, Buford was to attempt with his brigade, but in light of the most recent estimates that Stuart's force now numbered close to 20,000 men Buford's orders were cancelled on June 6. Instead, Hooker and Pleasonton prepared a larger effort designed to confront Stuart's reported numbers on a more equal footing. Col. William Mann did send a patrol from the 1st Vermont Cavalry to Thoroughfare Gap at Buford's request, but they found no evidence that the enemy had crossed the upper Rappahannock in strength.[19]

On the fifth, Hooker had advised Lincoln that he intended to attack the rear of Lee's army once he was certain that Lee was indeed on the move north. Hooker also suggested that in light of the developing crisis it would be best if all of the troops in the regions threatened by Lee were placed under his command. The following day he was more pointed in his approach, requesting that Stahel be tasked with holding the fords of the Rappahannock, while Pleasonton's cavalry engaged Stuart in Culpeper County. Still, Hooker did not trust Stahel and he requested that Stahel "not be informed of the object" of Pleasonton's mission. Heintzelman saw Hooker's request as a threat to his own command. "I fear that he is trying to get my cavalry," he confided to his diary on the seventh, but "He won't." Still, Heintzelman intended to cooperate with Hooker. As Hooker massed his cavalry for a confrontation with Stuart, Stahel relieved Pleasonton of his responsibilities along the railroad.[20]

To prevent the possibility of an attack launched from the Shenandoah Valley and down the corridor from Leesburg, Heintzelman directed Stahel, on the sixth, to send a reconnaissance beyond the Blue Ridge and into the heart of the valley. Maj. Melvin Brewer, 1st Michigan, was given the task, leaving Fairfax Court House at four P.M. on June 7 with about 170 men from his command as well as a detachment from the 2nd Pennsylvania Cavalry, led by Capt. Stephen Hanson. After spending the night at Gainesville, Brewer proceeded the next morning to Waterloo Bridge, driving off an enemy picket party and tearing up the bridge before continuing through Chester Gap to the outskirts of Front Royal, which he reached about 10 P.M. There he encountered a force of about 300 men. When they were challenged the Wolverines replied, "Sixth Virginia Cavalry," which, aided by darkness and their dust-covered uniforms, completely confounded the Confederates within the town. The Yankees were soon bombarded with questions concerning the military situation, while several Southern officers reportedly accompanied the Federals through the town. It was not until they were challenged at a crossing of the Shenandoah River that their deception fell apart but the alert outpost, numbering just 20 men, was quickly overrun by Brewer's advance guard led by Lt. George Maxwell. The Wolverines then continued to Winchester where they remained for several days with Milroy's command. Brewer had earlier detached Hanson's force to scout the eastern slope of the Blue Ridge north of Barbee's Crossroads. Hanson scoured the area as far as Upperville before turning east, and returning through Middleburg and Aldie, picking up eight prisoners along the way. When Brewer filed his report from Winchester on the eighth he noted, accurately, that Ewell's corps was camped just north of Culpeper, and that the fords of the Rappahannock and Shenandoah rivers were strongly guarded.[21]

Late morning on the seventh Halleck advised Hooker that while much of Stahel's division was "out scouting," Stahel would cooperate with Pleasonton "as far as he has means." In a message of the same date, but without the time noted, Maj. Gen. Daniel Butterfield, Hooker's chief of staff, informed Pleasonton that his request for support from Stahel had gone unanswered, telling the cavalryman, "You will not be able to count upon any assistance from [Stahel]." Hooker, who had misused his cavalry in the Chancellorsville campaign and then hung the blame for his failure upon their commander, used this perceived lack of cooperation on the part of Halleck, Heintzelman and Stahel as a key piece of evidence in his own defense when called before the Committee on the Conduct of the War months later. Specifically he attributed much of his most recent failure to the fact that Stahel's cavalry was not sent to his assistance in a timely fashion, claiming that his cavalry corps was left "numerically too weak to cope with the superior numbers of the enemy." Hooker testified that Stahel's division numbered 6,100 sabers, though the effective strength was less than half of that. Hooker further stated, sarcastically, that these men were tied up chasing Mosby's 200 guerrillas. He conveniently ignored the fact that half of Stahel's division was occupied in securing the Orange and Alexandria Railroad, that was reopened for the sole purpose of supplying Hooker's army, while the other half had consistently responded to every request for assistance emanating from his headquarters. After the war John Mosby was happy to follow Hooker's lead, and took full credit for tying up Stahel's division, claiming that his operations against the railroad "had created [such] great uneasiness in Washington," that the Federals were afraid to release any of the security force guarding the line. In truth Mosby's most recent attempt to interdict the supply line appears to have generated little, if any, additional concern within the larger context of the anticipated raid.[22]

Hooker and Mosby also forgot or chose to overlook Stahel's response of that evening in which he stated his intent to depart at three o'clock in the morning with "the whole of my available force here [Fairfax Court House] and on the Orange and Alexandria Railroad," with the aim of holding the river crossings behind Pleasonton, once he moved into Culpeper. As William Martin, 18th Pennsylvania observed, every man who had a horse "had to go," but at Hooker's request they did not know where they were headed. Still, Stahel left only a nominal force to hold the approaches out of Loudoun County.[23]

Stahel was at Kettle Run, along the railroad three hours after departing and in communication with Pleasonton. The corps commander now informed Stahel that he was to disregard his earlier request to secure the river crossings. Instead, Stahel was to remain along the railroad, sending out small scouting parties and picket details to the posts vacated by Pleasonton's troopers. Pleasonton confirmed Stahel's full compliance to Hooker later that morning, as Stahel's troopers arrived at Warrenton Junction in time to see Pleasonton's men depart. All of them knew that something was in the wind, and "it was provoking to stand there & see Buford's division move towards the Rappahannock," but, as William O'Brien,

7th Michigan, concluded, "we had to submit to it." Edwin Havens, who watched for two hours as Buford's men moved up to the river, noted, "I felt like a school boy condemned to the confinement of the schoolroom while he saw his mates enjoying themselves on the 'Fourth' or some other grand holiday." O'Brien and his comrades rode through the deserted campsites and could not believe the amount of property, including "carbines revolvers sabres & cartridges burned & destroyed in a shameful manner" by Buford's men. The Wolverines were able to salvage so much of the discarded equipment that they, in turn, cast the surplus aside.[24]

The following morning, June 9, Pleasonton crossed the Rappahannock River with three mounted divisions, sparking the largest cavalry battle of the war. For 14 hours the echo of the combat rolled back across the river, infuriating Stahel's men who were "deprived of the privilege of participating." Late in the day Pleasonton requested that Stahel advance to Bealeton, a measure that "immediately" improved their "spirits." They set out promptly, "eager for a brush" with the vaunted Stuart, only to have their hopes dashed again, when they were tasked with guarding Pleasonton's wagon train and his prisoners. "Let me say here," O'Brien declared, "that if the accursed Brigadier Gens & some of the Major Gens were kicked out of the service it would be the most patriotic move Lincoln could make for it seems they stumble into every error & avoid every chance to gain victory."[25]

In the early evening, Pleasonton fell back across the river, having sustained almost 1,000 casualties while inflicting over 500 casualties among Stuart's legions. Hours later O'Brien had reason to visit Pleasonton's headquarters. Bitterly disappointed at having missed the battle, his tone was more reserved as he described the scene. "I expected to see something pretty nice but judge my surprise on entering to see the officers of Pleasonton's staff tumbled promiscuously over the dirty floor ... a dirtier set of men I never saw." O'Brien, who did not state his reason for being there, met with Pleasonton's chief of staff, Col. Andrew Alexander, who gave him an overview of the fighting. O'Brien found Alexander "sitting at a table writing his dress consisted of a pair of drawers & shirt he was minus boots socks, hat coat vest & pants ... his face was very dirty his hair ... covered with dust his manner reserved & of a business nature." Clearly this was not what the young, uninitiated solder expected. After the battle much would be made of Pleasonton's claim to have broken up the intended raid by Stuart, but O'Brien, who wrote his account that night, was shown evidence by Alexander that supported Pleasonton's claim. Arriving back at Bealeton Station O'Brien concluded, "the loss of life is immense" as he watched three trains loaded with dead and wounded head toward Washington, with one entire car reserved for dead officers. After the trains pulled out he "passed thirty ambulances loaded with wounded soldiers" just arriving from the battlefield. Once the wounded had been placed on cars bound for the capital the prisoners were placed aboard a train bound for Alexandria. Thirty-five to 40 prisoners were herded into each rail car with a like number of soldiers to guard them. The train made at least one stop so surgeons could treat the wounded prisoners and "to cut off a great many arms and legs." O'Brien, who had been so provoked at missing the battle only hours earlier, must have now said a silent prayer of thanks that he had been so lucky.[26]

As O'Brien and others had surmised, Stahel's men might have made a difference on the battlefield that day. That they did not was a question for Hooker and Pleasonton to answer, not Heintzelman or Stahel. Not for the first time Hooker displayed his reluctance to share credit with another command. If he could have absorbed Stahel's division into his army prior to the battle, perhaps it might have played a more decisive role, but neither Hooker nor Pleasonton could fairly complain that any request for assistance was not complied with in a most expeditious manner. By 6 P.M., June 10, Stahel had his command back on the road, and Pleasonton again assumed the security of the railroad as far as Catlett Station. Stahel arrived at Fairfax Court House by noon on the eleventh, after a march through dust so thick "that it was impossible to see the man ahead." O'Brien hoped for "a month to recruit our horses," only to be disappointed when he was sent out on picket duty that afternoon.[27]

On June 7 Captains William Boyd and Ezra Bailey, 1st New York (Lincoln) Cavalry led an expedition of 100 men into "Mosby's Confederacy," from their base in the Shenandoah Valley. Crossing the mountains at Snicker's Gap, the Yankees moved south, through the Crooked Run valley, searching houses and rounding up prisoners. In a brief skirmish near Piedmont Station on the eighth, one of the Federals was killed and two were listed as missing. Pushing on, the New Yorkers reached Salem where they learned that Mosby, along with his family, was at the home of James and Elizabeth Hathaway, south of Middleburg. In the early hours of June 9, the Yankees surrounded the house and demanded entry. The searchers seized his spurs and one of his horses, but the "Gray Ghost" eluded them.[28]

The following day, June 10, Mosby officially mustered in 60 men as Company A, 43rd Battalion Virginia Cavalry, at Rector's Crossroads. Observing the ceremony were about 30 men from Capt. William Brawner's Company H, 15th Virginia Cavalry, known as the Prince William Rangers. Frank Stringfellow, one of Stuart's most trusted scouts, was also present. Once the formality of electing the company officers was completed Mosby led his command north toward the Potomac River, with the intention of attacking a squadron from the 6th Michigan encamped at Seneca, Maryland, near Rowser's Ford.[29]

Mosby had yet to conduct any operations in Maryland and the timing of this first effort is interesting. It was Stuart's intention to cross the Rappahannock River on the morning of June 9, and to provide a screen for Longstreet's and Ewell's infantry as they moved north along the line of the Blue Ridge Mountains. Pleasonton's attack and the grueling battle that resulted delayed Stuart's plan, and he did not resume his move north until the fifteenth. Exactly where Stuart had intended to cross the Potomac River is unknown, but the timing of Mosby's Seneca raid suggests that it may have been made at Stuart's request. Though Mosby said little about his rationale for the timing of the raid, Frank Stringfellow did. Stringfellow claimed that he had been sent by Stuart to scout the river crossings below Harpers Ferry in connection with an eventual crossing of the river by Stuart. Stringfellow's biographer has linked this mission with Mosby. Much would eventually influence Stuart's route to the Potomac River and a strong argument can also be made against a direct correlation, but the possibility cannot be ignored that Mosby opted to attack the camp of the 6th Michigan Cavalry at Seneca as a means of aiding an anticipated crossing by Stuart shortly thereafter.[30]

Early on the tenth, Col. Albert Jewett, commanding a Union brigade posted along the north bank of the Potomac River, forwarded a report from a woman in Dranesville that Mosby, hauling "some pieces of artillery" had been in the area the previous day. Mosby no longer possessed any artillery but several of his scouts may have been in the area scouting an approach to the river, as well as the defenses along the far shore. The woman reported the information to the commanding officer at Seneca, who then put his men on alert throughout the day and night. General Stahel, who had not yet returned from assisting Pleasonton, was tasked with investigating the report, though he could do little beyond alerting the sentinels from the 5th and 6th Michigan who had remained in Fairfax County to secure the Virginia side of the river.[31]

With the weight of evidence increasingly pointing to an invasion of the north by Lee, as well as the continuing threat of a cavalry raid, Heintzelman sent one of his aides, Capt. Henry Norton, to inspect the picket line on the north side of the upper Potomac, from Great Falls, just above the mouth of Difficult Run, to the confluence of the Monocacy. Writing his report on the tenth, Norton advised that the area around Rowser's Ford was held by the 10th Vermont Infantry, whose pickets were stationed too far apart, as the regiment tried to compensate for a lack of men. Still, Norton was confident that hourly cavalry patrols would prevent any sizable force from crossing undetected. Norton closed by stating his belief that "no organized guerrillas" were operating in that sector. Five days later Mortimer Moulden, the provost marshal for Montgomery County, made his own report, referring to the citizens as "disloyal" in general. Of more concern was that "men having little or no sympathy for our Government" controlled that section of the Chesapeake and Ohio Canal, including the lock at Seneca. "It is true there is a company of cavalry stationed at the Falls, but with the aid of disloyal citizens who know every curve of the river, what chance would our pickets have to give the alarm?" Moulden asked.[32]

Mosby planned to make a night attack against Capt. Charles Deane's Company I, 6th Michigan Cavalry, which was stationed along the river and attached to Jewett's brigade. He was delayed when his guide got lost, forcing him to cross "after daylight." The identity of the guide remains unknown but one of Deane's men accused Lewis Cross, who resided near the Union camp, of aiding Mosby by the use of signal lights displayed in an upper window of his home. Mosby also believed that the Yankees had been "apprised of my movement" and were thus formed to receive him when he launched his attack, but Mosby was mistaken. The partisans had captured several pickets and one four-man patrol along the canal resulting in several shots being fired which alerted the Union pickets down the line. These men awakened the camp "just at daylight," by firing on the head of the gray column, giving the 40 or so men in camp just enough time to get mounted. One of the sentinels further aided his comrades by turning the bridge that crossed the canal, delaying Mosby still longer. Outnumbered, Deane opted to make his stand on the far side of Seneca Bridge from where they fought "briskly," once Mosby made his appearance. Yet when their "pistols and carbines were empty" Mosby gave them no opportunity to reload, sending his men across at three points in an effort to cut off their line of retreat. Deane successfully extricated his Wolverines and retreated two miles toward Poolesville before attempting to make another stand, but Mosby never gave him a chance. Spurring his tired horses, Mosby drove Deane from this position as well, before his horses began to give out and the partisan called off the chase. Deane lost four men killed, two wounded, both of whom were captured and twelve others taken prisoner. Mosby lost two officers killed: Captain Brawner of the Prince William Rangers and George Whitescarver, who had been elected as a lieutenant in Company A the previous day. At least two other men were wounded.[33]

One of Deane's pickets not caught up in the rout went back to the river and began firing his weapon in an attempt to draw the attention of the men manning the outpost at the mouth of Difficult Run. Albert Sawyer, 1st Vermont Cavalry, who was stationed nearby, confirmed the warning, but he admitted that the news was not relayed to his headquarters in a timely manner. The Vermonters remained unconcerned until word arrived from another frightened picket that Mosby was now attacking their camp at Freedom Hill. Colonel Gray, who had ignored the first warning, soon had his men mounted and racing toward the river before he determined this second alarm to be false.[34]

Word of the attack also reached a Union cavalry camp just outside the capital when a courier from Heintzelman arrived in a lather with orders for Col. Charles Russell Lowell, 2nd Massachusetts Cavalry, to respond with a detachment from both the 2nd Massachusetts Cavalry and the 11th New York Cavalry. Lowell arrived at the scene of the fight, 16 miles distant, to find it "a mass of smouldering ruins," and pushed on for Poolesville, where he halted for a few hours. Resuming the march at two A.M., Lowell crossed the Potomac at White's Ford at dawn in a dense fog. No word had reached the infantry pickets that Lowell would be entering their lines, and when they heard the column approaching they took cover in a blockhouse. Luckily the officer in command was not afflicted with the jitters and ordered the men to hold their fire. As Lowell passed within a few hundred feet of the blockhouse the foot soldiers moved to a bluff overlooking the troopers and challenged them before learning their identity. As one wrote, "If we had fired into them Jewett could not have blamed our Captain." Shortly after crossing the river Lowell recovered a man from the 10th Vermont, who had been captured the previous day, and then paroled by Mosby near Leesburg. Allowing the men a brief rest outside of Leesburg, Lowell telegraphed for orders, advising his superiors that Mosby had been at Ball's Mill along Goose Creek earlier that morning. He indicated his intention to move south, checking the fords along Goose Creek, and hopefully driving the guerrillas into other Union patrols moving up from the south. "Go where you please in pursuit of Mosby," was the reply. Lowell followed the trail as it crossed the winding stream several times before striking the Little River Turnpike near Aldie. He had just selected his best 200 horses, with which to continue the chase, when he encountered a patrol, led by Maj. John Hammond, 5th New York, arriving from Middleburg. Concluding that Mosby had passed through the area the previous day and "immediately disbanded," Lowell gave up his pursuit.[35]

The news of Mosby's latest incursion reached General Stahel minutes after he arrived at Fairfax Court House. Tired and covered in dust, the general quickly attempted to coordinate a response to the Southern incursion. He telegraphed Colonel DeForest, who had remained with his brigade along the railroad, to send Major Hammond with 450 men to Aldie and Middleburg, to "catch or break up [Mosby's] band." Stahel then telegraphed Maj. Melvin Brewer, who was still in Winchester, to return at daylight by way of Leesburg. After insuring that both Hammond and Brewer were aware of the other patrols they might encounter, Stahel set out with a detachment of Wolverines who had just returned from assisting Pleasonton. He arrived at Freedom Hill that evening and allowed the men to rest briefly while he conferred with Colonel Gray and Major Taggart about the incident, that was, again, believed to be the opening salvo of Stuart's "*anticipated* raid into Maryland." This was based on initial erroneous reports that Mosby had remained on the Maryland side of the river, possibly to hold the crossing point for Stuart. Stahel then headed his column toward Chantilly and Centreville.[36]

Hammond departed from Kettle Run at 3 A.M. with troops from his own 5th New

York as well as the 1st West Virginia. He pursued a course through Haymarket, Thoroughfare Gap and White Plains before striking the corridor through Middleburg to Aldie. Once word was received that Mosby had disbanded near Middleburg Hammond was directed to search the houses in and around the town closely for "arms and ammunition," and to take into custody "all men known to be disloyal and leave no horses which can be used by guerrillas." Hammond was then to return through Brentsville, searching the town just as thoroughly. The result was the arrest of seven men, six of whom were from Mosby's command, including James Foster, who had just been elected captain, William Rose, who was described as "a bushwhacker of the worst kind," and Frank Stringfellow. With his prisoners in tow Hammond arrived at Kettle Run near midnight, after a grueling 70-mile ride. George Crosby, 1st Vermont Cavalry, referred to two of the "bush whackers" brought in that day as "old offenders but we have caught them at last, they will be hanged or shot."[37]

Major Brewer had his battalion on the road by sunrise on the twelfth, entering Loudoun County through Snicker's Gap. Brewer reached Fairfax Court House at midnight, having marched 65 miles. He secured four men in the guardhouse, two troopers captured while home on furlough and two citizens who refused to take the oath of allegiance.[38]

Stahel had cast his net as quickly as possible, with the hope that one of the patrols would encounter the guerrillas and drive them toward the other columns. In the end, he simply could not react fast enough, however, given that he was not even aware of the raid until he arrived at Fairfax Court House hours after the event. By one estimate his orders went out four hours after Mosby had dispersed his men. The best opportunity to intercept the raiders had been the warning shouted across the river while Mosby was still chasing Deane, but it was ignored, first by the pickets of the 1st Vermont and later by Colonel Gray. Victor Comte expressed the frustration felt by many men in the Federal camps. "I must tell you that Moseby ... kept us busy these past 6 days. Five times he tried to break through our pickets.... This keeps us constantly armed and the horses are always saddled ... which makes it impossible for us to obtain any rest. But worst of all is when we arrive on the spot he's 2 or 3 miles farther away hidden in the woods where even the devil couldn't dislodge him." Still, the young soldier remained hopeful for an opportunity to "force this cursed guerrilla-soldier to come out of the woods and fight.... We're determined to finish it all with him."[39]

Mosby had taken one of his biggest risks to date crossing the river, knowing that he could be cut-off or cut-up attempting to return. When his brief report reached Stuart, the general took notice of his "brilliant service," and recommended that he be promoted. But in his haste to get back across the river Mosby had been forced to leave his dead on the field; that both men were officers made this particularly galling, especially to Julia Brawner, sister of Captain Brawner. Julia held Mosby personally responsible for her brother's death. Brawner "was leading his men and those of Mosby's who were not too busy gathering up plunder to follow. I shall attach some blame to Mosby for lagging behind — if he & his men had kept up, the Yankees in all probability would not have turned & fired the fatal shot. I do not like the man, to praise him as others do. He was cowardly then, & that is enough for me." In her grief she could not understand how his comrades had time to remove some of her brother's personal affects but had then abandoned his body. "I think they might have [recovered his body].... He would have done it for another." As soon as she was able Julia Brawner hired an undertaker in Alexandria to recover her brother's remains, and to inter him in a family plot in Alexandria.[40]

The point in the battle at which the Union camp was plundered is uncertain, though it is likely that Julia Brawner received her information directly from men in her brother's company who were present. Mosby never specifically addressed Julia's accusation, stating only that the Michiganders abandoned the site along with "all their camp equipage and stores." John Scott, however, in an account that Mosby reportedly vetted, states clearly, "Mosby ordered his command to halt and destroy the camp," before proceeding to attack the Union position at the bridge. A number of men "not understanding the order," continued the pursuit to the bridge, where "the fight was continued until Mosby came up." Lieutenant Whitescarver was killed just after crossing the span, and it was shortly thereafter that Mosby ordered the chase abandoned. Mosby did state, however, that Brawner and several men failed to obey his order and pressed the matter until Brawner was killed. If this was the case then his body was in advance of Mosby's main force and abandoned by his own men who had only enough time to recover a few personal effects.[41]

21

June 12–June 21, 1863

"Tomorrow perhaps we will be on the war path"

Lee had now been on the move for nine days, and Ewell's corps was nearing Winchester. The city of Pittsburgh, Pennsylvania, was being fortified against a possible attack and plans were formulated to defend the line of the Susquehanna River in the event of a strike against the state capital at Harrisburg, yet Hooker and the Army of the Potomac remained along the Rappahannock. From his headquarters Hooker badgered Pleasonton for accurate, timely information upon which he could formulate a plan to counter Lee. The army commander believed that he could thwart Lee by launching an attack either against the rear of his army, or by advancing directly on Richmond, though neither option was palatable to Lincoln. Pleasonton did little to alleviate the problem, opting instead to rest, review, and reorganize his corps, following the battle at Brandy Station. Rather than send his own men in search of the information requested by his commander, Pleasonton was content to send in unreliable information gleaned from deserters, prisoners and contrabands, none of which satisfied Hooker.[1]

Pleasonton did consider the possibility of bribing John Mosby, discussing the idea briefly on June 12, with Brig. Gen. Rufus Ingalls, the army's chief quartermaster. How, when and with whom the thought first percolated is unknown, but the limited information available suggests that it was Pleasonton's idea. But why, and why at this point in the campaign? A logical explanation was that both Pleasonton and Hooker were still seeking a means by which they could expand the cavalry corps. The cavalry chief saw this expansion as necessary if he was to obtain his second star. Hooker believed that Stahel's division was being squandered under Heintzelman, and could be put to better use if transferred to his army. Hooker also believed that it was only a fear of Mosby that prevented this transfer. Thus if Mosby could be removed from the equation, Stahel's division would become available in time for the coming campaign. Money was the motivating force for many of the men who rode with Mosby and Pleasonton might have suspected that it was the main incentive for their commanding officer as well, but he could not have been more wrong as Mosby repeatedly refused a share of the spoils.[2]

A second possibility is that it was simply a random thought conveyed over the telegraph between two friends and thus recorded for posterity. Pleasonton had been a year behind Ingalls at West Point and their friendship is evidenced by the numerous unofficial telegrams that passed between them. On the twelfth Ingalls had sent the cavalry chief a brief note stating, "Send me some news. The General is anxious," and it was possibly in reply that

Pleasonton suggested the scheme to bribe the partisan. The idea appears to have died a quick death, however, and Mosby remained unaware of it until after the war.[3]

On June 13 Hooker finally ordered his army to begin moving north, again relying upon the Orange and Alexandria Railroad, and with an initial concentration point at Centreville. Several elements of the army were to follow an interior line along the Telegraph Road toward Alexandria. Pleasonton was immediately assailed with a flurry of orders and requests to advance his cavalry as a screen for the troops moving along the railroad while also maintaining the picket line along the Rappahannock so as to conceal the movement for as long as possible. Hooker viewed the Loudoun Valley and the gaps in Bull Run Mountain as the most likely avenue by which Lee could attack his army before it could be concentrated. Tasked with preventing such a move, Pleasonton sent one brigade to Thoroughfare Gap, and a second to Warrenton while a third brigade maintained the picket line along the Rappahannock. Claiming that he was now stretched to the breaking point, Pleasonton immediately sought relief from the requirement to hold Thoroughfare Gap, requesting that Stahel handle the job instead. Pleasonton then sought to abdicate his responsibility entirely, suggesting that Stahel should be tasked with locating Lee's army.[4]

Brig. Gen. Alfred Pleasonton, controversial commander of the Cavalry Corps, Army of the Potomac. Along with army commander Joseph Hooker, Pleasonton waged a bitter and ultimately successful campaign to have Stahel's cavalry division transferred to his command (USAMHI).

Pleasonton's lack of cooperation left Hooker to plead for assistance from Halleck, who refused him. Growing weary of Hooker's pleas, Halleck declared, "There is no possibility of sending you more cavalry." Rebuked, Hooker attempted to circumvent the chain of command and sent his requests directly to Stahel, who would have been unable to assist, but for the fact that in their search for Mosby his columns were then converging on the very area that concerned Hooker. Stahel replied promptly, but his message was routed through the War Department, presumably to keep his own superiors aware of the situation, and did not reach Hooker until late the next morning, prompting a terse second request for the same information. In the interim Stahel was summoned to Washington by Heintzelman, presumably to discuss Hooker's continuing attempts to purloin his division as well as to confer in person about the developing campaign. In Stahel's absence a staff officer reiterated to Hooker that no enemy troops had been encountered in the Loudoun Valley by any of the recent patrols. Gen. Benjamin Kelley, commanding the Department of West Virginia and based at Harpers Ferry, also had patrols in the northwestern section of Loudoun County. No enemy troops had been encountered, but Kelley warned that Lee was "on his way to drive Milroy out of Winchester."[5]

By June 14, Hooker knew that an enemy force (A.P. Hill's Corps) still held the line along the Rappahannock, while the bulk of the Southern army was moving north between Culpeper and Winchester, leaving the Union commander facing the possibility of an enemy thrust either from the Shenandoah Valley into Maryland and Pennsylvania, or out of the Loudoun Valley against Washington. Once in motion however, the Army of the Potomac moved quickly in a race to place itself between Lee and the capital. The men sweltered under a blistering sun and staggered through choking dust but by that evening the western arm of the army was concentrating around Centreville, while the van of the eastern arm had crossed the Occoquan River into Fairfax County.[6]

Late on the fourteenth, Pleasonton was advised to concentrate his corps at Centreville, to be "gotten ready for vigorous service." All of the dismounted troopers who were awaiting horses at Dumfries were now instructed to march to Alexandria for their remounts, as the supply depots to the south were abandoned. Those men who had just received fresh horses were to head for Fairfax Station by easy marches as the horses had yet to be shod. With much of the infantry now ahead of Pleasonton's cavalry, requests for assistance continued to be sent directly to Stahel, including an appeal from Maj. Gen. Oliver O. Howard, commanding the Eleventh Corps, that Stahel again scout the approach out of Aldie. Undeterred by Stahel's insistence that there was no threat from that region, Howard persisted until Stahel sent 200 men from the 1st Michigan to recheck the ground. North of the Potomac River, Colonel Jewett remained skittish in the wake of Mosby's recent incursion. He reported that 200 cavalry were observed moving toward the river from Leesburg "in great haste." Jewett also warned that the river was so low as to provide "but slight impediment," and he sought to concentrate his reduced force at Edward's Ferry. The route followed by the 1st Michigan is uncertain, but after scouting the Aldie-Middleburg corridor, they may have swung north to Leesburg, giving rise to Jewett's report.[7]

In the early evening of the fourteenth, Pleasonton provided the most ominous news of the day, when he reported that his scouts had heard distant firing, possibly near Harpers Ferry. Hours later, Pleasonton updated this report, placing the location of the firing near Winchester. Though he had no idea what the reports portended, they supported what others already suspected, that Milroy was on the brink of defeat, and, indeed, that was the case as Ewell overwhelmed Milroy's command in a series of actions at Berryville, Winchester and Martinsburg. In this same report Pleasonton placed Stuart, with 15,000 men, at Upperville, an erroneous claim that was supposedly based on the observation of his own scouts who he claimed had gone as far as Ashby's Gap, immediately west of Upperville. The cavalry commander also opined that Longstreet was in supporting distance of Stuart, while Ewell and A.P. Hill remained south of the Rappahannock. Nothing could have been more inaccurate. In the words of one nervous diarist in Washington, "the rebel army ... spreads in all directions, and takes the offensive. We do not even know positively where Lee is going, where he will appear and strike."[8]

Halleck called Pleasonton's reports "contradictory" and "very unsatisfactory." Frustrated, Halleck turned to Stahel for help, but Stahel had not had men out to the Blue Ridge in several days and so could do little to erase the confusion. Pleasonton continued to fill the telegraph wires with conjecture and supposition, suggesting to Stanton that the units guarding the crossing points along the Potomac near the Monocacy be bolstered to block Stuart's advance. In fact, Stuart was many miles to south and just resuming his move north that had been interrupted on the ninth. For several days Pleasonton had resisted the less glamorous work of picket and scouting duty, in favor of holding his command together in the event an opportunity arose for another climactic battle. Pleasonton's lack of cooperation soon set the infantry commanders to complaining that their flanks remained unprotected as they moved along the line of the railroad. Pleasonton immediately sought to saddle Stahel with this task as well. This prompted a curt response from Maj. Gen. John Reynolds, commanding the left wing of the army, that Pleasonton's cavalry was still responsible for screening the infantry, and he reminded Pleasonton, "I have no control of Stahel." Still, Pleasonton continued to focus entirely on his command, though he wisely changed his concentration point to the railhead at Manassas Junction rather than Centreville. He also diverted the recently remounted men from Fairfax Station to Manassas Junction.[9]

Beyond misleading his own superiors, Pleasonton's reports were also causing concern north of the river. His report that Stuart was at Upperville, bent on crossing the Potomac near the Monocacy added to the strain felt by Colonel Jewett, who determined to concentrate his infantry and cavalry as a defensive measure. His small brigade included the 10th Vermont and 23rd Maine, the 10th Massachusetts Battery, Captain Deane's squadron of the 6th Michigan Cavalry and three companies of the 11th New York Cavalry, under the command of Maj. Joseph Kenyon, totaling 1,700 effectives. Jewett was allowed to concentrate his men on more defensible ground, but they were the only troops guarding the Chesapeake and Ohio Canal and could not be completely withdrawn. His superiors attempted to reassure him, telling him they understood the "difficult" nature of his position, while explaining "it is impossible to send you more troops now. Something must be risked to save the canal." Adding to Jewett's concerns were recent reports that Lige White was planning to make a raid through his lines "tonight (June 15) or in the morning." After he was counseled to "make up by activity for lack of numbers," and "Cover all approaches to your position by cavalry patrols," Jewett set his men to digging earthworks.[10]

Meanwhile Stahel was irritated at having to continually defend his reports that the Loudoun Valley was free of Southern troops, except for those of Mosby and White. The citizens that his men spoke with knew nothing of Lee's intentions, nor did Stahel think Stuart had crossed or planned to cross the river near the Monocacy, "as I would be aware of it," he added with a touch of annoyance. He found himself again fielding entreaties from Howard that he establish a picket line of some "10 or 12 miles" to secure the infantry's flank against an attack from troops that only Pleasonton believed to be in the region. Stahel agreed to increase his mounted patrols in the vicinity but could do little else. Another request from Howard sought to pull men from the 200-man patrol force of the 1st Michigan to assist a signal officer in establishing a post atop Bull Run Mountain at Aldie. General Abercrombie had been "ordered to arrest all stragglers from the Army of the Potomac," and he immediately sought to siphon off another detachment of Stahel's cavalry to assist him. Struggling to meet these demands, Stahel sought to concentrate his command by pulling in several of his outposts. Heintzelman refused to allow him to withdraw the troopers guarding the approaches from the Occoquan, but he did grant permission to pull DeForest's brigade into Fairfax County from its position along Kettle Run.[11]

By morning on the sixteenth the military situation was reaching a crisis point; Pleasonton's failures, combined with the many wild rumors and reports generated throughout a rapidly expanding region, left Hooker and Halleck at their wit's end and at each other's throats. Hooker sought to shift his army to the northwest, to Leesburg where the fords of the Potomac River were the shallowest. Not only would this be the easiest point at which to cross the river but it would also close the distance to Harpers Ferry where the garrison was again believed to be in danger of attack. In response to reports from the governor of Pennsylvania that Confederate forces had entered the state and were advancing in three columns on Chambersburg, Gettysburg and the coal mine region, Hooker offered to send his entire cavalry force into Maryland and Pennsylvania ahead of the army, but only if he could retain the services of Stahel's division.[12]

Hooker closed his message to the President with a prescient observation, in which he warned that should the enemy "hold the [mountain] passes stoutly, he can cause me delay. You may depend upon it, we can never discover the whereabouts of the enemy, or divine his intentions, so long as he can fill the country with a cloud of cavalry. We must break through that to find him." How Hooker intended to accomplish this went unstated, especially if he was considering sending his cavalry corps into Pennsylvania and away from the army. By way of reply, Halleck, who was losing patience with Hooker, counseled that neither he nor Hooker had enough accurate information upon which to base their next move, and before Hooker sent his cavalry into Pennsylvania he should employ them in determining exactly where Lee was and where he was going. "Unless your army is kept near enough to the enemy to ascertain his movements, yours must be in the dark or on mere conjecture." This was possibly the only point upon which the two men were in agreement. The dilemma was in the solution, as Hooker and Pleasonton were still trying to create a situation in which Halleck would have to relent and transfer Stahel's division to the army. Sending Pleasonton into Pennsylvania had been their latest ploy, and it had just failed.[13]

At 8 A.M., June 16, Hooker queried Stahel as to how his division was deployed and Stahel promptly replied. Four hours later Stahel was at Hooker's headquarters offering advice on the road network, as well as the bridges and streams, throughout western Fairfax County and eastern Loudoun County that would facilitate the movement of the army over the next couple of days, and he agreed to provide troopers to guide the infantry commands as needed. The orders directing the army to Leesburg did not address the cavalry corps, though Pleasonton told both Gregg and Buford to be ready to move at 3 o'clock the next morning, the same hour at which the army was to move. As the day closed Heintzelman, who disliked Hooker intensely, wondered, "What can Hooker be doing?" Recognizing that the army commander was in a quandary as to Lee's location and intentions, Heintzelman opined, "He could learn that by going nearer and sending out his cavalry."[14]

Before the campfires flickered out for the night men again put pen to paper. Alfred Ryder, 1st Michigan, told his friends, "These are action times something is going to tell on the war before long.... I'm tired of lingering." In a letter to a hometown newspaper a trooper in the 6th Michigan observed, "We are having exciting times here now. All eyes are turned to the Army of the Potomac." One of Stannard's Vermonters explained that he had watched the army march by him for two days. "It fairly makes my head sick to see them, dusty dirty worn out looking men as I ever saw."[15]

The campfires outside Hooker's headquarters at Fairfax Station burned brightly throughout the night, even as those in the camps around him waned. Few of his aides got a good night's rest, nor did his telegraph operator as a steady stream of messages flowed between his headquarters and Washington. Secretary of War Stanton, who was himself frustrated with the deteriorating military situation as well as the constant bickering between Hooker and Halleck, was also up throughout the night, reviewing the messages between the two men. He finally intervened, warning Hooker. "The very demon of lying seems to be about these times, and generals will have to be broken for ignorance before they will take the trouble to find out the truth of reports."[16]

But the bitter disappointment of the spring campaign, in which Hooker sent the majority of his cavalry on a raid toward Richmond, still haunted the army commander. Hooker had stumbled blindly through the wooded terrain around Chancellorsville without his cavalry, and he would forever fault his mounted arm for his own lack of foresight. Unwilling to make the same mistake a second time, Hooker refused to send his cavalry toward the Shenandoah Valley in search of Lee. Instead, Pleasonton was hold his corps near Aldie, allowing only one regiment to make an extended reconnaissance of the Loudoun Valley. That regiment would then rejoin the command near Leesburg on the eighteenth, near the point where Hooker planned to cross the Potomac.[17]

Stahel, who had spent much of the night with Hooker, returned to Fairfax Court House at 3 A.M. on the seventeenth, to find a message from Heintzelman, inquiring about the results of a reconnaissance that Heintzelman had ordered earlier. Stahel informed his superior that he had not complied with the order as all the roads were clogged with troops and supply trains from the Army of the Potomac, but added that he had scouts with each of the columns. That afternoon Stahel received a request from the army commander to concentrate his division in the event that Hooker needed it. This was followed by a second request from Hooker that Stahel send two regiments to reconnoiter beyond Warrenton to the Rappahannock River, searching for the tail of Lee's army. Stahel responded immediately, sending Colonel DeForest, with the 1st Vermont and 18th Pennsylvania. The troopers left Fairfax Court House that evening, but marched only as far as Centreville before halting.[18]

At 3 A.M. on the seventeenth Pleasonton ordered David Gregg to have his division on the road in two hours, and to encamp that night at Aldie. Exactly how far Pleasonton was to advance the main body of his corps that day is unclear. In March 1864, he gave testimony before the Committee on the Conduct of the War that has always been viewed as self-serving and patently unreliable, but a careful reading of several documents confirms Pleasonton's account. He stated that Hooker had initially directed him to reconnoiter the Loudoun Valley on the seventeenth, but during the march Capt. Ulric Dahlgren arrived with a new directive from Hooker, instructing Pleasonton to halt where he was, for Hooker now intended "to receive battle from the enemy in that position at Manassas." Pleasonton remonstrated, sending Dahlgren back to Hooker with word that he thought it best to advance beyond the mountains at Aldie. Pleasonton then ordered his lead brigade "to go on immediately, and not stop until we got through" Aldie Gap. The uncertainty that gripped Hooker at this key point in the campaign appears to have survived a face-to-face meeting with his cavalry chief the previous night in which Pleasonton almost certainly urged the same course of action.[19]

According to Dahlgren, his meeting with Pleasonton occurred prior to one o'clock that afternoon, when Pleasonton was between Sudley Springs and Aldie. Pleasonton was to hold the cavalry corps at Gum Springs, east of Aldie, but the captain confirms that Pleasonton recommended advancing the main body through the gap. Both men recognized that, regardless of whether the cavalry corps pushed deeper into the Loudoun Valley the following day, the only sensible move on this day was to move beyond the gap, so that they did not have to fight for it in the future, especially since the clouds of dust thrown up by thousands of horses had broadcast their location to the enemy. Dahlgren then rode as far as the telegraph key in Centreville to send Pleasonton's request to Hooker and waited for a reply. When the wire arrived at Fairfax Station, Hooker's chief of staff, Maj. Gen. Daniel Butterfield instructed Pleasonton, "Under no circumstances advance the main body of your cavalry beyond [Aldie]." Butterfield informed the cavalry chief that the infantry would be holding their positions for the night, and asked that scouting parties be sent through Snicker's Gap as well as toward Leesburg, in an attempt to locate with certainty the enemy infantry now believed to be along the upper Potomac River. Butterfield also referred to DeForest's pending reconnaissance to the Rappahannock River, by way of Warrenton. To insure that there was no misunderstanding the general sent the message with one of Hooker's staff officers, Maj. William Sterling, rather than by return wire. Capt. Benjamin Fisher, acting chief signal officer for the army, accompanied Sterling in the event an observation post could be established in the mountains.[20]

The officers never arrived, but Hooker's adjutant, Brig. Gen. Seth Williams, wisely sent a similar message by wire, though it is unknown when Pleasonton received it. Williams confirmed that in response to new information indicating that the majority of Lee's army was still in Virginia, Hooker had tempered his orders to his infantry commanders. Instead of sending half of the army all the way to Leesburg, the infantry would avoid moving during the killing afternoon heat, and the lead elements would advance no closer to the river than Dranesville and Guilford Station. Williams confirms that Dahlgren had been sent with verbal orders instructing Pleasonton to make "easy marches," placing "the main body of your command in the vicinity of Aldie," while sending only scouting parties "toward Winchester, Berryville and Harpers Ferry." But then Williams confuses the matter. Dropping his cautious, matter of fact approach, he exhorted Pleasonton to "Drive in pickets, if necessary, and get us information. It is better that we should lose men than to be without knowledge of the enemy, as we now seem to be." One could not fault Pleasonton if he was uncertain as to how he was to proceed.[21]

Judson Kilpatrick, commanding a brigade in David Gregg's division was to provide the scouting force for the corps that day. Recently promoted to the rank of brigadier general, Kilpatrick left his camp near Union Mills with orders to march, initially, to Aldie, from where he could control the vital pass through Bull Run Mountain, including the turnpikes leading into the Shenandoah Valley as well as the Old Carolina Road, tracking north south along the line of Bull Run Mountain and Catoctin Mountain. Nine miles from his destination, and following the meeting between Pleasonton and Dahlgren, Kilpatrick received new instructions, ordering him "to push on through Aldie across the mountains into the Valley and join the Cavalry Corps [the following day] at [Noland's Ferry]—reporting from time to time such information as I might gain from the enemy." Prior to departing that morning, Kilpatrick or Gregg, at Pleasonton's direction, dispatched Col. Alfred Duffie and his 1st Rhode Island Cavalry to march due west, through Thoroughfare Gap, and to hold the town of Middleburg that night. On the eighteenth, Duffie was to make a circuit north through Union, Snickersville and Purcellville, rejoining the brigade at Noland's Ferry, above Leesburg and near the mouth of the Monocacy River, the point where Hooker was planning to erect a pontoon bridge across the Potomac River. Hooker remained unwilling to risk another battle without his cavalry corps by his side.[22]

Pursuant to his new instructions, Kilpatrick continued to Aldie, where he collided with a brigade of Southern cavalry. This was completely "unexpected as the enemy was not supposed to be on the south side of the mountains." Having held his command in Culpeper County following the battle at Brandy Station on June 9, Stuart had resumed his march north on June 15, sending Fitz Lee's brigade, under the temporary command of Col. Thomas Munford, to screen Longstreet's advance. Munford crossed the Rappahannock the following day, bivouacking below Upperville on the evening of the sixteenth. Following Munford were the brigades of Beverly Robertson and Rooney Lee, with Grumble Jones and Hampton's brigades bringing up the rear of the division. On the morning of June 17, Munford advanced through Upperville, accompanied by Stuart as far as Middleburg, before continuing to

Aldie, where he was to hold the gap through Bull Run Mountain. It was his pickets who clashed with Kilpatrick's advance east of the town, touching off six days of often desperate fighting for control of the Loudoun Valley.[23]

Stuart intended to screen the advance of Longstreet and A.P. Hill by blocking access to the Loudoun Valley. To accomplish this he ordered Munford to hold Aldie Gap, and Col. John Chambliss, in temporary command of Rooney Lee's brigade, to block Thoroughfare Gap, while Robertson held his brigade near Rectortown, a point from which he could support either Munford or Chambliss. Stuart set up his headquarters in Middleburg, at the center of a road network connecting all three points. John Mosby met with Stuart briefly that morning at Yew Hill, the home of Miss Kitty Shacklett, south of Piedmont Station [modern day Delaplane]. There Mosby presented his friend and benefactor with a horse captured in the Seneca raid, and gave him what information he could pertaining to the position of Hooker's army. The two men separated but met again that afternoon in Middleburg. With Stuart now en route for the Potomac River and neither man expecting another delay, Mosby received permission to again strike the cavalry outpost at Seneca.[24]

Leaving Stuart at Middleburg, Mosby headed toward the Potomac, with between 30 and 40 men, and stopped several miles north of Aldie at the home of James Gulick for some refreshment against the blistering heat of the afternoon. While there, he heard the sounds of the developing battle between Munford and Kilpatrick, and he elected to cancel his plan to raid the outpost at Seneca in favor of moving toward the sound of the guns and sowing confusion behind the Union lines. Avoiding the roads Mosby moved to a point on the Little River Turnpike five miles east of Aldie, whence he could monitor the steady passage of Union cavalry. With three men he passed through this cordon until he observed a home with several horses tied up outside and guarded by a couple of Union orderlies. The horses belonged to Major Sterling and Captain Fisher, who had stopped for dinner at the home of Mr. Almond Birch, a Union sympathizer, prior to delivering the orders they carried to Pleasonton. Mosby seized the orderlies about 10 o'clock. Minutes later the two officers exited the house and were captured as well. After hustling the captives to a safer location, Mosby requested the dispatches that he knew the officers were carrying, thanks to a talkative orderly. Terming these orders the "'open sesame' to Hooker's army," Mosby scribbled out a note of explanation and then gave the papers to one of his men to carry back through the Union lines to Stuart. By daybreak Stuart knew exactly what Hooker's plans were, the manner in which his army was deployed and what he could expect from both Pleasonton and Stahel over the next couple of days.[25]

Kilpatrick's clash with Munford lasted several hours, ending as the sun was going down, and left his brigade badly battered, but thanks to the timely arrival of reinforcements, along with an assist from Duffie, the young general remained in possession of the field. Duffie's arrival in Middleburg had taken Stuart and his staff completely by surprise and forced them to beat a hasty retreat to Rectortown. As he departed Stuart sent one of his aides to Munford, ordering him to fall back to meet this latest threat, the dimensions of which were then unknown. Munford grudgingly complied, giving Kilpatrick a costly tactical victory. Once in Middleburg, Duffie attempted to comply with his orders that he hold the town that night, even though he knew that he was in the midst of at least two Southern brigades. With daylight waning, Stuart met Robertson near Rectortown and ordered an immediate attack against Duffie that forced the Yankees to abandon the town and retire several miles to the south. The bloody fighting left Hooker's plan, such as it was, in tatters.[26]

Following Milroy's defeat at Winchester General Ewell, who was to lead the army into Maryland and Pennsylvania, requested the assistance of Lige White's 35th Battalion as a personal scouting force. The request was granted but White asked that he be allowed to make a strike against Point of Rocks, Maryland, where he hoped to encounter his old nemesis Samuel Means. This request was also granted and on the morning of the seventeenth White led his battalion through Snicker's Gap and across northern Loudoun County to Grubb's Ford, three miles above Point of Rocks. Once across the river White sent Lt. Joshua Crown with Company B toward the rear of the town, while he continued with the remaining five companies along the towpath toward the other end of town. Crown encountered and defeated a detachment of Col. Henry Cole's Maryland Cavalry, driving them for several miles before Crown determined to break off the chase and return to assist White. Crown found White enjoying his own success, having routed a force of the Loudoun Rangers and seizing several supply wagons and an eighteen-car train. Once the men satisfied their wants the train was burned, the track destroyed and telegraph wires were pulled down. White then led his men back across the river and spent the night near Hillsboro before joining Ewell on the eighteenth. According to Stahel, one of his scouting patrols encountered a party of White's men in the vicinity of Leesburg and recovered some horses and mules taken in the raid.[27]

Though the intent of White's raid was strictly personal, the timing and location could not have been worse from a Northern viewpoint. Since White had been relatively inactive for several months, some of the preliminary reports gave the credit to John Mosby. The proximity of the raid to Hooker's planned crossing point at Noland's Ferry raised concerns that Stuart was intending to cross at or near the same location and units were sent racing to hold the crossing before Stuart could arrive. A dismounted cavalry contingent, numbering 1,000 foot-sore men from eight regiments under the command of Capt. Samuel McKee, was sent from Alexandria and was in position by 4 A.M., June 18. Trailing the cavalry was a battalion of engineers and the pontoon train, moving by way of the canal. As to the fate of any guerrillas who might be taken by the advancing troops, they were to be killed and then tried in the opinion of General Butterfield.[28]

On the eighteenth, Pleasonton, still hamstrung by Hooker's over-riding reluctance to risk his cavalry regardless of what the army commander said to the contrary, advanced only in brigade strength along three separate avenues into the Loudoun Valley. John Buford and David Gregg were to sweep the upper region of the county before reuniting at Noland's Ferry in the evening. There they would join General Slocum and his Twelfth Corps, to hold the river crossings in advance of the army. But by five o'clock that morning Pleasonton had a better understanding of the severity of the fighting at Aldie and the toll the battle had exacted in Gregg's division. He also knew that Duffie was cut off at Middleburg, surrounded by enemy cavalry in his front and rear, all of which forced him to alter his plans. Rather than striking for the river, Pleasonton sent Col. Tom Devin and his brigade to Thoroughfare Gap in an effort to relieve Duffie, while Col. William Gamble was instructed to push his brigade to Snicker's Gap and send scouting parties into the Shenandoah Valley. Col. John Irvin Gregg, whose brigade had seen only limited fighting the previous day, would continue the advance toward Middleburg and Ashby's Gap.[29]

Arriving in Middleburg, Gregg learned that Duffie's beleaguered regiment had been driven out of the town during the night. It was later determined that the command had been routed by the 9th Virginia Cavalry that morning, with the survivors, including Duffie, fleeing across Bull Run Mountain to safety. The true extent of his loss would not be realized for several more days, but more than 230 men had been killed, wounded or captured. Colonel Gregg moved quickly through Middleburg until he reached a ridge one mile west of the town, now known as Mount Defiance, where Stuart dug in his heels and the Union advance came to a halt. Stuart's staunch defense coupled with the continuing indecision from Hooker left Pleasonton unwilling to hold his advanced position throughout the night. He elected to retire to Aldie. Gamble, who had skirmished his way to within sight of Snicker's Gap, also opted to retire to Aldie when Munford refused to yield any further ground.[30]

Clearly Pleasonton had not accomplished all that he had hoped to that day. He had not cleared the Loudoun Valley, nor was his command in position along the Potomac River as planned. Moreover he had surrendered most of the ground he had gained during the day, while the loss of the 1st Rhode Island left Kilpatrick's brigade next to useless. Again, it is easy to hold Pleasonton solely accountable for these failures. He stated that Gregg had withdrawn when it appeared that Stuart was trying to draw him away from his supports and onto his infantry, but it is also clear that Hooker was still looking to give battle along the Bull Run-Catoctin-South Mountain line, and he may have tethered Pleasonton to the gaps at Thoroughfare and Aldie as he had done the previous day. In light of the losses he had incurred Pleasonton sought to have Captain McKee's command, the equivalent of an additional brigade, released from their responsibilities along the river and ordered to join him. Without horses, however, they would be of no immediate benefit and they remained near the river for several more days before returning to the remount depots near Washington.[31]

Colonel DeForest's reconnaissance to the Rappahannock had come up short as well. Leaving Centreville that morning, 800 to 1,000 men strong, and after a halt in Gainesville, DeForest resumed the march that afternoon under threatening skies. Based on the information captured by Mosby, Jeb Stuart had alerted Wade Hampton to the Union probe, and the South Carolinian posted his pickets in the gap east of New Baltimore, while holding his main force around Warrenton. In the midst of a violent thunderstorm the Yankees pushed the Southern sharpshooters beyond New Baltimore before flashes of lightening defined Hampton's main line drawn up to oppose any further advance. As one of the Green Mountain boys later admitted, "The heavy thunder and sharp lightening as we sat in the face of the enemy made one feel rather anxious." Once the storm began to abate, DeForest resumed his advance, clearing a line of woods with a squadron from the 1st Vermont. With night now upon him, however, and a force estimated at several thousand attempting to turn his flanks the colonel "did not think it safe to go into the town." Calling in his skirmishers DeForest returned to Centreville.[32]

Pleasonton made another attempt on the nineteenth to force his way across the Loudoun Valley, again sending David Gregg's division through Middleburg to Ashby's Gap and Buford toward Snicker's Gap. With four of his brigades now in position across the valley Stuart rebuffed both efforts after heavy fighting, especially in Gregg's front along the Ashby's Gap Turnpike. Three days of battle had borne little fruit, and Pleasonton was only midway across the Loudoun Valley, having driven Stuart less than a mile that day. Increasingly "apprehensive," and with no hope of a quick penetration of the Blue Ridge, it was Hooker who now, in a reversal of the situation two days earlier, struggled to keep Pleasonton focused on the task of breaking through Stuart's screen.[33]

Increasingly frustrated, Hooker ordered Stahel to abandon his picket lines and to concentrate his division. He intended to send the cavalryman into Maryland searching for the head of Lee's army, while Pleasonton confronted Stuart. Heintzelman concurred that Stahel should now concentrate his division but he insisted that Stahel maintain his picket line. Heintzelman also deflected attempts by Hooker to send his infantry from positions holding Poolesville, Maryland, and Noland's Ferry to the seize the South Mountain Pass. Irritated by Heintzelman's intransigence, the army commander requested clarification from Halleck as to his authority to issue orders directly to the troops under Heintzelman's command. Halleck did little to alleviate the deteriorating relationship between himself and Hooker by waiting several days before replying, and then the answer was not what the army commander wished to hear. Hooker could continue to send orders directly to Heintzelman, but the department commander was under no obligation to comply when those orders were in conflict with his own. In that event Heintzelman would confer with Halleck, and the general-in-chief would make the final decision.[34]

That day, as they listened to the sounds of battle to the west, Stahel's troopers broke down their camps, shipping their excess baggage to Washington as they eagerly awaited orders that would end their months of enforced monotony along the picket line. Several hundred fresh horses were distributed throughout the division, and the men in the 18th Pennsylvania finally received Burnside carbines to replace the inferior weapons they had carried for months. Watching as the ranks swelled with men returning from hospitals and detached service, William Martin believed the invasion was "the best move that the rebs ever made for our cause as it is generally thought that they can never escape." William Wilkins, 1st West Virginia, predicted, "tomorrow perhaps we will be on the war path."[35]

On the morning of June 20, Hooker, still anticipating an attack through the gaps in Bull Run Mountain, ordered Maj. Gen. Winfield Scott Hancock, commanding the Second Corps, to hold Thoroughfare Gap and Gainesville. Col. Tom Devin's cavalry brigade was then relieved of its responsibility for holding the gap and rejoined Buford's division. Hancock's troops did not arrive until the following day so Pleasonton was forced to leave Col. John Taylor's brigade, which had been supporting Devin, in place until the infantry arrived. Now aware that Stuart had his entire division of five brigades blocking his line of advance, Pleasonton sought all of the help that he could muster. Unable to recall Taylor, the general attempted to have the 8th Pennsylvania relieved from its assignment as an escort for the Second Corps but was rebuffed. The general was also under the mistaken impression that he was facing mounted infantry. To counter this possibility Hooker ordered Maj. Gen. George Meade to assist the cavalry with a division from his Fifth Corps.[36]

While the cavalry fought their way across the Loudoun Valley, Lee was willing to receive an attack near the line of the Blue Ridge, and he had directed Longstreet to advance slowly along the eastern slope of the mountains, while A.P. Hill moved north along the west side of the mountains through the Shenandoah Valley. No fighting of consequence took place on June 20, but Hooker did not wish to yield his position covering the capital until both Longstreet and Hill could be located. As Ewell's position was established north of the Potomac and Longstreet's location fixed with some certainty along the Blue Ridge Hooker needed only to determine the position of Hill's corps, a point he reiterated with Pleasonton shortly after five o'clock that afternoon. Thinking that Hill might be tailing Longstreet,

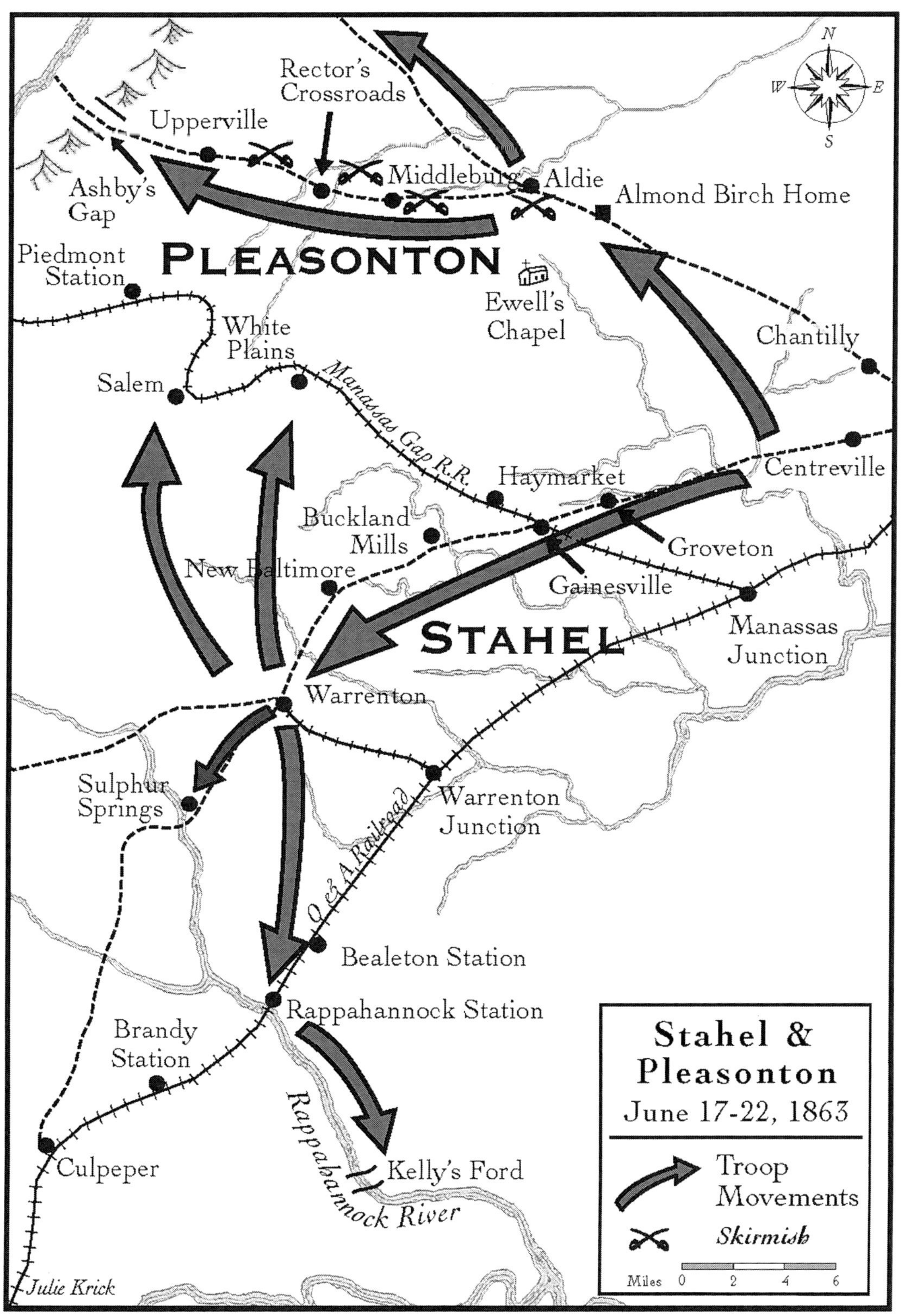

Rector's Crossroads
Upperville
Ashby's Gap
Middleburg
Aldie
Almond Birch Home
Piedmont Station
PLEASONTON
Ewell's Chapel
White Plains
Salem
Chantilly
Manassas Gap R.R.
Haymarket
Centreville
Buckland Mills
Groveton
New Baltimore
Gainesville
STAHEL
Manassas Junction
Warrenton
Sulphur Springs
Warrenton Junction
O. & A. Railroad
Bealeton Station
Rappahannock Station
Brandy Station
Culpeper
Kelly's Ford
Rappahannock River
Julie Krick
Stahel & Pleasonton
June 17-22, 1863
Troop Movements
Skirmish
Miles 0 2 4 6

Hooker directed Stahel to make a reconnaissance across Prince William County to insure that Hill was not a threat to the left flank of his army.[37]

Hooker desired that two separate reconnoitering parties sweep the county. The first, numbering 300 men, was to proceed to Catlett Station, returning through Dumfries and Wolf Run Shoals. A smaller force was to move inside the first column and check the interior of the region, including Brentsville and Maple Valley before returning across Wolf Run Shoals. In the end only the 1st Michigan, led by Lt. Col. Peter Stagg, made the reconnaissance. Stagg departed Centreville at noon and marched to Bristoe Station before halting for the night. The Wolverines resumed the march in the morning passing through Catlett Station, Brentsville and Dumfries. Once they were beyond the army the men found the ride enjoyable, but when they encountered roads still blocked by troops and supply trains "it was very disagreeable and fatiguing."[38]

The men of General Copeland's brigade continued to strip their camps as they came in from the now abandoned picket lines. They had watched for several days as the veterans marched by, "and it was a pity to see the poor fellows go along some dropping by the wayside from exhaustion." The tired, dirty souls were followed by the wounded troopers coming in from the fighting at Aldie and Middleburg, all of which led the Wolverines to believe that Hooker was retreating and they were being called to his relief. Edwin Havens refused to speculate as to where they might be headed. All he knew for sure was that the men had three days rations in their haversacks and two days worth on their wagons, "our blacksmiths are busy shoeing all horses that need it, our revolvers have been emptied of the old loads, thoroughly cleaned and reloaded, ammunition issued and our sabres ground" to a razor's edge. William Rockwell warned his wife, "We are to leave every thing behind and you may not hear from me for some time. But trust in God and have patience." He would not have an opportunity to write her again for nineteen days.[39]

22

June 21–June 24, 1863

"To disperse about 100 guerrillas"

Alfred Pleasonton may not have slept on the night of June 20 as he finalized his plans for battle in the morning. At 3 A.M. he sent off another message to army headquarters, expressing his opinion as to the location of Lee's army. The whereabouts of A.P. Hill's Third Corps remained the unknown. The cavalry chief was correct in recognizing that Hill had been the last element of the army to abandon his lines along the Rappahannock, but by moving behind a screen provided by both Stuart and Longstreet, Hill had dropped out of sight. Pleasonton could only speculate as to Hill's location, telling Seth Williams that Hill had either not yet crossed the Rappahannock, or was "on the way up the valley." His second assumption was correct as Hill was holding the key road junction at Berryville by the afternoon of the twenty-first. After sending his message to Williams, Pleasonton returned to planning his next attempt to pierce Stuart's cavalry screen, an attempt that would focus on Ashby's Gap and result in the second largest cavalry battle of the war to date. Williams, however, could not ignore Pleasonton's remark that Hill might be lingering behind, "guarding" the line of the Rappahannock, and he turned again to Julius Stahel. The Hungarian was to "make without delay a reconnaissance in force in the direction of Warrenton and the Upper Rappahannock." If he encountered Hampton's brigade, believed to still be in the vicinity of Warrenton he was to destroy it. Most important, he was to "make every effort to ascertain the whereabouts of the enemy's forces, and particularly of the corps commanded by A.P. Hill," determining if he had "passed up the Shenandoah Valley." He was also to ascertain if the railroad bridge at Rappahannock Station had been repaired.[1]

When Stahel received these orders is unknown, but Williams sent them at eight thirty-five on the morning of the twenty-first. The division, minus Stagg's 1st Michigan, was on the move by 10 A.M., by which time the men had been listening to the sound of Pleasonton's battle, west of Middleburg, for two hours. The men were "wild with joy," at the prospect of joining the fight, finally "measuring their strength with the greybacks." Taking the field for the first time in months were brigade commanders, Joseph Copeland and R. Butler Price. Before departing, George Telling, 6th Michigan, dashed off a hurried letter to his brother explaining that a bulletproof vest he ordered had just arrived. Telling, who had immediately put the device to a test by firing his revolver at it, remarked, "I am satisfied that no shot will penetrate it," and he predicted, "The next time you hear from me will be in Pennsylvania or Maryland and no doubt [I will have] had some hard fighting." But as they turned toward Centreville and Gainesville the spirits of the men sank as they realized, once again, they were to play only a secondary role to the Cavalry Corps.[2]

The division was through Centreville by 3 P.M., but Stahel remained there, communicating with army headquarters and attempting to determine Stagg's location, lest the two forces mistakenly engage each other along the route. After leaving instructions for Stagg, who had already re-entered the lines at Wolf Run Shoals, Stahel set out to rejoin the division. Brig. Gen. Gouverneur Warren, Hooker's chief topographical engineer, was in the area examining the road network in the event another battle might take place along Bull Run. He encountered Copeland's brigade resting near Groveton. Warren was incensed, and wrote a highly critical report with lasting repercussions for both Copeland and Stahel. Warren was especially critical of the former judge, depicting a man in an apparent state of confusion. "A General Copeland introduced himself; stated that he was waiting orders from Gen. Stahel at Centreville; enquired where Bull Run was, which he had crossed a short time previous; he was laboring under the erroneous supposition that Cub Run was south of Bull Run and was in a quandary about watering the horses which he had neglected to do at the right place." Disgusted, Warren left the cavalry behind and continued on to Gainesville.[3]

Warren most certainly understood the urgency of the situation as well as the importance of Stahel's expedition and was furious with the lack of haste exhibited by the cavalry. The situation was only made worse when Warren encountered a "newspaper boy" who had been accosted "by a force of 150 rebel cavalry" earlier that afternoon near Groveton. These men were from the Phillips Legion, detached from Hampton's brigade, and were the same troops who routed a patrol from the 8th Pennsylvania Cavalry earlier that day near New Baltimore. Stahel's cavalry finally arrived at eight-thirty, bivouacking between Buckland and New Baltimore. By the time Warren's report reached headquarters, Hooker was aware that Stahel had taken his wagon train with him. Believing that the wagons would impede Stahel's rate of march, Butterfield urged him to continue without them. This perceived error in judgment became another nail in Stahel's coffin, but it appears that in his haste to depart Fairfax Court House, as quickly as possible, Stahel did not distribute a sufficient forage ration to be carried by the men. As the men had previously cooked three days rations and distributed ammunition, Stahel took the field leaving the wagons to bring up the additional forage when they could. The wagons did not reach Gainesville until the morning of the twenty-second after an all night march, and there they remained following Butterfield's reprimand. This left the horses with but one ration of fodder beyond the grass they grazed at night and adversely affected Stahel's ability to stay in the field.[4]

Stahel believed, based on the reports from DeForest following his skirmish near Warrenton on the eighteenth, that he would encounter Hampton's brigade in the same vicinity. He sent scouting parties out during the night and intended to attack Hampton in the morning, unaware that Hampton had already joined Stuart and had been heavily involved in the fighting between Middleburg and Upperville during the day. At 3 A.M., June 22, Stahel sent Capt. Ulric Dahlgren with a small detail from the 6th Michigan into Warrenton, following with the entire command three hours later. Informed by Dahlgren that the town was unoccupied, Stahel dispatched large scouting parties from Copeland's brigade to the outskirts of Fredericksburg as well as to Bealeton Station and Kelly's Ford, with one detachment crossing the Rappahannock River and probing to the west for several miles. Smaller details examined the country toward White Plains and Salem. Each returned reporting no sign of the enemy. Stahel noted that the railroad bridge at Rappahannock Station had not been repaired and concluded that the remainder of Stuart's cavalry had passed through the area by the nineteenth. More important, Stahel established with certainty that no Confederate infantry remained in Fauquier County or along the Rappahannock, but any plans that he had to examine the upper region of Culpeper County and lower Rappahannock County in an effort to locate Hill were now negated by events beyond his control.[5]

John Mosby made several claims after the war about his effectiveness in tethering Stahel's division to the defensive lines around the capital when it might have done better service attached to the army. Several of these claims can be challenged but the last is entirely justified, reflecting a contribution to the campaign that the partisan could not have been aware of at the time. Following his capture of Major Sterling and Captain Fisher on the night of June 17, Mosby found the Little River Turnpike a hive of activity as hundreds of supply and sutler's wagons moved between Fairfax Court House and the troops at Aldie and Gum Spring. Two wagons had been looted along the road on the eighteenth, while Mosby continued to move through the Union columns with impunity. During the early hours of the nineteenth Mosby captured a teamster out of a cherry tree, reportedly within two hundred yards of First Corps headquarters. "The Gray Ghost's" omnipresence left one officer with the impression that the country around Aldie was "full of guerrillas," and he suggested that all "couriers should have escorts of ten or twelve men."[6]

Taking advantage of the fact that they now held the heart of his territory in strength, the Federals made several attempts to end Mosby's career. On the twentieth, while the cavalry corps was refitting prior to their attack the following day, Pleasonton directed David Gregg to arrest any and all men found in and around Middleburg on the belief that they either "belong to or are implicated with Mosby." Gregg's troopers seized seven partisans, but that night a second wagon train was attacked along the turnpike. The following night General Meade received information that Mosby and a group of his men would pass Dunblane, the home of Dr. Jesse Ewell, late that night or early on the morning of the twenty-second. Ewell's home sat along a seldom-used path over Bull Run Mountain that allowed Mosby to avoid the heavy Union traffic along the turnpike. Meade rushed to implement an ambush, sending 136 men from the 14th U.S. Infantry and the 17th Pennsylvania Cavalry to the Ewell home. It was daylight before the troops were in place after a difficult march under a steady rain. The men had just settled in when the guerrillas rode into view, but when the order to fire was given most of the weapons failed to discharge on account of wet powder. Still, three Rangers were wounded, and one Union soldier was killed as Mosby ordered his men to charge through the ambush to safety. In reporting the incident that morning General Meade concluded, "the prettiest chance in the world to dispose of Mr. Mosby was lost."[7]

On June 21, Meade intended to send a train of 20 wagons from Aldie to a supply point between Chantilly and Jermantown. Hoping to avoid another attack he asked Pleasonton if he would also be sending back any wagons and if so Meade suggested that they be combined into one train. Meade also requested a cavalry escort to discourage the Rangers, but following the heavy fighting that day Pleasonton was not in a position to assist, and Meade, whose infantry had supported the cavalry throughout the day, apparently held the train until the next day, when it was sent through unescorted. After escaping the ambush and seeing to his wounded, Mosby led a group of 30 men back to the Little River Turnpike and intercepted Meade's wagons "near the junction of the Leesburg road" [present day Gilbert's Corner]. His men were in the process of unhitching the mules when a detachment from the 12th Illinois Cavalry rode up and dispersed the raiders, capturing a handful of men and recovering some of the mules. This minor affair, however, combined with the knowledge that a second Southern force (two companies of the Phillips Legion) was within the Union lines, and responsible for the attack on the 8th Pennsylvania Cavalry near New Baltimore as well as the robbery of the newsboy near Groveton, left the Union high command uneasy.[8]

Maj. Gen. Winfield Hancock notified Hooker about the attack near New Baltimore at 6:20 P.M. on June 22. Forty minutes later Hancock was notified of the attack on the supply train near Chantilly. In that message Butterfield warned that Hancock should not send in any additional wagon trains until Stahel was recalled and could escort them. In a second telegram to Hancock, received at the same hour, Butterfield directed that Stahel "return without delay, to dispose his forces so as to catch the party inside our lines if possible." Hancock quickly dispatched two riders "by different routes" to Stahel with the orders that he return. Butterfield also diverted Stagg, who was en route to rejoin Stahel, and sent him instead by way of Chantilly "to try and capture the band that are prowling inside our lines." Stagg had his men back in the saddle by dark, though after the long march of the previous few days he moved slowly, reaching Fairfax Court House just before daylight. There he rested again until noon when he set out on a twelve-hour ride scouring the region to the Potomac River and back.[9]

When Stahel received the recall order is unknown. A newspaper account stating that the command started back "early Monday morning," and linking it to the raid on the wagon train is incorrect. Due to events of the next week Stahel never wrote a complete report of the reconnaissance, and it was not until the following year that he addressed the conclusion of his expedition. "Just as I was about to cross the Rappahannock with two Brigades, one of my Brigades being already across ... I received the [order to return]. It was with feelings of bitter regret and disappointment that I received this order inasmuch as.... All of Lee's supplies had to pass up between the Rappahannock and Blue Ridge or cross into the Shenandoah Valley and my force was sufficient to have destroyed his entire trains.... There would have been hardly any obstacle in my way ... but I was compelled to abandon my movement ... to disperse about 100 guerrillas." What Stahel could have accomplished by pushing his division across the Rappahannock and going after Lee's supply lines is a matter of conjecture, as the lack of forage for his horses would have told before long, but there were no troops to intercept him. If he had quickly located and attacked Hill's supply train he would have, almost certainly, delayed Lee or forced him to alter his plans. John Mosby believed that Stahel "might have done much damage on Gen. Lee's line of communication, as it was entirely uncovered." After the war the aging partisan was critical of Hooker for making the same mistake that he accused others of making, that being "keeping this large force [Stahel] to watch my small one." Stahel's aborted reconnaissance was a factor, however, in the decision by Lee and Stuart to leave two brigades in the Loudoun Valley when the cavalry chief began his controversial ride to Pennsylvania a couple of days later.[10]

Stahel, unlike Hooker and Pleasonton, understood the futility of chasing Mosby, and saw the recall as an irrational response based on panic. At issue was the manner in which Stahel and Hooker understood the initial orders given to Stahel on the morning of the twenty-first, because once he departed Centreville that afternoon he would be beyond telegraphic communication and forced to rely upon couriers and his own discretion and interpretation. The orders, as written by Seth Williams, do not state the size of the force that

Stahel was to take with him, but Stahel clearly believed he was to take his entire division based on previous instructions to abandon his picket lines and concentrate his command. Stahel was then directed to make "a reconnaissance in force in the direction of Warrenton and the Upper Rappahannock," establishing his headquarters in Warrenton, which he did. He was tasked with examining the lower fords of the river, to include the crossing at Rappahannock Station, which he did. If he located Hampton's brigade near Warrenton he was to "attack, destroy, capture, or disperse it," but as Hampton had already joined Stuart at Middleburg, Stahel focused on the final aspect of the instructions, to "make every effort to ascertain the whereabouts of the enemy's forces, and particularly of the corps commanded by A.P. Hill. It is important to ascertain whether or not they have passed up the Shenandoah Valley." Stahel appears to have followed the orders to the letter, electing to act decisively where he was given the latitude. Thus when the recall order arrived he was either moving or planning to move in strength across the Rappahannock in search of Hill. But in communicating with Heintzelman directly on June 22, Hooker placed an entirely different twist on the orders, stating only that Stahel was "to make a reconnaissance with his *disposable* cavalry in the direction of Warrenton, where I had reason to believe the enemy held a brigade of cavalry." There was no mention of scouting the Rappahannock crossings or searching for Hill, and Hooker concluded, "Unless he should fall in with the enemy, I shall look for his return to-night." If this was truly what Hooker believed he then had every reason to expect that Stahel was in position to pursue Mosby promptly, but Hooker also had every reason to be deceptive, when communicating with Heintzelman, as he continued to stretch the limits of his authority over the troops in Heintzelman's department.[11]

Beyond this issue, however, as well as the obvious point that Mosby had dispersed his men long before Butterfield issued the recall order, was the fact that Pleasonton had by then concentrated his entire corps around Aldie. He had withdrawn from the line of the Blue Ridge on the morning of the twenty-second, and it was troopers from Buford's division who had broken up the attack on the train that afternoon. Pleasonton had sustained close to 1,000 casualties and lost many hundreds of horses in the recent fighting, but Col. John Taylor's brigade was fresh, having been only lightly engaged that morning in covering Pleasonton's withdrawal. Though it is impossible to create an accurate timeline for the events of the twenty-second, it was Taylor's brigade that should have been sent after Mosby, rather than Stahel. But this did not fit Pleasonton's overall scheme. He continued to covet Stahel's division, sending in another request that afternoon "that my force may be augmented by some regiments drawn from other commands," in the hope of accomplishing this goal.[12]

Once he received the recall order there is nothing to suggest that Stahel did anything but comply as quickly as he could call in his scattered brigades, but events conspired against him. Late on the twenty-second, Hancock, whose corps remained near Thoroughfare Gap, reported that he continued to lose men within Stahel's lines. But Stahel had not established a picket line nor had he been told to. While there is every reason to believe that Stahel was still in Warrenton that day, it is difficult to determine exactly the manner in which his men were dispersed. Stahel's preliminary report, dated June 23, from Gainesville, suggests that his men crossed the river near Sulphur Springs, raising the possibility that at least two detachments had already crossed the river, as Copeland had troopers across the river farther south. Regardless, Stahel's focus was to the south and west of Warrenton, with only a cursory effort made to scout the region to the north as Pleasonton had been in the area for several days. Hancock's assumption was based on an earlier assertion from Butterfield that Stahel had cleared the region of enemy troops the previous day. When none were found, however,

Stahel moved his focus to the south and west, while Hancock relaxed, believing, as Butterfield had assured him, "There cannot be much danger to your command or rear while [Stahel] is there in such force as he is." On June 23, as his losses mounted and his infamous temper reached a boiling point, Hancock engaged Stahel in a debate over responsibility for the loss of his men. Then the infantryman asked Stahel for the loan of 200 men to assist the 8th Pennsylvania Cavalry, which was already attached to his corps. Aside from the fact that the request may have been improper, Stahel knew only that he had been ordered back with his entire division and refused Hancock's request. Indignant, Hancock dropped the entire matter on Hooker's desk, "but the reply I received was such as to deter me from asking again." While this should have alerted Hancock to the urgent need for cavalry elsewhere, the timing of the dispute did not bode well for Stahel.[13]

The extent to which Pleasonton was aware of this dispute is unknown but he was certainly aware that Stahel had been in the field for several days and was in no way accountable for Mosby's recent attacks on the wagon trains. Nor was Stahel accountable for the capture of the two officers at the Birch home on the seventeenth, which occurred well beyond Stahel's former picket line. But that night Pleasonton sat down with one of his aides, Capt. Elon Farnsworth, to bring the matter of Stahel's division before Congressman John Farnsworth, Pleasonton's friend and benefactor and Elon's uncle. Pleasonton sought to incorporate Stahel's division within his corps as a means of gaining his second star and reaching parity with the other corps commanders. Furthermore that Stahel was already a major general meant that he was an obstacle to be removed entirely before Pleasonton could succeed. "With regard to General *Stahel* he ranks me & if put over me I shall retire," the corps commander groused. Pleasonton then challenged Stahel's ability and competence, stating he "has not shown himself a cavalryman & it is ruining cavalry to place it under him." Addressing the events of the previous day Pleasonton claimed disingenuously, "the guerrillas under *Mosby* are burning trains ... & Stahel's force is watching empty air down about Washington." This was a canard of the first magnitude, but Pleasonton continued, telling Farnsworth "if the President prefers General *Stahel*, let him have all the cavalry, *but concentrate it*, or when the shock comes between the two armies he will painfully [realize] the truth of what I now tell him." Mimicking his superior, Captain Farnsworth also hung responsibility for Mosby's recent successes entirely around Stahel's neck. "Trains passing between here and Fairfax C.H. are burned by Bushwhackers and dispatches intercepted and yet Stahel does nothing. *Now* if you [were] to get the cavalry consolidated and Stahel left out for Gods sake do it." Hoping to insure the congressman's aid Pleasonton suggested that he would recommend Elon for promotion to brigadier with a commensurate command in the expanded corps. "I am sadly in want of officers with the proper dash to command cavalry.... Do assist us until we get ahead of the rebs." Pleasonton had been recommended for promotion to major general on June 18, a fact that he was probably aware of. What he was probably not aware of at this time was that the request had been approved effective June 22.[14]

Stahel had his troopers headed back to Fairfax Court House by 6 A.M. on the twenty-third. Copeland, who started from Bealeton Station, rejoined Stahel and Price at Gainesville, where they gained a few hours rest before resuming the march at three o'clock the next morning. When he reached Fairfax six hours later, Lt. Col. Ebenezer Gould told his wife, "We have been out three days and nights in the saddle nearly all the time.... I do not think I slept during the time over five hours." There would be no further rest, however, as they found a fresh set of marching orders awaiting them, directing that they "be ready to move in one hour."[15]

23

June 22–June 25, 1863

"We may have stirring times for a while now"

Pleasonton's cavalry, advancing in two columns and aided by infantry during the morning and early afternoon of the twenty-first, had driven Stuart to the outskirts of Upperville. When on the verge of finally penetrating the Southern cavalry screen, Pleasonton had found his way blocked by Southern infantry and artillery at Ashby's Gap. Realizing that he could not force the gap without incurring significant casualties, the Union commander elected to retire on the twenty-second. Light skirmishing continued throughout the morning, as Stuart maintained close contact with the Federals during their retrograde movement. At least one spirited attack was made against a Union regiment just as it went into camp west of Aldie, but by afternoon the beauty of the valley was again apparent as the clouds of dust and gun smoke dissipated. The lines were much as they had been on the night of June 17, as the tired, dusty men dropped to the ground for some well-deserved rest. The Yankees believed they had given Stuart a good thrashing, especially the previous day when they had driven him back upon his infantry supports in Ashby's Gap. The extent of the intelligence garnered during the prolonged fighting remains open to question however. Reluctant to risk losing his cavalry, Hooker had only grudgingly assented to Pleasonton's request to seize "one the gaps in the Blue Ridge." The Federals could not establish any foothold in Ashby's Gap, however, as Longstreet succored Stuart in his hour of need, throwing a wall of artillery and infantry into the breech. Still, Pleasonton was able to draw a reasonably accurate picture of the manner in which Lee's army was dispersed. With two-thirds of the Confederate army still in Virginia, Hooker could not be certain that the next battle would not be fought near one of the mountain gaps bordering the Loudoun Valley. However, once it became apparent that Pleasonton was no longer intent on continuing his offensive, Longstreet resumed his march to the Potomac, which he began crossing on June 25. A.P. Hill, who had not been delayed by the recent fighting, had begun crossing the river on the twenty-fourth. Once Longstreet resumed his march to the river, Hooker was free to abandon any plans for a battle in Virginia and push his troops across the river as well.[1]

On June 19, Hooker had elected to move the crossing point from Noland's Ferry to nearby Edward's Ferry, and the first of two pontoon bridges was completed across the Potomac River at that location on the morning of the twenty-first. In the midst of his battle that day Pleasonton had been instructed to send a regiment to aid General Slocum's infantry holding the crossing near Leesburg, but it was not until the twenty-fourth that he reluctantly released the 10th New York Cavalry to assist Slocum. Clashes in the streets of Frederick,

Maryland, on Saturday and Sunday also raised concerns for the safety of the northern end of the span, and Capt. Samuel McKee was instructed, "to drive out the marauders."[2]

These marauders were a battalion of the 1st Maryland Cavalry led by Capt. George Emack and Maj. Harry Gilmor. On Saturday afternoon, Gilmor sent a scouting party into the city that captured three members of the 1st Connecticut Cavalry. They also paroled the Union soldiers found in a local hospital. On Sunday, Gilmor returned with a larger force intent on burning a bridge over the Monocacy River. About 2 P.M. the Southerners began skirmishing with Capt. George Vernon's company of Cole's Maryland (Federal) Cavalry around South Market Square in a clash that residents thought "was quite exciting," as troopers in blue and gray raced through the city "at a furious rate and made the bullets whistle in every direction." Vernon, recognizing that he was outnumbered eventually withdrew. Gilmor, though greeted by an effusive crowd, was equally cautious and remained but a short time before making an unsuccessful attempt to destroy the bridge. Shortly before three o'clock, a detachment from the 2nd U.S. Cavalry had arrived from McKee, but finding the city again quiet it also withdrew.[3]

At Poolesville, Col. Albert Jewett received orders directing him to march to Harpers Ferry with the troops then under his command. Jewett initially balked at the directive, referring it to Heintzelman who approved the move on the twenty-fourth. Jewett's recalcitrance forced Hooker to again request that Heintzelman's troops be instructed to "obey promptly any orders they may receive from me." While ordering that other troops would now obey any orders from the army commander Halleck ignored the request as it pertained to Heintzelman, telling Hooker, "No other troops can be withdrawn from the Defenses of Washington." Heintzelman was, in fact, telling his commanders to "comply" with Hooker's orders promptly and report "them afterwards," but Jewett was apparently unaware of this edict. Jewett arrived at Harpers Ferry on the morning of June 26, at which time his brigade became part of a garrison force led by Maj. Gen. William French. Thoroughly disgusted, Heintzelman complained, "I have lost all the troops I had beyond the entrenchments."[4]

Well to the south Lt. Col. Edward Platt, a member of Hooker's staff, conducted an inspection of the defenses along the Occoquan River on June 22, and men from the 12th, 13th and 14th Vermont regiments were soon set to felling more trees and throwing more dirt in a continuing effort to shore up the defenses, especially those at the several fords between the mouth of the river and Union Mills. The move to the old line was unpopular, as was the menial labor, but the men, whose terms of enlistment were about to expire, accepted it grudgingly. "I don't like the move much," Lt. Col. Roswell Farnham complained, "but I suppose I can stand it about as long as we shall be in the service unless the Gov't persuades the men to stay longer." The following day he told his wife, "We have had an invitation to join Hooker's Army & remain six months longer!" But in an attempt to reassure her he added, "You need not be alarmed for there are not a hundred men in the brigade who will do it.... We have been here nine months & have done no fighting & are going home just as the exciting times are coming on." On June 23, however, the matter was settled as the army resumed moving north and Stannard was informed that his brigade had been transferred to the First Corps, Army of the Potomac. He was told to remain along the river until the army was gone and then follow. "It is quite probable," one infantryman surmised, "that we may have stirring times for a while now."[5]

General Stahel also found orders awaiting him upon his return to Fairfax Court House, directing that he march with his entire command to join General French at Harpers Ferry.

He was instructed to ford the river at Young's Island, downstream from Edward's Ferry, which would lessen the congestion at the pontoon bridge. The ford at Young's Island was "practicable" for his wagons and artillery. Unfortunately for the men who crossed at Young's Island the information concerning the conditions at the ford was incorrect: the water ran four feet deep. Once across the river, Stahel was "to drive away and destroy any rebel force of cavalry now on the north side of the Potomac" as well as examine the gaps at South Mountain.[6]

During their brief respite at Fairfax, Stahel's troopers were allowed to unsaddle and feed their horses, "but not undue our things as we may have to march again before night," noted a weary trooper. In the few hours they were granted to recover from their just completed mission they gathered two days rations for their horses and restocked their saddlebags with three days rations for themselves. An additional four days rations were loaded onto the wagons. By six o'clock that evening they were again on the move, marching to Dranesville that night.

In the morning, June 25, having apparently missed the directive to cross at Young's Island or because he realized that the condition of the ford made it barely practicable, Stahel continued to Edward's Ferry, only to find the crossing point choked with the infantry and wagons of the Eleventh Corps. This irritated Maj. Gen. Oliver O. Howard, commanding the corps, since he expected that the two commands would cross at separate points, and that Stahel would then lead his infantry through Maryland. Stahel's arrival "in a covered spring wagon drawn by four white mules" did little to enhance his standing with Howard. An agreement was apparently reached, however, and Colonel Price was crossing the pontoon bridge by eight-forty that morning. The other two brigades waited at the ferry for up to three hours before they backtracked to Young's Island, with DeForest in the van. Andrew Buck, 7th Michigan, probably spoke for the men in both brigades, when he complained, "our boots filled with water and our pants soaked to our knees added none to our comfort," as they waded through water up to the shoulders on their animals. Exceedingly tired and chilled by a "drizzling rain" the men went into bivouac well after dark: Price at Urbana, where the men stood to horse through the night, DeForest at Licksville and Copeland at Poolesville. Copeland's wagons remained in Virginia that night, guarded by a squadron of the 5th Michigan led by Maj. Crawley Dake. Dake would not complete his crossing until the twenty-seventh. Hooker charged Stahel with gathering "information of incalculable value" as to the location of the enemy. "The future movements of" the Army of the Potomac now rested upon Stahel's shoulders.[7]

General Howard made no mention of Stahel or the confusion at Edward's Ferry in his autobiography, but he did refer to an incident that took place on the twenty-fourth when he believed that he was almost captured by Mosby and "his peculiar force of guerrillas." Days earlier the general reported the capture of some stragglers by either "guerrillas or Mosby's cavalry." Now, Howard spoke of the "bushwhackers" that invested the region as "scouts, spies, and all partisan insurgents who were never really made part of the Confederate army. They penetrated our lines ... picked off our aids and messengers ... and circulated every sort of false story that might be made use of to mislead us." It is unclear, based on his description of the incident, exactly how he became aware of his brush with capture near Goose Creek that day. Stating that the guerrillas were concealed in a thicket near the road he wrote, "They saw horsemen approaching, at first at a slow pace, but we outnumbered them, so their leader decided not to attack."[8]

Following his strike against the wagon train on June 22, Mosby continued to scout the Union lines, determining that Hooker had briefly halted the movement of his army while he waited to see if Lee would give battle south of the Potomac. Stuart had maintained contact with Pleasonton's cavalry as it fell back from Upperville on the twenty-second, and now made his headquarters at the home of Clinton Rector at Rector's Crossroads. It was here that Stuart discussed with Mosby his plan to exit the Loudoun Valley through one of the gaps in Bull Run Mountain with three of his brigades and move north to the Potomac River, all the while skirting the Union army, which he believed to be holding in place. At Stuart's request, Mosby made another pass through the Union lines to confirm this fact. Finding the situation unchanged, Mosby sent one of his men back to notify Stuart, while he continued to gather intelligence.

On the evening of June 24, Stuart ordered the three brigades now led by Fitz Lee, John Chambliss and Wade Hampton, along with James Breathed's battery of horse artillery to rendezvous at Salem. They departed under cover of darkness, intent on passing through Glascock's Gap without being observed by the Union troops scattered throughout the region. The plan went awry almost immediately when they encountered Hancock's Second Corps near Haymarket, and Stuart could not resist the urge to shell the Union column with his artillery. Finding the roads clogged with Union troops and having just announced his presence Stuart abandoned the plan to meet Mosby at Gum Spring, which was also Hancock's destination. With his timetable already in shambles, and with clear evidence before him that the Army of the Potomac was again in motion, Stuart elected to turn loose his horses, deemed "already worn and jaded," to graze while he considered his options. Realizing that he could no longer follow his preferred route to the Potomac, Stuart opted to swing farther south and east, moving entirely around Hooker rather than slicing through his army. Thus on June 26, he moved his column through Brentsville, halting for the night west of Wolf Run Shoals.[9]

Occupied though he was defending and protecting his department from Hooker's continuing attempts to pick it clean of troops, Heintzelman, like Hooker days earlier, showed a prescient concern for the crossing at Wolf Run Shoals. For months he had maintained a military presence at the ford for fear that Stuart would lead a raid against the capital from that point. Hooker, too, had ensured that it was held until the last instant by Stannard's brigade, but the Vermonters had begun evacuating the defenses on the twenty-fourth. That day Heintzelman sent one of his staff officers to examine the strength of the defenses, warning the officer to abandon the mission "if there is the least possibility of your being attacked." When the 12th Vermont departed the next morning, Lt. Col. Roswell Farnham observed, "there was nothing to prevent the Rebels coming into our rear as we marched from the Shoals." Hooker, as well, continued to view the crossing as an unguarded back door, and on June 25, he ordered Capt. Julius Mason, commanding the 5th U.S. Cavalry, to "send a scouting party" to the ford, with instructions to remain throughout the night "to give timely notice should the enemy attempt to cross at that point." Mason was to observe the approaches to the depot at Fairfax Station with the remainder of his command, and then follow the army as a rear guard the following day. He was to be supported at Fairfax Station by a regiment from the Sixth Corps but both efforts were a day or two too early, and Stuart's arrival went undetected.[10]

On June 24 Hooker sent a note to Pleasonton asking if he could not "devise some way to capture Moseby and his party." By way of reply the cavalry chief said only, "I shall try Mosby tomorrow." At about the same time Meade learned that "Mosby's gang will rendezvous in the mountains ... to-night." Meade, who cared not a wit for the cavalry and may have held them responsible for the failure against Mosby a couple of days earlier, opted to rely solely upon his Regulars for this attempt. He sent Capt. Henry W. Freedley, 3rd U.S. Infantry, with 100 men in an "endeavor to entrap" the guerrilla leader. The next morning, still intent on meeting Stuart at Gum Spring, Mosby stopped for breakfast along the route. As he later recounted the incident, "Two men had been sent forward on a picket; but they had scarcely got a hundred yards before a volley was fired; and the bullets whistled all around us. We sprang upon our horses; but, as the men did not return, we knew they must have been killed or captured." Mosby learned that Meade was responsible for this second "ambuscade," and questioned, "if he would have called this *bushwhacking*." One of the two pickets was captured, while the other apparently escaped. Making "a *detour*" around the Union troops in the vicinity Mosby continued toward the rendezvous point only to find Union infantry moving along all the roads. Just one or two nights earlier Mosby had captured two Union soldiers along the heavily traveled Little River Turnpike and with them on either side he rode the length of a Union wagon train, "a mile or so in length," and through an escorting column of cavalry as he "was anxious to get to Stuart that night." Now, the man whose reputation rested in large measure on his ability to pass through enemy lines found that he could not, and he assumed that if he could not then Stuart could not either and thus had abandoned his venture. Mosby, who had just survived a second attempt to end his career by ambush in three days, concluded to abandon his attempts to reach Stuart as well. Nor did he attempt to reach any element of the main army with the information he had gleaned over the last couple of days. Instead, on June 28, Mosby headed west into the Shenandoah Valley and then north making his own brief incursion into Pennsylvania, returning with several hundred head of cattle and horses as well as twelve Negroes.[11]

24

June 25–June 30, 1863

"Washington was again like a city besieged as after Bull Run"

By the time Stahel reached the Maryland shore his orders had changed. Rather than reporting to General French at Harpers Ferry, he was now to send only a "sufficient escort" to aid the general while reporting with his division to Maj. Gen. John Reynolds, who held a temporary wing command that included his First Corps as well as the Third and Eleventh Corps. Stahel was to immediately send one brigade to seize Crampton's Gap and Turner's Gap in South Mountain and hold them until infantry and artillery from the Eleventh Corps could arrive. He assigned this task to Colonel DeForest. With the remainder of his division, Stahel was to screen the advance of Reynolds' infantry "in the direction of Frederick, [Maryland] and Gettysburg, [Pennsylvania]." He was to push his troopers as far to the east as necessary to "drive from that country every rebel in it."[1]

DeForest moved through Adamstown, Jefferson and Burkittsville, before passing through Crampton's Gap and on to Rohrersville, where he spent the night of June 26, in advance of the infantry that held the gaps in South Mountain. Stahel arrived in Frederick about noon to find "the stars & stripes ... floating from nearly every window & door." Many of the citizens poured into the streets "waving Union flags and making other demonstrations of joy" as the troops marched past, and by five o'clock that afternoon one overawed resident estimated that ten thousand horse soldiers had passed through. Stahel sent Price to Middletown to support DeForest, while a couple of regiments went to Lewistown to hold the roads north of Frederick.[2]

Stahel took dinner at the home of Lawrence Brengle and wrote a message to Reynolds, in which he detailed the military situation, as he understood it, as well as outlining what his men had accomplished during the day. He then rode ten miles west to meet with Price at Middletown and assess the situation at South Mountain. He returned to Frederick sometime after 7 P.M. Late that evening Sgt. Charles Phelps, 5th New York, was summoned to the Dill Hotel to meet with Stahel. Phelps, who was one of Stahel's scouts, stated that the meeting took place after eleven o'clock and that he found Stahel, and several other officers, marking enemy positions on a map and outlining routes for the division to follow in the morning. Considering the many miles that he had ridden over the last week, the mule drawn spring-wagon that drew snickers from many observers may have provided Stahel the only opportunity to get a few minutes of rest. Regardless, the many miles were taking a toll on the saddle-weary command.[3]

Unused to the rigors of constant campaigning, Stahel's men and horses quickly con-

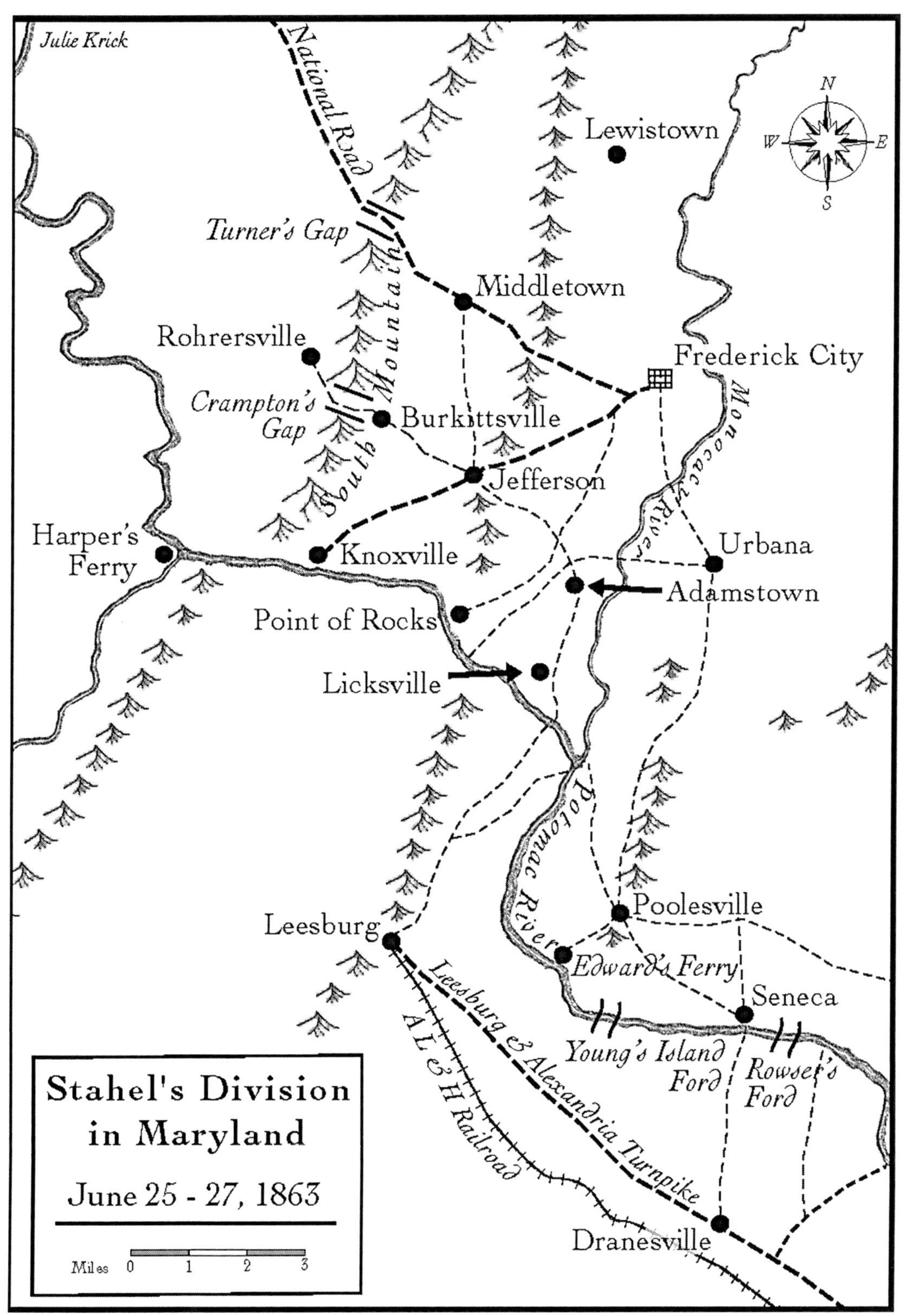
Julie Krick
National Road
Lewistown
N
W
E
S
Turner's Gap
South Mountain
Middletown
Rohrersville
Frederick City
Crampton's Gap
Burkittsville
Monocacy River
Jefferson
Harper's Ferry
Knoxville
Urbana
Adamstown
Point of Rocks
Licksville
Potomac River
Leesburg
Poolesville
Edward's Ferry
Seneca
Leesburg & Alexandria Turnpike
AL & H Railroad
Young's Island Ford
Rowser's Ford
Dranesville
Stahel's Division in Maryland
June 25 - 27, 1863
Miles 0 1 2 3

sumed the rations they carried. Without sufficient time to recover from the expedition to the Rappahannock or to forage along the route to Frederick, and with the division's supply train delayed at the river, the horses began to falter that evening. More important, Stahel must have been near the point of total exhaustion, as evidenced by the fact that after writing his report to Reynolds at three o'clock that afternoon he had no idea where to send it. Thus the report languished on his desk until five-thirty the following afternoon. If Reynolds was not hearing from Stahel, he was getting an earful from Howard, who remained angry over the confusion at the river and the resulting delay that left some of the cavalry moving behind his infantry, rather than out front protecting and expediting his advance. Ignoring the fact that DeForest's men were now well to his front, Howard credited his own headquarters escort for scouting the gaps in South Mountain. Hearing nothing to the contrary from Stahel, Reynolds assumed, "The cavalry sent out by Stahel does nothing. They go into camp behind the infantry, and send out small squads from [there]." When these reports reached Hooker he sent a note to Halleck requesting, in language remarkably reminiscent of that used earlier by Pleasonton in his letter to Congressman Farnsworth, that Stahel be transferred, claiming, "His presence here as senior major-general will much embarrass me and retard my movements."[4]

Earlier that afternoon Pleasonton, whose own troopers had been resting and refitting for four days, dismissed a report from Hancock that "a body of several thousand cavalry" had been detected near Gainesville. Pleasonton ignored the possibility that Stuart intended to pass through the Union army or to swing entirely around it. Instead, he assumed that Stuart was going to make a strike against the army and Pleasonton cavalierly reassured Butterfield, "My dispositions cover that." When Pleasonton sent this message shortly before one o'clock on the afternoon of the twenty-sixth he closed by stating, "I shall remain here [Leesburg] until the crossing is accomplished." He then changed his mind, advising shortly after five o'clock, "Shall be over to see the General in a short time." Three hours later, and possibly with Pleasonton by his side, Hooker sent his note to Halleck requesting that Stahel be removed.[5]

The unease felt by Heintzelman and his staff, as well as other officers tasked with guarding the capital was clearly evident by the twenty-fifth when Heintzelman cautioned Halleck, "As all my cavalry has been taken from [Virginia], should the Army of the Potomac move from my front, the first indication of the approach of the enemy would be their appearance at our works." A warning was issued to his subordinates demanding "that unusual precautions be taken to be advised of the approach of the enemy on our uncovered front." John Barnard, chief engineer of the defensive line around the city, was just as nervous, reminding Heintzelman that the men in the forts could not hold the city by themselves. Without troops to hold the entrenchments connecting the forts, "A considerable body of cavalry might ... dash into and destroy Washington," and he urged the immediate organization of a militia force. On June 26, Heintzelman estimated that he had lost the services of "at least 30,000 veteran soldiers" in the last two weeks and called upon Halleck to authorize a militia or home guard. All troops still in the city were relieved from their guard duties and readied "to move at a moment's notice" in the event the enemy appeared in front of the forts. Civilian employees from the Quartermaster and Commissary departments were ordered to handle the security assignments until the crisis was over.[6]

Col. Charles Lowell, who had moved his 2nd Massachusetts to Poolesville following Jewett's departure, was instructed to "watch carefully" the river crossings near the capital from the Maryland side, and to attack without hesitation any "guerrilla or irregular cavalry [who] show themselves near your line, if you can do so with a reasonable chance of success." As a final precaution Heintzelman ordered Col. James Swain, 11th New York Cavalry, to send a squadron from Washington to Centreville to observe the roads east of Bull Run Mountain as the army departed. Swain's command was scattered throughout the region; three companies were with Jewett at Harpers Ferry, one company was assigned as the President's bodyguard, and two were serving as orderlies for several officers in the capital, including Halleck. The remaining companies did patrol and picket duty. These included Companies B and C, numbering 87 officers and men. About four-thirty on the afternoon of June 26, Maj. Seth Pierre Remington led this squadron across the Potomac at Georgetown, arriving at Fairfax Court House about six hours later where they bivouacked for the night. The men got little rest, however, as recently abandoned campfires continued to smolder all around them, sparking and flaring and giving the illusion of "persons flitting by and around some of these fires" before they finally flickered out. What the men remembered may not have been an illusion. In his haste to comply with his orders sending his division into Maryland, Stahel had abandoned a vast amount of military stores, including "hospital tents, ordinance and other property." The quantity was such that Brig. Gen. Rufus Ingalls was forced to detail contrabands to police the abandoned cavalry camps. Local residents may have also scavenged the camps during the night.[7]

Julia Wheelock recalled that orders had been received on the twenty-fourth "to break up our hospitals" at Fairfax Court House, which now included the Gunnell home, referred to since March 9, as the "Stoughton House," and that the sick were removed early the next morning but Wheelock and many of the staff remained. "Oh how lonely and desolate everything appeared! Tents struck, blankets, pillows, and dishes scattered about." Foremost on the minds of the nurses and doctors who remained was John Mosby. "I had made up my mind that I should not get away that day, and was trying to fix up some nice little speech to make to his excellency, Mr. Moseby, in case he should give me a call," recalled Wheelock. Mosby never appeared, and "my little speech was never made, for about three o'clock transport came to remove the hospital stores.... No fears now of 'Moseby and Co.'"[8]

Jeb Stuart splashed across the Occoquan at the now unguarded Wolf Run Shoals ford early on June 27. He led two brigades directly to Fairfax Station, while Fitz Lee took the road to Burke Station and Annandale, protecting Stuart's right flank until they reunited that evening. Work had proceeded at a furious pace through the twenty-fifth, to insure that all military property was removed from the depot at Fairfax Station, and that anything that could not be removed was burned before the depot was abandoned by the Union troops. Still, when the Confederates arrived Stuart allowed the men to scavenge the site, recovering what they could, including badly needed corn and oats for the horses. As a precaution a party of 20 men was sent up the road toward the courthouse, while Stuart and his staff relaxed and allowed their famished mounts a chance to feed on Yankee corn.[9]

That morning Major Remington ordered his men west toward Centreville, stopping briefly to water their horses at a branch of Accotink Creek immediately west of the courthouse. Proceeding to Centreville they searched the abandoned campsites for salvageable property and scouted the approaches from Bull Run Mountain. Satisfied that there was no sign of the enemy, Remington began the return march to Washington. As they came in sight of the courthouse the men observed movement off to the south, in the direction of

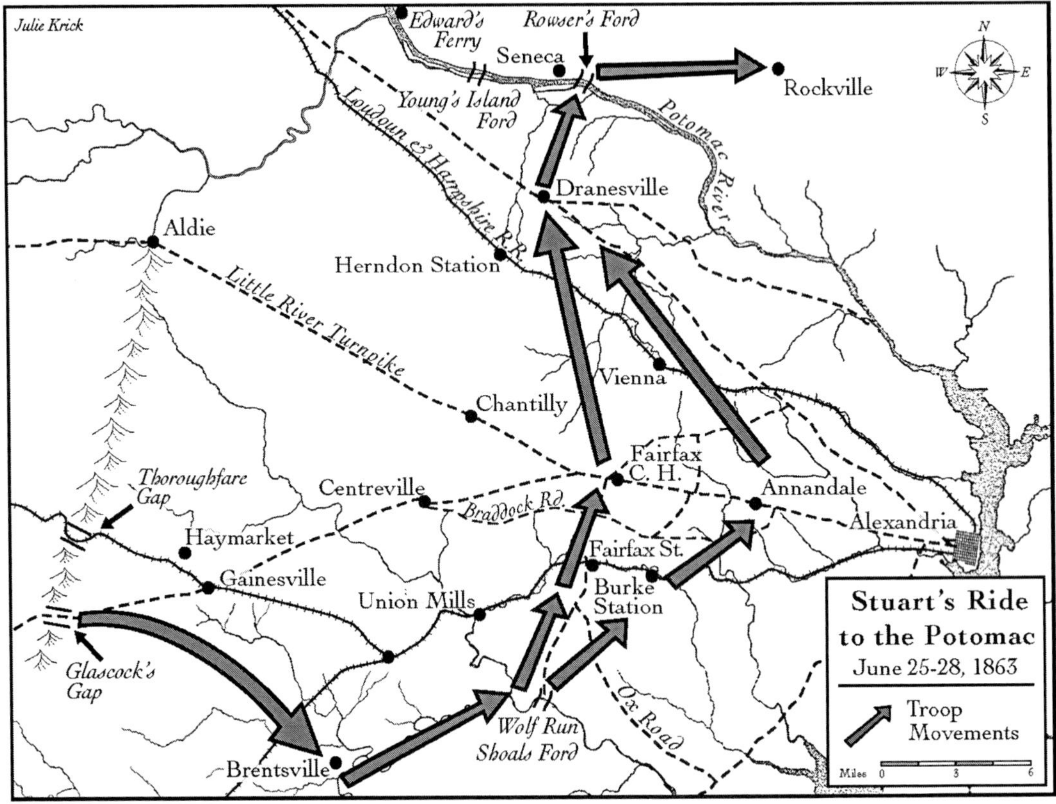

Fairfax Station but could not distinguish with the naked eye the nature of the activity. The major chose not to investigate any further, opting instead to gain the east side of the courthouse as quickly as possible. Near Jermantown the New Yorkers were fired upon from the woods alongside the road.[10]

Believing that bushwhackers or a party of Mosby's men confronted him, Remington sent a squad into the woods on foot as skirmishers. Then one of the led horses broke loose and set off at a gallop for the courthouse, pursued by Lt. George Dagwell. The lieutenant chased the runaway animal past his own advance guard on the outskirts of the village. These men had passed the enemy patrol unopposed and were then examining the wagons of several civilians who were scrounging the property abandoned by the army. Just beyond them, and along the same branch of Accotink Creek where the men had watered their horses that morning, Dagwell reined his horse to a halt as he observed their campsite of the previous night swarming with enemy soldiers. Still believing the Southerners were from Mosby's command, Dagwell jerked his horse around to the right and raced away. Reaching a high point he signaled furiously in an attempt to draw Remington's attention. He was soon joined by the men of the advance guard, followed shortly thereafter by the major with the main body.[11]

After a consultation, Remington and Dagwell elected to attack, following the course of the stream south toward Fairfax Station. While the officers formed their men for the charge they were under continuous fire from the Confederates drawn up below them, but sustained no casualties. Once Remington ordered the charge, however, the Confederates broke and ran, some heading for the woods while others took the Ox Road back to Fairfax

Station. The road, which had been corduroyed the previous winter, was now in terrible condition and made, in Dagwell's opinion, "one of the most undesirable race courses I ever undertook to catch Johnny Rebs on." The chase continued to a clearing overlooking the depot at Fairfax Station where Dagwell again reined to an abrupt halt as it became painfully apparent that it was not a party of guerrillas they were chasing but Stuart's cavalry.[12]

For the second time in ten days a Union cavalry force had surprised Stuart while he and his staff "quietly lounged about." Alerted by distant but rapidly approaching gunfire, the Southern officers observed the men of their advance guard emerging from the woods, firing at their pursuers. Wade Hampton also heard the skirmish and rode up at the head of the 1st North Carolina Cavalry, which was led that day by Maj. John Whitaker. Stuart ordered Hampton and Whitaker to develop the situation while he and his officers bridled their mounts. Lt. Theodore Garnett, one of Stuart's aides, was better prepared than his fellow officers and joined the Carolinians as they raced off through the woods on what he termed a "fox chase." Emerging into a clearing, they observed Remington's squadron "in beautiful order, sabres flashing and uniforms glittering in the bright sunlight, under the full headway of a gallant and well ordered charge."[13]

As the Confederates entered the clearing, Dagwell realized just how quickly the situation had turned. He looked at the few men around him, and their exhausted horses, legs quivering and heads drooping as they sought to regain their wind, and he pondered briefly the tight position they were now confronting. Dismounting, he gave his animal a brief respite until Remington arrived. Dagwell tried to convince him to turn back but Remington ordered the men again into line. As the Carolinians approached, the New Yorkers could hear their

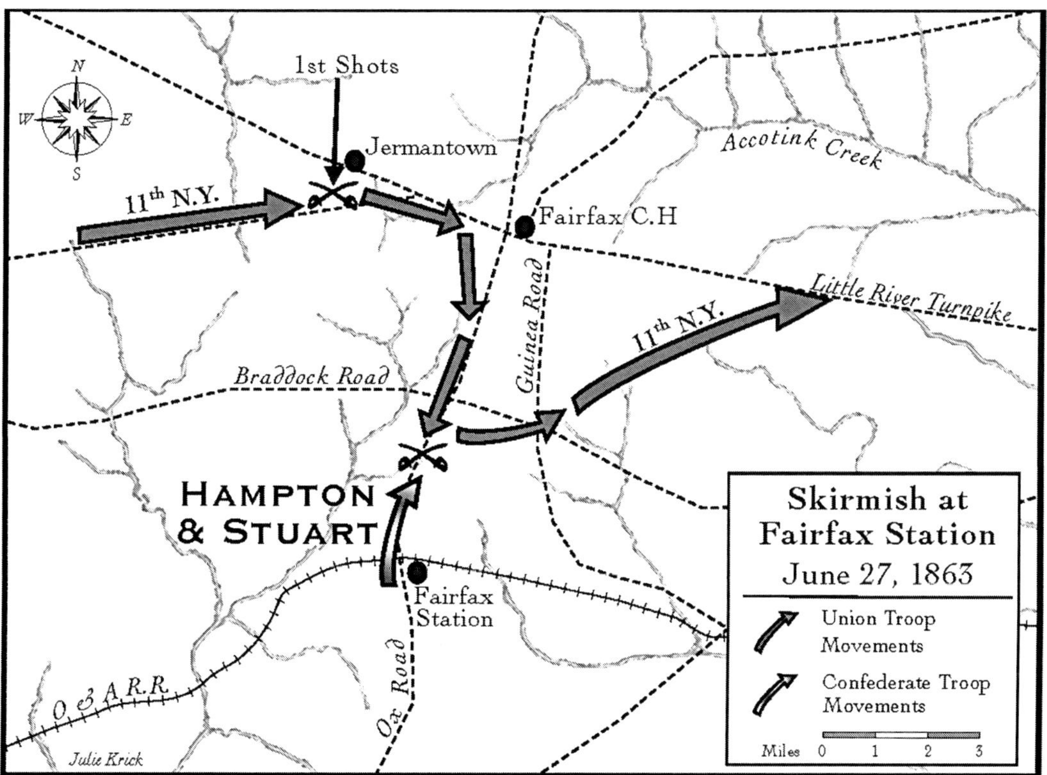

officers issuing commands. Dagwell believed that Whitaker's men were refusing his orders to advance, though several opened fire. When Remington ordered the charge his men quickly closed the distance, emptying their revolvers before drawing their sabers. Whitaker, "a brave and accomplished officer," was mortally wounded as the outnumbered Yankees fought "with terrible desperation," driving the Southerners in confusion before the weight of numbers and the exhausted condition of their horses began to tell. Soon it was Remington's men who broke and headed for the safety of the trees but Hampton immediately sent a fresh squadron to cut them off. Believing themselves surrounded those still able abandoned the contest and fled in a race to safety. Dagwell along with a handful of men made it as far as Annandale, where they were cut off and captured by Fitz Lee's brigade after a brief resistance during which Dagwell was shot in the shoulder. At least three men were killed, one mortally wounded, fourteen wounded and captured and nineteen others captured. Four men who were too seriously wounded to move were paroled on the field, and left at a home near the courthouse, while the able-bodied and walking wounded were herded across the Potomac and later paroled in Brookville, Maryland. Major Remington, whose horse had been shot twice, made it to the defensive lines outside the capital with the survivors.[14]

The Southern cavalry "took possession of" Fairfax Court House about nine o'clock that morning, and the men scavenged the abandoned campsites during another respite of several hours. Stuart then headed his two brigades to Dranesville, where he again allowed Chambliss to rest, while Hampton continued to the Potomac River. After capturing several sutlers' wagons near Annandale, in addition to the men from the 11th New York, Fitz Lee rejoined Stuart at Dranesville. When Stuart and Lee approached their second river crossing that day luck was again on their side, as Hooker had ordered Colonel Lowell, late on the twenty-sixth, to move his command to Knoxville, Maryland, twenty miles upstream.[15]

Hooker chose not to inform Heintzelman, who remained unaware of the move until notified by Lowell the next morning. The men from the Bay State were long gone, however, by the time an infuriated Heintzelman received the message and ordered Lowell to ignore any instructions from Hooker until confirmed by "these headquarters." A rider reached Lowell to order him back too late: by 3 A.M., June 28, Stuart's command was across the river at Rowser's Ford, "the very ford I was especially to watch," groused Lowell. It is doubtful that Lowell could have prevented the crossing, but he certainly could have caused Stuart further delay and possibly driven him farther upstream where he might have encountered Union infantry. Lowell concluded that he was "disgraced forever;—in consequence of my regiment being removed and of Hooker's neglecting to picket [the river] with another regiment." In fact, as Lowell later admitted, he had instigated the move by personally visiting Hooker in an attempt to obtain a more active role in the campaign, and Hooker, desperate for troops in general and cavalry especially was only too happy to oblige. For his part Hooker remained defiant, ordering Lowell to Harpers Ferry, while Heintzelman and Halleck urged him to pursue Stuart. Aware that the problem was of his own creation, Lowell opted to follow the orders from Heintzelman, but even then he did so only because they were co-signed by Halleck. By then it was too late, another opportunity was lost.[16]

When Colonel Swain heard the accounts of the fight at Fairfax Station he sent a note to Brig. Gen. Gustavus De Russy, commander of the defenses south of the Potomac, at Arlington House. "I deem that a portion of my command has been sacrificed ... [though] I do not question the correctness or discretion of the order, which precipitated a handful of men upon a regiment of the enemy. I respectfully request permission to gather the fragments of my regiment to pursue the rebels and avenge my officers and men." The general declined, as he needed the men for other assignments. One company was sent to the Signal Corps leaving Swain with less than 60 available effectives (the entire regiment numbering only 240 men) and De Russy immediately dispatched them into Fairfax County in search of Stuart's column. Proceeding northwest toward Bailey's Crossroads the reconnaissance force split off following three separate routes to the Little River Turnpike in an attempt to clarify the rumors that had come in throughout the day, especially those regarding Fitz Lee's activities around Annandale. Capt. Horace Ellsworth was eventually able to confirm that Lee had captured four sutlers, and eleven employees of the quartermaster department along with Lieutenant Dagwell and as many as eighteen men who were with him. The estimates of the enemy force, however, gave the erroneous impression that Stuart had upwards of 10,000 men, but with the Confederates long gone the Federals were still left guessing as to their objective.[17]

With the exception of Col. William Mann's 7th Michigan, which was detached to assist Colonel Price and tasked with scouting toward Hagerstown, the majority of Stahel's command enjoyed their first day of rest in over a week, bedding down early on the twenty-sixth. Several recalled waking up "much refreshed, with horses well fed and groomed and haversacks replenished," either through the generosity of Howard or as a result of spending the night in lush meadows where the horses found an abundance of grass. Later that afternoon DeForest fell back through Crampton's Gap, passing through Frederick and moving north along the road to Emmittsburg. Copeland's Wolverines were the most active, moving early that morning toward Emmittsburg, and seeking permission to continue on to the crossroads town of Gettysburg, in southern Pennsylvania, where skirmishing had erupted the previous afternoon.[18]

Ranging ahead of Ewell's infantry, Lige White and men of his 35th Battalion traded shots with members of the Pennsylvania militia northeast of the town, and Stuart's veterans, "more amused than abused," charged, uttering "barbarian yells" and easily drove off the militia. Later that afternoon White's men encountered a picket post manned by two soldiers in the 21st Pennsylvania Cavalry. In another brief exchange of shots one of the Yankees was killed, a scant two miles from his home. Behind White came the foot soldiers, who held the town of Gettysburg overnight before continuing east on the morning of June 27. Whether word of this incursion reached Stahel and Copeland is unknown, but at three-thirty that afternoon Butterfield was seeking permission for Stahel to head in that direction, advising Hooker that the 5th and 6th Michigan were already en route.[19]

Unbeknownst to Stahel, however, his tenure with the army had already come to an end. At noon Halleck sent word to Hooker that the cavalryman was relieved, with orders to report immediately to Maj. Gen. Darius Couch at Harrisburg, where he was to "organize and command the cavalry in the Department of the Susquehanna." The proud Hungarian, who had played the political game to his personal advantage the previous winter, was now the victim of Hooker's and Pleasonton's own version of the same game. While he remained in the field, striving to meet every demand placed before him by both officers, he was doubtless unaware of the machinations taking place behind his back until it was too late, but his head was just the first of several yet to fall.[20]

The last elements of the Army of the Potomac were across the river that evening, and Jacob Engelbrecht and the other residents of Frederick stood in the streets and watched as the infantry and artillery filed past. While Engelbrecht tallied the troops he also noted the senior officers as they were pointed out, but one man who was not to be seen was Joseph Hooker. As the last elements of the army entered Maryland and the bridges at Edward's Ferry were taken up, Hooker opted to force his increasingly contentious dispute with Halleck over the matter of reinforcements. Butterfield had just returned from a personal interview with both the President and Halleck, during which he had been allowed to inspect the books as to troop strengths within the Department of Washington. Both Lincoln and Halleck had reiterated that no further troops would be pulled from the lines around the capital or Baltimore. Hooker's last option was to abandon Harpers Ferry, using those troops, now led by William French, to bolster his army. Seeking to finally settle the question as to his authority to act without first gaining Halleck's approval, Hooker instructed French to abandon his position and join the army. Hooker, who was with French at the time, then waited while French wired Halleck for approval, as he was bound to do and as Hooker knew that he would. When Halleck instructed French to ignore the order Hooker submitted his request to be relieved. Eight hours after approving Hooker's appeal that Stahel be removed, Halleck accepted the army commander's request, and named Maj. Gen. George Meade as his replacement. Of the three men most affected by the day's events, Hooker, Meade and Stahel, only Hooker had an inkling of what had transpired.[21]

Meade's Fifth Corps went into bivouac on the outskirts of Frederick on the twenty-seventh, and Meade rode into the city hoping to meet with Hooker and discuss the military situation, but the commander had not yet returned, and Meade returned to camp. At three o'clock the next morning, June 28, Meade was awakened and informed of the change in command. He met with Hooker several hours later to complete the formalities.[22]

As Meade prepared for this meeting, Stahel forwarded a message from Copeland, then near Emmittsburg, reporting the presence of enemy troops in and around Gettysburg, and advising that Copeland would head there in the morning. Copeland approached the town as Hooker and Meade concluded their meeting. Between noon and one o'clock, and with the 5th Michigan in the lead, the Wolverines rode into Gettysburg, where the townsfolk greeted them with a heart-felt reception. As James Kidd later described, "The freedom of the city was extended. Every door stood open, or the latch-string hung invitingly out." With their horses covered in flowers and their hands full of eatables, the men followed their officers into fields east of town ripe with clover that "made the poor, famished animals fairly laugh." Copeland ensured that the roads into the town were secured and that the latest intelligence, including "an intercepted dispatch from Gen'l Ewell to Gen'l Early," was promptly forwarded to Stahel, while those men lucky enough to escape picket duty relaxed and enjoyed the hospitality of the citizenry. At some point that evening, 30 miles to the south, Joseph Hooker stepped up into a spring wagon for a short ride to the Frederick train station and away from the army.[23]

Unbeknownst to Copeland a series of orders emanated from army headquarters on June 28, announcing the change in command and the reorganization of the cavalry corps. Following the publication of Special Orders, Number 174, that made official Stahel's transfer and the assignment of his division to the cavalry corps, Pleasonton submitted a plan for the reorganization of the corps, to include a third division. He recommended that Judson Kilpatrick be placed in command of the new division. Then, in the vein of his earlier letter to Congressman Farnsworth, Pleasonton added, "I shall require three brigadier generals, able competent men, capable of commanding cavalry & ... I urgently recommend the following named officers for promotion & appointment as brigadiers, for these commands. *Cavalry must have able commanders with dash & spirit* or it will inevitably fail. The officers I mention have proven themselves by their brilliant & distinguished conduct at *Beverly Ford ... Aldie* ... and at Middleburg & Upperville ... to be suitable selections for cavalry commander." With the stroke of his pen Pleasonton then altered the image of the Union cavalry for the remainder of the war, nominating Elon Farnsworth, George Custer and Wesley Merritt for elevation to brigadier, as well as selecting John Tidball to command his horse artillery and Col. John McIntosh to supercede Col. John Taylor in command of his brigade. "These appointments are urgent necessities at this time to enable me [to] organize & fight the cavalry corps as it should be done." He concluded by requesting that an additional brigade of horse artillery be ordered to report to him from the artillery reserve to further bolster his force. In the first special order to appear over his signature George Meade approved the request in all respects, and while Meade's order did not specifically mention either Tidball or McIntosh both were elevated as Pleasonton desired. With Meade's approval in his pocket Pleasonton announced the reorganization just as quickly, uniting the four Michigan regiments into one brigade under the command of George Custer. Wesley Merritt, whom Pleasonton had singled out for promotion on June 22, took over the Reserve Brigade in Buford's division and McIntosh assumed command of Taylor's brigade in Gregg's division. Elon Farnsworth was also elevated to brigade command. Colonel Price was relegated to command of his 2nd Pennsylvania, which was then assigned to provost duty at army headquarters. Othneil DeForest returned to the 5th New York Cavalry, and Joseph Copeland was assigned to David Gregg's division with no specific responsibility.[24]

A satisfied Pleasonton then held a brief review of the cavalry that both Stahel and Custer attended. Though he was most likely confused and angry, Stahel was gracious as he took leave from his division. Thanking his officers and men for the manner in which they had "raised the standard of the command and greatly increased its efficiency," Stahel declared his pride in what they had accomplished together, and concluded, "Confident that you will be as true to your new commander as you have been to me and feeling assured that all your energies will be devoted to the single object of terminating this war and resting peace to our country, I bid you farewell." Heintzelman, who was truly disappointed with the change, complemented Stahel on the "splendid ... condition & efficiency" of the command and assured him "that I parted with you & them with many regrets." After saying his goodbyes, Stahel was escorted by four members of his personal escort to the train station. Samuel Gillespie, Company A, 1st Ohio Cavalry, had remarked earlier in the spring that the Buckeyes were "pleased with our General ... notwithstanding our natural aversion to foreigners." Now, having spent several months as a member of the general's escort detail, he observed Stahel's departure with sadness.[25]

Joseph Copeland learned of his removal from command the following day on the road back to Emmittsburg, when a courier rode up and handed him a dispatch from Pleasonton, instructing that he turn over his brigade to the next senior officer and report himself to General Gregg at Frederick. Arriving there, Copeland learned that Gregg had moved to Middleburg, Maryland, northwest of Frederick, but when he arrived there Gregg was gone. Copeland did not locate Gregg until July 1, and it was only then that he learned his brigade had been taken from him and that he "had been assigned to an inferior brigade in Gen'l Gregg's Division." In conference, the two men determined that Copeland was Gregg's senior and thus Gregg suggested that Copeland discuss the matter with Pleasonton. This meeting may have taken place at Meade's headquarters on the battlefield, where Pleasonton told him, "that while he intended no disrespect nor reflection on me, he must insist on giving the command to those best known to himself." The former judge was incensed, telling a friend days later, "To this, on the eve of Battle, in the face of the Enemy, thirty-two miles in advance of our army, [to] have my command taken from me ... is an indignity and disgrace that I should not and cannot quietly submit to." But there was little he could do, and on July 11, he was assigned to the draft depot at Annapolis Junction, Maryland. Months later, he still bristled as he recalled learning that his brigade "had been conferred upon a Lieut. and staff officer of Gen'l Pleasonton's, who on the same occasion had summarily been made a Brig. General for the purpose."[26]

As Hooker and Stahel took their leave from the army, others, namely George Custer and Elon Farnsworth, had reason to celebrate, but time was short. Capt. Andrew Cohen, of Pleasonton's staff, sent a note to fellow aide, Capt. John Spangler, advising, "The Gen'l Comd'g directs that you hurry back as we most probably move tomorrow. Custer & Farnsworth are Brigadiers & wish you to christen the star in four (4) five (5) gallon kegs of best whiskey. I hold the vouchers." The extent to which the officers imbibed is unknown, but certainly the revelers did not consume all of the whiskey. Farnsworth did not live long enough to say anything concerning these events, and Custer, who by all accounts no longer consumed alcohol, made no mention of the celebration. But liquor was clearly present as evidenced by numerous references to drunken soldiers within the city of Frederick the next day. The mayhem reached such a level that Colonel Price was ordered to clear the city "of drunken and straggling soldiers." That George Crosby, 1st Vermont, described his "whole brigade [as] drunk" suggests the extent of the problem, which another soldier attributed to "an abandoned restaurant and wine cellar that the boys discovered."[27]

While Pleasonton celebrated his good fortune at Frederick, Heintzelman had plenty of reason to regret the loss of his cavalry that Sunday morning as Jeb Stuart moved into Maryland. Beyond the remnants of the 11th New York the crusty commander of the Department of Washington now had no cavalry to clarify the confusion generated by Stuart's passage through Fairfax County. Halleck was equally frustrated. "There is not a cavalry picket on the line of the Potomac below Edwards Ferry, and we have none here to send out."[28]

The only mounted force known to be near the capital on the morning of the twenty-eighth was a contingent of freshly remounted men that departed from either Washington or Alexandria the previous morning en route to the army. Numbering 565 men and led by Maj. William Fry, 16th Pennsylvania Cavalry, these troopers came from several regiments, including 50 from the 2nd New York Cavalry. Just one week earlier Cohen had complained that he had never seen "a more unruly, insubordinate set of people than these." Further, the men were unarmed. The troopers explained that their weapons had been left with their respective regiments, but Cohen suspected that they were undependable shirkers, who may have ditched their weapons to avoid the trials of frontline duty. If they had departed as noted by Captain Cohen at 6:30 A.M. on June 27, they should have been well north of the capital the following morning, but at least one officer in the 16th Pennsylvania thought Fry to be "utterly inefficient as a horseman," and a man who owed his rank to "influence rather than ability."[29]

After crossing the Potomac Stuart's troopers captured and burned a number of barges along the Chesapeake and Ohio Canal before pressing on toward Rockville, Maryland.

Beyond the canal, Colonel Chambliss encountered Fry's freshly mounted Yankees. According to Col. Richard Beale, 9th Virginia Cavalry, a quartermaster's detail was foraging in advance of the brigade when they were observed and pursued by Fry's force. Lt. James Pollard then advanced with Company H, 9th Virginia, to investigate. Once he had the Yankees in sight he charged without waiting for further support. His attack convinced Fry to fallback toward the capital, "but," not before, as Stuart later described, "the speed of their horses deprived us of the usual results in captures." Theodore Garnett, however, recalled seeing several prisoners pass by "with bloody heads, showing that the sabre had been at work." Staff officer Frank Robertson rightly described the Yankee column as "the 'pack ups,' gathered around Washington and being sent to the front," and who were in "a very hilarious" mood right before they were hit by the Virginians and sent as Robertson recalled, back to the capital "with much celerity."[30]

At half past noon the Southern cavalry reached Rockville. The column charged through the town at a gallop led by a squadron of the 2nd South Carolina. Stuart's legions were now just 15 miles from the White House. While tearing down the telegraph line the Southerners spotted a wagon train moving north from the capital. Capt. Henry Page was escorting the 140 wagons to the army, including the ambulance train for Abercrombie's Division. Page was two miles south of Rockville when he was accosted by a frightened man, yelling, "'the rebels are upon you!'"[31]

Captain Page may have been near the point of exhaustion. He had been ordered to escort a wagon train from Fairfax Station to Gainesville on June 22, and upon his return he was left in charge of dismantling the depot at Fairfax Station. He worked through the night on the twenty-fifth, under a constant harangue from Ingalls, and to whom he vowed at one point that he would not burn anything "as long as there is a ghost of a chance to save property. I would sooner go to Richmond than fail to do my duty." After removing the depot at Fairfax Station, he was ordered to report to Lt. Col. Charles Sawtelle at Alexandria. On June 26, Sawtelle sent Page to General Buford for assignment with his division. On his way to Buford he was tasked with leading the supply train out of the capital.[32]

The captain was now in no mood for the frightened civilian, and had him arrested and placed under guard to prevent a panic. When a preacher confirmed that the Rebels did indeed hold the town, Page and several others rode to the brow of a hill from where they observed a skirmish line followed by a heavier column advancing rapidly in their direction. The Yankees remained until they came under fire, at which time Page ordered the teamsters to turn the wagons back to Washington. "Then," in the opinion of one observer, "commenced the greatest confusion I ever saw," as the cavalry pursued them "with lightening speed ... firing as they came. The teams at the head of the train which turned first came down at a thundering rate of speed upon those in the act of turning, taking off wheels, breaking tongues, upsetting sometimes a half dozen wagons, and then themselves becoming a total wreck." Robertson termed it, "A circus ... that I have never seen paralleled." In contrast to Southern reports that the entire train was captured, a writer for the Lancaster, Pennsylvania, *Daily Evening Express,* who was riding with Page when the attack commenced claimed that "about fifteen or twenty" of the wagons escaped into the capital. Still, it was "quite a serious loss," in his view as "at least eight hundred mules swapped hands in an hour this morning." The writer opined, "Someone should be held to savage responsibility" for the debacle. A wildly different account appeared in the Washington *Evening Star,* stating that just two Confederate soldiers captured the entire train without a shot being fired. In this account Page was toward the middle of the train and escaped by jumping his horse over a fence and fleeing into the capital.[33]

As the wagons, containing by one reckoning just one bale of hay and two bags of grain each, were secured along with the prisoners and the damaged wagons destroyed, Stuart considered his options, including a dash into the capital. Deeming an attack that day "extremely hazardous," he elected to continue north, cut the line of the Baltimore and Ohio Railroad and rejoin the army. Stuart paroled his 400 prisoners in Brookeville, and pressed on to the railroad.[34]

Montgomery Meigs, the prickly quartermaster-general, was incensed when he learned of the loss. He assumed that Major Fry could have prevented the debacle, and rightly questioned the ill-considered decision to allow Fry to head north to the army on the twenty-seventh with near 600 men, while allowing the wagons to make the same trek the following day unescorted. While it made perfect sense to pair the troopers with the wagon train, Meigs assumption that a relatively untried officer in command of a force thrown together at a remount camp and riding raw horses would have beaten off an attack by Stuart's veterans was hasty and his anger and sarcasm misdirected. Speaking for many within the capital, Meigs closed one of several blistering telegrams to Rufus Ingalls by stating, "All the cavalry of the Defenses of Washington was swept off by the army, and we are now insulted by burning wagons 3 miles outside Tennallytown. Your communications are now in the hands of General Fitzhugh Lee's brigade." Following his berating from Meigs, Ingalls instructed Sawtelle to not send any more supplies "until you know the way is clear."[35]

"The city is full of strange, wild rumors of rebel raids," observed secretary of the navy Gideon Welles. "They are doubtless exaggerations, yet I think not without some foundation.... The War Department is wholly unprepared for an irruption here, and J.E.B. Stuart might have dashed into the city to-day with impunity."[36]

Meade, who Welles termed more of "a 'smooth bore' than a rifle," was now racing to familiarize himself with his new duties and responsibilities while trying to react promptly and properly to the rapidly changing situation that he found himself confronted with. When he was advised of the attack on the wagon train Meade recognized that there was little he could do as he focused his attention on Lee and his infantry. Pleasonton instructed David Gregg to send two brigades east to Ridgeville in an effort to secure the railroad, but Meade was confronted with conflicting reports that placed Stuart to the west near Williamsport, to the south in Fairfax County and now at Rockville. Realizing that it was too late for accusations and second-guessing, Meade informed Halleck the next morning that he would move the army to Westminster and Emmittsburg. Once he could determine the validity of the many reports concerning Stuart he would send his cavalry to deal with him, but until then he intended to go after Lee and "submit to the cavalry raids around me."[37]

A now constant "chattering of Stuart" and his cavalry roaming, virtually unmolested, along the approaches to the capital on both sides of the Potomac River left those within the city wondering if the long-rumored raid had finally arrived. In diarist Adam Gurowski's opinion, Hooker "took all [the troops] he could and all he met on the way," leaving "not two hundred cavalry" to aid in the defense of the city. Ignoring the fact that he had approved the move, Halleck also blamed the deposed Hooker for having "carried away all of General Heintzelman's cavalry." While waiting for Colonel Lowell to return with the 2nd Massachusetts, Halleck was left to rely upon the cavalry "we have picked up from Pleasonton's command," referring to Major Fry's remounts, as well as any men still waiting to be mounted, and he instructed Heintzelman to assume command of all of the cavalry from the army then within the department "and use them until further orders." Fry's contingent would be temporarily added to Lowell's command upon his return but Halleck wrote them off as "too weak to do much." Brig. Gen. John Slough, military governor of Alexandria, was ordered to round up all the troopers within the city of Alexandria and hold them for emergency service. Placed in command of this "fire brigade" was Col. Percy Wyndham, who was in the capital recovering from a wound received at Brandy Station. In the returns for June 30, this force numbered 2,600 officers and men present for duty. Wyndham organized his command into three detachments, led by Lt. Col. David Clendenin, 8th Illinois, Lt. Col. John Thompson, 1st Rhode Island and Lt. Col. Robert Johnstone, 5th New York. Lowell's 2nd Massachusetts would also fall under Wyndham's command when it arrived.[38]

That evening, with the safety of the capital still very much in doubt, Secretary of the Navy Gideon Welles sent orders for a couple of gunboats to steam up the Potomac River. Railroad superintendents were queried as to how many laborers could be spared "immediately to work on defenses north of Washington," while the garrison troops south of the river were instructed to clear all the brush within one hundred feet of their forts.[39]

The battalion of the 11th New York sent to aid De Russy remained at Arlington House under his control until the crisis passed, but De Russy continued to confuse the situation. None of the patrols sent out between June 27 and 29 had reported the presence of any enemy cavalry in the region extending from Alexandria through Fairfax to the Potomac, but De Russy continued to report otherwise, telling both General Slough and Heintzelman on the twenty-ninth that Southern cavalry was still reconnoitering the "defenses of Alexandria."[40]

Among the troopers gathered in Alexandria were 300 men of the 1st Rhode Island, only a third of whom were "mounted and fit for service," after their regiment's battering near Middleburg. A reconnaissance party of 60 men was pulled together from the regiment and, under the command of Capt. George Bliss, sent to scout the country between Alexandria and Edward's Ferry. Arriving at Seneca Creek at 8:30 P.M., June 30, Bliss met Lt. Col. Augustus Pruyn and 160 men of the 4th New York Cavalry along with a detachment of engineers guarding the canal and repairing the damage wrought by Stuart. Bliss again confirmed that Stuart and his men had vacated the region immediately around the capital and were no longer a threat to the city, but he would not make this information known until his return to the capital the next day. Meanwhile, Stuart had moved beyond Westminster, Maryland, after brushing aside a valiant attack by the 1st Delaware Cavalry the previous day. On the thirtieth, while Bliss was marching to the Potomac River, Stuart again clashed with Union cavalry at Hanover, Pennsylvania. Still, the residents of Washington remained on edge, and Edwin Stanton implored Halleck to "see that every possible means of security is adopted against any sudden raid or incursion of the enemy." In the opinion of one observer, "Washington was again like a city besieged as after Bull Run."[41]

25

History's Dusty Attic

John Mosby had waged his brand of guerrilla warfare in Northern Virginia for almost six months by the time the two great armies met at Gettysburg. His first victims had been veterans, as were many of the horse soldiers who manned the outposts around the Union capital, yet their experience meant little when they were confronted by Mosby's style of warfare. Within days of these first skirmishes, or raids, Mosby was striking outposts up and down the picket lines in Northern Virginia, and it was not long before he encountered men fresh from civilian life, men with no concept of traditional warfare, much less guerrilla warfare. All of these men soon learned that experience meant nothing; the training manuals were useless. They also learned there was no glory to be garnered along the picket lines. The warfare these men learned as they stood watch over the Union capital was ugly. Regardless of what others may have thought, these sentinels never viewed it as anything but bushwhacking and simple murder. In time, some of these men gained a measure of revenge against the partisans, at places like at Catlett Station, Warrenton Junction and Greenwich. But, as the last days of June slipped away, others were still seeking a chance to test their mettle on an open field in a fair fight. All would have to wait for their next meeting with John Mosby, but none of these men had to wait long before enduring their own personal challenges on the battlefield.

At Hanover, Hunterstown, East Cavalry Field and the many engagements that followed, the men who had struggled to endure the months of boredom, as well as the solitary moments of terror along the picket lines, finally gained a share of the success and distinction they had long despaired of ever achieving. But that fame, such as it was, came at a bloody cost in lives lost and dreams shattered. Some of these men would again test themselves against John Mosby in some of the darkest days of the war, days that saw women and children forced to watch as their homes were put to the torch, nights during which men were executed along dark lonely roads and a day where others were hanged in the street. But by then many of the soldiers who had been there at the beginning of this war, when the seeds of bitterness and hate were strewn, were long gone.

Richard Butler Price remained colonel of the 2nd Pennsylvania until the last months of the war but never again led men in battle. His regiment was assigned to provost duty with army headquarters, to guard prisoners during the battle of Gettysburg and to sweep the torn fields for stragglers when the armies departed. Not until October did the regiment return to full duty with the cavalry corps. Price did not remain with his regiment. In late July he went to Pennsylvania on recruiting duty, where he remained through the fall of 1863. He then returned to Washington, serving on several military commissions until he left the service on February 1, 1865. He had resisted several requests to return to his regiment, including an appeal in November 1864, when the regiment was under the command of a captain whose term of service had expired, but who could not be mustered out until a suitable replacement could be found. In January 1865, a note was attached to a document outlining Price's career that stated in part, "the service will be benefited by his being mustered out. He has always managed to keep away from his regt., and stood in the way of the promotion of a meritorious officer viz Lt. Col. [Joseph] Brinton. The officers of this regt. and the commander of the brigade has more than once petitioned the War Dept. to remove this officer, being of no use to the service and standing in the way of meritorious officers." He returned to Philadelphia after the war and died in 1876.[1]

Too little information remains about Price to make a fair and accurate assessment of his career. The documents in his military files, though few, suggest that he may have recognized that he was too old for the demands of active campaigning and had taken advantage of every opportunity to avoid frontline duty. Still he took it upon himself to judge men, often many years his junior, and sometimes men of whom he had no personal knowledge, and to judge them severely. He ruined careers and branded several men as cowards. By tying up the colonelcy of the regiment but avoiding duty in the field, he adversely influenced the lives and careers of men with whom he was familiar and hampered the effectiveness of the regiment he had raised.[2]

Edwin Hall Higley returned to the 1st Vermont in the summer of 1863, and saw action throughout the Bristoe Campaign, serving the latter part of the year on the staff of General Custer. He survived the disastrous Kilpatrick-Dahlgren Raid in early 1864, during which he was in command of a section of guns and briefly shelled the city of Richmond. He was captured that spring at Stony Creek Station during the Wilson-Kautz Raid, and remained a prisoner until his exchange in March 1865. In the fall of 1865, he returned to school and completed his education at Middlebury College in Vermont. He spent the remainder of his life teaching, and died on May 5, 1916. If he ever again spoke of the St. Patrick's Day fight at Herndon Station, and his subsequent struggle to clear his name, no reference has been found. In 1867 he received brevet promotions to captain and major. In adding his personal endorsement to these increases in grade, William Wells, who had achieved the rank of brigadier general with a brevet to major general, described Higley as "a capable, honest and brave officer."[3]

George Bean moved to Alabama following the war and resumed his pre-war occupation as a blacksmith. Following his exchange Franklin Huntoon entered the United States Navy. The severity of the wound sustained by Josiah Grout on April 1, 1863, ended his military career. He later entered politics and served a two-year term as governor of the state. The 1st Vermont Cavalry, which had driven home the final charge at Greenwich, continued to redeem its reputation, first at Hanover, Pennsylvania, on June 30, and again in a very controversial charge against Southern infantry on July 3, which resulted in the death of Brig. Gen. Elon Farnsworth.[4]

The 15th Vermont Infantry was mustered out of service and returned to Vermont in late July 1863. On August 3, 1863, Governor Holbrook directed that a new regiment, the 17th Vermont, be raised, and former lieutenant Eldin Hartshorn again answered the call, enlisting as a private. His company soon elected him captain, and he served to the end of the conflict. Following the war he moved to Iowa, where he entered politics. He closed his political career as governor of the state. He then moved to Kensington, Maryland, where in died in 1926. He and his wife are buried in Arlington National Cemetery.[5]

Lt. Col. Robert Johnstone, 5th New York Cavalry, did not accompany his men to Pennsylvania; he remained in Virginia assisting Col. Percy Wyndham and supervising a camp of convalescents. He was placed under arrest shortly after the armies returned to Virginia that summer. While under arrest he was called before an examination board to determine his competency to remain in his position, but he refused to appear while still facing charges. In October 1863, and with the Army of the Potomac near Centerville, Johnstone made his way to a dismount camp near Washington. He was arrested a second time and charged with a breach of arrest and being absent without leave. He was tried, convicted and cashiered from the service.[6]

The life and career of Col. Percy Wyndham remains surrounded by mystery. After returning to his regiment in March 1863, Wyndham again ran afoul of his superiors that spring and was briefly placed under arrest by General Stoneman. He was released on May 25, without charges being filed, but he received a letter of censure that was recorded by general order. In the letter, General Pleasonton, who had recently replaced Stoneman, wrote, "The offense he committed of allowing his command to go on picket without being with it, and neglecting to join it after being ordered to do so, is of the gravest character. The higher an officer's rank, the greater the obligation resting upon him to discharge all his duties with fidelity and exactness. Soldiers cannot repose confidence in an officer who does not share their privations, exposures and dangers, and without first obtaining the confidence and respect of his men, an officer cannot properly command them."[7]

While recovering in the capital from a wound received at Brandy Station, Wyndham was tasked with gathering what cavalry he could and to provide for the defense of the city until the threat posed by Stuart and his cavalry had passed. By his count he gathered up 2,500 men within a week, saw that they were mounted and equipped as quickly as possible and began returning them to their units once the danger had passed. He then established a cavalry depot that he named Camp Wyndham, and from which he continued to remount and refit men on his own accord, prior to funneling them back to the army. In late July he was aggrieved to learn that he was to be superseded and returned to his regiment at Pleasonton's request. In a letter to Stanton he pleaded, "that Camp Wyndham be not broken up; *and that I not be deprived of this command until at any rate my wound has closed sufficiently to enable me to take the field.*" He then submitted a doctor's statement that the wound, in the calf of his right leg, would prevent him from returning to active duty for at least thirty days and he requested that Pleasonton allow him "to continue the equipment of the men under my command."[8]

A series of events then occurred in rapid succession that cloaked Wyndham's last days with the army in an aura of intrigue. First, he overstayed his leave and was reported by Pleasonton on September 3, as being "away from his command without authority." Then a letter appeared in the New York *Herald*, of September 16, in which he answered at length an allegation that he was a fraud. One Percy S. Wyndham, M.P., leveled the charge, disputing among other points the colonel's claim to the name of Percy Wyndham. In attempting to establish his own bona fides and prove his accuser a "falsifier," he laid out his life's history and his military resume, submitting documents attested to by, among others, Secretary of State William Seward. He described himself as "but a humble soldier (call me a soldier of fortune if you will)," and then stated, "Some men make a name for themselves; others die contemplating the parents who gave them their name." In explaining his "right to use a title" he concluded, "I have rarely or never used it. Others have associated it with my name. I prefer to let my acts speak for themselves."[9]

During his absence he again sought promotion to the rank of brigadier and submitted a letter of recommendation from General Hooker attesting to his "high character" and "professional reputation." Hooker further declared, "I found him capable, prompt and efficient in the execution of orders, and with an enemy in his front enterprising and brave." When Wyndham did not return to the army until the second of October, however, he was charged with being absent without leave. On that same day Edwin Stanton sent a telegram to General Meade stating, "Information received [at the War Department] indicates that Colonel Percy Wyndham should not be permitted to have a command or come within the lines of your army at present." The colonel had already rejoined his command when the message arrived, however, and Meade was forced to seek further "instructions." Stanton directed that Wyndham be relieved from any "military duty, and ordered to proceed to Washington, but not in arrest." The colonel quickly sought a court of inquiry to investigate the matter and followed with another request that he be allowed to return to the army as a volunteer aide.[10]

An undercurrent of suspicion had dogged Wyndham's tenure with the army since the debacle at Harrisonburg, in June 1862, when a correspondent speculated that he might be "tinctured with Secesh." That December, when he had first sought elevation to the rank of brigadier, a J.M. Baldwin asserted, "There are many men who doubt his loyalty and I have it from a field officer of cavalry that Wyndham said to him ... that he would as [soon] fight for the Confederates as for the Union and he would if our Gov't did not give him what he wanted." But there the matter had lingered and now his career hung in limbo. He continued to draw his pay and made several attempts to return to active duty. In late June 1864 he did return to the army on his own accord, only to be taken into custody and returned to Washington, under the supervision of Maj. James Walsh, 3rd Pennsylvania Cavalry. Walsh turned his "prisoner" over to Col. Edward Townsend at the Adjutant General's Office, on the first of July. The major later stated that Townsend refused to accept several documents proffered by Wyndham or to listen to anything that he had to say, but "reminded [Wyndham] on each occasion that he had no business to go the Army of the Potomac." On July 5, 1864, Percy Wyndham was mustered out of the army.[11]

He engaged in several business ventures over the next few years and served a brief stint on the staff of General Giuseppe Garibaldi during a conflict in Europe in 1866 and 1867. By one account he was later "reduced to great poverty, and had pawned his jewels and decorations to get money to pay his debts." His last venture involved giving "exhibition ascensions" in a balloon of his own construction. On January 27, 1879, near Rangoon, India, the balloon, with Wyndham on board and after rising to a height of several hundred feet burst and fell into a lake. His body was recovered within minutes but attempts to revive him were unsuccessful. A local newspaper closed its account of the incident by stating, "Thus ended a singular and adventurous career."[12]

If Wyndham was ever fully aware of the reason for his termination he made no mention of it in the documents that have been located. After his death, however, an item appeared in the Chicago *Tribune* that purported to explain the circumstances that led to his "indefinite leave of absence [ordered] by Secretary Stanton." Shortly before his own death in 1869, Stanton had told a confidant within the War Department the reason behind Wyndham's dismissal "under promise of solemn secrecy during [Stanton's] lifetime." Stanton had received information from "informers" whose identity he had agreed to protect, "that Wyndham had entered into a negotiation with the Confederate Government to surrender his command for the sum of $300,000." Bound by his agreement to protect his sources Stanton was unable to try the colonel and thus his only alternative was to allow him to be mustered out of the service."[13]

The War Department investigated the allegations, but the detective found nothing to indicate that anyone had ever directly approached Wyndham about allowing himself and his men to be captured by Confederate forces or that he was in anyway aware of or complicit with the plan. Nor is it clear that the Confederate government ever sanctioned the plan. What is clear is that Henry De Ahna, a disgruntled former Union officer, who had been court-martialed earlier in the war following a confrontation with Maj. Gen. Charles Fremont, was the driving force behind the plot. His purpose, including the question of whether he was working for the Confederate government or purely for himself remains uncertain. The detective who investigated the matter termed De Ahna "a most consummate scoundrel and a dangerous man to be at large." The same detective informed his superiors that he was "not in possession of any information prejudicial to [Wyndham's] character." Still, it appears that he was the only man to suffer as a result of the allegations. The truth of this allegation may never be fully known, but it becomes even more curious when considered with General Heintzelman's comment of May 20, 1863, that the expected Rebel raid against the capital was to be aided by a disloyal Union colonel. In the same vein but referring to the capture of Edwin Stoughton, De Ahna reportedly alleged that Wyndham "has once already allowed himself to be strangely surprised."[14]

Despite the lack of verifiable evidence the conflict between Wyndham and Mosby, while brief, appears to have been an intensely personal affair, beginning with Mosby's charge that Wyndham threatened to put the town of Middleburg to the torch. Mosby's disdain for his Union antagonist is best seen in light of the fact that in John Scott's account of Mosby's career, which Mosby reportedly vetted, each chapter is written as a letter, addressed to "Dear Percy."

William Mann retained command of the 7th Michigan Cavalry until he resigned his commission effective March 1, 1864. During his tenure, his relationship with his officers remained less than friendly. In mid–June an unidentified soldier from the regiment had complained to Governor Austin Blair about the conduct of several of the senior officers, including the colonel. The governor then wrote to Lt. Col. Allyne Litchfield inquiring as to the merits of the complaints. In a rather damning reply Litchfield agreed with most of the accusations, "even to cowardice," and affirmed that Mann "is regarded with hatred and utter contempt." Blair suggested that Litchfield file charges so as to bring the matter before a military court but Litchfield refused, telling the governor that such a course of action would be viewed "as a move for personal ends." In the fall of 1863, while Mann was on leave, a majority of the senior officers, including Litchfield, signed a petition to the governor, charging Mann with cowardice, incompetence and conduct unbecoming an officer. Several other officers then submitted a second petition in support of the colonel. When Mann returned he met with each of the disgruntled men individually. Following these interviews a third letter was sent to the governor, in which the original petitioners asked that he drop the entire matter, claiming that they had signed the initial letter based on a false rumor. Though Litchfield did not attach his name to this last missive, he did notify the governor that "the conduct of Col. Mann has been such since his return ... and the feelings of the officers ... so different from their expressions in petition sent you for his removal, that I desire no action on your part in response to the petition.[15]

In October 1863, Mann proposed to the War Department that he would raise a brigade of veteran soldiers to serve as mounted infantry. He envisioned that the brigade would follow the "regular infantry organization," traveling in wagons, "eighty to the regiment, eight to the company ... with storage under the seats" for all of the implements necessary to conduct "extensive raids into the rich country of the enemy, destroying his depots of supplies, harassing his rear & cutting his lines of communication." This plan, for what Litchfield derisively termed a "Buggy Brigade," was approved by his superiors in the army but was rejected by the War Department. Mann had also designed a cartridge box, which incorporated both the cartridge and cap boxes into one unit, worn in the center of the chest so as to reduce injuries caused by wearing the current models on the waist. He resigned his commission so that he could lobby the War Department to purchase the boxes and to manage the production of the equipment. By the end of the war he had delivered close to 40,000 sets to the army.[16]

Following the conflict Mann was involved in numerous ventures, both profitable and controversial, several of which kept him in the news and the courtroom. He was involved in an oil swindle in 1865. He was arrested and tried in New York, but he escaped conviction when the judge determined that the charges should have been brought against him either in Ohio or Pennsylvania, where Mann claimed to have struck oil. He was later embroiled in a fraud, slander and perjury case in New York City, which was front-page news for months.[17]

While these matters have long since passed into history's dusty attic, Mann will be forever linked to the famed Michigan Cavalry Brigade. It was, arguably, his idea to raise a regiment of mounted rifles that was the genesis of the brigade. He had foreseen a need to target the Confederacy's guerrilla units but he had little opportunity to test his mettle against John Mosby or any guerrilla unit during his career. Mann had insisted that the regiment should be armed with, perhaps the most iconic firearm of the war, the Spencer repeating rifle, but the weapon had proved a failure, as did all carbines in confrontations with Mosby's command. Mosby relied on the revolver, of which his men generally carried several, and he favored a lightning fast attack in which he closed quickly with the enemy. The reliance on speed and close-in fighting overcame any perceived advantage that breech-loading or repeating weapons might have provided. The carbines, and especially the more cumbersome rifles, were next to useless on horseback and forced the Union troopers to engage the enemy from a standstill, thus surrendering the initiative as well as the "shock" of the charge to their opponent. As a result Mosby and his men prevailed on most every field. Still, the shift to the modern weapons did revolutionize the use of cavalry on the battlefield, as the troopers were now able to hold ground effectively. As such they became more like the mounted infantry that Mann envisioned, while the saber and revolver continued to let the troopers transition quickly to the more traditional role of cavalry.[18]

Allyne Litchfield was captured on March 1, 1864, near Atlee's Station, Virginia, during the Kilpatrick-Dahlgren Raid. As a result of the controversy attached to the raid Litchfield claimed that he was treated as a criminal rather than a prisoner of war until his exchange in March 1865. He along with five other officers and four black soldiers were confined in an unlit, "dungeon" in the basement of Libby Prison that measured, by his recollection, "7 feet by 11 feet." Following the war he received a brevet promotion to brigadier, but he never recovered from his time as a prisoner. He entered several fields of endeavor, including a ten-year stint as Consul General at Calcutta, India, but his mind began to deteriorate. By the turn of the century, friends and family deemed him to be insane. He died in 1911, and is buried in Massachusetts.[19]

Edwin Havens served with the 7th Michigan throughout the remainder of the war. He was commissioned a lieutenant in May 1865, and traveled west with the brigade before he was discharged that December. He lived in Wisconsin and Michigan, where he was employed by the state Lands Division. He died in Lansing, Michigan, in 1931.[20]

Joseph Copeland never returned to active campaigning. He closed out his career in command of the military post and prison at Alton, Illinois. He resigned on November 8, 1865, having missed entirely the fame earned by the brigade that he had led throughout the spring of 1863. Combined with Copeland's old 1st Michigan and under the command of George Custer, few units achieved more renown than the Michigan Brigade. The last commander of the brigade was Peter Stagg, who was elevated to the rank of colonel in August 1864, and to brigadier by brevet on March 13, 1865. Promoted to brigadier by brevet on the same date was James Kidd. Ebenezer Gould was wounded above the right ankle at Hagerstown on July 12, 1863. The wound troubled him for months, and though he was finally promoted to colonel in the fall of 1864 he was discharged due to disability that November.[21]

On the afternoon of July 3, in the fields of the Rummel Farm east of Gettysburg, George Custer cast aside any lingering reservations about his youth and ability and led the men from Michigan to enduring success and fame. Referring to the final cavalry charge of the afternoon, one chronicler declared, "The First Michigan had passed safely through months of neglect and mismanagement to launch a counterattack that has passed into history as one of the most gallant of the war." Never taking their renown for granted the men of the brigade cemented their place in history on field after field throughout the war, but the cost was staggering. By one tabulation "the Brigade had sustained the highest percentage of loss of any brigade in the mounted service, and of the four mounted regiments that lost the most men killed or fatally wounded in action the First, Fifth, and Sixth Michigan ranked second, third and fourth."[22]

Among the many thousands of young men who failed to return from Pennsylvania were Alfred Ryder, Frank Barbour, John Farnill and George Telling. Both James Kidd and Gershom Mattoon were wounded during the campaign. Frederick Schmalzried died of disease on June 28, 1863, a disease almost certainly contracted during his time in a Southern prison camp or a Northern parole camp following his capture in February.

Julius Stahel, like so many other officers, quickly faded from the pages of history. Though angered by his abrupt transfer in June, Stahel carried out his new assignment to the full satisfaction of his superior, Maj. Gen. Darius Couch. When Stahel was again transferred in March 1864, Couch thanked him for his service, "cheerfully given under every and all circumstances," and he noted, "I shall follow your future career with great interest, and permit me to wish you every success for the future." Stahel was reunited with General Sigel in the spring of 1864, and again took command of a cavalry division until he was wounded in the left shoulder at Piedmont, Virginia, on June 5, 1864. The wound prevented him from returning to active duty, however, and he resigned his commission on February 8, 1865. The general was later awarded the Medal of Honor for his actions at Piedmont. Like many other aging veterans Stahel may have sought the award for himself, though he engaged an attorney to contact the war department on his behalf. The affidavit in support of his claim is very brief and there are no supporting documents from witnesses in the file. Nor are there any details of the action at Piedmont. It is interesting, however, that much of the short letter deals with his expedition of late November 1862, and, but for the wound received at Piedmont he may have received the award for the earlier affair or it may have been denied.[23]

Following the war Stahel served as United States Consul to Japan, and closed out his government service as Consul-General at Shanghai, China, resigning due to poor health in 1895. Ironically John Mosby held a similar position in Hong Kong during this period, and

Stahel may have had occasion to communicate with the man who had been his nemesis throughout the spring of 1863. Stahel died on December 4, 1912.[24]

Samuel Heintzelman was relieved as commander of the Department of Washington on October 14, 1863, in part, because of the increasing frequency of attacks by John Mosby and other guerrillas operating in Northern Virginia. In August, Mosby began a series of operations in Fairfax County that drew the ire of both Stanton and Halleck, including two attacks on the outskirts of Annandale on August 11. Mosby then struck a detachment of the 2nd Massachusetts in the same location on the twenty-fourth. Though Mosby was wounded in this skirmish the depredations continued. Following an incident in which a bridge was burned across Pope's Run, in Fairfax County, in late September, Stanton ordered Heintzelman to give his "personal superintendence to" the problem, and Heintzelman took the field immediately to review the security precautions that his men had instituted. When guerrillas struck again on October 1, burning another bridge near Alexandria, Halleck blistered Heintzelman for an explanation. In his journal the defiant general wrote, "If they are not satisfied with my administration of this department, why don't they relieve me. I am satisfied that I know my duty and have done it. If I have not, neither the Secretary of War or General Halleck can teach me it." Rumors immediately took hold that he would be relieved, and on October 6, he remarked, "A few days will develop the matter." On October 13 he was informed by his replacement, Maj. Gen. Christopher C. Auger, that the decision had been made, and it was announced in orders the following day.[25]

Heintzelman remained in the capital on other administrative duties and served as an honorary pallbearer for John Buford in December. He was posted to Texas for reconstruction duty following the war and retired from the army in 1869. He returned to Washington, D.C., late in life, where he passed away on May 1, 1880.[26]

When the Army of the Potomac returned to Virginia in mid–July, John Mosby was waiting for it. The men in the cavalry corps were now seasoned veterans, hardened by the grueling campaign across Maryland and Pennsylvania. The ineffective brigade and regimental commanders had, in large measure, resigned or been replaced by younger, more aggressive men who were willing and eager to meet their enemy on any field, but Mosby would continue to frustrate them for the remainder of the war. As the long columns of men and supply wagons moved south through Loudoun and Fauquier counties that summer, they were continually harassed by "guerrillas and bushwhackers," and specifically, as one infantry commander noted, by "Mosby's guerrillas." Yet with his force becoming ever larger Mosby increasingly turned his efforts toward targets of more strategic value than the small picket details that he had harassed so effectively during the first six months of his career as a partisan.[27]

Jeb Stuart and John Mosby, each had brilliant careers in the service of the Confederacy. Both men continue to garner the acclaim and attention of historians, and justifiably so. Stuart's proven ability to raid deep within and behind Union lines created near-constant anxiety within the administration and the military, and it is a sad irony that when a Confederate force did finally launch an attack against the fortifications ringing the city on July 12, 1864, he was not alive to appreciate it or to participate, having been mortally wounded two months earlier.

Stuart and Mosby held a special bond, a bond to which both men remained true to their dying day. Jeb Stuart sanctioned Mosby's career as a partisan, mentored him throughout and stood by him when others sought to bring his service as such to an end. Stuart counseled Mosby early on to avoid referring to his men by names that had already fallen into disrepute, and his communications often stressed Mosby's value as a scout as opposed to a guerrilla to further distance him from the outlaw bands that fueled the debate in the South over the need for and effectiveness of guerrillas.

During the first six months of 1863 the senior officials within the Federal government and the military saw Stuart, rather than Mosby, as the greater threat to the safety of the capital, but that would change. In time, those who ignored Mosby did so at their peril, as Samuel Heintzelman learned later that year. The Union sentinels who manned the picket lines, however, were always aware of John Mosby. These soldiers, who may have shown little appreciation for the larger aspects of the Union war effort, clearly understood that the men of the many guerrilla bands who roamed the region posed the most direct threat to their lives and their freedom. By the summer of 1863 John Mosby was the face of the guerrilla war in Northern Virginia. Though these Union soldiers hated the manner of warfare that he prosecuted, their letters home suggest a grudging admiration for the man they often referred to as Mr. Mosby.

In August 1863 Colonel Mann had led his 7th Michigan "on a hunt for the far-famed guerrilla." In closing his account of the expedition Andrew Buck concluded, "I can say one thing to the credit of this private hero, and that is that he is *surprisingly humane*." Indeed when the conflict between the guerrillas and the Wolverines began escalating out of control in September 1864, it was John Mosby who took the critical first step to end the ugly cycle of retribution and execution. Thanks in large measure to Mosby's leadership the guerrilla war in Northern Virginia never degenerated to the outlaw warfare that consumed other regions of the country.[28]

Appendix

Thc Order Captured by John Mosby, June 17, 1863

Hdqrs Army Potomac
June 17, 1863

Genl. [Pleasonton]
Commdg. Cavalry Corps

General

Under no circumstances advance the Main body of your cavalry beyond [Aldie] until further information is received of the movements of the enemy. If the position you should occupy tonight should offer advantages for grazing your horses, it will be well to hold on there until your scouts can furnish us with further information. We have reason to believe that Ewells and Longstreets corps passed up the valley with a heavy Cavalry force and if so the presumption is that they are still near the Upper Potomac. The[y] must have come for an object and until we know where they are we cannot devise it. It will be advisable for the Infantry to remain where they will be tonight until further orders. Send a small detachment in the direction of Leesburg and should it fall in with no considerable force of the enemy, direct them to connect with Capt. [McKee's] Cavalry tonight at the mouth of the Monocacy and have them ordered to join you.

Direct the force sent to Snickers Gap to penetrate if possible into the valley and ascertain what force the enemy have or had there, and also the direction of their departure, if they have left. The General feels the worth of reliable information in that direction and desires that you spare no labor to obtain it. Also send a Detachment to Thoroughfare Gap and beyond if practicable for the same object. If you should be in want of supplies before the completion of this, send me timely notice in order that the proper Department may have you provided. We shall endeavor to have a couple of Regiments from [Stahel's] command go to Warrenton and Sulphur Springs and penetrate in that direction.
A Signal Officer will join you and it is reported that from a point of observation on the Blue Ridge near Snickers Gap, the whole Country beyond can be observed without difficulty. Give timely notice of any want of supplies to the proper Staff Departments, that they may be furnished you.

Very Respy. Your obt. Sevt.
Daniel Butterfield
MG C of Staff[1]

Abbreviations

ARAGSNY	Annual Report of the Adjutant General State of New York
BACA	Baltimore *American and Commercial Advertiser*
CMU	Central Michigan University, Clarke Historical Library
CHS	Connecticut Historical Society
DAT	Detroit *Advertiser & Tribune*
DFP	Detroit *Free Press*
DPL	Detroit Public Library, Burton Collection
DU	Duke University, William R. Perkins Library
GU	Georgetown University, Lavinger Library
GHS	Georgia Historical Society, Savannah Georgia
GRDE	Grand Rapids *Daily Eagle*
GRPL	Grand Rapids Public Library, Grand Rapids, Michigan
HSP	Historical Society of Pennsylvania, Philadelphia, Pennsylvania
HSWP	Library and Archives Division, Historical Society of Western Pennsylvania, Pittsburgh, Pennsylvania
KPP	Kingston *People's Press*
LC	Manuscript Division, Library of Congress
MSU	Michigan State University, Conrad Hall
MWR	*Mosby's War Reminiscences*
NARA	National Archives and Records Administration, Washington, D.C.
NC	Navarro College, Corsicana, Texas
NYSLA	New York State Library and Archives, Albany, New York
NYT	New York *Tribune*
OR	*The War of the Rebellion: A Compilation of Official Records of the Union and Confederate Armies*. 128 vols. Washington, D.C., 1890–1901. All cites refer to Series I unless noted.
ORS	*Supplement to the Official Records of the Union and Confederate Armies,* edited by Janet B. Hewett, Noah Andre Trudeau and Bryce A. Suderow (Wilmington, 1994), Part I, Reports. All cites refer to Part I unless noted.
PL	*Partisan Life with Col. John S. Mosby*
PI	Philadelphia *Inquirer*
PWT	*Philadelphia Weekly Times*
RDUA	Rochester *Daily Union & Advertiser*
RDA	Rochester *Democrat & American*
SAM	State Archives of Michigan, Lansing, Michigan

TNYT	*The New York Times*
USMA	United States Military Academy, West Point, New York
USAMHI	United States Military History Institute, Carlisle, Pennsylvania
UC	University of California, Davidson Library, Santa Barbara, California
UG	University of Georgia, Athens, Georgia
UMBL	University of Michigan, Bentley Historical Library
UMCL	William L. Clements Library, University of Michigan
UNC	University of North Carolina, Lewis Round Wilson Library
UV	University of Vermont, Bailey/Howe Library
UVA	University of Virginia, Alderman Library
VHS	Vermont Historical Society, Barre, Vermont
VSL	Virginia State Library
WES	Washington *Evening Star*
WMU	Western Michigan University
WSU	Wichita State University, Department of Special Collections

Chapter Notes

Introduction

1. *The Oxford American Desk Dictionary and Thesaurus* (New York, 2001), p. 594; Richard Berleth, *The Twilight Lords: An Irish Chronicle* (New York, 1978), p. 19.

2. U.S. War Department, *The War of the Rebellion: The Official Records of the Union and Confederate Armies*, 128 volumes (Washington, D.C., 1890–1901), Series I, volume 19, Part 2, p. 242. Hereinafter cited as *OR*. All references are to Series I unless otherwise noted.

Chapter 1

1. George B. McClellan, *McClellan's Own Story* (New York, 1887), pp. 536–537.

2. Jackson [Michigan] *Eagle*, September 6, 1862; *NYT*, September 1, 1862. Emphasis in the original.

3. Worthington C. Ford, *A Cycle of Adams Letters 1861–1865*, 2 volumes (Boston, 1920), volume 1, pp. 177–181; *OR*: 12:3:802, 807 and 19:2:604–605; Elizabeth Lindsay Lomax, edited by Lindsay Lomax Wood, *Leaves from an Old Washington Diary 1854–1863* (New York, 1943), p. 210; Margaret Leech, *Reveille in Washington 1860–1865* (Alexandria, 1980 edition), p. 240; James M. McPherson, *Crossroads of Freedom: Antietam* (New York, 2002), pp. 102–104.

4. *OR*: 12:2:45, 12:3:736–737, 797 and 51:1:787, 789, 800; *DFP*, September 11, 1862; *DAT*, September 22, 1862.

5. *OR*: 51:1:797, 801, 870, also 19:2:242; Roger D. Hunt and Jack R. Brown, *Brevet Brigadier Generals in Blue* (Gaithersburg, 1990), p. 492; Samuel Bates, *History of Pennsylvania Volunteers 1861–1865*, 14 volumes (Wilmington, 1993 edition), volume 3, pp. 320–321.

6. Edward G. Longacre, *Custer and His Wolverines: The Michigan Cavalry Brigade, 1861–1865* (Conshohocken, 1997), pp. 15, 29–30, 39–41, 59–64; OR: 12:2: 564 and 12:3:589–590; John Hennessy, *Return to Bull Run: The Campaign and Battle of Second Manassas* (New York, 1993), pp. 40–46; John Mosby, *MWR*, pp. 245–247; Charles Wells Russell, editor, *Gray Ghost: The Memoirs of Colonel John S. Mosby* (New York, 1992 edition), pp. 103–104; J.E.B. Stuart to My Dear Wife, August 19, 1862, in Adele H. Mitchell, *The Letters of Major General James E. B. Stuart* (Fairfax, 1990), pp. 260–261; Jeffery D. Wert, *General James Longstreet: The Confederacy's Most Controversial Soldier—A Biography* (New York, 1993), p. 164; John Scott, "The Black Horse Cavalry," *PWT*, May 25, 1878.

7. Frederick H. Dyer, compiler, *A Compendium of the War of the Rebellion*, 3 volumes (Des Moines, 1908), volume 3, p. 1655. Two companies of the 1st West Virginia remained with the Army of the Potomac and saw action at Antietam in September 1862.

8. Dyer, *A Compendium of the War of the Rebellion*, volume 3, p. 1374; Louis N. Boudrye, *Historic Records of the Fifth New York Cavalry, First Ira Harris Guard* (Albany, 1865), pp. 17–18, 37–38; Roger D. Hunt, *Colonels in Blue, Union Army Colonels of the Civil War, New York* (Atglen, 2003), p. 102. The history of the 1st Vermont will be examined in depth in a later chapter.

9. Dyer, *A Compendium of the War of the Rebellion*, volume 3, pp. 1647–1648; Horace K. Ide, *History of the First Vermont Cavalry Volunteers in the War of the Great Rebellion*, edited by Elliott W. Hoffman (Baltimore, 2000), pp. 13–21.

10. Myles Keogh, "John Buford, Etat de Service," John Buford Papers, USMA; J.E.B. Stuart to My Darling One, September 4, 1862 in Mitchell, *The Letters of General Stuart*, p. 263. As in almost all cases throughout the war the casualty figures for the regiment vary, and trying to achieve an accurate tabulation is an inexact science. The total given here is based on a comparison of lists published after the battle, a parole list published at the time and the post war regimental roster. The exact number of men with the regiment that morning is uncertain but one published source puts the figure at 300. See *DAT*, September 16, 1862; Aaron Bliss, *Record of Service of Michigan Volunteers in the Civil War 1861–1865, 1st Cavalry* (Kalamazoo, 1905); Rob L. Wagner, "Mortally wounded Colonel Thornton Brodhead left behind two blood-smeared letters denouncing his superiors," *America's Civil War*, May 1998, p. 70. The figures for the remainder of the Union regiments, including the 4th New York, which fought alongside Buford but was not assigned to his brigade, were compiled from the following sources: H.D. to Editor, Chain Bridge, Virginia, September 8, 1862, *KPP*, September 18, 1862; *OR*: 12:2:253, 274, 738; Patrick Hughs to Editor, Camp Parole, September 20, 1862, Monroe [Michigan] *Commercial*, October 9, 1862; William Wilkins to Dear Wife, Alexandria, Virginia, September 7, 1862, "The Civil War Letters of William Porter Wilkins," Civil War Miscellaneous Collection, USAMHI; A. E. Matthews to Mr. Ryder, September 7, 1862, Alfred Ryder Letters, UMBL; D. O. Pickard, "The Death of Col. Brodhead," *National Tribune*, October 15, 1885. The figure given for Buford's brigade includes one man killed and eight captured or missing from the 1st Vermont, though it is not believed that this regiment was directly involved in the fight. It is believed that Buford had assigned them the task of holding the fords and that these men were lost in the confusion that followed Buford's defeat. He may also have held them back as a reserve or rally force but never had the opportunity to bring them into the fight.

11. Alfred Ryder to Dear Friends, Cumberland, Maryland, September 7, 1862, Ryder Letters, UMBL; *DAT*, September 17, 1862 and October 7, 1862; *DFP*, September 16, 1862 and September 30, 1862; Bliss, *Record of Service of Michigan Volunteers in the Civil War 1861–1865, First Cavalry*, p. 12; Maj. William Atwood resigned his commission in November 1862 while still a paroled prisoner and it was accepted in January 1863, see Atwood to Adjutant General, Detroit, March 16, 1863, in Atwood's VSR File, RG 94, Entry 496, NARA.

12. *OR*: 12:1:579–580; DFP, August 14, 1862; Bliss, *Record of Service, First Cavalry*, p. 49; DAT, September 22, 1862.

13. HD [Henry Delamater] to Dear Sir, Hall's Farm, September 27, 1862, *KPP*, October 9, 1862; Charles Johnson to Dear Mother, Alexandria, October 10, 1862, Charles Johnson

Letters, UC; Col. E. B. Sawyer to Gen. Meigs, October 15, 1862, 1st Vermont Letter and Order Books, RG 94, and Gen. Nathaniel Banks to Col. James Hardie and Capt. Richard Irwin to Gen. Samuel Heintzelman, October 11, 1862, RG 107, M504, NARA.

14. *OR*: 19:2: 3–4; Charles Johnson to Dear Mother, Camp First Michigan Cavalry, September 28, 1862, Johnson Papers, UC; Henry Smith to Dear Mother Sisters and Brothers, Alexandria, September 24, 1862, Henry A. Smith Letters, VHS; Nancy Chappelear Baird, editor, *Journal of Amanda Virginia Edmonds, Lass of the Mosby Confederacy, 1857–1867* (Stephens City, 1984), p. 117.

15. Frank J. Welcher, *The Union Army, 1861–1865: Organization and Operations volume I: The Eastern Theater* (Bloomington, 1989), pp. 512, 546–553. A comprehensive study of the history of this command is beyond the scope of this narrative. When the Army of Virginia and the Army of the Potomac were consolidated several corps designations changed, including Banks' II Corps which became the XII Corps and Franz Sigel's I Corps, Army of Virginia, which became the XI Corps, Army of the Potomac on September 12, 1862. When McClellan moved into Maryland he left behind 47,000 men who had until recently been assigned to either the Army of Virginia or the Army of the Potomac. These men were in addition to the troops that garrisoned the forts and their supporting infantry, for a total of 73,000 men. By the end of October, however, McClellan had pulled nearly 65,000 of these troops for service with the army.

16. *OR*: 19:2:220, 227–228, 237, 253, 497; Samuel Peter Heintzelman Journal, LC. Several conflicting dates are given for when Heintzelman actually assumed command of the Defenses of Washington. According to his journal it happened on November 13.

17. Ezra J. Warner, *Generals in Blue: Lives of the Union Commanders* (Baton Rouge, 1964), p. 227–228; Patricia L. Faust, editor, *Historical Times Illustrated Encyclopedia of the Civil War* (New York, 1986), p. 356; *DAT*, October 21, 1862; William B. Styple, editor, *Letters from the Peninsula: The Civil War Letters of General Philip Kearny* (Kearny, 1988), p. 91; Walter H. Hebert, *Fighting Joe Hooker* (Lincoln, 1999) p. 72; Jerry Thompson, *Civil War to the Bloody End: The Life & Times of Major General Samuel P. Heintzelman* (College Station, 2006), pp. xiii, 263–264.

18. Charles Johnson to Dear Mother, Alexandria, October 10, 1862, Johnson Papers, UC; Regimental Order No. 42, October 30, 1862, RG 94, 1st Michigan Regimental Letter and Order Books, and Charles Town's Commission Branch File, RG 94, M1064, NARA; J. H. Kidd, *Personal Recollections of a Cavalryman with Custer's Michigan Cavalry Brigade in the Civil War* (Alexandria, 1983 edition), p. 24, Longacre, *Custer and His Wolverines*, p. 37.

19. Col. Town to Adjt. Gen. Robertson, November 14, 1862, Petition of December 7, 1862, Town to Robertson, December 15, 1862, and Town to Robertson, August 19, 1864, Regimental Service Records, 1st Michigan Cavalry, SAM; Longacre, *Custer and His Wolverines*, p. 65.

20. *OR*: 19:2:106, 518, 545; Samuel P. Heintzelman Journal, LC.

21. Ted Alexander, "Antietam Horsepower or, Greasy Heel and the Dead Colonel's Mount," *Blue & Gray*, volume 20, number 1 (2002), p. 12; Silas Mason to Respected Parents, November 8, 1862, Silas Mason Letters, NYSLA; Nelson Taylor, *Saddle and Saber: The Letters of Civil War Cavalryman Corporal Nelson Taylor*, compiled by Dr. Gray Nelson Taylor (Bowie, 1993), p. 74. That Stuart's cavalry was plagued by the same outbreak of disease is confirmed by Lee in *OR*: 19:2:701 and 709–710, as well as Charles W. Ramsdell, "General Robert E. Lee's Horse Supply, 1862–1863," *American Historical Review*, volume 35, number 4 (1930), p. 762.

22. Gen. Heintzelman to Gen. Sigel, November 19, 1862 and Heintzelman to Maj. Leavitt Hunt, November 21, 1862, and Heintzelman to Hunt, November 22, 1862, RG 107, M504, NARA.

23. Col. Price to Maj. Hunt, November 24, 1862, RG 393, Part 2, Entry 6744, Letters Received and Sent, March to December 1862, NARA; Alfred Ryder to Dear Friends, Dranesville, November 23, 1862, Ryder Letters, UMBL.

24. *OR*: 21:12, 801; Gen. Sigel to Gen. Burnside, November 26, 1862, RG 107, M504, NARA.

25. Gen. Heintzelman to Gen. Sigel and Heintzelman to Anson Stager, November 26, 1862, Capt. Carroll Potter to Gen. Burnside, November 28, 1862, RG 107, M504, Heintzelman to Sigel, November 26, 1862, Potter to Maj. Hunt, November 28, 1862, RG 393, Pt.1, Entry 5379, and Col. Price to Hunt, Report of November 24, 1862, RG 393, Pt. 2, Entry 6744, also Lt. Col. Platt to Gen. Bayard, November 25, 1862 and Gen. Parke to Bayard, November 26, 1862, RG 393, Pt. 2, Entry 1449, NARA. The guerrilla problem around Accotink eventually became such a concern that a Home Guard force of about fifty men was recruited to supplement the troops posted there in October 1863, see RG 94, Entry 496, NARA.

26. *OR*: 19:2:478; *TNYT*, December 3, 1862; Capt. Wilbur Bentley to his wife, Fairfax Court House, December 2, 1862, *Western New Yorker*, December 11, 1862, in Conrad B. Bush, *Ninth New York Cavalry (Veteran,) Stoneman's Cavalry or Westfield Cavalry: News Articles from Wyoming County Newspapers* (privately printed, 2000), p. 40; Report of Lt. James Burrows, December 1, 1862 in Helen Mathews, compiler, *Civil War Letters: 1st Lt. James Baldwin Burrows, 9th New York Cavalry, 1861–1864*, Civil War Miscellaneous Collection, USAMHI; Newel Cheney, *History of the Ninth Regiment New York Cavalry* (New York, 1901), p. 67; *NYT*, December 3, 1862; *ARAGSNY* (Albany, 1894), volume 2, pp. 1075, 1182; H.D. to Dear Sir, Chantilly, November 20, 1862, *KPP*, December 11, 1862; *PI*, December 4, 1862.

27. *TNYT*, December 3, 1862; *PI*, December 4, 1862; *NYT*, December 3, 1862.

28. Frank Myers, *The Comanches: A History of White's Battalion, Virginia Cavalry, Laurel Brig., Hampton's Div., A.N.V., C.S.A* (Gaithersburg, 1987 edition), p. 132; *TNYT*, December 3, 1862.

29. *TNYT*, December 3, 1862; Bentley Letter, *Western New Yorker*, December 11, 1862, in Bush, *Ninth New York Cavalry*, p. 41; Boudrye, *Historic Records of the Fifth New York Cavalry*, p. 42; Delevan Arnold, edited by Helen Everett Wood, *A Kalamazoo Volunteer in the Civil War* (Kalamazoo, 1962), p. 37; *OR*: 21:18.

30. Myers, *The Comanches*, p. 137; Boudrye, *Historic Records of the Fifth New York Cavalry*, p. 43; *TNYT*, December 3, 1862; *NYT*, December 3, 1862; Fredonia Censor, December 17, 1862. The accounts that at least two unit flags or guidons were captured are too numerous to discount but not confirmed by records in the National Archives. This suggests that they were either company guidons or that they were not turned over to the government.

31. Myers, *The Comanches*, pp. 134–135; William N. McDonald, *A History of the Laurel Brigade, Originally the Ashby Cavalry of the Army of Northern Virginia and Chew's Battery*, edited by Bushrod C. Washington (Gaithersburg, 1987 edition), p. 107. White had been shot during a skirmish in Leesburg on September 17.

32. Samuel S. Moore, "Through the Shadow: A Boy's Memories of the Civil War in Clarke County," *Proceedings of The Clarke County Historical Association*, volume 24, 1989–1990, p. 2; *OR*: 21:19; Cheney, *History of the Ninth Regiment*, p. 67.

33. *OR*: 21:20; Cheney, *History of the Ninth Regiment*, p. 67; Burrows' report in Mathews, *Civil War Letters*, USAMHI; *PI*, December 4, 1862; *NYT*, December 3, 1862.

34. Capt. W. G. Bentley Letter, Fairfax Court House, December 2, 1862, *Western New Yorker*, December 11, 1862 in Bush, *Ninth New York Cavalry*, p. 41; *TNYT*, December 1 and December 3, 1862; *NYT*, December 3, 1862.

35. *NYT*, December 3, 1862; *OR*: 21:19; George M. Neese, *Three Years in the Confederate Horse Artillery* (Dayton, 1988 edition), pp. 135–136; Michael Mahon, editor, *Winchester Divided: The Civil War Diaries of Julia Chase & Laura Lee* (Mechanicsburg, 2002) pp. 68–69.

36. Cheney, *History of the Ninth Regiment*, p. 67; Burrows' report in Mathews, *Civil War Letters*, USAMHI.

37. *OR*: 21: 20; Myers, *The Comanches*, p. 137; *NYT*, December 3, 1862.

38. *OR*: 21:18, 20; Myers, *The Comanches*, p. 136; *NYT*, December 3, 1862; *TNYT*, December 1, 1862 and December 3, 1862.

39. *TNYT*, December 3, 1862; Capt. W. G. Bentley Letter, Fairfax Court House, December 2, 1862, *Western New Yorker*, December 11, 1862, in Bush, *Ninth New York Cavalry*, p. 41; Myers, *The Comanches*, p. 138.

Chapter 2

1. Warner, *Generals in Blue*, p. 92; *DFP*, April 22, 1862.

2. Bliss, *Record of Service, First Cavalry*, p. 123; William O. Lee, *Personal and Historical Sketches and Facial History of and by Members of the Seventh Regiment Michigan Volunteer Cavalry, 1862–1865* (Detroit, 1990 edition), pp. 22, 24; Longacre, *Custer and His Wolverines*, p. 15, 82; Joseph Copeland's Report, U.S. Army Generals' Reports of Civil War Service, 1864–1887, RG 94, M1098, and Copeland's Commission Branch File, RG 94, M1064, NARA; William Mann to Edwin Stanton, Washington, D.C., June 21, 1862, Austin Blair Papers, Burton Historical Collections, Detroit Public Library, cited hereafter as Blair Papers, DPL.

3. Capt. William Mann to Secretary of War Edwin Stanton, June 21, 1862, Austin Blair Papers, DPL; Joseph Copeland File, RG 94, M1064, NARA; *DFP*, August 14, 1862; Jackson *Eagle*, August 23, 1862. John Hunt Morgan had just made a three-week raid through Kentucky that July.

4. Capt. Mann to Gov. Blair, June 21, 1862, Blair Papers, DPL; Copeland file, RG 94, M1064, NARA.

5. Lee, *Personal and Historical Sketches*, pp. 22–23; *DFP*, August 23, 1862; J. K. Lowden, "Michigan's 5th Cavalry in the Latter Period of the War," *National Tribune*, July 16, 1896.

6. George S. May, *Michigan and the Civil War Years, 1860–1866: A Wartime Chronicle* (Lansing, 1964), pp. 28–29; Gregory J. W. Urwin, "'Come On, You Wolverines!' Custer's Michigan Cavalry Brigade," *Military Images*, volume 7, number 1, July-August 1985, pp. 7–8; Lee, *Personal and Historical Sketches*, pp. 23–25.

7. C to Editors, Camp Kellogg, October 3, 1862, Mecosta County [Michigan] *Pioneer*, October 16, 1862. C was Jacob Osborn Coburn.

8. C to Editors, Camp Kellogg, October 1862, Mecosta County *Pioneer*, October 23, 1862; Edwin Havens to Dear Father and Mother, Camp Kellogg, September 30, 1862, Edwin Havens' Letters, MSU; Frederick Baird to Dear Brother, Virginia, May 23, 1863, The Baird Family Papers, UMBL; Kidd, *Personal Recollections*, p. 53; Ebenezer Gould to Hon. A. Gould, Fairfax Court House, April 26, 1863, Amos Gould Papers, CMU.

9. Kidd, *Personal Recollections*, p. 53; *DFP*, October 12, 1862; George Custer to Gov. Blair, Washington, D.C., January 31, 1862, Blair Papers, DPL. In his *Recollections*, Kidd recalled that many of the officers were not in favor of Gray, but in a war date letter he speaks only of himself as preferring "a regular army officer," see James Kidd to Dear Father, Ionia, September 25, 1862, the James Kidd Letters, UMBL.

10. Capt. Custer to Gov. Blair, Washington, D.C., Jan. 31, 1862, Blair Papers, DPL.

11. Adjutant General Robertson to Gen. Meigs, August 6, 1862, Robertson to Gen. Ripley, August 6, 1862 and Robertson to Gov. Blair, August 19, 1862, Letters Sent by the Adjutant General, Entry 174, Acc. 59–14, SAM; Col. Copeland to C. W. Foster, Asst. Adjt. General, October 24, 1862, RG 94, Muster Rolls, Returns and Regimental Papers, 5th Michigan Cavalry, NARA.

12. Wiley Sword, "'Those Damned Michigan Spencers': Colonel Copeland's 5th Michigan Cavalry and Their Spencer Rifles," *Man at Arms*, volume 19, number 5, September/October 1997, pp. 24–29; Col. Copeland to AAG Foster, October 24, 1862, RG 94, Muster Rolls, Returns, Regimental Papers, 5th Michigan Cavalry, NARA.

13. *DFP*, September 13, 1862 and December 5, 1862, *DAT*, December 6, 1862.

14. James G. Genco, *Arming Michigan's Regiments, 1862–1864* (privately printed, 1982), p. 96; Sword, "'Those Damned Michigan Spencers,'" p. 31; Joseph Bilby, "Carbines — Yesterday," *The Civil War News*, December 1992, p. 51; Berkeley R Lewis, *Notes on Cavalry Weapons of the American Civil War 1861–1865* (Washington, D.C., 1961), p. 12.

15. *DFP*, October 19, 1862 and October 22, 1862; *DAT*, November 17, 1862; Lee, *Personal and Historical Sketches*, pp. 24–26. Urwin, "'Come On, You Wolverines!': Custer's Michigan Cavalry Brigade," p. 9.

16. *DAT*, November 4, 1862; Genco, *Arming Michigan's Regiments*, pp. 99–101; John D. McAulay, *Carbines of the U.S. Cavalry, 1861–1865* (Lincoln, 1996), pp. 32, 46; Edwin Havens to Dear Father, Mother and Nell, Camp Kellogg, November 28, 1862, Havens Letters, MSU.

17. *DFP*, February 10 and 21, 1863; *DAT*, November 4, 1862, January 27 and 29, 1863; Edwin Havens to Brother Nell, Bristow Station, April 27, 1863, Havens Letters, MSU.

18. Francis Kellogg to Edwin Stanton, October 21, 1862, Copeland File, RG 94, M1064, NARA; *DAT*, November 4, 1862.

19. Gershom Mattoon to Dear Brother and Sister, Camp Kellogg, November 21, 1862, Mattoon Family Papers, MSU; John Morey to Dear Cousin, Camp Banks, November 23, 1862, John R. Morey Papers, UMBL.

20. Edwin Havens to Nell, undated letter, Edwin Havens to Brother Nell, Camp Kellogg, November 20, 1862, Havens Letters, MSU; John Morey to Dear Cousin, November 23, 1862, Morey Papers, UMBL; Rebecca Richmond Diary, GRPL; Gershom Mattoon to Dear Brother and Sister, November 21, 1862, Mattoon Family Papers, MSU.

21. Gov. Blair to Gen. Halleck, November 26, 1862, Letters From the Adjutant General, SAM; *DFP*, November 29, 1862 and January 16, 1863; John Farnill to My Dear Sister, Camp Kellogg, December 5, 1862, John S. Farnill Letters, CMU; Kidd, *Personal Recollections*, p. 71; Richmond Diary, GRPL.

22. *DFP*, December 5, 1862; Lee, *Personal and Historical Sketches*, p. 23; Col. Mann to Gen. Halleck, November 13, 1862, Copeland File, RG 94, M1064, NARA.

23. H. Baros to Edwin Stanton, November 12, 1862, Copeland File, RG 94, M1064, NARA. Emphasis in the original.

Chapter 3

1. Alfred Ryder to Dear friends, Dranesville, December 6, 1862, Ryder Letters, UMBL; Charles Johnson to Dear Mother, Dranesville, December 3, 1862, Johnson Letters, UC; Capt. Potter to Maj. Hunt, December 4, 1862, Gen. Sickles to Col. Beckwith, December 4, 1862, RG 107, M504; Col. Town to Maj. Hunt, December 4, 1862, RG 393, Part 2, Entry 6744, NARA; *OR*: 21:819. This particular pontoon train may never have left Alexandria — See *OR*: 21:840.

2. John Fortier, *15th Virginia Cavalry* (Lynchburg, 1993), pp. 90–93, 117–118; Lee A. Wallace, Jr., *A Guide to Virginia Military Organizations, 1861–1865* (Lynchburg, 1986), pp. 56–57; Louis H. Manarin, compiler, *North Carolina Troops, 1861–1865, A Roster*, 14 volumes (Raleigh, 1968), volume 2, 74; Charlotte *Western Democrat*, March 31, 1863.

3. *OR*: 21:61–62, 842–843, 860; T.A. Case to Dear Editors, Aquia Creek, December 18, 1862, Fredonia *Censor*, December 31, 1862; Gen. Heintzelman to Gen. Sigel, December 10, 1862, RG 107, M504, NARA.

4. *OR*: 21:846; Maj. Hunt to Gen. Sigel, December 11, 1862, RG 393, Part 1, Entry 5379, Gen. Halleck to Gen. Heintzelman, December 11, 1862, RG 393, Part 1, Entry 5382, Letters Received, Department of Washington, NARA.

5. William Plum, *The Military Telegraph During the Civil War in the United States,* 2 volumes (Chicago, 1882), volume 1, p. 355; Gen. Sigel to Gen. Slocum, December 12, 1862, RG 107, M504, NARA.

6. R. Jackson Ratcliffe, *This Was Prince William* (Leesburg, 1978), pp. 42–43.

7. Ford, *A Cycle of Adams Letters*, volume 1, pp. 200–201; Bohemian to Editors, Dumfries, November 19, 1861, Richmond *Dispatch*, November 26, 1861; JMS to Messrs. Editors, Brook's Station, December 10, 1862, Bucks County Intelligencer, December 23, 1862. Bohemian was the pen name assumed by Dr. William Shepardson.

8. Ezra J. Warner, *Generals in Gray: Lives of the Confederate Commanders* (Baton Rouge, 1959), pp. 122–123; *OR*: 21:1067.

9. *OR*: 21: 690; U.R. Brooks, *Butler and His Cavalry in the War of Secession, 1861–1865* (Camden, 1989 edition), p. 85.

10. *OR*: 21: 690; Brooks, *Butler and His Cavalry*, p. 86.

11. *OR*: 21: 690–691; Brooks, *Butler and His Cavalry*, p. 86; *WES*, December 14, 1862.

12. *OR*: 21: 689, 850; Stephen W. Sears, editor, *On Campaign with the Army of the Potomac: The Civil War Journal of Theodore Ayrault Dodge* (New York, 2001), p. 108.

13. Gen. Stoughton to Capt. Scott, December 14, 1862, RG 393, Part 1, Entry 3966, Letters Sent by General Casey, and Col. Price to Stoughton, December 19, 1862, RG 107, M504, NARA; Charles Cummings to My Dear Wife, Fairfax Court House, December 14, 1862, Cummings' Letters, VHS; *OR*: 21:870.

14. Letter signed GSM, December 12, 1862, Windsor *Vermont Journal*, January 31, 1863; Samuel H. Merrill, *The Campaigns of the First Maine and First District of Columbia Cavalry* (Portland, 1866), p. 41; Col. David Thomson to his daughter, Fairfax Court House, October 2, 1862, *Yearbook: The Historical Society of Fairfax County, Virginia*, volume 20, 1984–1985, pp. 86–88.

15. George C. Benedict, *Army Life in Virginia: Letters from the Twelfth Vermont Regiment and Personal Experiences of Volunteer Service in the War for the Union, 1862–63* (Burlington, 1895), pp. 85, 89; James P. Brady, compiler, *Hurrah for the Artillery! Knap's Independent Battery "E," Pennsylvania Light Artillery* (Gettysburg, 1992), p. 187; Milo M. Quaife, editor, *From the Cannon's Mouth: The Civil War Letters of General Alpheus S. Williams* (Lincoln, 1995 edition), pp. 153–154; Ezra D. Simons, *A Regimental History: The One Hundred and Twenty-Fifth New York State Volunteers* (New York, 1988), p. 52; *OR*: 21: 854.

16. Quaife, *From the Cannon's Mouth*, p. 154; Alexander Hays to Dear Annie, Washington, December 15, 1862, Gilbert Hays Collection, HSWP.

17. Col. Gregg to Capt. Scott, December 16, 1862, RG 393, Part 1, Entry 3966, NARA; Letter signed G. R. B., Washington, D.C., December 12, 1862, *DFP*, December 18, 1862.

18. Brady, *Hurrah For The Artillery!*, pp. 184–185; David Thackery, *A Light and Uncertain Hold: A History of the Sixty-Sixth Ohio Volunteer Infantry* (Kent, 1999), pp. 115–116.

19. *OR*: 21:695; William Deloney to My Dear Rosa, Culpeper, December 17, 1862, William Deloney Letters, UG; Adjt. George Kennedy to Capt. Wier, December 29, 1862, RG 94, Muster Rolls, Returns, and Regimental Papers, 10th New York Cavalry, NARA.

20. *OR*: 21:695,853; *RDUA*, December 23, 1862; Zack Miller to Dear Father, Dumfries, December 14, 1862, Helen King Boyer Collection, GU.

21. *OR*: 21:693, 696; Col. Rush to Maj. Hunt, December 20, 1862, RG 393, Part 1, Entry 5382, NARA.

22. *OR*: 21: 693, 696; Col. Rush to Maj. Hunt, December 20, 1862, RG 393, Part 1, Entry 5382, NARA; *RDUA*, December 23, 1862; Eric J. Wittenberg, *Rush's Lancers: The Sixth Pennsylvania Cavalry in the Civil War* (Yardley, 2007), p. 14.

23. *OR*: 21:696; Col. Rush to Maj. Hunt, December 20, 1862, RG 393, Part 1, Entry 5382, NARA.

24. Beverly Barrier Troxler and Billy Dawn Barrier Auciello, *"Dear Father": Confederate Letters Never Before Published* (North Billerica, 1989), p. 99; Col. Rush to Maj. Hunt, December 20, 1862 and December 21, 1862, RG 393, Part 1, Entry 5382, NARA; *OR*: 21:696; NSP to Mr. Editor, Camp Rapidan, Virginia, December 25, 1862, Augusta *Daily Constitutionalist*, January 3, 1863.

25. *OR*: 21: 694, 873, 876; Col. Rush to Maj. Hunt, December 20, 1862 and December 21, 1862, Entry 5382, NARA; H.P. Moyer, *History of the Seventeenth Regiment, Pennsylvania Volunteer Cavalry: or One Hundred and Sixty-second in the Line of Pennsylvania Volunteer Regiments, War to Suppress the Rebellion, 1861–1865* (Lebanon, 1911), p. 31. The sutler that Rush was concerned about may have been Charles Johnson, from Loudoun County — see Chamberlin and Souders, *Between Reb and Yank*, pp. 157–158.

26. Benedict, *Army Life in Virginia*, pp. 91–99; Elna Rae Zeilinger and Larry Schweikart, editors, "'They Also Serve ...': The Diary of Benjamin Franklin Hackett, 12th Vermont Volunteers," *Vermont History*, Spring 1983, volume 51, number 2, p. 95. It was reported that two members of the 12th Vermont were shot and one of them killed on the 17th at a forward picket post between Bull Run Bridge and Blackburn's Ford, but if the incident occurred the men must have been from a unit other than the 12th Vermont. See report of J. Smith Brown Adjutant of the 126th New York to Capt. Shriber, December 18, 1862, as quoted in Kevin C. Ruffner, *"Tenting on the Old Camp Ground": The Civil War History of Union Mills, Fairfax County, Virginia, Part One: The Historical Record* (Fairfax County, 1992), p. 69. None of the reports concerning Lige White can be substantiated. Other reports place him in the Shenandoah Valley following a recent raid against a Union outpost in Poolesville, Maryland. Still, it was White who was dominating the concerns of the men manning the forward outposts.

27. Alfred Ryder to Dear Father, Dranesville, December 21, 1862, Ryder Letters, UMBL; Baird, *Journals of Amanda Virginia Edmonds*, p. 129; Gen. Abercrombie to Gen. Heintzelman, December 18, 1862, RG 393, Part 2, Entry 659, Letters Sent September 1862 to December 1863, Abercrombie's Command, NARA.

Chapter 4

1. George Kilborn to Reuben McArthur, Dranesville, December 23, 1862, George Kilborn Letters, UMBL; Alfred Ryder to Dear Mother, Dranesville, December 24, 1862, Ryder Letters, UMBL; Darius Maynard to My own precious Nell, Near Washington, December 26, 1862, Maynard Letters, WSU. Kilborn is listed in the roster as Kilburn but signed his letters Kilborn.

2. Letter signed B, December 25, 1862, Fairfax Court House, Rutland [Vermont] *Herald*, in Donald H. Wickman, editor and compiler, *Letters to Vermont From Her Civil War Soldier Correspondents to the Home Press,* 2 volumes (Bennington, 1998), volume 1, p. 134; John H. Williams Diary, VHS.

3. Emory Thomas, *Bold Dragoon: The Life of J.E.B. Stuart* (New York, 1986), p. 192; Robert J. Trout, *With Pen & Saber: The Letters and Diaries of J.E. B. Stuart's Staff Officers* (Mechanicsburg, 1995), p. 128; Heros Von Borcke, *Memoirs of the Confederate War for Independence* (Gaithersburg, 1985 edition), p. 329; *OR*: 21: 1075–1076.

4. *OR*: 21:731,738; Robert McClellan to Dear Willy, Beckham's Farm, December 25, 1862, the Gordon Family Papers, GHS.

5. Col. Price to Col. Wyndham, December 23, 1862, and Gen. Sigel to Gen. Slocum, December 24, 1862, RG 107, M504, NARA; *OR*: 21: 880, 886–887, 891.

6. R. Channing Price to Dear Sister, Fredericksburg, January 2, 1863, in Trout, *With Pen & Saber*, p. 135; *OR*: 21:731. Stuart states that his command spent the night at Morrisville, ten miles southwest of Bristersburg; however, he wrote his report in February 1864, while Price detailed the raid on January 2, 1863.

7. Letter signed J.S.H., 10th Virginia Cavalry, Port Royal,

January 3, 1863, Richmond *Daily Dispatch*, January 9, 1863; OR: 21: 723–724, 730–731, 742. All accounts refer to Stith Bolling as a captain leading a squadron of cavalry, however, the regimental roster indicates that his promotion to captain did not become official until January 17, 1863. Estimates of when the fighting started range from 10:30 A.M. to 2 P.M. JSH may have been John S. Hopkins, 10th Virginia Cavalry.

8. *OR*: 21: 723–728, 731; Price letter in Trout, *With Pen & Saber*, p. 135; Richmond *Sentinel*, July 13, 1863. About 24 of Cook's men bolted during the day, arriving at the regimental camp at Hall's Farm by January 1, where they reported that the command had met with a disaster — See Col. Kielmansegge to Capt. Cook, January 1, 1863, RG 107, M504, NARA.

9. *OR*: 21: 729, 732, 742. The *OR* shows John Clybourn's name as Clybourne. I have used the spelling from his Compiled Service Record.

10. *OR*: 21: 729, 732, 738, 741; Samuel M. Blackwell, *In the First Line of Battle: The 12th Illinois Cavalry in the Civil War* (DeKalb, 2002), p. 61.

11. *OR*: 21: 719; Hiram L. Leister's Compiled Service Record, RG 109, M270, Compiled Service Records of Confederate Soldiers Who Served in Organizations from the State of North Carolina, NARA.

12. *OR*: 21: 732, 738–739, 741, William Carter Diary, VSL; Price letter in Trout, *With Pen & Saber*, p. 136; Theodore Wilder, *The History of Company C, Seventh Regiment, O.V.I.* (Oberlin, 1866), p. 34; Richmond *Dispatch*, February 20, 1863. While James Drake is consistently referred to as colonel in the Confederate reports, the regimental roster suggests that he held the rank of major at this time. Col. Rosser writing on March 15, 1863, spoke of the attack by the 5th Virginia as a success, stating that 50 or 60 of his men "charged the enemy's line of skirmishers, driving them back and capturing & killing fifteen or twenty of the enemy," see Col. Rosser to Gen. Seth Cooper, March 15, 1863, RG 109, M324, NARA.

13. *OR*: 21:727–728, 730, 732–733; Price letter in Trout, *With Pen & Saber*, p. 136; Alexandria *Gazette*, January 1, 1863; Carter Diary, VSL.

14. *OR*: 21: 736.

15. *OR*: 21: 708, 736–737; Letter signed J.S.H. Port Royal, January 3, 1863, Richmond *Daily Dispatch*, January 9, 1863.

16. *OR*: 21:706, 891–892, Capt. Scott to Gen. Stoughton, December 27, 1862, and Gen. Sigel to Gen. Stahel, December 27, 1862, RG 107, M504, NARA; Quaife, *From the Cannon's Mouth*, p. 155; John Keatley, "Across the Occoquan, How Raider Stuart Dodged an Ambush and Laid Waste the Country," *National Tribune*, March 18, 1897.

17. Lt. Col. Peter Stagg to Col. Price, December 27, 1862, RG 107, M504, NARA; *OR*: 21:708; Letter signed E, Camp 2nd Pennsylvania Cavalry, January 10, 1863, Lancaster [Pennsylvania] *Daily Express*, January 16, 1863.

18. Benedict, *Army Life in Virginia*, p. 102; *WES*, December 29, 1862.

19. Price letter in Trout, *With Pen & Saber*, p. 136; *OR*: 21: 736–737.

20. *OR*: 21: 708–711, 736; Letter Signed E, Lancaster *Daily Express*, January 16, 1863; *WES*, December 31, 1862.

21. *OR*: 21: 709, 711

22. Price letter in Trout, *With Pen & Saber*, p. 137; U. R. Brooks, *Stories of the Confederacy* (Camden, 1991 edition), p. 124; *OR*: 21: 711, 733; Carter Diary, VSL.

23. Letter signed E, Lancaster *Daily Express*, January 16, 1863.

24. *OR*: 21: 711–712, 741; Letter signed E., Lancaster *Daily Express*, January 16, 1863; Carter Diary, VSL. In March 1863 Col. Rosser recommended Lt. James Bayley for promotion based on his valor during this raid. Rosser stated that Bayley led his command across the Occoquan "in the face of the most deadly fire, and by thus dashing over a wide and rocky ford succeeded in dispersing and capturing the force which had dismounted and lined the banks confident of checking the advance of the entire cavalry brigade," see Col. Rosser to Gen. Seth Cooper, March 15, 1863, RG 109, M324, NARA.

25. *OR*: 21: 712–713, 740; Bates, *History of Pennsylvania Volunteers*, volume 3, pp. 322, 326–355 and volume 8, pp. 1009–1041; *WES*, December 31, 1862. The published roster of the 2nd Pennsylvania is very incomplete and virtually useless in this case.

26. *OR*: 21: 733, 736–737; Price letter in Trout, *With Pen & Saber*, p. 137.

27. *OR*: 21: 737.

28. Brady, *Hurrah for the Artillery!*, pp. 187–188; *OR*: 21: 738. The Union troopers may have been from the 1st Maine Cavalry, Company M, attached to Geary's Division.

29. *OR*: 21: 736–738; Price letter in Trout, *With Pen & Saber*, p. 137.

30. *DFP*, January 6, 1863; Col. Price to Gen. Stoughton, December 28, 1862, and Lt. Col. Stagg to Picket guards at Wolf Run Shoals, December 28, 1862, RG 107, M504, NARA; H. B. McClellan, *The Life and Campaigns of Major General J.E.B. Stuart* (Little Rock, 1987 edition), p. 201.

31. Col. Price to Col. Wyndham, December 28, 1862, RG 107, M504, NARA; *OR*: 21:713, 715.

32. Capt. Potter to Gen. Abercrombie, December 28, 1862, RG 107, M504, and Gen. Heintzelman to Gen. Parke, Roll 57, and Maj. Hunt to Abercrombie and Hunt to Gen. Slough, December 28, 1862, RG 393, Part 1, Entry 5379, NA; *OR*: 21: 706–708.

33. *OR*: 21: 714, Thomas West Smith, *The Story of a Cavalry Regiment: "Scott's 900" Eleventh New York Cavalry from the St. Lawrence River to the Gulf of Mexico, 1861–1865* (Chicago, 1894), p. 50; Franklin McGrath, *The History of the 127th New York Volunteers, "Monitors" in the War for the Preservation of the Union — September 8th, 1862, June 30th, 1865* (no publisher, 1898), p. 30; MLS Jackson Diary, USAMHI.

34. John E. Morris to Dear Uncle John, On Picket, December [30], 1862, John E. Morris Papers, CHS.

35. *OR*: 21: 707,716, 894; Gen. Heintzelman to Gen. Stoughton, December 28, 1862, RG 107, M504, NARA.

36. Benjamin Hatch to My dear old Lucina, December 28, 1862, Fairfax Court House, Benjamin Hatch Letters, UV; *OR*: 21: 716–717; Quaife, *From the Cannon's Mouth*, pp. 155–156; Henry Jillson to Dear Father, December 30, 1862,Henry Jillson Letters, and Walcott Mead to My Dear beloved friends, Fairfax Court House, December 29, 1862, Walcott Mead Letters, VHS; Letter signed J.C.W. January 1, 1863, Fairfax Court House, Rutland *Herald*, January 8, 1863, in Wickman, *Letters to Vermont*, volume 1, pp. 156–157.

37. Letter signed B, January 2, 1863, Fairfax Court House, Rutland *Herald*, January 7, 1863, in Wickman, *Letters to Vermont*, volume 1, pp. 137–139; Benedict, *Army Life in Virginia*, p. 104.

38. *OR*: 21: 715–716; William F. LeMunyon Reminiscences, p. 12, USAMHI.

39. Price letter in Trout, *With Pen & Saber*, p. 137; Kenneth L. Stiles, *4th Virginia Cavalry* (Lynchburg, 1985), p. 22; *OR*: 21: 734, 897; *WES*, January 2, 1863.

40. Price letter in Trout, *With Pen & Saber*, pp. 137–138; Albert Greene to Dear Father, January 1, 1863, Albert R. Greene Letters, and Roswell Farnham to Sister Laura, Fairfax Court House, December 31, 1862, Roswell Farnham Letters, UV; Charles Wellington Reed to Dear Mother, Fort Ramsey, Virginia, January 1, 1863, in Eric Campbell, editor, *"A Grand Terrible Dramma": From Gettysburg to Petersburg: The Civil War Letters of Charles Wellington Reed* (New York, 2000), p. 64.

41. Benedict, *Army Life in Virginia*, pp. 103, 108–109; Ralph O. Sturtevant, *Pictorial History: The Thirteenth Regiment Vermont Volunteers, 1861–1865* (Burlington, 1911), pp. 107–109; *OR*: 21: 714; Charles Stone Diary, UV. Abercrombie in his report, *OR*: 21:1:714, refers to Erhardt as Urquhart.

42. Roswell Farnham to Sister Laura, Fairfax Court House, December 31, 1862, Farnham Letters, UV; Benedict, *Army Life in Virginia*, pp. 104–105, 109.

43. Sturtevant, *Pictorial History*, p. 105; Farnham to Sister Laura, Fairfax Court House, December 31, 1862, Farnham Letters, UV; Benedict, *Army Life in Virginia*, p. 106; Letter signed

B, Fairfax Court House, January 2, 1863 in Wickman, *Letters to Vermont,* volume 1, p. 138; John Yale to Dear Mother & Sister, Fairfax, December 29, 1862, John L. Yale Papers, UV.

44. John Yale to Dear Mother & Sister, Fairfax, December 29, 1862, Yale Letters, UV; Unsigned letter in the Rutland *Herald,* January 15, 1863; Walcott Mead to My Dear beloved friends, Fairfax Court House, December 29, 1862, Mead Letters and Roswell Farnham to Sister Laura, Fairfax Court House, December 31, 1862, Farnham Letters, UV; Gen. Heintzelman to Lt. Col. Richmond, December 29, 1862, RG 107, M504, NARA; Robert T. Hubard Jr., *The Civil War Memoirs of a Virginia Cavalryman,* edited by Thomas P. Nanzig (Tuscaloosa, 2007), p. 73. Sgt. Elliot Fishburne, 1st Virginia Cavalry, claimed, in a letter written in 1886, that it was his colonel, James Drake who met the truce party — see David and Audrey Ladd, *The Bachelder Papers: Gettysburg in Their Own Words,* 3 volumes (Dayton, 1994), volume 2, p. 1285.

45. Henry Jillson to Dear Father, Fairfax Court House, December 30, 1862, Jillson Letters, VHS; Benedict, *Army Life in Virginia,* p. 106; Roswell Farnham to Sister Laura, Fairfax Court House, December 31, 1862, Farnham Letters, UV; *OR*: 21: 718; Price Letter in Trout, *With Pen & Saber,* p. 138. The prisoner may have been George Nicholas, 3rd Virginia, who deserted during the night, as noted in Thomas P. Nanzig, *3rd Virginia Cavalry* (Lynchburg, 1989), p. 120.

46. Henry Jillson to Dear Father, Fairfax Court House, December 30, 1862, Jillson Letters, VHS; Letter signed B, Fairfax Court House, January 2, 1863 in Wickman, *Letters to Vermont,* volume 1, p. 139; Benedict, *Army Life in Virginia,* p. 108; Unsigned letter in the Rutland *Herald,* January 15, 1863.

47. Price Letter in Trout, *With Pen & Saber,* p. 138; Carter Diary, VSL; John Morris to Dear Uncle John, December [30], 1862; Morris Letters, CHS.

48. Carter Diary, VSL; *WES,* December 31, 1862.

49. *OR*: 21: 713–714, 898; Capt. Potter to Gen. Abercrombie, December 29, 1862, RG 107, M504, and Maj. Hunt to Gen. Stoughton, and Hunt to Gen. Slough, December 29, 1862, RG 393, Part 1, Entry 5379, NARA; *WES,* December 31, 1862; Stone Diary, UV; Smith, *The Story of a Cavalry Regiment,* p. 50.

50. Letter signed J.S.H., near Port Royal, January 3, 1863, Richmond *Daily Dispatch,* January 9, 1863; *OR*: 21: 735, 897; Gen. Stoughton to Capt. Scott, December 29, 1862, RG 393, Part 1, Entry 3966, and Col. D'Utassy to Gen. Casey, December 29, 1862, RG 393, Part 2, Entry 676, Telegrams Sent and Received, September 1862 to April 1863, Casey's Division, NARA.

51. Col. Price to Maj. Hunt, January 1, 1863, *OR*: 21:710. The emphasis is in the original copy in the Archives but removed from the copy in the *Official Records.*

52. Quaife, *From the Cannon's Mouth,* pp. 155–156.

53. John O. Williams, *Life in Camp: A History of the Nine Months' Service of the Fourteenth Vermont Regiment, From October 21, 1862 When it was Mustered into the U.S. Service, to July 21, 1863, Including the Battle of Gettysburg* (Claremont, 1864), p. 62; W. A. Mead to Dear Cousin, Fairfax Court House, December 30, 1862, Mead Letters, VHS.

54. *OR*: 21:734–735, 741.

55. Letter signed Phi to Editor, Belle Plain, December 29, 1863, Indianapolis *Daily Journal,* January 8, 1863.

Chapter 5

1. Heintzelman Journal, LC; *OR*: 21: 895–897.

2. *OR*: 21: 901–902; Heintzelman Journal, LC.

3. *OR*: 21: 923; Ford, *A Cycle of Adams Letters,* volume 1, pp. 225–228.

4. Ford, *A Cycle of Adams Letters,* volume 1, pp. 228–229; Benjamin W. Crowninshield, *A History of the First Regiment of Massachusetts Cavalry Volunteers* (Baltimore, 1995 edition), p. 107.

5. Price Letter in Trout, *With Pen & Saber,* pp. 138–139.

6. Mosby, *MWR,* p. 29; John S. Mosby, "A Bit of Partisan Service," in Robert U. Johnson and Clarence C. Buel, editors, *Battles and Leaders of the Civil War,* 4 volumes (New York, 1956 edition), volume 3, p. 148.

7. Keen and Mewborn, *43rd Battalion Virginia Cavalry Mosby's Command,* p. 1; Jeffry D. Wert, *Mosby's Rangers* (New York, 1990), pp. 25–26; Michael Marshall, "The 'Grey Ghost' at Virginia: The Story of a Rebel Expelled," *University of Virginia Alumni News,* volume LXXIV, number 4 (March/April 1986), pp. 10–11.

8. Marshall, "The 'Grey Ghost' at Virginia," pp. 11–12.

9. Wert, *Mosby's Rangers,* p. 27.

10. W. W. Blackford, *War Years with Jeb Stuart* (Baton Rouge, 1993 edition), pp. 14–15; Robert J. Driver, Jr., *1st Virginia Cavalry* (Lynchburg, 1991), p. 9.

11. H. B. McClellan, "The Invasion of Pennsylvania in '63," *PWT,* July 20, 1878; Wert, *Mosby's Rangers,* p. 29; Mosby to Dr. A. Monteiro, January 22, 1895, in Adele Mitchell, *The Letters of John S. Mosby* (Stuart-Mosby Historical Society, 1986), p. 73.

12. *OR*: 12:1:417. In his report of March 31, 1862 Stuart recommended Mosby for promotion, and though his commission as 1st Lt. came through on April 2nd there does not appear to be any connection between Stuart's recommendation and the actual date of the commission, which was dated to February 17, 1862.

13. Horace Mewborn, "A Wonderful Exploit, Jeb Stuart's Ride Around the Army of the Potomac," *Blue & Gray,* volume XV, issue 6, p. 9; *OR*: 11:1: 1040.

14. Daniel Sutherland, "Guerrilla Warfare, Democracy, and the Fate of the Confederacy," *The Journal of Southern History,* volume 68, number 2, May 2002, pp. 264–266, 270.

15. Sutherland, "Guerrilla Warfare," pp. 275–279.

16. Sutherland, "Guerrilla Warfare," pp. 281–286.

17. Keen and Mewborn, *43rd Battalion Virginia Cavalry,* p. 13; "Mosby and the War," Richmond *Dispatch,* May 6, 1894; *OR*: 51:2:594.

18. "Mosby and the War," Richmond *Dispatch,* May 6, 1894. His exchange, for Lt. C.A. Bayard, 5th Wisconsin Infantry, was listed in an order dated 8–27–62, in *OR,* Series 2:4:442. The incident at Verdiersville is referred to in Chapter 1.

19. Mosby, *MWR,* p. 28.

20. Gen. Stuart to Gen. Jackson, July 19, 1862, in Mitchell, *The Letters of General J.E.B. Stuart,* p. 258; Mosby, "A Bit of Partisan Service," pp. 148–149; *OR*: 21:923.

Chapter 6

1. Charles Johnson to Dear Mother, Dranesville, January 15, 1863, and Johnson to Dear Mother, Dranesville, January 3, 1863, Johnson Letters, UC.

2. "Movements of the 5th New York Cavalry," Lewis Leigh Collection, USAMHI; Lt. Col. Robert Johnstone to Gen. Wyndham and Gen. Stoughton, RG 107, M504, and Johnstone to Stoughton, January 1, 1863, RG 393, Part 2, Entry 676, NARA; Hiram Earl to Dear Father, German Town, January 15, 1863, in B. Conrad Bush, *Articles from Wyoming County Newspapers and Letters from Soldiers of the 5th New York Cavalry* (privately printed, 2000), pp. 77–78; ARAGSNY, volume 2, pp. 20, 316; Col. Wheelock Veazey to My Darling Wife, January 4, 1863, Wheelock Veazey Letters, VHS.

3. Col. Johnstone to Commanding Officer 1st West Virginia Cavalry, January 4, 1863, Col. Candy to Gen. Slocum and Candy to Gen. Stahel, January 4, 1863, and Gen. Heintzelman to Col. Wyndham, January 4, 1863, RG 107, M504, NARA; *OR*: 21:942.

4. Compiled Service Record of Michael Carver, 1st Connecticut Cavalry, RG 94, NARA; Robert K. Krick, *9th Virginia Cavalry* (Lynchburg, 1982), p. 105.

5. Michael Carver's Compiled Service Record, RG 94, NARA; WES, January 6, 1863. For the most part the troops

assigned to the forts along the inner defensive line appear to have been unconcerned with much of what occurred along the outer lines, much less with the main army. They largely ignored more famous incidents like the Stoughton Raid in their letters home but this incident did resonate with them. See Charles Wellington Reed to Dear Sister Helen, Fort Ramsey, Virginia, January 9, 1863, as quoted in Campbell, "A *Grand Terrible Dramma,*" p. 68.

6. Ebenezer Gould to Dear Brother, Washington City, January 4, 1863, Gould Papers, CMU; Statement from Surgeon J. P. Wilson, February 19, 1863, Washington, D.C., and Charges and Specifications filed against Norvell by Maj. Noah Ferry, February 20, 1863 in Freeman Norvell's Compiled Service Record, also 5th Michigan Cavalry Letter and Order Books, RG 94, NARA.

7. Ebenezer Gould to Dear Wife, January 5, 1863, Gould Papers, CMU; Capt. Potter to Col. Wyndham, January 5, 1863, RG 107, M504, NARA.

8. James Kidd to Dear Father, December 27, 1862, continued on January 5, 1863, Kidd Letters, UMBL.

9. ARAGSNY, volume 2, 5th New York Cavalry Roster; Boudrye, *Historic Records of the Fifth New York Cavalry*, p. 47.

10. Mosby, *MWR*, p. 30; John Scott, *PL*, p. 22. Though it is often assumed that Scott rode with Mosby, his Compiled Service Record suggests that he did not, with the possible exception of a brief period in 1865.

11. Don Rickey, Jr., *Forty Miles a Day on Beans and Hay: The Enlisted Soldier Fighting the Indian Wars* (Norman, 1963), p. 279.

12. Scott, *PL*, p. 22; Boudrye, *Historic Records of the Fifth New York Cavalry*, pp. 48, 212; Captain James Penfield, *The 1863–1864 Civil War Diary of Captain James Penfield, 5th New York Volunteer Cavalry, Company H* (Crown Point, 1999), p. 20; "Movements of the 5th New York Cavalry," Leigh Collection, USAMHI; Scott, *PL*, pp. 21–22; Horace Mewborn, "The Operations of Mosby's Rangers," *Blue & Gray*, volume XVII, issue 4, p. 8. The accounts are contradictory as to the number of men taken in each of these incursions, along with the exact dates that the attacks occurred. Scott wrote that this raid occurred on January 10, but Union accounts, as well as service records confirm that it occurred on January 5, 1863. Contemporary and modern accounts suggest that twelve to thirteen men were captured on the two nights from the 5th New York. In his regimental narrative Reverend Boudrye states that "quite a number of men were captured" on the fifth and that "several were captured and one wounded" the following night near Cub Run. In a later tabulation Boudrye totals seven men captured at Frying Pan on the fifth and four men at Cub Run on the sixth. Capt. James Penfield totaled the losses as five on the fifth and eight on the sixth. Mosby himself totaled the number of men captured in these attacks at 20 — see Mosby, *MWR*, p. 30. An attempt to reconcile the many different accounts suggests that the first men captured by John Mosby were Cpl. William Barrows, Joseph Ozier, Albert Shattuck, Charles Smith, John Starks and George Whaley, all of Company H. The roster hints that if any of these men were wounded it was John Starks, but his service record does not confirm this. The men taken the second night were from two different companies, Peter Fero and Edward Ward from Company B and Royal Austin and Lorenzo Davis from Company E. Peter Fero was shot in the abdomen on the second night. The information concerning Union casualties has been gathered from the roster in Boudrye, *Historic Records of the Fifth New York Cavalry* and ARAGSNY, as well as Compiled Service Records.

13. Mosby, *MWR*, pp. 30–31; Scott, *PL*, pp. 22–24 Alexandria *Gazette*, January 8, 1863; George Ewens Compiled Service and Pension Records, RG 94, NARA. The earliest account for these events is Scott's, but he was not present, and there are several errors with his version, including the dates, which he gives as January 10 and 12, 1863. There are, however, problems confirming several of Mosby's early raids through Union regimental rosters, but other contemporary records generally confirm each of these attacks. The problem might be poor record keeping or the manner in which the men were or were not officially paroled. The regimental roster for the 1st Vermont does not list any men captured from the regiment during the month of January, and though this is by no means conclusive, it is surprising that no mention of this affair is recorded in regimental records. Forty-four-year-old Pvt. George Ewens, 1st Vermont, was shot in the hand while on picket near Dranesville on the fourth. Though not indicated in his records, Ewens may have been shot during this incident. He contracted tetanus and died later that month.

14. Mewborn, "The Operations of Mosby's Rangers," p. 8; Keen and Mewborn, *43rd Battalion, Virginia Cavalry, Mosby's Command*, p. 8.

15. *WES*, January 7, 1863; Col. Wyndham to Gen. Heintzelman, January 6, 1863, Col. Johnstone to Capt. Peter Penn Gaskell, January 6, 1863, and Johnstone to Comd'g Officer 5th New York Pickets, January 6, 1863, RG 107, M504, NARA. Cyrus James, 9th New York Cavalry, was also captured on the 6th between Dumfries and Stafford C.H. while serving as a courier and paroled the same day. James is one of several men credited with being the first Union soldier killed at Gettysburg.

16. Col. Wyndham to Gen. Heintzelman, January 6, 1863, and Capt. Potter to Wyndham, January 7, 1863, RG 107, M504, NARA; Publication Committee, *History of the Eighteenth Regiment of Cavalry, Pennsylvania Volunteers (163rd Regiment of the Line) 1862–1865* (New York, 1909), p. 34; Hugh St. Clair, *Hugh St. Clair of Crawford County, Pennsylvania Civil War Diary, 1 January to 31 December 1863, 18th Pennsylvania Regiment of Mounted Volunteers*, transcribed by Patricia Ann St. Clair Ostwald (Boulder, 1993), p. 2. Jermantown is mistakenly shown on some period maps as Germantown, but it was named after the Jerman family who lived there and remains Jermantown today.

17. Col. Price to Maj. Hunt, January 7, 1863, RG 393, Part 1, Entry 5383, Letters Received, Department of Washington, 1863–1867, NARA; Boudrye, *Historic Records of the Fifth New York Cavalry*, p. 48.

18. Benedict, *Army Life in Virginia*, p. 111. Benedict was referring to Lincoln's Emancipation Proclamation.

19. Moyer, *History of the Seventeenth Regiment*, p. 33; Col. Price to Maj. Hunt, January 7, 1863, RG 393, Part 1, Entry 5383, NARA.

20. Col. D'Utassy to Gen. Stoughton, January 6, 1863, and Col. Price to Col. Wyndham, January 10, 1863, RG 107, M504, NARA; *OR*: 21: 750. There are several problems that confuse the date of the fight in Brentsville. Averell, in *OR*: 21: 750 states that Lt. Maxwell set out on January 8, and the best date for the fight in which he was captured is the 9th. It is unlikely, however, that such a small patrol would have been expected to stay out over night, suggesting that Maxwell left on the 9th and very possibly in response to Candy's telegram.

21. Stiles, *4th Virginia Cavalry*, p. 140; E. Prioleau Henderson, *Autobiography of Arab* (Oxford, 1991 edition), pp. 62–63; *Record of Service 1st Michigan Cavalry*, p. 199; 1st Michigan Cavalry Regimental Letter and Order Books, RG 94, NARA; "Editorial Paragraph," *Southern Historical Society Papers*, volume 3, 1877, p. 96; *OR*: 21:751 and 51:1:971. The details of this affair are sketchy and confusing. Henderson's history, while very good, contains few if any dates and the date of this fight remains unclear. Sgt. Wilcox is listed in the roster as being killed on January 7 and in the Regimental Books as killed on January 9. Charles Hicks is listed in the roster as killed at Ft. Scott on Jan. 12, but in the regimental books as killed on January 7, at Brentsville. Henderson claims that five Federals were killed but the regimental records do not support this. No Union account of the fight has been located, though Colonel Candy claimed that all but one of the Wolverines was dismounted at the time Mickler attacked and he accused Maxwell of being captured "whilst reading a newspaper." George Maxwell was a remarkable soldier, as evidenced by his rise from corporal to Lt. Colonel with a brevet to colonel, and possibly to brigadier. His outstanding record belies the accusations made by Col.

Candy. Unfortunately his military records have been either lost or misplaced.

22. *OR*: 21:749; WES, January 13, 1863; Sears, *On Campaign with the Army of the Potomac*, p. 144.

23. *OR*: 21: 749–751, 961–962; Stiles, *4th Virginia Cavalry*, p. 122. As Lt. Maxwell and the other two men were recovered before being formally paroled there is no record of their capture in the regimental records.

24. *OR*: 21:750–751.

25. Capt. Scott to Gen. Stoughton, January 9, 1863, RG 107, M504, NARA.

26. Warner, *Generals in Blue*, p. 482; Edwin Stoughton's Compiled Service Record, RG 94, NARA; Howard Coffin, *Nine Months to Gettysburg: Stannard's Vermonters and the Repulse of Pickett's Charge* (Woodstock, 1997), pp. 23, 119–120.

27. *OR*: 19:2:583; Charles Cummings to Dear Wife, Camp Vermont, November 16, 1862, Cummings Letters, VHS; Henry S. Willey Reminiscences, pp. 6–7, LC; Williams Diary, VHS; Edward Clark to My Dear Mary, Fairfax Court House, January 10, 1863, Edward P. Clark Letters, Missouri Historical Society.

28. Henry Smith to Dear Mother, Lewinsville, January 9, 1863, Henry Smith Letters, VHS; William Martin to Dear Wife, Fairfax Court House, January 9, 1863, William Martin Letters, Harrisburg Civil War Roundtable Collection, USAMHI; F. S. Dickinson, "Fifth New York Cavalry at Fairfax," *The Maine Bugle*, July 1895, pp. 225–226.

29. Regimental Order #9, January 10, 1863, 5th Michigan Cavalry Regimental Letter and Order Books, RG 94, NARA; Ebenezer Gould to Dear Brother, Camp Copeland, January 11, 1863, Gould Papers, CMU; Frank L. Klement, editor, "Edwin B. Bigelow: A Michigan Sergeant in the Civil War," *Michigan History Magazine*, September 1954, p. 201; John Farnill to My Dear Father, Washington, January 10, 1863, Farnill Letters, CMU; George Harrington Diary, WMU.

30. General Hays to Capt. Scott, January 11, 1863, RG 393, Part 1, Entry 3966, Scott to Hays, January 11, 1863 RG 107, M504, and Hays to Col. D'Utassy, January 11, 1863, RG 393, Part 2, Entry 3935, Letters Sent, Casey, Hays and Abercrombie's Commands, NARA.

31. Annie Hays to Dear Rachel, Union Mills, January 12, 1863 and Annie Hays to My Dear Agnes, Union Mills, January 13, 1863, Hays Letters, HSWP; Letter from J. N. Brown, Centreville, March 28, 1863, *RDUA*, April 6, 1863; Lewis Crandell Diary, Lewis Crandell Papers, NC.

32. Gen. Hays to Capt. Scott, January 13, 1863, RG 393, Part 1, Entry 5382, NARA.

33. "The Wyndham Question Settled," New York *Herald*, September 16, 1863; Wyndham to Heintzelman, December 3, 1862, M1064, NARA; Ella Lonn, *Foreigners in the Union Army and Navy* (Baton Rouge, 1952), pp. 293–294.

34. Samuel Toombs, *New Jersey Troops in the Gettysburg Campaign from June 5 to July 31, 1863* (Orange, 1888), p. 403; George Van to Editor, Camp Custis, March 11, 1862, [New York] *Tri-States Union*, March 21, 1862; *PI*, February 20, 1862; C.M.M. to Editors, Alexandria, March 19, 1862, Bucks County Intelligencer, March 25, 1862; Jersey City *Courier & Advertiser*, June 12, 1862; *OR*: 12:1:679–680.

35. *TNYT*, June 14, 1862; *NYT*, June 12, 1862 as quoted in Francis C. Kajencki, *Star on Many a Battlefield, Brevet Brigadier General Joseph Karge in the American Civil War* (Cranbury, 1980), pp. 53–55; Charles Coffman to Joseph Barnsley, Mt. Jackson, Virginia, June 13, 1862, Bucks County Intelligencer, July 1, 1862; M to Editors, Manassas, June 26, 1862, Bucks County Intelligencer, July 8, 1862; Member of Stonewall Jackson's Staff, "The Death of General Turner Ashby," *The Old Guard*, August 1866, volume 4, issue 8. Jacob Chrisman and Holmes Conrad both claim to have captured Wyndham. See Richard Armstrong, *7th Virginia Cavalry* (Lynchburg, 1992), pp. 129 and 131. Conrad claimed that after he galloped after Wyndham, who was by himself, he also realized that none of his men were with him either. See Holmes Conrad to Jedediah Hotchkiss, September 5, 1896, Jedediah Hotchkiss Papers, LC, as quoted in Peter Cozzens, *Shenandoah 1862: Stonewall Jackson's Valley Campaign* (Chapel Hill, 2008), p. 436.

36. Samuel J. Bayard, *The Life of George Dashiell Bayard* (New York, 1874), p. 241.

37. Col. Wyndham to Gen. Heintzelman, December 3, 1862 and J.M. Baldwin to Gen. Halleck, December 13, 1862, M1064, NARA; Wyndham to Secretary of War, December 14, 1862, RG 94, M619, Letters Received by the Office of the Adjutant General, NARA. Emphasis in the original.

38. Col. Wyndham to Gen. Heintzelman, January 6, 1863 and Col. Price to Wyndham, January 10, 1863, RG 107, M504, NARA; WES, January 21, 1863.

39. Windsor *Vermont Journal*, January 10, 1863; Petition to General Heintzelman, January 3, 1863, Wyndham's Compiled Service Record, RG 94, NARA. Wyndham made his headquarters during this period at the home of Cornelia Stuart known as Chantilly and from which the local area took its name. The home was destroyed by fire, though the actual date and circumstances are uncertain. In her diary entry for January 17, 1863, Elizabeth Blair Lee states that a shell fired into the home during a skirmish with Stuart at the end of his Christmas Raid caused the fire. Other accounts suggest that it burned in early February while still serving as Wyndham's headquarters. Whether it burned by accident or arson, as some accounts suggest, is unknown. Numerous Northern troops reported, erroneously, that the home was associated with Jeb Stuart's family. The diary entry is in Virginia Jean Lass, *Wartime Washington: The Civil War Letters of Elizabeth Blair Lee* (Urbana, 1991), p. 233. News accounts concerning the fire can be found in the Alexandria *Gazette* of February 19 and 21, 1863 as well as March 5,1863.

40. Heintzelman memorandum of January 20, 1863 in Wyndham's Compiled Service Record, RG 94, NARA; *Captain James Penfield*, p. 22; *WES*, January 21, 1863.

41. Nathaniel Richmond Compiled Service Record, RG 94, M508, and his Volunteer Service Record, RG 94, Entry 496, NARA. Richmond resigned again later that year for medical reasons.

Chapter 7

1. Alfred Ryder to Dear Mother, near Occoquan River, January 14, 1863, Ryder Letters, and George Kilborn to Reuben McArthur, Fort Scott, January 16, 1863, Kilborn Letters, UMBL.

2. Charles Tewksbury to Dear Brothers, Sisters & Parents, Fairfax Court House, January 15, 1863, Charles C. Tewksbury Letters, UV.

3. Charles Johnson to Dear Mother, Dranesville, January 15, 1863, Johnson Letters, UC.

4. William Martin to Dear Wife, January 16, 1863 Martin Letters, USAMHI; *Captain James Penfield*, p. 25; Col. D'Utassy to Lt. R. C. Schriber, January 16, 1863, and D'Utassy to Capt. Scott, January 16, 1863, RG 107, M504, NARA; Publication Committee, *History of the Eighteenth Regiment of Cavalry*, p. 35. In his diary Hugh St. Clair places the number of men captured at 17. The regimental itinerary registers a loss of 9 men on the 15th, though none can be identified through the regimental roster, and it mistakenly attributes the loss to Mosby, who was still south of the Rappahannock.

5. Letter signed Phi, Belle Plain, January 16, 1863, Indianapolis *Daily Journal*, January 22, 1863; Averell to Gen. Parke, January 13, 1863, RG 107, M504, NARA.

6. *OR*: 21:1094; Col. Candy to Lt. Col. Theodore Meysenberg, January 17, 1863, RG 107, M504, and Gen. Hays to Capt. Scott, January 28, 1863, RG 393, Part 2, Entry 3935, NARA.

7. *OR*: 21:937, 968–969, 974–976, 981; Gen. Slocum to Gen. Burnside, January 16, 1863, Col. Candy to Slocum, January 10, 1863, Slocum to Burnside, January 18, 1863 and Candy to Slocum, January 19, 1863, RG 107, M504, NARA.

8. Gen. Stoughton to Capt. Scott, January 27, 1863, RG

393, Part 1, Entry 3966, and Gen. Casey to Stoughton, January 19, 1863, RG 393, Part 2, Entry 675, Letters Sent, Casey's Division, September 1862 to April 1863, NARA.

9. Roswell Farnham to Dear Laura, Near Wolf Run Ford, January 22, 1863, Farnham Letters, UV; Quaife, *From the Cannon's Mouth*, p. 159.

10. Roswell Farnham to Dear Laura, Near Wolf Run Ford, January 22, 1863, Farnham Letters, UV.

11. Manley Stacy Diary, Stacy Papers, and Crandell Diary, NC; Annie Hays to My dear Father, Union Mills, January 21, 1863, Hays Letters, HSWP; *OR*: 51:1:975; Gen. Casey to Gen. Hays, and Hays to Lt. Col. Crandall, January 19, 1863 and Casey to Capt. Potter, January 20, 1863, RG 393, Part 2, Entry 675, NARA.

12. *OR*: 21:953 and 51:1:972; Ebenezer Gould to Dear Wife, Camp Copeland, January 18, 1863, Gould Letters, CMU.

13. Ebenezer Gould to Dear Wife, Camp Copeland, January 18, 1863, Gould Letters, CMU; WES, January 19, 1863, and January 22, 1863.

14. Frank Brown to Dear Father, Camp Copeland, January 20, 1863, Frank Brown Letters, UMBL; *DFP*, January 22, 1863; Asa Isham, *An Historical Sketch of the Seventh Regiment Michigan Volunteer Cavalry, From Its Organization, in 1862, To Its Muster Out, in 1865* (Huntington, 2000 edition), p. 12.

15. Darius Maynard to Dearest Nellie, Camp 1st Michigan Cavalry, Maynard Letters, WSU.

16. Charles Chapin to Dear Brother, Lewinsville, January 18, 1863, Charles Chapin Letters, USAMHI; George C. Benedict, *Vermont in the Civil War: A History of the Part Taken by the Vermont Soldiers and Sailors in the War for the Union 1861–1865*, 2 volumes (Burlington, 1888), volume 2, p. 581.

17. Stacy Diary and Crandell Diary, NC; *Captain James Penfield*, pp. 26–27; "Movements of the 5th New York," USAMHI; Boudrye, *Historic Records of the Fifth New York Cavalry*, p. 49.

18. Richard Kenwell to Dear Parents, [Jermantown], January 24, 1863 in Bush, *Articles from Wyoming County Newspapers*, p. 79.

19. William Martin to Dear Wife, January 24, 1863, Martin Letters, USAMHI.

20. Joel Craig, editor, *Dear Eagle: The Civil War Correspondence of Stephen H. Bogardus, Jr., to the Poughkeepsie Daily Eagle* (Wake Forest, 2004), p. 64; Fortier, *15th Virginia Cavalry*, pp. 117–118. It is possible that William Brawner and his Prince William Rangers, Company H, 15th Virginia Cavalry, had been released to conduct guerrilla operations in their home territory, but nothing has been found to confirm this.

21. Gen. Stahel to Lt. Col. Lathrop, April 5, 1863, RG 107, M504, and the Loudoun County Census for 1860, NARA; *NYT*, May 6, 1863; Windsor *Vermont Journal*, May 30, 1863. According to the census Moran would have been at least 48 in 1863, but documents in his Compiled Service Record indicate that he was only 42 when he was paroled in 1865 — see RG 109, M324, NARA.

22. *OR*: 21: 998–999, 1004–1005.

23. Keen and Mewborn, *43rd Battalion*, p. 8; Wynne C. Saffer, *Mount Zion Cemetery, Aldie, Virginia* (Lovettsville, 1997), p. ii.

24. Mosby, "A Bit of Partisan Service," p. 149.

25. William Martin to Dear Wife, near Fairfax Court House, February 2, 1863 and Martin to Dear Wife, January 26, 1863, Martin Letters, USAMHI; Mewborn, "The Operations of Mosby's Rangers," p. 11; Publication Committee, *History of the Eighteenth Regiment of Cavalry*, p. 35. Postwar Confederate sources state that 11 men were captured but a parole list in the National Archives confirms ten men captured, from four companies, and lists their names. See RG 249, Office of the Commissary General of Prisoners, Misc. List of Federal Prisoners, 1861–1865, NARA. The regimental roster indicates the loss of only two men. John Scott's account of this affair is, again, off by two days.

26. *Captain James Penfield*, p. 31, Boudrye, *Historic Records of the Fifth New York Cavalry*, p. 50; *OR*: 25:1:5; "Movements of the 5th New York," USAMHI. Both Krom and Waugh had signed the petition against Wyndham.

27. *Captain James Penfield*, p. 31.

28. Keen and Mewborn, *43rd Battalion Virginia Cavalry*, p. 23; Mewborn, "The Operations of Mosby's Rangers," p. 11; *WES*, January 30, 1863; William Martin to Dear Wife, near Fairfax Court House, February 2, 1863, Martin Letters, USAMHI. Penfield's brief, cryptic entries leave the location of this skirmish in some doubt as to whether it occurred west of Middleburg or east, near Aldie, and if they captured the last three men as a result of the skirmish or as they returned through Aldie.

29. *OR*: 25:1:5; *Captain James Penfield*, p. 31; Col. Price to Col. Wyndham, January 27, 1863, RG 107, M504, and the 1860 Loudoun County Census, NARA; *WES*, January 30, 1863; *DAT*, February 2, 1863; Charles W. Belknap Diary, USAMHI.

30. Col. Candy to Gen. Slough, January 24, 1863, RG 107, M504, NARA; *WES*, January 26, 1863.

31. Alfred Ryder to Dear Parents, near Occoquan, January 27, 1863, Ryder Letters, UMBL.

32. Col. D'Utassy to Capt. Scott, January 26, 1863, RG 107, M504, NARA; Mary Farnham to Brother Henry, Wolf Shoals Creek, January 27, 1863, Farnham Letters, UV.

33. Carl Sandburg, *Abraham Lincoln, The War Years*, 4 volumes (New York, 1939), volume 2, p. 4.

34. Adam Gurowski, *Diary, From November 18, 1862, to October 18, 1863*, Two volumes (New York, 1864), volume 2, pp. 109–111; Heintzelman Journal, LC; Thompson, *Civil War to the Bloody End*, pp. 272–273; *OR*: 25:2:3.

35. Gen. Copeland to Capt. Scott, January 28, 1863, RG 393, Part 1, Entry 3966, NARA; Ebenezer Gould to Dear Brother, Camp Copeland, January 26, 1863, Gould Letters, CMU.

36. *DFP*, February 6, 1863; Gen. Heintzelman to Gen. Schenck, January 31, 1863, RG 393, Part 1, Entry 5382, NARA.

37. Col. Wyndham to Capt. Potter, Fairfax Court House, January 28, 1863, RG 393, Part 1, Entry 5382, NARA.

38. Capt. Potter to Col. Wyndham, January 30, 1863, RG 107, M504, NARA.

39. Macomber Diary, CMU; Charles Johnson to Dear Mother, Camp Buford, February 7, 1863, Johnson Letters, UC; *OR*: 25:1:5. One historian has interpreted Macomber's account to mean that Mosby captured 25 men of the 1st Michigan on this date, but this is incorrect, see Longacre, *Custer and His Wolverines*, p. 103. Macomber is in error when he states that Mosby had 25 men under his command at this time, if in fact, Mosby was involved.

Chapter 8

1. Edwin Havens to Dear Father and Mother, Camp Kellogg, November 15, 1862, and Edwin Havens to Dear Father, Mother, and Nell, Camp Kellogg, November 28, 1862, Havens Letters, MSU.

2. Edwin Havens to Dear Brother Nell, Camp Kellogg, December, 14, 1862, Edwin Havens to Brother Nell, Camp Kellogg, December 18, 1862, Edwin Havens to Dear Nell, Lee Barracks, December 21, 1862, and Edwin Havens to Dear Brother Nell, Lee Barracks, January 1, 1863, Havens Letters, MSU. Lee Barracks replaced the name Camp Kellogg in mid-December.

3. Edwin Havens to Brother Nell, Lee Barracks, January 21, 1863, Havens Letters, MSU.

4. Edwin Havens to Brother Nell, Lee Barracks, January 29, 1863, Havens Letters, MSU.

5. Edwin Havens to Brother Nell, Lee Barracks, January 21, 1863 and Edwin Havens to Dear Father and Mother, February 1, 1863, Havens Letters, MSU.

6. Mosby, *MWR*, p. 32; Scott, *PL*, pp. 27–29; Keen and Mewborn, *43rd Battalion Virginia Cavalry*, pp. 23–24.

7. *OR*: 25:1:5; Scott, *PL*, pp. 28–29; Mosby, *MWR*, pp.

33–36. In speaking of this raid in his reminiscences Mosby makes no mention of a trap, saying only that he encountered some Union cavalry on the ride home who fired several shots at him, but that he avoided them by taking another route. That Mosby does not confirm Scott's account suggests that Scott embellished the facts. The outpost systems employed by the cavalry of both sides during the war were similar, including a reserve force, or grand guard, and a string of pickets, sentries or videttes positioned forward of the reserve as the eyes and ears of the main body. The duties of Union soldiers assigned to outpost duty were clearly defined in a document titled *Instructions for Officers on Outpost and Patrol Duty*. This pamphlet prescribed how a picket line was to be positioned in both daylight and darkness, as well as the responsibilities of the men assigned to the forward positions and those in the reserve or grand guard positions. When confronted by an enemy force the forward pickets were instructed to fire their weapons and retire on the reserve. The officer in command of the reserve would then send riders to notify the other reserve posts, as well as the main body, before advancing to meet the threat. Officers commanding the reserve posts were cautioned, however, that in few circumstances would it "be practicable to advance farther than the chain of Vedettes," so as not to be overwhelmed by a larger enemy force. This appears to be exactly the scenario that occurred in this case; the reserve heard the sound of Sergeant Headlee and his companion galloping toward them followed by gunfire and rode to investigate. Finding the post captured, and possibly the sergeant's body, the officer in command terminated his pursuit as instructed, rather than risk riding blindly into an unknown force of the enemy — see U. S. War Department, *Instructions for Officers on Outpost and Patrol Duty*, 1862, pp. 13–14, in the Farnham Papers, UV.

8. *Instructions for Officers on Outpost and Patrol Duty*, p. 7, Farnham Papers, UV.

9. William Martin to Dear Wife, Fairfax Court House, February 2, 1863, Martin Letters, USAMHI.

10. *Captain James Penfield*, pp. 34–35; *Movements of the 5th New York Cavalry*, USAMHI; Boudrye, *Historic Records of the Fifth New York Cavalry*, p. 50; Col. D'Utassy to Lt. R.C. Schriber, February 3, 1863, RG 107, M504, NARA; *WES*, February 4, 1863. There is some disagreement as to when the patrol left Centreville in these accounts, with Penfield suggesting they left on the morning of February 3.

11. Scott, *PL*, p. 27. If Wyndham issued his threats in writing the documents have not been found. These threats were seldom carried out, but the residents of Middleburg were undoubtedly aware that the small town of Haymarket had been burned several months earlier due to guerrilla activity. That arson was not sanctioned by proper authority and several officers responsible were held accountable.

12. *OR*: 25:1:6.

13. *OR*: 25:2:42.

14. *OR*: 25:2:51.

15. *Captain James Penfield*, pp. 35–36.

16. *Captain James Penfield*, pp. 36–37; Lt. Col. Robert Johnstone to Capt. Potter, February 6, 1863, RG 107, M504, NARA; New York *Herald*, February 8, 1863. In *Ranger Mosby*, p. 80, author Virgil C. Jones, locates this incident at the home of Washington Vandevener near Wheatland, and mentions that one of the women and two of the Rangers were wounded. Washington Vandevener lived closer to Leesburg, while members of the McCarty family, which Penfield identifies by name, lived just north of Aldie along the Snickersville Turnpike. Jones may have confused this incident with one that did occur at the Vandevener home in Feb. 1864. Jones also mistakenly credits the Loudoun Rangers as the unit that captured the men. Each of the six men was detached from the 1st Virginia Cavalry. The roster for the regiment states that Williams was wounded and captured on Feb. 8, near Delaplane, which is incorrect.

17. Mosby, *MWR*, pp. 63–65; Lt. Col. Johnstone to Capt. Potter, February 6, 1863, RG 107, M504, and RG 249, Office of the Commissary General of Prisoners, NARA; Theodore S. Peck, *Revised Roster of Vermont Volunteers and Lists of Vermonters Who Served in the Army and Navy of the United States During the War of the Rebellion, 1861–1866* (Montpelier, 1892), pp. 232, 257–259; Stone Diary, UV. Ball's Mill no longer stands but was located at the crossing of the Old Carolina Road and Goose Creek.

18. Lt. Frank Evans to Major Wells, February 2, 1863 and William Wells to Brother Fred, Dranesville, February 6, 1863, William Wells Papers, UV; Charles Johnson to Dear Mother, Camp Buford, February 7, 1863, Johnson Letters, UC. Emphasis in the original.

19. J. Somerville to Editor, February 2, 1863, *GRDE*; Letter signed Occasionally, Camp Gray, February 3, 1863, *GRDE*, February 8, 1863.

20. Col. Gray to Lt. Richard Baylis, February 7, 1863, RG 393, Part 1, Entry 5382 and RG 393, Part 1, Entry 5381, Register of Letters Received, NARA; John Farnill to My Dear Father, Washington, D.C., February 7, 1863, Farnill Letters, CMU.

21. John Farnill to My Dear Father, Washington, D.C., February 7, 1863, Farnill Letters, CMU; *OR*: 25:1:10–11 and 25:2 59, 61; Capt. Potter to Gen. Hays, February 8, 1863, and Lt. Frank Evans to Lt. Col. Stagg, February 8, 1863, RG 107, M504, also the pension records of Lt. Pius English, RG 94, NARA; William H. Beach, *The First New York (Lincoln) Cavalry From April 19, 1861 to July 7, 1865* (Annandale, 1988 edition), p. 211; Moyer, *History of the Seventeenth Regiment Pennsylvania Volunteer Cavalry*, pp. 34–35.

22. Klement, "Edwin B. Bigelow: A Michigan Sergeant in the Civil War," p. 205; Ebenezer Gould to Dear Brother, Washington, D.C., February 16, 1863, Gould Letters, CMU.

23. Ebenezer Gould to My Dear Brother, Washington, D.C., February 13, 1863, Gould Letters, CMU; Noah Ferry to Dear Bro, Camp Copeland, February 13, 1863, Blair Papers, DPL. Ferry claimed that a total of $18,000 was seized but that the men "gobbled" $10,000 for themselves.

24. Baird, *Journals of Amanda Virginia Edmonds*, pp. 132–133.

25. Ebenezer Gould to My Dear Brother, Washington, D.C., February 13, 1863, Gould Letters, CMU; Noah Ferry to Dear Bro, Camp Copeland, February 13, 1863, Blair Papers, DPL.

26. Samuel Harris, *Personal Reminiscences of Samuel Harris* (Chicago, 1897), pp. 13–14; Statements of George Dutcher, Samuel Harris and William Williams in Dutcher's Pension File, RG 94, NARA; Klement, "Edwin B. Bigelow: A Michigan Sergeant in the Civil War," p. 205. Harris later compounded his fabrication when he included a claim that Dutcher received a second wound in the same hand during the affair from a saber.

27. Baird, *Journals of Amanda Virginia Edmonds*, pp. 132–133.

28. Ebenezer Gould to Dear Brother, Washington, D.C., February 16, and February 13, 1863, Gould Letters, CMU; Klement, "Edwin B. Bigelow: A Michigan Sergeant in the Civil War," p. 205; Noah Ferry to Dear Bro, Camp Copeland, February 13, 1863, Blair Papers, DPL.

29. Col. Price to Maj. Hunt, February 14, 1863, RG 393, Part 1, Entry 5383, NARA; Stone Diary, UV; Samuel Gillespie, *A History of Company A, First Ohio Cavalry, 1861–1865* (Washington Court House, 1898), p. 132; Victor Comte to Dear Elise, Washington, February 17, 1863; Victor Comte Letters, UMBL; Augustus Paddock to Dear Friends, Mud Grove, February 15, 1863, Augustus Paddock Letters, UV; Ide, *History of the First Vermont Cavalry*, p. 90.

30. Victor Comte to Dear Elise, Washington, February 17, 1863, Comte Letters, UMBL; Augustus Paddock to Dear Friends, Mud Grove, February 15, 1863, Paddock Letters, UV.

31. *Captain James Penfield*, pp. 38–39; Col. Wyndham to Capt. Potter, February 11,1863, RG 393, Part 1, Entry 5384, Telegrams Received 1863–1864, NARA; "Movements of the 5th New York Cavalry," USAMHI. Three Confederates were captured in Warrenton, two from the former Dixie Artillery and a conscript from Fauquier County, who were assisting William H. Chapman, former commander of the battery before

it was disbanded and later Lt. Colonel in the 43rd Battalion on a recruitment effort — see RG 109, War Department Collection of Confederate Records, Entry 199, Union Provost Marshal's File, Confederate Prisoners, NARA. Chapman, at the time, was a recruiting officer in Fauquier County. At least two men from Co. H, 4th Virginia were captured — Henry Lee and Sands Smith.

32. Ebenezer Gould to My Dear Wife, Washington, D.C., February 12, 1863, and Gould to My Dear Children, Washington, D.C., February 15, 1863, Gould Letters, CMU. Alexander Davis was a true, outspoken, Connecticut Yankee, who lived with his wife and three children near Mt. Zion Church just east of Aldie. He was arrested several times by Southern authorities early in the war and acquitted each time. The attack at his home took place on the night of June 17, 1862, and as he recounted the event to Gould, four of his attackers were believed killed or seriously wounded and he was gravely wounded. When he recovered he served as a guide for Union troops operating in the region.

33. *OR*: 25:2:621–622, 649.

34. Col. Price to Maj. Hunt, February 14, 1863, RG 393, Part 1, Entry 5383, NARA; Ebenezer Gould to Dear Brother, Washington, D.C., February 16 and February 23, 1863, Gould Letters, CMU. Gould's signature does appear on any of the documents.

35. Col. Price to Maj. Hunt, February 10, 1863, RG 393, Part 1, Entry 5383, NARA; Alexander Hays to Dear Wife, Union Mills, February 9, 1863, Hays Letters, HSWP.

36. Col. Price to Maj. Hunt, February 10, 1863, RG 393, Part 1, Entry 5383, and Col. Price to Lt. Col. Stagg, February 11, 1863, RG 107, M504, NARA.

37. Macomber Diary, CMU; Frederick Schmalzried to Dear brother, Annapolis, February 22, 1863, Frederick Schmalzried Letters, UMBL; Henderson, *Autobiography of Arab*, pp. 65–67; Charlotte [North Carolina] *Western Democrat*, March 31, 1863. Like the earlier fight in Brentsville there is some confusion about the date of this skirmish. The *OR* places it on the 14th, even though the only report is dated the 13th. And while the date given for casualties is generally the 14th, other contemporary accounts suggest that it took place on the 13th. James W. Moore, 2nd S.C. Cavalry, places the fight on the 12th, see Henry W. Moore, *"Chained to Virginia While Carolina Bleeds," The Civil War Correspondence of Henry Woodbury Moore and James Washington Moore* (Waterboro, 1996), p. 146. Handley was later arrested and charged with being a Federal spy. He was convicted and sentenced to be shot, but the sentence was reversed, see Manarin, compiler, *North Carolina Troops, 1861–1865: A Roster*, volume 2, p. 74.

38. Henderson, *Autobiography of Arab*, pp. 67–68; Charlotte *Western Democrat*, March 31, 1863. For another, rather fanciful, version of this fight, in which three of the Iron Scouts ride into Brentsville and challenge the Federals to a fight in a face to face meeting see U. R. Brooks, *Butler and His Cavalry*, pp. 96–99. Once goaded into a fight the Yankees are led into the ambush where 17 of 21 men are killed. Hugh Scott, the author of the account and a member of the Iron Scouts who claimed to have been there, states that the Union officer in charge was a member of Gen. Crawford's staff. Crawford had not yet returned to the field after being wounded at Antietam.

39. Henderson, *Autobiography of Arab*, pp. 69–71; Charlotte *Western Democrat*, March 31, 1863.

40. Frederick Schmalzried to Dear Brother, Annapolis, February 22, 1863, Schmalzried Letters, UMBL. Charlotte *Western Democrat*, March 31, 1863.

41. Gen. Hays to Capt. Scott, Union Mills, February 13, 1863, RG 393, Part 1, Entry 5383, NARA; Hays to Dear Wife, Union Mills, February 14, 1863 and Hays to Dear Wife, Union Mills, February 17, 1863, Hays Letters, HSWP.

42. Alfred Ryder to Dear Father, near Bull Run, February 18, 1863, Ryder Letters, UMBL; Benjamin Clark to Dear Brothers and Sister, Union Mills, March 3, 1863, Benjamin Clark Letters, CMU. Casualty figures range from 17 to 21, with dates ranging from February 13 to 16. Several men are listed as both missing in action and killed in different tabulations but no deaths have been confirmed.

43. William Martin to Dear Wife, February 19, 1863, Martin Letters, USAMHI. Martin was not present, but his is the only contemporary account found of this incident.

44. Howard Thomson and William K. Rauch, *History of the "Bucktails": Kane Rifle Regiment of the Pennsylvania Reserve Corps (13th Pennsylvania Reserves, 42nd of the Line)* (Dayton, 1988 edition), pp. 246–248. The men of this regiment were armed with breechloading Sharps Rifles, making them a good choice for this kind of mission, if it occurred. In their history Thomson and Rauch identify the cavalry detachment as being from the 1st Rhode Island. This is almost certainly inaccurate as that unit was attached to the Army of the Potomac and well south of the area in question.

45. Scott, *PL*, pp. 30–31; Willard Glazier, *Three Years in the Federal Cavalry* (New York, 1874), p. 148; Untitled John Mosby Document pertaining to the March 2, 1863 fight at Aldie, p. 5, John S. Mosby Papers, DU. Ratcliffe was a friend of Jeb Stuarts. She may have met Mosby for the first time when the men stopped at her home near Herndon Station on December 29, 1862. According to Scott it was while the two men were at the Ratcliffe home that Stuart first hinted at his intention to leave Mosby and a small party of men behind to protect the "good Southern people" living in the area, and he asked Laura "to do all you can for" Mosby — see Scott *PL*, p. 20. While a consistent theme runs through each of these accounts, two of which were penned well after the war, there are inconsistencies or problems with each. At this late date it may be impossible to determine with certainty when this event took place and exactly what happened.

The Bucktails had just arrived from the Army of the Potomac, following an arrangement, in which Hooker and Heintzelman exchanged a like number of Pennsylvania troops. Though several Pennsylvania units later claimed the title of Bucktails during the war, it originated with the 13th Pennsylvania Reserves, which was one of the regiments involved when the Third Division, First Corps, referred to collectively as the Pennsylvania Reserves, was transferred to the Department of Washington. The three brigades were posted at Minor's Hill, Upton's Hill and Fairfax Court House. The 13th Reserves arrived on February 7, and spent four days near Alexandria before taking a train for Fairfax Station. The unit history states only that the Bucktails were involved in scouting duty by the fifteenth of February. In early March, Lt. Col. Robert Johnstone did approach the regiment about volunteering to support his pickets, telling Price on the sixth, "I have induced some 50 Bucktails to volunteer," though he deemed that another 50 would be necessary for the task. He explained to Price that he planned to use them to aid the 18th Pennsylvania Cavalry in the area between Frying Pan and Chantilly Church, where Mosby had been so active, and the same area where the ambush was attempted. The Pennsylvania troopers were still too new, Johnstone explained, and "their arms bad & horses imperfectly broken. The material of the regt. cannot be better. With infantry supports to fall back on they will do good service. I hope Heintzelman will permit the Bucktails whose arms [Sharps Rifles] & habits qualify them for this service to act with us." According to Captain Penfield, the Bucktails were on the front lines as early as March 3, when they went out to Thompson's Corner, just a few days after Mosby captured a reserve post of the 18th Pennsylvania at that location, see Thomson and Rauch, *History of the "Bucktails,"* p. 246; Gen. Butterfield to Gen. Heintzelman, February 8, 1863, and Lt. Col. Johnstone to Col. Price, March 6, 1863, RG 107, M504, NARA; *OR*: 21: 877–878 and 25:2: 49, 53–54, 69, 87, 90, 118 also 51:1:985–986; Alexander Hays to Dear Wife, Union Mills, February 11, 1863, Hays Letters, HSWP; *Captain James Penfield*, p. 49. The 1st Reserves were sent to the front lines ahead of the other units in the command, but arrived in a mutinous mood, and it is doubtful that they would have been used in a scheme like the one described.

46. Scott, *PL*, pp. 31–32; Stone Diary and Augustus

Paddock to Dear Father, Dranesville, February 28, 1863, Paddock Letters, UV. One man from the regiment who had other ideas was Pvt. Peter Rock, who deserted from the Lewinsville outpost on or about the eighteenth of February. John Mosby paroled Rock under the alias of Rote, nine days later. Shortly thereafter he was arrested, possibly in Martinsburg, where he used the alias of Thomas Burnham, and identified himself as a member of Lige White's 35th Battalion. His identity was discovered after he arrived at Fort Delaware as a prisoner of war. His true intentions remain unknown, but he may have been attempting to join White in the Shenandoah Valley with the idea of leading White against his former comrades, see Peter Rock's Compiled Service Record, RG 94, NARA.

47. William Martin to Dear Wife, February 19, 1863, Martin Letters, USAMHI.

Chapter 9

1. Gen. Casey to Capt. Potter, February 16, 1863, RG 94, Muster Rolls, Returns and Regimental Papers, 5th Michigan Cavalry, and Col. Jewett to Capt. Potter, February 20, 1863, RG 107, M504, NARA; Stephen Aldrich to Editor, Rockville, Maryland, April 19, 1863, *GRDE*, April, 25, 1863; *DAT*, March 23, 1863; George Briggs to Friend Mary, Washington, February 19, 1963, Farnill Letters, CMU. The rotation fostered a rumor that Captain Simonds's company of the 5th Michigan had been captured and that the two companies of the 6th had been sent "to get them back."

2. *DAT*, February 21, 1863; Edwin Havens to Dear Father, Mother and Nell, Washington, D.C., February 28, 1863, Havens Letters, MSU.

3. Stephen Aldrich to Editor, Rockville, Maryland, April 19, 1863, *GRDE*, April 25, 1863; Benedict, *Army Life in Virginia*, pp. 118–121; James C. Mohr, *The Cormany Diaries: A Northern Family in the Civil War* (Pittsburgh, 1982), p. 298; James Aiken Diary, VHS; Charles Hampton Diary, CMU; Henry Norton, *Deeds of Daring, or History of the Eighth N.Y. Volunteer Cavalry* (Norwich, 1889), p. 56; Victor Comte to Dear Elise, Washington, February 24, 1863, Comte Letters, UMBL.

4. Norton, *Deeds of Daring*, p. 57; Gen. Seth Williams to Gen. Stoneman, February 18, 1863, RG 393, Part 1, Entry 3964, Letters Sent and Received, Army of the Potomac, June 1861–June 1865, NARA.

5. Benedict, *Army Life in Virginia*, p. 119; Stacy Diary, NC; Silas Mason to Dear Parents, Camp Harris, February 21, 1863, Mason Letters, NYSLA; Victor Comte to Friend Elise, Washington, February 24, 1863, Comte Letters, UMBL.

6. Col. Price to Maj. Hunt, February 17, 1863, RG 94, Muster Rolls, Returns and Regimental Papers, 5th Michigan Cavalry, and Ernest Yager's Scouting Report, February 26, 1863, RG 393, Part 1, Entry 3980, Miscellaneous Letters, Reports and Lists Received, 1861–1865, NARA; *OR*: 25:2:99–100.

7. *OR*: 25:2:623,627, 631, 642, Lee to Stuart, undated telegram, James Ewell Brown Stuart Papers, Henry E. Huntington Library, San Marino, California. The reports concerning Gen. Hays, listed as Hazen in the *OR*, most likely came from the prisoners captured near Brentsville on the fourteenth.

8. Lee to Stuart, February 17, 1863, Stuart Papers, Huntington Library; *OR*: 25:2:623; Carter Diary, VSL. On the 18th Maj. Samuel Chamberlain, 1st Mass. Cavalry, had found the men of a picket post manned by the 16th Pennsylvania and under the command of Lt. Henry Cranville in a discussion with enemy pickets. Cranville had allowed his men to leave their weapons, and unbridle their horses while they met with the Southern pickets. Cranville was arrested and dismissed from the army two days later without a trial. One could ask if it was during this visit that the crucial intelligence was passed that led to this incursion. Years later his record was cleared by an act of Congress. See Lt. Henry Cranville's file RG 94, Entry 496, NARA.

9. *OR*: 25:1:25 and 2:642; Gen. Averell to Gen. Butterfield, February 25, 1863, RG 107, M504, NARA.

10. GB to Dear Union, Waugh Point, Virginia, February 25, 1863, *RDUA*, March 3, 1863; *OR*: 25: 2:103,106,108.

11. *OR*: 25:2:100, 102, 106; Capt. Scott to Gen. Copeland, February 25, 1863, RG 393, Part 2, Entry 675, and Copeland to Scott, February 26, 1863, RG 393, Part 1, Entry 5382, and Col. Price to Col. Wyndham, February 26, 1863, RG 107, M504, NARA; *GRDE*, March 12, 1863. It is possible that Hooker's request was transcribed incorrectly.

12. Col. Price to Colonel, February 26, 1863, RG 393, Part 1, Entry 5383, NARA.

13. Col. Wyndham to Capt. Potter, February 26, 1863, Fairfax Court House, RG 393, Part 1, Entry 5384, NARA; William Martin to Dear Wife, Chantilly, February 27, 1863, Martin Letters, USAMHI. That Stuart and Mosby might have coordinated their efforts is not beyond the realm of possibility.

14. Keen and Mewborn, *43rd Battalion Virginia Cavalry*, p. 27; Scott, *PL*, pp. 35–36; Wyndham to Potter, February 26, 1863, Fairfax Court House, RG 393, Part 1, Entry 5384, Col. Clinton MacDougall to Gen. Hays, February 26, 1863, Centreville, RG 393, Part 1, Entry 5382, NARA; *OR*: 25:1:37. The several postwar Southern accounts of this affair, as well as a letter written by William Martin, on February 27, vary widely in the manner in which the attack was conducted, and specifically as to whether the sentry's weapon fired or misfired. I have elected to base this account on Mosby's report written on February 28, 1863, as his is the only account from an actual participant, and Martin, who was a member of the relief party. Both Mosby and Martin indicate that the men were in more than one building. The buildings sat near the present intersection of West Ox Road and Thompson Road.

15. William Martin to Dear Wife, Chantilly, February 27, 1863, Martin Letters, USAMHI; Hugh St. Clair Diary, p. 14; *OR*: 25:1:37; Col. MacDougall to Gen. Hays, February 26, 1863, RG 393, Part 1, Entry 5384, and Col. Price to Col. Lathrop, March 9, 1863, RG 94, Entry 496, NARA. Hugh St. Clair, who took a regular turn at the Thompson picket post, mentioned that only three men were captured. Gilmer's name is spelled Gilmer on war-date official documents. In postwar rosters it became Gilmore and most accounts of his tenure with the regiment use Gilmore.

16. Lt. John Nelson, Service and Pension Records, RG 94, NARA. In a telegram, thought to be dated Feb 28, Price reported that Gilmer captured ten members of the 4th Virginia Cavalry — see Price to Col. Lathrop, RG 393, Part 1, Entry 5382, NARA — a claim not substantiated by the regimental roster.

17. Capt. Potter to Gen. Hays, February 26, 1863, Col. Price to Comd'g Officer Cavalry, and Price to Lt. Col. Johnstone, February 26, 1863, Johnstone to Price, February 26, 1863, RG 107, M504, and Price to Capt. Potter, March 12, 1863, RG 94, Entry 496, NARA; *NYT*, February 27, 1863. Price filed his report of this affair three days after Mosby captured Gen. Stoughton. The resulting embarrassment and criticism may have affected the manner in which Price concluded his investigation into Nelson's conduct.

18. Lewis Scheuch-Evans, " Sir Percy Wyndham, Personality Profile" *Military History*, Vol. 22, No. 9, December 2005, p. 24; Stacy Diary, NC; Lt. E. Lehermerhorn to Capt. Potter, Fairfax Court House, February 26, 1863, and Col. Wyndham to Potter, Centreville, February 26, 1863, RG 393, Part 1, Entry 5384, NARA.

19. Ebenezer Gould to Dear Brother, Washington, February 26, 1863, Gould Letters, CMU: *OR*: 25:1:39; Freeman Norvell's Compiled Service Record, RG 94, NARA.

20. Chaplain Sixth Mich. Cavalry to Editor, Washington, February 26, 1863, *GRDE*, March 9, 1863; Kidd, *Personal Recollections of a Cavalryman*, pp. 88–89; *OR*: 25:1:39; Victor Comte to Dear Elise, Washington, March 4, 1863, Comte Letters, UMBL.

21. *GRDE*, March 12, 1863; Charles Emmons Diary, Em-

mons Family Collection, UMBL; Ebenezer Gould to Dear Brother, Washington, March 4, 1863, Gould Letters, CMU; Kidd, *Personal Recollections of a Cavalryman*, p. 91.

22. *OR*: 25:1:38–39; *GRDE*, March 12, 1863, *DAT*, March 23, 1863. Though Col. Gray states that he "deviated to his right" upon leaving Warrenton, it is more likely, considering Wyndham's route due south, that Gray took an interior line to the left.

23. *OR*: 25:1:38–39; "Movements of the 5th New York Cavalry," USAMHI; *WES*, March 6, 1863; Emmons Diary, UMBL. A third prisoner listed as James W. James, 11th Virginia Cavalry, may have later enlisted with Mosby as J. Wright James. Though Wyndham blamed the forage problem on the Michiganders who he said failed to bring forage, other accounts confirm that the men carried two days feed with them, but that their wagons were sent back on the second day on account of the terrible condition of the roads, leaving the men without food.

24. *OR*: 25: 1:40; Brig. Gen. Lorenzo Thomas to Gen. Hooker and to the Governor of New Jersey, February 28, 1863, Col. Wyndham to Brig. Gen. Seth Williams, March 1, 1863, and Unknown to Col. Wyndham, March 9, 1863, Percy Wyndham's Volunteer Service File, RG 94, Entry 496, NARA. Wyndham makes no mention of his resignation in his report, and his actual letter of resignation has not been located. Until that letter is found the identity of the superior officer in question can only be surmised. R. Butler Price appears to be the logical choice. Price did not have the military resume that Wyndham had crafted, nor had a foreign head of state bestowed a title upon him. Worse he was hide-bound, content to spend the war behind a desk, while passing judgment upon those who labored in the field, the exact opposite of the impulsive Wyndham, who must have bristled that they were military equals by rank.

25. *OR*: 25: 1:40; Ebenezer Gould to Dear Brother, Washington, March 4, 1863, Gould Letters, CMU; Kidd, *Personal Recollections of a Cavalryman*, pp. 95–96; *GRDE*, March 12, 1863; James Kidd to Dear Mother, Washington, March 6, 1863, Kidd Letters, UMBL; Petition dated May 5, 1863 in the Blair Papers, DPL.

26. *OR*: 25:2:106, 108,109; Stacy Diary, NC; Albert Sawyer to Dear Mary, Lewinsville, February 27, 1863, Albert Sawyer Letters, UV; Gen. Kelley to Col. Jewett, Col. Wyndham and Gen. Stoughton, Harpers Ferry, February 27, 1863, RG 107, M504, NARA; William Martin to Dear Wife, Chantilly, March 5, 1863, Martin Letters, USAMHI.

27. Ide, *History of the First Vermont Cavalry*, p. 91; Lt. Col. E. A. Woodyard to Col. H. G. Sickles, Fairfax Court House, February 28, 1863, RG 393, Part 1, Entry 5384, NARA.

28. Heintzelman Journal, LC; Capt. Potter to Gen. Hays and Gen. Stoughton, March 1, 1863, Gen. Heintzelman to Col. Wyndham, March 1, 1863, Col. Price to Comd'g Officer Cavalry at Jermantown, March 1, 1863, Lt. Col. Johnstone to Wyndham, undated in March 1863, and Price to Johnston, March 1, 1863, RG 107, M504, NARA.

29. *OR*: 25:2:114–115.

30. *OR*: 25:2:113, 115; Heintzelman Journal, LC; Gen. Hays to Gen. Stoughton, March 1, 1863, Col. Clinton MacDougall to Capt. Schriber, March 1, 1863, Col. Price to Comd'g Officer at Jermantown, March 1, 1863, Price to Lt. Col. Stagg, March 1, 1863, and Lt. Col. Johnstone to Capt. Potter, undated, RG 107, M504, NARA. Though undated this last telegram contains information confirming that it was sent on March 1.

31. Macomber Diary, CMU; *OR*: 25:1:41 and 2:117; *Captain James Penfield*, p. 48; "Movements of the 5th New York Cavalry," USAMHI; JHP to Editor, March 5, 1863, Windsor *Vermont Journal*, March 14, 1863; William Martin to Dear Wife, Chantilly, March 5, 1863, Martin Letters, USAMHI; Col. Price to Comd'g Officer at Jermantown, March 1, 1863, RG 107, M504, NARA.

32. James J. Williamson, *Mosby's Rangers* (Alexandria, 1981 edition), pp. 28–30.

33. James F. Ames, Compiled Service Record, RG 94, NARA; Williamson, *Mosby's Rangers*, pp. 28–30, 80; Scott, *PL*, pp. 32–33; Mosby, *MWR*, p. 67. The accounts pertaining to exactly when Ames first rode with the Rangers vary widely, and at least one historian doubts the accuracy of this account, but Williamson includes a narrative by Frankland that I have opted to follow, in part because it is a first person account in which several key details are corroborated by Union accounts, and because Mosby confirms the account in his *Reminiscences*.

34. Williamson, *Mosby's Rangers*, pp. 31–32.

35. William Martin to Dear Wife, Chantilly, March 5, 1863, Martin Letters, USAMHI; Scott, *PL*, p. 40; Untitled John Mosby Document, p. 6, Mosby Papers, DU; *OR*: 25:1:41; Keen and Mewborn, *43rd Battalion*, p. 28.

36. Untitled John Mosby Document, pp. 6–8, Mosby Papers, DU; Mosby, *MWR*, pp. 32, 48–49; Jones *Ranger Mosby*, p. 78.

37. Franklin Huntoon and John Woodward Compiled Service Records, RG 94, NARA; Benedict, *Vermont in the Civil War*, Vol. 2, p. 581.

38. *OR*: 25:1:41; JHP to Editor, Letter of March 5, 1863, Windsor *Vermont Journal*, March 14, 1863, William Martin to Dear Wife, Chantilly, March 5, 1863, Martin Letters, USAMHI; Hugh St. Clair Diary, p. 11.

39. Untitled John Mosby Document, p. 9, Mosby Papers, DU; JHP to Editor, Letter of March 5, 1863, Windsor *Vermont Journal*, March 14, 1863; Report of Maj. William Collins to Col. Price March 2, 1863, in Franklin Huntoon's Volunteer Service Record, RG 94, Entry 496, NARA.

40. Untitled John Mosby Document, p. 10, Mosby Papers, DU.

41. *OR*: 25:1:41; JHP to Editor, Letter of March 5, 1863, Windsor *Vermont Journal*, March 14, 1863; Keen and Mewborn, *43rd Battalion Virginia Cavalry*, p. 29; Benedict, *Vermont in the Civil War*, volume 2, p. 583; Benedict, *Army Life in Virginia*, pp. 129–130; Maj. Collins to Col. Price, March 2, 1863, Franklin Huntoon's Volunteer Service Record, RG 94, Entry 496, NARA. Turner was from Prince George's County, Maryland and known as "Prince George's Tom" to help distinguish him from the several other William Turners in the command.

42. Peck, *Revised Roster of Volunteers*; Benedict, *Vermont in the Civil War*, volume 2, p. 583; *Captain James Penfield*, p. 48; William Martin to Dear Wife, Chantilly, March 5, 1863, Martin Letters, USAMHI; Lt. Col. Johnstone to Capt. Potter, March 4, 1863, RG 107, M504, and Franklin Huntoon's Volunteer Service Record, RG 94, Entry 496, NARA; Keen and Mewborn, *43rd Battalion Virginia Cavalry*, p. 30; Rutland *Daily Herald*, February 25, 1862.

43. Col. Sawyer to Edwin Stanton, February 2, 1863, Special Order 31, of December 25, 1863, undated statements of Capt. Huntoon and Capt. Parsons, and Special Order 1, January 2, 1866, in Franklin Huntoon's Volunteer Service File, RG 94, Entry 496, NARA. Other factors may have motivated Sawyer's actions, and they are discussed in a later chapter. The fact that Huntoon's case was adjudicated after Stoughton's capture on March 9 could not have helped his cause either. Emphasis in the original.

44. Crandell Diary, NC; Calvin Haynes to My Dear Wife, Centreville, March 2, 1863, Calvin Haynes Letters, NYSLA; Simons, *A Regimental History*, p. 60; *OR*: 25:2:117–118; Col. MacDougall to Gen. Hays, March 2, 1863, and Capt. Potter to Gen. Hays, March 2, 1863, RG 107, M504, NARA; Septem to Editor, Union Mills, Letter of March 4, 1863, *RDA*, March 11, 1863.

45. Gen. Slocum to Col. Creighton, March 2, 1863, Slocum to Gen. Seth Williams, March 3, 1863, RG 107, M504, Gen. Stoneman to Seth Williams, March 4, 1863, and Stoneman to Gen. Pleasonton, March 4, 1863, RG 393, Part 2, Entry 1449, Seth Williams to Stoneman, March 4, 1863, RG 393, Part 1, Entry 3964, NARA; *OR*: 25:2:122.

46. Genesee to Editor, Stafford Court House, Letter of March 7, 1863, *RDUA*, March 13, 1863; Capt. V. M. Smith to Editor, Hope Landing, Letter of March 7, 1863, *RDA*, March 14, 1863; Hampton Diary, CMU; Norton, *Deeds of Daring*, p.

58; Richmond *Dispatch*, March 12, 1863. The reports indicate that as many as 17 men and as few as six were captured in this instance. The regimental roster confirms that at least ten were captured, but differentiating which men were lost on which night is difficult, as the roster appears to combine the losses from both nights under one date, while other accounts break it down differently. In the one Southern account of this fight, as well as another attack referred to in Chapter 12, Farrow is listed as Richard Farrow, Capt. Farrar, R. S. Farrell and Capt. Farrand, but attempts to verify any of these names have been unsuccessful. He is also linked to both Virginia and South Carolina units.

47. *OR*: 25:1:42; Gen. Slocum to Gen. Butterfield, March 5, 1863, RG 107, M504, NARA.

48. Gen. Williams to Gen. Stoneman, March 6, 1863, RG 393, Part 1, Entry 3964, NARA; Hampton Diary, CMU; *OR*: 25:2:128; Augustus C. Weaver, *Third Indiana Cavalry: A Brief Account of the Actions in Which They Took Part* (Greenwood, 1919), pp. 3–4; Samuel Gilpin Diary, LC. Gen. Slocum placed Col. Candy back in command at Dumfries as a result of this skirmish; replacing Col. Creighton, see Charles E. Slocum, *The Life and Services of Major-General Henry Warner Slocum* (Toledo, 1913), p. 68.

49. General Order #4, March 6, 1863, 1st Rhode Island Letter and Order Books, RG 94, NARA.

50. Col. Devin to Lt. Col. Taylor, March 7, 1863, RG 393, Part 2, Entry 1449, NARA; Committee on Regimental History, Hillman Hall Chairman, *History of the Sixth New York Cavalry (Second Ira Harris Guard)* (Worcester, 1908), pp. 94–95.

51. Lt. Col. Johnstone to Capt. Potter, March 4, 1863, Potter to Col. Wyndham, March 6, 1863, RG 107, M504, Lt. Col. Stagg to Col. Price, March 7, 1863, RG 393, Part 1, Entry 5384, and Gen. Hays to Capt. Scott, March 7, 1863, RG 393, Part 2, Entry 3935, NARA; *OR*: 25:2:128; Dexter Macomber Diary, CMU. One of the prisoners captured from the 1st Michigan was probably Reuben Farwell, who is listed as captured at Wolf Run Shoals on March 3. If a second was taken he has not been identified.

52. Col. Price to Gen. Schimmelfennig, March 8, 1863, and Lt. Col. Johnstone to Col. Price, March 8, 1863, RG 107, M504, NARA; Gurowski, *Diary*, volume 2, p. 168; Charles Chapin to Dear Wilbur, Lewinsville, March 7, 1863, Chapin Papers, USAMHI.

53. Benedict, *Army Life in Virginia*, p. 122; Alexander Hays to Dear Wife, Union Mills, March 8, 1863, Hays Letters, HSWP; Herman A. Post Diary, UV; Aiken Diary and the Royal D. King Diary, VHS.

Chapter 10

1. Mosby, "Mosby and the War," Richmond *Dispatch*, May 6, 1894; Jones, *Ranger Mosby*, p. 90; *OR*: 25:1:1121, 2:114.

2. *OR*: 25:1:1121–1122; Col. Price to Comd'g Officer at Jermantown; March 5, 1863, and Lt. Col. Johnstone to Price, March 6, 1863, RG 107, M504, also Johnstone to Capt. Potter, March 6, 1863, RG 393, Part 1, Entry 5382, NARA. Initially the Federals believed Mosby passed through the pickets of the 1st Vt. near Herndon Station, see Col. MacDougall to Gen. Hays, March 9, 1863, M504, NARA.

3. *OR*: 25:1:1121–1122; Mosby, "Mosby and the War," Richmond *Dispatch*, May 6, 1894. Mosby remained consistent on the time of his arrival, while other accounts generally vary by no more than an hour, putting him in town by 2:30 or 3 A.M.

4. *OR*: 25:1: 1122; Scott, *PL*, pp. 45–46; Keen and Mewborn, *43rd Battalion Virginia Cavalry*, p. 34.

5. Mosby, "Mosby and the War," Richmond *Dispatch*, May 6, 1894; Keen and Mewborn, *43rd Battalion Virginia Cavalry*, p. 34; Sturtevant, *Pictorial History*, p. 135; *DAT*, March 21, 1863; Scott, *PL*, p. 48. The now famous version of how Mosby awakened Stoughton and their conversation first appeared in the Richmond *Dispatch*, March 13, 1863, but Mosby himself did not adopt this story until many years after the war. His earliest accounts of the incident are very direct, and avoid the dramatic confrontation and conversation depicted by the press.

6. *OR*: 25:1:1122; Keen and Mewborn, *43rd Battalion Virginia Cavalry*, pp. 35–36; Gillespie, *A History of Company A, First Ohio Cavalry*, p. 134. According to R. B. Short, some of the men captured from the 1st Ohio may have also been employed in controlling some of the captured horses—see Gillespie, p. 135.

7. *OR*: 25:1:1122; Mewborn, "The Operations of Mosby's Ranger," p. 15; Zeilinger and Schweikart, editors, "'They Also Serve ...': The Diary of Benjamin Franklin Hackett," p. 96.

8. Richmond *Enquirer*, March 17, 1863; Mewborn, "The Operations of Mosby's Rangers," p. 15; Gillespie, *A History of Company A, First Ohio Cavalry*, p. 135; Col. MacDougall to Gen. Hays, March 9, 1863, RG 393, Pt. 1, Entry 5382, NARA.

9. Richmond *Sentinel*, March 17, 1863.

10. Col. Price to Lt. Col. Johnstone, March 9, 1863 and Price to Capt. Potter, March 9, 1863, RG 107, M504, NARA.

11. *Captain James Penfield*, p. 50; Gen. Abercrombie to Capt. Potter, March 9, 1863, RG 393, Pt. 1, Entry 5384, and Col. Candy to Gen. Slocum, March 9, 1863, RG 107, M504, NARA; *WES*, March 14, 1863.

12. Roswell Farnham to Sir, Wolf Run Shoals, March 10, 1863 and Farnham to Dear Laura, Wolf Run Shoals, March 9, 1863, Farnham Letters, UV; Benedict, *Army Life in Virginia*, p. 124; Benjamin Hatch to Lucina, Near Wolf Run, March 9, 1863, Hatch Letters, UV; *DAT*, March 21, 1863; Capt. Scott to Gen. Stoughton, date uncertain, RG 107, M504, NARA.

13. Willey Reminiscences, p. 1, LC; Walcott Mead to Dear Sister, Fairfax Station, March 31, 1863, Mead Letters, VHS; Edward Clark to My Dear Mary, Wolf Run Shoals, March 9, 1863, Clark Papers, Missouri Historical Society; Alfred Ryder to Dear Friends, Near Bull Run, March 12, 1863, Ryder Letters, UMBL.

14. Alexander Hays to Dear Wife, Union Mills, March 9, 1863, and Hays to Dear Sir, Union Mills, March 11, 1863, Hays Letters, HSWP; Capt. Robert Scott to Col. Asa Blunt, March 9, 1863, RG 393, Part 2, Entry 676, NARA; Benedict, *Army Life in Virginia*, p. 125. Emphasis in original.

15. *DAT*, March 21, 1863; St. Johnsbury, Vermont, *Caledonian*, March 20, 1863; Charles Cummings to My Dearest Wife, near Fairfax Station, March 17, 1863, and Cummings to My Dear Wife, near Fairfax Station, March 21, 1863, Cummings Letters, VHS.

16. Williams Diary, and Wheelock Veazey to unknown recipient, Fairfax Station, March 9, 1863, Veazey Letters, VHS; *WES*, March 14, 1863; *OR*: 25:2:664, 856–858.

17. *OR*: 25:2:856–858.

18. Williams Diary, VHS; *WES*, March 14, and 16, 1863; Keen and Mewborn, *43rd Battalion Virginia Cavalry*, p. 39; Ernest B. Furgurson, *Freedom Rising: Washington in the Civil War* (New York, 2004), pp. 229–232, 263; *NYT*, March 18, 1863.

Chapter 11

1. Capt. Potter to Col. Wyndham, March 10, 1863, RG 107, M504, NARA; Edwin Havens to Dear Brother Nell, Washington, March 13, 1863, Havens Letters, MSU; *OR*: 25: 2: 127–128, 136–137, 656–661.

2. *OR*: 25:2:127–128, 135–136; Gen. Seth Williams to Gen. Stoneman, March 11, 1863, RG 393, Part 2, Entry 1449, NARA.

3. *OR*: 25:2:139; Capt. Potter to Col. Wyndham, March 10, 1863, RG 107, M504, NARA; Ebenezer Gould to Dear Brother, Washington, March 14, 1863, Gould Letters, CMU. That Gould wrote this account on the 14th, before events developed along the Rappahannock, lends credence to his version.

4. *OR*: 25:2:139–140.

5. *OR*: 25:1:47; Col. Wyndham to Lt. Col. Lathrop, March 12, 1863, RG 107, M504, NARA.

6. James Kidd to Dear Mother, Washington, D.C., March 21, 1863, Kidd Letters, UMBL.

7. Mosby, *MWR*, p. 45.

8. Col. MacDougall to Gen. Hays, March 13, 1863, RG 393, Part 1, Entry 3966, and Capt. Scott to Col. Blunt, March 13, 1863, RG 393, Part 2, Entry 676, NARA. The emphasis is MacDougall's.

9. John Skinker to Col. Sharpe, March 13, 1863, RG 393, Part 1, Entry 3980, Lt. Col. Stagg to Col. Price, March 13, 1863 and Price to Stagg, March 13, 1863, RG 107, M504, NARA.

10. *OR*: 25:2:137; Lt. Col. Stagg to Col. Price, March 14, 1863 and Col. MacDougall to Gen. Hays, March 16, 1863, RG 107, M504, also Col. Francis Randall to Gen. Hays, March 14, 1863, and Col. MacDougall to Capt. Potter, March 16, 1863, RG 393, Part 1, Entry 5384, NARA; Macomber Diary, CMU; Stacy Diary, NC.

11. Col. Randall to Gen. Hays, Col. Blunt to Gen. Casey, and Col. Wyndham to Capt. Potter, March 14, 1863, RG 393, Part 1, Entry 5384, Col. MacDougall to Gen. Hays, RG 393, Part 2, Entry 676, NARA; Emmons Diary, UMBL; Klement, "Edwin B. Bigelow: A Michigan Sergeant in the Civil War," p. 210.

12. *OR*: 25:1:45–46; Thomas B. Kelley to Dearest Mary, On Patrol from Dumfries to the Occoquan River, March 15, 1863, Kelley Letters, Dr. James Milgram Collection; Abner Hard, *History of the Eighth Cavalry Regiment Illinois Volunteers, During the Great Rebellion* (Dayton, 1984 edition), pp. 225–226.

13. *OR*: 25:1:45–46; Edwin F. Palmer, *The Second Brigade; or Camp Life* (Montpelier, 1864), pp. 134–135.

14. *OR*: 25:2:667; Mosby, *MWR*, p. 69; Scott, *PL*, pp. 54–55; Edwin Higley Volunteer Service File, RG 94, Entry 496, NARA. While post war Southern accounts state that Mosby rode with 40 men, war date Union accounts from the captured officers list the size of his party at 50.

15. William Wells to unknown recipient, Dranesville, March 17, 1863, Wells Letters, UV; Rutland *Herald*, March 26, 1863, J.H.P. to Editor, Letter of March 21, 1863 Windsor *Vermont Journal*, March 28, 1863; Mosby, *MWR*, p. 70.

16. William Wells to Brother Charles, on Road to Richmond, March 17, 1863, Wells Letters, UV; J.H.P. to Editor, Letter of March 21, 1863, Windsor *Vermont Journal*, March 28, 1863; Rutland *Herald*, March 26, 1863; St. Johnsbury *Caledonian*, March 27, 1863; Mosby, *MWR*, pp. 70–71.

17. William Wells to Brother Charles, on Road to Richmond, March 17, 1863, Wells Letters, UV; William A. Brent, *The Civil War Reminiscences of William A. Brent (1842–1904)*, p. 15, Fauquier Heritage Society Library, Marshall, Virginia.

18. Mosby, *MWR*, pp. 71–72; Rutland *Herald*, March 26, 1863. Mosby returned to the home several weeks later and apologized to Kitty Hanna for the shooting that had taken place on St. Patrick's Day, see Chuck Mauro, "Mosby's raid fills Herndon house with bullets, fear," Washington *Times*, March 15, 2008.

19. Allen M. Ward, "Edwin Hall Higley, an American Classicist: The Intersections of Geography, Biography, and History," *New England Classical Journal*, volume 33, number 1, 2006, pp. 58–71; "An Address in Memory of Major Edwin Hall Higley delivered by The Rev. Sherrard Billings in Groton School Chapel June 4, 1922 on the occasion of the unveiling of a tablet to Major Higley," p. 5, Edwin Higley Papers, Middlebury College Special Collections and Archives, Middlebury College Library, Middlebury, Vermont.

20. Mosby, *MWR*, pp. 72–73; Edwin Higley Volunteer Service File, RG 94, Entry 496, NARA; J.H.P. to Editor, Letter of March 21, 1863, Windsor *Vermont Journal*, March 28, 1863.

21. William Wells to Brother Charles, on Road to Richmond, March 17, 1863, Wells Letters, UV; Russell, *Gray Ghost*, p. 144; Scott, *PL*, p. 57; Baird, *Journals of Amanda Virginia Edmonds*, p. 135.

22. J.H.P. to Editor, Letter of March 21, 1863, Windsor *Vermont Journal*, March 28, 1863; *OR*: 25:1:65; Benedict, *Vermont in the Civil War*, volume 2, p. 585; Edwin Higley Volunteer Service File, RG 94, Entry 496, NARA.

23. Edwin Higley Volunteer Service File, RG 94, Entry 496, NARA.

24. Edwin Higley Volunteer Service File, RG 94, Entry 494, NARA. Taggart was "a very intimate personal" friend of Price who described Taggart on one occasion as "a man of merit and sterling integrity," and on another as "a first rate fellow and as brave as Julius Caesar." Thus Higley's slur against his bravery would not have earned him any sympathy from Price. Taggart was transferred to Stahel's staff immediately in the wake of disastrous affair at Miskell's Farm on April 1, 1863. See Col. R. Butler Price to Governor Curtin, Philadelphia, November 17, 1861 and Price to Dear Colonel, Philadelphia, November, 3, 1861, Records of the 2nd Pennsylvania Cavalry, RG 19, Pennsylvania State Archives, Harrisburg, Pennsylvania. The order in which Stahel announced his staff can be found in the 1st Vermont Letter and Order Books, RG 94, NARA. Emphasis in the original.

25. Edwin Higley Volunteer Service File, RG 94, Entry 496, NARA.

26. Edward Sawyer to William Wells, Head Quarters 3rd Cavalry Brigade, May 22, 1863, Wells Letters, UV.

27. Edwin Higley Volunteer Service File, RG 94, Entry 494, NARA.

28. Augustus Paddock to Dear Father, Fort Scott, March 18, 1863, Paddock Letters, UV; The Burlington, Vermont, *Daily Free Press*, March 23, 1863; Richmond *Sentinel*, March 26, 1863.

Chapter 12

1. Heintzelman Journal, LC; *OR*: 51:1:995–996.

2. *OR*: 25:2:51,70–71; Stephen D. Engle, *Yankee Dutchman: The Life of Franz Sigel* (Fayetteville, 1993), pp. 156–158; Roy Basler, editor, *The Collected Works of Abraham Lincoln*, 9 volumes (New Brunswick, 1953), volume 6, p. 5, 55,79–80,93; Carl Schurz to President Lincoln, January 25, 1863, news clipping, Julius Stahel Papers, LC.

3. Engle, *Yankee Dutchman*, pp. 156–158.

4. Military biography of Julius Stahel, and Gen. Heintzelman to Gen. Stahel, March 13, 1863, Julius Stahel Papers, LC; Basler, *The Collected Works of Abraham Lincoln*, volume 6, p. 135; *OR*: 25:2:150.

5. Warner, *Generals in Blue*, p. 469; *DFP*, September 2, 1862.

6. H.D. to Dear Sir, Aldie, November 17, 1862, *KPP*, December 4, 1862; Annie Hays to Dear Rachel, Centreville, June 12, 1863, Hays Letters, HSWP; Edwin Havens to Brother Nell, Fairfax C.H., April 2, 1863; Havens Letters, MSU; Kidd, *Personal Recollections of a Cavalryman*, p. 97.

7. Gen. David Hunter to Gen. Halleck, May 22, 1864, RG 94, M1064, NARA; *OR*: 37:1:614.

8. Gen. David Hunter to Gen. Halleck, May 22, 1864, RG 94, M1064, NARA; *TNYT*, October 14, 1862.

9. *OR*: 19:2:81–82, 97–98, 417–419, 426–427; *ORS*: 3, pp. 591–592, 595–596, 598, 601–603; *TNYT*, October 14, 16, 18, 20 and 21, 1862; Cheney, *History of the Ninth Regiment*, p. 62–63; *Western New Yorker*, October 23, 1862, in Bush, *Ninth New York Cavalry*, p. 36; Gen. Stahel to Gen. Sigel and forwarded to Banks and Heintzelman, October 17, 1862, Stahel to Sigel and forwarded to Banks, October 19, 1862, RG 107, M504, NARA.

10. Maj. Charles Knox to Gen. Stahel, March 19, 1863, Stahel Papers, LC.

11. Heintzelman Journal, LC; *OR*: 25:2:146, and 51:1: 994–995.

12. Mosby, *MWR*, p. 82; Gen. Silas Casey to Col. John Kelton, December 27, 1862, RG 393, Part 2, Entry 675, NARA.

13. Lt. Col. Stagg to Col. Price, March 21, 1863, RG 107, M504, also Col. Blunt to Gen. Casey and Col. Farnham to Capt. Scott, March 22, 1863, RG 393, Part 2, Entry 676, NARA; Stacy Diary, NC; *OR*: 25:1:67–70; Palmer, *The Second Brigade*, p. 137; R. Shepard Brown, *Stringfellow of the Fourth* (New York, 1960), pp. 181–182; Alexandria *Gazette*, March 26, 1863; Edith M. Sprouse, compiler, *Fairfax County in 1860: A Collective Biography* (Privately Published, 1996), volume 6, pp.

2043–2044. Mrs. Violett's home stood near the present intersection of Lorton Road and Furnace Road. The widow of Thompson Violett, Elizabeth was referred to throughout the war as the widow Violet, with her last name generally misspelled. Some of the reports speculated that the party crossed both times at Selectman's Ford, but it seems improbable that they avoided the pickets at that location prior to the attack but then encountered them on the way back after the fight. In Brown's account Frank Stringfellow attributes the motive for the attack to the "murder" of two of his friends. They had been guarding two Union prisoners but fell asleep, allowing the prisoners to escape after killing the two men while they slept. He gives a very colorful account of this fight.

14. *OR*: 25:1:67–70; Lt. Col. Johnstone to Col. Price, March 25, 1863, RG 107, M504, NARA; Heintzelman Journal, LC. The wounded man, thought to have been the leader of the Southern force is identified as Richard Farrow, Capt. Farrar, R. S. Farrell and Capt. Farrand in different accounts, but attempts to verify any of these names have been unsuccessful.

15. Col. Price to Lt. Col. Stagg, March 22, 1863, RG 107, M504, NARA; *OR*: 25:1:69; Genesee to Editor, Dumfries, Letter of March 25, 1863, *RDUA*, April 1, 1863; Heintzelman Journal, LC.

16. Col. Price to Lt. Col. Stagg, March 23, 1863, RG 107, M504, NARA; Sturtevant, *Pictorial History*, pp. 137–139. It was possibly in response to this raid that the 13th Vermont was shifted to a point closer to Occoquan in early April.

17. Capt. Brinton to Col. Price, March 23, 1863, RG 393, Part 1, Entry 5382, Price to Lt. Col. Johnstone, March 23, 1863, Gen. Stahel to Price, March 23, 1863, and Johnstone to Price, RG 107, M504, NARA; Charles Johnson to Dear Mother, Union Mills, March 24, 1863, Johnston Letters, UC; Macomber Diary, CMU.

18. Mosby, *MWR*, pp. 84–88; Scott, *PL*, pp. 59–60; Williamson, *Mosby's Rangers*, p. 59; *OR*: 25:1:71–72; Boudrye, *Historic Records of the Fifth New York Cavalry*, p. 53. Mosby's boast that he made this attack knowing that a division of Union cavalry was camped two miles away is inaccurate. On that date there were no more Federals in the vicinity than there had been at any other time since he had commenced operating against their lines.

19. Mosby, *MWR*, pp. 88–89; *OR*: 25:1:71–72; Brent, *The Civil War Reminiscences of William A. Brent*, p. 16.

20. *OR*: 25:1: 71; Mosby, *MWR*, p. 89; Edward Winters to Dear Mother, Camp Parole, April 15, 1863, in Bush, *Articles from Wyoming County Newspapers*, p. 87; Brent, *The Civil War Reminiscences of William A. Brent*, p. 17.

21. *OR*: 25:1: 71–72; ARAGSNY, volume 2, Roster of the 5th New York; Marvin Wight to Friend Ameliar, Fairfax Court House, March 29, 1863, Horace Mewborn Collection, New Bern, North Carolina; Boudrye, *Historic Records of the Fifth New York Cavalry*, p. 53.

22. William Rockwell to My Dear Wife, Camp Copeland, March 23, 1863; William Rockwell Letters, WMU; Ebenezer Gould to Dear Brother, Washington, D.C., March 24, 1863, Gould Letters, CMU; Gen. Hays to Col. MacDougall, March 22, 1863, RG 107, M504, NARA; Edwin Havens to Dear Brother, Camp Kellogg, March 24, 1863, Havens Letters, MSU.

23. Klement, "Edwin B. Bigelow: A Michigan Sergeant in the Civil War," p. 211; James Kidd to Dear Mother & Father, Vienna, Virginia, March 30, 1863, Kidd Letters, UMBL; *DFP*, April 15, 1863.

24. Col. Price to Col. Wyndham, March 15, 1863, Price to Lt. Col. Johnstone, Johnstone to Lt. Col. Lathrop, March 22, 1862, Johnstone to Price, March 24, 1863, and Price to Johnstone, March 24, 1863, RG 107, M504, NARA; *OR*: 25:2:153; William Martin to Dear Wife, March 30, 1863, Martin Letters, USAMHI; Williams, *Life in Camp*, p. 99; L.N.B. to Editor, Centreville, April 7, 1863, *RDA*, April 13, 1863; Alexander Hays to Dear Wife, Union Mills, March 24, 1863, Hays Letters, HSWP.

25. Lt. Col. Johnstone to Capt. Potter, March 25, 1863, RG 107, M504, and Gen. Heintzelman to Comd'g Officer 1st Brigade, Pennsylvania Reserves, RG 393, Part 1, Entry 5379, NARA; Sturtevant, *Pictorial History*, p. 139.

26. Col. Price to Lt. Col. Stagg, March 25, 1863, Col. Randall to Stagg, March 27, 1863, RG 107, M504, also Provost Marshal to Capt. Potter, March 25, 1863, RG 393, Part 1, Entry 5384, NARA; Macomber Diary, CMU.

27. Edwin Havens to Dear Nell, Fairfax Court House, March 29, 1863, Havens Letters, MSU; Gen. Copeland to Gen. Stahel, March 27, 1863, Lt. Col. Johnstone to Copeland, March 27, 1863, Capt. Scott to Col. Fessenden, Scott to Col. Blunt, March 28, 1863, and Johnstone to Gen. Hays, March 29, 1863, RG 107, M504, and Gen. Heintzelman to Gen. Hooker, March 28, 1863, RG 393, Part 2, Entry 1449, Maj. Hunt to Gen. Abercrombie, March 28, 1863, and Heintzelman to Gen. Butterfield, March 28, 1863, RG 393, Part 1, Entry 5379, also March 29, 1863 Circular, RG 393, Part 2, Entry 659, NARA; Jackson Diary, USAMHI.

28. Lt. Thomas Kennedy to Capt. Potter, and Kennedy to Col. Johnstone, March 29, 1863 and Col. Price to Gen. Stahel, March 29, 1863, RG 107, M504, NARA; Stacy Diary, NC.

29. Andrew Buck to Brother & Sister, Fairfax Court House, April 3, 1863, Buck Family Correspondence, and John Farnill to My Dear Father and Mother, Camp in the Woods, March 29, 1863, Farnill Letters, UMBL; Ebenezer Gould to Dear Brother, Fairfax Court House, March 29, 1863, Gould Letters, CMU, Allyne Litchfield to My Dear Wife, Allyne Litchfield Letters, UMCL; Lee, *Personal and Historical Sketches*, p. 106.

30. *OR*: 25:2:169; Capt. Potter to Gen. Abercrombie and Potter to Gen. Stahel, March 30, 1863, RG 393, Part 1, Entry 5379, Gen. Stahel to Heintzelman, March 31, 1863, RG 393, Part 1, Entry 5384, and Maj. Brewer to Lt. Col. Stagg and Col. Price, March 30, 1863, RG 107, M504, NARA; Stacy and Crandell Diaries, NC; Jackson Diary, USAMHI.

31. *OR*: 25:2:684, 693–694.

32. George Morton to Gen. Heintzelman, March 24, 1863, RG 393, Part 1, Entry 5382, NARA. See also Capt. Merritt to Lt. Col. Lathrop, March 30, 1863, same cite for an inspection report of the troops guarding the Potomac River in Montgomery County.

33. Arabella M. Willson, *Disaster, Struggle, Triumph: The Adventures of 1000 "Boys in Blue," From August, 1862, to June, 1865* (Albany, 1865), p. 138; L.N.B. to Editor, Centreville, April 7, 1863, *RDA*, April 13, 1863; Charles Tewksbury to Dear Parents, Brothers & Sisters, Wolf Run Shoals, March 28, 1863, Tewksbury Letters, UV; Special Order 34, March 19, 1863, Headquarters Department of Washington, RG 94, Muster Rolls, Returns and Regimental Papers, 15th Vermont Infantry, NARA.

34. Hampton Diary, CMU; ARAGSNY, volume 2, 8th New York Cavalry Roster; Maj. Pope to Lt. Parsons, March 28, 1863, RG 393, Part 2, Entry 1449, NARA.

35. Maj. Pope to Lt. Parsons, March 29, 1863, RG 393, Part 2, Entry 1449, NARA; Norton, *Deeds of Daring*, p. 58.

36. *OR*: 25:1:74–75; Maj. Pope to Captain, March 30, 1863, RG 393, Part 2, Entry 1449, NARA. Lee was complaining at the same time, to Secretary of War James Seddon, of the difficulty his scouts were having penetrating the Union pickets which were "posted within 50 steps of each other," see *OR*: 25:2:691.

37. Capt. Farnsworth to Lt. Col. Clendennin, March 31, 1863, RG 393, Part 2, Entry 1449, NARA.

38. Farnsworth to Clendennin, March 31, 1863, RG 393, Part 2, Entry 1449, and James Dulin's Compiled Service Record, RG 109, M267, NARA; Henderson, *Autobiography of Arab*, pp. 73–76; Ron Crawley, "Roster of General Wade Hampton's 'Iron Scouts,'" from http:www.schistory.net/ironscouts. Though both Farnsworth and Henderson mention that Towles escaped, he is listed as captured on March 31, 1863 in Stiles, *4th Virginia Cavalry*, p. 140, taken to Old Capitol Prison and not exchanged until May. A more sinister and thus more compelling story later developed around this incident and it is often cited today in outlines of Farnsworth's career. The story is attributed to U. R. Brooks in his *Butler and His Cavalry*, pp.

129, 488–492. Brooks states that five of six Dulin brothers entered Southern service, three with the 49th Virginia Infantry, one, James, with the 2nd S.C. Cavalry and William with "the famous black horse company of cavalry." The service of the first four is easily verified. The fifth, William, was supposedly "shot down in cold blood ... in Warrenton by a Captain Farnsworth," while pinned under his horse in the street and "in a semi-conscious condition." James then supposedly swore to never "give or ask quarter, and that he would take a hundred lives to pay for the life of his murdered brother." William Dulin's service however cannot be verified.

Chapter 13

1. *OR*: 25:1:72; Scott, *PL*, p. 65; Benedict, *Vermont in the Civil War*, volume 2, p. 585. The idea that Mosby was fighting the best men from the best regiment in the Union command has been expanded upon by modern writers, for example see James A. Ramage, *Gray Ghost: The Life of Col. John Singleton Mosby* (Lexington, 2000), p. 80; Peter A. Brown, *Mosby's Fighting Parson: The Life and Times of Sam Chapman* (Westminster, 2001), p. 107.

2. Ide, *History of the First Vermont Cavalry*, pp. 17–19; Benedict, *Vermont in the Civil War*, volume 2, p. 539.

3. Benedict, *Vermont in the Civil War*, volume 2, pp. 533–534, 542; Col. Lemuel Platt to Brig. Gen. Stoneman, Burlington, Vermont, November 19, 1861; Muster Rolls, Returns and Regimental Papers, 1st Vermont Cavalry, RG 94, NARA.

4. Benedict, *Vermont in the Civil War*, volume 2, pp. 542–543.

5. Benedict, *Vermont in the Civil War*, volume 2, pp. 543–544; *OR*: 12:3:17.

6. Benedict, *Vermont in the Civil War*, volume 2, pp. 544–545; *OR*: 12:3:52; Thomas P. Lowry, *Curmudgeons, Drunkards & Outright Fools: Courts-Martial of Civil War Colonels* (Lincoln, 1997), p. 195.

7. Benedict, *Vermont in the Civil War*, volume 2, p. 536, 551; Ide, *History of the First Vermont Cavalry*, pp. 36, 300 and 305. Tompkins had achieved a measure of notoriety on June 1, 1861, when he led his detachment of the 2nd U. S. Cavalry in a charge through Fairfax Court House. He was awarded a Medal of Honor for the action after the war, though at the time some questioned his sobriety, see *OR*: 2:60–64; Ide, *History of the First Vermont Cavalry*, p. 36; Donald R. Pfanz, *Richard S. Ewell: A Soldier's Life* (Chapel Hill, 1998), p. 128.

8. Charles H. Blinn Diary, UV; Benedict, *Vermont in the Civil War*, volume 2, p. 556; Charles H. Tompkins, "With the Vermont Cavalry, 1861–2, Some Reminiscences by Brig. Gen. Charles H. Tompkins, U.S.A.," *The Vermonter*, volume 17, number 4, April 1912, pp. 506–507.

9. Benedict, *Vermont in the Civil War*, volume 2, pp. 546, 556–567; Ide, *History of the First Vermont Cavalry*, pp. 38–44; *The* [Burlington] *Free Press*, May 29, 1862; *OR*: 12:1:585–593. Casualty figures vary among the sources. The figures listed are compiled from several sources.

10. Benedict, *Vermont in the Civil War*, volume 2, p. 568.

11. Ide, *History of the First Vermont Cavalry*, pp. 52–53; Benedict, *Vermont in the Civil War*, volume 2, pp. 571, 575.

12. Benedict, *Vermont in the Civil War*, volume 2, pp. 575, 580; Ide, *History of the First Vermont Cavalry*, pp. 59–61.

13. Benedict, *Vermont in the Civil War*, volume 2, p. 579; Ide, *History of the First Vermont Cavalry*, pp. 64–68; Montgomery Meigs to Edwin Stanton, Washington, September 11, 1862, RG 94, Entry 496, NARA.

14. Ide, *History of the First Vermont Cavalry*, pp. 68–69; *OR*: 12:1:587–593, E. B. Sawyer to Maj. William Wells, Washington, November 28, 1863, Wells Papers, UV.

15. Ide, *History of the First Vermont Cavalry*, pp. 70–75; Capt. Joel Erhardt to Hon. Edwin M. Stanton, January 28, 1863, Joel Erhardt's Compiled Service Record, RG 94, NARA.

16. Ide, *History of the First Vermont Cavalry*, pp. 75–77; Joel Erhardt's Compiled Service Record, RG 94, NARA.

17. Charles Chapin to Dear Brother, Lewinsville, January 18, 1863, Chapin Papers, USAMHI; William L. Greenleaf, "From the Rapidan to Richmond," *Vermont War Papers and Miscellaneous States Papers and Addresses for Military Order of the Loyal Legion of the United States*, volume 54 (Wilmington edition, 1994), p. 3; Ramage, *Gray Ghost*, p. 80. The degree to which sickness and disease contributed to the problems at this outpost is unknown, but it was almost certainly an issue. For an examination of the general health problem, including the degree to which static armies were more prone to sickness than armies on the move see Michael A. Cooke, "The Health of the Union Military in the District of Columbia, 1861–1865," *Military Affairs* volume 48, number 4, October 1984, pp. 194–199.

18. Benedict, *Vermont in the Civil War*, volume 2, pp. 581–582.

19. Ide, *History of the First Vermont Cavalry*, p. 92; Darius Maynard to Dear Nell, Near Washington, D.C., March 29, 1863, Maynard Letters, WSU; Victor Comte to Dear Elise, Fairfax Court House, April 1, 1863, Comte Letters, UMBL.

20. *OR*: 25:1:72; Mosby, *MWR*, pp. 98–103; Keen and Mewborn, *43rd Battalion Virginia Cavalry*, pp. 44–45; Samuel Chapman, "Memories of 'Mosby's Men,' The Dranesville Raid," *Religious Herald*, January 16, 1902, in Horace Mewborn, editor, *"From Mosby's Command": Newspaper Letters & Articles by and about John S. Mosby and His Rangers* (Baltimore, 2005) p. 91. Horace Mewborn provided the information that the name of the farm was that of the tenant who was farming the property in a letter of August 6, 2007. There is a Thomas Miskell listed on the 1860 Census for that district who was a farmer.

21. Col. Price to Maj. Harvey Baldwin Jr., undated report of April 1863, *ORS*: 1:4:531, 533; Ide, *History of the First Vermont Cavalry*, p. 58,78; Benedict, *Vermont in the Civil War*, volume 2, p. 585; Ramage, *Gray Ghost*, p. 80. Bean had been summarily dismissed the previous spring when it was alleged that he pretended to be captured during the disastrous attack in May. This verdict was later overturned, but he would not survive a second allegation against his character. See Bean's Volunteer Service file, RG 94, Entry 496, NARA. The six companies were A,B,C,D,G and I. For references to his force being picked volunteers or the best and the bravest see Williamson, *Mosby's Rangers*, p. 52; Scott, *PL*, p. 65; Brown, *Mosby's Fighting Parson*, p. 107. For mention that the men were simply all that was available see OR: 25:1:72.

22. *ORS*: 1:4:534; Mosby, *MWR*, p. 104; Keen and Mewborn, *43rd Battalion Virginia Cavalry*, pp. 45–46; Josiah Grout, *Memoir of Gen'l William Wallace Grout and Autobiography of Josiah Grout* (Newport, 1919), pp. 218–241, as reproduced at vermontcivilwar.org/units/ca/grout.php. Scott, in *PL*, p. 65, credits Flint with commenting as he left the Green home, "All right, boys; we will give Mosby an April fool!" Though it makes a nice story and is often cited in other accounts one should question where it came from and how Scott can attribute it to Flint. Mosby in *MWR*, p. 110, gives a more likely version, crediting a similar comment to a Union captive.

23. Mosby, *MWR*, pp. 104–105; *ORS*: 1:4:531–534; *OR*: 25:1:72, 77; Vermont *Chronicle*, April 14, 1863; *The* [St. Johnsbury] *Caledonian*, April 10 and April 17, 1863; Ide, *History of the First Vermont Cavalry*, p. 93, 95; Grout, *Autobiography of Josiah Grout*, pp. 218–241. An account in the Rutland *Daily Herald*, April 11, 1863, states that Flint left Bean with 100 men and attacked with the remaining 35 men.

24. Mosby, *MWR*, p. 105; Scott, *PL*, p. 67; Williamson, *Mosby's Rangers*, p. 54; Ramage, *Gray Ghost*, p. 81; Ide, *History of the First Vermont Cavalry*, p. 95. The extent to which carbines could have influenced the fight is open to question. Each of the six companies would have averaged 30 men, and, according to Grout, only the men in Companies D and I were armed with carbines — single shot Sharps.

25. Ide, *History of the First Vermont Cavalry*, p. 93; Keen and Mewborn, *43rd Battalion Virginia Cavalry*, p. 46, *ORS*: 1:4:534; Benedict, *Vermont in the Civil War*, volume 2, p. 586; Ide, *History of the First Vermont Cavalry*, p. 93. Emphasis is in the original.

26. Grout, *Autobiography of Josiah Grout*, pp. 218–241; Chapman, "Memories of 'Mosby's Men,'" in Mewborn, "*From Mosby's Command*," p. 91; Alexandria *Gazette*, April 4, 1863; The *Caledonian*, April 10, 1863.

27. Grout, *Autobiography of Josiah Grout*, pp. 218–241, Ide, *History of the First Vermont Cavalry*, p. 95.

28. Grout, *Autobiography of Josiah Grout*, pp. 218–241; Mosby, *MWR*, pp. 106–108; *OR*: 25:1:72.

29. *ORS*:1:4:53; Ide, *History of the First Vermont Cavalry*, p. 93; Vermont *Chronicle*, April 14, 1863; Grout, *Autobiography of Josiah Grout*, pp. 218–241.

30. Mosby, *MWR*, pp. 107–108; *OR*: 25:1:72; Vermont *Chronicle*, April 14, 1863; Grout, *Autobiography of Josiah Grout*, pp. 218–241; Edmund Pope, Jr., to Dear Father, Near Fairfax Court House, April 7, 1863, Edmund Pope Papers, VHS.

31. Cordelia Grantham Sansone, editor, *Journey to Bloomfield: Lives and Letters of 19th Century Virginia Families* (Fairfax, 2004), p. 181; *OR*: 25:1:72; Peck, *Revised Roster of Vermont Volunteers*, pp. 214–265; Vermont *Chronicle*, April 14 and 21, 1863. The regimental roster does not confirm the higher casualty figures given by Mosby in his report and used in later accounts.

32. *OR*: 25:1:78; Benedict, *Vermont in the Civil War*, volume 2, pp, 587–588.

33. Grout, *Autobiography of Josiah Grout*, pp. 218–241.

34. William P. Buck, editor, *Sad Earth, Sweet Heaven: The Diary of Lucy Rebecca Buck During the War Between the States, Front Royal, Virginia, December 25, 1861—April 15, 1865* (Birmingham, 1973), p. 176; Mosby, *MWR*, p. 103; *OR*: 25:1:79; *Journal of the Congress of the Confederate States 1861–1865* (Washington, D.C., 1904), volume 2, p. 121.

35. *OR*: 25:1:78; Benedict, *Vermont in the Civil War*, volume 2, pp, 587–588; Rutland *Daily Herald*, April 6, April 8 and April 11, 1863; Ide, *History of the First Vermont Cavalry*, pp. 95, 319; Col. Price to Maj. Baldwin, undated report of April 1863; *ORS*: 1:4:532. James Kelley was among the men captured.

36. Ebenezer Gould to Dear Brother, Fairfax Court House, April 1, 1863, Gould Letters, CMU.

37. Allyne Litchfield to My Dear Wife, Fairfax, April 3, 1863, Litchfield-French Letters, UMCL; Edwin Havens to Brother Nell, Fairfax Court House, April 2, 1863 and Edwin Havens to Dear Father, Fairfax Court House, April 5, 1863, Havens Letters, MSU.

Chapter 14

1. William Martin to Dear Wife, Fairfax, April 3, 1863, Martin Letters, USAMHI; Lt. Col. Lathrop to Maj. Gen. Stahel, April 2, 1863, RG 393, Part 1, Entry 5379, NARA; PML to Editor, Fairfax, April 6, 1863, *GRDE*, April 15, 1863.

2. Col. Price to Lt. Col. Stagg, April 3, 1863, RG 107, M504, NARA; *DFP*, April 15, 1863; William Martin to Dear Wife, Fairfax, April 6, 1863, Martin Letters, USAMHI; *Hugh St. Clair Diary*, p. 16; PML to Editor, Fairfax, April 6, 1863, *GRDE*, April 15, 1863.

3. Randolph to Editor, Fairfax Court House, April 6, 1863, *DAT*, April 13, 1863; PML to Editor, Fairfax, April 6, 1863, *GRDE*, April 15, 1863, James Kidd to Dear Father, Fairfax Court House, April 7, 1863, Kidd Letters, UMBL.

4. *DFP*, April 15, 1863; James Kidd to Dear Father, Fairfax Court House, April 7, 1863, Kidd Letters, UMBL; Scott, *PL*, pp. 70–71.

5. *DFP*, April 15, 1863; James Kidd to Dear Father, Fairfax Court House, April 7, 1863, Kidd Letters, UMBL; Scott, *PL*, pp. 70–71; Albert Dimond Pension Record, RG 94, NARA; Ebenezer Gould to Dear Brother, Fairfax Court House, April 8, 1863, Gould Letters, CMU.

6. Randolph to Editor, Fairfax Court House, April 6, 1863, *DAT*, April 13, 1863; James Kidd to Dear Father, Fairfax Court House, April 7, 1863, Kidd Letters, UMBL.

7. Randolph to Editor, Fairfax Court House, April 6, 1863, *DAT*, April 13, 1863; Mosby, *MWR*, p. 122.

8. X to Editor, Middleburg, April 1863, Richmond *Sentinel*, April 18, 1863. The most likely candidate for the officer identified as Col. Johnson is Lt. Col. Robert Johnstone of the 5th New York, but sources for that regiment don't confirm that he accompanied Copeland.

9. *OR*: 25:1:80; Maj. Gen. Stahel to Lt. Col. Lathrop, April 5, 1863, RG 107, M504, NARA; *NYT*, April 10, 1863; Emily G. Ramey and John K. Gott, *Years of Anguish: Fauquier County, Virginia 1861–1865* (Fauquier, 1965), p. 39; Ebenezer Gould to My Dear Wife, Fairfax Court House, April 5, 1863 and Gould to Dear Brother, Fairfax Court House, April 8, 1863, Gould Letters, CMU; David M. Cooper, *Obituary Discourse on Occasion of the Death of Noah Henry Ferry, Major of the Fifth Michigan Cavalry, Killed at Gettysburg, July 3, 1863* (New York, 1863), p. 13.

10. Gen. Stahel to Lt. Col. Lathrop, April 5, 1863, RG 107, M504, NARA; Tabor Parcher to Sadia, Conrad's Ferry, April 5, 1863, Tabor Parcher Letters, UV.

11. Capt. Granville Johnson to Lt. Col. Lathrop, April 6, 1863, RG 393, Part 1, Entry 5382, NARA; Scott, *PL*, p. 73

12. Col. Price to Hd Qrs 2nd Brigade, April 10, 1863, Capt. Robert Scott to Col. Blunt, April 12, 1863, RG 107, M504, NARA; *DFP*, April 15, 1863; Edwin Havens to Dear Nell, Wolf Run Shoals, April 12, 1863, Havens Letters, MSU.

13. Alexander Hays to Dear Wife, Centreville, April 13, 1863 and April 15, 1863, Hays Letters, HSWP; *OR*: 25:2:210, 224, 257 and 51:1:1002–1003, 1007; Lt. Col. Lathrop to Gen. Stahel, April 11, 1863, and Gen. Heintzelman to Gen. Stahel, April 14, 1863, RG 393, Part 1, Entry 5379, Gen. Stahel to Maj. Harvey Baldwin, April 11, 1863 and Col. Bryan to Col. Price, April 14, 1863, RG 94, M504, and Special Order 12, April 16, 1863, 1st Vermont Letter and Order Books, RG 94, NARA; McGrath, *The History of the 127th New York*, p. 37; MLS Jackson Diary, USAMHI.

14. *OR*: 25:2:223, 741; Richmond *Sentinel*, April 24, 1863; Stiles, *4th Virginia Cavalry*, p. 26; Hard, *History of the Eighth Cavalry Regiment*, p. 230; Alexander Dixon Payne Memorandum Book, Virginia Historical Society, Richmond, Virginia. The regimental historian relates that Southworth was almost killed, but nothing in the captain's records suggests that he was ever wounded or injured in the field. Southworth was eventually transferred, at his request, to the Invalid Corps but for medical reasons related to malaria contracted on the Peninsula in 1862.

15. Herman Haupt to A. Anderson, April 17, 1863 and Capt. Potter to Gen. Stahel, April 17, 1863, RG 107, M504, also Gen. Heintzelman to Stahel, Potter to Stahel and Potter to Heintzelman, April 17, 1863, RG 393, Part 1, Entry 5379, NARA; *OR*: 25:2:222.

16. Scott, *PL*, p. 74; *OR*: 51:1:177

17. *BACA*, April 21, 1863; Letter from Taylor Chamberlin to author, March 28, 2006; Washington *Daily Morning Chronicle*, February 14, 1863; Charles Chapin to Dear Brother, Freedom Hill, April 19, 1863, Chapin Letters, USAMHI; Smith, *The Story of a Cavalry Regiment*, p. 66; Gen. Copeland to Col Gray, and Gray to Maj. Baldwin, April 21, 1863, RG 393, Part 2, Entry 1449, NARA; Heintzelman Journal, LC; E-mail to author from Taylor Chamberlin, Waterford, Virginia, March 28, 2006.

18. Albert Greene to Dear brother, April 18, 1863, Greene Letters, UV.

19. Ide, *History of the First Vermont Cavalry*, p. 99.

20. James Kidd to Dear Father, Freedom Hill, April 18, 1863, Kidd Letters, UMBL.

21. Ford, *A Cycle of Adams Letters*, volume 1, pp. 283–284.

22. Robert C. Wallace, edited by John Carroll, *A Few Memories of a Long Life* (Fairfield, 1988 edition), pp. 20–25; Scott, *PL*, p. 72; *DAT*, April 28 and April 29, 1863; Keen and Mewborn, *43rd Battalion Virginia Cavalry*, p. 50. Scott confirms that Wallace was remembered by the "citizens of Fauquier and Loudoun from his gentlemanly deportment when on raids ... and when it was known that he had been captured, many regrets were expressed that, instead of him, it had not been one of

those brutal creatures who sometimes wore and always disgraced the uniform of a Federal officer."

23. John Farnill to Dear Father and Mother, April 19, 1863, Farnill Letters, CMU; Emmons Diary, UMBL; Charles Chapin to Dear Brother, Freedom Hill, April 19, 1863, Chapin Letters, USAMHI; Scott, *PL*, p. 72; GWA to Editor, Fairfax Court House, April 20, 1863, *DAT*, April 28, 1863. GWA was most likely Capt. George W. Alexander. Emphasis in the original.

24. Thackery, *A Light and Uncertain Hold*, p. 129; *OR*; 25:2:217,235; Col. Candy to Capt. Elliott, April 16, 1863, Gen. Slocum to Candy, April 16, 1863, and Gen. Pleasonton to Gen. Butterfield, April 17, 1863, RG 107, M504, NARA; Slocum, *The Life and Services of Major-General Henry Warner Slocum*, p. 71.

25. *OR*: 25:2:198 and 51:1:1008; Warner, *Generals in Blue*, p. 471; George S. Maharay, *Vermont Hero: Major General George J. Stannard* (Shippensburg, 2001), p. 20; George Hagar to Dear Sarah, Headquarters 12th Vermont, April 22, 1863, George Hagar Letters, and Charles Tewksbury to Dear Brother, Camp Carusi, April 25, 1863, Tewksbury Letters, UV; Edwin Clark to My Dear Father & Mother, Wolf Run Shoals, April 28, 1863, Clark Papers, Missouri Historical Society; Edwin Hall to Dear Father, Union Mills, May 31, 1863, Edwin Hall Letters, VHS.

26. Capt. Potter to Gen. Abercrombie, April 20, 1863, and April 23, 1863, Gen. Stahel to Maj. Baldwin, April 21, 1863, Gen. Stannard to John Devereux and Stannard to Gen. Abercrombie, April 23, 1863, RG 107, M504, also Gen. Heintzelman to Gen. Haupt and Heintzelman to Gen. Stahel, April 21, 1863, Heintzelman to Gen. Stoneman, April 22, 1863, and Lt. Col. Lathrop to Stahel, April 23, 1863, RG 393, Part 1, Entry 5379, NARA; Heintzelman Journal, LC; *OR*: 25:2:245; Charles Brigham to Brothers and Sisters, April 28, 1863, Lewis Leigh Collection, USAMHI, in Ruffner, "*Tenting on the Old Camp Ground": The Civil War History of Union Mills*, p. 113.

Chapter 15

1. Ernest Yager to Col. Sharpe, April 24, 1863, RG 393, Part 1, Entry 3980, NARA; Edwin C. Fishel, *The Secret War for the Union: The Untold Story of Military Intelligence in the Civil War* (Boston, 1996), p. 292; *OR*: 25:2:700, 703, 721, 724–725, 730.

2. *OR*: 25:2:738, 740–741; Fortier, *15th Virginia Cavalry*, p. 26. Brawner's Company H, 15th Virginia Cavalry, had initially been enlisted as a partisan ranger company, and may have conducted some guerrilla operations in Prince William and Fairfax Counties over the winter, in cooperation with the Iron Scouts and the Black Horse Cavalry, though this remains uncertain.

3. *OR*: 25:2:745, 749–750, 860; Gen. Lee to Gen. Stuart, April 22, 1863, Stuart Papers, The Henry E. Huntington Library.

4. *OR*: 25:2:860.

5. *OR*: 25:2:242–243; Superintendent J. H. Devereux's Report for January to July 1863 in RG 92, Entry 1528, Military Railroad Reports 1863–1866, NARA.

6. *OR*: 25:2:238, 251, 253, 257.

7. *OR*: 25:2:257; Lt. Col. Lathrop to Gen. Stahel, April 25, 1863, RG 393, Part 1, Entry 5379, NARA; Allyne Litchfield to Dear Wife, Occoquan, April 26, 1863, Litchfield Letters, UMCL.

8. Alfred Ryder to Dear Friends, Fairfax, April 25, 1863, Ryder Letters, UMBL; Bradford Smith Hoskins Diary, *PI*, June 5, 1863, in Mewborn, "*From Mosby's Command*," p. 17; Taylor M. Chamberlin and John M. Souders, *Between Reb and Yank: A Civil War History of Northern Loudoun County, Virginia* (Jefferson, 2011), p. 175.

9. Scott, *PL*, p. 73; Ramey and Gott, *The Years of Anguish*, pp. 39–44, 70–71.

10. Capt. Potter to Gen. Stahel, April 26, 1863, and Lt. Col. Lathrop to Stahel, RG 393, Part 1, Entry 5379, NARA; *OR*: 25:2:257,261.

11. Edwin Havens to Dear Nell, Bristoe Station, April 27, 1863, Havens Letters, MSU; Allyne Litchfield to Dear Susie, Bristoe Station, April 28, 1863, Litchfield Letters, UMCL.

12. Lt. Col. Lathrop to Gen. Stahel, April 25, 1863, RG 393, Part 1, Entry 5379, and Lt. Col. A. J. Alexander to Gen. Gregg, April 27, 1863, RG 393, Part 2, Entry 1449, NARA; Edwin Havens to Dear Nell, April 27, 1863, Bristoe Station, Havens Letters, MSU. Brentsville's reputation as a haven for guerrillas had not gone unnoticed by Stoneman either, and when Mann returned through the town that afternoon he encountered a patrol from the 2nd New York Cavalry. The New Yorkers had been specifically tasked with scouting the country between the Orange and Alexandria Railroad and the Occoquan for "guerrillas," and Lt. Col. Henry Davies had been provided with "a list of suspected persons living in and about Brentsville." Davies was instructed to divide his command "into small parties for the purpose of more thoroughly scouring the country," and urged to prosecute his orders "with the utmost energy & vigor," however, the results of his expedition are unknown.

13. Macomber Diary, CMU; William Martin to Dear Wife, Fairfax, April 30, 1863, Martin Letters, USAMHI; J. W. Jackson to Editor, Fairfax Court House, May 8, 1863, Wyoming County *Mirror*, in Bush, *Articles from Wyoming County Newspapers*, p. 91; *DFP*, May 2, 1863; *NYT*, May 2, 1863; Scott, *PL*, p. 78.

14. Scott, *PL*, p. 79; Keen and Mewborn, *43rd Battalion*, p. 51; Jackson Letter in Bush, *Articles from Wyoming County Newspapers*, p. 92; Mosby, *MWR*, p. 122. It was on this expedition that Mosby recalled the Yankees capturing "a man named Hutchison, who," Mosby claimed, "was 70 years old, and had always used crutches," but who was accused by a member of the 1st Vermont as "leading the charge in the fight at Miskel's farm." Whether another man named Hutchison was captured is unknown but Lycurgus Hutchison was not seventy years old in 1863. Shortly after his exchange he enlisted with Mosby on June 10, 1863 and served with him throughout the war.

15. Jackson Letter in Bush, *Articles from Wyoming County Newspapers*, p. 92; *NYT*, May 2, 1863; Scott, *PL*, p. 79; Richmond *Sentinel*, June 3, 1863; Mosby, *MWR*, pp. 119–121; David M. Jordan, "*Happiness Is Not My Companion": The Life of General G. K. Warren* (Bloomington, 2001), p. 92.

16. *NYT*, May 2, 1863; William Martin to Dear Wife, Fairfax, April 30, 1863, Martin Letters, USAMHI; Mosby, *MWR*, pp. 119–120.

17. Macomber Diary, CMU; Movements of the 5th New York Cavalry, USAMHI; Scott, *PL*, pp. 80–81; Mosby, *MWR*, p. 122; Baird; *Journals of Amanda Virginia Edmonds*, pp. 140–141. The accounts are rather confusing but it does not appear that Stahel took his entire force toward Upperville, and no Union account confirms Scott.

18. *NYT*, May 2, 1863.

19. Mosby, *MWR*, pp. 123–125; Scott, *PL*, pp. 78, 81–83; Jackson Letter in Bush, *Articles from Wyoming County Newspapers*, p. 92; Ramey and Gott, *The Years of Anguish*, pp. 41–44; William Martin to Dear Wife, Fairfax, April 30, 1863, Martin Letters, USAMHI.

20. Ramey and Gott, *The Years of Anguish*, pp. 41–44.

21. Jackson Letter in Bush, *Articles from Wyoming County Newspapers*, p. 92; *Hugh St. Clair Diary*, p. 21; Mosby, *MWR*, pp. 125–126; Scott, *PL*, p. 83; *NYT*, May 2, 1863.

22. Jackson Letter in Bush, *Articles from Wyoming County Newspapers*, p. 92; Richmond *Sentinel*, June 3, 1863; Macomber Diary, CMU; Charles Johnson to Dear Mother, Fairfax Court House, May 2, 1863, Johnson Letters, UC.

23. Jackson Letter in Bush, *Articles from Wyoming County Newspapers*, p. 92; *Hugh St. Clair Diary*, p. 21; *NYT*, May 1 and May 2, 1863, Mosby, *MWR*, p. 122.

24. Mosby, *MWR*, p. 125; Scott, *PL*, pp. 81–82; William Martin to Dear Wife, Fairfax, April 30, 1863, Martin Letters, USAMHI; *NYT*, May 2, 1863; Richmond *Sentinel*, June 3, 1863.

25. *NYT*, May 2, 1863; Richmond *Sentinel*, June 3, 1863.

26. *OR*: 25:2:273, 315; Gen. Heintzelman to Gen. Butterfield and Lt. Col. Lathrop to Gen. Stahel, April 30, 1863, RG 393, Part 1, Entry 5379, NARA.

27. Gen. Abercrombie to Lt. Col. Lathrop, April 27, 1863, RG 393, Part 1, Entry 5382, Capt. Potter to Abercrombie, April 29, 1863, RG 393, Part 1, Entry 5379, NARA; Stacy Diary, NC; Simons, *A Regimental History*, pp. 70–71; Belknap Diary, USAMHI; William Martin to Dear Wife, May 4, 1863, Martin Letters, USAMHI. Emphasis in original.

Chapter 16

1. Gen. Haupt to F. P. Lord, May 1, 1863, RG 107, M504, Capt. Potter to Gen. Stahel, May 1, 1863, Maj. Hunt to Gen. Abercrombie, May 1, 1863, RG 393, Part 1, Entry 5379, Col. Mann to Lt. Col. Litchfield, May 1, 1863, RG 94, 7th Michigan Cavalry Letter and Order Books, NARA; Heintzelman Journal, LC; Movements of the 5th New York Cavalry, USAMHI.

2. Roswell Farnham to My Dear Wife, Warrenton Junction, May 4, 1863 and Farnham to Dear Mary, Warrenton Junction, May 5, 1863, Farnham Letters, UV.

3. Col. Gregg to Col. Blake, May 2, 1863, RG 107, M504, NARA; *OR*: 25:2:356; Allyne Litchfield to My Dear Wife, Bristoe Station, May 2, 1863, Litchfield Letters, UMCL; "Movements of the 5th New York Cavalry," USAMHI. Emphasis in the original.

4. Ramey and Gott, *The Years of Anguish*, p. 71; Hoskins Diary in Mewborn, "*From Mosby's Command*," p. 19; Mosby, *MWR*, pp. 130–131.

5. Samuel Chapman, "Memories of 'Mosby's Men,' The Fight at Warrenton Junction (Calverton)," *Religious Herald*, January 23, 1902, in Mewborn, "*From Mosby's Command*," p. 94; Scott, *PL*, p. 84.

6. Roswell Farnham to My Dear Wife, Warrenton Junction, May 4, 1863, Farnham Letters, UV; Zeilinger and Schweikart, editors, "'They Also Serve ...': The Diary of Benjamin Franklin Hackett," p. 96; Henderson, *Autobiography of Arab*, p. 87.

7. Emmons Diary, UMBL; William Wilkins to Dear Friend, Fairfax Court House, June 2, 1863, Athens [Ohio] *Messenger*, June 18, 1863, Wilkins Letters, USAMHI; Scott, *PL*, p. 85; *OR*: 25:2:1105. As in most all instances the estimates of numbers involved in this fight vary widely. In his report (OR: 25:2: 861) Mosby claimed to have captured "nearly the whole of their regiment (about 300 officers and men.)" Stahel in *OR*: 25:1:1104 listed the size of the detachment at fifty, while Gen. Abercrombie said it numbered "about 100," in his report *OR*: 25:1:1105. Wilkins states there were 70 men from the regiment, while later news accounts held firm at 80 men. Likewise Union estimates of Mosby's force vary from a high of 1,000 men in Maj. Chamberlain's report, *OR*: 25:1:1106, to a more accurate 110 in the Wilkins' letter.

8. Ramage, *Gray Ghost*, p. 84; Scott, *PL*, p. 85; William Wilkins to Dear Friend, Fairfax Court House, June 2, 1863, Wilkins Letters, USAMHI; New York *Herald*, May 7, 1863.

9. Keen and Mewborn, *43rd Battalion*, p. 373; New York *Herald*, May 7, 1863; Letter signed Ned, May 6, 1863, Windsor Vermont *Journal*, May 16, 1863; William Martin to Dear Wife, Fairfax, May 4, 1863, Martin Letters, USAMHI. Templeman was said to have had a pass signed by General Heintzelman in his pocket.

10. Scott, *PL*, p. 85, Edwin Havens to Our Dear Folks, Warrenton Junction, May 5, 1863, Havens Letters, MSU; Henderson, *Autobiography of Arab*, p. 88.

11. New York *Herald*, May 7, 1863; Scott, *PL*, pp. 85–86; Keen and Mewborn, *43rd Battalion*, p. 55; Chapman, "Memories of 'Mosby's Men,'" in Mewborn, "*From Mosby's Command*," p. 95. Henderson, *Autobiography of Arab*, p. 88. Chapman recalled that Mosby issued the order to burn the house just after the four men got inside, and that the timing convinced the men to surrender quickly.

12. Henderson, *Autobiography of Arab*, pp. 88–89; Chapman, "Memories of 'Mosby's Men,'" in Mewborn, "*From Mosby's Command*," pp. 95–96.

13. Henderson, *Autobiography of Arab*, p. 90; Jackson Letter in Bush, *Articles From Wyoming County Newspapers*, p. 93; Benedict, *Army Life in Virginia*, p. 142; Scott, *PL*, p. 86; *OR*: 25:2:860. Edwin Havens, who was stationed at Warrenton Junction as of May 4, stated that the New Yorkers were camped "about 50 rods" away, or less than 1000 feet, but this seems unlikely. See Edwin Havens to Our Dear Folks, Warrenton Junction, May 5, 1863, Havens Letters, MSU. Boudrye in his history of the 5th New York denies that the 1st Vermont played any role in this fight, but the weight of evidence suggests otherwise.

14. Jackson Letter in Bush, *Articles From Wyoming County Newspapers*, p. 93; John W. Munson, *Reminiscences of a Mosby Guerrilla* (New York, 1906), pp. 66–67; Boudrye, *Historic Records of the Fifth New York Cavalry*, p. 55; Edwin Havens to Our Dear Folks, Warrenton Junction, May 5, 1863, Havens Letters, MSU; New York *Herald*, May 7, 1863; Chapman, "Memories of 'Mosby's Men,'" in Mewborn, "*From Mosby's Command*," p. 96; Abram Krom's Compiled Service and Pension Records, RG 94, NARA.

15. Chapman, "Memories of 'Mosby's Men,'" in Mewborn, "*From Mosby's Command*," p. 96; Keen and Mewborn, *43rd Battalion*, p. 55; P.C. to Editor, Alexandria, Virginia, May 12, 1863, New York *Sunday Mercury*, May 17, 1863, in William B. Styple, *Writing and Fighting the Civil War: Soldier Correspondence to the New York Sunday Mercury* (Kearny, 2000), p. 190.

16. Chapman, "Memories of 'Mosby's Men,'" in Mewborn, "*From Mosby's Command*," p. 96; Keen and Mewborn, *43rd Battalion*, p. 55; P.C. to Editor, Alexandria, Virginia, May 12, 1863, New York *Sunday Mercury*, May 17, 1863, in Styple, *Writing and Fighting the Civil War*, p. 190; Benedict, *Army Life in Virginia*, pp. 143–144; Roswell Farnham to My Dear Wife, Warrenton Junction, May 4, 1863, Farnham Letters, UV.

17. New York *Herald*, May 7, 1863; William Martin to Dear Wife, Fairfax, May 4, 1863, Martin Letters, USAMHI; Edwin Havens to Our Dear Folks, Warrenton Junction, May 5, 1863, Havens Letters, MSU; Edwin Hall to Dear Father, Union Mills, Virginia, May 6, 1863, Hall Letters, VHS; Gen. Stahel to *Tribune* Room, Washington and Stahel to *Herald* Room, Washington, May 3, 1863, RG 107, M504, and John Krepps and William McCoy's Compiled Service Records, RG 94, M508, as well as McCoy's Pension Record, NARA; Roswell Farnham to My Dear Wife, Warrenton Junction, May 4, 1863, Farnham Letters, UV.

18. New York *Herald*, May 7, 1863; William Martin to Dear Wife, Fairfax, May 4, 1863, Martin Letters, USAMHI; Edwin Havens to Our Dear Folks, Warrenton Junction, May 5, 1863, Havens Letters, MSU; Gen. Stahel to *Tribune* Room, Washington and Stahel to *Herald* Room, Washington, May 3, 1863, RG 107, M504, and John Krepps and William McCoy's Compiled Service Records, RG 94, M508, as well as McCoy's Pension Record, NARA.

19. Edwin Havens to Our Dear Folks, Warrenton Junction, May 5, 1863, Havens Letters, MSU.

20. Scott, *Partisan Life*, p. 88; Chapman, "Memories of 'Mosby's Men,'" in Mewborn, "*From Mosby's Command*," p. 96; Mohr, *The Cormany Diaries*, p. 310; *OR*: 25:2: 860–861; Mosby, *MWR*, pp. 133–135.

21. Baird, *Journals of Amanda Virginia Edmonds*, pp. 142–145.

22. Lt. Thomas Kennedy to Gen. Hays, May 3, 1863, RG 107, M504, also Gen. Heintzelman to Gen. Stahel and Maj. Hunt to Gen. Abercrombie, May 3, 1863, RG 393, Part 1, Entry 5379, NARA; Stacy Diary, NC; Benedict, *Army Life in Virginia*, p. 147; Heintzelman Journal, LC; J. N. Brown to Editor, Centreville, May 6, 1863, *RDA*, May 13, 1863.

23. *OR*: 51:1:1037; Capt. Slipper to Gen. Stannard, Stannard to Gen. Abercrombie, Stannard to Lord and Stannard to Col. Blunt, May 5, 1863, RG 107, M504, and Gen. Heintzelman to Gen. Stahel, May 5, 1863, RG 393, Part 1, Entry 5379, NARA; Roswell Farnham to Dear Mary, Warrenton Junction,

May 5, 1863, Farnham Letters, UV. The bridge at Rappahannock Station was in a state of disrepair and unable to carry rail traffic, but the Federals did not need to take trains across the river. They wanted to insure that Southern cavalry did not use the bridge as an avenue of attack. See Roswell Farnham to My Dear Wife, Rappahannock Bridge, May 11, 1863, Farnham Papers, UV. As the size of the security force along the railroad increased so to the number of trains increased. This is suggested by a request made by General Stannard to the Assistant Superintendent of the railroad on the fifth in which he asked that one car be sent with supplies to the 12th Vermont below Warrenton Junction, and that seven cars be dispatched with supplies and forage for the 7th Michigan Cavalry. Stannard also asked that one platform car be left with Farnham's detachment of the 12th Vermont, to assist in shuttling timber for the construction of blockhouses. The official refused to leave a car for any period within the disputed area, but told Stannard that once he had the timber cut and ready for transport that he would send a train to move it. This information is noted in the sources listed above.

24. Gen. Stannard to Col. Blunt, Stannard to Abercrombie, Stannard to F. P. Lord, and Capt. Hazard to Lord, May 6, 1863, RG 107, M504, also Gen. Heintzelman to Gen. Stahel, and Capt. Potter to Col. Jewett, May 6, 1863, RG 393, Part 1, Entry 5379, NARA; Roswell Farnham to Dear Mary, Warrenton Junction, May 6, 1863, Farnham Letters, UV; Heintzelman Journal, LC; Edward Clark to My Dear Wife, In camp on the shore of the "Rappahannock," May 8, 1863, Clark Letters, Missouri Historical Society.

25. Allyne Litchfield to Dear Wife, Warrenton Junction, May 5, 1863, Litchfield Letters, UMCL; Gen. Stahel to Gen. Heintzelman, May 3, 1863, RG 107, M504, NARA.

26. Edwin Havens to Our Dear Folks, Warrenton Junction, May 8, 1863, Havens Letters, MSU.

27. Gen. Stahel to Gen. Heintzelman, May 8, 1863 and Capt. McMasters to Col. DeForest, May 8, 1863, RG 107, M504, NARA; Boudrye, *Historic Records of the Fifth New York Cavalry*, p. 57; Stiles, *4th Virginia Cavalry*, pp. 27, 136. The captured trooper was John Dowd, though his capture is not mentioned in the regimental roster. The soldier who drowned was Sgt. Michael Murphy.

28. Roswell Farnham to My Dear Wife, Rappahannock Bridge, May 8, 1863, Farnham Letters, UV; Gen. Butterfield to Gen. Pleasonton, May 7, 1863, RG 393, Part 1, Entry 3964, and Gen. Abercrombie to Gen. Stannard, May 7, 1863, RG 107, M504, NARA.

29. *OR*: 25:2:440,450; Capt. Potter to Gen. Stahel, Stahel to Col. DeForest and Gen. Stannard to Capt. Slipper, May 8, 1863, RG 107, M504, and Potter to Stahel, May 8, 1863, RG 393, Part 1, Entry 5379, NARA. Some of the first news of Stoneman's Raid came from Gen. Stoughton who was still in Richmond at the time, but was exchanged and returned to Washington prior to Stoneman rejoining the army. Abercrombie sent four companies of the 13th Vermont Infantry to aid DeForest's cavalry.

30. Gen. Stahel to Col. DeForest, May 9, 1863, RG107, M504, NARA; Edwin Havens to Our Folks, Warrenton Junction, May 13, 1863, Havens Letters, MSU; Allyne Litchfield to My Dear Wife, May 9, 1863, Litchfield Letters, UMCL.

31. Special Order Number 78, May 9, 1863, 1st Vermont Cavalry Letter and Order Books, RG 94, NARA.

Chapter 17

1. Gen. Stahel to Lt. Col. Lathrop, May 10, 1863, RG 107, M504, NARA.

2. Mosby, *MWR*, p. 137; Scott, *PL*, p. 89; Hugh Henry to Dear Mother, Union Mills, May 15, 1863, Hugh Henry Letters, UV; *OR*: 25:2:861. Mosby may be the only period source for claims that a train derailed. However, in an undated telegram that appears to refer to this incident, Herman Haupt informed Hooker that attempts were made to burn three bridges, "rails loosened and ties piled on track but we lost but one car." This is not confirmed by the men who were on the train. See Haupt to Hooker, no date, RG 107, M504, NARA.

3. Hugh Henry to Dear Mother, Union Mills, May 15, 1863, Henry Letters, UV.

4. OR: 25:2:861; Scott, *PL*, p. 89; Ramage, *Gray Ghost*, p. 84. An extensive search was made of the records for the military railroad, specifically the Orange and Alexandria Railroad for the month of May 1863 in an attempt to verify this claim. This included train registers, as well as construction and bridge repair logs and nothing was found to support Mosby's claim, nor is there mention of guerrilla activity in general. The most promising collection is RG 92, Entry 1581, Conductor Reports, but the massive size of this collection as well as the fact that it is completely unarranged as to date and railroad has, so far, prevented the locating of the pertinent reports. In Superintendent Devereux's report for the period of January to July 1863 (RG 92, Entry 1528) he mentions that a total of four engines were damaged "by raids or the effect of rail-ripping," during the first half of the year, only one of which can be attributed with certainty to Mosby.

5. Gen. Stahel to Col. DeForest, May 10, 1863, Gen. Stannard to Lt. Slipper, May 11, 1863, Stannard to Cols. Blunt and Proctor, May 11, 1863, Gen. Heintzelman to Gen. Abercrombie, forwarded to Stannard, May 11, 1863, RG 107, M504, also Lt. Col. Lathrop to Abercrombie, Heintzelman to Stahel, and Heintzelman to Gen. Hooker, May 11, 1863, RG 393, Part 1, Entry 5379, NARA; Heintzelman Journal, LC.

6. Capt. Potter to Gen. Stahel and Stahel to Col. DeForest, May 11, 1863, RG 107, M504, NARA.

7. Allyne Litchfield to My Dear Wife, Warrenton Junction, May 11, 1863, Litchfield Letters, UMCL.

8. Edwin Havens to Our Folks, Warrenton Junction, May 13, 1863, Havens Letters, MSU.

9. Allyne Litchfield to Dear Wife, Warrenton Junction, May 13, 1863, Litchfield Letters, UMCL; Edwin Havens to Our Folks, Warrenton Junction, May 13, 1863, Havens Letters, MSU.

10. Richard E. Crouch, "The Mobberly Mysteries: The Strange Life and Death of Loudoun County's Exceedingly Romantic Bastard (?) / Hero (?)," *Civil War Quarterly*, volume 7, 1986, pp. 32, 38; John E. Divine, *35th Battalion Virginia Cavalry* (Lynchburg, 1985), p. 99; Keen and Mewborn, *43rd Battalion*, p. 349; John Divine, Bronwen Souders and John Souders, editors, *"To Talk is Treason": Quakers of Waterford, Virginia on Life, Love, Death & War in the Southern Confederacy* (Waterford, 1996), p. 79; Gen. B. F. Kelley to Lt. Col. Chesebrough, no date, RG 107, M504, NARA.

11. Gen. Morris to Lt. Col. Chesebrough, May 11, 1863, Gen. Schenck to Gen. Milroy, May 12, 1863 and Chesebrough to Morris, May 12, 1863, RG 107, M504, also the 1860 Virginia Census, NARA; *OR*: 25:2:472, 475; *NYT*, May 14, 1863.

12. *OR*: 25:2:1107–1108.

13. *OR*: 25:2:1108. I have relied on the official report for this description as it was written the same day that Boyd returned. Both regimental histories (Stevenson and Beach) suggest that this affair took only two days, with the skirmishing around Upperville taking place on the 13th. Stevenson, in his account, pp, 169–170, goes out of his way to place Mosby directly in the fighting around Upperville and credits him with killing one of the horses with a pistol shot, but no Southern accounts place Mosby at the scene.

14. Myers, *The Comanches*, pp. 155–156.

15. Col. Jewett to Capt. Potter, Potter to Jewett, and Gen. Stahel to Potter, May 13, 1863, RG 107, M504, also Potter to Stahel, May 13, 1863, RG 393, Part 1, Entry 5379, NARA; *OR*; 51:1:1041; *NYT*, May 16, 1863.

16. Gen. Stahel to Capt. Potter, May 13, 1863, RG 107, M504, and Potter to Stahel, May 13, 1863, RG 393, Part 1, Entry 5379, NARA.

17. *OR*: 25:2:469,474–475, 480; Gen. Buford to Col. Alexander, Deep Run, May 12, 1863, RG 393, Part 2, Entry 1449, NARA; Samuel L. Gracey, *Annals of the Sixth Pennsylvania Cavalry* (Lancaster, 1996 edition), p. 153.

18. *OR*: 25:2:468–469, 474–475, 513; Frank Dickerson to Dear Father, Brooks Station, Virginia, May 23, 1863, Frank Dickerson Papers, Civil War Miscellaneous Collection, US AMHI; Gen. Sickles to the Sec. of War, May 17, 1863, Pleasonton's Commission Branch File, RG 94, M1064, NARA.

19. Darius Maynard to My Dear Nell, Fairfax Court House, May 12, 1863, Maynard Letters, WSU. Emphasis in the original.

20. Victor Comte to Dear Elise, Cavalry Outpost, May 12, 1863, Comte Letters, UMBL.

21. Ebenezer Gould to Dear Brother, Fairfax Court House, May 12, 1863, Gould Letters, CMU.

22. Ebenezer Gould to Dear Brother, Fairfax Court House, May 12, 1863, Gould Letters, CMU; Gen. Copeland to Gen. Heintzelman, Washington, D.C., February 23, 1863, Norvell Freeman's Compiled Service Record, RG 94, NARA. Companies F and M of the 1st Vermont remained in Fairfax County when the remainder of the regiment moved to Prince William County.

23. Ebenezer Gould to Dear Brother, Fairfax Court House, April 19, 1863, Gould Letters, CMU; Gould to Gov. Blair, April 28, 1863, Blair Papers, DPL. Emphasis in the original.

24. Ebenezer Gould to Dear Brother, Fairfax Court House, April 26, 1863, and Ebenezer Gould to Dear Brother, Fairfax Court House, May 3, 1863, Gould Letters, CMU; Gen. Pleasonton to Gov. Blair, including Gen. Hooker's endorsement, May 30, 1863, Gen. Stahel to Gov. Blair, including Gen. Heintzelman's endorsement, Fairfax Court House, April 20, 1863, and Petition to Blair, Fairfax Court House, May 5, 1863, Blair Papers, DPL; Gen. Copeland to John Robertson, Fairfax Court House, May 9, 1863, Regimental Service Records, 5th Michigan Cavalry, Box 121, SAM. In their petition the officers referred to the disastrous expedition to Falmouth and without naming Wyndham directly, they cited him, erroneously, as being a regular army officer and wanted no part of another. For references to Gould's political position see undated petition from ten citizens to Blair, as well as Gould to Hon. A. Gould, Fairfax Court House, March 29, 1863, Blair Papers, DPL. For a detailed account of the February expedition, including the actions taken by Ferry and the inaction of Gould see Noah Ferry to Dear Bro, Camp Copeland, February 13, 1863, Blair Papers, DPL.

25. Kidd, *Personal Recollections of a Cavalryman*, p. 54; Aaron T. Bliss, *Record of Service of Michigan Volunteers in the Civil War, 1861–1865: Sixth Michigan Cavalry* (Kalamazoo, 1905), p. 14; Russell Alger to Governor Austin Blair, Corinth, Mississippi, July 21, 1862 and Alger to Blair, Grand Rapids, Michigan, August 7, 1862, Blair Papers, DPL.

26. Russell Alger to Governor Blair, January 8, 1863, Washington, Alger to Blair, May 4, 1863, Freedom Hill, and Alger to Blair, June 15, 1863, Fairfax Court House, Blair Papers, DPL.

27. Alfred Ryder to Dear Father, Fairfax Court House, April 18, 1863, Ryder Letters, UMBL; Col. Town to Maj. Baldwin, Fairfax Court House, May 14, 1863, 1st Michigan Cavalry Letter and Order Books, RG 94, NA. Emphasis in the original.

Chapter 18

1. Edwin Havens to Dear Nell, Warrenton Junction, May 16, 1863, Havens Letters, MSU; Allyne Litchfield to Dear Wife, Near Warrenton, May 15, 1863, Litchfield Letters, UMCL; *OR*: 25:1:1109; Isham, *An Historical Sketch*, pp. 18–19; Asa Isham, "The Story of a Gunshot Wound," *Sketches of War History 1861–1865, Papers Prepared for the Ohio Commandery of the Military Order of the Loyal Legion of the United States 1890–1896* (Wilmington edition, 1991), volume 4, p. 429.

2. Isham, *An Historical Sketch*, pp. 18–19; Asa Isham, "The Story of a Gunshot Wound," p. 429.

3. Henderson, *Autobiography of Arab*, pp. 80, 93; *OR*: 33: 267–268; Capt. James Long to Sir, Catlett Station, April 12, 1864, RG 94, M1064, NARA; Timothy J. Reese, *Sykes' Regular Infantry Division, 1861–1864: A History of Regular United States Infantry Operations in the Civil War's Eastern Theater* (Jefferson, NC, 1990), pp. 295–296. Several members of the Marsteller family lived near Nokesville. The 1860 and 1870 Census records help but do not entirely clarify where this occurred. Arrelton or Arelton was a family home owned by Philip Marsteller, who would have been 62 in May 1863. He had two daughters and two sons. The 1870 Census shows LeClaire A. Marsteller, then 30, as the head of household with two other adults then in their fifties, living next door to Margaret Marsteller, then 37 who had three other women in the house then aged 21, 19 and 18. A similar incident occurred at the home in April 1864, when several Union officers approached the home to visit the daughters. They were attacked from ambush and one officer was killed and two captured.

4. Report of Surgeon E. Donnelly, Alexander McClain's Compiled Service Record, RG 94, NARA; Lee, *Personal and Historical Sketches*, pp. 129–132. In 1894 Isham sought a Medal of Honor for this incident. The award was denied, but in his explanation of the events Isham stated that they approached the house with the intention of searching for concealed weapons — see Isham to Daniel Lamont, Cincinnati, November 24, 1894, RG 94, Entry 496, NARA. According to Litchfield, McCain was shot in the back near the spine while attempting to flee. One of the other men was shot in the corner of his mouth, with the "ball literally cutting his throat and coming out the back of his neck, laying it open all the way round,," see Litchfield to Dear Wife, Near Warrenton, May 15, 1863. Though Litchfield does not identify this soldier, it was most likely Aaron Kitchen. One of the men who may have frequented the home was Colonel Mann. One month after this incident an unnamed "soldier" from the regiment wrote an inflammatory letter to Michigan governor Austin Blair. The soldier was particularly upset with the conduct of the regimental officers, including the colonel. He accused Mann of being at "ease with wine and women" and, without including any names, dates or locations, he spoke of a situation in which Mann was holding "a Rebel prisoner of a confessed Rebel family the rest all in the Rebel army." When the prisoner's sister rode into camp she met with Mann and "after a short conference he put the prisoner on a horse and let him go and he [Mann] mounted his own steed and rode off with the [sister]. Governor Blair sought to investigate the soldier's complaints further and he asked Lt. Colonel Litchfield for his views on the grievances. Litchfield was equally concerned about the manner in which the colonel comported himself and wrote a rather damning letter in reply. Though he disabused the claim that Mann was intemperate, he confirmed that Mann was a womanizer. "All that is said about women in connection with the Col is true the [Marstella] case was a very [aggravating] one and caused some words between the Col & myself," see A Soldier to Governor Austin Blair, Fairfax, Virginia, June 12, 1863 and Lt. Col. Allyne Litchfield to Blair, Boonsboro, Maryland, July 9, 1863, Blair Papers, DPL. No further particulars related to this incident have been found but it seems reasonable that the young women of the family were comfortable luring foolish Union soldiers into a situation in which they were easily ambushed.

5. Lee, *Personal and Historical Sketches*, pp. 129–132; Edwin Havens to Dear Nell, Warrenton Junction, May 16, 1863, Havens Letters, MSU; Allyne Litchfield to Dear Wife, Near Warrenton, May 15, 1863, Litchfield Letters, UMCL. Walden Raymond, who held the rank of corporal at the time, may have been the trooper who killed the member of the Marsteller family in the bushes, see Lee, p. 209, where Raymond claimed the distinction "of being the first member of the Regiment to down a Rebel, which took place at the Marstella Farm."

6. William O'Brien to Dear Mother, Warrenton Junction, May 1863, O'Brien Family Letters, UMBL; Surgeon Donnelly's Report, McClain Compiled Service Record, RG 94, NARA; Letter from Asa Isham, Washington, D.C., June 28, 1863, *DAT*, July 3, 1863; Edwin Havens to Dear Nell, Warrenton Junction, May 16, 1863, Havens Letters, MSU; Allyne Litchfield to Dear Wife, May 15, 1863, Litchfield Letters, UMCL. The previously transcribed copy of the O'Brien letter carries a date of May 11,

1863, suggesting that it was misdated either by O'Brien or the person who transcribed it, or he started the letter on one date and continued it after this incident, which was not uncommon.

7. Edwin Havens to Dear Nell, Warrenton Junction, May 16, 1863, Havens Letters, MSU. Several Marstellers were enlisted in the 4th Virginia Cavalry.

8. Benedict, *Vermont in the Civil War*, volume 2, pp. 435–436; Palmer, *The Second Brigade*, p. 155; Sturtevant, *Pictorial History*, p. 167; J.B. Chamberlin to Dear Father & Mother, Camp Carusi, May 16, 1863, Chamberlin Letters, UV; Gen. Abercrombie to Lt. Col. Lathrop, May 15, 1863, RG 107, M504, NARA; *OR*: 25:2:499.

9. *OR*: 25:1: 138, 145; Gen. Morris to Gen. Schenck, Schenck to Gen. Milroy and Lt. Col. Chesebrough to Morris, May 16, 1863, also Schenck to Gen. Kelley and Milroy to Schenck, May 17, 1863, RG 107, M504, NARA; *PI*, May 25, 1863; Armstrong, *7th Virginia Cavalry*, p. 52; Beach, *The First New York (Lincoln) Cavalry*, pp. 225–226.

10. *PI*, June 5, 1863, in Mewborn, "*From Mosby's Command*," p. 21; Mosby, *MWR*, p. 137; Scott, *PL*, p. 90; *OR*: 25:2: 861.

11. Maj. Claude White to Lt. Col. Alexander, Dumfries, May 21, 1863, RG 393, Part 2, Entry 1449, and Col. Gregg to Col. Blake, May 2, 1863, Blake to Gen. Williams, May 3, 1863, Blake to Capt. Cohen, May 9, 1863, RG 107, M504, NARA. Emphasis in original.

12. Maj. Claude White to Lt. Col. Alexander, Dumfries, May 21, 1863, RG 393, Part 2, Entry 1449, NARA.

13. Maj. Claude White to Lt. Col. Alexander, Dumfries, May 21, 1863, RG 393, Part 2, Entry 1449, NARA; Keen and Mewborn, *43rd Battalion*, pp. 58–59;

14. Mosby, *MWR*, pp. 137–138; Maj. White to Lt. Col. Alexander, Dumfries, May 21, 1863, RG 393, Part 2, Entry 1449, NARA.

15. Col. Mann to Gen. Stahel, May 19, 1863, RG 107, M504, NARA; Allyne Litchfield to My Dear Wife, Kettle Run, May 19, 1863, Litchfield Letters, UMCL; *OR*: 25:2:511. Emphasis in original.

16. *OR*: 25:2:493, 498; Col. Kielmansegge to Gen. Gregg, May 18, 1863, RG 393, Part 2, Entry 1449, NARA.

17. *OR*: 25:2:499–500, 503–506.

18. Gen. Stannard to John Devereux, May 17, 1863 and Stannard to Gen. Abercrombie, May 18, 1863, RG 107, M504, NARA; Silas Mason to Respected Mother, Bristoe Station, May 18, 1863, Mason Letters, NYSLA.

19. Crandell Diary, NC; Heintzelman Journal, and Willard Family Papers, Orders dated May 11 and May 20, 1863 LC; Maj. Williams to Col. Lathrop, May 20, 1863, RG 393, Part 1, Entry 5383, and Capt. Potter to Gen. Slough, May 24, 1863, RG 393, Part 1, Entry 5379, NARA; *OR*: 25: 2: 515,517; Ramage, *Gray Ghost*, p. 177; Roswell Farnham to My Dear Wife, Bristoe Station, May 26, 1863, Farnham Letters, UV; Noah Brooks, *Washington in Lincoln's Time* (New York, 1895), p. 58; Darius Maynard to My Dear Nell, Fairfax Court House, May 24, 1863, Maynard Letters, WSU. Though Mosby is often linked with the order for the planks of the bridge to be removed, there is no mention of Mosby's name in any of the official references — those being the orders cited here and one dated July 6, 1864 relative to Gen. Jubal Early's advance on Washington, see *OR*: 37:2:83. An editorial in the *NYT* of May 28, 1863 also attributes the order solely to the expected raid, making no mention of John Mosby. James Kidd links the order to "a projected invasion by Stewart," without reference to Mosby, even though he was posted along the picket line, see James Kidd to Dear Mother and Father, June 1, 1863, Kidd Letters, UMBL. The size of the force alone cited by Heintzelman suggests that it was not a guerrilla raid that gave rise to the order. A brief item in the Alexandria *Gazette* of May 27, 1863 does connect both Stuart and Mosby to the suspected raid but makes no mention of the bridges across the Potomac. Gen. Hooker would later link the removal of the planks to Mosby in his testimony before the Joint Committee on the Conduct of the War in early 1864, though the actual reason, as stated at the time, was a matter beyond his official purview in the spring of 1863, see U. S. Congress, *Report of the Joint Committee on the Conduct of the War*, 9 volumes (Wilmington edition, 1999), volume 4, pp. 162–163. Though he was aware of the possibility of a raid there is no evidence that he was consulted with in reference to the actions taken by Heintzelman. Still, his comments remain unchallenged, when, in fact, there appears to be no official basis for his assertion.

20. Col. Mann to Maj. Harvey Baldwin, May 21, 1863, 7th Michigan Regimental Letter and Order Books, RG 94, NARA; Allyne Litchfield to My Dear Wife, Bristoe Station, May 24, 1863, Litchfield Letters, UMCL; Edwin Havens to Brother Nell, Kettle Run, May 25, 1863, Havens Letters, MSU.

21. Allyne Litchfield to My Dear Wife, Bristoe Station, May 24, 1863, Litchfield Letters, UMCL; Edwin Havens to Brother Nell, Kettle Run, May 25, 1863, Havens Letters, MSU; Roswell Farnham to My Dear Wife, Bristoe Station, May 24, 1863, Farnham Letters, UV; Stiles, *4th Virginia Cavalry*, p. 141; *OR*: 25:2:519; *PI*, June 5, 1863 in Mewborn, "*From Mosby's Command*," p. 22. Though Havens believed that the Confederates belonged to the Black Horse, their identity is unclear. Neither he nor Litchfield mention that any prisoners were taken on the twenty-third, but the roster of the 4th Virginia reflects that James Waddle was captured that day near Warrenton.

22. Heintzelman Journal, LC; Capt. Potter to Gen. Stahel, May 24, 1863, RG 107, M504, NARA; *OR*: 25:2:513–514; Allyne Litchfield to My Dear Wife, Kettle Run, May 26, 1863, Litchfield Letters, UMCL.

23. Julia Wheelock, *The Boys in White: The Experience of a Hospital Agent in and Around Washington* (New York, 1870), p. 100.

24. *OR*: 25:2:819; Gen. Stahel to Lt. Col. Lathrop, May 26, 1863, RG 107, M504, NARA.

25. William Martin to Mr. James Davidson, Camp Fairfax, May 26, 1863, Martin Letters, USAMHI; *OR*: 25:2:519, 566; Gen. Stahel to Lt. Col. Lathrop, May 26, 1863, RG 107, M504, and Stahel to Lathrop, May 26, 1863, RG 393, Part 2, Entry 732, Letters and Telegrams Sent by Stahel's Cavalry Division, NARA.

26. Gen. Stahel to Capt. Potter, May 27, 1863, RG 107, M504, NARA.

27. *OR*: 25:2:514–516, 521–522, 524–525; Gen. John Buford to Capt. Andrew Cohen, May 27, 1863, RG 393, Part 2, Entry 1449, NARA.

28. Gen. Stahel to Capt. Potter, May 27, 1863, RG 107, M504, NARA.

29. Allyne Litchfield to My Dear Wife, Kettle Run, Virginia, May 26, 1863, and Litchfield to My Dear Wife, Bristoe, Virginia, May 29, 1863, Litchfield Letters, UMCL; Edwin Havens to Brother Nell, Bristoe Station, Virginia, May 31, 1863, Havens Letters, MSU; William O'Brien to Dear Brother, Bristoe Station, Virginia, May 30, 1863, O'Brien Letters, UMBL; *OR*: 25:2: 528; Col. William Mann to Maj. Harvey Baldwin, May 27, 1863, RG 107, M504, NARA.

30. Edwin Havens to Brother Nell, Bristoe Station, Virginia, May 31, 1863, Havens Letters, MSU; Allyne Litchfield to My Dear Wife, Bristoe, May 29, 1863, Litchfield Letters, UMCL; William O'Brien to Dear Brother, Bristoe Station, Virginia, May 30, 1863, O'Brien Letters, UMBL; Rutland *Herald*, June 4, 1863; *OR*: 51:1:1042.

31. Gen. Stahel to Gen. Heintzelman, May 3, 1863, and Stahel to Lt. Col. Lathrop, May 26, 1863, RG 107, M504, NARA; *OR*: 25:2: 862.

32. Edwin Havens to Brother Nell, Bristoe Station, May 31, 1863, Havens Letters, MSU; Hoskins Diary, *PI*, June 5, 1863, in Mewborn, "From Mosby's Command," p. 22; Robert J. Trout, *They Followed the Plume: The Story of J.E.B. Stuart and His Staff* (Mechanicsburg, 1993), pp. 102–114. An item in the *NYT*, June 1, 1863 identified "Capt. Farley" as a member "of Gen. Stuart's staff." William Farley, often referred to as "Will," was mortally wounded at Brandy Station on June 9, 1863. Henry served with Stuart through September 1863.

Chapter 19

1. Col. Mann to Maj. Harvey Baldwin, and Gen. Buford to Capt. Cohen, May 27, 1863, RG 107, M504, also Capt. Potter to Gen. Stahel, RG 393, Part 1, Entry 5379, and RG 92, Entry 1584, Northern Virginia Miscellaneous, Bridge Repair Logs 1863–64, May 27, 1863, NARA; *OR*: 25:1:144.

2. Gen. Gregg to Capt. Cohen, May 28, 1863, RG 107, M504, NARA; *OR*: 25:2:536–537.

3. *OR*: 25:2:533–534, 538.

4. *OR*: 25:2:538, 543; Gen. Buford to Gen. Seth Williams, Buford to Capt. Cohen, and Buford to Col. Daniel Rucker, May 28, 1863, RG 107, M504, NARA.

5. *OR*: 25:2:535–536, 542–543.

6. Gen. Stahel to Gen. Hooker, May 28, 1863, RG 393, Part 2, Entry 732, NARA.

7. *NYT*, May 28, 1863; Hebert, *Fighting Joe Hooker*, p. 233.

8. William Rockwell to My Dear Wife, Cavalry Headquarters, May 28, 1863, Rockwell Letters, WMU.

9. Major Luther Trowbridge to Colonel, Camp of Cavalry Outposts, May 28, 1863, RG 94, Musters Rolls, Returns and Regimental Papers, 6th Michigan Cavalry, NARA.

10. Heintzelman Journal, LC.

11. *OR*: 25:2:566; Gen Stahel to Gen. Heintzelman, May 29, 1863, RG 107, M504, and Heintzelman to Stahel, May 29, 1863, RG 393, Part 1, Entry 5379, NARA.

12. Edwin Havens to Brother Nell, Bristoe Station, May 31, 1863, Havens Letters, MSU; Lee, *Personal and Historical Sketches*, pp. 91–92.

13. Mosby, *MWR*, p. 142; Chapman, "Memories of "Mosby's Men," *Religious Herald*, February 6, 1902, in Mewborn, "*From Mosby's Command*," p. 97–98; Scott, *PL*, p. 92. Scott is the only reference to the men spending the night near Marsteller's. The other accounts are much more vague. None of the Mosby accounts mention that he scouted the line that evening. Several Union accounts credit Mosby with two howitzers but they are incorrect.

14. Alexandria *Gazette*, June 1, 1863; Benedict, *Vermont in the Civil War*, volume 2, p. 436; Edwin Hall to Dear Father, Union Mills, May 31, 1863, Hall Letters, VHS; General Stannard's report, May 31, 1863, RG 393, Part 2, Entry 6833, Letters Sent, December 1862 to June 1863, Defenses of Washington, Stoughton, Casey and Abercrombie, and RG 92, Entry 1584, Entry for May 30, 1863, NARA; Russell, *Gray Ghost, The Memoirs of Colonel John S. Mosby*, p. 152; Scott, *PL*, p. 92. Mosby stated that it was a train of 12 cars. Reasonable estimates of the size of the guard force vary between 25 and 50, with Stannard putting it at 25. Scott used a badly inflated estimate of 200 men.

15. Mosby, *MWR*, p. 143; Munson, *Reminiscences of a Mosby Guerrilla*, p. 68. General Buford estimated that the wire was cut at 7:30 that morning — see *OR*: 25:2:571.

16. Edwin Havens to Brother Nell, Bristoe Station, May 31, 1863, Havens Letters, MSU; Allyne Litchfield to My Dear Wife, Bristoe Station, May 31, 1863, Litchfield Letters, UMCL; General Stannard's report, RG 393, Part 2, Entry 6833, NARA. In a postwar letter to John Munson, Elmer Barker, 5th NY, confirmed Havens's account that the train stopped at their camp. See Munson, *Reminiscences of a Mosby Guerrilla*, p. 71. Reports of the time when the first shot was fired vary from near eight o'clock to ten thirty. Havens wrote an account in later life in which he stated that he was examining the spot where the shooting had occurred earlier and that he watched the train go by and that it was still in view when it derailed. See Lee, *Personal and Historical Sketches*, p. 92.

17. Alexandria *Gazette*, June 1, 1863; Mosby, *MWR*, p. 144; Chapman, in Mewborn, "*From Mosby's Command*," p. 99; Scott Laughlin to Dear Friend John, Catlett Station, June 13, 1863, in the John S. T. Wallace Letters, VHS. Ranger John Munson also states that the train came to a stop without derailing but he was not present.

18. Chapman, in Mewborn, "*From Mosby's Command*," p. 99; Scott Laughlin to Dear Friend John, Catlett Station, June 13, 1863, Wallace Letters, and Edwin Hall to Dear Father, Union Mills, May 31, 1863, Hall Letters, VHS; Nelson Rogers to Dear Friend Mrs. Farnham, Union Mills, May 31, 1863, Farnham Letters and George Hagar to Dear Sarah, Union Mills, May 31, 1863, George Hagar Letters, UV; Heintzelman Journal, LC; RG 92, Entry 1571, Train Registers, Union Mills & Brandy Station volume, NARA. A Court of Inquiry was impaneled and a hearing was held to investigate Hartshorn's conduct at his own insistence. Col. Farnham was the president of the panel and he makes several references to the hearing in his letters home. In his letter of June 10, he mentions that the panel had just concluded examining witnesses, including a visit to the hospital to interview the young boy whose leg was broken, but that is his last mention of the court, as other events appear to take precedence. See Farnham to My Dear Mary, June 10, 1863, Union Mills, Farnham Letters, UV. The findings were approved as of June 18 — see RG 393, Part II, Entry 6834 reference the court being impaneled and RG 393, Part II, Entry 659, reference it being impaneled at Hartshorn's insistence as well as the findings being approved. To date I have been unable to find the records of the court to determine the findings. Emphasis in the original.

19. General Stannard's report, RG 393, Part 2, Entry 6833, NARA. Edward Clark, 12th Vermont, also concluded that Mosby had two howitzers, see Edward Clark to My Dear Mary, Union Mills, May 31, 1863, Clark Papers, Missouri Historical Society.

20. *OR*: 3:2:709–710; Chapman, in Mewborn, "*From Mosby's Command*," p. 99; General Stannard's report, RG 393, Part 2, Entry 6833, NARA.

21. John Jackson to Dear Editor, Fairfax Court House, June 4, 1863, Wyoming *County Mirror*, June 10, 1863, in Bush, *Articles From Wyoming County Newspapers*, p. 93; Munson, *Reminiscences of a Mosby Guerrilla*, p. 71; Ide, *History of the First Vermont Cavalry*, p. 101; Allyne Litchfield to My Dear Wife, Bristoe Station, May 31, 1863, Litchfield Letters, UMCL; Edwin Havens to Brother Nell, Bristoe Station, May 31, 1863, Havens Letters, MSU; Mosby, *MWR*, p. 147; *OR*: 25:1:1117; General Stannard's report, RG 393, Part 2, Entry 6833, NARA.

22. Ide, *History of the First Vermont Cavalry*, p. 101; *NYT*, June 5, 1863; Jackson Letter in Bush, *Articles From Wyoming County Newspapers*, pp. 93–94; Mosby, *MWR*, p. 146.

23. Munson, *Reminiscences of a Mosby Guerrilla*, p. 72; Allyne Litchfield to My Dear Wife, May 31, 1863, Litchfield Letters, UMCL; Boudrye, *Historic Records of the Fifth New York Cavalry*, p. 59

24. Munson, *Reminiscences of a Mosby Guerrilla*, pp. 72–73; Joseph Worster and George Jenkins Pension Files, RG 94, NARA; Jackson Letter in Bush, *Articles From Wyoming County Newspapers*, p. 94; Mosby, *MWR*, pp. 147–148.

25. Mosby, *MWR*, p. 148; Chapman in Mewborn, "*From Mosby's Command*," pp. 99–100; Jackson in Bush, *Articles from Wyoming County Newspapers*, p. 94.

26. Munson, *Reminiscences of a Mosby Guerrilla*, p. 73; Jackson Letter in Bush, *Articles From Wyoming County Newspapers*, p. 94; Ide, *History of the First Vermont Cavalry*, pp. 101–102; Edwin Havens to Brother Nell, Bristoe Station, May 31, 1863, Havens Letters, MSU; Chapman in Mewborn, "*From Mosby's Command*," p. 101; Allyne Litchfield to My Dear Wife, Bristoe Station, May 31, 1863, Litchfield Letters, UMCL; Joseph D. Collea, Jr., *The First Vermont Cavalry in the Civil War: A History* (Jefferson, NC, 2010), pp. 152–153. Benedict later stated that Preston's men also charged to within 20 feet of the muzzle as well, but an estimate given at the time was 50 yards. See Benedict, *Vermont in the Civil War*, volume 2, p. 590, and Stahel, *OR*: 25:1:1117.

27. *OR*: 25:1:1117; Edwin Havens to Brother Nell, Bristoe Station, May 31,1863, Havens Letters, MSU; Alexandria *Gazette*, June 1, 1863; Col. Mann to Maj. Baldwin, June 2, 1863, RG 107, M504, NARA; Allyne Litchfield to My Dear Wife, Bristoe Station, June 2, 1863 and Allyne Litchfield to

Dear Susie, Bristoe Station, June 5, 1863, Litchfield Letters, UMCL; Mosby, *MWR*, p. 155.

28. Allyne Litchfield to My Dear Wife, Bristoe Station, May 31, 1863, Litchfield Letters, UMCL; Edwin Havens to Brother Nell, Bristoe Station, May 31, 1863, Havens Letters, MSU; Col. Mann to Maj. Baldwin, and Gen. Stahel to Lt. Col. Lathrop, May 30, 1863, RG 107, M504, also Stahel to Gen. Heintzelman, Fairfax Court House, May 31, 1863, RG 393, Part 2, Entry 732, NARA; *OR*: 25:1:1118; *PI*, June 4, 1863; Mosby, *MWR*, p. 151. The cannon is on display at the 45th Infantry Museum in Oklahoma City, Oklahoma. James Rose, a trooper in the 7th Michigan, claimed that the gun was dubbed the "Little Moseby," see James Rose, "Famous Custer Cavalry of Civil War," *National Tribune*, September 29, 1929.

29. Edward Clark to My Dear Mary, Union Mills, May 31, 1863, Clark Letters, Missouri Historical Society.

Chapter 20

1. *OR*: 25:2:568–569, 571; Gen. Hays to Gen. Stahel, May 30, 1863, Stahel to Hays and Gen. Butterfield to Gen. Haupt, May 30, 1863, RG 107, M504, NARA; Edward Clark to My Dear Mary, Union Mills, May 31, 1863, Clark Letters, Missouri Historical Society.

2. Fishel, *The Secret War for the Union*, pp. 421–422.

3. Darius Maynard to My Dearest Nell, Fairfax Court House, May 31, 1863, Maynard Letters, WSU.

4. *OR*: 25:1:593; Lt. Col. J. A. Haskin to Col. Lowell and Lt. W. G. Fitch to Lt. Col. J. H. Taylor, June 1, 1863, RG 393, Part 1, Entry 5382, also Maj. J. C. Williams to Capt. Potter, June 1, 1863, RG 393, Part 1, Entry 5383, NARA.

5. Col. Lathrop to Gen. Stahel, June 1, 1863, RG 393, Part 1, Entry 5379, NARA; *NYT*, June 5, 1863. There was a supply depot of some size maintained at Accotink and two companies of infantry had been assigned to guard the depot since April 20, 1863. See references to this detail in RG 393, Part 2, Entry 3935, NARA.

6. William Martin to Dear Wife, Fairfax Court House, June 1, 1863, Martin Letters, USAMHI; Gen. Stahel to Col. Gray, May 29, June 1, and June 14, 1863, RG 109, M345, Union Provost Marshal's File of Papers Relating to Individual Civilians, and Order 491, June 3, 1863 in RG 393, Part 2, Entry 642, Letters Sent, Department of Washington, NARA. Nothing has been found concerning the charges against Thompson in either case.

7. McClellan, *The Life and Campaigns*, p. 261; *OR*: 25:2:479, 516, 528, 792, 820; Fishel, *The Secret War for the Union*, p. 418.

8. *OR*: 25:2:820, 826–28, 832–833.

9. *OR*: 25:2:834, 836, 844; Fishel, *The Secret War for the Union*, p. 426, 428–429.

10. Gen. Buford to Col. Alexander, June 1, 1863, RG 393, Part 2, Entry 1449, NARA; *OR*: 25:2:849–850.

11. *OR*: 27:1:29, 902,1048–1049; Col. Wyndham to Capt. H. G. Weir, June 3, 1863, RG 393, Part 2, Entry 1449, NARA; Crowninshield, *A History of the First Regiment of Massachusetts Cavalry*, pp. 125–127; Ford, *A Cycle of Adams Letters*, volume 2, pp. 26–28; Carter Diary, VSL; Nanzig, *3rd Virginia Cavalry*, p. 35. Gleason sought a Medal of Honor after the war, in part for his involvement in this fight but his application was denied.

12. *OR*: 27:3:3; John Skinker to Col. Sharpe, June 3, 1863, RG 393, Part 1, Entry 3980, NARA; Williams Diary, VHS.

13. Edwin Havens to Dear Father and Mother, Kettle Run, June 3, 1863, Havens Letters, MSU.

14. Mosby, *MWR*, p. 155; Scott, *PL*, p. 96; *OR*; 27:2:777.

15. Victor Comte to Dear Elise, Headquarters Outpost, June 6, 1863, Comte Letters, UMBL; Mosby, *MWR*, p. 155.

16. Frederick Corselius to Dr. Mother, Chantilly, June 5, 1863, Frederick Corselius Letters, UMBL; Allyne Litchfield to Dear Wife, Bristoe Station, June 6, 1863, Litchfield Letters, UMCL.

17. Mosby, *MWR*, pp. 155–156; Frederick Corselius to Dr. Mother, Chantilly, June 5, 1863, Frederick Corselius Letters, and Victor Comte to Dear Elise, Headquarters Outpost, June 6, 1863, Comte Letters, UMBL; John Farnill to Dear Parents, Fairfax, June 11, 1863, Farnill Letters, CMU; Randolph to Editor, Fairfax Court House [June] 9, 1863, *DAT*, June 16, 1863. The man wounded by Underwood and his men in the opening skirmish is listed in the accounts as a member of Company M, 5th Michigan, but he cannot be identified. He received a grazing wound to the head or neck.

18. Col. Jewett to Lt. Col. Taylor, June 4, 1863, RG 107, M504, NARA; Roswell Farnham to My Dear Wife, Union Mills, June 7, 1863, Farnham Letters, UV.

19. *OR*: 27:1:30–31, 33, 1049–1050 and 27:3:8,10, 13, 18–19; Fishel, *The Secret War for the Union*, p. 428; George Crosby Diary, VHS.

20. *OR*: 27: 1:30, 33; Heintzelman Journal, LC.

21. Col. Mann to Maj. Harvey Baldwin, June 6, 1863, RG 107, M504, and Col. Figyelmesy to Gen. Heintzelman, June 8, 1863, RG 393, Part 1, Entry 5383, NARA; *OR*: 27:2:785, and 27:3:18; *DAT*, June 18, 1863; *DAT*, July 8, 1863; Macomber Diary, CMU.

22. *OR*: 27:3:25–26,28, 242; *Report of the Joint Committee on the Conduct of the War*, volume 4, pp. 162–163; John S. Mosby, *Stuart's Cavalry in the Gettysburg Campaign* (Gaithersburg, 1987 edition), p. 10

23. *OR*: 27:3:31; William Martin to Dear Wife, Fairfax Court House, June 9, 1863, Martin Letters, USAMHI; Klement, "A Michigan Sergeant in the Civil War," p. 218.

24. *OR*: 27:3:33–35; Gen. Stahel to Lt. Col. Taylor, June 8, 1863, RG 107, M504, NARA; William O'Brien to Dear Brother, Warrenton Junction, June 8 and 9, 1863, O'Brien Letters, UMBL; Edwin Havens to Dear Nell, Warrenton Junction, June 9, 1863, Havens Letters, MSU.

25. William O'Brien to Dear Brother, Warrenton Junction, June 8 and 9, 1863, O'Brien Letters, UMBL; Ebenezer Gould to My Dear Wife, Fairfax Court House, June 12, 1863, Gould Letters, CMU; *OR*: 27:3:37–39. A detailed description of the battle of Brandy Station is beyond the scope of this work.

26. *OR*: 27:3:37–39, 45; William O'Brien to Dear Brother, Bealeton, June 9 and 10, 1963, O'Brien Letters, UMBL; Roswell Farnham to Dear Mary, Union Mills, June 10, 1863, Farnham Letters, and Benjamin Hatch to Lucina, Union Mills, June 11, 1863, Hatch Letters, UV; Gen. Stahel to Superintendent Devereux, Stahel to Gen. Pleasonton, Stahel to Col. Mann, June 9, 1863, Col. Sharpe to Gen. Pleasonton, June 10, 1863, RG 107, M504, NARA. The evidence in question was a letter from a soldier to his father, advising that Stuart was planning "a raid into the [enemy's] country." See Bill to My Dear Father, June 4, 1863, in the Joseph Hooker Papers, Huntington Library.

27. Gen. Pleasonton to Gen. Stahel, June 11, 1863, RG 107, M504, NARA; William O'Brien to Dear Brother, Bealeton, June 9 and 10, 1863, and O'Brien to unreadable, Fairfax, June 11, 1863, O'Brien Letters, UMBL. In March, Hooker had refused Wyndham's plan for a combined attack across the Rappahannock. He then modified the plan using only troops from the army with less success than might otherwise have been achieved.

28. James H. Stevenson, *"Boots and Saddles": A History of the First Volunteer Cavalry of the War, Known as the First New York (Lincoln) Cavalry, and also as The Sabre Regiment* (Harrisburg, 1879), pp. 180–182; Beach, *The First New York (Lincoln) Cavalry*, p. 228; Ramage, *Gray Ghost*, pp. 89–90; Mewborn, *43rd Battalion*, pp. 65–66; Gen. Benjamin Kelley to Lt. Col. Donn Piatt, June 9, 1863, RG 107, M504, Roll 163, NARA. The dates of this expedition as well as the incident at the Hathaway home are often given erroneously, and Mosby never mentioned it. Horace Mewborn has unraveled the correct time line and, along with Ramage, gives the most accurate account.

29. Mosby, *MWR*, pp. 157–158; Scott, *PL*, p. 97; Mewborn, *43rd Battalion*, pp. 64–65; Ramage, *Gray Ghost*, p. 90. Confederate soldiers were allowed by law to elect their officers, but Mosby controlled the election by submitting only one name for each position, allowing his candidates to be elected unanimously.

30. McClellan, *The Life and Campaigns*, p. 262; Mosby, *MWR*, pp. 158–159, 162; Mosby, *Stuart's Cavalry in the Gettysburg Campaign*, p. 92; Jeffry Wert, *Cavalryman of the Lost Cause: A Biography of J. E. B. Stuart* (New York, 2008), p. 262; Brown, *Stringfellow of the Fourth*, p. 197, 205–206. After meeting with Stuart on June 17, and with Stuart now in close proximity to the river, Mosby again intended to attack the Union camp at Seneca. This attack by Mosby, as well as a crossing by Stuart, was again delayed by a confrontation with Union cavalry. When Mosby and Stuart discussed Stuart's route to Maryland the partisan suggested that Stuart cross the river at Seneca.

31. Col. Albert Jewett to Lt. Col. J. H. Taylor, and Gen. Stahel to Col. Philip Figyelmesy, June 10, 1863, RG 107, M504, NARA; *OR*: 27:3:50.

32. Capt. Norton to Lt. Col. Taylor, June 10, 1863, RG 393, Part 1, Entry 5383, NARA; *OR*: Series 3:3:363. Several members of the extended White family owned property in the area, but at the time of the war Lige White did not. On which of these farms the incident occurred is unknown.

33. *OR*: 27:2:786–787 and Series 3:3:363; [Cpl. J. Osborn] Coburn to Editor, Seneca Locks, Maryland, June 14, 1863, Mecosta County [Michigan] *Pioneer*, July 2, 1863; Scott, *PL*, p. 99; Ezekiel to Sister Mary, White's Ford, June 13, 1863, Farnham Letters, UV.

34. Albert Sawyer to Brother Micah, Liberty Hill, June 12, 1863, Sawyer Letters, UV.

35. T.H.M to Editors, Near Washington, D.C, June 22, 1863, Alta *Daily Californian*, July 17, 1863, in Larry Rogers and Keith Rogers, *Their Horses Climbed Trees, A Chronicle of the California 100 and Battalion in the Civil War, from San Francisco to Appomattox* (Atglen, 2001), pp. 149–152; Ezekiel to Sister Mary, White's Ford, June 13, 1863, Farnham Letters, UV; *OR*: 27:3:74–75; Col. Lowell to Lt. Col. Haskin, June 12, 1863, RG 107, M504, NARA.

36. *OR*: 27:3:50, 64–66; Gen. Stahel to Col. DeForest, Stahel to Maj. Brewer, Brewer to Stahel, June 11, 1863, and Col. Jewett to Lt. Col. Taylor, June 12, 1863, RG 107, M504, NARA; Albert Sawyer to Brother Micah, Liberty Hill, June 12, 1863, Sawyer Letters, UV; Allyne Litchfield to My Dear Wife, Fairfax Court House, June 11, 1863, Litchfield Letters, UMCL; Edwin Havens to Dear Nell, Near Chantilly, June 13, 1863, Havens Letters, MSU. Hammond was in command as orders were received at the same time from Heintzelman ordering Stahel to place Col. DeForest under arrest. The nature of the charges against DeForest have not been determined, and the matter was dropped the following day. See Capt. Potter to Gen. Stahel, June 11, 1863, RG 107, M504, also Lt. Col. Taylor to Stahel, June 12, 1863, RG 393, Part 1, Entry 5379, NARA.

37. *Captain James Penfield*, p. 63; Wilkins Letters and Diary, USAMHI; *OR*: 27:3:75; Descriptive Roll of Prisoners, June 15, 1863, RG 94, M797, NARA; Crosby Diary, VHS.

38. Charles Johnson to Dear Mother, Fairfax Court House, June 14, 1863, Johnson Letters, UC; Macomber Diary, CMU; Descriptive Roll of Prisoners, June 15, 1863, RG 94, M797, NARA.

39. John Louiselle to Dear Wife, Monocacy, June 12, 1863, Green-Louiselle Papers, UV; *OR*: 27:3:95; Victor Comte to Dear Elise, Headquarters Outpost, June 12, 1863, Comte Letters, UMBL.

40. *OR*: 27:2:788; Sansone, *Journey to Bloomfield*, pp. 42, 187–188. At least one soldier in the 10th Vermont sent a scrap of Brawner's shirt home to a friend, see William White to Dear Friend Jacob, Camp Heintzelman, June 14, 1863, William White Letters, VHS.

41. Mosby, MWR, pp. 160–161; Scott, *PL*, p. 100.

Chapter 21

1. Hebert, *Fighting Joe Hooker*, p. 235; *OR*: 27:70–71, 80.

2. *OR*: 27:3:72; Mosby, *Reminiscences*, p. 158.

3. Gen. Ingalls to Gen. Pleasonton, June 12, 1863, RG 107, M504, NARA. It seems most likely that Hooker was anxious for news on Lee's army, but the casual nature of the request and the fact that it came from Ingalls, the army's quartermaster, may have led Pleasonton, who had been reviewing and reorganizing his command and had little information regarding Lee's army to throw out the idea to a friend. No other reference to this has been found.

4. *OR*: 27:1:38, 2:185, and 3:75, 82–92.

5. *OR*: 27:1:36–37 and 27:3:75, 91; Maj. Baldwin to Gen. Hooker, and Gen. Kelley to Lt. Col. Piatt, June 13, 1863, RG107, M504, NARA.

6. *OR*: 27:1:38–39 and 3:85, 101, 103; Gen. Abercrombie to Lt. Col. Taylor, June 14, 1863, RG 107, M504, NARA; Sturtevant, *Pictorial History*, p. 173; F. Vogl, "Who Laid the Pontoons?" *National Tribune*, October 11, 1888.

7. *OR*: 27:3:106, 114–115; Gen. Butterfield to Capt. McKee, Lt. Col. Meysenberg to Gen. Stahel, Stahel to AAG, Howard's Corps (Meysenberg), Maj. Baldwin to Gen. Howard, June 14, 1863, and Col. Jewett to Lt. Col. Taylor, June 14, 1863, RG 107, M504, NARA; Macomber Diary, CMU.

8. *OR*: 27:3:103, 114; Gurowski, *Diary*, volume 2, p. 245.

9. *OR*: 27:1:41–42, 2:687, and 3:115–117,119; Col. Alexander to Capt. McKee, June 15, 1863, RG 107, M504, NARA.

10. *OR*: 27:3:121; Col. Jewett to Lt. Col. Taylor and Taylor to Jewett, June 15, 1863, RG 107, M504, also Jewett to Lt. Col. Taylor, June 27, 1863, RG 393, Part 1, Entry 5382, NARA.

11. *OR*: 27:3:121; Gen. Stahel to Lt. Col. Taylor, Lt. Col. Meysenberg to Maj. Baldwin and Gen. Abercrombie to Stahel, June 15, 1863, RG 107, M504, also Taylor to Stahel, June 15, 1863, RG 393, Part 1, Entry 5379, NARA; Wilkins Letters and Diary, USAMHI.

12. *OR*: 27:1:44–46 and 3:131,148–149, 151–152.

13. *OR*: 27:1:45.

14. *OR*: 27:3:146–147, 150–151; Heintzelman Journal, LC.

15. Alfred Ryder to Dear friends, Fairfax Court House, June 16, 1863, Ryder Letters, UMBL; James Parsons to Joseph King, Fairfax Court House, June 16, 1863, [Flint, Michigan] *Wolverine Citizen*, July 11, 1863; Edwin Hall to Dear Father, Between Bristoe and Manassas Junction, June 16, 1863, Hall Letters, VHS.

16. *OR*: 27:1:47–48.

17. *OR*: 27:1: 48, and 3:171–172.

18. *OR*: 27:1:52, and 3:172,175–176; Crosby Diary, VHS.

19. *OR*: 27:3:171; *Report of the Joint Committee on the Conduct of the War*, vol. 4, pp. 32–33; David S. Sparks, editor, *Inside Lincoln's Army: The Diary of General Marsena Rudolph Patrick, Provost Marshal General, Army of the Potomac* (New York, 1964), p. 260; Gen. Pleasonton to Gen. Ingalls, June 16, 1863, RG107, M504, NARA. In this message Pleasonton requests a train to carry him from near Bull Run Bridge to Fairfax Station, presumably to meet with Hooker. In a second message, Ingalls orders a train to return Pleasonton to his headquarters, suggesting that the meeting did take place.

20. Capt. Dahlgren to Gen. Butterfield, June 17, 1863, RG 107, M504, NARA; Ulric Dahlgren Diary/Memo Book, John Dahlgren Papers, LC; Butterfield to Gen. Pleasonton, June 17, 1863, Charles Venable Papers, Southern Historical Collections, University of North Carolina, Chapel Hill, North Carolina. The complete order is found in an appendix.

21. *OR*: 27: 3: 151–152, 171–172. Guilford Station was in modern-day Sterling, Virginia, along what is known today as the Washington and Old Dominion Regional Railroad Park.

22. Gen. Kilpatrick to Col. di Cesnola, June 16, 1863, RG 107, M504, NARA; Kilpatrick's Report for the Battle of Aldie, Joseph Hooker Papers, Huntington Library; *OR*: 27:1:962, and 3:179.

23. Kilpatrick's Report, Hooker Papers, Huntington Library; *OR*: 27:2:687; Carter Diary, VSL. A detailed account of these battles is beyond the scope of this work.

24. *OR*: 27:2:688; Mosby, *MWR*, p. 163

25. Mosby, *MWR*, pp. 163–167; *OR*: 27:2:689 and 3:192, 210.

26. *OR*: 27:1:962–963 and 2:688, 741.

27. *OR*: 27:2:770–771 and 3:176; Myers, *The Comanches*, pp. 188–191. According to White, Stuart at first refused the request that he be allowed to join Ewell. It was only after a second request was made that Stuart relented. See White to Hon. John H. Alexander, Leesburg, April 17, 1906, in Mosby, *Stuart's Cavalry in the Gettysburg Campaign*, p. 156.

28. Capt. McKee to Gen. Williams, June 18, 1863, RG 107, M504, NARA; Heintzelman Journal, LC; *OR*: 27:3:179, 182, 191, 193–197, 209 and 51:1059; Theodore Case to Editor, Monocacy, Maryland, June 20, 1863, Fredonia *Censor*, July 1, 1863.

29. *OR*: 27:1:907 and 3:178, 193.

30. *OR*: 27: 1:908–909 and 3:193; Frederic Denison, *Sabres and Spurs: The First Rhode Island Cavalry in the Civil War* (Baltimore, 1994 edition), p. 239.

31. *OR*: 27:1:51, 908 and 3:210–212; Theodore Case to Editor, Alexandria, June 22, 1863, Fredonia *Censor*, July 1, 1863. Pleasonton was given permission to order McKee to join him, once McKee could do so without placing his men at risk, but it does not appear that Pleasonton issued such an order, see *OR*: 27:3:209–210. Hooker specifically mentioned the gaps in South Mountain but his ordering officers from the artillery to scout for firing positions at Gainesville, Haymarket and Gum Springs indicates his willingness to give battle along the length of the mountain chain from Thoroughfare Gap northward into Maryland.

32. *OR*: 27:1:910, 2:689 and 3:208; Crosby Diary, VHS; Charles Chapin to Dear Brother, Fairfax, June 24, 1863, Chapin Letters, USAMHI; Albert Greene to Dear Brother, Fairfax, June 21, 1863, Greene Letters, UV; Elizabeth Dunbar Murray, *My Mother Used to Say: A Natchez Belle of the Sixties* (Boston, 1959), p. 174; Gen. Stahel to Lt. Col. Taylor, June 19, 1863 RG 393, Part 2, Entry 732, NARA; Benedict, *Vermont in the Civil War*, volume 2, p. 591.

33. *OR*: 27:3:211.

34. *OR*: 27:1:52,54 and 3:210–211, 214–215.

35. William Martin to Dear Wife, Fairfax, June 19, 1863, Martin Letters, USAMHI; Wilkins Diary, USAMHI; *OR*: 27:3:225–226; Gen. Stahel to Gen. Rucker, June 19, 1863, RG 107, M504, NARA; John Farnill to Dear Parents and Relations, Fairfax, June 20, 1863, Farnill Letters, CMU.

36. *OR*: 27:1:32 and 3:223–224, 227–229; Francis A. Walker, *History of the Second Army Corps in the Army of the Potomac* (Gaithersburg, 1985 edition), p. 259; Committee on Regimental History, *History of the Sixth New York Cavalry*, p. 130; Regimental History Committee, *History of the Third Pennsylvania Cavalry, Sixteenth Regiment Pennsylvania Volunteers in the American Civil War, 1861–1865* (Philadelphia, 1905), p. 254; William P. Lloyd, *History of the First Reg't Pennsylvania Reserve Cavalry, From Its Organization, August, 1861, to September, 1864, with List of Names of All Officers and Enlisted Men* (Philadelphia, 1864), p. 57. Pleasonton's conclusions were supported by reports from one of Duffie's men who had been captured and then recovered, as well as several infantry stragglers who were captured. While Pleasonton is often ridiculed for this conclusion, John Buford had made the same assumption earlier in the month.

37. *OR*: 27:2:306 and 3:225, 228.

38. *OR*: 27:3:225–226; Gen. Stahel to Lt. Col. Stagg, June 21, 1863, RG 107, M504, NARA; Macomber Diary, CMU; James Rowe Reminiscences, Rowe Family Papers, UMBL.

39. Edwin Havens to no addressee, Fairfax Court House, June 20, 1863, Havens Letters, MSU; John Farnill to Dear Parents, Fairfax, June 20, 1863, Farnill Letters, CMU; William Rockwell to My Dear Wife, June 20, 1863, Rockwell Letters, WMU; Victor Comte to Dear Elise, Fairfax, June 21, 1863, Comte Letters, UMBL.

Chapter 22

1. *OR*: 27:2:613 and 3:244–245.

2. *OR*: 27:3:244–245; Gen. Stahel to Lt. Col. Stagg, June 21, 1863, RG107, M504, NARA; Crosby Diary, VHS; Victor Comte to Dear Elise, Fairfax, June 21, 1863, Comte Letters, UMBL; George Telling to Dear Brother William, Fairfax, June 21, 1863, Telling Letters, USAMHI; Wilkins Letters and Diary, USAMHI; William Martin to Dear Wife, Fairfax, June 24, 1863, USAMHI; *NYT*, June 26, 1863.

3. Gen. Abercrombie to Lt. Col. Taylor, June 21, 1863, RG 107, M504, NARA; Roswell Farnham to My Dear Wife, Wolf Run Shoals, June 21, 1863, Farnham Letters, UV; "Report of Reconnaissance by General Warren, June 21, 1863 of the country around Chantilly and Gainesville," Gouverneur K. Warren Papers, NYSLA.

4. Report of Reconnaissance, Warren Papers, NYSLA; *OR*: 27:1:974 and 3:247,255–256, 270; Brooks, *Stories of the Confederacy*, p. 161; Ulric Dahlgren Diary/Memo Book, LC; Andrew Buck to Brother & Sister, Gainesville, June 22, 1863, Buck Letters, UMBL; Emmons Diary, UMBL; James Kidd to Dear Father, Emmittsburg, June 28, 1863, Kidd Letters, UMBL; Wilkins Diary, USAMHI. The newsboy was en route to deliver the Sunday paper to Brig. Gen. Albion Howe's division of the Fifth Corps at Bristoe Station. It is ironic that Warren would play a role in ending the tenure of Copeland and Stahel with the army, for their failure to act with proper urgency only to be relieved himself in the last days of the war for a similar lack of urgency at a key point on the battlefield.

5. *OR*: 27:3:250, 269–270; *NYT*, June 26, 1863; James Kidd to Dear Father, Emmittsburg, June 28, 1863, Kidd Letters, UMBL; Allyne Litchfield to Dear Susie, Gainesville, June 23, 1863, Litchfield Letters, UMCL; *DAT*, June 26, 1863.

6. Keen and Mewborn, *43rd Battalion*, p. 70; Mosby, *MWR*, pp. 169–172; Stephen Minot Weld, *War Diary and Letters of Stephen Minot Weld, 1861–1865* (Boston, 1979), p. 220; Scott, *PL*, p. 106; *OR*: 51:1:1062. The man or men captured in the cherry tree took place near the home of John Coleman. Scott states that the men were from the 5th NY Cavalry, however that cannot be confirmed in the regimental roster. Weld, a staff officer attached to the First Corps, also places the incident near the Coleman home but states that it was the head teamster for the corps who was captured.

7. Keen and Mewborn, *43rd Battalion*, p. 70; Wert, *Mosby's Rangers*, p. 91; Lt. Col. Locke to Gen. Pleasonton, June 20, 1863, RG 393, Part 2, Entry 1449, NARA; *OR*: 27:1:641–643 and 3:229, 255; Mosby, *MWR*, pp. 169–170. The primary sources, Mosby, Scott and others speak of this period with either few actual dates given or dates that are clearly incorrect. I have relied on Keen and Mewborn's *43rd Battalion* for the date of the first attack on the wagons. The second attack is mentioned in the Locke document of June 20, though it is not entirely clear if this was a separate incident or if in fact the first attack actually took place on the 20th.

8. Maj. Gen. David Birney to Gen. Williams, June 22, 1863, RG 393, Part 1, Entry 3980, and Lt. Col. Locke to Gen. Pleasonton, June 20, 1863, RG 393, Part 2, Entry 1449, also Descriptive List of Prisoners, Including the Circumstances of Their Capture, June 22, 1863, RG 109, Entry 183, NARA; Mosby, *MWR*, pp. 170–171.

9. *OR*: 27:3:256–257; Gen. Butterfield to Gen. Abercrombie, June 22, 1863, RG 107, M504, NARA; Macomber Diary, CMU.

10. *NYT*, June 26, 1863; *DAT*, June 26, 1863; Report of General Julius Stahel, RG 94, M1098, NARA; Mosby, *MWR*, p. 172; *OR*: 27:3:923.

11. *OR*: 27:3:244–245, 254. The emphasis is the authors.

12. *OR*: 27:3:258–259; Gen. Pleasonton to Gen. Ingalls, June 26, 1863, RG 107, M504, NARA. A squadron from the battered 6th Pennsylvania, which was refitting at Fairfax Station, was also sent after Mosby — see Clement Hoffman to Dear Mother, Fairfax Court House, June 23, 1863, Clement Hoffman Letters, USAMHI.

13. *OR*: 27:3:245, 255, 257–258, 267–270; *NYT*, June 26, 1863; *DAT*, June 26, 1863. Beyond his message of June 23, advising that he would "scout the whole country from Bull Run Mountain toward Fairfax Court House," there is nothing in the record to confirm that Stahel actually attempted to locate Mosby, but instead moved his division directly to the courthouse — see *OR*: 27:3:270.

14. Alfred Pleasonton to My Dear General, Head Quarters Cavalry Corps, June 23, 1863, and Elon Farnsworth to Dear General, Head Quarters Cavalry Corps, June 23, 1863, Alfred Pleasonton Papers, LC; *OR*: 27:1:51, 90; Gen. Pleasonton to Adjutant General, June 25, 1863, RG 94, M1064, NARA. The emphasis is in the original letters. John Farnsworth was an attorney in Chicago before the war and a friend of Lincoln, who raised and led the 8th Illinois Cavalry, before rising to a brigade command and the rank of brigadier in late 1862. He was elected to Congress from Illinois in the critical election that November and resigned his commission on March 4, 1863. See Hard, *History of Eighth Cavalry Regiment*, pp. ii–iv.

15. Harrington Diary, WMU; Ebenezer Gould to Dear Wife, Fairfax, June 24, 1863, Gould Letters, CMU.

Chapter 23

1. Gen. Butterfield to Gen. Pleasonton, June 21, 1863, RG 393, Part 1, Entry 3964, NARA; *OR*: 27:2:358, 613.

2. *OR*: 27:3:209, 246; N. D. Preston, *History of the Tenth Regiment of Cavalry New York Volunteers, August, 1861 to August, 1865* (New York, 1892), p. 102.

3. John C. Babcock to Dear Col. [Sharpe], Frederick City, June 22, 1863, RG 393, Part 1, Entry 3980, NARA; Robert J. Driver, Jr., *First and Second Maryland Cavalry, C.S.A.* (Charlottesville, 1999), p. 51; Harry Gilmor, *Four Years in the Saddle* (New York, 1866), pp. 92–94; Frederick *Union*, June 26, 1863; Frederick *Examiner*, July 1, 1863; William R, Quynn, editor, *The Diary of Jacob Engelbrecht* (Frederick, 2001), p. 971.

4. Edwin M. Haynes, *A History of the Tenth Regiment Vermont Volunteers with Biographical Sketches of the Officers Who Fell in Battle and a Complete Roster* (Lewiston, 1870), pp. 33–34; Col. Jewett to Lt. Col. Taylor, June 24, 1863 and Taylor to Jewett, June 24, 1863, RG 107, M504, also Jewett to Taylor, June 27, 1863, RG 393, Part 1, Entry 5382, NARA; *OR*: 27:1:56–57, and 3: 260, 271, 293, 445; Heintzelman Journal, LC.

5. *OR*: 27:3:259; Aiken Diary, VHS; Roswell Farnham to My Dear Wife, Union Mills, June 20, 1863 and Farnham to My Dear Wife, Wolf Run Shoals, June 21, 1863, Farnham Letters, UV; Benedict, *Army Life in Virginia*, pp. 159–160; Unaddressed letter of Edward Clark, Union Mills, June 20, 1863, Clark Papers, Missouri Historical Society. Though this letter is unaddressed Clark confirms in his diary that he wrote a letter to his wife this day.

6. *OR*: 27:3:283, 287–289, 291–292, 312; Gen. Seth Williams to Gen. Reynolds, June 24, 1863, RG 393, Part 2, Entry 3582, Letters Received, 1862–1864, also Unknown to Gen. Stahel, June 24, 1863, RG 393, Part 1, Entry 3964, and Stahel's Report of Service, RG 94, M1098, NARA.

7. John Farnill to Dear Parents, Fairfax, June 24, 1863, Farnill Letters, CMU; Allyne Litchfield to Dear Susie, Fairfax Court House, June 24, 1863, Litchfield Letters, UMCL; Macomber Diary, CMU; Klement, "Edwin B. Bigelow: A Michigan Sergeant in the Civil War," p. 219; Andrew Buck to Editor, South Mountain, June 27, 1863, *GRDE*, July 10, 1863; Isham, *An Historical Sketch of the Seventh Regiment*, p. 20; Publication Committee, *History of the Eighteenth Regiment of Cavalry*, p. 38; Boudrye, *Historic Records of the Fifth New York Cavalry*, 63; Kidd, *Personal Recollections*, p. 115; *DAT*, July 8, 1863; Morey Diary, UMBL; *OR*: 27:3:291, 311. Samuel Gillespie claimed that the water at the ford "barely wet the skirts of our saddles," see *A History of Company A, First Ohio Cavalry*, p. 145.

8. Oliver O. Howard, *Autobiography of Oliver Otis Howard, Major General United States Army* (New York, 1908) volume 1, pp. 390–391; *OR*: 51:1:1061–1062.

9. Mosby, *MWR*, pp. 173–180; *OR*: 27:2:691–693, Wert, *Cavalryman of the Lost Cause*, p. 264. A detailed examination of Stuart's controversial ride to Gettysburg is beyond the scope of this work. One has to wonder, however, if any of his superiors ever questioned Stuart as to the condition of his horses and their ability to complete the venture then being considered. Once started, Stuart was forced to rest his horses several times, further complicating his ability to complete his task in a timely manner, namely to cross the Potomac River as quickly as possible. It is likely, however, that the condition of his horses was discussed, but the campaign had advanced to such a point that Lee needed his cavalry regardless of their condition. There simply was no time to rest them as Stuart had done after Brandy Station.

10. Capt. Potter to Capt. E. S. Johnson, June 24, 1863, RG 393, Part 1, Entry 5379, and Unknown to Capt. Julius Mason, June 25, 1863, RG 393, Part 1, Entry 3964, also Gen. Ingalls to C. B. Stowe, June 25, 1863, RG 107, M504, NARA; Roswell Farnham to My Dear Wife, Centreville, June 25, 1863, Farnham Letters, UV.

11. Unknown to Gen. Pleasonton, June 24, 1863, RG 393, Part 1, Entry 3964, NARA; *OR*: 27:3:289 and 51:1:1062–1063; Mosby, *MWR*, pp. 176–181; Keen and Mewborn, *43rd Battalion*, p. 72; Williamson, *Mosby's Rangers*, pp. 79–80. The emphasis appears in the original. In Edward P. Tobie, *History of the First Maine Cavalry, 1861–1865* (Gaithersburg, 1987 edition), p. 174–175 there is an account of several severely wounded Union troopers who were left behind, presumably at Alexander Davis' barn east of Aldie, when the cavalry corps moved out. The account refers to them being warned that Mosby was aware of their presence and intended to send them to Richmond. The surgeon was able to get a message through and two hundred men from the 2nd Massachusetts Cavalry escorted several ambulances in an attempt to recover the men. Mosby then attacked the ambulances before being driven off by the escort. No dates are given and it is impossible to reconcile this with other accounts. Douglas Southall Freeman disputes Mosby's claim that he was to meet with Stuart, stating that he was instead ordered to proceed to the Potomac River and select a crossing point, see Freeman, *Lee's Lieutenants, Gettysburg to Appomattox* (New York, 1944), volume 3, p. 58.

Chapter 24

1. *OR*: 27:3:305–308, 312–313.

2. Boudrye, *Historic Records of the Fifth New York Cavalry*, p. 63; *Captain James Penfield*, p. 67; Macomber Diary, CMU; Col. Russell Alger's Gettysburg Report, RG 94, Union Battle Reports, NARA; Publication Committee, *History of the Eighteenth Regiment of Cavalry*, p. 38; *DAT*, July 8, 1863.

3. *OR*: 27:3:334–335; Charles Phelps' Compiled Service Record, and the 1860 U.S. Census for Maryland, NARA; Quynn, *The Diary of Jacob Engelbrecht*, p. 971; Boudrye, *Historic Records of the Fifth New York Cavalry*, p. 276.

4. *OR*: 27:1:58 and 3:334–335, 337–338.

5. *OR*: 27:3:333; Gen Pleasonton to Gen. Williams, June 26, 1863, RG 107, M504, NARA.

6. *OR*: 27:3:323, 331–332, 339–340, 345–346.

7. *OR*: 27:1: 1037, and 3:324; Smith, *The Story of a Cavalry Regiment*, pp. 73, 76, 85; Col. Swain to AAG, June 27, 1863, RG 94, 11th New York Letter and Order Books, Gen. Ingalls to Gen. Rucker, June 25, 1863, and Capt. Page to Ingalls, June 25, 1863, RG 107, M504, NARA.

8. Wheelock, *The Boys in White*, pp. 104–109.

9. *OR*: 27:2:693; Theodore S. Garnett, Jr., "Cavalry Service with Gen. Stuart," *PWT*, February 8, 1879; Gen. Ingalls to C. B. Stowe and Capt. Henry Page, June 25, 1863, RG 107, M504, NARA.

10. Smith, *The Story of a Cavalry Regiment*, p. 77. Smith includes an account of this fight by George Dagwell, as well

as other accounts by men from the regiment that were written postwar. Dagwell's is the most complete. It appears to be based entirely on an account that appeared in the *WES*, June 29, 1863.

11. Smith, *The Story of a Cavalry Regiment*, pp. 77–78. Of the several accounts included by Smith, only George Dagwell's is helpful in trying to pin down the location, though it is still rather confusing. He mentions that the fight began near the stream where they watered their horses that morning, and describes it as being west of the town, orienting it with Fairfax Station as well. He later places the scene of the opening shots near the intersection with the Little River Turnpike (which he erroneously identifies as the Alexandria and Leesburg Turnpike), stating that they were still about three miles from the courthouse. Taken together these identifiers suggest that the opening shots were fired near the intersection at Jermantown. The nearest stream west of the courthouse is a branch of Accotink Creek that does point toward Fairfax Station, and it was there that Dagwell was fired on. The men may have also followed a branch of Popes Head Creek, from a point south of the courthouse toward Fairfax Station.

12. Smith, *The Story of a Cavalry Regiment*, pp. 78–80.

13. Garnett, "Cavalry Service with Gen. Stuart," *PWT*, February 8, 1879.

14. Smith, *The Story of a Cavalry Regiment*, pp. 80–83, 90–97; Garnett, "Cavalry Service with Gen. Stuart," *PWT*, February 8, 1879; Brooks, *Stories of the Confederacy*, p. 162; *OR*: 27:1:1037. The figures given are compiled from the roster in Smith as well as the roster in *ARAGSNY*, volume 3. Two names listed in Smith's narrative as captured do not appear as casualties in either roster and are not reflected above.

15. Richmond *Dispatch*, July 2, 1863; *OR*: 27:2:693 and 3:354; Carter Diary, VSL; Garnett, "Cavalry Service with Gen. Stuart," *PWT*, February 8, 1879; Driver, *1st Virginia Cavalry*, p. 63; Edward Waldo Emerson, *Life and Letters of Charles Russell Lowell* (Columbia, 2005 edition), pp. 267–269.

16. *OR*: 27:3:358–359; Emerson, *Life and Letters of Charles Russell Lowell*, pp. 267–269.

17. Gen. De Russy to Adjutant General, Dept. of Washington, June 28, 1863, RG, 393, Part 1, Entry 5382, Col. Swain to AAG, June 27, 1863, RG 94, 11th New York Letter and Order Books, NARA.

18. *OR*: 27:3:350, 353; Isham, *An Historical Sketch of the Seventh Regiment*, p. 20; Kidd, *Personal Recollections*, p. 116; Klement, "Edwin B. Bigelow: A Michigan Sergeant in the Civil War," p. 219.

19. *OR*: 27:3:353; Gary Kross, "Attack from the West," *Blue & Gray*, volume 27, number 5, Campaign 2000, p. 9; Myers, *The Comanches*, p. 192.

20. *OR*: 27:1:59, 926.

21. *OR*: 27:1:59–60 and 3:353, 355–358, 369; Quynn, *The Diary of Jacob Engelbrecht*, p. 972; Stephen W. Sears, "Meade Takes Command," *North & South*, volume 5, number 6, September 2002, pp. 12–20; Hebert, *Fighting Joe Hooker*, pp. 231–245; John F. Marszalek, *Commander of All Lincoln's Armies, A Life of General Henry W. Halleck* (Cambridge, 2004), pp. 172–175.

22. George Meade, *The Life and Letters of George Gordon Meade, Major-General United States Army* (Baltimore, 1994 edition), volume 2, pp. 1–3.

23. *OR*: 27:3:370, 377; Longacre, *Custer and His Wolverines*, p. 126; John Robertson, compiler, *Michigan in the War* (Lansing, 1882), p. 574; Klement, "Edwin B. Bigelow: A Michigan Sergeant in the Civil War," p. 220; Joseph Copeland to Col. Ritter, Washington D.C., July 9, 1863, Simon Gratz Autograph Collection, HSP; Hebert, *Fighting Joe Hooker*, p. 246.

24. *OR*: 27:1: 913 and 3:373–376, 396; Gen. Pleasonton to Gen. Williams, June 28, 1863, RG 393, Part 1, Entry 3986, "Two or More Name File," 1861–1865, NARA. Emphasis in the original. Custer later wrote that he was notified of the promotion "about three P.M." and that it was confirmed by the Secretary of War in a telegram that arrived "about 9 P.M.," see George Custer to Judge Christiancy, Amissville, Virginia, July 26, 1863, Henry Clay Christiancy Papers, UV.

25. Macomber Diary, CMU; Boudrye, *Historic Records of the Fifth New York Cavalry*, p. 63; Stahel Farewell Order, June 28, 1863, and Gen. Heintzelman to Gen. Stahel, Washington, July 11, 1863, Stahel Papers, LC; Gillespie, *A History of Company A, First Ohio Cavalry*, pp. 139, 147.

26. Joseph Copeland to Col. Ritter, Washington, D.C., July 9, 1863, Simon Gratz Autograph Collection, HSP; *OR*: 27:3:656; Joseph Copeland's General's Report, RG 94, M1098, NARA. George Custer's rank at this time remains a matter of some confusion. While Pleasonton held the rank of brigadier Custer held the rank of lieutenant, but following Pleasonton's promotion to major general Custer was elevated to the rank of captain, and it is as a captain that Pleasonton refers to him in the documents and orders that day. See Custer's comment concerning his rank in Marguerite Merington, editor, *The Custer Story, The Life and Intimate Letters of General Custer and His Wife Elizabeth* (New York, 1950), p. 56. In his letter to Judge Christiancy of July 26, 1863, Custer confirms almost verbatim Pleasonton's stated reason for relieving Copeland.

27. Capt. Cohen to Capt. Spangler, June 28, 1863, RG 107, M504, and Gen. Williams to Col. Price, June 29, 1863, RG 393, Part 1, Entry 3964, NARA; Frederick *Union*, July 2, 1863; *OR*: 27:3:398; Sparks, *Inside Lincoln's Army*, p. 266; David L. and Audrey J. Ladd, *The Bachelder Papers, Gettysburg in Their Own Words*, 3 volumes (Dayton, 1994) volume 1, p. 52; Crosby Diary, VHS; Gillespie, *A History of Company A, First Ohio Cavalry*, p. 147.

28. Heintzelman Journal, LC; *OR*: 27:1:63; Gen. De Russy to Adjutant General, Dept. of Washington, June 28, 1863, RG, 393, Part 1, Entry 5382, NARA.

29. Unaddressed note from Captain Cohen, June 27, 1863, RG107, M504, and Cohen to Gen. Pleasonton, June 21, 1863, RG 393, Part 2, Entry 1449, NARA; Mohr, *The Cormany Diaries*, pp. 260–261, 552–553; *OR*: 25:1:57; Charles H. Miller, compiler, *History of the 16th Regiment Pennsylvania Cavalry for the Year Ending October 31st 1863* (Philadelphia, 1864), pp. 37–38. While Cormany depicts Fry as indolent and content to exercise his authority at remount facilities thereby avoiding the dangers associated with front-line duty, other accounts suggest otherwise. In his report of the fight at Kelly's Ford, John Irvin Gregg, then in command of the regiment, singled out Fry for special notice after he had led a charge of 30 men that "drove a squadron of the enemy from the woods immediately in my front." Later that spring Fry was temporarily given the reins to the regiment following Gregg's elevation to brigade command, but he was passed over a short time later for the lieutenant colonel's vacancy in favor of a captain, and Fry remained a major throughout his term of service. Cormany may well have had a personal dispute with Fry that shaped his opinion. Some of Fry's time at the remount facility in Washington, D.C. was necessitated by a bout with hemorrhoids, a common complaint in the cavalry. Fry, along with three other officers, was captured near Winchester in September 1864, by men of Mosby's command, and released in February — see Keen and Mewborn, *43rd Battalion Virginia Cavalry Mosby's Command*, p. 175. When he returned to the regiment on April 16, Cormany implied that he was a coward, returning only after the "danger is over." See also Fry's Compiled Service Record and Volunteer Service Record, RG 94, Entry 496, NARA.

30. *OR*: 27:2:694 and 3:379; Driver, *1st Virginia Cavalry*, p. 63; R.L.T. Beale, *History of the Ninth Virginia Cavalry in the War Between the States* (Amissville, 1981 edition), p. 78; Garnett, "Cavalry Service with Gen. Stuart," *PWT*, February 8, 1879; Heintzelman Journal, LC; Trout, Robert, editor, *In the Saddle with Stuart: The Story of Frank Smith Robertson of Jeb Stuart's Staff* (Gettysburg, 1998), p. 76. Beale believed he had encountered the 11th NY and mentioned that Pollard accounted for "eleven dead and wounded" in that unit. In his report Stuart identifies the enemy force as the 2nd NY Cavalry, which seems more likely given that Fry's command included a contingent of 50 men from that unit on fresh horses. Meigs, who gave

several estimates for the size of Fry's command, tabulated his loss as "about 16" men in two skirmishes. Heintzelman stated that Fry lost 20 men and captured two. I have opted to rely on Cohen's specific tally for the size of his force.

31. McClellan, *The Life and Campaigns*, p. 324; Trout, editor, *In the Saddle with Stuart*, p. 76; *OR*: 27:2:694; Lancaster [Pennsylvania] *Daily Evening Express*, July 1, 1863; Simons, *A Regimental History*, pp. 78–79.

32. Gen. Ingalls to Capt. Page, June 22 and 25, 1863, Page to Ingalls, June 25, 1863 and Ingalls to Lt. Col. Sawtelle, June 26, 1863, RG 107, M504, NARA.

33. McClellan, *The Life and Campaigns*, p. 324; Trout, editor, *In the Saddle with Stuart*, p. 76; *OR*: 27:2:694; Lancaster *Daily Evening Express*, July 1, 1863; Simons, *A Regimental History*, pp. 78–79; *WES*, June 29, 1863. A detailed discussion of Stuart's "Ride to Gettysburg," as well as the continuing controversy concerning his decision to burden himself with these wagons, is beyond the scope of this work. A July 29, 1878 letter from Wade Hampton to H. B. McClellan suggests the accuracy of the *WES* account. In attempting to reconcile the several accounts and the different Southern units taking claim for the capture of the train it may be helpful to consider the length of the train and that several units may have been involved along that distance. For Hampton's letter see Hampton to My Dear Major, July 29, 1878 in the H. B. McClellan Papers, Virginia Historical Society, Richmond, Virginia.

34. *OR*: 27:2:694; *WES*, June 29, 1863. In contrast to the account quoted, Col. Richard Beale stated, postwar, that the wagons were loaded down with everything from oats to whiskey and hams to cutlery, see Beale, *History of the 9th Virginia Cavalry*, p. 80.

35. *OR*: 27:3:378–379, 381–382; Gen. Ingalls to Lt. Col. Sawtelle, June 28, 1863, RG 107, M504, NARA.

36. Gideon Welles and John T Morse, Jr., *Diary of Gideon Welles, Secretary of the Navy Under Lincoln and Johnson*, 3 volumes (Boston, 1911), volume 1, p. 350.

37. *OR*: 27:1:61–67, and 3:396; Welles, *Diary of Gideon Welles*, volume 1, p. 349.

38. James G. Smart, editor, *A Radical View: The "Agate" Dispatches of Whitelaw Reid, 1861–1865* (Memphis, 1976), volume 2, p. 8; Gurowski Diary, volume 2, p. 253; *OR*: 27:1:62,64, 66 and 3:384, 392–393, 407, 440, 442; Gen. Heintzelman to Gen. Slough, Capt. Potter to Slough and Potter to Gen. De Russy, June 28, 1863, RG 393, Part 1, Entry 5379, NARA.

39. Heintzelman Journal, LC; General Order Number 21, June 28, 1863, RG 393, Part 2, Entry 6752, General Orders and Circulars, August 1862 to August 1865, Defenses South of the Potomac, also Col. McCallum to Devereaux and Anderson, June 27, 1863, RG 107, M504, NARA.

40. *OR*: 27:3:397,406–407.

41. *OR*: 27:3: 428–429, 482; Gen. Slough to Lt. Col. Taylor, June 29, 1863, RG 107, M504, and Capt. Bliss to Col., July 1, 1863, RG 393, Part 1, Entry 5382, NARA; Smart, *A Radical View*, volume 2, p. 8.

Chapter 25

1. Sparks, *Inside Lincoln's Army*, pp. 267,269; Bates, *History of Pennsylvania Volunteers*, volume 3, p. 323; Capt. George Eckert to Maj. Vincent, November 12, 1864 and note signed HD and dated January 18, 1865 in Richard Butler Price's Volunteer Service File, RG 94, Entry 496, NARA; Francis B. Heitman, *Historical Register and Dictionary of the United States Army, From its Organization, September 29, 1789, to March 2, 1903* (Gaithersburg, 1988 edition), p. 807

2. For a different view of Price see George A. Rummell III, *Cavalry on the Roads to Gettysburg: Kilpatrick at Hanover and Hunterstown* (Shippensburg, 2000), p. 104.

3. Ward, "Edwin Hall Higley, an American Classicist," pp. 58–71; "An Address in Memory of Major Edwin Hall Higley delivered by The Rev. Sherrard Billings in Groton School Chapel June 4, 1922, on the occasion of the unveiling of a tablet to Major Higley," p. 5, Higley Papers, Middlebury College; Lewis Francis to the Hon. George Edmunds, January 2, 1867, RG 94, M1064, NARA; Jacob G. Ullery, *Men of Vermont: An Illustrated Biographical History of Vermonters & Sons of Vermont* (Brattleboro, 1894), Part 3, p. 83.

4. George Bean Compiled Service Record, RG 94, and the U.S. Census for 1880, NARA; Prentiss C. Dodge, *Authentic Biographical Sketches of the Representative Men of Vermont and Sons of Vermont in Other States* (Burlington, 1912), p. 49.

5. Coffin, *Nine Months to Gettysburg*, pp. 258, 277; Eldin Hartshorn's Compiled Service Record, RG 94, NARA; Eldin Hartshorn Obituary in the Frederick *Post*, January 19, 1926, as cited at vermontcivilwar.org/units/15/obits.

6. Lt. Col. Robert Johnstone's Compiled Service Record, RG 94, NARA. The nature of the charges governing his initial arrest has not been determined.

7. General Order Number 13, May 25, 1863, Col. Percy Wyndham's Compiled Service Record, RG 94, NARA.

8. Col. Wyndham to Stanton, July 29, 1863, Letter dated August 1, 1863 from Surgeon John Higgins, and Wyndham to Lt. Col. Taylor, August 3, 1863, Col. Percy Wyndham's Compiled Service Record, RG 94, NARA. Emphasis in the original.

9. Gen. Pleasonton to Gen. Seth Williams, September 3, 1863, Percy Wyndham's Volunteer Service File, RG 94, Entry 496, NARA; New York *Herald*, September 16, 1863.

10. Gen. Hooker to President Lincoln, September 26, 1863, RG 94, M1064, and Charges and Specifications against Percy Wyndham, Maj. James Hardie to Gen. Meade, October 2, 1863, Unsigned Telegram to Maj. Hardie, and Hardie to Meade, October 3, 1863 and notes dated October 8 and 12, 1863, Percy Wyndham's Volunteer Service File, RG 94, Entry 496, NARA.

11. Bucks County Intelligencer, July 1, 1862; J. M. Baldwin to Gen. Halleck, December 13, 1863, RG 94, M1064, File W628CB1863, also Col. Wyndham to Gen. Thomas, February 24, 1864, Wyndham to Col. Hardie, May 30, 1864, Gen. Meade to Adjutant General, June 28, 1864 and Special Order 227, July 5, 1864, Percy Wyndham's Volunteer Service File, RG 94, Entry 496, and Maj. James Walsh to Capt. Schuyler, July 6, 1863, Wyndham's Compiled Service Record, RG 94, NARA.

12. Toombs, *New Jersey Troops in the Gettysburg Campaign*, pp. 404–406. The news account quoted in Toombs is from the Rangoon (India) *Gazette*, of January 27, 1879, and it states that Wyndham ignored concerns that the condition of the balloon had deteriorated to the point that it was unsafe.

13. Percy Wyndham to President Abraham Lincoln, February 8, 1864, and Henry C. De Ahna to Lincoln, January 31, 1864, Abraham Lincoln Papers, LC, at http://memory.loc.gov/ammem/alhtml/malhome.html; Chicago *Tribune*, March 6, 1879. If this account is accurate, and if the account mentioned in Chapter 18, that a Union colonel was going to provide the password to aid a Southern raiding force in an attack against the capital, is also accurate, one can question if Wyndham was the officer involved in both events.

14. Detective Chris Hogan to Edwin Stanton, October 23, 1863, and undated statement of Capt. George Bru, RG 94, Entry 179, Case Files of Investigations by Levi C. Turner and Lafayette C. Baker, 1861–1866, NARA; Heintzelman Journal, and Henry C. De Ahna to President Abraham Lincoln, January 31, 1864, Abraham Lincoln Papers, LC. Henry Halleck once said of De Ahna, "I would rather trust my dinner to a hungry dog.... I have not the least doubt he would take pay on either side and fight on none," see Lowry, *Curmudgeons, Drunkards, and Outright Fools*, p. 86.

15. Col. William Mann to Gen. Thomas, October 5, 1863, Summary of Military Service for Col. Mann, March 10, 1906, William Man Volunteer Service File, RG 94, Entry 496, NARA; A Soldier to Governor Austin Blair, Fairfax, Virginia, June 12, 1863, Lt. Col. Allyne Litchfield to Blair, Boonsboro, Maryland, July 9, 1863, Petitions dated September 5 and 8, 1863, as well as an undated petition to Governor Blair, Litchfield to Blair, Gainesville, Virginia, October 24, 1863, and Col.

William Mann to Blair, November 8, 1863, Blair Papers, DPL.

16. Col. William Mann to Gen. Thomas, October 5, 1863, Summary of Military Service for Col. Mann, March 10, 1906, William Man Volunteer Service File, RG 94, Entry 496, NARA; Allyne Litchfield to My Dear Wife, Fordsville, October 8, 1863, Litchfield Letters, UMCL; John Kuhl, "The Mystery of the Mann Accoutrements: Where have all the boxes gone?" *Military Images*, volume 17, number 5, March-April 1996.

17. *TNYT*, June 27, July 18 and July 26, 1865, also January 28, 1906; *National Tribune*, February 1, 1906. Mann's postwar life is well documented in Andy Logan, *The Man Who Robbed the Robber Barons* (Pleasantville, 2001 edition).

18. *OR*: 27:2:787. In August 1864 Capt. Richard Blazer was put in command of 100 men whose sole purpose was to hunt down and destroy Mosby's battalion. To facilitate their efforts the men were issued either Spencer carbines, and though they enjoyed some initial success, Mosby ultimately defeated the command.

19. Allyne Litchfield Pension File, RG 94, NARA; Hunt and Brown, *Brevet Brigadier Generals in Blue*, p. 360.

20. Edwin Havens Compiled Service Record and Pension file, RG 94, NARA

21. Warner, *Generals in Blue*, p. 93; Heitman, *Historical Register*, pp. 596, 914; Note from Surgeon E. G. Gale, October 12, 1863, Gould Papers, CMU; Bliss, *Record of Service of Michigan Volunteers*, 5th Michigan, p. 61. Stagg's Compiled Service Record has, unfortunately, been lost, making it difficult to develop the career of a most deserving officer.

22. Francis F. McKinney, "Michigan Cavalry in the Civil War," *Michigan Alumnus Quarterly Review* 43, 1957, p. 138; Michael Phipps, "*Come On, You Wolverines!" Custer at Gettysburg* (Gettysburg, 1995), pp. 42–51.

23. Warner, *Generals in Blue*, pp. 469–470; Stahel Papers, LC, Maj. Gen. Darius Couch to Stahel, Chambersburg, March 21, 1864, In Stahel's pension file, RG 94 and Simon Wolf to Daniel Lamont, Secretary of War, Washington, D.C., November 3, 1863, RG 94, Entry 496, NARA.

24. Warner, *Generals in Blue*, pp. 469–470; Stahel Papers, LC; Scott, *PL*, p. 83.

25. *OR*: 29:2:322; Keen and Mewborn, *43rd Battalion Virginia Cavalry*, pp. 77–78; Heintzelman Journal, LC.

26. Heintzelman Journal, LC; Warner, *Generals in Blue*, p. 228; *WES*, May 1, 1880; Thompson, *Civil War to the Bloody End*, p. 286.

27. *OR*: 27:1:710.

28. Andrew Buck to Editor, Warrenton Junction, August 10, 1863, *GRDE*, August 20, 1863.

Appendix

1. Maj. Gen. Daniel Butterfield to Brig. Gen. Alfred Pleasonton, June 17, 1863, Charles S. Venable Papers, Southern Historical Collection, University of North Carolina.

Select Bibliography

Manuscript Collections

- **Central Michigan University, Clarke Historical Library**

Benjamin Clark Letters
John Farnill Letters
Amos Gould Papers
Charles Hampton Diary
Dexter Macomber Diary

- **Connecticut Historical Society**

John E. Morris Letters

- **Detroit Public Library, Burton Collection**

Austin Blair Papers

- **Duke University, William R. Perkins Library**

John S. Mosby Papers

- **Fauquier Heritage Society Library, Marshall, Virginia**

The Civil War Reminiscences of William A. Brent (1842–1904)

- **Georgetown University, Lavinger Library**

The Helen King Boyer Collection

- **Georgia Historical Society**

Gordon Family Papers

- **Grand Rapids Public Library, Grand Rapids, Michigan**

Rebecca Richmond Diary

- **The Henry E. Huntington Library, San Marino, California**

The Joseph Hooker Papers
The James Ewell Brown Stuart Papers

- **Historical Society of Pennsylvania**

Simon Gratz Autograph Collection

- **Historical Society of Western Pennsylvania, Library and Archives Division**

Gilbert Hays Collection

- **Library of Congress**

John Dahlgren Papers
Samuel Gilpin Diary
Samuel Peter Heintzelman Papers
Hickey Family Papers
Alfred Pleasonton Papers
Julius Stahel Papers
Willard Family Papers
Henry S. Willey Reminiscences

- **Horace Mewborn Collection, New Bern, North Carolina**

Marvin Wight Letter of March 29, 1863

- **Michigan State University, Archives and Historical Collections, Conrad Hall**

Edwin Havens Letters
Mattoon Family Papers

- **Middlebury College**

Edwin Hall Higley Papers

- **Dr. James Milgram Collection, Chicago, Illinois**

Thomas Benton Kelley Letters

- **Missouri Historical Society**

Edward P. Clark Papers

National Archives and Records Administration

United States Census, 1860

- **Record Group 92 — Records of the Office of the Quartermaster General**

Entry 1528, Military Railroad Reports 1863–1866
Entry 1552, Foreman Reports of Repairs 1863
Entry 1571, Train Registers
Entry 1581, Conductor Reports
Entry 1584, Bridge Repair Logs
Entry 1616, Telegrams Sent to Conductors and Engineers as well as Train Orders and Dispatcher Books

- **Record Group 94 — Records of the Adjutant General's Office**

Case Files of Investigations by Levi C. Turner and Lafayette C. Baker — Microcopy M797

Compiled Service Records of Volunteer Union Soldiers
Compiled Service Records of Volunteer Union Soldiers Who Served in Organizations From the State of West Virginia — Microcopy M508
Descriptive Roll of Prisoners — Microcopy M797
Entry 492, Letters Sent, 1861–1869, Volunteer Service Division
Entry 496, Union Officer Volunteer Service Records
Entry 729, Union Battle Reports
Letter and Order Books, 1st Michigan Cavalry
Letter and Order Books, 5th Michigan Cavalry
Letter and Order Books, 7th Michigan Cavalry
Letter and Order Books, 11th New York Cavalry
Letter and Order Books, 1st Rhode Island Cavalry
Letter and Order Books, 1st Vermont Cavalry
Letters Received by the Commission Branch, 1863–1870 — Microcopy M1064
Letters Received by the Office of the Adjutant General (Main Series), 1861–1870 — Microcopy M619
Muster Rolls, Returns and Regimental Papers, 1st Vermont Cavalry
Muster Rolls, Returns and Regimental Papers, 5th Michigan Cavalry
Muster Rolls, Returns and Regimental Papers, 6th Michigan Cavalry
Muster Rolls, Returns and Regimental Papers, 10th New York Cavalry
Muster Rolls, Returns and Regimental Papers, 11th New York Cavalry
Muster Rolls, Returns and Regimental Papers, 15th Vermont Infantry
Pension Files of Union Soldiers
U.S. Army Generals' Reports of Civil War Service, 1864–1887, Microcopy M1098

• **Record Group 107 — Records of the Office of the Secretary of War**
Telegrams Collected by the Secretary of War (Unbound) — Microcopy 504

• **Record Group 109 — War Department Collection of Confederate Records**
Compiled Service Records of Confederate Soldiers from South Carolina — Microcopy 267
Compiled Service Records of Confederate Soldiers From North Carolina — Microcopy 270
Entry 183, Miscellaneous Documents
Entry 199, Union Provost Marshal's File of Confederate Prisoners
Union Provost Marshal's File of Papers Relating to Individual Civilians — Microcopy 345

• **Record Group 249 — Office of the Commissary General of Prisoners**
Miscellaneous File 377

• **Record Group 393, Part 1 — Records of the U.S. Army Continental Commands**
Entry 3964, Letters Sent and Received, Army of the Potomac, June 1861–June 1865
Entry 3966, Letters Sent by General Casey Commanding at White House, Va., June 1862.
Entry 3980, Miscellaneous Letters, Reports and Lists Received, 1861–1865
Entry 3986, Two or More Name File
Entry 5379, Telegrams Sent, Sept. 1862–Dec. 1863, Department of Washington
Entry 5381, Register of Letters Received
Entry 5382, Letters Received, Department of Washington
Entry 5383, Letters Received, Department of Washington
Entry 5384, Telegrams Received, Department of Washington, 1863–1864

• **Record Group 393, Part 2 — Records of the U.S. Army Continental Commands**
Entry 642, Letters Sent, Department of Washington
Entry 659, Letters Sent, September 1862 to December 1863, Abercrombie's Command
Entry 675, Letters Sent, Casey's Division, September 1862 to April 1863
Entry 676, Telegrams Sent and Received, September 1862 to April 1863, Casey's Division
Entry 732, Letters and Telegrams Sent by Stahel's Cavalry Division, March — June 1863
Entry 1449, Letters, Telegrams, Reports, and Lists Received by the Cavalry Corps, 1861–1865
Entry 2198, Letters Received, Feb. — Mar. 1862, Banks' Division
Entry 3582, Letters Received, 1862–1864
Entry 3935, Letters Sent, Casey, Hays and Abercrombie's Commands
Entry 5444, Letters, Telegrams, Orders and Lists Received by Gen. John W. Geary
Entry 6744, Letters Received and Sent, March to December 1862, Defences of Washington
Entry 6745, Telegrams Received and Sent, September to December 1862, Heintzelman's Command
Entry 6752, General Orders and Circulars, August 1862 to August 1865, Defenses South of the Potomac
Entry 6833, Letters Sent, December 1862 to June 1863, Defenses of Washington, Stoughton, Casey and Abercrombie
Entry 6834, General Orders, Abercrombie's Division, October 1862–July 1863

• **Navarro College, Pearce Civil War Collection**
Lewis Crandell Papers
Stacy (Manley) Papers

• **New York State Library and Archives**
Calvin Haynes Letters

Silas Mason Letters
Gouverneur K. Warren Papers

• **Pennsylvania State Archives**
RG 19 Regimental Records

• **State Archives of Michigan**
Letters Sent by the State Adjutant General
Regimental Service Records, 1st Michigan Cavalry
Regimental Service Records, 5th Michigan Cavalry

• **United States Military Academy**
John Buford Papers

• **United States Military History Institute**
Civil War Miscellaneous Collection
James Baldwin Burrows Collection
Charles W. Belknap Diary
Charles Chapin Letters
Frank Dickerson Papers
M.L.S. Jackson Diary

William F. LeMunyon Reminiscences
Dexter Macomber Letters
The Civil War Letters of William Porter Wilkins

Civil War Miscellaneous Collection, 2nd Series
George Telling Letters

Harrisburg Civil War Roundtable Collection
William Martin Letters
Clement Hoffman Letters

Lewis Leigh Collection
Movements of the 5th New York Cavalry

• **University of California, Santa Barbara, Davidson Library**
Charles H. Johnson Papers

• **University of Georgia, Hargrett Rare Book and Manuscript Library**
William Deloney Letters

• **University of Michigan, Bentley Historical Library**
Baird Family Papers
Frank Brown Letters
Buck Family Correspondence
Victor Comte Letters
Frederick Corselius Letters
Emmons Family Collection
James Kidd Collection
George Kilborn Letters
John R. Morey Diary and Letters
O'Brien Family Papers
James Rowe Reminiscences
Alfred Ryder Letters
Frederick Schmalzried Letters

• **University of Michigan, William L. Clements Library**
Litchfield — French Letters

• **University of North Carolina, Lewis Round Wilson Library**
Charles S. Venable Papers

• **University of Vermont, Bailey/Howe Library**
Charles H. Blinn Diary
J. B. Chamberlin Letters
Roswell Farnham Letters
Albert Greene Letters
Greene-Louiselle Family Papers
George Hagar Letters
Benjamin Hatch Letters
Hugh Henry Letters
Augustus Paddock Letters
Tabor H. Parcher Letters
Herman A. Post Diary
Albert Sawyer Letters
Charles Stone Diary
Charles C. Tewksbury Letters
William Wells Papers
John L. Yale Papers

• **University of Virginia, Alderman Library**
Henry Clay Christiancy Papers

• **Vermont Historical Society**
James Aiken Diary
George Crosby Diary
Charles Cummings Letters
Edwin C. Hall Letters
Henry Jillson Letters
Royal D. King Diary
Walcott Mead Letters
Edmund Pope Papers
Henry A. Smith Letters
Wheelock Veazey Letters
John S. T. Wallace Letters
William White Letters
John H. Williams Diary

• **Virginia Historical Society**
Alexander Dixon Payne Memorandum Book
Henry B. McClellan Papers

• **Virginia State Library**
William Carter Papers

• **Western Michigan University, Archives and Regional History Collections**
George Harrington Diary
William Rockwell Collection

• **Wichita State University, Department of Special Collections**
Darius G. Maynard Letters

Newspapers

Alexandria *Gazette*
Augusta *Daily Constitutionalist*

Baltimore *American and Commercial Advertiser*
Bucks County Intelligencer
Burlington *Free Press*
Charlotte *Western Democrat*
Chicago *Tribune*
Detroit *Advertiser & Tribune*
Detroit *Free Press*
Flint *Wolverine Citizen*
Frederick *Examiner*
Frederick *Union*
Fredonia *Censor*
Grand Rapids *Daily Eagle*
Indianapolis *Daily Journal*
Jackson *Eagle*
Jersey City *Courier & Advertiser*
Kingston *People's Press*
Lancaster *Daily Evening Express*
Mecosta County *Pioneer*
Monroe *Commercial*
National Tribune
New York *Herald*
New York *Tribune*
New York *Tri-States Union*
Philadelphia *Inquirer*
Richmond *Daily Dispatch*
Richmond *Enquirer*
Richmond *Examiner*
Richmond *Sentinel*
Rochester *Daily Union & Advertiser*
Rochester *Democrat & American*
Rutland *Daily Herald*
St. Johnsbury *Caledonian*
The *New York Times*
Vermont *Chronicle*
Washington *Daily Morning Chronicle*
Washington *Evening Star*
Washington *Evening Star*
Windsor *Vermont Journal*

Periodicals

Alexander, Ted. "Antietam Horsepower or, Greasy Heel and the Dead Colonel's Mount." *Blue & Gray*, volume 20, number 1, 2002.

Bilby, Joseph. "Carbines — Yesterday." *The Civil War News*, December 1992.

Cooke, Michael A. "The Health of the Union Military in the District of Columbia, 1861–1865." *Military Affairs*, volume 48, number 4, October 1984.

Crouch, Richard E. "The Mobberly Mysteries: The Strange Life and Death of Loudoun County's Exceedingly Romantic Bastard (?) / Hero (?)." *Civil War Quarterly*, volume 7, 1986.

Dickinson, F.S. "Fifth New York Cavalry at Fairfax." *The Maine Bugle*, July 1895.

"Editorial Paragraph." *Southern Historical Society Papers*, volume 3. Richmond: The Southern Historical Society, 1877.

Garnett, Theodore S., Jr. "Cavalry Service with Gen. Stuart." *Philadelphia Weekly Times*, February 8, 1879.

Greenleaf, William A. "From the Rapidan to Richmond." *Vermont War Papers and Miscellaneous States Papers and Addresses for Military Order of the Loyal Legion of the United States*, volume 54. Wilmington, NC: Broadfoot, 1994 edition.

Isham, Asa. "The Story of a Gunshot Wound." *Sketches of War History 1861–1865, Papers Prepared for the Ohio Commandery of the Military Order of the Loyal Legion of the United States 1890–1896*. Wilmington, NC: Broadfoot, 1991 edition.

Keatley, John. "Across the Occoquan, How Raider Stuart Dodged an Ambush and Laid Waste the Country." *National Tribune*, March 18, 1897.

Klement, Frank L., editor. "Edwin B. Bigelow: A Michigan Sergeant in the Civil War." *Michigan History Magazine*, September 1954.

Kross, Gary. "Attack from the West." *Blue & Gray*, volume 27, number 5, Campaign 2000.

Kuhl, John. "The Mystery of the Mann Accoutrements: Where Have All the Boxes Gone?" *Military Images*, volume 17, number 5, March-April 1996.

Lowden, J.K. "Michigan's 5th Cav. in the Latter Period of the War." *National Tribune*, July 16, 1896.

Marshall, Michael. "The 'Grey Ghost' at Virginia: The Story of a Rebel Expelled." *University of Virginia Alumni News*, volume LXXIV, number 4, March/April 1986.

Mauro, Chuck. "Mosby's raid fills Herndon house with bullets, fear." Washington *Times*, March 15, 2008.

McClellan, H.B. "The Invasion of Pennsylvania in '63." *Philadelphia Weekly Times*, July 20, 1878.

McKinney, Francis F. "Michigan Cavalry in the Civil War." *Michigan Alumnus Quarterly Review* 43, 1957.

Member of Stonewall Jackson's Staff. "The Death of Turner Ashby." *The Old Guard*, August 1866, volume 4, issue 8.

Mewborn, Horace. "The Operations of Mosby's Rangers." *Blue & Gray*, volume XVII, issue 4.

_____. "A Wonderful Exploit, Jeb Stuart's Ride Around the Army of the Potomac." *Blue & Gray*, volume XV, issue 6.

Moore, Samuel S. "Through the Shadow: A Boy's Memories of the Civil War in Clarke County." *Proceedings of The Clarke County Historical Association*, volume 24, 1989–1990.

Mosby, John S. "A Bit of Partisan Service." Robert U. Johnson, and Clarence C. Buel, editors, *Battles and Leaders of the Civil War*, volume 3. New York: Castle Books, 1956 edition.

_____. "Mosby and the War." Richmond *Dispatch*, May 6, 1894.

Pickard, D.O. "The Death of Col. Brodhead." *National Tribune*, October 15, 1885.

Ramsdell, Charles W. "General Robert E. Lee's Horse Supply, 1862–1863." *American Historical Review*, volume 35, number 4, 1930.

Rose, James A. "Famous Custer Cavalry of Civil War." *National Tribune*, September 29, 1929.

Scheuch-Evans, Lewis. " Sir Percy Wyndham, Personality Profile." *Military History*, volume 22, number 9, December 2005.

Scott, John. "The Black Horse Cavalry." *Philadelphia Weekly Times*, May 25, 1878.

Sears, Stephen W. "Meade Takes Command." *North & South*, volume 5, number 6, September 2002.

Sutherland, Daniel E. "Guerrilla Warfare, Democracy, and the Fate of the Confederacy," *The Journal of Southern History*, volume 68, number 2, May 2002.

Sword, Wiley. "'Those Damned Michigan Spencers' Colonel Copeland's 5th Michigan Cavalry and Their Spencer Rifles." *Man at Arms*, volume 19, number 5, September/October 1997.

Tompkins, Charles H. "With the Vermont Cavalry, 1861–2, Some Reminiscences by Brig. Gen. Charles H. Tompkins, U.S.A." *The Vermonter*, volume 17, number 4, April 1912.

Urwin, Gregory J.W. "'Come On, You Wolverines!' Custer's Michigan Brigade." *Military Images*, volume 7, number 1, July-August 1985.

Vogl, F. "Who Laid the Pontoons?" *National Tribune*, October 11, 1888.

Wagner, Rob L. "Mortally Wounded Colonel Thornton Brodhead Left Behind Two Blood-smeared Letters Denouncing His Superiors." *America's Civil War*, May 1998.

Ward, Allen M., "Edwin Hall Higley, an American Classicist: The Intersection of Geography, Biography, and History." *New England Classical Journal*, volume 33, number 1, 2006.

Yearbook: The Historical Society of Fairfax County, Virginia, volume 20. 1984–1985.

Zeilinger, Elna Rae, and Larry Schweikart, editors. "'They Also Serve ...': The Diary of Benjamin Franklin Hackett, 12th Vermont Volunteers" *Vermont History*, Spring 1983, volume 51, number 2.

Published Sources

Annual Report of the Adjutant-General of the State of New York. Albany: James B. Lyon, State Printer, 1895.

Armstrong, Richard L. *7th Virginia Cavalry*. Lynchburg: H.E. Howard, 1992.

Arnold, Delevan. *A Kalamazoo Volunteer in the Civil War*. Edited by Helen Everett Wood. Kalamazoo: Kalamazoo Public Museum Publication, 1962.

Baird, Nancy Chappelear, editor. *Journals of Amanda Virginia Edmonds, Lass of the Mosby Confederacy 1857–1867*. Stephens City: Commercial Press, 1984.

Basler, Roy, editor. *The Collected Works of Abraham Lincoln*. New Brunswick: Rutgers University Press, 1953.

Bates, Samuel P. *History of Pennsylvania Volunteers 1861–5*. Wilmington, NC: Broadfoot, 1993 edition.

Bayard, Samuel J. *The Life of George Dashiell Bayard*. New York: G.P. Putnam & Sons, 1874.

Beach, William H. *The First New York (Lincoln) Cavalry, From April 19, 1861 to July 7, 1865*. New York: The Lincoln Cavalry Association, 1902.

Beale, George W. *A Lieutenant of Cavalry in Lee's Army*, Baltimore: Butternut and Blue, 1994 edition.

Beale, R.L.T. *History of the Ninth Virginia Cavalry in the War Between the States*, Amissville: American Fundamentalist, 1981 edition.

Benedict, George G. *Army Life in Virginia, Letters from the Twelfth Vermont Regiment and Personal Experiences of Volunteer Service in the War for the Union, 1862–63*, Burlington: Free Press Association, 1895.

_____. *Vermont in the Civil War, A History of the Part Taken by the Vermont Soldiers and Sailors in the War for the Union 1861–1865*. Burlington: The Free Press Association, 1888.

Berleth, Richard. *The Twilight Lords, An Irish Chronicle*. New York: Alfred Knopf, 1978.

Blackford, W.W. *War Years with Jeb Stuart*. Baton Rouge: Louisiana State University Press, 1993 edition.

Blackwell, Samuel M. *In the First Line of Battle: The 12th Illinois Cavalry in the Civil War*. DeKalb: Northern Illinois University Press, 2002.

Bliss, Aaron T. *Record of Service of Michigan Volunteers in the Civil War 1861–1865, First Cavalry*. Kalamazoo: Ihling Brothers & Everhard, 1905.

_____. *Record of Service of Michigan Volunteers in the Civil War 1861–1865, Fifth Cavalry*. Kalamazoo: Ihling Brothers & Everhard, 1905.

_____. *Record of Service of Michigan Volunteers in the Civil War 1861–1865, Sixth Cavalry*. Kalamazoo: Ihling Brothers & Everhard, 1905.

_____. *Record of Service of Michigan Volunteers in the Civil War 1861–1865, Seventh Cavalry*. Kalamazoo: Ihling Brothers & Everhard, 1905.

Boudrye, Louis N. *Historic Records of the Fifth New York Cavalry, First Ira Harris Guard*. Albany: J. Munsell, 1865.

Brady, James P., compiler. *Hurrah for the Artillery! Knap's Independent Battery "E," Pennsylvania Light Artillery*. Gettysburg: Thomas, 1992.

Brooks, Noah. *Washington in Lincoln's Time*. New York: Century, 1895.

Brooks, U.R. *Butler and His Cavalry in the War of Secession 1861–1865*. Camden: J.J. Fox, 1989 edition.

_____. *Stories of the Confederacy*. Camden: J.J. Fox, 1991 edition.

Brown, Peter A. *Mosby's Fighting Parson: The Life and Times of Sam Chapman*. Westminster: Willow Bend Books, 2001.

Brown, R. Shepard. *Stringfellow of the Fourth*. New York: Crown, 1960.

Buck, William P, editor. *Sad Earth, Sweet Heaven: The Diary of Lucy Rebecca Buck During the War Between the States, Front Royal, Virginia, December 25, 1861—April 15, 1865*. Birmingham: The Cornerstone, 1973.

Bush, B. Conrad, editor. *Articles from Wyoming County Newspapers and Letters from Soldiers of the 5th New York Cavalry*. privately printed, 2000.

_____, editor. *Civil War Letters of Captain Daniel Wade Lapham Co. A & K, 9th NY Volunteer Cavalry*. privately printed, 2003.

_____, editor. *Ninth New York Cavalry (Veteran) Stoneman's Cavalry or Westfield Cavalry, News Articles from Wyoming County Newspapers*. privately printed, 2000.

Campbell, Eric, editor. "*A Grand Terrible Dramma:*" *From Gettysburg to Petersburg: The Civil War Letters of Charles Wellington Reed*. New York: Fordham University Press, 2000.

Chamberlin, Taylor M., and James D. Peshek. *Crossing the Line: Civilian Trade & Travel Between Loudoun County, Virginia, and Maryland During the Civil War*. Waterford: Waterford Foundation, 2002.

Chamberlin, Taylor M., and John M. Souders. *Between Reb and Yank: A Civil War History of Northern Loudoun County, Virginia*. Jefferson, NC: McFarland, 2011.

Cheney, Newel. *History of the Ninth Regiment New York Volunteer Cavalry*. New York: Martin Merz & Son, 1901.

Coffin, Howard. *Nine Months to Gettysburg: Stannard's Vermonters and the Repulse of Pickett's Charge*. Woodstock: The Countryman Press, 1997.

Collea, Joseph D., Jr. *The First Vermont Cavalry in the Civil War: A History*. Jefferson, NC: McFarland, 2010.

Committee on Regimental History, Hillman Hall, Chairman. *History of the Sixth New York Cavalry (Second Ira Harris Guard)*. Worcester: The Blanchard Press, 1908.

Cooper, David M. *Obituary Discourse on Occasion of the Death of Noah Henry Ferry, Major of the Fifth Michigan Cavalry Killed at Gettysburg, July 3, 1863*. New York: John F. Trow, 1863.

Cozzens, Peter. *Shenandoah 1862: Stonewall Jackson's Valley Campaign*. Chapel Hill: University of North Carolina Press, 2008.

Craig, Joel, editor. *Dear Eagle: The Civil War Correspondence of Stephen H. Bogardus, Jr. to the Poughkeepsie Daily Eagle*. Wake Forest: The Scuppernong Press, 2004.

Crowninshield, Benjamin W. *A History of the First Regiment of Massachusetts Cavalry Volunteers*. Baltimore: Butternut and Blue, 1995 edition.

Denison, Frederic. *Sabres and Spurs: The First Rhode Island Cavalry in the Civil War*, Baltimore: Butternut and Blue, 1994 edition.

Divine, John E. *35th Battalion Virginia Cavalry*. Lynchburg: H. E. Howard, 1985.

Divine, John, Bronwen Souders, and John Souders. "*To Talk Is Treason*": *Quakers of Waterford, Virginia on Life, Love, Death & War in the Southern Confederacy, from Their Diaries & Correspondence*. Waterford: The Waterford Foundation, 1996.

Dodge, Prentiss C. *Authentic Biographical Sketches of the Representative Men of Vermont and Sons of Vermont in Other States*. Burlington: Ullery, 1912.

Driver, Robert J. *First and Second Maryland Cavalry, C.S.A.* Charlottesville: Rockbridge, 1999.

_____. *1st Virginia Cavalry*. Lynchburg: H.E. Howard, 1991.

Dulany, Ida Powell. *Civil War Diary of Ida Powell Dulany*. privately printed, no date.

Dyer, Frederick H., compiler. *A Compendium of the War of the Rebellion*. 3 volumes. Des Moines: Dyer, 1908.

Emerson, Edward Waldo. *Life and Letters of Charles Russell Lowell*. Columbia: University of South Carolina Press, 2005 edition.

Engle, Stephen D. *Yankee Dutchman: The Life of Franz Sigel*. Fayetteville: University of Arkansas Press, 1993.

Faust, Patricia L., editor. *Historical Times Illustrated Encyclopedia of the Civil War*. New York: Harper & Row, 1986.

Fishel, Edwin C. *The Secret War for the Union, The Untold Story of Military Intelligence in the Civil War*. Boston: Houghton Mifflin, 1996.

Ford, Worthington C. *A Cycle of Adams Letters 1861–1865*. Boston: Houghton Mifflin, 1920.

Fortier, John. *15th Virginia Cavalry*. Lynchburg: H.E. Howard, 1993.

Freeman, Douglas Southall. *Lee's Lieutenants*. New York: Scribner's, 1944.

Furgurson, Ernest B. *Freedom Rising: Washington in the Civil War*. New York: Alfred A. Knopf, 2004.

Genco, James G. *Arming Michigan's Regiments 1862–1864*. privately printed, 1982.

Gillespie, Samuel. *A History of Company A, First Ohio Cavalry*. Washington Court House: Press of Ohio State Register, 1898.

Gilmor, Harry. *Four Years in the Saddle*. New York: Harper & Brothers, 1866.

Glazier, Willard. *Three Years in the Federal Cavalry*. New York: R. H. Ferguson, 1874.

Gracey, Samuel L. *Annals of the Sixth Pennsylvania Cavalry*. Lancaster: VanBerg, 1996 edition.

Gurowski, Adam. *Diary, From November 18, 1862, to October 18, 1863*. New York: Carleton, 1864.
Hard, Abner. *History of the Eighth Cavalry Regiment Illinois Volunteers, During the Great Rebellion*. Dayton: Morningside House, 1984 edition.
Harris, Samuel. *Personal Reminiscences of Samuel Harris*. Chicago: Rogerson Press, 1897.
Haynes, Edwin M. *A History of the Tenth Regiment Vermont Volunteers with Biographical Sketches of the Officers Who Fell in Battle and a Complete Roster*. Lewiston: The Tenth Vermont Regimental Association, 1870.
Hebert, Walter H. *Fighting Joe Hooker*. Lincoln: University of Nebraska Press, 1999 edition.
Heitman, Francis B. *Historical Register and Dictionary of the United States Army, From its Organization, September 29, 1789, to March 2, 1903*. Gaithersburg: Olde Soldier Books, 1988 edition.
Henderson, E. Prioleau. *Autobiography of Arab*. Oxford: The Guild Bindery Press, 1991 edition.
Hennessy, John. *Return to Bull Run: The Campaign and Battle of Second Manassas*. New York: Simon & Schuster, 1993.
Howard, Oliver O. *Autobiography of Oliver Otis Howard, Major General United States Army*. New York: Baker & Taylor, 1908.
Hubard, Robert T., Jr. *The Civil War Memoirs of a Virginia Cavalryman*. Edited by Thomas P. Nanzig. Tuscaloosa: University of Alabama Press, 2007.
Hunt, Roger D. *Colonels in Blue: Union Colonels in the Civil War, New York* Atgleg: Schiffer, 2003.
_____, and Jack R. Brown. *Brevet Brigadier Generals in Blue*. Gaithersburg: Olde Soldier Books, 1990.
Ide, Horace K. *History of the First Vermont Cavalry Volunteers in the War of the Great Rebellion*. Edited by Elliott W. Hoffman. Baltimore: Butternut and Blue, 2000.
Isham, Asa. *An Historical Sketch of the Seventh Regiment Michigan Volunteer Cavalry, from Its Organization, in 1862, to Its Muster Out, in 1865*. Huntington: Blue Acorn Press, 2000 edition.
Jones, Virgil C. *Ranger Mosby*. Chapel Hill: University of North Carolina Press, 1944.
Jordan, David M. *"Happiness Is Not My Companion": The Life of General G.K. Warren*. Bloomington: Indiana University Press, 2001.
Journal of the Congress of the Confederate States 1861–1865, volume 2. Washington, D.C.: Government Printing Office, 1904.
Kajencki, Francis C. *Star on Many a Battlefield: Brevet Brigadier General Joseph Karge in the American Civil War*. Cranbury: Fairleigh Dickinson University Press, 1980.
Keen, Hugh C., and Horace Mewborn. *43rd Virginia Battalion Virginia Cavalry Mosby's Command*. Lynchburg: H. E. Howard, 1993.
Kidd, J.H. *Personal Recollections of a Cavalryman with Custer's Michigan Cavalry Brigade in the Civil War*. Alexandria: Time Life Books, 1983 edition.
Krick, Robert K. *9th Virginia Cavalry*. Lynchburg: H. E. Howard, 1982.
Laas, Virginia Jeans, editor. *Wartime Washington; The Civil War Letters of Elizabeth Blair Lee*. Urbana: University of Illinois Press, 1991.
Ladd, David, and Audrey Ladd, editors. *The Bachelder Papers: Gettysburg in Their Own Words*. Dayton: Morningside House, 1994.
Lee, William O. *Personal and Historical Sketches and Facial History of and by Members of the Seventh Regiment Michigan Volunteer Cavalry, 1862–1865*. Detroit: Detroit Book Press, 1990 edition.
Leech, Margaret. *Reveille in Washington 1860–1865*. Alexandria: Time Life Books, 1980 edition.
Lewis, Berkeley R. *Notes on Cavalry Weapons of the American Civil War 1861–1865*. Washington, D.C.: The American Ordinance Association, 1961.
Lloyd, William P. *History of the First Reg't Pennsylvania Reserve Cavalry, from Its Organization, August, 1861, to September, 1864, with List of Names of All Officers and Enlisted Men*. Philadelphia: King & Baird, Printers, 1864.
Logan, Andy. *The Man Who Robbed the Robber Barons*. Pleasantville: The Akadine Press, 2001 edition.
Lomax, Elizabeth Lindsay. *Leaves from an Old Washington Diary 1854–1863*. Edited by Lindsay Lomax Wood, New York: E.P. Dutton, 1943.
Longacre, Edward G. *Custer and His Wolverines: The Michigan Cavalry Brigade, 1861–1865*. Conshohocken: Combined Publishing, 1997.
Lonn, Ella. *Foreigners in the Union Army and Navy*. Baton Rouge: Louisiana State University Press, 1952.
Lowry, Thomas P. *Curmudgeons, Drunkards & Outright Fools: Courts-Martial of Civil War Colonels*. Lincoln: University of Nebraska Press, 1997.
Mahon, Michael G., editor. *Winchester Divided: The Civil War Diaries of Julia Chase & Laura Lee*. Mechanicsburg: Stackpole Books, 2002.
Maharay, George S. *Vermont Hero: Major General George J. Stannard*. Shippensburg: White Mane Books, 2001.
Manarin, Louis H., compiler. *North Carolina Troops, 1861–1865: A Roster*. volume 2. Raleigh: North Carolina State Department of Archives and History, 1968.
Marszalek, John F. *Commander of All Lincoln's Armies: A Life of General Henry W. Halleck*. Cambridge: The Belknap Press of Harvard University Press, 2004.
May, George S. *Michigan and the Civil War Years, 1860–1866: A Wartime Chronicle*. Lansing: Michigan Civil War Centennial Observance Commission, 1964.

McAulay, John D. *Carbines of the U.S. Cavalry, 1861–1905*. Lincoln: Andrew Mowbray, 1996.

McClellan, George B. *McClellan's Own Story*. New York: Charles L. Webster, 1887.

McClellan, H.B. *The Life and Campaigns of Major-General J.E.B. Stuart*. Little Rock: Eagle Press of Little Rock, 1987 edition.

McDonald, William N. *A History of the Laurel Brigade, Originally the Ashby Cavalry of the Army of Northern Virginia and Chew's Battery*. Edited by Bushrod C. Washington. Gaithersburg: Olde Soldier Books, 1987 edition.

McGrath, Franklin. *The History of the 127th New York Volunteers "Monitors" in the War for the Preservation of the Union—September 8th, 1862, June 30th 1865*. No publisher, 1898.

McPherson, James M. *Crossroads of Freedom: Antietam*. New York: Oxford University Press, 2002.

Meade, George. *The Life and Letters of George Gordon Meade, Major-General United States Army*. Baltimore: Butternut and Blue, 1994 edition.

Merington, Marguerite, editor. *The Custer Story: The Life and Letters of General Custer and His Wife Elizabeth*. New York: Devin-Adair, 1950.

Merrill, Samuel H. *The Campaigns of the First Maine and First District of Columbia Cavalry*. Portland: Bailey & Noyes, 1866.

Mewborn, Horace, editor. *"From Mosby's Command": Newspaper Letters & Articles by and about John S. Mosby and his Rangers*. Baltimore: Butternut and Blue, 2005.

Miller, Charles H., compiler. *History of the 16th Regiment Pennsylvania Cavalry for the Year Ending October 31st 1863*. Philadelphia: King & Baird, Printers, 1864.

Mitchell, Adele H., editor. *The Letters of General J.E.B. Stuart*. Fairfax: The Stuart—Mosby Historical Society, 1990.

_____, editor. *The Letters of John S. Mosby*, Fairfax: The Stuart—Mosby Historical Society, 1986.

Mohr, James C. *The Cormany Diaries, A Northern Family in the Civil War*. Pittsburgh: University of Pittsburgh Press, 1982.

Moore, Henry W. *"Chained to Virginia While Carolina Bleeds.": The Civil War Correspondence of Henry Woodbury Moore and James Washington Moore*. Columbia: privately printed, 1996.

Mosby, John Singleton. *Mosby's War: Reminiscences and Stuart's Cavalry Campaigns*. Harrisburg: The Archive Society, 1995 edition.

_____, *Stuart's Cavalry in the Gettysburg Campaign*. Gaithersburg: Olde Soldier Books, 1987 edition.

Moyer, H. P. *History of the Seventeenth Regiment Pennsylvania Volunteer Cavalry or One Hundred and Sixty-Second in the Line of Pennsylvania Volunteer Regiments, War to Suppress the Rebellion, 1861–1865*. Lebanon: Sowers Printing, 1911.

Munson, John W. *Reminiscences of a Mosby Guerrilla*. New York: Moffat, Yard, 1906.

Murray, Elizabeth Dunbar. *My Mother Used to Say: A Natchez Belle of the Sixties*. Boston: Christopher Publishing House, 1959.

Myers, Frank. *The Comanches: A History of White's Battalion, Virginia Cavalry, Laurel Brig., Hampton's Div., A.N.V., C.S.A.* Gaithersburg: Butternut Press, 1987 edition.

Nanzig, Thomas P. *3rd Virginia Cavalry* Lynchburg: H. E. Howard, 1989.

Neese, George M. *Three Years in the Confederate Horse Artillery*. Dayton: Morningside House, 1988 edition.

Norton, Henry. *Deeds of Daring, or History of the Eighth N.Y. Volunteer Cavalry*. Norwich: Chenango Telegraph Printing House, 1889.

Palmer, Edwin F. *The Second Brigade; or Camp Life*. Montpelier: E.P. Walton, 1864.

Peck, Theodore S., compiler. *Revised Roster of Vermont Volunteers and Lists of Vermonters Who Served in the Army and Navy of the United States During the War of the Rebellion, 1861–1866*. Montpelier: Press of the Watchman, 1892.

Penfield, James. *Captain James Penfield, 1863–1864 Civil War Diary, 5th New York Volunteer Cavalry, Company H*. Crown Point: The Penfield Foundation, Press of America, 1999.

Pfanz, Donald C. *Richard S. Ewell: A Soldier's Life*. Chapel Hill: University of North Carolina Press, 1998.

Phipps, Michael. *"Come On, You Wolverines!" Custer at Gettysburg*. Gettysburg: Farnsworth House Military Impressions, 1995.

Plum, William R. *The Military Telegraph During the Civil War in the United States*. Chicago: Jansen, McClurg, 1882.

Preston, N.D. *History of the Tenth Regiment of Cavalry New York Volunteers, August, 1861 to August, 1865*. New York: D. Appleton, 1892.

Publication Committee. *History of the Eighteenth Regiment of Cavalry Pennsylvania Volunteers (163d Regiment of the Line) 1862–1865*. New York: Wynkoop Hallenbeck Crawford Co., 1909.

Pyne, Henry R. *Ride to War: The History of the First New Jersey Cavalry*. New Brunswick: Rutgers University Press, 1961.

Quaife, Milo M., editor. *From the Cannon's Mouth: The Civil War Letters of General Alpheus S. Williams*. Lincoln: University of Nebraska Press, 1995 edition.

Quynn, William R., editor. *The Diary of Jacob Engelbrecht*. Frederick: Historical Society of Frederick County, 2001.

Ramage, James A. *Gray Ghost: The Life of Col. John Singleton Mosby*. Lexington: University Press of Kentucky, 1999.

Ramey, Emily G., and John K. Gott. *The Years of*

Anguish: Fauquier County, Virginia 1861–1865. Fauquier: The Fauquier County Civil War Centennial Committee, 1965.

Ratcliffe, R. Jackson. *This Was Prince William.* Leesburg: Potomac Press, 1978.

Reese, Timothy J. *Sykes' Regular Infantry Division, 1861–1864: A History of Regular United States Infantry Operations in the Civil War's Eastern Theater.* Jefferson, NC: McFarland, 1990.

Regimental History Committee. *History of the Third Pennsylvania Cavalry, Sixteenth Regiment Pennsylvania Volunteers in the American Civil War, 1861–1865.* Philadelphia: Franklin, 1905.

Rickey, Don, Jr. *Forty Miles a Day on Beans and Hay: The Enlisted Soldier Fighting the Indian Wars.* Norman: University of Oklahoma Press, 1963.

Robertson, John, compiler. *Michigan in the War.* Lansing: W.S. George & Co., 1882.

Rogers, Larry, and Keith Rogers. *Their Horses Climbed Trees, A Chronicle of the California 100 and Battalion in the Civil War, From San Francisco to Appomattox.* Atglen: Schiffer, 2001.

Ruffner, Kevin C. "*Tenting on the old Camp Ground*": *The Civil War History of Union Mills, Fairfax County, Virginia, Part One: The Historical Record.* Fairfax: Fairfax County History Commission, 1992.

Rummell, George A., III. *Cavalry on the Roads to Gettysburg: Kilpatrick at Hanover and Hunterstown.* Shippensburg: White Mane Books, 2000.

Russell, Charles Wells, editor. *Gray Ghost: The Memoirs of Colonel John S. Mosby.* New York: Bantam Books, 1992 edition.

Saffer, Wynne C. *Mount Zion Cemetery, Aldie, Virginia.* Lovettsville: Willow Bend Books, 1997.

St. Clair, Hugh. *Hugh St. Clair of Crawford County, Pennsylvania Civil War Diary, 1 January to 31 December 1863, 18th Pennsylvania Regiment of Mounted Volunteers.* transcribed by Patricia Ann St. Clair Ostwald. Boulder: Privately Published, 1993.

Sandburg, Carl. *Abraham Lincoln, The War Years.* New York: Harcourt, Brace, 1939.

Sansone, Cordelia Grantham, editor. *Journey to Bloomfield, Lives and Letters of 19th Century Virginia Families.* Fairfax: AlphaGraphics Printshops of the Future, 2004.

Scott, John. *Partisan Life with Col. John S. Mosby.* New York: Harper & Brothers, 1867.

Sears, Stephen W., editor. *On Campaign with the Army of the Potomac: The Civil War Journal of Theodore Ayrault Dodge.* New York: Cooper Square Press, 2001.

Simons, Ezra D. *A Regimental History: The One Hundred and Twenty-Fifth New York State Volunteers.* New York: privately printed, 1888.

Slocum, Charles E. *The Life and Services of Major-General Henry Warner Slocum.* Toledo: Slocum, 1913.

Smart, James G., editor. *A Radical View: The "Agate" Dispatches of Whitelaw Reid 1861–1865.* 2 volumes. Memphis: Memphis State University Press, 1976.

Smith, Thomas West. *The Story of a Cavalry Regiment: "Scott's 900" Eleventh New York Cavalry from the St. Lawrence River to the Gulf of Mexico 1861–1865.* Chicago: W.B. Conkey, 1894

Sparks, David S., editor. *Inside Lincoln's Army: The Diary of General Marsena Rudolph Patrick, Provost Marshal General, Army of the Potomac.* New York: Thomas Yoseloff, 1964.

Sprouse, Edith M., compiler. *Fairfax County in 1860: A Collective Biography.* Privately Published, 1996.

Stevenson, James H. "*Boots and Saddles*": *A History of the First Volunteer Cavalry of the War, Known as the First New York (Lincoln) Cavalry, and also as The Sabre Regiment. Its Organization, Campaigns and Battles.* Harrisburg: Patriot, 1879.

Stiles, Kenneth L. *4th Virginia Cavalry.* Lynchburg: H. E. Howard, 1985.

Sturtevant, Ralph O. *Pictorial History: The Thirteenth Regiment Vermont Volunteers, 1861–1865.* Compiled by Eli N. Peck. Burlington: Thirteenth Vermont Regiment Association, 1911.

Styple, William B., editor. *Letters from the Peninsula: The Civil War Letters of General Philip Kearny.* Kearny: Belle Grove, 1988.

_____, editor. *Writing and Fighting the Civil War: Soldier Correspondence to the New York Sunday Mercury.* Kearny: Belle Grove, 2000.

Supplement to the Official Records of the Union and Confederate Armies. Edited by Janet B. Hewett, Noah Andre Trudeau and Bryce A. Suderow. Wilmington, NC: Broadfoot, 1994.

Taylor, Nelson. *Saddle and Saber: The Letters of Civil War Cavalryman Corporal Nelson Taylor.* Compiled by Dr. Gray Nelson Taylor. Bowie: Heritage Books, 1993.

Thackery, David. *A Light and Uncertain Hold: A History of the Sixty-Sixth Ohio Volunteer Infantry.* Kent: Kent State University Press, 1999.

Thomas, Emory. *Bold Dragoon: The Life of J.E.B. Stuart.* New York: Harper & Row, 1986.

Thompson, Jerry. *Civil War to the Bloody End: The Life & Times of Major General Samuel P. Heintzelman.* College Station: Texas A&M University Press, 2006.

Thomson, Howard, and William K. Rauch. *History of the "Bucktails": Kane Rifle Regiment of the Pennsylvania Reserve Corps (13th Pennsylvania Reserves, 42nd of the Line).* Dayton: Morningside House, 1988 edition.

Tobie, Edward P. *History of the First Maine Cavalry, 1861–1865.* Gaithersburg: Ron R. Van Sickle Military Books, 1987 edition.

Toombs, Samuel. *New Jersey Troops in the Gettysburg Campaign from June 5 to July 31, 1863.* Orange: The Evening Mail Publishing House, 1888.

Trout, Robert J. *In the Saddle with Stuart: The Story of Frank Smith Robertson of Jeb Stuart's Staff.* Gettysburg: Thomas, 1998.

_____, *They Followed the Plume: The Story of J.E.B. Stuart and His Staff.* Mechanicsburg: Stackpole Books, 1993.

_____, *With Pen & Saber: The Letters and Diaries of J.E.B. Stuart's Staff Officers.* Mechanicsburg: Stackpole Books, 1995.

Troxler, Beverly Barrier, and Billy Dawn Barrier Auciello. *"Dear Father" Confederate Letters Never Before Published.* North Billerica: Privately Published, 1989.

Ullery, Jacob G. *Men of Vermont: An Illustrated Biographical History of Vermonters & Sons of Vermont.* Brattleboro: Transcript, 1894.

U.S. Congress. *Report of the Joint Committee on the Conduct of the War.* Wilmington, NC: Broadfoot, 1999 edition.

U.S. War Department. *Instructions for Officers on Outpost and Patrol Duty.* Washington, D.C: Government Printing Office, 1862.

_____. *The War of the Rebellion: The Official Records of the Union and Confederate Armies.* Washington, D.C.: Government Printing Office, 1880–1901.

Von Borcke, Heros. *Memoirs of the Confederate War for Independence.* Philadelphia, 1867; Gaithersburg: Butternut Press, 1985 edition.

Walker, Francis, A. *History of the Second Army Corps in the Army of the Potomac.* Gaithersburg: Butternut Press, 1985 edition.

Wallace, Lee A. *A Guide to Virginia Military Organizations, 1861–1865.* Lynchburg: H.E. Howard, 1986.

Wallace, Robert C. *A Few Memories of a Long Life.* Edited by John Carroll. Fairfield: Ye Galleon Press, 1988.

Warner, Ezra J. *Generals in Gray: Lives of the Confederate Commanders.* Baton Rouge: Louisiana State University Press, 1959.

_____, *Generals in Blue, Lives of the Union Commanders.* Baton Rouge: Louisiana State University Press, 1964.

Weaver, Augustus C. *Third Indiana Cavalry: A Brief Account of the Actions in Which They Took Part.* Greenwood: Privately Published, 1919.

Welcher, Frank J. *The Union Army, 1861–1865, Organization and Operations, volume I, The Eastern Theater.* Bloomington: Indiana University Press, 1989.

Weld, Stephen Minot. *War Diary and Letters of Stephen Minot Weld, 1861–1865.* Boston: Massachusetts Historical Society, 1979.

Welles, Gideon, and John T Morse, Jr. *Diary of Gideon Welles, Secretary of the Navy Under Lincoln and Johnson.* 3 volumes. Boston: Houghton Mifflin, 1911.

Welsh, Jack D. *Medical Histories of Union Generals.* Kent: Kent State University Press, 1996.

Wert, Jeffry. *Cavalryman of the Lost Cause: A Biography of J.E.B. Stuart.* New York: Simon & Schuster, 2008.

_____. *General James Longstreet: The Confederacy's Most Controversial Soldier—A Biography.* New York: Simon & Schuster, 1993.

_____. *Mosby's Rangers.* New York: Simon & Schuster, 1990.

Wheelock, Julia. *The Boys in White. The Experience of a Hospital Agent in and Around Washington.* New York: Lange & Hillman, 1870.

Wickman, Donald H., editor and compiler. *Letters to Vermont from Her Civil War Soldier Correspondents to the Home Press.* Bennington: Images from the Past, 1998.

Wilder, Theodore. *The History of Company C, Seventh Regiment O.V.I.* Oberlin: J.B.T. Marsh, Printer, 1866.

Williams, John O. *Life in Camp: A History of the Nine Months' Service of the Fourteenth Vermont Regiment, From October 21, 1862, When it was Mustered into the U.S. Service, to July 21, 1863, Including the Battle of Gettysburg.* Claremont: Claremont Manufacturing, 1864.

Williamson, James J. *Mosby's Rangers.* Alexandria: Time Life Books, 1981 edition.

Willson, Arabella M. *Disaster, Struggle, Triumph: The Adventures of 1000 "Boys in Blue," from August, 1862, to June, 1865.* Albany: Argus, 1870.

Wittenberg, Eric J. *Rush's Lancers: The Sixth Pennsylvania Cavalry in the Civil War.* Yardley: Westholme, 2007.

Electronic Sources

Crawley, Ron. Roster of General Wade Hampton's "Iron Scouts," from http://schistory.net/iron scouts.

Grout, Josiah. *Memoir of Gen'l William Wallace Grout and Autobiography of Josiah Grout* (Newport, 1919), pp. 218–241, from vermontcivilwar.org/units/ca/grout.php.

Hartshorn Obituary in the Frederick *Post,* January 19, 1926, from vermontcivilwar.org/units/15/obits.

Lincoln Papers, LC, accessed at http://memory.loc.gov/ammem/alhtml/malhome.html.

Reference

The Oxford American Desk Dictionary and Thesaurus, New York: Berkley Books, 2001.

Index

Page numbers in ***bold italics*** indicate illustrations.